A Long Cold War

A LONG COLD WAR

A CHRONOLOGY OF AMERICAN LIFE
AND CULTURE
1945 TO 1991

JERRY CARRIER

Algora Publishing
New York

Library of Congress Cataloging-in-Publication Data —

Names: Carrier, Jerry, 1948- author.
Title: A long Cold War: a chronology of American life and culture 1945 to
    1991 / Jerry Carrier.
Other titles: Chronology of American life and culture 1945 to 1991
Description: New York: Algora Publishing, [2018] | Includes bibliographical
    references and index.
Identifiers: LCCN 2018012391 (print) | LCCN 2018016304 (ebook) | ISBN
    9781628943207 (pdf) | ISBN 9781628943184 (soft cover: alk. paper) | ISBN
    9781628943191 (hard cover: alk. paper)
Subjects: LCSH: United States—History—1945-—Chronology. | Popular
    culture—United States—History—20th century—Chronology. | United
    States—Civilization—1945- | Cold War—Influence.
Classification: LCC E741 (ebook) | LCC E741 .C266 2018 (print) | DDC
    973.918—dc23
LC record available at https://lccn.loc.gov/2018012391

Printed in the United States

This book is dedicated to Mom and Dad and my Grandparents,
who lived in these times,
and to Neal so he will know.

Table of Contents

FOREWORD

This is a cultural history of the Cold War from 1945-1991, written in an almanac or journal form. It is a reference to give the reader a complete sense of what it would have been like to live in these times as they happened. These were the headlines of the day, the fads, the weather and a few sporting events. Most entries are important in shaping American culture, however some entries are about forgotten fads or facts that seemed important at the time but that have faded in importance now. This book can be used as a historical reference, timeline or as a good read for the nostalgic or casual reader. It can be read in its entirety, in sequence or in parts, year by year to get a sense of the specific times.

Significant events (sometimes two or three per date) are recorded in mostly one or two sentences, as you may have read the headlines at the time. Some major events are expanded to a paragraph or a page to give the reader a sense of their complexity, impact and their importance. The entries include scientific, political, cultural, military, sports, inventions, fads, major calamities and weather events. Some dates have no entries because the author determined that no significant events or interesting trivia took place. The events included are purely the judgment of the author. At the end of each year there is an economic summary of consumer prices and incomes for that year and there are also summaries of the movies, radio/television, music and literature.

This is the story of America at her peak, competing with the USSR and China while enjoying a casual and affluent lifestyle that looked like an attractive model to many people around the world. This book gives a detailed look daily American life during those times.

> "When I said that American fighter-bombers had shot up my tanks
> with 40mm shells, the Reichsmarschall, who felt himself touched by this,
> said: 'That's completely impossible. The Americans only know how to make

razor blades.' I replied: 'We could do with some of those razor blades, Herr Reichsmarshal.'"

—Field Marshal Erwin Rommel

"I fear all we have done is awaken a sleeping giant and fill him with a terrible resolve."

—Admiral Isoroku Yamamoto, after the successful attack on Pearl Harbor

"In the councils of government, we must guard against the acquisition of unwarranted influence, whether sought or unsought, by the military-industrial complex. The potential for the disastrous rise of misplaced power exists and will persist."

—Dwight Eisenhower

"There is an English expression which is purported to be an ancient Chinese curse: 'May you live in interesting times.' The twentieth century is probably the most "interesting" period mankind has ever known."

—Robert Kennedy

INTRODUCTION: V IS FOR VICTORY

At the end of WWII the nation state version of the last man standing was the United States of America. The industrial capacity of Europe and Asia were completely destroyed by the war and the only nation of significant power that had any major industrial capacity was the United States. Even the civilian populations of the combatants in Europe, Asia and the Pacific were devastated while the American civilian population was left relatively unscathed. The US homeland, with the exception of Pearl Harbor and a few insignificant attacks, was largely untouched by the war. The US was the only major industrial power that was not destroyed.

In the summer of 1945 this manufacturing capacity, coupled with America's dominate military might and the discovery and use of the atomic bomb made the US the unquestioned world power. The only armies strong enough to compete with the US were that of the USSR and to a lesser extent China in a very limited regional capacity in Korea. This post war rise to power also saw the US become the new leader of the English speaking world as the United Kingdom's power declined and Britain became an appendage to American power. This was a bitter pill for the British to swallow as they watched the sun setting on the once vast British Empire where they had once fondly boasted that the sun never set. They were now forced to recognize that they owed their WWII victory to American and Soviet power and that they were now secondary players in a new Cold War.

The Western European powers and Japan pledged their allegiance to the US as they saw and feared the Soviet Union's domination of Eastern Europe and Communist China's rising dominance in East Asia. After the war, the Europeans appeared powerless stop the demise of their colonies in Asia, Africa, and Latin America as independence movements arose. The colonial powers quickly sought to preserve some of their colonies with American assistance. America's rivalry and subsequent Cold War competition with the Soviets and China was used by the Western Europeans to persuade

America to assist them in retaining their colonial powers as this nationalist freedom movement was frequently labeled (or mislabeled) "communist." America then became a primary hindrance to these movements. The colony of French Indo-China (Vietnam) was the most calamitous engagement for the US, as the US replaced the French as the colonial power, but there were many other American interventions with disastrous results. America's foreign policy in the last half of the 20th century was consumed by these movements and their fear they would tilt toward communism or socialism. President Eisenhower and the two brothers, John Foster Dulles his Secretary of State and Allan Dulles the head of the CIA were the primary proponents of this anti-nationalist contingency in the US. They called it the domino theory. If one fell, the others would follow. They saw the USSR and China as competition to dominate and spread their influence over the former colonies. Eisenhower and the Dulles brothers labeled most freedom movements as communistic or socialistic and they fought their cold war over this "Third World."

In 1949 when China became communist and the USSR created the atomic bomb, the US feared that communism would overrun the globe with nations falling to Sino-Soviet communism again like a of a row of toppling dominoes. Communism was expanding in the post colonial world, but it was more a reaction against their colonial masters than the success of a Sino-Soviet master plot as the Americans and Western Europeans claimed. China, Vietnam and even Korea were never Soviet puppet states, as the US maintained. Communism never really threatened the US and these fears of a communist takeover of the US were mostly paranoia and/or propaganda. Americans became xenophobic, they feared the other. In 1945 Americans were just entering this Cold War, a long and sometimes violent war that would last for about forty-seven years.

In the wake of WWII and the Great Depression, America was also hungry for consumer goods. Now that the industrial powerhouses of Europe had been destroyed, Americans with their unchallenged industrial capacity were about to experience their best economic times. They would see the creation of new consumer products that would revolutionize the world. This is the story of America in those times, the prosperity, the paranoia and the power. It was America's time.

A Note about the Cold War

Most look at 1945, the end of WWII, as the beginning of the Cold War. However, some disagree. Europe and America's distrust of communists dates back to at least the late 19th century — and then WWI and the Russian civil war that began as the war with Germany was nearing an and. The October Revolution ignited in 1917. The main invasion took place in Vladivostok and was called the Siberian Expedition. The allies occupied the port and surrounding areas; the last of them withdrew in 1922, finally concluding that Czarist Russia would not return. The Americans, British, French and Canadians also invaded Northern Russia in the Archangel Campaign and occupied parts of Northern Russia until 1920. Some historians mark these invasions as the real beginning of the Cold War between the Soviets and the West.

In October 18, 2008, Nick Holdsworth (reporting for the British newspaper *The Telegraph*) reported that secret documents showed that Stalin made an offer to the British, Poles and French in August of 1939, just before war broke out with Germany, to put a million Soviet troops in Poland on the German border to smother Hitler's ambitions. It was ignored by the Allies. The primary reason given for the British, French and Poles rejecting Stalin's offer was that some felt that Stalin was as ambitious as Hitler and would occupy Eastern Europe, including Poland, and that the million Soviet troops would never leave. Two weeks later Stalin signed his notorious treaty dividing Poland with Germany, and Hitler invaded Poland, starting WWII. Some see this reluctance to ally with the Soviet Union against Germany in 1939 as the start of the Cold War.

Chapter 1. 1945: Peace at Last, the American Boys Came Home

Germany surrendered on May 7, 1945. The first atomic bomb was dropped on Hiroshima on August 6, 1945 and the second at Nagasaki on August 9, shortly after Japan notified the Americans of their desire to surrender. They formally did so on August 10, with the condition that the status of Emperor Hirohito would remain unchanged. The Americans refused the following day. Fearing more atomic bombs, the Japanese felt they had no choice and agreed to an unconditional surrender three days later.

Sensing an opportunity and at the urging of the US who feared an invasion of Japan was imminent, the USSR declared war on Japan on August 8, two days after the bomb was dropped on Hiroshima. That same day the Soviets moved into North Korea and set up a communist government. On August 15, Korea was declared liberated, ending thirty-five humiliating years of Japanese rule. On August 17, Korea was divided by the US and USSR along the 38th parallel separating the "Hermit Kingdom" in two parts and beginning a war that would blow hot and cold into the twenty-first century. In 1945 most Americans didn't notice or care. By August 15, they were celebrating in the streets that the war was over. Americans were more excited that the US government had just announced the end of war time gas rationing. Americans ceased to care what was happening far away. They were celebrating so frenetically in San Francisco that a riot broke out.

On August 17, the Indonesians took the opportunity to announce their declaration of independence from the Dutch. It was the beginning of the end of the "Dutch East Indies." It was the first of many of the European colonies in the post war period to seek to overthrow their European colonial rulers.

In 1945 the American people were more concerned with domestic and economic issues. They now cared more about baseball and football than in foreign affairs. On August 18, the big news was that the scheduled demonstrations at Polo Grounds and Ebbets Field to end segregation in organized baseball had been called off and that baseball would resume. On the following day most Americans eagerly heard on the radio or read in their newspapers that thirty-seven-year-old pitcher Jimmy Foxx pitched seven innings to win. Americans celebrated the following day when seventeen-year-old Tommy Brown hit a home run for the Brooklyn Dodgers, becoming the youngest player to ever do so in Major League Baseball. Americans were thrilled that August when Bob Feller returned home from the Navy to strike out a dozen for the Cleveland Indians. On August 30, the NFL All Star Game featured the Green Bay Packers defeating the College All Stars 19 to 7 in Chicago before an unheard of crowd of over 92,000. After the wartime pause major league sports were finally coming back to full strength and the Americans were hungry for them.

On September 2, Japan formally signed their surrender while most Americans were already turning inward to domestic things. They were too busy to notice or care that Ho Chi Minh led a coup in Vietnam on August 22 and declared Vietnam free from French colonialism. Ho's declaration started a war with France, with the Americans becoming the occupying enemy when the French were defeated by the Vietnamese at Dien Bien Phu in 1954.

At home, the issue of desegregating the public schools was a hot issue. On August 18, over a thousand Whites walked out of the schools in Gary, Indiana, to protest desegregation, and also on that day that the Chicago Cubs clinched the National League Pennant.

Baseball was much more exciting for most Americans than the fact that on August 25, Jewish immigrants were permitted to leave Mauritius for Palestine. This was a new current in the Jewish Exodus that was taking place to build the state of Israel that was officially created in 1948. Americans had become war weary and short-sighted.

Americans in their war weariness had no apparent concerns or understanding that a man named Kim Il Sung had just returned to Korea from the Soviet Union on September 9, to become the communist dictator of North Korea. Americans were also unaware and deliberately kept in the dark that the first German Nazis, rocket scientists, SS Intelligence Agents, and Nazi medical doctors who performed torture and mind control experiments were brought into the US on September 20, as part of Operation Paperclip. The infamous Operation Paperclip would bring hundreds of German Nazis, many of them war criminals to the United States, and unlike what they told the president and American public, very few of them were "anti-Nazi rocket scientists." The American Office of Strategic Services, (OSS) the forerunner of the CIA and the Catholic Church began to organize the Rat Lines to give Nazi war criminals shelter in the US, Latin America and other parts of the world.

September 12-20, the Homestead Hurricane hit Florida with winds up to 130 MPH, killing 26 people and doing $60 million in damage.

October 10, War weary Americans were preoccupied with the World Series, where the Detroit Tigers beating the Chicago Cubs to care or notice the next day when the Chinese Civil War between Chiang Kai-shek and Mao Zedong began again where it left off before the Japanese invasion.

October 14, the Chicago Cardinals football team ended a record 29 game losing streak by beating the Chicago Bears.

October 15, it was announced that the 1945 baseball season had set a new attendance record of over ten and a quarter million people as Americans breathed a welcome sigh of relief that their domestic life and pastimes had returned.

October 18, the Nuremburg Trials started in Germany.

October 29, ballpoint pens began replacing fountain pens. Invented by a Hungarian, László Biró, the new tool was successfully commmmercialized by BIC, a French company.

October 30, Branch Rickey signed Jackie Robinson to a contract with the Montreal Royals which began the desegregation of baseball and major league sports.

October 24, the United Nations Charter became effective and France, the United Kingdom, the USSR, China, and the US were named the five permanent members of the Security Council.

October 25, at the behest of the US the Japanese surrendered Taiwan to General Chiang Kai-shek. The island became "Nationalist China" when the General lost his civil war on the mainland to Mao.

November 1, the first issue of Ebony Magazine was sold.

Also on November 1, Americans saw the Army at West Point with the number one college football team beat the number two team, Notre Dame, 48 to 0.

November 10, the Indonesians began a violent war against the returning Dutch colonialists.

On November 13, Truman appointed a panel to look into the resettlement of the Jewish refugees in Palestine. In August of 1945 President Truman, had received the Harrison Report which detailed the horrific plight of the Jews in Europe. Under growing pressure from the American Jewish community, Truman decided to do something to find a safe haven for the Jews. The news was not met with any enthusiasm by the British who controlled Palestine.

November 16, Yeshiva University was founded and became the first Jewish University in the United States.

November 20, twenty-four Nazi leaders were put on trial at Nuremburg for "crimes against humanity."

November 21, General Motors workers, whose wages had been frozen during the war, went on strike for higher wages.

November 22, Jim Benton of the Cleveland Rams set a football record of 303 receiving yards in a game.

November 23, Americans celebrated as the war time food rationing of meat and butter came to an end.

November 27, General George Marshall was named envoy to China as their civil war became more intense, with Mao leading the communists and Chiang Kai-shek leading the US-supported Nationalists.

November 29, Yugoslavia was declared a socialist Republic.

December 4, Doc Blanchard, who played college football for Army won the Heisman Trophy.

December 5, Flight 19 consisting of five Navy bombers was lost in the "Bermuda Triangle" giving Americans a new mystery to ponder.

December 10, Americans were excited when Preston Tucker, who had built race cars for Ford prior to the war, announced his plans for a new kind of car that could travel at 150 MPH.

December 16, the Cleveland Rams in a controversial game won the NFL championship defeating the Washington Redskins 15 to 14 in sub zero temperatures in Cleveland before more than 32,000 fans who braved the sub-zero cold.

December 20, the government announced that war time rubber and tire rationing had ended.

December 27, the World Monetary Fund was created to foster global monetary cooperation, secure financial stability, facilitate international trade, promote high employment and sustainable economic growth, and to reduce poverty around the world.

December 28, the Congress announced that they were officially recognizing the Pledge of Allegiance. This began the habit of American public schools starting their day by having the students recite the Pledge. Congress wanted to show their patriotism.

December 31, the ratification of the United Nations Charter was completed.

Domestic life was not easy in 1945. Despite the end of war time rationing, there were still shortages of many things. Most of America's industrial production had gone into the war effort and it took some time to retool factories for the production consumer goods. There was a critical shortage of housing and most people lived in fairly cramped conditions. It wasn't uncommon for children to sleep two or three in a bed. These shortages would last a few years.

The average annual wage in 1945 was about $2,400. However, prices were somewhat reasonable. A new house, if you could find one, averaged $4,600 or about two years of the average wage and rents averaged only $60 per month.

The price of a new car, if you could find one, was little over a thousand dollars and gasoline was just fifteen cents per gallon. The US inventory of automobiles was severely aged in 1945. Out of the twenty-five million registered vehicles well over half were more than ten years old. It would take Detroit some time to gear up from military vehicles to civilian auto production.

The movies of 1945 reflected a new peace time reality. A popular military movie was *Anchors Aweigh*, a musical starring Frank Sinatra and Gene Kelly about two sailors on liberty in Los Angeles. Other popular films were Billy Wilder's *Lost Weekend*, the first movie to take a substantial look at the problems of alcoholism. It starred Ray Milland and won four Oscars that year including Best Picture and Best Actor. *The Paleface* was a comedy starring Bob Hope with Jane Russell, and included the song *Buttons and Bows* which won the Oscar for Best Song. *National Velvet* was the movie that made a young Elizabeth Taylor famous. She starred in the film with Mickey Rooney and the movie won two Oscars and was nominated for three others. Alfred Hitchcock's psychological thriller *Spellbound* set in a mental hospital was another popular movie. It starred Gregory Peck and Ingrid Bergman. The film was nominated for seven Oscars and won two.

Radio was still the most popular media. The Oscars were broadcast in their entirety for the first time in 1945 on the radio as millions listened. The radio programs with the highest ratings in 1945 were *The Bob Hope Show*, *Fiber McGee and Molly*, and *The Bing Crosby Show*. The radio comedies and dramas would soon find their way to television and the sit-com and soap opera which became staples of television owed their invention to radio. Within about five years many of the popular radio shows would find their way to television.

The most popular songs of 1945 were Sammy Kaye's *Chickery Chick*, Harry James' *Its Been a Long, Long Time*, Johnny Mercer's *Ac-cent-Tchu-Ate the Positive* along with his *On the Atcheson, Topeka and the Santa Fe*. Other popular tunes included: *Sentimental Journey* and *My Dreams are Getting Better All the Time* by Les Brown, and Perry Como's *Til the End of Time*.

The popular books of 1945 included: *Animal Farm* by George Orwell, *Cannery Row* and *The Pearl* by John Steinbeck, *Brideshead Revisited* by Evelyn Waugh, *Black Boy* by Richard Wright, *Stuart Little* by E.B. White, *The Glass Menagerie* by Tennessee Williams, *The Egg and I* by Betty MacDonald, *The Age of Reason* by Jean Paul Sartre, *Lark Rise to Candleford* by Flora Thompson, and *Pippi Longstocking* by Astrid Lindgrin.

Chapter 2. 1946: The Best Years of Our Lives

In 1946 Samuel Goldwyn released the movie *The Best Years of Our Lives* about three WWII vets and their difficult adjustment returning to civilian life. It was almost three hours in length and starred Fredric March, Myrna Loy, Dana Andrews, and Harold Russell. The movie captured the essence of the times and won nine Oscars, including Best Picture, Best Director and Best Actor. Myrna Loy would also win the Best Actress Award at the Brussels World Film Festival for her role. In Britain it won the British Academy Film Award (BAFTA) for Best Picture. It also won Best Picture at the Golden Globe Awards in 1947.

Harold Russell a disabled Army veteran who lost both hands in an Army training accident won two Oscars for Best Supporting Actor and a special Award for "Bringing aid and comfort to disabled veterans." Russell also won a special award at the Golden Globe Awards. In 1992 a destitute Russell was forced to auction off his two Oscars to pay for his wife's medical care.

The Best Years of Our Lives sold over fifty-five million tickets in the US and another twenty million in Britain. It became the highest grossing and most attended film in the US and Britain and still remains one of the highest when adjusted for inflation. The movie grossed over twenty-three million dollars in the US, a record at the time, with well over eleven million in profits for the studio. It remains one of the most critically acclaimed and successful films in US history.

The computer age began in January of 1946 when ENIAC the first computer was finished on New Year's Day.

January 3, according to the *New York Times* Mafia mobster Charles "Lucky" Luciano had his prison sentence commuted by New York's Governor Thomas E. Dewey for the Mafia's cooperation with the OSS during the war. As part of the agreement Luciano was deported to Italy. During the War the Mafia assisted with intelligence inside Italy, helped plan the Allied invasions and provided waterfront security against the Nazis on the waterfront of the East

Coast during the war. It was a secret deal that would not come to light for many years. It would also lead to later CIA and Mafia operations.

January 7, Cambodia became independent of France and was no longer part of "French Indo-China."

January 11, Bert Bell became the second NFL Commissioner and moved the NFL offices from Chicago to Philadelphia. The following day he approved the controversial move of the NFL Champion Cleveland Rams to Los Angeles. Bell was the co-founder and co-owner of the Philadelphia Eagles. He is credited with creating the NFL Draft and later for bringing the NFL to television making NFL Football America's favorite sport replacing baseball. He is an original member of the NFL Hall of Fame. He served as Commissioner until his death in 1959.

January 22, at the urging of his military and intelligence advisors President Truman signed the National Security Act of 1947 establishing the Central Intelligence Agency to replace the Office of Strategic Services (OSS). The National Security Act charged the CIA with coordinating the nation's intelligence activities and correlating, evaluating and disseminating intelligence affecting national security. Truman would later state in his biography, *Plain Speaking*, that it was the greatest mistake of his life.

February 1, Trygve Lie, a Norwegian Socialist, became the first UN Secretary General. His election began conservative and right-wing America's hatred of the United Nations. American's fear/hate of socialism was never rational as some of Roosevelt's popular New Deal Programs such as Social Security were socialistic.

February 2, the US established the South Korean dictatorial government of Sygnman Rhee.

February 21, more European colonies began to rebel, and anti-British demonstrations took place in Egypt.

On February 24, Juan Peron was elected President of Argentina.

On February 26, two were killed and ten were wounded in a race riot in Columbia, Tennessee. America was on the verge of the Civil Rights Movement.

March 2, Ho Chi Minh was elected the President of Vietnam. That same day the Dutch invaded East Bali to try to re-establish their Dutch East Indies colony.

March 5, In Fulton, Missouri, Winston Churchill gave his "Iron Curtain" speech, coining that term as a call to arms for a Cold War with the USSR.

March 6, the French recognized Vietnam as a state, but only within their colony of French Indo-China. Newly elected Vietnamese President Ho Chi Minh vowed Vietnamese independence.

March 9, Dutch troops invaded Batavia and Semarang to re-establish their colony.

March 12, Finland was forced to give part of its Petsamo Province to the USSR in reparations for siding with Germany against Russia. Stalin began immediately deporting thousands of Finns from the province to Siberia.

March 14, knowing that Britain lacked the military power to keep India as a colony, British Prime Minister Clement Atlee agreed to India's right to independence.

March 19, France agreed to make Guadeloupe, French Guiana, Martinique and Reunion into "overseas departments" of France giving them more independence.

Also on March 14, Kenny Washington joined the Los Angeles Rams and became the first Black player in the NFL since 1933.

March 22, Britain agreed to independence for Jordan.

Also on March 22, the Space Age began when the US successfully launched the first rocket to leave the Earth's atmosphere in White Sands, New Mexico. On April 16, the US modified and launched a captured GermanV2 rocket. July 30, another rocket at White Sands achieved an altitude of a hundred miles. October 24, a camera mounted on another modified V-2 rocket took the first pictures of Earth from space. Later in October, other German rocket scientists, working for the USSR, also began work on the Soviet Space Program. It was the beginning of the US-Soviet space race.

March 28, if there is such a thing as a declaration of Cold War it happened on this day when the US State Department issued the Acheson-Lilienthal Report. It was a plan to keep nuclear weapons from the USSR and to preserve the US military superiority over the USSR.

April 1, saw 400,000 mineworkers, whose wages were frozen during the war, go on strike.

Also on April 1, war-time food rationing had ended the year before and Americans began over consuming. Some Americans began to worry about gaining too much weight and on this day Weightwatchers was created.

Also on this date an earthquake in the Aleutian Islands caused a tsunami that struck Hawaii.

In another event on April 1, the British reorganized their colonies on the Malay Peninsula into what they called the Malayan Union. The Malays disliked that the British gave citizenship to many residents of Chinese and Indian ancestry, whom the Malays hated for their ethnicity and religious differences. The Malays were mostly Muslim and the Chinese and Indians were mostly Buddhists and Hindus. The Chinese and Indian residents of the Malay Peninsula were also merchants and they had a significant control of the Malay economy which caused rivalry and jealousy. As a consequence the Malay refused to participate in the Union and within two years Britain relented and formed the Federation of Malay which eventually led to independence and the creation of Malaysia.

In April Truman's committee to investigate the resettlement of European Jews in Palestine came to a conclusion and unanimously recommended that the Jews be re-settled in Palestine. Truman then began a plan to do so. However, the Joint Chiefs of Staff and the British convinced Truman that Jewish communists could take over the region and threaten the vital Mideast oil resources. They managed to convince Truman to hold off for another two years.

On April 7, France notified Syria it would grant independence; this officially took place on April 17. On the same day the Soviets annexed part of Prussia.

April 13, Eddie Kemp, a White pitcher signed by the defending Negro Baseball League Champion Cleveland Buckeyes, was officially banned from playing baseball in Birmingham, Alabama for playing in the Negro League. On April 18, Jackie Robinson broke the Whites only barrier in baseball and made his debut as a second baseman for the Montreal Royals.

April 18, the US formally recognized Tito's communist government of Yugoslavia and received a pledge of neutrality from Tito in the new cold war between the USSR and the US.

April 21 and 22, the East German Socialist Party was formed.

April 29, twenty-eight Japanese war time leaders were indicted as war criminals. On May 3, their trial began.

May 2-3, there was a prison revolt at Alcatraz. Two guards and three prisoners were killed and about a dozen were wounded. Two prisoners were later given the death penalty for their roles in the revolt and the murder of the two guards.

May 5, a civil war in Greece flared as the communists and British-backed monarchists clashed. May 26, the communist party won the elections in Czechoslovakia. October 27, the communists won the elections in Bulgaria.

May 8, two Estonian school girls blew up the Soviet memorial in Tallinn. They were part of a group that became known as the Forest Brethren, a guerilla army of freedom fighters from the Baltic states of Latvia, Estonia and Lithuania who opposed the USSR occupation. They fought their guerilla war with the USSR until they were exterminated in 1951. It is estimated that 34,400 rebels died during the five year conflict.

The Forest Brethren weren't the only guerillas fighting the Soviets. The Ukrainian Insurgent Army was created October14, 1942. It formed in the Carpathian Mountains and fought against the Nazi occupation of the Ukraine. Shortly after the Nazis were defeated they began fighting the Soviets and their puppet government in the Ukraine. They were eventually defeated by the Soviet Army in 1949. The Polynational War Memorial estimates that the number of Ukrainians killed in this conflict was about 60,000.

May 7, in Japan, the Tokyo Telecommunications Engineering Company was formed it was later renamed Sony.

May 9, the first one hour television show, NBCs *Hour Glass* aired. It was a variety show. However, except for New York City and a small number of sets in a few other large East Coast cities, television was still an unknown commodity. In this year coaxial cable connections allowed television stations of the same network, NBC and Du Mont, to show the same shows in cities such as New York, Boston, Philadelphia and Washington DC at the same time and created the first television season. It was extremely limited as the network shows only aired in New York and the other three cities. In June NBC televised the first sport show, a boxing match between Joe Lewis and Billy Conn from Madison Square Garden. A record 131,000 saw the match mostly on televisions that had been installed in bars as the sets were too expensive for most consumers.

That fall the first television season operated from 7:00 PM to 10:30 PM. The most prominent feature was boxing shown every Monday for three hours and another two and a half hours every Friday on NBC. It was called *The Gillette Cavalcade of Sports* and the show lasted until 1960. The DuMont network had a new half hour live drama show that began October 2, called *Faraway Hill*. This show was the first soap opera on television. In September Chicago's WBKB-TV which is now WBBM-TV became the first television station outside of the Eastern Time Zone. RCA produced 10,000 television sets in 1946 at price of $352 which was too steep for the average household. Most televisions were installed in bars to watch the boxing matches.

May 13, the War Time Tribunals in Nuremburg sentenced to death fifty-eight Nazis who had overseen the concentration camps.

On May 17, in their first post war election, the Dutch elected a majority of communists to their parliament. The incident frightened the US and some other western European nations.

Also on May 17 President Truman seized control of the US railroads to prevent a national railroad strike that would have shut down the growing post-war economy.

May 19, the Dutch Cooperation for Sexual reform went into effect which allowed prostitution in Amsterdam. It was the start of the infamous Amsterdam Red Light District.

June 2, the Italians chose a republic over a monarchy.

June 3, the first bikini bathing suit went on sale in Paris. Western dress was becoming more casual and women's clothing more revealing.

On June 5, a fire in the LaSalle Hotel bar in Chicago killed 61 people, another hotel fire killed 19 on June 9, in Dubuque, Iowa, and on June 21, ten more died in a hotel in Dallas. December 7, a hotel fire in Atlanta killed 119. These fires prompted a review of fire exits for hotels and public buildings and brought about modern day fire and building codes and regular inspections.

June 6, the Basketball Association of America formed and would soon become the National Basketball Association (NBA). They started with eleven professional teams, six of which still play in the NBA today.

June 7, the modern Civil Rights Era began when the Supreme Court banned discrimination on interstate travel.

June 10, the Italian Republic was established.

June 13, commercial air travel was becoming more available and the first one day round trip transcontinental air flight occurred from California to Maryland. July 26, Aloha Airlines began regular service from Honolulu to California. The pilots trained by the military and the technical improvements made to aircraft during the war made Airline passenger service boom in the post war years. America was entering the Auto-Air era, bringing many changes.

Prior to this time, most people were born, lived and died within a very small geographic space, many never left their community. There were migrations prior to this era, like the migration from rural to urban and the great migration of Blacks and Whites out of the South and into the industrialized Northeast and Midwest using the railorads, but even these migrations were later greatly enhanced by the new highways, freeways and airlines of the post-war period.

The Auto-Air Era began the great migration of Puerto Ricans to New York and other destinations. It began the migration of Latinos out of the Southwest and into the rest of America. It began the movement of Easterners and Midwesterners to the West, particularly to California, and from the Frost Belt to the Sun Belt to destinations like California, Arizona, New Mexico, Texas and Florida. It increased the movement from rural to urban. Americans became much more mobile. They moved for new jobs, new opportunities or just because they could do it easily and cheaply.

The Auto-Air Era also destroyed the passenger trains. Passenger trains became unprofitable and the federal government through AMTRAK had to rescue them. Americans wanted speed and individual choices on where to go and when to stop. Trains were too slow and confined to tracks and schedules. Planes could take you from New York to California in a matter of hours not days. Cars could take you anywhere and allow you to choose when to stop and what to see and were and were faster than trains.

June 16, the British conflict with the Jews in Palestine came to violence as the Jewish underground military unit, the Palmach, blew up eight road and rail bridges between Palestine and neighboring countries. The Jewish militant group the Irgun captured six British officers. Two escaped, two were released by the Irgun and two were later traded in exchange for the commutation of the death sentences to life in prison by of two Irgun members who were held by the British. The British responded to the Jewish uprising en masse and approximately 25,000 British Troops conducted surprise raids against the Jews during the Jewish Holy Sabbath on June 29. It became known as "Black Sabbath." About 2,700 Jews were arrested and held in prison, among them future Israeli Prime Minister Moshe Sharett.

The British called it Operation Agatha. It was an extensive military operation with British planes circling Jerusalem, army roadblocks set up at major crossroads stopping and searching all vehicles for weapons and contraband. Trains were flagged down, and all the Jewish passengers were evacuated and escorted home by the Army. Special licenses were required for the operations of emergency vehicles and strict curfews were imposed.

The British tactics were draconian and many British troops openly displayed their anti-Semitism by shouting Heil Hitler at the Jews and scrawling Swastikas on walls in Jewish areas. In some Jewish settlements the Jews were rounded up and put in cages reminiscent of the Nazis. This all happened as the Nuremburg Trials were making the news and the international press was aghast as Jewish women prisoners in Palestine began to rip their clothing to show the press their concentration camp tattoos. American and world opinion quickly went against the British. Operation Agatha was only successful in the short term as world opinion began to side with the Jews.

June 17, Southwestern Bell introduced the first mobile telephone service for autos in St. Louis.

June 22, Gandhi called on the South African White Apartheid government to stop their racist "hooliganism." The next day White South Africans responded by violently attacking passive Indian protestors in South Africa.

July 1, the US exploded an atomic bomb as a test at the Bikini atoll in the South Pacific, and on July 25 they exploded another.

Also on July 1, the Communicable Disease Center (CDC), now the Centers for Disease Control and Prevention, opened its doors and occupied one floor of a small building in Atlanta. Its first mission was simple but highly challenging: prevent malaria from spreading across the nation.

Anti-Semitism flared on July 4, in Kielce, Poland, where 42 Jews were murdered in anti-Jewish riots.

Also on July 4, the US granted the Philippines their independence.

July 8, the Major League Baseball set a minimum player salary of $5,000.

July 14, Dr. Spock's *Common Sense Book on Baby and Child Care* was published. The book would be the child rearing bible for many mothers of the Baby Boom generation.

July 16, 46 Nazis were sentenced to death before the War Crimes tribunal for crimes against humanity at the Dachau Concentration Camp. Later on September 22, 22 more Nazis were convicted of war crimes and Joachim Von Ribbentrop and Herman Goering were sentenced to death. On October 1, 12 more Nazi war criminals were convicted. October 16, ten Nazis were hung for their war crimes.

The Jewish terrorist organization the Irgun sought revenge for Operation Agatha. On July 23, they bombed the King David Hotel, the headquarters of the British government in Palestine. The attack was planned by future Israeli Prime Minister Menachem Begin.

July 25, a new comedy team of Dean Martin and Jerry Lewis gave their first performance in Atlantic City.

July 26, in what would be one of the bravest political acts ever undertaken, President Truman, a Missouri politician, desegregated the United States Armed Forces and endured the wrath of segregationists who still seemed to be in the majority among American Whites. Truman also later issued Executive Order #9808 on December 5, creating The Committee on Civil Rights to look at desegregating other government and public venues.

August 13, Britain diverted a ship full of Jewish holocaust survivors bound for Palestine to detainment in Cyprus.

August 16, religious riots between Muslims and Hindus erupted in Calcutta and about 4,000 died in the violence.

August 17, George Orwell's anti-communist novel *Animal Farm* was published in Britain.

September 2, Nehru formed a government in India. On that same day Greece voted to return to a monarchy.

September 8, Bulgaria ended their monarchy in favor of communism.

September 20, Churchill proposed a "United States of Europe," which ultimately led to the discussions that would produce the European Union decades later.

Also on September 20, the first Cannes Film Festival was held.

September 29, an independence party was formed in the Latin American colony of Dutch Surname.

October 8, Chiang Kai-shek proclaimed himself President of China while fighting a civil war with Mao.

October 9, US industry was finally producing large quantities of consumer goods. The first electric blanket was produced and sold for $39.50.

October 14, the Dutch and Indonesians declared a cease fire in their war for Indonesian independence.

On October 22, the first actual battle of the Cold War occurred when communist Albania fired on two British warships that trespassed in their territorial waters, which Albania declared was an act of war. It was called the Corfu Channel Incident. The two British warships were severely damaged, one beyond repair, and forty-four British sailors were killed and another forty-two wounded. The incident went to the World Court where Albania was directed to pay Britain for the damage to their ships.

November 9, President Truman ended the war time wage and price freezes.

November 10, the US and Western Europe became alarmed as French Communists won a significant number of seats in the parliamentary elections in France.

November 15, the US House Committee on Un-American Activities (HUAC) became concerned about communist subversives in the United States. They interrogated Astronomer Harlow Shapley. Joe McCarthy claimed Shipley was a communist who worked for the State Department. Shapely had no connection whatsoever to the State Department and was not a communist. Despite this he had to defend himself in the press and did so by calling McCarthy a bully and a liar. Shipley was a friend and supporter of former Vice President Henry Wallace, who was a socialist, and Shipley had befriended other socialists. During this time, which become known as the "McCarthy Era," being friends with socialists or communists was very problematic and frequently led to charges of being "a fellow traveler," meaning that anyone associating with socialists or communists must also be a communist and therefore anti-American.

November 23, in reaction to the Vietnamese independence movement the French Navy fired on Haiphong killing an estimated 6,000 Vietnamese.

December 3, the US reversed its support of the Spanish dictator Francisco Franco and asked the United Nations to order Franco out of Spain. Franco ignored them and on December 11, the United Nations announced that membership for Spain was suspended. The US had previously recognized Spain's Franco government in 1939, on the same day that Pope Pius XII personally congratulated and approved Franco and his fascist government.

December 8, the Bell X-1 secret rocket plane made its first powered flight. It would ultimately lead to the first supersonic aircraft. These experiments would also lead to the first space plane the X-15 and ultimately led to the Space Shuttle.

December 11, Tide laundry detergent was introduced to the American market and became an American favorite.

December 12, John D. Rockefeller Jr. gave six blocks of Manhattan to the United Nations as a gift, and on December 14, the UN voted to place its headquarters in New York City.

December 19, in retaliation for the French Naval bombardment killing 6,000 Vietnamese, Ho Chi Minh's communist forces declared war and attacked the French in Hanoi.

December 24, the U.S. Military granted 800,000 "minor" Nazis amnesty. According to Anne Jacobsen in *Operation Paperclip*, and other authors, most were not so minor Nazis. Those granted amnesty included many senior SS Nazi officers that the OSS/CIA and the US military wanted to use in their intelligence, mind control, biological and chemical weapons research, and rocket programs.

The Mafia began to build Las Vegas in 1945 and on December 26, Bugsy Siegel, a California mobster, opened the Flamingo Hotel. It was hailed as "The West's greatest resort hotel." Siegel named it after his girl friend Virginia Hill, whom he had called the "Flamingo" because of her long skinny legs. It was the first hotel on what was to become the famous Las Vegas Strip. Siegel was later killed by the Mafia for skimming money from the building fund and gambling operations at the expense of his Mafia partners. Virginia Hill fled to Switzerland with over two million dollars of the skimmed money.

During 1946 there were severe shortages of food and medicine in most parts of the world. There were many people going hungry in Europe and an estimated 30 million people facing starvation in China. There were still shortages of many things in the US as well.

In Italy the first Vespa motor scooter was produced — a highly affordable new form of transportation — and would soon become popular in America and around the world.

In the movies *The Best Years of Our Lives* and Disney's *Song of the South* were the two most popular movies. Other notable films were *Gilda* and *The Post Man Always Rings Twice*. One of the most lasting movies of the year, *It's a Wonderful Life*, which premiered on December 21, 1946.

Some of the best books of 1946 were: John Hersey's *Hiroshima*, Robert Pen Warren's *All the Kings Men*, and Eugene O'Neil's play *The Iceman Cometh*. O'Neill became the first playwright to win the Nobel Prize for Literature. Another book, *Thomas the Tank Engine*, by Wilbur Awdry, became very popular with children and their parents.

The most popular songs of 1946 were: *The Gypsy* by the Ink Spots, *Let it snow, Let It Snow, Let It Snow* by Vaughn Monroe, and *Prisoner of Love* by Perry Como. Como had three songs in the Top Forty that year as did Bing Crosby.

Performers with two songs in the Top Forty were: The Ink Spots, Frank Sinatra, Frankie Carle, Stan Kenton, Sammy Kaye, Freddy Martin, Johnny Mercer, Dinah Shore and Les Brown. The Big Band sound was still dominant.

The Baby Boom also began in 1946 and American birthrates sky-rocketed. Between 1946 and 1964 76 million children were born in America.

CHAPTER 3. 1947: THE HUNGER WINTER

January 1, due to shortages and the dire need for winter fuel, Britain nationalized its coal industry on New Year's Day.

January 2, Mahatma Gandhi began a peace march in East Bengali for Indian independence from the British.

January 8, General George Marshall became Secretary of State under Truman. Marshall warned that the massive shortages of food and fuel — caused by deliberate destruction of Europe's infrastructure, industry and agriculture — could lead Europe to "face economic, social, and political deterioration of a very grave character" and he called for the creation of what would become known as the Marshall Plan. It was a $13 billion aid program that would help prevent sixteen European nations from starvation and cold-related deaths after the devastating war. It was justified to the Congress by claiming that this aid would also keep these countries from turning to communism.

The winter of 1947 was very cold and the snowiest on record. There were over twenty-five million homeless people in Europe and the cold weather was particularly brutal causing many deaths. Hundreds of Germans did die of cold and hunger in what was called the "Hunger Winter." Even in Ireland over 600 people died of the cold and hundreds more of cold related illnesses such as pneumonia and tuberculosis. That winter was also cold in North America and on February 3, Snag, Yukon recorded a temperature of minus eighty-one degrees Fahrenheit, which is still the record low for North America.

January 10, Britain stopped two ships filled with Jewish immigrants on their way to Palestine. Many were survivors of the concentration camps.

January 18, a Yangtze River boat sank in China killing more than 400.

February 7, Arabs and Jews rejected the British proposal to split Palestine.

February 12, a large meteorite struck eastern Siberia.

February 17, the Cold War heated up as the US began their "Voice of America" propaganda broadcasts into the USSR.

February 20, the British appointed Earl Mountbatten of Burma as the Viceroy of India. He would be the last British ruler of India.

February 20, a Greek passenger ship struck a mine left over from the war, killing 392 people.

Also on February 20, a mistake in mixing chemicals at a factory in Los Angeles caused an explosion that destroyed 42 blocks of the city.

February 20, the first self-developing instant camera was demonstrated in New York City by Edwin Land. The Polaroid Land Camera went into production with the first models sold the following year.

February 23, General Eisenhower began a charity to raise $170 million in aid for European Jews.

February 28, a protest against General Chiang Kai-shek and his Kuomintang occurred in Taiwan. His army used deadly force to stop the demonstrations and over 30,000 were killed. On March 7, Chiang and Mao actively resumed their civil war for the control of China.

Early in March, a civil war broke out in Paraguay. Paraguayans seeking more democracy and freedoms attacked the military government. The revolt was put down by the Army with a key role played by Lieutenant Colonel Alfredo Stroessner who would later take control of the military dictatorship in Paraguay. Over 4,000 were killed in the rebellion. Stroessner strengthened his military by importing Nazi advisors smuggled into the country by the Catholic Church's ratline. Paraguay then became a haven for Nazi war criminals.

March 6, the XB-45, the first US jet aircraft was tested in California. The aircraft was reverse engineered from a captured German jet aircraft.

March 12, the Truman Doctrine was announced. This policy held that the United States would seek to obstruct any expansion of the influence of the Soviet Union by providing political, military and economic assistance to all nations under threat from external or internal communism.

March 15, John Lee was appointed the first Black officer in the US Navy.

March 21, Truman signed Executive Order #9835 requiring all federal employees to pledge loyalty oaths to the United States. America was becoming more xenophobic and anti-communist.

March 29, the people of Madagascar revolted against the French colonial government. About 11,000 people were killed in the violence. The French suffered only 180 deaths in the revolt. The French also arrested and convicted another 6,000 who were either imprisoned or executed.

April 1, a ship carrying Jewish immigrants managed to avoid the British Navy and arrived at Port Eilat. Most were concentration camp survivors.

April 8, the largest sunspot event occurred. Over 7,000 sunspots were observed. Radio transmissions were affected by the event.

April 9, a tornado struck west Texas and Oklahoma, killing 169 and injuring over 1,300.

April 16, a French freighter exploded in Texas City, Texas. The blast was heard 150 miles away. Between about 600 people were killed, over 3,000 were wounded and many buildings were flattened. The blast triggered other blasts at nearby chemical factories. Fires burned for several days. The ship's one and a half ton anchor was flung into the air and landed two miles away, embedding itself ten feet in the ground near a refinery.

April 17, Jackie Robinson appeared in the starting lineup for the Brooklyn Dodgers and became the first Black player in US Major League Baseball.

April 28, anthropologist Thor Heyerdahl and a crew of five built a raft called the Kon-tiki and sailed from Peru to Polynesia to prove his theory that ancient South Americans could have had contact with the Polynesians. Although his adventure was followed with enthusiasm by the press and the public, his theories were not taken seriously in academia.

May 1, the first radar was made available for commercial and private planes.

May 3, the new Japanese constitution went into effect. As part of this constitution Japan renounced militarism and stated that it would only permit enough military to defend its shores. On May 7, General MacArthur the American commander in Japan approved the Constitution.

May 5, as a result of the record snowfall that winter, the Mississippi River flooded and killed 16 people and caused $850 million in damage.

May 11, B.F. Goodrich announced the first tubeless auto tire.

May 22, the US first implemented the Truman Doctrine, stamping out any move toward communism, by giving assistance to Greece and Turkey. The Greek resistance which had fought the Nazis during the war began to clash with the right-wing government imposed by Britain after the war. The majority of the people of Greece were supporting the resistance, whose leadership included some communists. The US heavily supported the rightwing military government against the resistance. The OSS became involved, and in July when the CIA was created, the agency became very active in providing intelligence, funding and arms for the Greek military government. The Greek civil war resulted in about 154,000 deaths and destroyed the Greek economy. In 1949 the US-backed military government triumphed over the resistance. It was a hollow victory, as Greece has had many problems ever since, and the Greeks blame most of these problems on the US.

Also on May 22, the US test fired the first ballistic missile.

May 31, the Communists came to power in Hungary.

June 4, the Taft Hartley Act was passed by the House of Representatives limiting the power of labor unions and beginning the decline of labor unions in the US. President Truman vetoed Taft-Hartley on June 20, but the Congress overrode his veto on June 23, making it law.

June 14 and 15, the first major league night baseball games were played in Chicago and Detroit and night baseball games became common.

June 16, the Dumont network began the first TV national network news from Washington, DC. One of the first news stories was that Pravda, the Soviet news agency, had just denounced the Marshall Plan as American imperialism.

June 17, Pan American Airlines was chartered and became the first world-wide passenger airline.

June 24, a pilot spotted flying saucers over Mount Rainer, setting off the UFO craze. On July 8, rumors begin that a an alien UFO crash landed in Roswell, New Mexico and the UFO phenomenon became a nation-wide fad. During the previous year flying saucers had been reported over Scandinavia. Swedish radar tracked the objects and later notified the US Air Force that they thought they might be aircraft of Soviet origin. The Swedes, after discounting that they were of Soviet origin, began to investigate the possibility that they were extraterrestrial craft but came to no conclusion. The USAF initiated Project Bluebook to study this phenomenon. It was operational from 1947 to 1969. Project Bluebook came to no conclusions and the public was given this inconclusive statement as to why it was ended: "further study of UFOs could not be justified on grounds of scientific advancement."

June 25, the *Diary of Anne Frank* was published.

July 3, a record 252,288 people passed through Grand Central Station in Manhattan. US passenger trains were at their zenith, but they would decline rapidly in the auto-and-air era of the 1950s and 60s. The peak ridership occurred in 1944 when US rail passengers racked up an astonishing 98 billion passenger miles. By the 1960s, railroads were struggling with huge financial losses on their passenger lines. In 1971 Amtrak, a federal government nonprofit corporation, took over the long-distance passenger train service from the railroads.

July 6, one of the most used rifles of the post WWII era, the AK-47, went into production in the Soviet Union. The design was based on the German Sturmgewehr 44 assault rifle which was modified by Mikhail Kalashnikov. The rifle is also referred to as the Kalashnikov rifle.

July 9, in a questionable election Spain became a monarchy with dictator General Francisco Franco elected King.

July 18, the British seized a ship of 4,500 Jewish refugees, including men women and children that were mostly concentration camp survivors on their way to Palestine. The ship was called the Exodus and writer Leon Uris would later use this event and to name his book *Exodus* about the creation of Israel. British destroyers surrounded the ship and three Jews were killed and dozens were shot and wounded as the British took possession of the unarmed ship. The passengers of the Exodus were forced onto three British transport ships which brought them to Toulon, France. The Jews refused to disembark and the French authorities refused the British request to use force to make them disembark. The three British ships then brought them to Hamburg, Germany, where British troops physically forced them to disembark and forced them into detainment camps, to the outrage of many. The Jews began a hunger strike;the world press and public opinion came down hard on the British who were being compared to Hitler's Nazis. People in Europe and the United States staged protests and sympathy hunger strikes. It was a turning point. Britain, whose sympathy was strongly with the Arab Palestinians, began to realize that world opinion, and especially that of the United States, was now firmly on the side of the Jews and that world opinion seemed to favor the creation of a Jewish homeland.

July 18, the partition of India was set forth by the British in the Indian Independence Act 1947 and resulted in the dissolution of the British Indian Empire and the end of the British Raj. It divided the occupied British lands into India and Pakistan. This partition resulted in a struggle for land and power between the newly constituted states of Hindu and Buddhist India and Islamic Pakistan. The conflict displaced up to 12.5 million people. Deaths were estimated between 300,000 and a 1,000,000. The violent nature of the partition created a permanent atmosphere of hate, hostility and occasional violence between India and Pakistan that continues to plague the two nations.

July 25, the US Department of Defense was formed. On September 28, the Army Air Corps was separated from the Army and formally became a separate and equal branch of the military, the "US Air Force." As part of the reorganization, the National Security Act was passed and the CIA was created. President Truman would later call the creation of the CIA the greatest mistake of his presidency.

According to Anne Jacobsen in *Operation Paperclip*, the CIA began immediately expanding the OSS black operations. The OSS had been busy cleansing Nazi war criminals records and bringing many of them to the US and using Nazi SS Officers as intelligence agents in Germany and Eastern Europe against the Soviets. The Catholic Church was also busy assisting Nazis escape prosecution. The original efforts were called "the Rat Line." The CIA called it Operation Paperclip and greatly expanded the OSS operation.

In the beginning US intelligence officers had been quiet observers of the Catholic Church's Draganović ratline that was smuggling Nazi war criminals out of Europe, but this changed in the summer of 1947. They became partners and also began their own ratlines. A now declassified US Army intelligence report called the *History of the Ratlines* from 1950 laid out in detail the history of the OSS/CIA's Nazi smuggling operation. According to the report, from the summer of 1947 throughout the 1950s the US forces had also begun to use the Catholic Church's Draganović network to evacuate its own "visitors." The report states these were "visitors who had been in the custody of the 430th CIC and completely processed in accordance with current directives and requirements, and whose continued residence in Austria constituted a security threat as well as a source of possible embarrassment to the Commanding General of USFA, since the Soviet Command had become aware that their presence in the US Zone of Austria and in some instances had requested the return of these persons to Soviet custody."

The worst of these American sponsored Nazis was S.S. General Reinhard Gehlen. Major General Reinhard Gehlen was Hitler's spy master. He had overseen a large organization of more than thirty-five hundred Nazi spies scattered throughout Eastern Europe and the Soviet Union. His top officers were Nazi zealots who had committed some of the most atrocious crimes of the war in the concentration camps and in the prisoner of war camps. They were vicious and had proven their effectiveness in their efforts to torture, drug and trick information from prisoners. They became masters of mind control and breaking the human spirit. They were also accomplished at inserting their agents into Russia.

The records and techniques that Gehlen amassed during the Nazi regime were deemed invaluable to the Allies, especially to a select group of very interested Americans, the OSS, and later the CIA led by Allan Dulles who had knew Gehlen. The right-wing OSS men were already preparing for a cold war with the Soviets midway through the war. At the end of the war Gehlen was confident that a suitable arrangement with the Americans could be made for himself and his organization. There were many in the OSS like the Allen Dulles who had extensive pre-war connections and sympathies with Nazi Germany. Dulles was the OSS Station Chief in Switzerland during the war and he knew of Gehlen's work.

Gehlen had been planning this move for months as he watched Germany collapse. He used his connections to Allen Dulles to execute it. He noted in his memoirs that, "Early in 1944 I told my more intimate colleagues that I considered the war lost and we must began thinking of the future and plan for the approaching catastrophe."

In a pre-planned and negotiated move on May 22, 1945, Major General Gehlen surrendered to the US Army in Bavaria. He was brought to what had previously been an interrogation center for the German Air Force. In 1945 the United States Army also began to use this place as their interrogation center and intelligence post. They named it Camp King.

Gehlen was a known commodity to both Bill Donovan, the head of the OSS as well as Dulles. They were both eager to interrogate him because of his knowledge and contacts inside the Soviet Union. They were also aware of his mind control and interrogation techniques, and they were interested in knowing more. He offered them his intelligence methods, his archives and his network of contacts in exchange for his liberty and the liberty of his senior Nazi colleagues imprisoned in American POW camps in Germany. He also brazenly offered to work for them, an offer they quickly accepted. The OSS quietly removed Gehlen and his commanders from the official lists of American POWs and more ominously removed them from the war crimes lists where most of them were wanted for their atrocious crimes against humanity. They "sanitized" their war records and transferred seven of Gehlen's senior officers to Camp King. Gehlen's intelligence archives were then unearthed and brought to the camp for examination.

William Donovan and Allen Dulles made the deal with Gehlen to formally work for American intelligence. On 20 September 1945 Gehlen and three other high ranking Nazi officers were secretly flown to the United States to be prepared for their secret work for the OSS.

Immediately Gehlen tried to prove his worth by exposing a number of American OSS officers who he claimed were secret members of the US Communist Party. In retrospect their guilt has since been highly suspect as it is now believed that Gehlen likely accused the innocent Americans to impress his new bosses. It was just the beginning of Gehlen's and his Nazi officers many lies and deceptions. Many would become double agents and worked for the Soviets as well. They were spies for hire.

President Truman was also lied to during this time. The OSS told the president that only a handful of "rocket scientists" were brought to the United States, but that "none of them were real Nazis." The called it "Operation Paperclip." The operation not only included German rocket scientists, but physicists working on the German nuclear weapons program, Nazi Intelligence officers like Gehlen, most of whom were SS and Gestapo, and Nazi scientists who had performed some of the most atrocious human experiments ever conducted. All of these men had committed war crimes. Even the rocket scientist Werner Von Braun, the father of the American space program, was a member of the Nazi Party and a member of the SS who was linked to the deaths of thousands of concentration camp prisoners. He was also guilty of using slave labor in his rocket program. Von Braun proudly wore his SS Uniform to work every day in Germany.

Many of the other Nazi scientists that were recruited by the OSS had studied torture and mind control and most of these had been identified as war criminals during the Nuremberg Trials. When the CIA replaced the OSS several secret US government mind control projects grew out of Operation Paperclip. These projects included Project Chatter in 1947, and Project Bluebird in 1950, which was renamed Project Artichoke in 1951. Ultimately they all became part of the infamous Project MK-ULTRA. Their purpose was to study mind control, interrogation, torture and behavior modification in order to develop superior torture and interrogation techniques, and to use mind control to create "human robots" who would later be subject to the commands of the CIA. These human under mind control could be used as unwitting spies, thieves, terrorists, couriers and assassins. They became commonly known as the "Manchurian Candidates."

The modification of the records of these Nazis to hide their heinous crimes was a chore in itself. The records were "sanitized" by removing all records of atrocities and giving the guilty either clean records or new identities. According to Anne Jacobsen in her book *Operation Paperclip*, two of the more interesting Americans helping in this sanitation of records were Henry Kissinger and Richard Nixon.

August 5, under pressure from the United Nations to end the bloodshed in Indonesia, the Netherlands was forced to seek a political solution and possible independence for Indonesia.

August 23, President Truman's daughter Margaret began her singing debut. Her career was short-lived as the press and the critics were harsh in their criticism of her. President Truman called her critics "SOBs" in the press and received backlash for his crude terminology.

September 15, a typhoon hit Japan, killing over 1,900 and severely injuring another 1,600 and set back efforts to rebuild the country.

October 1, the first civilian use of a helicopter began as an express air mail service in Los Angeles.

October 5, President Truman gave the first ever televised presidential address. Television cameras were set up in the White House for this event.

On October 9, Americans were wowed with the first telephone conversation from a car to a plane.

October 11, under pressure and to curry favor with the US, Chile and Brazil broke diplomatic relations with the USSR.

October 14, Chuck Yeager made the first supersonic flight in the Bell XS-1.

October 20, the House Committee on Un-American Activities and Senator Joe McCarthy began an investigation into communists in Hollywood. This investigation and subsequent hearings would damage the reputations of hundreds of innocent writers and actors. One of those assisting the Committee in their nefarious work as an informer was actor Ronald Reagan, who began reporting on his fellow actors. Most were people Reagan disliked and who were not communists.

October 30, the US and 22 nations signed the General Agreement on Tariffs and Trade. GATT would serve to control and regulate international trade until it was replaced in 1995 with the World Trade Organization.

November 16, over 15,000 people demonstrated in Brussels against the lenient sentences given to most Nazis at the War Trials.

November 29, the UN General Assembly partitioned Palestine into Jewish and Arab sections with the British Mandate to end the following year. Violence between the Jews and Arabs began the next day as Jewish settlements were attacked. The British, who were supposed to maintain order, ignored their duties. Many British units were pro-Arab and began giving weapons and equipment to the Arab Palestinians. Other Arab nations also began to give aid and support to the Arab Palestinians. Over 4,000 people would be killed during this year in these conflicts.

December 6, the Everglades National Park was dedicated in Florida.

December 14, the National Association for Stock Car Racing, NASCAR, was founded in Daytona Beach, Florida.

December 17, a blizzard struck New York, covering parts of the state with twenty-seven inches of snow.

December 26, the entire Northeast was hit with heavy snowfalls and this time New York City was covered in about twenty-five inches of snow. That same day Los Angeles saw a record high for December at 84°F.

December 23, the transistor was invented at Bell Labs.

December 30, King Michael of Romania was forced to abdicate the throne as the communists came to power.

Although there were still housing and consumer shortages, Americans were starting to enjoy "peace time" life. Wages rose but so did prices. The average annual wage was $2,850. The price of a new house was $6,600. A new car averaged $1,300 and gas was 15 cents per gallon.

By 1947 there were 40 million radios but only about 44,000 televisions. Almost 70% of all televisions, about 30,000, were in the New York City area. However, in 1947 television began to spread outside of New York. That year Washington DC saw the opening of three television stations. KTLA the first station west of the Mississippi in Los Angeles began broadcasting. Stations in St. Louis, Cleveland, Baltimore, Detroit and another in Philadelphia all began in 1947. October 27, *You Bet Your Life* with Groucho Marx began on radio, but it would soon find its way to television. November 20, the news show, *Meet the Press*, began on NBC. On December 27, a new children's program, *The Howdy Doody Show*, also premiered on NBC. November 20, the first television was installed on a ship.

Radio was still the king of the airwaves and it was announced on October 20, that the radio rights for the Word Series sold for $475,000 for the next three series.

The House Committee on Un-American activities found ten people guilty of contempt of Congress for refusing to cooperate with the Committee's investigation into communism in Hollywood. The ten refused to answer questions about themselves or their Hollywood friends, saying it wasn't the government's business. "The Hollywood Ten" were given fines of $1,000 and a year in prison, which caused a world-wide protest. About this same time the Senate charged civil rights leader William L. Patterson with contempt of Congress after he refused to answer further committee questions about his "socialist leanings" after he was called "a Black son of a bitch" and was threatened with violence at his Senate hearing.

Despite the hearings Hollywood was enjoying its golden age. The top movies of 1947 were: *Unconquered* with Gary Cooper and Paulette Goodard; *The Bachelor and the Bobby Soxer* starring Cary Grant, Myrna Loy and Shirley Temple; *The Egg and I* with Fred MacMurray and Claudette Colbert; *Mother Wore Tights* starring Betty Grable; and *Life with Father* with William Powell, Irene Dunn, and Elizabeth Taylor. Another American classic Christmas movie, *Miracle on 34th Street* made its debut.

The top songs of 1947 were: Frances Craig's *Near You*, The Harmonicat's *Peg O' My Heart*, Ted Weem's *Heartaches*, Ray Noble and Buddy Clark's *Linda*, and Tex William's *Smoke, Smoke, Smoke that Cigarette*.

The bestselling books of 1947 included: nonfiction books like Arnold Toynbee's *Study of History*, Betty MacDonald's *The Egg and I* which enjoyed new success because of the popularity of the movie, and *The Information Please Almanac*. It was a particularly good year for fiction with such titles as: Russell Janney's *The Miracle of Bells*, Thomas B. Constain's *The Money Man*, John Steinbeck's *The Wayward Bus*, Sinclair Lewis' *Kingsblood Royal*, Frank Yerby *The Vixens*, Laura Hobson's *Gentelmen's Agreement*, which was also made into the best attended movie of the previous year.

Chapter 4. 1948: A Year of Independence, India, Israel and Others

January 1, the first color newsreel was filmed in Pasadena, California, featuring the Rose Parade.

Also on this date British railroads were nationalized and became British Railways.

January 4, Burma declared its independence from Britain.

January 12, the U.S. Supreme Court found that the University of Oklahoma could not refuse admission to Ada Louis Sipuel, a Black woman, who applied to the law school. It was the case that set the precedent for the Court's future landmark case *Brown vs. The Board of Education* which would make "separate but equal" illegal in the United States.

Also on January 12, Mahatma Gandhi began his fast to death to stop the violence in the partition of India. On January 30, Gandhi was assassinated. He was shot three times in the chest at close range by a Hindu radical and died a short time later.

January 16, thirty-five Jews who were members of the militant Haganah group were ambushed and killed in Palestine.

January 17, the Netherlands and Indonesia agreed to a cease fire.

January 22, Britain proposed a union between Britain, France, Belgium, Netherlands and Luxembourg to oppose the Soviet Union. A treaty is signed in March and this union was the beginnings of the North Atlantic Treaty Organization, NATO.

January 26, Truman officially signed the Executive Order allowing Blacks to serve in all units of the U.S. Armed Forces.

January 27, the first commercial tape recorder went on sale.

In February the Somerset Light Infantry left India. They were the last British regiment to leave.

February 1, the Federation of Malaysia was formed in the former British colony.

February 4, the British colony of Ceylon, now Sri Lanka, declared their independence.

February 22, an Arab bomb attack killed 50 Jews in Palestine. In retaliation Jewish militants bombed a train, killing 27 British soldiers.

February 24, communists seized the government of Czechoslovakia.

February 28, in Accra the capital of the Gold Coast (now Ghana), a British West African colony, the British military violently broke up a peaceful demonstration by indigenous ex-servicemen who had served in the British military during the war. The ex-servicemen were attempting to deliver a petition to the government to obtain wartime pay that the British government had promised them. Three demonstrators were killed, including the leader of the demonstration, and many others were wounded. The killings sparked an independence movement.

In February of 1948 newspapers and magazines showed that Americans were more interested in domestic affairs and family and their ads featured Valentine's Day Houseware Fairs advertising electric household appliances with the electric utility cartoon spokesman, Reddy Kilowatt. Other ads showed: Greyhound was selling winter vacation packages; the Three Stooges were on a live appearance tour; and the Lone Ranger was now on television. *Life Magazine* featured articles on "What Does It Take to Be a Model Mother?" and another story "I love Him, I Love Him" on why Princess Anne still loved the newly abdicated King of Romania. Most of the magazine was devoted to consumer products with ads for things like Ford cars, Maytag appliances, Vaseline Hair Tonic "to cure dry scalp and to look good" and Borden's Sweetened Condensed Canned Milk with their recipe for "Magic Custard Pie." There was also a story for the growing baby boom on how baby's teething pain could be ended with Dr. Hand's Teething Lotion.

Another *Life Magazine* article in February, "*The Campus Revolution*," was about the GI Bill of Rights and asked "Why not college?" The GI Bill enacted by Congress allowed for payments to veterans to get further education. It could be used to get a General Education Diploma for those without high school educations, to go to trade school, or to go to college. The GI Bill covered the educational costs of hundreds of thousands of young men and some young women from the end of WWII to the end of Vietnam. This education was responsible for lifting millions of Americans out of the working class and into the lower middleclass. It was the only time in history where Americans saw such significant upward mobility. It was also partly responsible for the nation's growing prosperity. Congress began limiting the program after Vietnam, when compulsory service ended.

March 8, in a precedent-setting case, *McCollum vs. the Board of Education*, the US Supreme Court ruled that tax-supported public schools could not promote or aid religious instruction. The Court noted at the time that over 2,000 public schools were involved in required religious instruction affecting over one and a half million students. The decision paved the way for other separation of church and state cases.

March 9, a provisional Independent Indonesian government was set up in Batavia.

March 11, the Jewish Agency in Jerusalem was bombed by Palestinians.

March 12, a Costa Rican civil war began as the government decided to nullify the democratic presidential elections. During the next forty-four days over 2,000 people died in the revolt. A democratically-elected government was eventually installed.

March 17, the Hells Angels motorcycle gang was founded in California. It included many ex-servicemen.

March 18, the Dutch agreed to independence for their Caribbean colony of Aruba.

March 20, a newly independent Singapore held its first elections.

April 1, physicists Ralph Asher Alpher and George Gamow published their paper on the Big Bang Theory, forever altering concepts on the creation of the universe.

April 3, the Marshall Plan was signed into law.

Also on this day there was a revolt on Jeju Island in South Korea. The Koreans began to protest the split of their country into two parts governed by the US and USSR. The South Korean Army was used to put down the revolt. An estimated 30,000 people were killed by US-supported South Korean soldiers.

April 7, the World Health Organization was formed by the United Nations.

April 9, Jorge Eliécer Gaitán Ayala, the Liberal Party presidential candidate in Colombia, was assassinated by rightwing gunmen. His death sparked ten years of violence in Colombia between the rightwing fascists and liberals. These times are known in Colombia as "La Violencia."

Also on April 9, the Jewish terrorist organization the Irgun headed by Menachem Begin attacked the Arab Village of Deir Yassin to break through the Arab blockade of Jerusalem. Over 120 men, women and children were killed. The majority of the Jewish community was appalled and sent a letter of apology to King Abdullah of Jordan, but it was refused. The incident inflamed Arab resolve to force the Jews from Palestine.

April 10, the Jews repelled an attack to wipe out the Jewish settlement of Mishmar HaEmek.

April 13, a Jewish medical convoy was ambushed and attacked by Arabs in Palestine. Seventy-eight doctors, nurses and patients were killed. The bodies were then burned by the Arabs. British soldiers prevented the Haganah, the Jewish defense forces, from coming to the convoy's aid until the massacre was over and most of the bodies were burned.

April 14, the US performed a nuclear test at Enwetak in the Pacific Ocean.

April 18, the Social Democrats defeated the communists in the Italian elections. The CIA and their resources played a significant role in the victory over the communists.

April 18, the International Court of Justice opened at The Hague in the Netherlands.

April 19, newly independent Burma joined the United Nations.

April 20, United Auto Workers Union President Walter Reuther, a socialist, survived an assassination attempt at his home in Detroit. Reuther had just turned to speak to his wife and the shotgun blast hit his arm rather than his chest. His arm was shattered and permanently disabled from the blast. The assassins were never found, leading to speculation that it was management or the government behind the assassination attempt.

April 30, the Organization of American States, OAS, was created.

In May 1948 Stalin ordered the deportation of the Baltic peoples to Siberia to resume. During the years 1941 to 1953 more than 200,000 "uncooperative" Lithuanians, Latvians and Estonians were deported to Siberia, with an estimated 75,000 of them sent to the Gulags.

May 1, North Korea declared itself the People's Democratic Republic of Korea.

Also on this day, Eddie Arcaro, riding Citation, won the Kentucky Derby. The horse and rider would go on to win the Triple Crown.

Also on May 1, US Senator Glenn Taylor of Idaho was arrested in Birmingham, Alabama, for entering a meeting through a door marked "For Negroes."

May 3, the Pulitzer Prize was awarded to both James Michener and Tennessee Williams.

May 4, Lawrence Olivier's film *Hamlet* premiered in London. It would later win Oscars for Best Picture and Best Actor.

May 5, the first squadron of jet aircraft was placed aboard a US aircraft carrier.

May 10, Egyptian forces attacked Jews in Palestine.

May 14, the British forces permanently withdrew from Palestine. David Ben-Gurion appeared at an afternoon press conference and declared, "We hereby proclaim the establishment of a Jewish state in Palestine, to be called Israel." It was described as the first Jewish homeland in over 2,000 years. It was a bold statement as the Arabs throughout the Mideast had threatened to "chase the Jews out of Palestine and throw them into the sea." Although they were under heavy Arab attack at the time, the Jews began to celebrate when they learned that the United States had formally recognized the State of Israel, lending it legitimacy in international eyes.

May 15, the armies of Iraq, Syria, Lebanon, Jordan and Egypt attacked the Jews in Palestine. These Arab armies were joined by Saudi Arabia several days later. The Israelis outperformed these better equipped and much larger armies. The United Nations negotiated a ceasefire in 1949, leaving the Israel with the substantial part of Palestine. Hundreds of thousands of Palestinian Arabs left Israel as a result of the ceasefire, leaving a majority of Jews in the new nation. A strong bond developed between Israel and the United States, but it was at a cost of permanently alienating the Muslims of the Mideast.

On May 17, the USSR also recognized Israel.

May 26, Daniel François Malan was elected as the Prime Minister of South Africa and the era of apartheid began. This dark period of repression would last until 1991.

May 30, a dike on the Columbia River broke, flooding and obliterating the entire city of Vanport, Oregon. Fifteen people died and tens of thousands were homeless from the flood.

June 8, John Rudder became the first Black Marine Corps officer.

June 11, the first monkeys are sent into space from White Sands, New Mexico.

June 18, the newly created Malayan Union declared a state of emergency due to a communist guerilla insurgency.

June 20, the Deutsche mark was introduced as the currency in West Germany.

The first international crisis of the cold war began on June 19, when the USSR closed the single road and rail line through East Germany to Berlin. The USSR wanted to block food and other goods to Berlin to force their annexation to communist East Germany. On June 26, the US formally denounced the USSR blockade of Berlin. June 28, the US and Britain began the Berlin Airlift to bring food and supplies to the blockaded city by air. The blockade and the airlift would last until May of 1949. The blockade became an embarrassment to the Soviets as the Americans and British brought in more food and supplies to Berlin than had been transported by truck and rail before the Soviet blockade.

After the blockade ended, two German states were created. West German areas, controlled by the Americans and British, became the Federal Republic of Germany (also known as West Germany) and the areas controlled by the USSR became the German Democratic Republic (or East Germany). Berlin, located in East Germany, was split into two parts, West controlled by the US and Britain and the East controlled by the USSR.

June 24, Governor Thomas E. Dewey was nominated to be the presidential candidate of the Republican Party. Conventional wisdom held that Dewey would easily defeat President Truman in November.

June 28, *Oliver Twist*, a play based on the Charles Dickens' novel, premiered in London. The play was initially banned in the US because of its anti-Semitism.

July 5, Britain began the National Health Service Act to provide universal health care.

July 7, six women reservists were commissioned as the first women in the regular US Navy.

July 8, the 500th anniversary of the Russian Orthodox Church was celebrated in Moscow and elsewhere.

July 9, the great Negro League baseball legend, Satchel Page, at forty-two, made his pitching debut in Major League Baseball for the Cleveland Indians.

July 11, Jerusalem was bombed by Arabs.

July 14, Israel bombed Cairo.

July 15, Harry Truman was nominated by the Democrats for president, although many in his own party believed he would lose to Dewey in November. July 23, the Progressives nominated former Vice president Henry Wallace for president. This was also seen as a victory for Dewey as it was speculated that the Democratic vote would be split. Senator Strom Thurmond also ran on the Dixiecrat segregationist ticket which most thought would rob Truman of the Southern vote. Most newspapers predicted an easy Dewey victory in November.

July 17, the Republic of Korea was declared by a constitutional proclamation in the US-occupied southern part of the Korean peninsula. It would become known as South Korea. On July 24, the South Korean government was established under the despot President Syngman Rhee, who ruled with an iron fist until 1960. He was the choice of the Americans.

July 20, the President of the Communist Party USA and other Party members were arrested for being communists. The government ignored their constitutional rights by claiming that being communist was the same as advocating the violent overthrow of the government.

Also on July 20, President Truman declared a military draft for young men over eighteen years of age. The draft lasted until the end of the Vietnam War.

July 26, President Truman by Executive Order formally ended all racial discrimination in the US Armed Forces. It was a mixed blessing, as Black Americans were then subjected to the draft and were drafted in larger percentages than Whites.

July 31, Elizabeth Bentley appeared before the House Committee on Un-American Activities, HUAC, and implicated Whittaker Chambers. It was the beginning of the premier anti-communist event in the McCarthy witch hunt era. Chambers was a bright but disturbed man. He was later labeled a psychopath. He was born in Brooklyn, New York. His mother and father split up during his childhood. His mother cared for his mentally ill grandmother at their home during his childhood and his brother committed suicide in his teens. After high school he worked various jobs before enrolling at Williams College in 1920. A short time later he transferred to Columbia University, where he was well thought of for his writing and where many thought he would become a poet or novelist. In his sophomore year he wrote a play called *A Play for Puppets*, which was deemed blasphemous by the Columbia faculty, students, and even the New York press. Disillusioned, Chambers quit Columbia and joined the Communist Party in 1925, becoming an editor and writer of their publications. In the early 1930s he met and married Esther Shemitz, an artist and a leftwing pacifist. They had two children. He claimed to have become a Soviet spy in the 1930s, although much of what Chambers has claimed has since been disproven.

In the 1940s Chambers wrote to J. Edgar Hoover, claiming that he was a Soviet spy and that he had many homosexual affairs in the 1930s with important government officials as a spy. Chambers later told the FBI that he gave up homosexuality in 1938 when he left the Communist Party and became a Christian anti-communist. He wanted to cooperate with Hoover and the FBI to fight communism. He claimed that about a dozen of Roosevelt's New Deal appointees were communists, including Alger Hiss, an attorney who worked for the State Department. The FBI never wholly believed Chambers and didn't trust or believe him, but in 1948, when McCarthy began his anti-communist crusade, he eagerly used these dubious stories as testimony against others.

August 3, 1948 Chambers was asked by HUAC to testify against Alger Hiss. Chambers named Hiss as a member of the Communist Party. However in previous testimony he had not made any accusations of espionage against Hiss, leading many to suspect McCarthy had pushed him into to this accusation. When Hiss first testified before HUAC, he denied that he knew anyone by the name of Whittaker Chambers; later he changed his testimony before the committee. Upon seeing him in person, he said that he had known Chambers under the name "George Crosley." Hiss denied being a communist. The August 25, the HUAC Hiss hearing was televised and a young Congressman Richard Nixon, looking to make a name for himself and boost his US Senate run in California, took the most aggressive role in questioning Hiss. Despite the accusations from Chambers, the committee was forced to dismiss Hiss as Chambers had presented no evidence that Hiss was a communist.

At the encouragement of J. Edgar Hoover, Chambers and HUAC committee member Richard Nixon continued to accuse Hiss as a spy, although until October 1948 Chambers had repeatedly stated to the committee that Hiss had not engaged in any espionage. In a sudden reversal, Chambers gave the FBI and Nixon some notes in Hiss' handwriting and some microfilm of State Department memos from the 1930s, and Chambers then claimed that he and Hiss had been involved in espionage. He said he never passed these notes and documents to the Soviets but he claimed he hid these microfilmed documents in a pumpkin at his farm. These became known as the "Pumpkin Papers." On December 8, Nixon was rewarded for his aggressiveness in the Committee when Hoover to allowed him to present the Pumpkin Papers to the press at a news conference.

The supposed "important" microfilmed documents that had been allegedly photographed by Hiss were many years later revealed to be mostly blank with a few non-classified memos about things like life rafts and fire extinguishers. Only two documents were used at trial and these were documents referring to US and German relations in the 1930s.

Hiss and Chambers were never charged with espionage because the Committee said that the statute of limitations had expired. However, the real reason was that the evidence would have never stood up in a trial. The FBI went after Hiss and he was charged and tried for perjury. In his first trial in 1949 the jury was deadlocked and couldn't reach a decision. A second trial found Hiss guilty of two counts of perjury even though Chambers, the only witness, admitted that he had committed perjury in his testimony against Hiss and a psychiatrist testified for the defense that Chambers had a psychopathic personality and was also a pathological liar. Chambers was never charged with any crime although he admitted to both perjury and espionage in exchange for not being charged.

Chambers became the darling of the rightwing. He later became a writer for *Time*, *Look* and *Life* magazines. In 1952 he wrote a book, *Witness*, an autobiography which promoted anti-communism and proclaimed the horrors of the Soviet Union. *Witness* is still read and recommended among rightwing Americans. Chambers also worked as an editor and writer at William F. Buckley's conservative publication *National Review*. Chambers died in 1961. In 1984 President Ronald Reagan awarded Chambers the

Presidential Medal of Freedom posthumously for his role in "the century's epic struggle between freedom and totalitarianism," although Chambers was a self-confessed traitor and former communist. In 2001, members of the George W. Bush Administration held a private ceremony to commemorate the hundredth birthday of Whittaker Chambers and invited William F. Buckley Jr. as one of the speakers.

It was the Hiss trial that made McCarthy's false claims of communists in the government, the military and Hollywood believable to many. It was the Hiss trial and Hoover's support that helped Richard Nixon win a Senate seat and to go on to become Eisenhower's Vice President.

August 23, the World Council of Churches was formed.

September 9, Kim Il Sung was named the Prime Minister of the Democratic People's Republic of Korea, starting his family's totalitarian dynasty in North Korea that still rules as of this writing.

September 11, Muhammad Ali Jinnah, the founder of Pakistan, died. The following day, while Pakistan was in a state of shock, India invaded the State of Hyderabad and annexed it to India.

September 17, Swedish diplomat Folke Bernadotte, who had been chosen by the UN Security Council as the mediator to end the Arab–Israeli conflict, was assassinated in Jerusalem by the Jewish radical group the Stern Gang. One of the Stern Gang planners of this assassination was the future Prime Minister of Israel, Yitzhak Shamir. As part of his negotiations Bernadotte had proposed that Jerusalem be given to the Arabs. Ralph Bunche, the son of a Detroit barber and one of the first Black American diplomats, was confirmed as the acting mediator for the UN the following day. He received the Nobel Peace Prize for this work in 1950.

September 18, an uprising began in the Dutch East Indies.

September 24, the Honda Motor Company was founded in Japan.

October 1, the California Supreme Court voided a state statute forbidding inter-racial marriage.

October 3, uranium was discovered in the Belgian Congo, making the Western nations very interested in the colony's future.

October 6, the Ashgabat earthquake in Turkmenistan, USSR, killed about 110,000 people.

Also on October 6, paleontologist Mary Leakey found the first partial skull of *Proconsul africanus*, an ancestor to both apes and humans in Kenya. The find began to fill in the human evolutionary tree.

October 16, Russian Jews demonstrated in Moscow to honor Israeli Ambassador Golda Meir.

October 21, the United Nations rejected the USSR proposal to destroy all nuclear weapons.

October 22, while there was talk of a ceasefire, the Egyptian navy's flagship, the *King Farouk*, was sunk by Israel.

October 27, a temperature inversion caused heavy smog in Donora, Pennsylvania. By the time rain dissipated the smog on October 31, 20 people had died and over 7,000 were ill. Most of the pollution came from US Steel's Zinc Plant. Lawsuits were filed against US Steel, which never acknowledged responsibility for the incident, calling it "an act of God." A settlement was reached in 1951 for a sum of $235,000 to 80 complainants who barely recouped their legal costs. The mill closed in 1966.

October 29, the Arab village of Safsaf was taken by Israeli forces. The Israelis killed between 50 and 70 men who had surrendered.

November 1, the Chinese Red Army made major gains against Chiang Kai-shek. They took the city of Mukden in Manchuria. The Chinese Civil War had been ongoing since 1927 between the communists and the nationalist factions. The large American missionary community in China was a strong supporter of Chiang Kai-shek. Chiang had converted to Christianity and sang the praises of capitalism in order to receive US support. Chiang was never more than a corrupt warlord who lacked the support of the Chinese masses.

The missionaries in China cooperated with Chiang and the American rightwing to form what became known as the "China Lobby," a powerful group in US government and private business. The China Lobby included such notables as publisher Henry Luce and his wife Congresswoman and later Ambassador Clare Boothe Luce, Senator William Knowland of California, Senator Prescott Bush of Connecticut, Senator Joe McCarthy of Wisconsin, Senator Richard Nixon of California, and Congressman Walter Judd of Minnesota. The China Lobby relentlessly campaigned for arms, money and military support for Chiang in his attempt to unite China under his corrupt Nationalist banner.

During this civil war there was a ceasefire of sorts between the communists and nationalists when the Japanese invaded in 1937 and they each began independently fighting the Japanese Army. During WWII both Mao Zedong and Chiang Kai-shek coordinated their efforts with General "Vinegar Joe" Stilwell, the US commander in China. Toward the end of the war General Stilwell, the most knowledgeable American about China, who knew both Mao and Chiang, began to urge that the US support Mao and his Red Army over Chiang. Most of the US State Department personnel in China also endorsed Stilwell's recommendation. Stilwell reasoned that Chiang was corrupt and incompetent and stated that Mao had the support of the majority of the Chinese people. He stated that Mao would eventually win despite any US wishes. The General felt that Mao's communist China would serve as an ally and bulwark against Soviet expansion in Asia, as the USSR and China were rivals. In retrospect had Washington taken General Stilwell's advice, the US probably would not have gone to war in Korea and Vietnam.

However, because of his advice Chiang and the China Lobby eventually pressured the President to relieve General Stilwell of his command in 1944. Upon his return to the United States, Stilwell was ordered not to talk about China issues with the press. Stilwell died during surgery in 1946. In 1948 the general's prediction came true as the successive Chinese Red Army victories pushed Chiang and his Nationalist Army out of the Chinese mainland.

November 2, in a surprising upset, President Truman defeated Governor Thomas Dewey for president. Newspapers around the country had already printed headlines of Dewey's victory. In addition to former Vice President Henry Wallace running as a Progressive, Senator Strom Thurmond from South Carolina ran as a Dixiecrat against Truman and against his policies desegregating the US Armed Forces. Truman won with just over 24 million votes to Dewey's just under 22 million. Thurmond took four Southern states and had over a million votes. Wallace carried no states, but also had over a million votes.

November 4, the poet T.S. Eliot won the Nobel Prize for literature.

November 12, the Japanese War Crimes Tribunal sentenced former Japanese Premier Hideki Tojo to death.

November 24, a Venezuelan military junta took over the government. Venezuela had ten years of dictatorship after the junta.

December 3, the first US Army female officer not in the medical corps was commissioned.

December 12, during the Malayan communist insurgency the British Scots Guards killed twenty-four unarmed civilians and set fire to a village that was suspected of supporting communists.

Also on December 12, two brothers, Mac and Joe McDonald, revamped and opened their hamburger stand on E Street in San Bernardino, California. The new restaurant, complete with arches on top of the building, was called McDonald's.

December 28, a member of the Muslim Brotherhood, assassinated Egyptian Prime Minister Mahmud Fahmi Nokrashi.

December 29, the US announced that it had begun a study to put a satellite into Earth orbit.

In 1948 the housing shortage was still an issue in the US and the Congress enacted federal rent controls. A new house cost $7,700 but the average house (including the much larger market of existing houses) still sold at $1,751. Much of the new housing consisted of pre-fabricated structures built in the new suburbs. In 1948 inflation hit 7.74%. The average yearly wage was $2,950. The average price of a new car was $1,250 with gasoline selling at 16 cents per gallon. Popcorn became the favorite snack food and Scrabble was introduced and became the new popular board game. In 1948, polio was becoming an increasing health concern, particularly for the nation's baby boom. Polio was predominantly a childhood disease and it wreaked havoc every summer.

In 1948 television was the big news in America. Over thirty-one new television stations began in 1948, most of these in the South, Midwest and West. The ABC network expanded from radio to television and joined the NBC, CBS, and the DuMont television networks and they all began to provide expanded regular network programming. In January *Midwestern Hayride* in Cincinnati became the first country music television show. *Ted Mack's Original Amateur Hour* also premiered in January on the DuMont network. The first science show, *The Nature of Things*, debuted in prime time on NBC. In March the first live musical performance, by Eugene Ormandy, was aired on CBS. Also in March the game show *Stop the Music* premiered on the new ABC television network. In June, Ed Sullivan's *Toast of the Town* aired on CBS. In July the first Black television host, Bob Howard, appeared on CBS. Also in July professional wrestling became a staple of television and remained so through the 1960s when it seemed every town had their "World Champion." In August *Candid Camera* began on ABC. September saw Milton Berle began his television career on *The Texaco Star Theater*. In October NFL Football became the first regularly scheduled sports program on weekend television, and by the 1960s television propelled professional football past baseball to become the nation's favorite sport. In November *Hopalong Cassidy* and *Kukla, Fran and Ollie* made their television debuts.

The top songs of 1948 included *Mañana* by Peggy Lee, *Ballerina* by Vaughn Monroe, *I'm Looking Over a Four Leaf Clover* by Art Mooney, *Twelfth Street Rag* by Pee Wee Hunt, *Buttons and Bows* by Dinah Shore, *Nature Boy* by Nat King Cole, and *The Woody Woodpecker Song* by Kay Kyser. In June Columbia records introduced the Long Playing record (LP) at thirty-three and a third RPMs.

In addition to *Hamlet*, the movies in 1948 featured two Humphrey Bogart classics, *Treasure of the Sierra Madre* and *Key Largo*. The year also featured: *Red River* with John Wayne, *The Three Musketeers* with Gene Kelly and Lana Turner, *Homecoming* with Clark Gable and Lana Turner, *Johnny Belinda* with Jane Wyman and Lew Ayres, and *Easter Parade* with Fred Astaire and Judy Garland.

The top books of 1948 included: *Cheaper by the Dozen* by Frank Gilbreth Jr., *Cry, the Beloved Country* by Alan Paton, *Other Voices, Other Rooms* by Truman Capote, *The Ides of March* by Thornton Wilder, *Kon-Tiki* by Thor Heyerdahl, *The Naked and the Dead* by Norman Mailer, and *Sexual Behavior in the Human Male* by Alfred Kinsey.

Chapter 5. 1949: The People's Republic Won the Civil War in China and the USSR Developed the Bomb.

January 2, Louis Muñoz Marin became the first elected governor of Puerto Rico. During this time the first serious conversations were held about the territory of Puerto Rico becoming a state. It wasn't until 2012 that residents of the territory voted for statehood, which has still not been enacted by Congress.

January 5, the Netherlands ordered a ceasefire in Sumatra.

January 7, the first photograph of a gene was made at the University of Southern California.

January 10, RCA announced the 45 RPM record, and the "single" record became popular, particularly among older children — who were now commonly called "teenagers."

January 11, the first snowfall in Los Angeles was recorded.

January 14, racial unrest erupted in Durban, South Africa, as the Black Zulus rioted against Indians. The riots resulted in the massacre of 142 Indians. Another 1,087 people were injured and 58 shops, 247 homes and one factory were destroyed.

January 15, Mao and the Red Army captured Tientsin, the fourth largest city in China and an important industrial center.

January 19, Cuba recognized Israel.

January 20, in a bizarre gesture and inexplicably weird concern about her safety, J. Edgar Hoover gave the child actress Shirley Temple a concealed weapon, a tear gas fountain pen.

January 21, President Harry Truman's presidential inauguration was the first to be televised.

January 28, the UN Security Council condemned the Dutch violence in Indonesia.

January 29, Britain, Belgium, Luxemburg, the Netherlands, New Zealand, and Switzerland recognized Israel.

January 31, the first Volkswagen Beetle, the car named and championed by Adolf Hitler as an affordable car for regular folks, was imported into the US for the first time. By 1970, US buyers would purchase 570,000 of these vehicles.

February 4, an assassination attempt on the US- and British-supported Shah of Persia (now Iran) failed.

February 8, Hungarian Cardinal József Mindszenty was sentenced to life imprisonment by the communist government in Budapest. Mindszenty had opposed the Nazis during WWII and also opposed the communists coming to power. His trial and life sentence were condemned by the United Nations. He served eight years and was freed from prison during the Hungarian uprising in 1956. He was granted political asylum in the US Embassy in Budapest until 1971, when he was allowed to leave and live in exile in Vienna, Austria. He died there in 1975.

February 12, in a bizarre repeat of earlier US history, a panic riot occurred in Quito, Ecuador, when H.G. Wells' *War of the Worlds* aired on the radio. Like the American radio show in 1938, the listeners thought space aliens were actually invading.

February 19, fearing communist violence, India began massive arrests of communists.

February 24, Israel and Egypt signed an armistice agreement to end their conflict.

February 26, the Lucky Lady II, a USAF B-50 Superfortress bomber, began the first non-stop flight around the world from Fort Worth, Texas. On March 2, it returned successfully after a 94-hour flight covering 23,452 miles. America was demonstrating her military reach to the world.

March 4, the UN Security Council recommended Israel's membership to the United Nations.

March 29, Turkey became the first Muslim country to recognize Israel.

March 31, Newfoundland ceased to be a British colony and joined Canada as the tenth province.

April 3, Jordan signed an armistice agreement with Israel.

April 4, the North Atlantic Treaty Organization, NATO, agreement was signed in Washington, DC.

April 14, the Nuremberg Trials concluded.

April 18, the Republic of Ireland withdrew from the British Commonwealth.

April 23, Mao's People's Liberation Army (PLA) captured Nanking, the southern Chinese capital, from Chiang Kai-shek's "Nationalists."

April 24, Arthur Miller's play, *Death of a Salesman*, won the Tony Award. On May 2, Miller was also awarded the Pulitzer Prize for his play.

April 28, former Philippine First Lady Aurora Quezon was assassinated while en route to dedicate a hospital in memory of her late husband. Her entourage was attacked by 100 to 200 guerillas. Her daughter, son-in-law and nine others were also killed. The communists were accused, but they denied the killings. However the Catholic Church and the CIA under

General Ed Lansdale used the killings to unite the country in a war against the communists.

Legislative elections were held in Bolivia on May 1, 1949, and the conservative *Republican Union Party, Partido Union Republicana Socialista*, PURS, won 28 out of 56 seats in the Chamber of Deputies. The *National Revolutionary Movement, Movimiento Nacionalista Revolucionario*, a leftist group supporting workers and Indian rights, MNR, won 9 seats in the Chamber of Deputies. Ten individuals were killed in election-related violence. PURS President Enrique Hertzog temporarily turned over power to Vice-President Mamerto Urriolagoita on May 7, 1949. Acting President Mamerto Urriolagoita then declared a state of emergency and ordered the detention and exile of more than 200 labor leaders and MNR supporters on May 27, 1949.

May 5, the Council of Europe was formed. It was dedicated to democracy and human rights. Although it is a separate organization, the Council gave impetus for the European Union. No nation has ever been a member of the European Union without first becoming a member of the Council.

May 11, by a vote of 37 to 12, Israel was admitted as the 59th member of the United Nations.

Also on this date Siam changed its name to Thailand.

May 12, the US received the first woman ambassador from another country, Vijaya Lakshmi Pandit, from India.

May 14, President Truman signed a bill establishing a rocket launch center at Cape Canaveral, Florida. Also on that day the British produced their first jet bomber.

May 23, the Federal Republic of Germany was formally declared in West Germany.

May 25, Mao's Red Army swept across China and captured Shanghai.

May 30, the constitution of the German Democratic Republic in East Germany was formally approved.

Also on this day the new independent Republic of Suriname, formerly Dutch Guyana, a Dutch colony in South America, held their first elections.

June 1, the British gave independence to Cyrenaica (now the eastern part of Libya), a former Italian colony. They would remain an independent nation until joining Libya at the end of 1951.

June 2, Transjordan was officially named Jordan.

June 3, Wesley Anthony Brown became the first Black to graduate from the US Naval Academy.

June 9, Georgia Neese Clark became the first woman to be US Treasurer.

June 14, the French Colonial State of Vietnam was formed with Bao Dai named as Emperor.

June 20, President Truman formally signed the act creating the Central Intelligence Agency, CIA. He would later declare that it was his single greatest mistake as president.

June 23, the first woman graduated from Harvard Medical School, twelfth in her class.

June 29, the last US WWII combat troops left Korea, only to return with the outbreak of the Korean War.

Also on this day South Africa began administering apartheid by banning all mixed-race marriages.

June 30, the Dutch troops left Djakarta as the Netherlands gave up their colony in what was to become Indonesia.

June 6, a freakish weather phenomenon called a heat burst raised the temperature on the coast of Portugal from 100 degrees to 158 degrees Fahrenheit for two minutes.

July 10, the invention of the first rectangular television tube was announced. Prior to this they were round.

July 13, the Catholic Church formally declared war on communism. Pope Pius excommunicated all Catholic communists.

July 14, the USSR tested their first atomic bomb.

July 15, two Czech tennis stars, Jaroslav Drobny and Vladimir Cernik, defected to the United States.

June 19, Laos was created and became a part of the French Union colonies in Southeast Asia.

July 20, Israel's war for statehood against the Arabs ended.

July 29, the Soviets re-opened the road and rail line into Berlin and the Berlin Airlift was ended.

June 29, BBC radio began broadcasting.

June 30, the British warship the *Amethyst* escaped from Mao's Red Army down the Yangtze River in China.

July 31, lightning struck a baseball field in Florida, killing the shortstop and third baseman. Organized baseball began the practice of calling weather delays to prevent further fatalities.

August 3, the new Republic of Indonesia declared a ceasefire with the Netherlands.

August 4, the two professional basketball leagues, the Basketball Association of America and the National Basketball League, merged to form the modern National Basketball Association, NBA.

August 5, a large earthquake struck Quito, Ecuador, killing over 6,000 people.

August 8, Bhutan became an independent monarchy.

August 10, the US Department of Defense formally began operations.

August 14, a military coup took over the government in Syria.

August 28, a concert to raise funds for the Civil Rights Congress in Peekskill, New York, broke out into riots. Paul Robeson, a Black singer and actor and well known civil rights advocate and socialist who was to perform there, had been attacked in the media days before the event. Anti-communist and pro-segregation groups including the American Legion and the Ku Klux Klan arrived before the concert, protesting and chanting, yelling "dirty niggers, dirty commies, and dirty kikes." Then they attacked with baseball bats and rocks. They burned a large cross and hung Robeson in effigy.

Robison's driver, a local woman, noticed the crowd as she approached the concert venue and turned her car around despite Robeson's protests to go on. Her actions likely saved his and her lives. The police arrived late and did little to intervene. They later claimed it was outside their jurisdiction, and the state police claimed they were never called. Thirteen people were seriously injured. The commander of the American Legion said to the press the next day, "Our objective was to prevent the Paul Robeson concert and I think our objective was reached."

September 2, a fire in Chungking, China, killed an estimated 7,000 people.

September 6, in Camden, New Jersey, Howard Unrhu threatened to hit his mother with a wrench and she fled to a friend's house. He then killed thirteen neighbors including three children during a twelve-minute walk through his neighborhood. After that, he barricaded himself in his house and had a gun battle with the police for an hour. He was shot in the leg and surrendered. He gave only one nonsensical reason for these killings. He told the police that he thought the Hollywood actress Barbara Stanwyck was one of his neighbors.

September 17, NATO met officially for the first time.

September 23, President Truman announced that the US had proof that the USSR had detonated a nuclear weapon. The fear of nuclear war dominated the rest of the Cold War era.

On October 1, Mao Zedong officially proclaimed the People's Republic of China. On that same day Chiang Kai-shek formed the Republic of China on the Island of Formosa (Taiwan).

October 2, the USSR recognized the People's Republic of China.

October 4, the UN headquarters in New York City was dedicated.

October 14, fourteen Communist Party USA members were convicted of sedition. The CPUSA argued they were an American organization that sought to convert the US to socialism by free elections and were therefore protected by the First Amendment. However, the court found them guilty, saying that being communist was tantamount to advocating the violent overthrow of the US government. The Supreme Court later reversed this decision.

October 14, the Red Army captured Canton.

October 15, the Reverend Billy Graham began his ministry.

October 26, President Truman raised the minimum wage from forty cents to seventy-five cents.

November 2, the Netherlands recognized independent Indonesia.

November 6, the Greek Civil War ended. The war had broken out in the winter of 1943–44, after the collapse of the fascist government. The socialists and the democrats formed a coalition the National Liberation Front known as EAM. It would eventually have a fighting force known as the Greek Democratic Army, DSE. A rightwing military group comprised of former members of the fascist government formed the National Republican Greek League known as EDES. The DSE and the EDES began fighting for control of Greece. Britain supported the rightwing EDES, but it appeared that the more popular DSE would win the conflict in 1946. Fearing this win by the socialist democratic alliance, Britain called upon the US for assistance.

The US military and CIA went to work under the Truman Doctrine, shoring up the fascist EDES and forcing a victory over the DSE by late summer of 1949; the conflict ended in November. Over 80,000 Greeks lost their lives and 700,000 were left homeless. After the US-supported EDES won the war, they outlawed the communists and socialists. Many DSE were arrested and thousands fled to exile in Yugoslavia.

Greece remained under a fascist government for many years. In 1967, the US supported another military coup and Greece came under another military dictatorship until 1974. The two US interventions, especially the one in 1967, caused many Greeks to strongly dislike America and in particular the CIA.

November 7, King Farouk disbanded the Egyptian Parliament.

November 20, with the rapid migration of Jews to Israel after the declaration of statehood, the new country reached a population of over a million.

November 30, the Red Army captured Chungking.

December 7, Chiang was forced to flee to Formosa (Taiwan).

December 13, Israel transferred its capital to Jerusalem.

December 16, Sukarno became President of Indonesia.

Also on this date, the Saab the motor car company was founded in Sweden.

December 17, Burma recognized the People's Republic of China.

December 30, India recognized the People's Republic of China.

December 31, eighteen nations recognized Indonesia.

After the Great Depression and war time rationing, 1949 became a big consumer year as US production was now mostly dedicated to consumer products. Over 6,500,000 new cars were sold at an average price of $1,420. Gasoline was just 17 cents per gallon. The average wage was just under $2,950 per year and the economy roared, with virtually no inflation. The average cost of a new home was $7,450 as the suburbs grew rapidly. The De Havilland Comet, the first commercial passenger jet aircraft, made its first test flight in July.

1949 was another good year for television as forty-seven new stations began broadcasting and stations now covered most of the country. Included in the forty-seven new stations was the first UHF (ultra high frequency) station in Bridgeport, Connecticut. By August of 1949 there were two million television sets in use. Madison Avenue began paying close attention to television as the *Howdy Doody Show* sold over eleven million dollars in merchandise to children in 1949. RCA began the effort to develop a system to broadcast television in color.

In January the *Colgate Theater* premiered on NBC, *Arthur Godfrey and Friends* on CBS, and the first day time soap opera, *These are My Children*, debuted on NBC. In July *Dragnet* premiered on radio but as it became popular it switched to television two years later. Other television shows that debuted in 1949 were: *Cavalcade of Stars*, and *Captain Video* on the DuMont network, and *The Lone Ranger* on ABC, and *One Man's Family* on NBC. *The Goldbergs*, the first television sitcom premiered on CBS in January and ran until 1956. It was a show about the struggles of a New York Jewish-American family. Gertrude Berg who wrote and starred in the show won an Emmy in 1951.

On January 25, 1949 the first television Emmy Awards were held. *Pantomime Quiz* won for the most popular television show and Shirley

Dinsdale, a ventriloquist from KTLA in Los Angeles, won for best television personality.

1949 was also a good year for movies. Television had not yet begun to erode the movie theater market to any significant degree. The top movies included: *White Heat* with James Cagney, *All the King's Men* with Broderick Crawford, *The Heiress* with Olivia de Havilland, *Twelve O' Clock High* with Gregory Peck, *Adam's Rib* with Spencer Tracy and Katherine Hepburn, *I was a Male War Bride* with Gregory Peck, and *She Wore a Yellow Ribbon* with John Wayne. *All the Kings Men*, Broderick Crawford and Olivia de Havilland later won Oscars.

The top songs of 1949 included multiple hits by the same artist including three hits by Vaughn Monroe: *Riders in the Sky, Someday,* and *Red Roses for a Blue Lady.* Perry Como had three hits with: *Some Enchanted Evening, Forever and Ever,* and with the Fontaine Sisters *'A' You're Adorable.* Gordon Jenkins also had three hits: *Again, Don't Cry Joe,* and *I Don't See Me in Your Eyes Anymore.* Frankie Lane had a couple big hits with: *That Lucky Old Sun* and *Mule Train.*

The books of 1949 featured George Orwell's *1984,* Graham Green's *The Third Man,* Simone de Beauvoir's *The Second Sex,* John Gunther's *Death Be Not Proud,* Arthur Miller's *Death of A Salesman,* and one of the first books to raise environmental awareness, Aldo Leopold's *Sand County Almanac.* For children, Dr. Seuss' *Bartholomew and the Oobleck* was a hit. Another notorious book made its mark, *The Road Ahead, America's Creeping Revolution* by John T. Flynn. The book argued that a communist revolution in America was coming soon. Over a half million copies were printed and became a classic of the American rightwing. It greatly fanned the flames of America's paranoia and xenophobia during the Cold War.

CHAPTER 6. 1950: CREDIT CARDS, KOREAN WAR, McCARTHYISM, AND DUCK AND COVER

On January 1, 1950, Ho Chi Minh began his war for Vietnamese independence against the French. As a Vietnamese commander, he had been an American ally in WWII, recovering many downed American pilots before the Japanese could find them. He initially sought US assistance in his efforts for an independent Vietnam but on February 7, both the US and Britain recognized Bao Dai, the French puppet, as the head of Vietnam.

January 6, Britain recognized the government of The People's Republic of China. The US reacted in a fit of pique and, on January 14, recalled all consular officials from China.

January 12, the USSR reinstated the death penalty for espionage and treason.

January 15, over 4,000 attended the National Civil Rights Conference in Washington, DC.

January 16, Belgium, Luxemburg, and the Netherlands recognized Israel.

January 17, the "Crime of the Century" was committed when eleven men committed the largest robbery in US history at that time. A Brinks Security Truck in Boston was robbed of over two and a half million dollars in cash, checks and money orders. All eleven were eventually caught by the FBI.

January 26, India became a republic.

January 31, President Truman announced that the US had developed the much more powerful hydrogen bomb.

February 1, the USSR demanded that Emperor Hirohito of Japan be tried for war crimes. Defeated Japan came under American authority, and the US declined, honoring its surrender agreement with Japan.

February 3, Klaus Fuchs, a German Nazi scientist who was brought to the US during Operation Paperclip, was convicted of spying for the USSR. Fuchs was a key nuclear physicist in the development of both the atomic and hydrogen bombs. He was sentenced to fourteen years in prison, but was released after nine years. He emigrated to the German Democratic Republic in East Germany.

February 7, Joe McCarthy falsely asserted that there were many communist spies in the US State Department.

February 12, Albert Einstein warned against the dangers of the hydrogen bomb.

Also on February 12, Joe McCarthy falsely claimed to have a list of 205 communist employees in the US government. He was shown on television waving pages of paper supposedly containing these names. It was later discovered the pages were actually blank.

February 14, the USSR and China signed a peace treaty.

March 12, Pope Pius XII issued an encyclical condemning atheism. Americans and Catholics were encouraged to view atheism and communism as one and the same thing.

March 13, General Motors announced record sales of 656 million dollars.

March 14, the FBI began its "10 Most Wanted Fugitives" list.

March 27, the Netherlands recognized the People's Republic of China.

April 5, a communist government espionage trial against Catholic bishops and priests began in Prague, Czechoslovakia.

April 6, John Foster Dulles became an advisor to Secretary of State Dean Acheson.

April 11, a US bomber was shot down by the Soviets over Latvia, raising Cold War tensions.

April 24, President Truman, in response to McCarthy's statements, assured America that there were no communists spies in the US government.

Also on this day Israel formally annexed the West Bank, which was Palestinian territory located on the west bank of the Jordan River.

April 27, South Africa passed the Group Areas Act to physically separate and segregate the races.

May 1, the Mayor of Brussels banned the May Day parade for fear of communist uprisings.

May 8, Chiang Kai-shek asked the US for more advanced weapons to defend Formosa (Taiwan).

May 13, Diners Club issued the first credit cards and America began its love affair with buying on credit.

May 21, Ho Chi Minh's troops attacked the French in Cambodia.

June 5, the US Supreme Court ruled against separate but equal in *Sweatt v. Painter*, allowing Marion Sweatt to attend law school at the Whites-only University of Texas.

June 17, the first successful organ transplant, a kidney, was accomplished in Chicago.

Also on this day Egypt, Syria, Saudi Arabia, and Lebanon signed a security pact against Israel.

June 23, the Swiss Parliament refused to allow women the right to vote.

June 25, the Israeli airlines, El Al, began service.

Also on this date, upon strong advice from the military and the CIA, President Truman sent 35 senior US military advisors to aid the French in Vietnam.

Also on June 25, Kim Il Sung and his North Korean Army invaded South Korea, beginning the Korean War. On June 27, the North Koreans were at the edge of Seoul. On the urging of the US the UN condemned the North Korean attack and asked UN members to send assistance to South Korea. President Truman responded by ordering the US Air Force and Navy into the conflict. South Africa also sent ground troops. On June 28, the communists captured Seoul. General MacArthur, the Commander of US forces in Asia toured the Korean battle front and asked President Truman for US combat ground forces. June 1, the US immediately airlifted 407 combat ground troops to Korea. On June 3, they entered combat. July 8, General MacArthur was named the head of the UN forces in Korea. Although there were troops from other nations and it was officially a "UN police action," the war quickly became an American war.

In an overreaction to the communist invasion, Syngman Rhee ordered his army and special police to kill all the leftists and other government dissidents in South Korea. It was called the "Summer of Terror" and over 100,000 people were detained and killed. His troops were so busy finding and killing South Korean dissidents that the fight with North Korea became a secondary priority and the North Koreans advanced rapidly.

On July 8, just south of Seoul, the American ground forces clashed with the North Koreans for the first time in what has become known as the Battle for Osan. The Americans expected an easy victory but suffered 150 casualties and were forced to retreat. By July 21, the communist forces pushed the Americans and their allies to Daejon, a hundred miles south of Seoul. By August 4, things were looking bleak as the communists pushed the Americans and South Korean army into a toehold at the far southern end of the Korean peninsula called the Pusan Perimeter. It looked as if Korea would be lost to the communists.

MacArthur convinced the President that bold action was necessary and on August 4, he launched a massive amphibious assault with US Army and Marines at Inchon, far behind enemy lines near Seoul. The massive invasion surprised the communists and their supplies were cut off, forcing the communist army to retreat very rapidly or be cut off. Within a month, the US forces captured all of the South Korean territory that had been lost; they stopped at the original border of the 38th parallel as per President Truman's orders.

September 27, an overly confident MacArthur convinced the reluctant Truman to allow him to advance into North Korea, claiming he could take all of the North and still have his army home by Christmas. After MacArthur assured Truman that there was "little chance" that China would enter the war, Truman allowed MacArthur to advance as long as he did not encounter or antagonize Chinese or Soviet troops. Truman warned MacArthur that he didn't want a war with either China or the USSR.

On October 20, American troops took the North Korean capital at Pyongyang. US troops began celebrating and said that MacArthur had kept his word, as they thought they would all be home for Christmas. MacArthur openly bragged that if Truman gave him another division, he could march all the way to Beijing. Unknown to the Americans, the Chinese began sending tens of thousands of troops across the Yalu River into North Korea under the cover of darkness. They would then dig in and camouflage and conceal their positions before daybreak. Mao Zedong was fearful that if MacArthur took North Korea, he would convince Truman to attack China. Mao reasoned that if he had to fight the Americans, he would rather fight them in Korea.

In November the Chinese, numbering in the hundreds of thousands, attacked en masse, catching MacArthur off guard. The Americans suffered a string of humiliating defeats and were forced to retreat rapidly, losing most of North Korea in a short time. It was then apparent that it would become a long war and that the outcome was far from certain.

June 27, Truman authorized military aid to Taiwan.

August 1, Guam was made a US Territory.

August 7, the Birmingham, Alabama, police barred three White baseball players, Lou Chirban, Stan Mierko, and Frank Dyle from playing against the Birmingham Black Barons of the Negro League.

August 8, Florence Chadwick swam the English Channel in just over thirteen hours.

August 13, President Truman authorized increased military aid to the French in Indo China (Vietnam).

August 15, an earthquake in India killed between 20,000 and 30,000 people.

August 14, President Truman appointed Edith Sampson as the first American Black delegate to the United Nations.

August 25, with the country at war, President Truman ordered the US Army to take control of the US railroads to avoid a nationwide strike. As in WWI and WWII, all American railroad workers were then "frozen" in their jobs for the duration of the war.

September 4, a typhoon struck Japan killing 250 people.

Also on this date the first NASCAR race was held on Labor Day at the Darlington Raceway in South Carolina.

September 9, France began a massive arrest of French communists.

September 12, Belgium fired all communist government workers.

September 16, Ho Chi Minh's army attacked French military outposts in Vietnam.

September 19, the UN rejected the membership of the People's Republic of China.

September 22, American Ralph Bunche was awarded the Nobel Peace Prize for helping to negotiate the peace in the Mideast. He was the first Black and person of color ever to win a Nobel Prize.

September 24, Operation Magic Carpet moved all Jews from Yemen to Israel.

September 28, Indonesia became the 60th member of the UN.

September 29, Bell Laboratories invented the telephone answering machine.

October 3, unable to support their troops, the French vacated their military post at Cao Bằng in Vietnam, after losing the outpost at Đông Khê. By the time the French had retreated, they had lost 4,800 troops with another 2,000 wounded, out of a total force of 10,000. They also lost a considerable amount of military supplies. The USSR, upon seeing the Vietnamese victory, began to supply Ho Chi Minh's Viet Minh Army in earnest.

October 21, China occupied Tibet.

October 26, the Dutch sent 630 volunteers to Korea.

November 1, two men who wished independence for Puerto Rico attempted to assassinate President Truman. One was killed by a police officer, who was also killed in the attempt, and a Secret Service agent shot and detained the second. President Truman was unharmed.

Also on November 1, Charles Cooper joined the Boston Celtics to become the first Black player in the NBA.

November 7, due to their losses to the Viet Minh, the French Army ordered all French women and children to leave the Hanoi and the Tonkin area.

November 8, the first ever jet plane battle occurred over Korea.

November 16, King Farouk ordered all British forces to leave Egypt.

November 19, General Dwight Eisenhower was named the Supreme Commander of NATO.

November 25, the UN gave the former Italian colony of Eritrea to Ethiopia.

December 30, Vietnam, Cambodia and Laos officially became "independent states" under the French Union.

In 1950, as American children were catered to and pampered, they also faced some serious concerns. The U.S. Government produced films warning about atomic bombs and the threat of nuclear war. They designed mandatory school civil defense programs and television ads demonstrating techniques for surviving an atomic attack. Children were taught to "duck and cover" in school in the event of a nuclear attack. The civil defense film *Duck and Cover* was shown to schoolchildren beginning in 1950 and was shown to millions of American school children well into the 1960s which caused a new illness in children called Nucleomituphobia, the fear of atomic war.

In the film a cartoon turtle called Bert, along with a cheerful theme song and the safety directives were supposed to reassure children who might worry about an atomic attack. Instead, the images of little boys and girls diving to the floor or under their desks and covering their heads convinced children that the bombs were going to fall at any moment and gave them nightmares. Duck and Cover also became a national joke, as these tactics would do little to protect anyone in a nuclear attack.

In 1950 the average annual wage was $3,210. New house prices averaged $8,450. The average new car cost $1,510 and gasoline was at 18 cents per gallon. Men's suits cost about $29 and women's cotton dresses a little over $3, and if you wanted to make your own clothes, a new Singer sewing machine cost $19.90. At the Woolworth's lunch counter you could buy a ham sandwich, a piece of pie and coffee for 65 cents, which included a dime tip. A sundae, banana split, malt or an ice cream soda was only 25 cents.

Consumer buying took over the economy and many new products were aimed at the children of the baby boom. New toys like Silly Putty were created and went on sale. America was much more interested in their children, new cars, shopping and watching television and less interested in the Korean War or foreign affairs.

Television became increasingly popular; the number of homes with televisions rose to over a million. More stations were added to the four growing networks: NBC, CBS, ABC and the network pioneer DuMont. The FCC approved CBS for the development of the first color television. In August ABC began the first Saturday morning programming exclusively for children. In September the laugh track was invented and began use in the sitcom and variety shows. Many of the laugh tracks still used on television today were made in the 1950s by many people who have since passed away. January 27, the second Emmy Awards were held. The Ed Wynn Show and Texaco Star Theater won the Emmys.

In February one of the all time classical comedies of television began. *Your Show of Shows* debuted with Sid Cesar and Imogene Coca. The writers of this classic comedy were Mel Brooks, Neil Simon and Woody Allen.

Other shows making their debuts in 1950 included: the *George Burns and Gracie Allen Show* and the *Jack Benny Show*, which both came over from radio. The game and quiz shows *What's My line*, *Beat the Clock*, and *Truth or Consequences*, along with the comedy/quiz show *You Bet Your Life* with Groucho Marx made their television debuts. The *Cisco Kid* made its debut along with the *Grand Ole Opry*. James Dean made his acting debut appearing in a Pepsi Cola commercial.

Radio was still very popular with households without televisions, but radio began a rapid decline in 1950 and it looked like a dying industry until later in the decade when the baby boomers with their Rock and Roll and transistor radios began to claim this media. Rightwing radio commentator Paul Harvey also made his debut on radio in 1950 bringing it a new niche called "talk radio."

Television was beginning to impact the movies in 1950, however the movies were still popular. The best movie that year was *All About Eve* with Bette Davis, Ann Baxter, and George Sanders. The picture won the Oscars for Best Picture, Best Director and Best Supporting Actor for George Sanders. Other top movies were: Walt Disney's *Cinderella*, *King Solomon's Mine* with Deborah Kerr and Stuart Granger, *Sunset Boulevard* with Gloria Swanson, *Father of the Bride* with Spencer Tracy, Joan Bennett and Elizabeth Taylor, *My Blue Heaven* with Betty Grable and Dan Dailey; *Harvey* with Jimmy Stuart and Josephine Hull who won Best Supporting Actress; and the comedy *At War with The Army* starring Dean Martin and Jerry Lewis.

The songs of 1950 were mostly cheerful ditties such as: *Good Night Irene* by Gordon Jenkins with the Weavers, *Music Music Music* by Teresa Brewer, *If I Knew You Were Coming I'd of Baked a Cake* by Eileen Barton. There were also the usual romantic tunes like: *Mona Lisa* by Nat King Cole, *Habor Lights* by Sammy

Kaye, *Sentimental Me* by the Ames Brothers, the *Tennessee Waltz* and *All My Love* by Patti Page, and *I Wanna Be Loved* and *I Can Dream Can't I* by the Andrew Sisters with Gordon Jenkins. And then there was the *Third Man Theme* which was so popular that two artists, Anton Karas and Guy Lombardo, made it into the top ten hits with this song.

The bestselling books of 1950 included: *The Cardinal* by Henry Morton Robinson, *Joy Street* by Frances Parkinson Keyes, *Across the River and Into the Trees* by Ernest Hemingway, *The Wall* by John Hersey, *Star Money* by Kathleen Winsor, and *The Parasites* by Daphne du Maurier.

Chapter 7. 1951: General MacArthur was Fired and the Korean Peace Negotiations Began

January 1, as Americans celebrated the New Year at home, Americans and the UN forces in Korea were overrun by waves of Chinese soldiers. By January 7, the Chinese took Seoul and drove the American and UN Forces south.

January 3, the Soviets discovered that nine Jewish physicians in the Kremlin were working as US and British spies.

January 9, the first "adults only" rated film, *Life After Tomorrow*, debuted.

January 10, the first official jet passenger service began.

January 14, the first NFL Pro Bowl took place after it had been cancelled because of the war in 1942. The Americans beat the Nationals 28-27.

January 16, Ho Chi Minh and his Viet Minh begin their assault to take Hanoi.

January 17, China declined UN efforts to negotiate a ceasefire in Korea as they continued south.

January 18, a "Cloud of Death" killed over 3,000 in Papua New Guinea when a volcanic eruption of Mount Lamington poured deadly hot smoke and steam into the valley below.

Also on January 19, the lie detector was first used in the Netherlands.

January 25 the UN forces began a counter offensive in Korea.

January 28, the US performed the first of 126 nuclear tests in Nevada. The tests would continue to take place until 1992.

January 30, Belgium outlawed communist speeches on television and radio.

February 1, the US showed a nuclear test explosion on television. On this same day the UN officially declared China "the aggressor" in the Korean War.

Also on this date a record cold gripped the US as New Mexico saw minus 50 degrees Fahrenheit and the next day Indiana saw a record minus 37 degrees, both records at that time.

February 6, a train crashed in New Jersey and killed 84 people.

Also on this date rightwing radio commentator Paul Harvey attempted to sneak into the Argonne National Laboratory, a US nuclear site, to prove how lax US security was against the communists. He was caught and arrested.

February 16, New York City passed an ordinance banning racial discrimination in public housing.

February 18, three college basketball players admitted to accepting bribes to throw games.

February 25, the first Pan American games were held in Argentina.

February 27, the Republicans succeeded in passing the 22nd Amendment, limiting the terms of presidents to two terms. The Amendment was largely a reaction against Roosevelt and the New Deal.

March 12, US and UN troops pushed the Chinese north and reclaimed Seoul. There were about 250,000 US troops in Korea.

March 14, as the Korean War raged, a Gallup poll showed that Truman's popularity had reached an all time low with an approval rating of just 26%. US deaths in Korea had reached about 50,000. According to the poll half of the people thought the war in Korea was a mistake; the other half wanted to be more aggressive and thought Truman was too weak in the fight against communism.

March 15, Persia (Iran) nationalized the Anglo-Iranian Oil Company.

March 21, Julius and Ethel Rosenberg were convicted of espionage and providing atomic secrets to the Russians.

March 31, the US Army pushed the Chinese across the 38th parallel into North Korea.

April 7, the US exploded an atomic bomb in the atmosphere above the Pacific Ocean.

April 11, President Truman relieved General Douglas MacArthur of his command. The press and the Congress were both shocked and angry. MacArthur had a large and growing ego and he disagreed and clashed publicly with Truman's policies as commander-in-chief. Eight months before, in August of 1950, MacArthur had been invited to speak at a national meeting of the Veterans of Foreign Wars, VFW, in Chicago. He declined due to his duties but sent a letter to be read aloud. In the letter he chastised Truman for his "appeasement" attitudes and his weak defense the Chinese nationalists. Truman discussed relieving MacArthur at the time but decided not to do so because his concern of demoralizing the troops, but he ordered the General to withdraw his statement. MacArthur did so, but the damage had already been done and their relationship was hostile.

Truman's Defense Secretary Louis A. Johnson was a strong MacArthur supporter. When MacArthur wanted to invade across the 38th parallel in 1950, Johnson and MacArthur assured Truman that China would never get involved. However, General Charles A. Willoughby, MacArthur's second in command, had written a report about the massing of Chinese troops on the border and their likely entry into the war. MacArthur ignored Willoughby's report and withheld it from Truman, which Truman later discovered.

Johnson and MacArthur told President Truman that he was being far too cautious. Johnson also clashed continuously with Secretary of State Dean Acheson over Far East issues. When the Chinese did enter the war and nearly defeated the UN and American forces, Truman became further dissatisfied with Johnson. Johnson continued his clashes with the State Department and Acheson. When General Willoughby's report was made available to Truman, he asked for and received Johnson's resignation.

Truman and MacArthur had met seven months before on Wake Island to discuss matters on October 15, 1950. MacArthur wanted to make a big show of it and asked if he could bring the press with him. The White House declined, saying that the usual White House press corps was enough. When Truman met MacArthur on the tarmac, disembarking from his plane, the General walked up and crudely shook the President's hand rather than saluting as is the protocol. Many saw this disrespectful move as MacArthur's attempt to prove he was the equal to the president. MacArthur's uniform, particularly his hat, was dirty and sloppy, which caused some offense with the president and his staff. Truman later remarked to his staff that MacArthur's "greasy ham and eggs hat looked as if it had been in use for twenty years." It was later learned that MacArthur staged the look because he wanted to appear to the press as if he had just been in combat, something that MacArthur rarely ever saw.

The president and others discussed all aspects of the Far East with General MacArthur, and then pressed him on the real issue. What were the odds of Chinese intervention in Korea if he was allowed to cross the 38th parallel and go into North Korea? The General replied, "Very little. The Chinese have 300,000 men in Manchuria. Of these only 100,000 to 115,000 are distributed along the Yalu River. Only 50,000 to 60,000 could be gotten cross the Yalu River... if the Chinese tried to get down to Pyongyang there would be the greatest slaughter." He also told Truman and General Bradley that he could send one of his divisions from Korea to Europe by the end of the year (1950).

It was a very poor assessment and patently untrue, particularly in the light of Willoughby's report stating the opposite. The Chinese had already moved 180,000 troops into North Korea.

It also became apparent to Truman that MacArthur wanted a wider war. He wanted to bomb China. On December 1, 1950, MacArthur was asked by a reporter if the restrictions on operations against Chinese forces on the far side of the Yalu River (China) were "a handicap to effective military operations." He replied that they were indeed "an enormous handicap, unprecedented in military history." He made similar remarks to the press on February 13, and on March 7, 1951.

Truman made a decision that he wanted a ceasefire with Korea and was willing to again divide Korea at the 38th parallel. He informed MacArthur of his decision. On April 9, in a brazen manner MacArthur defied the President and wrote a letter to the Republican House Minority Leader Joseph Martin disagreeing with Truman's orders, saying that Truman was appeasing the communists. It was after this that Truman and all his military advisors unanimously decided that MacArthur must go.

The day after MacArthur was relieved of command the Republicans in the Congress demanded the President's impeachment. Senator Richard Nixon demanded that MacArthur be immediately re-instated. In Europe and most of the rest of the world, MacArthur's termination was applauded as he was seen as a warmonger.

April 15, Michael Gossira became the independent head of state in the Dutch colony of Curacao. Curacao along with Bonaire, Saint Maarten, Saint Eustatius, and Saba were part of the Dutch Antilles colony in the Caribbean. On April 15, a new colonial government of the Dutch Antilles was formed by Da Costa Gomez.

Also on this date General Douglas MacArthur formally retired from the military with intention of running for president. On April 18, he arrived in San Francisco. It was the first time he and his family had been in the United States since 1937, having served primarily in the Philippines and Japan. His son, Douglas MacArthur IV, was thirteen and had never been in the United States. The family flew to Washington, DC, where he addressed Congress and defended his disagreement with the President. The Congress interrupted his speech with standing ovations fifty times. With this speech MacArthur had launched his presidential campaign.

He began a series of speaking engagements and public appearances around the country. He went everywhere and called press conference after press conference for the smallest reasons. He was accused by some of being "a ham." In the process he over exposed himself in the media, and both the press and the public grew tired of "his side of the story," especially after Truman started the peace negotiations.

Americans had moved on; they wanted peace. It became obvious even to the egotistical MacArthur that his time had passed. In 1952 he decided to support the conservative Senator from Ohio, Robert Taft, as the Republican presidential candidate. He had hoped that his endorsement would allow him to be named his vice presidential running mate. He was also the keynote speaker at the 1952 Republican Convention. Taft lost the nomination to Eisenhower and with Taft's loss, MacArthur's political ambitions ended. Eisenhower had no interest in MacArthur. Colonel Cole Kingseed wrote that Eisenhower had once served under MacArthur and said that he had "been beset on all sides by difficulties arising from [MacArthur's] personal ambition, personal glorification, and personal selfishness."

April 22, New York City threw a ticker tape parade for General MacArthur.

May 1, over 600,000 people marched for peace and freedom in Germany.

Also on May 1, Mickey Mantle hit his first home run in major league baseball.

May 8, the first men's suits made of the first man-made fiber, Dacron, went on sale.

May 12, the US exploded the first hydrogen bomb over the Pacific Ocean.

May 14, the apartheid government of South Africa denied the right to vote to all "colored people" of mixed races.

May 15, AT&T became the first company with a million stockholders.

Also on this date the Polish attaché for culture defected in Paris and asked for asylum.

May 16, the first regularly scheduled trans-Atlantic flight from New York's JFK Airport to Heathrow in London was started by the Israeli El Al Airlines.

May 24, racial segregation in Washington, DC, restaurants was ruled illegal by the courts.

May 27, the army of Tibet surrendered to the Chinese.

June 1, the first international cheese treaty was signed by most of Western Europe. The treaty provided guidelines for the naming and statement of origin of cheeses. A Roquefort cheese, for example, would now have to meet certain specifications to be packaged and sold as Roquefort cheese.

June 13, the UN and US forces reached Pyongyang. The Chinese and North Koreans proposed peace negotiations.

June 14, the first commercial computer, UNIVAC 1, went into operation for the US census.

June 18, after their retreat the French Army prevailed in their stand in the Red River Delta of Vietnam. They claimed to have killed over 10,000 Vietnamese communists in the fighting.

June 25, President Truman said publicly that he did not want a wider war and would be willing to enter into negotiations for peace with a divided Korea, with the boundary drawn again at the 38th parallel.

June 30, the NAACP began their campaign to end racial discrimination in public schools.

July 4, at a press conference it was announced that William Shockley of Bell Labs had invented the junction transistor. This invention lead to a variety of technical electronics companies forming in California in an area that would later become known as "Silicon Valley." In 1956 Shockley won the Nobel Prize for his work. The junction transistor made for improved computers, televisions, radio transmitters, mobile phones, and audio amplifiers.

July 10, the armistice talks to end the conflict in Korea began at Kaesong.

July 12, a large group of angry Whites rioted and tried to prevent a Black family from moving into a house in all-White Cicero, Illinois.

July 20, King Abdullah of Jordan was assassinated by a Palestinian as he attended prayers in Jerusalem.

July 31, Japan Air Lines was created.

August 5, there was an armed uprising at the Ambonezen Camp in Middelburg, South Africa. The Ambonezens are people of mixed Dutch and Indonesian ancestry.

August 6, as the peace negations started in Korea, flooding from a typhoon killed over 4,800 people in adjacent Manchuria (China).

August 7, a US Viking rocket went 130 miles into space and set a new record.

August 9, the Dutch volunteers fighting in Korea received a special Unit Citation for their brave service in Korea from the US.

August 11, the Mississippi River flooded over more than 100,000 acres in the Midwest.

August 13, Great Britain and Iraq signed an oil contract.

August 17, a hurricane struck Jamaica, grounding six large ships on the shore.

August 22, the Harlem Globetrotters played before a crowd of over 75,000 at the Olympic Stadium in Berlin.

August 26, the first artificial heart was demonstrated in Paris.

August 30, the US and the Philippines signed a mutual defense treaty.

September 2, the US, Australia, and New Zealand signed the ANZUS mutual defense treaty.

September 4, President Truman's speech opening the US–Japanese Peace treaty Conference became the first transcontinental television broadcast.

September 8, Japan signed peace treaties with 48 countries.

September 10, Britain began an economic boycott of Persia (Iran) to protest their government's intention to nationalize the country's oil industry. In revenge, on September 27, the Persian (Iranian) Army occupied a major oil refinery critical to British interests.

September 20, Swiss men voted against giving the vote to Swiss women.

September 24, the USSR conducted a large underground nuclear test.

September 29, NBC became the first to televise a football game in color.

October 1, the last segregated US Army unit, the all Black 24th Infantry Regiment, was deactivated.

October 6, Stalin formally announced that the USSR had the atomic bomb.

October 15, a Mexican chemist announced the creation of the first oral contraception, starting a new era of birth control and family planning.

Also on October 15, Egypt denounced the Suez Canal treaty. The treaty had provided that the British would control the Suez Canal for the next twenty years. The British had refused to give up the rights to the Canal with Egyptian independence.

October 18, the USSR performed another underground nuclear test.

October 20, Heisman Trophy candidate Johnny Bright, a Black quarterback from Drake University, played against Oklahoma A&M (now Oklahoma State) in Stillwater, Oklahoma. Although the University had supposedly integrated in 1949, Blacks remained unwelcome there. The all-White Oklahoma team targeted Bright in the game. The local and student newspapers quoted players saying that "Bright would not be around by the end of the game." The coach of Oklahoma A&M counseled his team on how to "get that nigger" and they practiced it for a week before the game.

Bright was derided by the crowd, who chanted "get the nigger." Bright was knocked unconscious three times by illegal blows to the head, but he continued playing despite the fact that the final one broke his jaw. He completed a touchdown pass despite the blow, but a few plays later he was too concussed and injured to continue to play. A series of photographs of the assaults on Bright during the football game later won a Pulitzer Prize and one photograph made the cover of *Life Magazine*.

October 22, an earthquake struck Formosa (Taiwan) killing over a hundred people.

Also on this same date the US exploded another nuclear test in Nevada. On October 30, the US performed yet another nuclear test in Nevada. Between 1951 and 1958 about 100 nuclear tests would be conducted about sixty miles north of Las Vegas in Nevada exposing many people in the Southwest to high doses of radiation.

October 25, the Korean peace talks resumed at Panmunjom.

October 26, after losing the post-WWII election, Winston Churchill was again elected British Prime Minister.

November 1, in New Mexico, US Army troops were ordered to dig in and occupy trenches during a nuclear explosion so that the Army could understand the effects on troops in the field. The experiment exposed the troops to high levels of radiation that later caused most of these men to develop severe medical problems.

November 10, the first long distance telephone call was made without the assistance of an operator. Most long distance calls would be made by area code direct dialing within a short time after.

November 18, as past of the continued conflict between the British and the Egyptians over the Suez Canal, Britain forcibly captured and occupied Ismailia, Egypt.

November 25, in a train crash in Woodstock, Alabama, seventeen people were killed.

November 27, the UN, China and the two Koreas signed a ceasefire at Panmunjom.

On this same day the US perfected the first surface to air missile when an experimental rocket hit a moving plane in a test at White Sands, New Mexico.

November 28, a military coup took control of Syria.

December 1, high winds in San Francisco caused the closure of the Golden Gate Bridge.

December 4, more than 500 people were killed in the Philippines during a volcanic eruption.

December 17, the Dutch passed a law forbidding communists from holding positions in the government.

December 23, Belgium announced that it had finally restored electricity to all communities that had lost it during WWII.

The first nationally televised football game was shown on this date, coast to coast, on the DuMont network. The Los Angeles Rams beat the Cleveland Browns in the NFL Championship Game 24 to 17.

December 24, *Amahl and the Night Visitor* became the first opera shown on television.

Also on this day the Kingdom of Libya was granted independence from Italy by the United Nations.

December 25, a cargo ship, *The Flying Enterprise*, sailing from Germany to the US with cargo and ten passengers, was struck by a storm in the English Channel and it suffered structural damage. On December 31, it began to list to one side. The passengers and crew were evacuated and one crewman lost his life. The ship sank ten days later on January 10, 1952, as it was being towed to port.

In 1951 Americans the average income was $3,510. Children and teens became the fastest growing consumer market. The average price of a new house was $9,000. New cars were flying off the car lots at an average price of $1,500, but things like turn signals were still an added luxury and many drivers continued to use hand signals to turn. Americans began buying foreign cars, particularly Volkswagens, and the British Austins were popular. Cars could also be purchased painted in two colors; they were called "two tones." Gasoline was 19 cents per gallon. Unemployment was about 3%.

Although you could direct dial long distance telephone calls without an operator, many homes still had party lines and shared their phone service with four other households. The number of rings designated whose call it was, but frequently nosey neighbors would listen to your phone calls anyway. And there were many conversations like: "Excuse me Mrs. Carter but you have been on the line for over thirty minutes and I have to call my husband." Or: "Can you please get off the line, Mrs. Carter, because we have an emergency" (and then there had better be an emergency, because Mrs. Carter was going to listen to your call). You could get a single user "private line" but they were generally more expensive.

Telephones still had exchange names rather than all numbers, which was why the rotary dial phones of the time had letters. Telephone numbers were given as Tuxedo (TU) 3-1142 and Liberty (LI) 5-0865. The use of multi-party lines and exchange names would continue into the 1960s.

In September NBC announced that it had sixty-one affiliated stations in their new "coast to coast" television network. The pioneering DuMont, which had started network television in 1946, began to experience problems as NBC, CBS, and ABC conspired to sign up television stations in the major cities often leaving DuMont with UHF stations that could not be received on most televisions at the time.

AT&T, who sent all the live network television transmissions from city to city via coaxial cable, had a limited capacity and allotted the distribution unfairly against DuMont. NBC and CBS were given over a hundred hours a week of prime time transmissions. They gave ABC 53 hours, and gave a miserly 37 hours to DuMont. It was the beginning of the end of the pioneer network of television. It didn't help that the Federal Communications Commission, FCC, regulators were biased toward the three former radio networks and their lobbyists with whom they had a long relationship. The FCC allowed this unfair division of transmission time. AT&T also forced the DuMont network to pay for radio transmission time to get their television transmission allocation even though DuMont had no radio stations. DuMont appealed this extra fee and after a long legal battle eventually DuMont eventually won, but it was too late.

The DuMont network terminated service in 1956 because they lacked enough stations and transmission time to compete with the three other networks. Most of the film of the Dumont shows, which were some of the very first of television shows, was destroyed in the 1970s and a good part of television history was lost, including the most popular show of its day, *Cavalcade of Stars*. This loss also includes most of the early television work that made Jackie Gleason a star.

In 1951 television was the medium that Americans turned to for news and entertainment. The TV antennae became a fixture on most American roof tops, unless the household was close enough to the television stations to use an indoor antenna called "rabbit ears." Although it was too expensive for the average home, color television became a reality. The first portable television camera was perfected by RCA and came into use in March of 1951. That year for the first time most Americans were able to watch both the World Series and the NFL Championship Game as they both were aired live from coast to coast.

The famous CBS Eye, one of the most recognized logos in America, made its debut in October. *I Love Lucy* made its debut and was the first national show filmed before a studio audience but it was not shown live. *Dragnet, Mr. Wizard, Amos & Andy, Roy Rogers*, the soap opera *Love of Life* which ran until 1980, and the longest running show on US television, *The Hallmark Hall of Fame* all made their debuts.

The longest running regularly scheduled show in US television history also began in 1951, the soap opera *Search for Tomorrow* made its debut and aired from 1951 to 1986. The show's sponsor was Proctor & Gamble and the two products that advertised on the show were Joy dishwashing liquid and Spic and Span household cleaner which is why they became known as "soap operas." Some of the show's more notable performers over the years included: Don Knotts, George Maharis, Larry Hagman, Susan Sarandon, Kevin Klein, Morgan Fairchild, Kevin Bacon, Olympia Dukakis, Lee Grant, Sandy Duncan, and Angela Basset.

Television began to have a negative impact on the movies. Theater attendance went down as television's popularity went up. The movie companies began catering to the children's Saturday matinee. Walt Disney's *Cinderella* was one of the most popular movies of 1951 as were the sci-fi and horror films *The Day the Earth Stood Still, The Thing from Another World, When Worlds Collide, The Man from Planet X*, and *Superman and the Mole Men*. There were some notable films as well including: *The African Queen* with Humphrey Bogart and Katherine Hepburn; *A Street Car Named Desire* with Marlon Brando, Vivian Leigh and Kim Hunter, Alfred Hitchcock's *Strangers on a Train*, and *American in Paris* with Gene Kelly and Leslie Caron.

The books of 1951 included some all time classics like: *Catcher in the Rye* by J.D. Salinger, *Catch 22* by Joseph Heller, *The Caine Mutiny* by Herman Wouk, *From Here to Eternity* by James Jones, and two classic sci-fi novels, *Foundation* by Isaac Asimov, and *The Illustrated Man* by Ray Bradbury.

The songs of 1951 included Nat King Cole's number one hit *Too Young*. Tony Bennett had two top ten songs with *Because of You* and *Cold, Cold Heart*.

Les Paul and Mary Ford had three big hits with *How High the Moon, The World is Waiting for the Sunrise* and *Mockin' Bird Hill* which was also a hit for Patti Page who had two other 1951 hits in the *Tennessee Waltz* and *Would I Love You?* Rosemary Clooney had a hit with *Come On-a My House.* Mario Lanza had two hit songs with *Be My Love* and *Lovliest Night of the Year.* The Weavers made the top ten with *On Top of Old Smokey* as did Perry Como with *If.*

Chapter 8. 1952: More War, the Eisenhower Election and the Birth of Rock and Roll

January 9, baseball great Ted Williams was re-called by the Marines for active duty in Korea.

January 12, the University of Tennessee admitted the first Black student.

January 14, *The Today Show* premiered on NBC with Dave Garroway and the show's mascot a chimpanzee named J. Fred Muggs. It was originally called the *Rise and Shine Revue* in production, but some thought the title was too long so it was named *The Today Show*. The news and feature show was the first of its genre and has held its slot as the most popular morning show for most of its history only losing out to ABCs *Good Morning America* in the late 1980s and early 1990s. Many of the show's anchors are a "who's who" of television news men and women, and two, John Chancellor and Tom Brokaw went on to be the primary news anchors for NBC.

January 14, a snowstorm in the Sierra Nevada Mountains killed twenty-six people.

January 19, the PGA approved of Black athletes participation in professional golf.

Also on January 19, the NFL took over the financially troubled New York Yanks football team and moved it to Texas to become the Dallas Texans. The team played for one year and then failed. It was the last NFL team to do so.

February 1, there was a general strike against the French colonial government in Tunisia.

February 4, Jackie Robinson became the first Black executive in television at WNBC in New York.

February 6, Queen Elizabeth succeeded King George VI to the British Throne.

February 15, King George was buried at St. George's Chapel at Windsor Castle.

February 19, the French launched an offensive against Ho Chi Minh and the Viet Minh Army in Hanoi.

February 20, major league baseball certified the first Black umpire.

February 26, Winston Churchill announced that Great Britain had the atomic bomb.

Also on this day the Netherlands and Indonesia began a peace and unity conference.

March 3, Puerto Rico approved their territorial constitution.

March 10, a US and CIA supported military coup led by General Fulgencio Batista took control of Cuba. US corporations and the Mafia ruled of most of Cuba during Batista's regime.

March 18, the peace talks stalled in Korea and the communists began a new offensive.

March 20, Japan was given its sovereignty by the US.

March 21, tornadoes across the South caused 343 deaths.

March 24, huge demonstrations against apartheid erupted in South Africa.

March 27, Sun Records in Memphis, Tennessee, began selling records.

April 8, President Truman nationalized the steel mills to prevent a crippling national strike during the Korean War.

April 9, following a popular uprising, Bolivia created a new democratic government which instituted agrarian reforms and nationalized the Bolivian tin mines. The US mining and business interests who had owned much of the mining industry claimed that communists were involved, and the CIA began to look at ways to overthrow the new democratic government.

April 11, the People's Republic of China and Chiang's Republic of China fought over the island of Nanri. Chiang's forces triumphed with massive military assistance from the US, but then abandoned the island to the mainland a short time later after looting all the island's resources.

April 15, was the first flight of the B-52 Stratofortress. This bomber became the main weapon of the Strategic Air Command and would be on permanent patrol in the skies awaiting the "go" orders to launch an attack on the USSR. They didn't stand down until 1991.

April 25, the American Bowling Congress approved the use of the automatic pin setter. Previous to this human pin setters were the rule as most bowling alleys were not automatic.

April 26, the US minesweeper Hobson accidently rammed the aircraft carrier Wasp and killed 176 sailors.

April 28, Dwight Eisenhower resigned as the NATO commander to run for president.

April 30, Mr. Potato Head became the first toy advertised on national television. The original toy was of plastic body parts and clothing that were pushed into a real potato for the body. However after many parents complained of rotting potatoes and health departments began to condemn the use of potatoes as a toy, a plastic body was made.

May 1, US Marines were ordered to take part in an atomic explosion test in Nevada to determine the effects on these men. It caused long term health problems for the Marines that were forced to participate.

Also on this day Trans World Airlines introduced its cheaper tourist class.

May 8, *Mad Magazine* debuted delighting boys and girls with their offbeat and irreverent humor and disgusting their parents.

May 13, Nehru became the premier of India.

May 16, National Educational Television, NET, the forefather of the Public Broadcasting System, PBS, began service with a grant from the Ford Foundation.

May 27, the European Defense Community plan was signed. The plan provided for a Western European Army to be formed in case of a conflict with the Soviet Union. Despite this signing the plan never took effect because Britain refused to join and NATO continued to provide this protection backed by American military power.

May 28, women were given the right to vote in Greece.

June 2, over 650,000 US metal workers went on strike.

June 12, the USSR declared their peace treaty with Japan was invalid. The US responded with a pledge of protection.

June 16, Russian Mig fighter jets shot down a Swedish flying boat used in rescue operations over the Baltic Sea. It was searching for survivors of an unarmed Swedish radio plane that had disappeared 48 hours earlier. It was later learned that the Russians had also shot the radio plane down and eight people were killed. However the five member crew of the flying boat were rescued from the sea by a German freighter.

June 23, as the Korean conflict continued, US planes heavily bombed areas along the Yalu River disrupting the movement of Chinese troops and supplies into Korea. The bombing was careful to not actually bomb across the Yalu into China.

July 11, General Eisenhower was nominated for President by the Republican Party. It was not as easy as later believed. "Mr. Conservative," Senator Robert Taft of Ohio nearly beat Eisenhower for the nomination. The convention turned rancorous as the Taft and Eisenhower campaigns fought. At the start of the convention the delegate counts were as follows: Eisenhower 595 delegates, Taft 500, Earl Warren 81, and MacArthur 10. The Eisenhower campaign claimed that the Taft campaign had refused to seat some rightfully elected Eisenhower delegates in Southern states, a claim that angered Taft. Eisenhower challenged the Southern delegations and won a vote at the convention called "Fair Play" that reassigned delegates as follows: Eisenhower 845, Taft 280, Warren 77, and MacArthur 4. Eisenhower then easily won. Governor Earl Warren had thought that the original near tie in delegates would deadlock the convention allowing him to be the acceptable alternative to both campaigns.

Taft was so angry over the convention manipulation that he only agreed to support Eisenhower after the General met with him personally and promised Taft that he would honor Taft's conservative pledge to "fight creeping domestic socialism in every field." The staunch anti-communist Senator, Richard Nixon, was recommended by conservatives as the vice presidential nominee to help mend Eisenhower's rift with Taft.

July 17, the British government invited CIA officer Kermit Roosevelt Jr., the grandson of Teddy Roosevelt, to London to discuss the British government's dissatisfaction of the nationalization of Persia's (Iran) oil. Out of this meeting Allan Dulles and Roosevelt created Operation Ajax that would over throw the democratic government of Persia. The Plan was carried out in 1953 with Roosevelt bribing the Shah of Iran with $1million to replace the prime minister with a Persian general who became a dictator that the Americans and British could manipulate.

July 19, the Olympic Games began in Helsinki, Finland.

July 21, the Democratic National Convention began. Competing for the democratic nomination were Governor Adlai Stevenson of Illinois, Senator Estes Kefauver of Tennessee, Senator Richard Russell of Georgia, and six other candidates. The battle came down to Stevenson and Kefauver with Russell playing the spoiler. Stevenson won after three ballots and chose Senator John Sparkman of Alabama as his vice presidential running mate to appease Russell and the Southern conservatives.

July 21, a powerful 7.8 earthquake hit Kern County, California, near Bakersfield. Fourteen people were killed.

July 22, Poland adopted a communist-imposed constitution.

July 23, the Egyptian military staged a coup and overthrew the Egyptian monarchy. King Farouk abdicated three days later.

July 24, President Truman settled the steelworkers strike.

July 25, Puerto Rico officially became a self-governing commonwealth of the United States with the proviso it may later vote and be accepted for statehood.

August 6, Satchel Page at 47 became the oldest pitcher to win a complete shutout.

August 8, US supported strongman, Syngman Rhee, was re-elected president of South Korea.

August 20, Joseph Stalin met the Chinese leader Zhou En-Lai to discuss mutual concerns.

August 22, France permanently closed its penal colony on Devil's Island.

August 26, the City of San Francisco became the first city to fluoridate their water.

September 6, Canadian television began broadcasting in Montreal.

September 11, West German Chancellor Adenauer signed a repatriation pact for Jews. The act also provided for German reparations to the Jews.

September 22, Charlie Chaplin left United States and was not permitted to return. In 1930s Chaplin had been disturbed by fascism and militarism growing in Europe. In 1940 he made a film, *The Great Dictator*, which satirized Hitler. The movie received five Academy Awards including Best Picture, Best Director and Best Actor. However, the movie was not appreciated by everyone. J. Edgar Hoover disliked the film and accused Chaplin of being a communist.

Hoover later defamed Chaplin in a paternity case where he had Chaplin charged with violations of the Mann Act. The charges were ridiculous and they were later dismissed by the court, but they greatly damaged Chaplin's reputation which was what Hoover had set out to do. Blood tests also proved that Chaplin was not the father of the child, but the judge, under pressure from the FBI, still found him to be the father and ordered Chaplin to pay for the child's care.

In 1947 Chaplin made a film, *Monsieur Verdoux*, which questioned and criticized capitalism. The original idea for the film came from Orson Welles. In 1947 after the film's premier, the FBI began investigating Chaplin as a communist subversive. Chaplin denied that he was a communist, saying that he was a "peacemonger," but he also further infuriated Hoover by speaking out against persecuting communists as a violation of the Bill of Rights. The rightwing members of Congress called for Chaplin to be deported.

Chaplin had just completed another movie, *Limelight,* in 1952 and left the US to premiere it in London where his movie took place. While he was out of the country the US Attorney General James P. McGranery notified Chaplin that the US would not issue a re-entry permit allowing him to come back to the US unless Chaplin agreed to an FBI interview and face charges for sedition. In 1980s the charges and documents were released; they contained no evidence that Chaplin was a communist or had committed any act detrimental to the US. Chaplin was born in London; he had come to the US at the age of 19 and was a US citizen.

In 1972 the Academy of Motion Picture Arts and Sciences awarded Chaplin an honorary Oscar for "the incalculable effect he has had in making motion pictures the art form of this century." In poor health and worried about re-entry problems, he initially was reluctant to return to the US, but he was reassured by the Academy that he would have no problems. In an emotional response he was given a twelve-minute standing ovation, the longest in Oscar history.

In 1975 he was given a knighthood by Queen Elizabeth. Chaplin died at his home in Switzerland in 1977.

September 23, Richard Nixon gave his "Checkers Speech" on national television. During the presidential campaign it was discovered that Richard Nixon had a private slush fund, funded by wealthy donors to pay his personal expenses during his congressional and senate campaigns and that the fund was still paying Nixon for personal expenses in the presidential campaign. Although not illegal, this secret account raised many ethical concerns about who Nixon was indebted to and who did he owe? Eisenhower considered removing him from the ticket, but Nixon pleaded for an opportunity to go on television and make his case. It was reputed to be Nixon's best speech.

In the speech Nixon admitted that his $18,000 fund was wrong but claimed, "Not one cent of the $18,000 or any other money of that type ever went to me for my personal use. Every penny of it was used to pay for political expenses that I did not think should be charged to the taxpayers of the United States. It was not a secret fund."

In the speech he also stated that he was not a rich man and that his wife did not have a fur coat, but had "a respectable Republican cloth coat." He claimed that the only gift he ever took for personal use was a little dog that was given to the family that his little daughter had named "Checkers." The speech worked and Nixon remained on the ticket to become Vice President.

October 3, Great Britain conducted their first atomic weapons test in Australia.

Also on October 3, the Black independence group the Mau Maus claimed their first victim in Kenya. This event began the Mau Mau uprising which lasted a decade. On October 21, Jomo Kenyatta, the president of the Kenya African Union was arrested along with 180 others by the British for the uprising. On October 30, as the uprising continued 500 more were arrested by the British. November 25, the British arrested 2,000 more suspected Mau Mau terrorists.

October 5, the highly publicized 19th Congress of the Soviet Communist Party began. It was the first Congress since WWII.

October 8, with the Korean peace talks stalled the Chinese launched another offensive.

October 30, "Ivy Joe" the first two stage thermonuclear weapon was tested in the pacific by the US. The US would have the first "ready to use" H-bomb the following year. These weapons were thousands of times more powerful than the atomic bombs that fell on Hiroshima and Nagasaki.

November 4, Dwight Eisenhower won the 1952 presidential election over Adlai Stevenson by 55 to 44%. Eisenhower carried 39 states but still lost most of the Democratic "solid South" which would later become Republican. The popular vote was 34 million for Eisenhower to 27 million for Stevenson. It was the first time the Democrats hadn't occupied the presidency since the 1932 election.

November 14, in a manipulated election, in which the CIA played a major role, military strongman General Papagos won the election in Greece.

November 19, a US F-86 Sabre Jet set the aircraft speed record of just under 700 MPH.

November 25, George Meany was appointed the Chairman of the American Federation of Labor.

November 26, the first 3-D movie, *Bwana Devil,* premiered in Hollywood.

November 29, President-elect Eisenhower visited Korea to assess the war.

December 3, the first television show was broadcast in Hawaii.

December 4, the killer fogs began in London and a new word, "smog," was created. By December 8, about 8,000 died from respiratory problems.

Also on December 4, labor leader Walter Reuther became the chairman of the Congress for Industrial Organizations (CIO).

December 6, the Czech government asked the Israeli ambassador to leave amid espionage charges, which sparked charges of anti-Semitism against the Soviet Bloc.

December 8, French troops fired upon independence demonstrators in Casablanca killing more than fifty.

December 15, in Denmark Christine Jorgenson, an American, became the first person to undergo a sex change operation.

December 28, the Detroit Lions beat the Cleveland Browns 17-7 in the NFL Championship before a large national television audience.

December 29, the first transistorized hearing aid went on sale.

December 30, the Tuskegee Institute reported that 1952 was the first year in seventy-one years without a Black lynching in the US.

In 1952 three out of five families now owned an automobile, two of three families had a home phone, and one in three homes had a television. Women were married on average by the age of 20 and very few women worked out of the home after marriage. A new car averaged $1,700. And for the first time more cars were produced with automatic transmissions than manual transmissions. Gas was 20 cents per gallon. The average wage was above $3,800. The average new home price was $9,050 and rental housing was still cheap with rents averaging $80 per month.

Life wasn't all good in the US. There were problems including continued discrimination against Blacks, Latinos and people of color, an estimated 50,000 people were afflicted with polio, and the Korean War continued.

In October the first television show was recorded using magnetic tape in Los Angeles. On October 7, *American Bandstand* premiered on local television in Philadelphia. Dick Clark would later join "*Bandstand*" in 1955 at first as a guest host before becoming the permant host.

Television shows making their debut in 1952 included; *Death Valley Days*, *I've Got A Secret*, *Adventures of Superman*, *Victory at Sea*, *The Bud Abbott and Lou Costello Show*, *American Bandstand*, *My Little Margie*, *The Adventures of Ozzie and Harriet*, and the radio soap opera *The Guiding Light* also premiered on television. On Thanksgiving Day CBS began a tradition by broadcasting live from New York the Macy's Thanksgiving Day Parade.

There were only 186,000 televisions in Canada, many of them in Toronto with antennas aimed at the Buffalo, New York television stations.

Movie theater attendance continued to decline. The movies of 1952 included: *The Quiet Man* with John Wayne and Maureen O'Hara, *Singing In the Rain* with Gene Kelly, Donald O'Connor and Debbie Reynolds, *The Greatest Show on Earth* with Jimmie Stewart, Charlton Heston, and Betty Hutton, *High Noon* with Gary Cooper and Grace Kelly, *Monkey Business* with Cary Grant, Marilyn Monroe and Ginger Rogers, and *Son of Paleface* with Bob Hope, Jane Russell, and Roy Rogers. *The Greatest Show on Earth* won the Oscar for Best Picture.

In March Allan Freed, the Cleveland radio disc jockey credited with creating the term Rock and Roll held the Moondog Coronation Ball at the Cleveland Arena which was later known as the first Rock concert. Allan freed was born in Johnstown, Pennsylvania, to a Russian-Jewish immigrant father and an American-Welsh mother. His family moved to Ohio where he spent his childhood, high school, and college years. He had a band called the Sultans of Swing. He became interested in radio while at college. In WWII he became a disc jockey for Armed Forces Radio. After the war he resumed his work as a disc jockey in Pennsylvania and then Ohio. Freed was interested in new music styles and he particularly liked rhythm and blues and the new pop sounds. He eventually coined a term for this new music, "Rock and Roll," and began promoting the music. Freed's show was called the Moondog House. In 1954 Freed moved his show to New York to a station that became the first around the clock top 40 Rock and Roll station. In the mid and late 1950s Freed guest starred in five Rock and Roll movies including *Rock Around the Clock* in 1956. In 1957 in addition to his radio show, Freed also hosted a television show called *Big Beat* which was the forerunner to shows like *American Bandstand.*

In 1958 Freed got in serious legal trouble for the Payola scandal where disc jockeys accepted bribes to play and promote records and recording stars by the record companies. It was also revealed that he was receiving royalties from some of the songs he promoted as a "co-writer" although Freed didn't actually co-write most of these songs. He had co-written the song *Sincerely* by the Moonglows, but accepting royalties while promoting the song on the air was still a conflict of interest. Freed was fired and lost his radio and television shows in the scandal. Freed moved to California and continued in radio in 1960 until his early death at 43 in 1965 from complications from alcoholism.

The popular songs of 1952 included four hits by Jonnie Ray: *Cry, Little White Cloud That Cried, Walkin' My Baby Back Home,* and *Please Mr. Sun.* Eddie Fisher had four hits with *Wish You Were Here, Anytime, I'm Yours,* and *Tell Me Why.* The Four Aces also had a hit with *Tell Me Why.* Jo Stafford had two with *You Belong to Me* and *Jambalaya.* Rosemary Clooney had a couple, with *Half As Much* and *Botch-a-me.* Kay Starr had the number two hit with *Wheel of Fortune* and Leroy Anderson the number one hit with *Blue Tango.*

On January 11, the Bollingen Prize for Poetry was awarded to Marianne Moore. Moore was a contemporary of Wallace Stevens and Ezra Pound, who were also awarded the prize in 1949 and 1950. Moore was also a contemporary of T.S. Eliot. She also encouraged and mentored Allen Ginsberg. On May 5, the Pulitzer Prize was awarded to Herman Wouk for *The Caine Mutiny.*

The books of 1952 included: the children's classic *Charlotte's Web* by E.B. White, *Old Man and the Sea* by Ernest Hemingway, *East of Eden* by John Steinbeck, *Foundation and Empire* by Isaac Asimov, *Invisible Man* by Ralph Ellison, *Kiss Me Deadly* by Mickey Spillane, *Waiting for Godot* by Samuel Beckett, *Giant* by Edna Ferber, *The Bridge Over the River Kwai* by Pierre Boulle, and the cartoon classic *I Go Pogo* by Walt Kelly.

Chapter 9. 1953: The Korean Conflict Ended, Americans in Vietnam, Communist Xenophobia Peaked, and Color Television

January 3, Frances Bolton and her son Oliver Bolton of Ohio took office in the new Congress. They were the first mother and son to simultaneously serve in the US Congress.

January 6, two passenger cruise ships, the *Willem Ruys* and the *Oranje* of the Netherland Line, collided in the Red Sea. It was the fashion of the day that when two passenger ships met at sea they would sail close to each other so that their passengers could greet each other as they passed. Unfortunately a miscommunication between the two ships caused one to turn into the other. No lives were lost, but this incident is the reason cruise ships no longer pass each other in close proximity.

January 9, a Korean ferry boat sank near Pusan and 249 passengers were killed.

January 12, nine Jewish doctors were arrested in Moscow as terrorists. This raised more Western charges of anti-Semitism against the Soviets.

January 13, Marshal Josip Tito became the president of Yugoslavia.

January 15, a runaway 16-car Federal Express train crashed in the station in Washington, DC.

Also on this day the East German Minister of Foreign Affairs, Georg Dertingen, was arrested as a spy for the west.

January 20, President Eisenhower delivered the first coast to coast live presidential inaugural address on television.

January 21, John Foster Dulles was appointed Secretary of State. On February 9, his brother Allen Dulles was appointed Director of the CIA. The brothers were from an old line Yankee family. Their grandfather had also served as Secretary of State. From 1937 until well after the US declared war on Germany in 1941 the Dulles brothers represented the Rockefellers, Prescott Bush and his father-in law George Herbert Walker (father and grandfather of George Herbert Walker Bush) and the Harrimans in many covert and illegal dealings with Nazi firms. Rather than divesting themselves of these tainted Nazi assets once America declared war on Germany, Prescott Bush, the Rockefellers and the Harrimans used Allen Dulles and his brother John Foster Dulles to help hide and conceal their ownership in these Nazi businesses.

It was this group along with their German business partners that financed Hitler's rise to power in exchange for Hitler outlawing the unions. John Foster Dulles was personally at the meeting in Germany where this was agreed. The Roosevelt Administration knew of these dealings but as America had no intelligence about Germany they desperately needed their help.

After the war none of these men were tried for their crimes except Prescott Bush who had allowed his father-in-law's German shipping line to be used for German espionage in the US prior to the war. He was charged with and convicted of "trading with the enemy." He was given a fine but no jail sentence. His conviction became an issue in his first run for Senate in 1950 which he narrowly lost. However, people seem to have forgotten, and he was elected to the Senate from Connecticut in 1952.

Allen Dulles was appointed as the Office of Strategic Services (OSS) Station Chief in Switzerland during the war. He was virtually the head of American intelligence for Germany. It was Dulles who cooperated with the Catholic Church after the war to create the ratlines and created Operation Paperclip to bring Nazi intelligence officers, scientists and others to America or into the employ of the Americans. It was Allen Dulles who recruited General Reinhard Gehlen and his Nazi SS Officers into the OSS/CIA despite their war crimes.

January 23, the NFL franchise rights for the defunct Dallas Texans were sold and they became the Baltimore Colts, now the Indianapolis Colts.

January 31, hurricane force winds stuck the Netherlands causing widespread floods as the ocean penetrated and overflowed the dykes. The floods badly damaged the country and killed 1,835 people. That same day a passenger ship, the *Princess Victoria*, capsized in the storm off the coast of Scotland killing 133 people.

February 6, the US government controls on wages and the remaining controls on consumer goods which were placed upon them during the war were finally cancelled.

February 11, President Eisenhower refused to grant clemency to the Rosenbergs to allow them to serve a life sentence rather than be executed for their espionage. In January 1950 the US discovered that Klaus Fuchs, a German physicist working for the British in the Manhattan Project, had provided key documents and information about the nuclear bomb program to the Soviets throughout the war. Fuchs identified his courier as Harry Gold, who was arrested on May 23, 1950. Gold confessed and to get a more lenient sentence identified Sergeant David Greenglass, a former machinist at Los Alamos, as an additional source. Greenglass under duress to get a more lenient sentence then accused his brother-in-law Julius Rosenberg and perjured himself to also implicate his sister, Rosenberg's wife. He did this as part of an agreement with the FBI that it would protect Greenglass' wife from any prosecution.

While it is true that Julius Rosenberg passed some US documents to the Soviets, what is also true is that at his trial the FBI used coercive measures to force witnesses to perjure themselves against him. He didn't receive a fair trial. Ethel Rosenberg was likely an innocent pawn caught up in the anti-communist xenophobia of the times and ruthless FBI agents and and over zealous prosecutors who wanted blood, innocent or not. There was also a significant amount of anti-Semitism that followed the Rosenbergs as they were brought to trial.

In 1995 the US government released a series of decoded Soviet cables which confirmed that Julius acted as a minor courier for the Soviets but contained no references to Ethel's involvement. The American government chose to single these two out for death sentences, even though all of the other atomic spies who were caught by the FBI in this incident, and who had actually committed larger crimes, were not executed (including Ethel's brother, David Greenglass). It was Greenglass and not Julius Rosenberg who supplied most of the documents stolen from Los Alamos. He was not given a death sentence and only served ten years of a fifteen year sentence. Harry Gold, who identified Greenglass served fifteen years in federal prison for being a courier like Julius. And the most culpable, the German scientist with British citizenship, Klaus Fuchs, the communist spy that headed this spy ring was sentenced to only fourteen years but served just a little over nine years.

Though he initially denied any involvement by his sister Ethel Rosenberg, Greenglass, under FBI coercion, then claimed that Ethel knew of her husband's dealings. He lied and said she had typed some documents for her husband although there was no other proof of this other than his coerced statement.

Greenglass became the key prosecution witness in the Rosenberg trial. He later recanted his testimony about his sister's involvement and said it had been forced by the FBI. He stated in an interview in 2001, "I don't know who typed it, frankly, and to this day I can't remember that the typing took place. I had no memory of that at all, none whatsoever." He said he gave false testimony to protect himself and his wife, Ruth, and said that he was coerced by the prosecution to do so. "I would not sacrifice my wife and my children for my sister." However, he also said that he didn't realize at the time that she would receive the death penalty.

The Rosenbergs were the only two American civilians ever to be executed for espionage during the entire Cold War. In sentencing them to death, Judge Irving Kaufman went over the top by saying that he held them responsible not only for espionage but also for all the deaths of the Korean War. He said, "I believe your conduct in putting into the hands of the Russians the A-Bomb years before our best scientists predicted Russia would perfect the bomb has already caused, in my opinion, the Communist aggression in Korea, with the resultant casualties exceeding fifty thousand and who knows but that millions more of innocent people may pay the price of your treason." It was an incredibly false statement that explodes with xenophobia.

Between the trial and the executions there were widespread protests and claims of anti-Semitism. The charges of anti-Semitism were widely believed, especially in Europe. Pope Pius XII appealed to President Eisenhower to spare the Rosenbergs' lives. However, Eisenhower with advice from his anti-communist Vice President Richard Nixon refused the Pope's request on February 11, 1953. All other appeals were also unsuccessful. Richard Nixon would later say that the evidence against Ethel was "tainted." "If I had known that at the time, if President Eisenhower had known it, he might have taken a different view with regard to her."

Julius and Ethel Rosenberg were executed in the electric chair at sundown on June 19, 1953. Julius Rosenberg died after the first electric shock, Ethel did not. After the normal course of three electric shocks, the doctors determined that Mrs. Rosenberg had not yet died and her heart was still beating. Two more electric shocks were applied, and at the conclusion eyewitnesses reported that smoke rose from her head in the chamber. The Rosenberg's had two small boys that paid a steep price. They were orphaned by the executions and no relatives adopted them. They were later adopted by a high school teacher. In later years they came to realize their father was as guilty as the others, but they believed that he was not as guilty as the others who were given relatively light jail sentences while their father was executed. They believe to this day that their mother, like them, was an innocent victim.

February 12, the USSR broke off diplomatic relations with Israel, claiming that it was coordinating Jewish espionage and terrorism in the Soviet Union.

February 19, baseball star and Marine pilot Ted Williams' plane was shot down in Korea. Williams was recovered uninjured.

February 21, Francis Crick and James Watson discovered structure of the DNA molecule, the double helix. The discovery led to breakthroughs in the genetic code and protein synthesis.

March 5, Joseph Stalin died of a cerebral hemorrhage. The next day Malenkov became the leader of the Soviet Union. On March 9, Stalin was buried.

March 8, there was growing awareness that the US family farm was fast disappearing. The US Census reported that almost a quarter of a million American families had given up farming in the past two years. Farms were becoming larger, corporate operations.

March 11, a US B-47 accidently dropped a nuclear bomb on South Carolina. Fortunately the bomb failed to detonate because of safety catches.

March 14, Nikita Khrushchev pushed Malenkov aside to become the leader of the Soviet Union.

March 18, an earthquake in Turkey killed 250 people.

On this day baseball's Boston Braves moved to Milwaukee and became the Milwaukee Braves. They later moved to become the Atlanta Braves.

March 26, Jonas Salk announced a vaccine to prevent polio. The disease had afflicted about 50,000 children the previous year.

March 27, twenty-one died in a train crash in Ohio.

March 31, the US Department of Health Education and Welfare was established.

Also on this day the UN nominated Dag Hammarskjold of Sweden as UN Secretary General. On April 7, he was elected.

April, the CIA Projects CHATTER, BLUEBIRD, and ARTICHOKE, the mind control and torture experiments that were started by the Nazis in WWII and whose doctors and scientists were brought to the US in Operation PAPERCLIP, were combined into one large mind control project called MK-ULTRA. Truman was told that the Soviets and the Chinese were working on mind control and that the US needed to do so or risk falling behind. The president was lied to by the CIA about the scope of the projects and he approved them as voluntary medical trials. They were not.

Once Project MK-ULTRA officially got underway in April, 1953, the experiments included administering LSD and many other harmful drugs to mental patients, prisoners, drug addicts and prostitutes, "people who could not fight back," as one agency officer put it. The most incredible was a project called Operation Midnight Climax conducted in several brothels in San Francisco. The prostitutes working for the CIA would spike the drinks of their johns with LSD, who would then be filmed by CIA agents behind one way mirrors as they participated in sex acts. The Johns were then blackmailed into further drug experiments, with the CIA threatening to show these films to the victim's wives, family, and employers.

Other forced experiments involved members of the military, the CIA, and prison inmates. In different experiments drugs, electric shocks, hypnosis, and torture was also used often to give the subjects multiple personalities or to totally erase minds or memories. Universities cooperated with the CIA program and did drug trials and mind control experiments on students. Ken Kesey the author of *One Flew Over The Cuckoo's Nest* admitted to being one of these students who was given tuition money in exchange for his participation. He was told that the drug trials were "safe." His experience left him with life-long mental problems. The worst of these experiments dealt with combining drugs, electric shock, hypnosis, sexual humiliation and other tortures on mental patients with mild disorders such as depression at a variety of mental hospitals and clinics in the US and Canada. Some of these alleged victims have included: Ted Kaczynski the Uni-bomber, Charles Manson, Jim Jones, and Sirhan Sirhan.

In addition to the forced and voluntary military programs, 44 colleges or universities, 15 research foundations, chemical and pharmaceutical companies including Sandoz (now Novartis) and Eli Lilly and Company, 12 hospitals or clinics and three prisons are known to have participated in the CIA's Project MK-ULTRA. There were thousands of victims. Some died, some were reduced to vegetative states and others became mentally damaged and deranged. These programs remained secret until the mid 1970s when a Senate Committee uncovered them.

It is one of the reasons that President Truman later said that his greatest mistake was signing the law that created the CIA.

April 9, Jomo Kenyatta was sentenced by the British to seven years in prison for his role in the Mau Mau uprising. Kenyatta would later become the first leader of independent Kenya.

April 10, in the 7th NBA championship the dominating Minneapolis Lakers lead by George Mikan won by beating the New York Knicks four games to one.

April 14, Ho Chi Minh's Viet Minh independence fighters launched an offensive against the French in Laos.

April 24, Winston Churchill was knighted by Queen Elizabeth.

April 27, In South America the British colony of British Guyana had their first general elections which began their path to independence.

May 2, King Hussein was installed as King of Jordan and King Feisal was installed in Iraq.

May 11, a tornado in Waco, Texas did $39 million in damages and killed 119 people.

Also on this day Winston Churchill severely criticized John Foster Dulles' for the Domino Theory.

May 19, a nuclear test explosion in Nevada caused a serious radiation problem in St, George, Utah.

May 22, President Eisenhower signed the Off-shore Oil Bill allowing oil companies to drill in off-shore waters.

May 23, Cliff Notes became available to US students.

May 25, the first non-commercial educational television station began in Houston, Texas.

May 29, Edmund Hillary and Tenzing Norkay, a Sherpa mountaineer in Nepal, were the first people to reach the summit of Mount Everest.

May 31, the Lebanese government disbanded.

June 2, the coronation of Queen Elizabeth took place in Westminster Abby.

June 5, the US vetoed the People's Republic of China's membership in the UN.

June 8, the US Supreme Court ruled that restaurants in Washington, DC, could not be segregated.

Also on this day tornadoes in Michigan and Ohio killed more than a hundred people.

June 14, President Eisenhower became increasingly angry with Senator Joe McCarthy and his communist witch hunt. McCarthy was being encouraged by J. Edgar Hoover and the FBI and began to target the military. In response the Administration began leaking detrimental information about McCarthy to the press, including that McCarthy tried to bully the military for a draft exemption for David Schine, one of his aides; and when that didn't work McCarthy tried to obtain preferential military duty for Schine. McCarthy had also launched a book-banning and book-burning campaign which included 300 titles such as: Thoreau's *Walden* with the essay *Civil Disobedience* and Steinbeck's book *The Grapes of Wrath*. On this day Eisenhower also condemned the book-burning campaign.

Also on June 14, Elvis Presley graduated from high school in Memphis, Tennessee.

June 17, people demanding re-unification rioted in East Germany.

June 18, a US Air Force transport plane crashed in Japan killing 129 servicemen.

June 26, in a continued power struggle within the Soviet leadership, Vice Premier Beria was arrested.

June 30, the first Chevy Corvette rolled off the assembly line in Detroit.

July 4, strikes and riots occur in the coal mines of Poland.

July 7, Ché Guevara set out on his motorcycle trip through South America that was chronicled in his *Motorcycle Diaries.*

July 14, the US dedicated a monument to George Washington Carver. It was the first US memorial to a Black American.

Also on this day the communists began a new offensive in Korea.

July 20, the USSR and Israel agreed to resume diplomatic relations.

July 26, Fidel Castro began a liberation movement to free Cuba from the Batista regime. His forces attacked a rural army outpost. The attack was unsuccessful and Castro was caught and sent to prison. Castro would then name his movement for the liberation of Cuba "The July 26 Movement."

July 27, the US and the United Nations, China and the two Koreas signed the Korean Armistice Agreement, ending the Korean Conflict. It ended where it first began with the two Koreas divided at the 38th parallel. On August 5, in Operation Big Switch the US exchanged prisoners of war with the Chinese. During the war over 2,500,000 Korean civilians died. The UN and South Korean forces killed were given at 178,476 including 33,629 Americans. Over 32,925 were also missing, and over 566,434 were wounded. Chinese and North Korean estimated casualties were 350,000 to 750,000 dead, and 686,000 to 789,000 wounded. It had been a very bloody and costly war for both sides with no real gains made by either side.

August 8, the USSR formally announced that it also had the hydrogen bomb.

August 12, a 7.2 earthquake destroyed most of buildings on some Greek islands in the Ionian Sea.

August 13, four million went on strike in France against the austerity measures.

August 18, the second Kinsey Report, *Sexual Behavior in the Human Female* was published.

August 19, the CIA overthrew the Persian (Iran) government and retained the Shah and a military government that was sympathetic to the US and British interests. The Shah would remain in power until 1980 when the Iranians revolted.

August 20, the US returned 382 ships captured during the WWII to West Germany.

Also on this day France ousted the King of Morocco and sent him into exile.

September 7, Soviet Premier Nikita Khrushchev consolidated his power by also becoming the head of the Soviet Central Committee.

September 25 a typhoon struck Southeast Asia killing over a thousand people.

Also on this day the first WWII German prisoners of war were returned from the Soviet Union to West Germany.

And on this date Britain finally ended their war time sugar rationing.

September 27, a typhoon stuck Japan causing massive damage.

September 29, the US gave France $385 million in military aid to continue fighting in Vietnam.

In October the Univac 1103 computer became the first commercial computer to use random access memory, RAM.

October 5, President Eisenhower appointed Republican Governor Earl Warren as the Chief Justice of the US Supreme Court. Vice president Richard Nixon gave a strong recommendation to appoint Warren who he said was a staunch conservative. Warren went on to lead one of the most liberal courts in US history and he would later be under constant pressure by the rightwing of the Republican Party and Southern segregationists to be impeached.

October 9, Konrad Adenauer was re-elected in West Germany.

October 10, the US signed a mutual defense treaty with South Korea pledging to protect it from future invasion.

October 14, President Eisenhower warned that he would fire any federal worker who was called before the House Committee for Un-American Activities who took the 5th Amendment to keep from testifying.

Also on this day the British performed another nuclear test in Australia.

October 30, General George Marshall and Albert Schweitzer, a medical missionary in Africa, were given the Nobel peace prize.

November 2, Pakistan became an Islamic republic.

November 3, the first live coast to coast color broadcast took place.

November 9, Cambodia declared their independence from France.

November 19, Vice president Nixon visited Hanoi to assure the French of strong American support in keeping their colony in Vietnam.

November 25, an earthquake and tsunami hit Japan.

November 29, American Airlines began the first regular non-stop cross continental air service from New York to Los Angeles.

Also on November 29, Laos erupted into civil war with the newly independent Kingdom of Laos fighting the communist Pathet Lao. The Cambodians also began fighting the French for their independence.

Also in a fateful move on November 29, French paratroopers took positions and fortified at Điện Biên Phủ in Vietnam.

December, Hugh Hefner began the sale of *Playboy Magazine*. The first issue sold over 54,000 copies and featured a nude photo of Marilyn Monroe as the first centerfold.

December 3, President Eisenhower rebuked Senator McCarthy's claim that there were communists in the Republican Party.

December 7, a visit to Iran by Vice president Nixon sparked riots as the Iranians protested the CIA backed military coup. Three students were shot and killed in the protests becoming martyrs and creating an event that has been observed annually ever since in Iran.

December 9, General Electric announced that all communist employees would be fired.

December 12, Chuck Yeager flew the Bell X-1A rocket plane to an altitude of 74,700 feet and reached an air speed of 1,620 miles per hour, both were records. Unfortunately he lost control of the aircraft which then began to spin out of control. Yeager was thrown about and broke the canopy of the aircraft with his helmet before he was able to get the plane under control.

December 14, the Brooklyn Dodgers signed pitcher Sandy Koufax.

December 16, the first televised White House Press Conference attracted 161 reporters.

December 23, in their continued leadership shake up the USSR formally announced that Beria had been executed.

December 24, a railroad bridge collapsed in a flood in New Zealand killing 166 people.

Also on this date in Czechoslovakia two express passenger trains collided head on and killed 103 passengers.

December 30 the first color television sets went on sale for $1,175.

December 1953, when unidentified flying objects, UFOs, sightings became more frequent the US government asked the CIA to deal with it. Their solution was to pass a joint Army-Navy-Air Force Regulation number 146 which made it a federal crime for military personnel to discuss classified UFO reports with unauthorized persons. Violators faced up to two years in prison and/or fines of up to $10,000. A panel of scientists, the Robertson Panel, was then assembled by the CIA to study and debunk UFOs. They did very little to study the phenomenon and instead focused on how to dissuade the public's interest. In their conclusion they felt that "unverifiable UFO reports were overloading intelligence channels." They suggested a campaign to discourage the UFO "craze" through their on-going Operation Mockingbird, an operation to manipulate the American press where they would seek "cooperative" mass media, psychologists, astronomers, and celebrities to ridicule the idea of UFOs and people who reported sightings, and put forward possible explanations for these UFOs. They also suggested that civilian UFO groups "should be watched because of their potentially great influence on mass thinking... The apparent irresponsibility and the possible use of such groups for subversive purposes should be kept in mind."

In 1955, the Air Force decided that Project Blue Book, the official US study of UFOs, should not actually investigate UFO reports but rather should be used to reduce the number of unidentified UFO reports to a minimum by classifying them as comets, weather balloons, weather phenomenon, or conventional aircraft.

The CIA's highly secret Operation Mockingbird to manipulate the press and the opinions of the American people was unfortunately very effective and in full bloom in 1953. Most of the Operation's efforts were to spread anti-socialist propaganda, and to discredit politicians, journalists, intellectuals and others who disagreed with the CIA's Cold War and political agenda. The CIA was in fact acting as a political police.

Operation Mockingbird was started by Allen Dulles of the CIA in 1950, by 1953 twenty-five major US newspapers and the wire services were in partial control of the CIA through Operation Mockingbird. They also controlled television media and had a major influence on movie production in Hollywood. The usual method of placing their disinformation was by placing reports developed by the CIA to witting or unwitting reporters. Those reports would then be repeated or cited by other cooperating reporters which in turn would then be cited throughout the media wire services and then taken as fact because they appeared to be confirmed by many media sources. Operation Mockingbird and its abuses would not be discovered by Congress until 1975 and would not be fully disclosed to the American public until 2007.

Buy now and pay later became the motto of 1953 as auto companies and lenders began granting longer payment periods for cars and other consumer goods. Americans began buying on credit. Furniture, cars, clothes, restaurant meals, televisions, appliances, encyclopedias, all could be bought on credit in 1952.

Union membership was at an all-time high and salaries and benefits reflected this. The unemployment rate was 2.9%. Average wages reached $4,000 a year and teachers averaged $4,254 per year. A new car averaged $1, 650 and gas was 20 cents per gallon. The average house price including existing homes was just above $2,000. However, new house prices rose to an average of $9, 550. In addition to the first color televisions, the first transistor radios went on sale. Radio was about to make a comeback with transistor radios and Rock and Roll music.

The popular songs of 1953 included: *Via Con Dios* by Les Paul and Mary Ford, *(How Much is) That Doggie in the Window* by Patti Page, *You, You, You* by the Ames Brothers. There were three hits by Perry Como, *No Other Love, Don't Let the Stars Get In Your Eyes*, and *Say You're Mine Again.* Joni James had three hits: *Why Don't You Believe Me?*, *Your Cheatin' Heart*, and *Have You heard?* Eartha Kitt had *C'est si Bon*, The Hilltoppers hit with *P.S. I Love You*, Jimmie Boyd with *I saw Mommy Kissing Santa Claus*, And Darrell Glenn with *Crying in the Chapel.*

In January 1953 about 68% of all US televisions watched *I Love Lucy* to see Lucy give birth to little Ricky. The following month Lucille Ball and Desi Arnaz signed an incredible $8 million contract to continue their show for two more years. In February the dramatized history show *You Are There* with Walter Cronkite began. *Romper Room* also premiered in February. In April *TV Guide* published its first issue. In June the Coronation of Queen Elizabeth became the big television event in the US and sales of new televisions rose sharply for this event. *Make Room for Daddy* with Danny Thomas began in September.

The top grossing picture of 1953 was Walt Disney's *Peter Pan.* Other hit movies included: *The Robe* with Richard Burton, *From Here to Eternity* with Burt Lancaster, Deborah Kerr, Frank Sinatra, and Donna Reed, *House of Wax* the 3D classic with Vincent Price, *Shane* with Alan Ladd, *Gentlemen Prefer*

Blondes with Marilyn Monroe and Jane Russell, *How to Marry a Millionaire* also with Marilyn Monroe, William Powell and Betty Grable, *Hondo* with John Wayne, *Roman Holliday* with Gregory Peck and Audrey Hepburn, and *Stalag 17* with William Holden. *From Here to Eternity* won the Oscar for Best Picture, Best Director, Best Supporting Actor for Frank Sinatra and Best Supporting Actress for Donna Reed. William Holden won Best Actor in *Stalag 17* and Audrey Hepburn won Best Actress in *Roman Holliday*.

On May 4, Ernest Hemingway won the Pulitzer Prize for *The Old Man and the Sea*. The popular literature of 1953 included Ray Bradbury's classic sci-fi *Fahrenheit 451*, Arthur Miller's *The Crucible*, Laura Ingalls Winder's book set, *The Little House Collection*, James Baldwin's *Go Tell It on the Mountain*, and *Junky* by William S. Burrows.

CHAPTER 10. 1954: VIETNAM, DISNEYLAND, THE DISGRACE OF JOE McCARTHY, AND THE STOCK MARKET FINALLY RETURNED TO THE PRE-CRASH 1929 HIGH.

January 1, the Rose Bowl and Cotton Bowl were telecast in color for the first time.

January 7, IBM and Georgetown University used an IBM 701 mainframe computer and gave a public demonstration of their computer's machine translation power by translating sixty Russian sentences into English.

January 11, an avalanche hit a train and killed ten people in Austria.

January 13, military rule took hold in Egypt and 318 Muslim Brotherhood members were arrested.

January 14, the Hudson Motor Company merged with the Nash-Kelvinator Company to form American Motors, AMC. It was at the time the largest corporate merger in US history. The two companies merged to be more competitive with the "Big Three" auto companies, General Motors, Ford, and Chrysler. AMC hired Michigan Governor George Romney as their executive. They eventually phased out their Nash and Hudson lines and created the Rambler which proved to be very popular.

Also on January 14, Marilyn Monroe and baseball great Joe DiMaggio were married.

January 20, the National Negro Network, a Black radio network was founded. It was the first national Black entertainment venue. It was started by a Chicago advertiser W. Leonard Evans Jr. and the network developed Black programs for 45 affiliate stations. Cab Calloway and Ethel Waters were two of the main producers of the network's shows. The network aired Black soap operas, music programs, and programs from Black colleges. Unfortunately television began taking most of the advertising revenues and radio was declining and this along with sponsor bias kept the network in the red. The network gave up after a year due to the lack of adequate revenues.

Also on January 20, a minus 70 degrees Fahrenheit was recorded in Rogers Pass, Montana becoming the record low for the contiguous 48 states.

January 21, the first nuclear submarine, the USS Nautilus, was launched in Connecticut. Its construction began in 1951. It had a long history and was decommissioned in 1980. In 1982 it was declared a Historic Landmark at the Museum of Submarine History in Gorton, Connecticut.

January 26, Disneyland began construction in Anaheim, California in what were large orange and walnut groves on land that was taken from Japanese farmers during their internment in WWII. It was open for business one year later at a cost of $17 million. In order to fund the park Walt Disney created the television show *Disneyland.*

January 30, Belgium canceled its trade agreements with the USSR.

February 10, President Eisenhower warned against US involvement in Vietnam.

February 14, Senator John Kennedy appeared on *Meet the Press.*

February 23, the first public inoculations of the Salk Polio Vaccine were in given in Pittsburgh.

February 25, Abdul Nasser was appointed the Egyptian Premier.

February 26, the first typesetting machine (photo engraving) was used in Quincy, Massachusetts.

Also on February 26, Republican Congresswoman Ruth Thompson of Michigan introduced legislation to ban the mailing of Rock and Roll records because they were "lewd, lascivious and filthy."

March 1, four radical Puerto Rican Nationalists sitting in the public galleries began firing guns at Congress. They fired 30 rounds before they were stopped. They wounded five congressmen who all later recovered. The four were tried and given long prison sentences.

Also on March 1, thirty people died in an independence rebellion in Khartoum, Sudan.

And on this date the US also exploded a nuclear weapon at the Bikini atoll in the South Pacific.

March 4, J. Earnest Wilkins Jr. became the first Black cabinet appointee when he became the Assistant Secretary of Labor. Wilkins was a child math whizz who completed a Bachelors degree in math at 17 and a Masters at 18. He was one of the mathematicians who worked on the Manhattan Project to create the atomic bomb.

Also on March 4, the first successful kidney transplant was announced in Boston, Massachusetts.

March 9, in a turning point for the nation the respected journalist Edward R. Murrow denounced Senator Joe McCarthy and his communist witch hunt on his television show, *See It Now.*

Also on March 9, the first color television commercial was aired in New York City.

On March 11, the U.S. Army charged that Senator McCarthy had been using "undue pressure tactics" against the U.S. Army.

March 13, Viet Minh General Vo Nguyen Giap began the assault on Diên Biên Phu. The French made a decision to create a fortified base at Diên Biên

Phu to draw the Viet Minh into a fight and kill their army with their superior firepower. Unknown to the French the Vietnamese with a remarkable effort had moved artillery and anti-aircraft weapons through heavy jungle and up steep terrain and had placed their artillery and men in tunnels on mountains surrounding and looking down on the French. These placements made the Vietnamese artillery impervious to French counter artillery.

When the Vietnamese artillery siege began the French Artillery commander Charles Piroth committed suicide because of his failure to prepare for this. Much of the French command was wiped out in the Vietnamese artillery onslaught. The French Legionnaire commander and his staff were killed that first evening. The Colonel commanding the Northern sector was killed a few minutes later. The Vietnamese launched an infantry assault and killed over 500 Legionnaires but also lost 600 of their own. The French were cutoff. The Viet Minh succeeded in knocking out the airstrip and took a French outpost. All supplies thereafter had to be delivered by parachute. The French counterattacked to retake the outpost and lost about a thousand men, but killed and equal amount of the Viet Minh. However the counterattack failed.

The attacks continued on the embattled French through the rest of March and April. The French dug in and their trenches were reminiscent of the trench warfare of WWI. On May 7, General Giap ordered an all-out attack to take Diên Biên Phu. By nightfall most of the French positions had been captured. Some of the French troops attempted to break out and run for Laos, but of these 1,700 troops only about 70 managed to escape. During the battle a US Congressional panel asked the Joint Chiefs of Staff if the US should intervene on behalf of the French. The Chairman of the Joint Chiefs Admiral Arthur W. Radford told them it was too late to save the French. President Eisenhower had also stated that "Nobody is more opposed to intervention than I am."

However, through the CIA, the Americans did covertly give air support to the French during the battle and 37 Air Force pilots and planes temporarily assigned to the CIA flew 682 secret combat sorties over Diên Biên Phu and two American pilots were killed. According to the Associated Press this was kept a classified secret until 2004, and in 2005 the seven remaining living US pilots were given the French Legion of Honor for their service.

On May 8, the French surrendered at Diên Biên Phu. The Viet Minh captured 11, 721 French troops of which 4,436 were wounded. The Vietnamese allowed the Red Cross to come in and treat the wounded and did release 858 seriously wounded French to the Red Cross. The remainder were taken prisoner and marched north to prison camps.

Diên Biên Phu cost the French a tenth of the total number of troops in Southeast Asia, but it was an even worse psychological defeat. It broke the French political will to keep Vietnam. The Geneva Conference opened on May 8, 1954 the day of the surrender. The result was that Vietnam was divided into a communist north with a French and US supported "Free South."

March 15, *the CBS Morning Show* debuted with Walter Cronkite and Jack Paar.

March 20, the first newspaper vending machine was used in Columbia, Pennsylvania.

March 25, RCA manufactured the first 12 and a half inch color television set to be sold for $1,000.

March 31, the US Air Force Academy in Colorado Springs was opened.

Also on this day the USSR offered to join NATO and was rebuffed.

April 1, an earthquake and tsunami killed 200 people and did major damage in the Aleutian Islands.

Also on this day the first US Army helicopter battalion was formed at Fort Bragg, North Carolina.

April 5, Elvis Presley debuted his first single, *That's Alright.*

April 6, the first TV dinner went on sale. It was produced by Swanson & Son's.

April 7, on the advice of John Foster Dulles and Allen Dulles, President Eisenhower went on television to warn about the "Domino effect" in Southeast Asia. The US began expanding covert operations to give aid to South Vietnam.

April 12, George Mikan and the Minneapolis Lakers won another NBA championship over Syracuse.

April 13, "the father of the Atomic Bomb" Robert Oppenheimer was accused of being a communist in a private hearing reviewing his security clearance. It was instigated by J. Edgar Hoover, who disliked Oppenheimer because of his growing opposition to nuclear weapons. Hoover began feeding rightwing Republicans misinformation that he was a communist because of some past associations. Oppenheimer had openly admitted being friendly with and knowing communists to the House Committee on Un-American activities in 1949, but had said he was not a communist.

Oppenheimer had his security clearance revoked in December, but rather than resign he insisted upon a public hearing. At the hearing Edward Teller, a nuclear physicist and Oppenheimer's rival testified that he did not think that Oppenheimer was a communist but damned him by saying," I feel that I would like to see the vital interests of this country in hands which I understand better, and therefore trust more. In this very limited sense I would like to express a feeling that I would feel personally more secure if public matters would rest in other hands."

The scientific community was outraged by Teller's self-interested comments and he was virtually shunned in the scientific community. Although many other scientists, government and military leaders testified on Oppenheimer's behalf his security clearance was not reinstated.

April 13, Hank Aaron played his first baseball game for Milwaukee.

April 14, a Soviet diplomat, Vladimir Petrov, asked for political asylum in Australia.

April 21, in a continuous shakeup of the Politburo in the USSR Gregori Malenkov became the new Premier of the USSR.

Also on this date the US Air Force flew a French Battalion to South Vietnam.

April 22, the US Army-McCarthy hearings began and were televised. McCarthy announced that it was his intent was to expose an alleged communist espionage ring within the US Army. McCarthy and the Army fought for over 188 hours most of which was aired on national television. The televised coverage of the hearing allowed the nation to witness the deceitfulness and cruelty of Joseph McCarthy. He failed to give any compelling evidence that even a single soldier was a communist or that there was as he had claimed a communist plot within the US Army. The hearing was the beginning of the end of McCarthy. He was exposed as a bully. It became apparent to the American people that McCarty's accusations of disloyalty, subversion, and treason lacked any regard for the truth and lacked any evidence.

April 24, Australia and the USSR broke off diplomatic relations over the defection of the Soviet diplomat.

April 25, British troops raided Nairobi, Kenya and arrested 25,000 more suspected Mau Mau.

Also on this day Bell Labs announced the creation of the first solar battery.

April 26, a nationwide test of the Salk polio vaccine was announced.

May 3, Charles Lindbergh Jr. won the Pulitzer Prize for his biography, *The Spirit of St. Louis*. It was Lindbergh's first return to prominence since falling from grace after his advocating on behalf of Hitler and the Nazis prior to WWII. Lindbergh accepted the Commander Cross Order of the German Eagle from Adolph Hitler about the time of Kristallnacht. He was also a close personal friend of the Nazi Air Corps Commander Herman Goering and he resigned his US Army Air Corps commission in a disagreement with President Roosevelt's stand against fascism. He also wrote a controversial article for *Readers Digest* about the intellectual superiority of the European White race over Blacks and others.

May 5, a military coup took place in Paraguay. General Alfredo Stroessner with help of the CIA took control of the country. The country became a refuge for former Nazi war criminals like Dr. Josef Mengele and other rightwing dictators like Juan Peron of Argentina.

May 6, Roger Bannister of Britain became the first person to break the four minute mile with a time of 3 minutes and 59 seconds.

May 17, in a landmark case the Supreme Court in *Brown v. Board of Education* unanimously ruled that "separate but equal" was illegal. Public schools were ordered to desegregate with "all deliberate speed." President Eisenhower had previously cautioned Chief Justice Warren, "These are not bad people. All they are concerned about is that their sweet little girls are not required to sit in school alongside some big Black buck." Immediately after the decision billboards saying "Impeach Earl Warren appeared across the country particularly in the South. Unfortunately ten years after the *Brown* decision only 1.2% of Black children in the Deep South attended school with White children. President Truman would later say, "If the fella that succeeded me had just given people a little leadership, there wouldn't have been all that difficulty over desegregating schools, but he didn't do it. He didn't use the power of the presidency to uphold a ruling of the Supreme Court of the United States, and I never did understand that."

May 19, the CIA, who had been reading all US telegrams to and from overseas and listening to overseas long distance phone calls, also began on this date to open and read the overseas mail of Americans.

May 21, an amendment to give 18 year olds the right to vote was defeated.

May 22, a Bar Mitzvah was given for Robert Zimmerman, a young singer and guitarist from Hibbing, Minnesota. In five years he would begin studying at the University of Minnesota. While there, he began performing folk music at the Ten O'Clock Scholar in Dinkytown and he began to call himself Bob Dylan.

May 24, a US rocket lifted off from White Sands, New Mexico and reached 150 miles into space.

On this same day IBM announced that it had created a computer with vacuum tubes capable of performing ten million operations per hour.

May 28, Arthur W. Murray beat Chuck Yeager's altitude record in a Bell X-1A rocket plane attaining a new record of 90,440 feet.

June 14, in a mixture of American jingoism and Christian fervor the Congress passed and President Eisenhower signed a bill adding "one nation under God" to the pledge of allegiance.

June 16, with the support of the CIA and the Catholic Church, Ngo Dinh Diem and the American CIA took temporary control of South Vietnam as the French gave up control. Diem was a Catholic monk and a staunch anticommunist. He had been an administrator for the French until he tried to get the Japanese to recognize a free Vietnam during their occupation. After the war, because of his collaboration with Japan, he was wanted as a traitor by the French. As the Japanese troops left they smuggled Diem out of the country dressed as a Japanese Army officer. After the war he lived in the US at Cardinal Spellman's seminary in New Jersey.

Diem was to serve as the leader of South Vietnam until the Vietnamese elections in 1955. Diem was popular with the American China Lobby. The rightwing of the Republican Party embraced Diem as a Christian anticommunist. Diem was very politically connected in the Catholic Church. His brother was a Bishop who had befriended and studied with the American, Francis Cardinal Spellman, who was also a friend of the Pope. Spellman also had the ear of many politicians in Washington, DC.

The problem for Diem was that the South Vietnam was about 90% Buddhist and all the Vietnamese Catholics lived in the communist North. According to the Geneva Accords the Vietnamese people were given a 300 day period in which they could freely move from the North to the South and vice versa. The US military and the CIA collaborated with the Catholic Church to move the Catholic population from the North to the South. At first the Northern Catholics were unwilling to move south even when their priests began to advise them to do so saying that the Catholics would be persecuted by the communists.

An odd agreement called Operation Passage to Freedom that was fashioned by Colonel Edward Lansdale of the CIA with Ho Chi Minh who also wanted to rid himself of this large Catholic opposition group. The CIA began to spread rumors that the US would drop an atomic bomb on the communists of Hanoi. At the same time the Catholic priests told their parishioners that if they stayed knowing this, that this was suicide and an unpardonable sin and told the Catholics they would be denied their "last rites." They also said that if they stayed all their possessions would be given to the communists. It was also rumored that Ho Chi Minh was allowing the Chinese communists to invade the northern part of the country where they were killing Catholic men and raping the women. The communists did their part by printing the atomic bomb rumors in their press. It worked.

Operation Passage to Freedom was accomplished using US naval ships to bring over 310,000 refugees, mostly Catholics, to the South. On some of these vessels the crew dressed as Catholic priests to make the naive and reluctant Vietnamese Catholics feel safe and come aboard.

With over 300,000 new Catholics Diem now had his support group and he began ruthlessly replacing all Buddhist political, civil service and military officers in South Vietnam with Catholics. He also ordered that the Vatican flag would be flown alongside the flag of South Vietnam. The majority Buddhist population began to protest the religious discrimination which was met with Diem's police brutality. It became a religious war.

Also during the 300 days of freedom Ho Chi Minh also took advantage and he moved a large number of his army south disguised as civilian refugees. They became guerillas and the backbone of the Viet Cong and the Southern insurgency. Some whole regular army units were also moved south disguised as civilian refugees and they began to create tunnel complexes and stockpiling weapons and supplies in remote areas from which they could fight the South Vietnamese and eventually the Americans.

Operation Passage to Freedom was distorted in the media through the CIA's Operation Mockingbird; it appeared in the world press that America was rescuing the pleading and frightened Christians from communist oppression. The press also played up the hundreds of thousands fleeing communism without mentioning that a large number of Vietnamese fled north to escape Diem and the Catholic controlled South.

June 27, the first atomic power station opened near Moscow.

Also on June 27, the CIA overthrew the government in Guatemala and forced the resignation of their democratically elected and very popular President Jacobo Árbenz Guzmán. When Árbenz came into office his country was desperately poor and about half of the arable land was owned by the powerful American corporation, the United Fruit Company, UFC. The UFC had planted about half their land in bananas and the rest was left unused. Árbenz proposed to buy this unused land back from UFC for Guatemalan farmers. The Guatemalan government took the unused UFC land and paid the corporation $600,000, which was the value that the company had self-declared it was worth on their Guatemalan tax statements. The UFC then counter-claimed the land was really worth $15,854,849.00. They had the

US State Department demand this amount in payment. Guatemala refused saying that this price was ridiculous and was counter to their claims in their tax statements. The UFC also knew that Guatemala could not pay this amount.

It is significant to know that Secretary of State John Foster Dulles and the Under Secretary of State Robert Hill were both large shareholders in UFC. The Cabot-Lodge family was also large shareholders and also had influence in US State Department and with President Eisenhower. CIA Director Allen Dulles and his predecessor at the CIA, Walter Bidell Smith, were also large shareholders. When Guatemala refused to pay the UFC their inflated price and confiscated the unused land for the $600,000 all these men wrongly convinced Eisenhower that Árbenz was a communist. The CIA attempted to start a Guatemalan revolution, but it failed because Árbenz had widespread popular support from the Guatemalan people. So the US Air Force bombed Guatemala and the US government threatened to bomb Guatemala to ruins and send in the Marines if the President Árbenz did not resign.

After seeing the devastation of the first bombing attack Árbenz feared his country would be reduced to rubble and he resigned and was forced into exile. The CIA and the UFC then put a military dictator, Carlos Castillo Armas, into power. He cancelled the land acquisition and the UFC and CIA then ran the country thereafter. In October 2011, long after Árbenz's death, the government of Guatemala formally apologized to Juan Jacobo Árbenz the son of President Jacobo Árbenz Guzmán and they named a highway in his honor for sacrificing himself to save his country from American bombs and invasion.

Guatemala was covered up in the press by the CIA's Operation Mockingbird who portrayed the incident as freedom loving Guatemalans overthrowing a communist dictator.

July 3, WWII food rationing finally ended in Britain.

July 4, in Ohio Dr. Sam Sheppard's wife was murdered and he was falsely accused of the crime. His fictionalized story was later made into a television series, *The Fugitive.*

July 12, President Eisenhower presented a plan for an Interstate Highway System. The bill authorizing the construction of the system would pass on June 29, 1956.

July 14, and 15, saw a record heat wave in the US. Three states set all time high temperatures: Missouri 118, Illinois 117, and Virginia with 110 degrees Fahrenheit.

Also on July 15, the Boeing 707 was tested and became the first standard US commercial jet transport plane.

July 20, in accordance with the Geneva agreements Vietnam was formally separated into North and South Vietnam.

June 22, the Virgin Islands adopted a constitution as a US territorial government.

July 3, a Cathay Pacific Airways passenger plane flying from British Hong Kong to Bangkok was shot down by Red Chinese fighter jets who mistook the plane for a Nationalist Chinese military attack plane. The tragedy was compounded when two US Navy planes searching for survivors were also fired on by the People's Republic planes thinking they were attacking. The two Chinese planes were shot down. The incident heightened already growing tensions in the South China Sea bringing the US and China close to war once again.

July 31, the first ascent of the Himalayan Mountain K-2 was achieved by an Italian expedition.

August 1, South Africa passed the Native Re-settlement Act which allowed the government to forcibly remove Blacks from areas adjoining Johannesburg.

August 3, the first Vertical Take-Off and Land aircraft, VTOL, the Bell X-14 was tested.

August 10, at Massena, NY, the ground-breaking for the St. Lawrence Seaway took place.

August 16, the first issue of *Sports Illustrated* went on sale.

August 19, the Nobel Prize winning American Ralph Bunche was named undersecretary of the UN.

August 24, President Eisenhower signed the Communist Control Act outlawing the communist party and making it a crime to be a communist. However, the Supreme Court of the United States has never ruled on the act's constitutionality and no administration has ever tried to enforce it. The provisions of the act "outlawing" the communist party have not been repealed. Nevertheless, the Communist Party of the USA continues to exist.

September 1, hurricane Carol struck Long Island and in Massachusetts killing 68 people, oddly on September 11, hurricane Edna following a similar path and caused another 20 deaths.

September 3, China began bombing the islands of Quemoy and Amoy held by Chiang Kai-shek. It appeared as if Communist China was preparing to launch an attack on Formosa (Taiwan). President Eisenhower warned the People's Republic that the US Seventh Fleet was prepared to defend Formosa. China and the US moved closer to war.

Also on September 3, the Espionage and Sabotage Act of 1954 was signed into law. The Act removed the previous ten year statute of limitations and made any acts of espionage or sabotage in the US punishable by death or life in prison.

September 6, a US Navy spy plane was shot down over Siberia. The US claimed the plane was in international waters and the Soviets claimed the plane was in Soviet air space. The plane crashed in the ocean just off Siberia where nine crew members were rescued, but a tenth crewman was apparently trapped in the sinking plane and died.

September 7, desegregation began in Baltimore and Washington, DC public schools.

September 8, the US and allies signed the Southeast Asia Treaty Organization, SEATO, to stop the spread of communism in the region.

September 9, an earthquake in Algeria killed over 1,700 people. The following day a second quake also killed many people.

September 11, the Miss America pageant was televised nationally for the first time. Nineteen-year-old Lee Meriwether from California was crowned.

September 14, the Soviets detonated a large nuclear test in Siberia.

September 20, one of the first computer programs FORTRAN began its first use.

September 26, a Japanese ferry boat sunk when a typhoon struck Japan and 1,172 people died.

September 27, *The Tonight Show* premiered. The host was Steve Allen.

October 1, the British Colony of Nigeria became an independent federation.

October 2, the French city colony of Chandernagore, now Chandannagar, on the Indian subcontinent was annexed to India.

October 10, Ho Chi Minh took formal possession of Hanoi as the French left.

October 14, in an act of revenge for an attack on Israel, the Israelis attacked Jordan and 53 people died.

October 15, Hurricane Hazel, was the third to hit the eastern US and Canada this season and 348 people died in the storm.

October 18, Texas Instruments announced the sale their first portable transistor radio.

October 19, Britain and Egypt signed a treaty and the British troops occupying Egypt left.

October 21, Indonesian troops invaded New Guinea.

October 23, West Germany joined NATO.

October 24, President Eisenhower pledged US support to the Republic of South Vietnam.

October 25, Chevrolet announced the creation of the new V-8 engine.

October 26, Trieste was returned to Italy.

October 27, Walt Disney premiered his first television show *Disneyland* on ABC.

Also on October 27, President Eisenhower offered an aid package to South Vietnam and sent the first "official" US military advisors.

In other news on this date Benjamin O. Davis Jr. became the first Black General in the US Air Force.

October 29, Colonel Nasser of Egypt disbanded and outlawed the Muslim Brotherhood.

October 31, the Algerian revolution against the French began.

November 1, with the assistance of the CIA and the US, General Fulgencio Batista was "elected" the President of Cuba and began his repressive regime. American business flourished in Cuba with the United Fruit Company and other American corporations treating Cuba as a colony. The American Mafia became entrenched in Havana running the city and its hotels, casinos, prostitution and drugs. Richard Nixon and his life-long friend Bebe Rebozo, the Mafia banker, became co-owners of a small hotel and casino in Havana.

November 2, Congressman Charles C. Diggs Jr. was elected Michigan's first Black member of Congress. Segregationist Senator Strom Thurmond of South Carolina became the first Senator ever elected with write-in votes.

November 12, the immigration station Ellis Island in New York was closed. It had been the busiest immigration station in US history. It opened in 1892 and over 12 million immigrants had come to the US through Ellis Island. It had also served as a detention and deportation facility.

November 22, the American Humane Association to protect animals became national and the headquarters was established in Denver, Colorado.

November 23, for the first time the US Stock Market closed above the peak that was set in 1929 before the crash that started the Great Depression.

November 24, the first Air Force One was designated. Previous to this the presidents flew on Air Force planes with regular flight numbers. There was a mix up in 1953 between an Air Force Flight 8610 with President Eisenhower aboard and an Eastern Airlines passenger flight also Flight 8610. Now any flight carrying the President of the US is designated as Air Force One.

Also on November 24, France sent 20,000 soldiers to put down the independence revolution in Algeria.

November 30, Liz Hodges of Oak Grove, Alabama became the first woman hit by a meteorite. The first man was hit in 1677 in Milan, Italy when a friar was struck and killed by a meteorite. A grapefruit-sized meteorite crashed through Hodges' roof, struck a wooden console radio cabinet and bounced off and hit her. She lived and donated the meteorite to the Alabama Museum of Natural History. In 1992 a small fragment of a meteorite also bounced off a tree and hit a Ugandan child.

On December 2, the US Senate admonished Senator Joseph McCarthy for his lies and slander. The Senate voted to "condemn" McCarthy on both counts by a vote of 67 to 22. All the Democrats voted against him and half the Republicans. The only Senator not voting was John Kennedy who was having back surgery at the time. Kennedy refused to say what his vote would have been. McCarthy was a Kennedy family friend. Bobby Kennedy had also worked for a time for McCarthy. The admonishment was the end of McCarthyism.

December 4, the first Burger King was opened in Miami, Florida.

December 10, Linus Pauling won the Nobel Prize in Chemistry. His work pioneered the field of molecular genetics. In 1962 he would also win the Nobel Prize for Peace for his anti-war activism. Also on December 10, Albert Schweitzer won the Nobel Peace Prize for his medical work in Africa.

In 1954 the median wage in was $4,700, the average cost of a new house rose to $10,250, but the average rent was still low at $80 per month. A new car averaged $1,700 and gasoline was at 22 cents per gallon. A Sylvania 17 inch black and white television cost $179.96. Tennis shoes were 98 cents a pair. Cigarettes were $1.67 per carton or 20 cents per pack. A cup of coffee at a café was 10 cents. The average cost of hamburger 25 cents. A quart of milk was 21 cents, a half gallon of ice cream was a dollar and a loaf of bread 15 to 17 cents.

The Emmy Awards were given to I Love Lucy for Best Television Show, to Donald O'Connor for Best Male Performer as the host of the Colgate Comedy Hour and Eve Arden as the Best Female Performer in Our Miss Brooks. In addition to The Tonight Show and Disneyland, other television shows debuting in 1954 included, *Lassie, Father Knows Best, Annie Oakley, Flash Gordon, The Adventures of Rin Tin Tin, Face the Nation,* and *The Secret Storm.* The top ten shows of 1954 included: *I love Lucy, Disneyland, Jack Benny, You Bet Your Life, December Bride, Toast of the Town, Dragnet, Ford Theater, The Jackie Gleason Show,* and the *George Goebel Show.*

The movies of 1954 included: *White Christmas* with Bing Crosby, Danny Kaye and Rosemary Clooney; *20000 leagues Under the Sea* with Kirk Douglas; Alfred Hitchcock's *Rear Window* with Jimmy Stewart and Grace Kelly; *The Caine Mutiny* with Humphrey Bogart and Fred MacMurray; *The Barefoot Contessa* with Humphrey Bogart and Ava Gardner; *Sabrina* with Humphrey Bogart and Audrey Hepburn; and *On the Waterfront* with Marlon Brando, Lee J. Cobb, Rod Steiger, and Eva Marie Saint. *On the Waterfront* won most of the Oscars with Best Picture, Elia Kazan for Best Director, Marlon Brandon for Best Actor, and Eva Marie Saint for Best Supporting Actress. It is worth noting that the movie *Godzilla* also premiered in Japan in November of 1954.

The top songs of 1954 featured: *Little Things Mean A Lot,* which was the number one hit sung by Kitty Kallen who also had another hit, *In the Chapel in the Moonlight.* Other hits included: *Wanted* and *Papa Loves Mambo* were hits for Perry Como; *Hey There* and *This Old House* by Rosemary Clooney; *Young at Heart* by Frank Sinatra; *That's Amore* by Dean Martin, *Secret Love* and *If I give My heart to You* by Doris Day, *Three Coins in the Fountain* and *Stranger in Paradise* by the Four Aces, Tony Bennett also had a hit with *Stranger in Paradise.* There were several Rock and Roll hits, *Rock around the Clock* by Bill Haley and the Comets, *Well All Right* and *Shake Rattle and Roll* by Big Joe Turner. *Shake Rattle and Roll* was Turner's biggest hit single. In 1954 Bill Haley and Elvis Presley in 1956 also had hit singles with their versions of *Shake Rattle and Roll.*

In October Ernest Hemingway won the Nobel Prize for Literature. The top books of 1954 included: *Lord of the Flies* by William Golding, *The Lord of the Rings* series by J.R.R. Tolkein, *Horton Hears a Who* by Dr, Seuss, *100 Selected Poems* by E.E. Cummings, *Live and Let Die* by Ian Fleming, *Twelve Angry Men* by Reginald Rose, *Sweet Thursday* by John Steinbeck, *Abraham Lincoln* by Carl Sandburg, *The Great Crash of 1929* by John Kenneth Galbraith, *The Man in the Gray Flannel Suit* by Sloan Wilson, *Nobody Knows My Name* by James Baldwin, *The Story of O* by Pailine Réage, *A Spy in the House of Love* by Anaïs Nin and *Ideas and Opinions* by Albert Einstein. *The Adventures of Augie March* by Saul Bellows won the 1954 National Book Award for fiction and *A Stillness at Appomattox* by Bruce Canton won for non-fiction.

CHAPTER 11. 1955: IN GOD WE TRUST, CIVIL DEFENSE, HURRICANES, DAVY CROCKETT, EMMET TILL AND ROSA PARKS

January, 2 President José Antonio Remón of Panama was assassinated by submachine gun fire at a race track by multiple unknown assailants. Remón and two of his bodyguards were killed. Two Americans, Martin Irving Lipstein and Roy Bettis, were initially detained as suspects but they were later released. At the time of his assassination Remón had been negotiating for more money and the return of some unused land from the US for their use of the Panama Canal. A Panamanian lawyer Rubén O. Miró confessed that he and José Ramón Guizado, who became President immediately after Remón, were part of the plot. Both men were released after serving only months in prison and without identifying the other plotters or the shooters.

January 6, President Eisenhower proposed a 20% wage increase for 1,300,000 federal workers.

January 7, Marion Anderson became the first Black singer to perform at the Metropolitan Opera in New York City.

January 20, in the Battle of Yijiangshan Islands the People's Liberation Army defeated Chain Kai-shek's forces and ejected them from the islands.

January 25, the USSR formally ended their war with Germany.

Also on this day Columbia University developed an atomic clock accurate to within one second in 300 years.

February 8, the turmoil in the leadership of the USSR continued as Malenkov resigned as premier and Bulganin replaced him.

February 9, the two largest American trade union federations agreed to merge and became the AFL/CIO.

February 12, the Soviets implemented plans for a space center to be built in Baikonur, Kazakhstan.

February 13, Israel acquired 4 of the 7 Dead Sea Scrolls. The Dead Sea Scrolls are a collection of 981 texts on scrolls that were discovered between 1946 and 1956 at Khirbet Qumran near the Dead Sea on the Israel's West

Bank. The texts are of great historical, religious, and linguistic significance because they include the earliest known surviving manuscripts (as early as 408 BCE) of works later included in the Hebrew Bible and from which came the religions of Judaism, Christianity and Islam.

February 15, the first synthetic diamonds were produced in a factory.

February 24, the Baghdad Pact, a mutual defense treaty, was signed between Britain, Turkey, Iran, Iraq, and Pakistan. It became known as the Central Treaty Organization, CENTO. The US and Secretary of Defense John Foster Dulles negotiated the treaty, but the US did not officially participate, but it played a major role behind the scenes. The pact was to prevent Soviet and communist expansion into the Mideast. It was weak from the beginning as the countries did not trust each other. Pakistan also wanted the partner countries to support it in its two wars with India. In 1979 CENTO dissolved.

March 1, an Israeli assault on Gaza killed 48 people.

March 3, Elvis Presley made his television debut on a televised version of the radio program *Louisiana Hayride*.

March 4, the first facsimile (fax) was sent across the country.

On March 11, the Civil Defense Administrator Val Peterson told a Senate Armed Services Subcommittee that all citizens should build some sort of underground shelter "right now," stocked with sufficient food and water to last 5 or 6 days. His recommendation was based on knowledge of what a hydrogen bomb might do when intercontinental guided missiles are perfected. When that happens, he said, "We had all better dig and pray. In fact, we had better be praying right now." It became the notice for Americans to build the backyard or basement fallout shelter.

March 15, the US Air Force unveiled the self-guided missile.

March 16, President Eisenhower stated that America would keep the option to use atomic weapons in war.

March 17, the Commissioner of the National Hockey League suspended Maurice Richard of the Montreal Canadians for the remainder of the year for acts of violence in the rink. French-Canadians strongly objected to his suspension and riots erupted in Montreal. Thirty-seven people were injured in the riots and over a hundred were arrested. Richard had to go on radio to plead with his fans to stop the violence before the rioting ended.

March 24, the first sea-going oil drill rig went into service.

Also on this day the British Army stopped regular patrols in Belfast, Northern Ireland.

March 25, the U.S. Customs Department confiscated 520 copies of Allen Ginsberg's poetry book *Howl*, which had been printed in England. Officials alleged that the poetry was obscene. Lawrence Ferlinghetti published the book in the fall of 1956 in San Francisco. The publication led to Ferlinghetti's arrest on obscenity charges.

Also on this day the German Democratic Republic (East Germany) was given semi-autonomy from the USSR and permitted to establish a German communist government.

March 26, the *Ballad of Davy Crockett* became the number one record in the US. The song was from a Disney film. Walt Disney made a live-action film starring Fess Parker about the life of Davy Crockett. Disney divided the movie in to three parts which were shown on television on December 15, 1954 and on January 26, and February 23, 1955. The television shows set off a craze among American children who all suddenly bought 45 RPM records and listened to the *Ballad of Davy Crockett*, bought artificial coonskin Davy Crockett hats and rubber Bowie knives, along with toy rifles named "Ol' Bess" to shoot at General Santa Ana's army as he charged the Alamo.

March 31, the Chase National Bank, the third largest in the US merged with the Bank of Manhattan, the 15th largest bank in the US, to form the Chase Manhattan Bank.

April 1, after withdrawing their troops from Egypt, the British decided to house these troops on Cyprus and to make that island the British base for the Mideast. Cypriots opposed this decision and on this date Cypriot independence fighters called EKOA began bombing British buildings and military targets.

Also on this day the Dutch used military force to break up a workers strike in Amsterdam.

April 3, a night passenger express train derailed in Guadalajara, Mexico and killed over 300 passengers.

April 11, an Air India plane, the Kashmir Princess, was bombed and crashed in a failed assassination attempt on Zhou Enlai by Chiang Kai-shek's Kuomintang. The plane flew from Bombay to Hong Kong and then on to Jakarta carrying diplomats and international press to a conference to end colonialism in Asia. Zhou Enlai was to be one of the diplomats aboard, but an emergency appendectomy cancelled his plans. The Hong Kong police determined that the bomber was Chow Tse-ming, who was working for the Kuomintang. Chow Tse-ming was smuggled out of Hong Kong on a CIA owned a Civil Air Transport plane back to Taiwan. The Hong Kong police tried to extradite him but were rebuffed by Chiang's government. Sixteen people died and three were rescued from the sea. The People's Republic of China accused the United States of involvement in the bombing. The CIA had proposed a plan to assassinate Zhou Enlai but Eisenhower had nixed it as too dangerous. The CIA then encouraged and assisted the Kuomintang to try and helped their bomber escape in the aftermath.

April 18, the first Walk/Don't Walk traffic signals were installed.

May 5, the Western Allied occupation of Germany ended. The Federal Republic of Germany became an independent sovereign state.

May 7, the USSR signed peace treaties with France and Great Britain.

Also on May 7, Reverend George Lee, a co-founder of the NAACP in Belonzi, Mississippi was shot and killed. Reverend Lee was the first Black to register to vote in Humphreys County. Lee's effort to register 100 Black voters in Humphreys County was likely the reason why he was murdered. He had received multiple death threats. When Medgar Evers and others tried to investigate his murder the county sheriff lied and said Lee was killed in an auto accident. The FBI attempted to bring murder charges, but they were blunted as the local prosecutor refused to cooperate.

May 9, the German Federal Republic joined NATO.

May 14, the Warsaw Pact, a mutual defense trearty, was signed by the Soviet Union, Albania, Bulgaria, Czechoslovakia, German Democratic Republic, Hungary, Poland, and Romania to counter NATO.

May 15, Britain, France, US and USSR signed the Austrian State Treaty to restore Austria's national independence.

May 25, a series of 19 tornadoes destroyed Udall, Kansas and Blackwell, Oklahoma.

May 31, Great Britain proclaimed a state of emergency due to a national railroad strike.

June 2, the USSR and Yugoslavia signed the Belgrade Declaration and normalized relations between the two countries Diplomatic relations had been discontinued in 1948.

June 13, a race car lost control at Le Mans, France and killed 77 spectators. Also on this day the first diamond mine (the Mir Mine) is discovered in the USSR.

June 15, when the Federal Civil Defense Administration staged Operation Alert in cities around the country, including in Washington, D.C. *The New York Times* observed on June 16, "This was the first Civil Defense test in which the Government actually left Washington and in which account was taken of the lethal and widespread effects of radioactive fall-out." The US was able to estimate the spread of fallout because it had exploded a hydrogen bomb on March 1, 1954, in the Bikini Atoll in the central Pacific Ocean. The test revealed that the fallout had spread 7,000 square miles over the Pacific. "On land," *The New York Times* said, "that fall-out would have killed virtually every exposed person in an area about the size of New Jersey."

The New York Times also noted that in such an explosion "the Federal Civil Defense Administration estimated assumed casualties at 5,000,000 killed and almost 5,000,000 injured. It also estimated that 10,000,000 persons had been made homeless, creating serious welfare problems."

In the targeted cities the participation of the public was reported as "spotty," as most people didn't participate or go to the shelters as they were requested. There were arrests around the nation of people who blatantly refused to participate or go to shelters when directed to do so by the police.

June 27, Illinois became the first state to enact an automobile seatbelt law.

July 9, the Russell-Einstein Manifesto was issued in London, by Bertrand Russell. Albert Einstein had co-authored the document and it was signed by some of the world's leading scientists calling for an end of nuclear weapons. Russell began the news conference in London by saying, "I am bringing the warning pronounced by the signatories to the notice of all the powerful Governments of the world in the earnest hope that they may agree to allow their citizens to survive."

Also on July 9, E. Frederic Morrow became the first Black executive on the White House staff.

July 11, in a mixture of American jingoism and Christian fervor the US Congress passed legislation for "In god we trust" to be placed on its most holy thing, the American currency.

July 14, lightning struck and killed two people and dazed many more at a racetrack in Ascot, England.

July 15, in a similar document to the Russell-Einstein Manifesto, Eighteen Nobel laureates signed the Mainau Declaration against nuclear weapons. It was later co-signed by thirty-four others. In part the document said, "All nations must decide voluntarily to refrain from violence as the last means of politics. If they are not prepared to do so, they will cease to exist."

July 17, the Disneyland theme park televised its grand opening on television.

Also on this day Arco, Idaho became the first American city with electricity from nuclear power.

July 22, Richard Nixon became the first Vice President to preside over a US cabinet meeting. Due to his age and health, Eisenhower began to assign his Vice president more duties. He asked Nixon to preside over these meetings in his absence.

July 27, Austria regained independence and autonomy.

Also on July 27, an Israeli El Al passenger plane on its weekly London to Tel Aviv flight changed course to avoid a serious thunderstorm and accidently strayed into Bulgarian air space and was shot down by two Mig-15 fighter jets. The seven member crew and 51 passengers died. Bulgaria admitted to shooting the plane down and later paid compensation to the families of the victims.

August 3, Hurricane Connie hit the East Coast and five days later Hurricane Diane followed in the same path. The two hurricanes caused widespread damage and flooding. In New York and New Jersey over a quarter million people lost power. In the aftermath five states were declared Federal Disaster Areas with over $700 million in damages.

August 4, President Eisenhower authorized an astonishing $46 million for a new CIA headquarters at Langley, Virginia.

August 8, A Geneva conference was held to discuss and promote the peaceful uses of atomic energy.

August 12, President Eisenhower raised the minimum wage from 75 cents to a dollar an hour.

August 13, Lamar Smith, a 63-year-old farmer and WWI veteran was shot and killed in front of the Lincoln County Courthouse in Mississippi. At the time of his death Smith was encouraging Blacks to register to vote. Three White suspects were charged but released because all the witnesses were too afraid to testify against them.

August 19, WINS radio in New York said it will no longer play the White cover versions of R&B records. They began by refusing to continue playing Pat Boone's version of Fats Domino's *Ain't It a Shame*. Other stations and DJs soon followed and Black artists began to be heard on mainstream radio.

August 20, hundreds were killed in anti-French and independence rioting in Algeria and Morocco.

August 25, the last Soviet forces left Austria.

August 27, the Guinness Book of World Records was first published.

August 28, a fourteen-year-old Black child from Chicago named Emmet Till went to visit his relatives in Money, Mississippi. On a dare he spoke to a 21-year-old White woman, Carolyn Bryant, who told her husband that a Black boy had talked to her when she was alone. Bryant's husband, a grocery store owner, and his brother went to the Till house and took him to a barn, where they beat and tortured the child, gouged out one of his eyes, and then shot him in the head. They tied a 70 pound weight around his neck with barbed wire and threw his body in the Tallahatchie River where it was recovered several days later. The trial attracted a significant amount of national press attention. In September 1955, Bryant and his brother were acquitted of Till's kidnapping and murder. After the trial, knowing they could not be tried again for the same crime, they bragged about what they had done in *Look Magazine*.

August 31, the first microwave television station began operation in Lufkin, Texas. Also on this day the first solar powered auto was demonstrated in Chicago.

September 1, two Egyptian fighter planes were shot down over Israel.

September 19, strongman Juan Peron of Argentina resigned and fled the country.

Also on this day hurricane Hilda stuck Mexico and killed over 200 people.

September 22, hurricane Janet killed over 500 in the Caribbean.

September 24, President Eisenhower suffered a heart attack and Richard Nixon became the first vice president to temporarily assume the duties of president.

September 30, Actor and cultural icon James Dean was killed in a car accident in California. He became the first actor to receive a posthumous Oscar nomination for Best Actor in *East of Eden*. He also won a posthumous Golden Globe Award for Best Actor in *East of Eden*. His movie *Rebel Without a Cause* was released after his death.

October 12-18, hurricane Hazel killed 1,191 people and caused $323 million in damages in the Caribbean and in the US from Virginia to New York, and then merged with a cold front to strike Canada as far inland as Toronto.

October 17, Miss America Lee Merriwether joined the *Today Show* cast.

October 18, two University of California physicists Emilio Sergé and Owen Chamberlain confirmed the existence of the antiproton. In 1959 they would win the Nobel Prize for Physics for this work.

October 25, the first microwave oven was sold.

October 26, the first edition of *The Village Voice* went on sale in New York City.

Also on this day the British occupied Saudi Arabian oil fields.

October 28, Saudi Arabia and Egypt signed a mutual defense treaty.

November 1, United Airlines Flight 629 from Denver to Portland was blown up by a time bomb. It was later determined that Jack Gilbert Graham, a man with an extensive criminal record, had planted the time bomb in his Mother's suitcase to collect her life insurance money.

November 7, the Maryland Supreme Court banned segregation in public recreational areas.

November 19, the ultra-conservative magazine, *The National Review* was published for the first time by William F. Buckley Jr.

November 22, RCA Victor paid $25,000 to Sam Phillips at Sun Records for the rights to Elvis Presley.

November 25, the *Interstate Commerce* Commission *banned racial segregation* on all interstate trains and buses.

November 26, British Governor General Sir John Harding declared a state of emergency in Cyprus because of the EOKA terrorist campaign against British forces.

December 1, Rosa Parks a 42-year-old seamstress was arrested for refusing to give up her seat to a White man on a Birmingham Bus. She later said, "When I made that decision I knew that I had the strength of my ancestors with me." In response to Ms Parks arrest a group named the Montgomery Improvement Association, composed of local Black activists and Black ministers organized a bus boycott. They chose a young Baptist minister, Martin Luther King, Jr., as their leader and spokesman. Inspired by Mrs. Parks' action, the boycott lasted 381 days, into December 1956 which almost bankrupted the municipal bus service. More than half the riders were Black. When the U.S. Supreme Court ruled that the segregation law was unconstitutional the Montgomery buses were integrated. The Montgomery Bus Boycott was the beginning of a new revolutionary era of Black non-violent mass protests in support of civil rights in the United States.

December 6, psychologist Dr. Joyce Brothers won the television show's *$64,000 Question* by answering a question about boxing.

December 12, British engineer Christopher Cockerell patented the hovercraft.

December 14, the Tappan Zee Bridge opened to traffic in New York.

December 26, RKO announced that it was selling its entire film library of movies to television.

December 31, the General Motors Corporation became the first corporation to earn over a billion dollars in a year.

In 1955 there was no real inflation. The average annual wage was $4,130. The average price of a new house was $10,950 with $87 for the average monthly rent. In 1955 almost 8 million new cars were sold at an average price of $1,900 with gasoline at 23 cents per gallon. These cars came with seat belts as required by the new laws. Seven out of ten American families now owned a car, and they used this new mobility to move to the suburbs in greater numbers. Fish Fingers appeared for the first time in 1955 along with the first cans of soda pop (Coke) which would eventually replace bottles. Ray Kroc bought the franchise rights to MacDonald's from the McDonald brothers and began to erect the hamburger stands nationwide. Emmet Till's beating and murder and Rosa Parks' refusal to give up her seat on a Montgomery Bus began a new era of civil rights. Rock and Roll swept the nation's youth, as did Davy Crockett, Disneyland, and *The Mickey Mouse Club.*

New black and white television set prices averaged under a hundred dollars, $99.95, and television sales increased dramatically. Many new shows made their debuts in 1955 including, *The Bob Cummings Show, The Lawrence Welk Show, Gunsmoke, Cheyenne, The Honeymooners* with Jackie Gleason, *The Millionaire, Alfred Hitchcock Presents, Sergeant Preston of the Yukon, Captain Kangaroo, The Mickey Mouse Club*, and the television show that began the quiz show craze, *The $64,000 Question.* The Emmys went to Danny Thomas and *Make Room for Daddy* and to Loretta Young. In March Mary Martin starred in the children's classic *Peter Pan* on television. Actor Steve McQueen also made his debut on *Goodyear Playhouse.*

In the movies *Marty* was the Oscar favorite taking Best Picture, the Best Director for Delbert Mann and the Best Actor for Ernest Borgnine. Many of the other films were World War II pictures including: *Mister Roberts* with Henry Fonda, James Cagney, and Jack Lemon; *Battle Cry* with Van Heflin and Aldo Ray; *To Hell and Back* with Audie Murphy; *The Sea Chase* with John Wayne; and a Cold War military movie, *Strategic Air Command* with Jimmy Stewart. Some teen movies also were successful such as the classic *Rebel Without a Cause* which starred James Dean, Natalie Wood, Sal Mineo, Dennis Hopper and Jim Backus, and *Blackboard Jungle* with Glenn Ford and Sidney Portier. *Guys and Dolls* won an Oscar for Best Musical with Marlon Brando and Frank Sinatra, and *Oklahoma* with Gordon McCrae and Shirley Jones was an equally popular musical. The Best comedy was *The Seven Year Itch* with Marilyn Monroe, Tom Ewell, and Jack Lemon. Walt Disney's *Lady and the Tramp* was the children's favorite. The classic *East of Eden* with James Dean, Julie Harris, and directed by Elia Kazan, also premiered.

Bill Haley's *Rock Around the Clock* was the number two hit of 1955, making Rock and Roll mainstream. The number one hit *Cherry Pink and Apple Blossom White* by Perez Prado was the top tune. Other hits included: *Unchained Melody* which was a hit for both Les Baxter and Al Hibbler, *Love is a Many Splendored Thing* by the Four Aces, *Sincerely* by the McGuire Sisters, *Ain't That a Shame* by Pat Boone, *Moments to Remember* by the Four Lads, *Mr. Sandman* by the Chordettes, *Let me Go Lover* by Joan Weber; *Sixteen Tons* by Tennessee Ernie Ford, and *The Ballad of Davy Crockett* was a hit for three different singers, Bill Hayes, Tennessee Ernie Ford, and Fess Parker who played Davy Crockett in the Disney film.

In May the Pulitzer Prize was awarded to Tennessee Williams for *Cat on a Hot Tin Roof.* Books of 1955 included: *Lolita* by Vladimir Nabokov (not published in the US until 1958), *Cat on a Hot Tin Roof* by Tennessee Williams, *The Talented Mr. Ripley* by Patricia Highsmith, *The Quiet American* by Graham Greene, *Moonracker* by Ian Fleming, *Andersonville* by MacKinlay Cantor, *Peyton Place* by Grace Metalious, *Profiles in Courage* by John F. Kennedy, *Marjorie Morningstar* by Herman Wouk, *No Man Is an Island* by Thomas Merton, *Run Silent, Run Deep* by Edward L. Beach, *The Angry Hills* by Leon Uris and *The Mouse That Roared* by Leonard Wibberley.

CHAPTER 12. 1956: SCHOOL DESEGREGATION VIOLENCE, EISENHOWER RE-ELECTED, THE HUNGARIAN REVOLT, AND ROCK AND ROLL IS HERE TO STAY

January 1, the Sudan declared its independence from Britain and Egypt.

Also on this day a panic at a religious event at the Yahiko Shrine in Japan caused a stampede and 124 people were trampled to death with many more wounded.

January 3, a fire damaged the top of the Eiffel Tower in France.

January 8, the Elvis Presley single record *Hound Dog* with *Don't Be Cruel* on the flip side rose to the number one spot on the music charts.

Also on January 8, five U.S. missionaries were killed by the Huaorani Indians in the eastern rainforests of Ecuador shortly after making contact with them. It was called Operation Auca to spread Christianity to a very remote tribe that had little contact with the outside world. The five became martyrs and galvanized American Christian missionary zeal. The event was covered in *Life* magazine and a 2006 movie was made about the event. The event also brought more missionaries to the Huaorani whose indigenous culture was eventually extinguished by the missionaries. In the process of saving their souls, they destroyed their culture and their tribe.

January 9, Abigail Van Buren's newspaper advice column, *Dear Abby* debuted.

January 16, Egyptian President Abdel Nasser pledged that Egypt would re-conquer Israel.

January 22, a train crash in Los Angeles killed 30 people.

January 30, after anonymous warnings for the young Black minister to stay out of politics, the home of the Reverend Martin Luther king Jr. was bombed in Birmingham, Alabama.

February 3, Autherine Lucy, a Black woman, and her Black friend classmate, decided to attend the University of Alabama in 1952. They were turned down. Lucy sought the help of the NAACP and was assigned lawyers who began legal action on her behalf. Autherine Lucy was "reluctantly allowed to register" at the University of Alabama but was barred from all dining areas and dormitories. On the third day of her classes a violent mob assembled to prevent her attendance. The University suspended Lucy saying that they could not protect her. She began legal action to get her suspension overturned and the University then used her legal action to say that Lucy was slandering the University and was no longer welcome as a student.

February 6, French Premier Guy Mollet was pelted with tomatoes in Algiers.

February 15, the Pittsburgh Pirates and the Kansas City A's exhibition baseball game in Birmingham was cancelled because of local ordinances barring Black players playing against Whites.

February 25, Khrushchev denounced Stalin at the 20th Soviet Communist Party Conference.

February 28, 13 died in a train crash in Massachusetts.

February 29, despite his age and health, President Eisenhower announced that he would seek a second term.

March 2, Morocco declared independence from France, with the official date of March 3, 1956.

March 5, the movie *King Kong* debuted on television.

March 9, the British made plans to exit Cyprus and leave the island to Greece. Archbishop Makarios of Cyprus objected on behalf of the Turkish population of Cyrus and was arrested and exiled to Seychelles. A day later the Turks on Cyprus declared a general strike to protest.

March 12, the DOW Jones Average posted above 500 for the first time.

Also on March 12, Senator Harry Byrd of Virginia convinced 101 of the 128 congressmen from the eleven Southern states of the old Confederacy, to sign "The Southern Manifesto on Integration." The document claimed that the United States Supreme Court's 1954 decision in *Brown v. Board of Education*, which declared racially segregated public education unconstitutional, constituted an abuse of power by the Court and negated state's rights in violation of federal law.

March 20, Tunisia gained independence from France.

Also on this day a 156 day strike against Westinghouse Electric ended.

May 3, a new mountain range was discovered in Antarctica with two peaks above 13,000 feet.

May 13, 1956, a sixteen-year-old Black girl, Annette Butler of Tylertown, Mississippi, was kidnapped and gang raped by four White men. The girl and her family reported the assault and the men were arrested, jailed, and tried for the crime. It was a rarity in Mississippi for White men to be charged with assaulting Black women. Despite their confession, an all-White jury refused to convict three of the four defendants, and the fourth was allowed to plead to a reduced charge in exchange for a reduced sentence.

May 27, French commandos landed in Algeria.

Also on May 27, US Treasury agents seized the Communist Party newspaper *The Daily Worker* for alleged nonpayment of taxes. At the same time they raided communist party offices in New York, Newark, Chicago, Detroit, Los Angeles, Philadelphia and San Francisco.

April 1, the violence between the French and the Algerians escalated with over 380 killed. On April 11, the French sent 200,000 reserve troops to Algeria.

April 8, six Marine recruits were killed in a training exercise in Paris Island, South Carolina.

April 11, singer Nat King Cole was attacked by the Ku Klux Klan in Birmingham while performing on stage. The leader of the Klansmen attack, Asa Earl Carter, became a noted western novelist and also wrote the screen play for *The Outlaw Joey Wales* starring Clint Eastwood.

April 18, Israel and Egypt agreed to a ceasefire.

May 2, the Methodist Church stopped racial segregation in their churches.

May 7, in a battle at Oran, Algeria over 300 were killed. On May 10, the French sent another 50,000 reserve troops to Algeria.

May 11, after hitting the charts in the US with several hits Elvis Presley got his first hit on the charts in Britain with *All Shook Up*.

May 12, East Pakistan (Bangladesh) was hit by a large cyclone and tidal waves.

May 16, Egypt recognized the People's Republic of China.

May 26, a fire aboard the aircraft carrier the USS Bennington killed 103 sailors off the coast of Rhode Island.

May 30, Blacks in Tallahassee, Florida began a bus boycott.

June 2, President Tito of Yugoslavia visited Moscow.

June 9, an earthquake in Afghanistan killed over 400 people.

June 13, after 72 years the British gave up their control of the Suez Canal to Egypt.

June 17, Golda Meir, formerly an American teacher from Milwaukee, Wisconsin, began her term as the Israeli Foreign Minister.

June 19, singer Dean Martin and comedian Jerry Lewis ended their partnership.

June 20, a Venezuelan passenger plane crashed in New Jersey killing 74 people.

June 21, the German Democratic Republic (East Germany) released about 19,000 prisoners taken at the end of WWII.

June 25, two passenger ships, the *Andrea Doria* and the *Stockholm* collided at night in the fog off the coast of Massachusetts killing 51 people.

June 28, in riots in Poznan, Poland 38 people were killed.

June 29, President Eisenhower signed the Highways Funding Act to begin construction of the American interstate system.

June 30, TWA and United passenger planes collided over the Grand Canyon killing 128 people.

July 5, the French people expressed outrage as France raised the tobacco tax by 20% due to the war in Algeria.

July 9, Dick Clark appeared for the first time as the host of *American Bandstand*.

July 10, over 650,000 American steel workers went on strike.

July 16, the Karelo-Finnish SSR officially became part of the Russian SFSR, which formally annexed what prior to the war had been part of Finland. Stalin had previously sent many Finnish residents of this area to Siberia.

July 19 and 20, the US and Britain refused to lend money to Egypt to build the Aswan Dam. The Soviets then gave Egypt $1.12 billion at 2% interest for the construction of the dam. The Soviets also supplied military weapons to Egypt angering both the US and Britain.

July 25, Jordan attacked the UN peace keeping forces on the West bank.

July 26, Egypt seized the Suez Canal. Israel, Britain and France planned an invasion of Egypt to take the canal. It began in October when Israel invaded the Sinai Peninsula and the British and French began bombing Cairo. The US and the USSR were both opposed to the action and applied pressure to the three invaders to stop their actions. The British and French forces withdrew by the end of the year under US pressure, but Israel remained in the Sinai until March of 1957 and prolonged the crisis. The Suez Canal did not re-open until the Israeli's withdrew. This event is sometimes cited as the end of Britain as a world power.

July 30, in another act of jingoistic Christian zeal Congress passed an Act replacing "E Pluribus Unum" the official US motto that had been adopted by Congress in 1782 with "In God We Trust."

August 6, the DuMont Network, unable to get its fair share of air time, made is final broadcast.

August 7, a train transporting dynamite in Colombia exploded and killed over 1,200 people.

August 8, a fire in a mine in Belgium killed 263 miners.

August 16, the Democratic National Convention was held in Chicago. Adlai Stevenson was again nominated. Stevenson's main competition was again Senator Estes Kefauver of Kentucky and Averell Harriman of New York. In the vice presidential balloting Kefauver was selected as Stevenson's running mate after three close ballots against John F. Kennedy. NBC newsmen Chet Huntley and David Brinkley co-anchored the convention coverage which proved so positive that the two men were then asked to co-anchor the NBC national nightly news.

August 17, in one of the largest anti-Apartheid demonstrations was staged in South Africa's history when 20,000 women marched in Pretoria to present a petition to the prime minister against the carrying of passes by women.

August 20, the Republican National Convention was held in San Francisco. Unlike 1952 there was no conservative challenger to Eisenhower. However in the spring of 1956 there was a lot of speculation that Nixon would not be on the ticket again. Eisenhower had wanted to go with a new vice president and had sounded Nixon out about a cabinet position but Nixon wasn't interested. In the end, with pressure from conservatives, Eisenhower decided to have Nixon serve again as his vice president. Richard Nixon and his conservative supporters had already decided that Nixon would run for President in 1960.

August 26, Black children, who later became known as the "Clinton Twelve," made history by walking down Foley Hill from Green McAdoo School where they registered and began attending classes at the public high school in Clinton, Tennessee. They were the first students to desegregate a state-supported public Tennessee high school and the first to do so in any southern state. Within a few days a crowd of angry Whites began to gather daily in front of the school to protest the Black students. By August 29, the crowds grew dramatically with between a thousand and two thousand angry Whites protesting outside the school. A federal judge issued a restraining order and when the crowd refused to disperse he had the leader arrested for contempt of court and gave him a year in jail. However the crowd continued to grow and became angry. On Labor Day weekend September 1-2, the crowd turned violent and overturned cars, smashed windows and threatened Blacks and Whites alike. They stopped and harassed Black motorists, including several service members going through town. The small Clinton police force was overwhelmed and the Mayor asked the Governor for help. Six hundred Guardsmen with tanks came to restore order. They were required to stay for all of September.

August 30, a violent White mob prevented the enrollment of Black students at a suburban Dallas high school in Mansfield, Texas.

September 2, a railroad bridge collapsed in India killing 120 people.

September 5, twenty people died in a train crash in New Mexico.

September 9, the African Party of Liberation of Guinea-Bissau and Cape Verde was formed to bring independence to these French West African colonies.

Also on September 9, Elvis Presley appeared on the Ed Sullivan Show for the first time.

September 10, the schools of Louisville, Kentucky integrated. However an elementary school in Clay, Kentucky barred the admission of Black students. On September 17, the Clay Elementary School was forced to admit Black students by the courts.

September 13, IBM introduced the first computer disk storage unit.

September 19, the first conference of international Black artists and writers was held at the Sorbonne in Paris.

September 25, the first trans-Atlantic telephone cable began service. Secretly the CIA tapped the cable to listen into all trans-Atlantic phone calls.

September 28, RCA reported that Elvis Presley had sold over 10 million records.

October 6, Dr. Albert Sabin announced the oral polio vaccine.

October 8, the Southdale shopping mall in Edina, Minnesota, opened on this day and became the first all indoor mall, starting a trend which began "the malling of America" and the decline of commercial downtowns. Although this mall and others that followed were anchored by large department stores, these malls along with the big box retailers like Wal-Mart and Target eventually contributed to the decline of the traditional Department Store.

October 16, the movie *Love Me Tender* starring Elvis Presley premiered.

Also on this day William J. Brennan Jr. was appointed to the Supreme Court.

October 17, England's first large scale nuclear power plant opened.

October 23-November 10, Hungary began a revolt against Soviet occupation. It began as a student revolt, when students tried to take over a radio station to demand freedom for Hungary. State security police fired on the students killing one. News spread of the killing, and disorder and violence erupted throughout Budapest. The government buildings were assaulted by thousands of people and the pro-Soviet government collapsed. The Hungarians then began forming militias and fighting with the occupying Soviet troops. A new government was formed and stated their intention was to declare independence and withdraw from the Warsaw Pact. On November 4, a large scale Soviet invasion of more than 200,000 troops destroyed the militias and dissolved the new government. During the revolt well over 2,500 Hungarians and 700 Soviet troops died. Over 200,000 Hungarians also fled the country. In the aftermath the Soviets arrested about 26,000 and imprisoned 13,000. They also executed more than 350 Hungarians.

October 24, Margaret Towner became the first woman ordained by the American Presbyterian Church setting off a controversy about women in the ministry.

November 3, *The Wizard of Oz* was aired for the first time on television.

November 6, Holland and Spain withdrew from the Olympics in protest to the Soviet Invasion of Hungary.

Also on November 6, in the US election Eisenhower defeated Stevenson 35 million votes to 26 million. Stevenson carried only seven "solid South" states.

November 18, Morocco gained independence.

November 22, the Olympic Games opened in Melbourne, Australia.

December 2, Fidel Castro returned to Cuba from exile in Mexico to begin his revolution in Cuba in the Sierra Maestra mountains.

December 6, Nelson Mandela and 156 others were arrested for their political activities in South Africa.

December 8, in preparation for a launch NASA began test firing the Vanguard Rocket to launch a satellite into space.

December 11, large anti-Soviet demonstrations occurred in Poland.

December 12, the Irish Republican Army began Operation Harvest, a guerilla war to free Northern Ireland from Britain and to unite it with the rest of Ireland. The war would last until 1962 when it ended in failure.

December 18, Japan was admitted as a member in the United Nations.

December 20, Montgomery, Alabama gave in to the bus boycott and removed all race based seating on the bus system.

December 25, Ku Klux Klan members bombed the Birmingham, Alabama, home of civil rights activist Reverend Fred Shuttlesworth. He was home at the time of the bombing with his family and two members of Bethel Baptist Church, where he served as pastor. The dynamite blast destroyed the home and caused damage to Shuttlesworth's church next door but miraculously no one inside the home suffered a serious injury. White supremacists would attempt to murder Shuttlesworth four more times during the next seven years, including one 1957 incident in which a White mob brutally beat Shuttlesworth with chains and bats and stabbed his wife after the couple attempted to enroll their daughters in a white high school.

December 28, snipers fired shots into a desegregated bus traveling through a Black neighborhood in Montgomery, Alabama. Rosa Jordan, a 22-year-old Black woman who was eight months pregnant, was shot in both legs while sitting in the rear of the bus. She was transported to the hospital, where doctors were hesitant to remove a bullet lodged in her leg, fearing it could cause Jordan to give birth prematurely. She was told she would have to remain in the hospital for the duration of her pregnancy.

In 1956 college became an option for many and one out of three high school graduates headed for college. Many young men were using their GI Bill educations benefits to attend college. Wages averaged almost $4,450 per year and consumer goods flew off the shelves. Disposable diapers appeared for the first time along with Tefal non-stick pots and pans. Inflation was very low although wages were high. The average new house price increased to $11,700 but rent prices were still low averaging $88 per month. The average price of a new car rose to $2,050 and gasoline averaged 22 cents per gallon. Car trips were easy and affordable. Food prices in 1956 were also low. Coffee was 69 cents per pound. Chuck roast was 33 cents and spare ribs were 39 cents per pound. Milk was 97 cents per gallon and bread 18 cents per loaf.

In January Rock and Roll era began in earnest. Elvis Presley recorded and released *Heartbreak Hotel*. Four days later Little Richard released *Tutti Frutti* and on January 20, Buddy Holly recorded *Black Days Black Night*. On January 28, Elvis Presley appeared for the first time on national television on the Dorsey Brother's *Stage Show* before a crowd of screaming teenage girls. On January 30, Elvis recorded *Blue Suede Shoes*. Rock and Roll was beginning to dominate the American music scene.

The music of 1956 was dominated by Rock and Roll and particularly by Elvis Presley who had five hits in the top fifteen, *Heartbreak Hotel, Don't Be Cruel*, which were the top two hits of 1956 along with *Hound Dog, I want You I need you I Love You*, and *Love Me Tender*. The Platters had three big hits with *My Prayer, You've Got the Magic Touch* and *The Great Pretender*. Carl Perkins also hit with *Blue Suede Shoes*. Jim Lowe with *Green Door*, The Four lads with *No Not Much* and *Standing on A Corner*, Frankie Lymon and The Teenagers with *Why Do Fools Fall In Love* which was also a hit for the Diamonds, Bill Haley and the Comets with *See You Later Alligator*, Fats Domino with *I'm in Love Again* and *Blueberry Hill*, Little Richard with *Long Tall Sally*, Gene Vincent with *Be-Bop-a-Lula*, and Patience and Prudence with *Tonight You Belong to Me*.

The older generation still managed to see some of their stars in the top 100 hits. Gogi Grant with *The Wayward Wind*, Doris Day with *Que Sera Sera*, Dean Martin with *Memories are Made of This*, Vic Damone with *On the Street Where You Live* and Patti Page with *Allegheny Moon*, Perry Como with *Hot Diggity* and *More*, and Frank Sinatra with *Hey Jealous Lover*.

In 1956 televisions were in 71% of American homes. It became the primary entertainment for most Americans as televisions were more affordable, and the number of programs, hours and stations grew. The first portable televisions were sold. The first videotape recorder was invented by Ampex in 1956. This year saw the quiz show become a staple in American television with the premier of *The $64,000 Question* and *Twenty-One*. The soap opera also became a staple as soap operas which had been fifteen minutes in length went to a half hour with the premier of two new soap operas, *As the World Turns* and *The Edge of Night*. Other shows that made their debuts in 1956 included: *Queen for a Day, My Friend Flicka, The Adventures of Jim Bowie, The Gayle Storm Show, Playhouse 90, The Nat King Cole Show,* and *The Price Is Right*.

Television was also making a serious dent in movie production. General attendance was down as Americans seemed to prefer the small screen to the large one. The top grossing movie of 1956 was *The Ten Commandments* starring Charlton Heston, Yul Brynner, Anne Baxter, and Edgar G, Robinson. *Around the World in Eighty Days* with David Niven and Shirley MacLaine was the second highest grossing film. Coming in third was *Giant* with Rock Hudson, Elizabeth Taylor, and James Dean. Other films of 1956 included: *War and Peace* with Audrey Hepburn and Henry Fonda, *The King and I* with Deborah Kerr and Yul Brynner, *The Searchers* with John Wayne, *Bus Stop* with Marilyn Monroe and Don Murray, *High Society* with Bing Crosby, Grace Kelly, and Frank Sinatra, *Anastasia* with Ingrid Bergman, *The Man Who Knew Too Much* with Jimmie Stewart and Doris Day, and *Love Me Tender* with Elvis Presley.

The Oscars were divided with no clear favorite. The Oscar for Best Picture went to *Around the World in Eighty Days*. Best Director went to George Stevens for *Giant*, The Best Actor went to Yul Brynner for *The King and I*, and the Best Actress for Ingrid Bergman in *Anastasia*.

The some of the most significant books of 1956 included: *Howl and Other Poems* by Alan Ginsberg, *The Fall* by Albert Camus, *The Art of Loving* by Erich Fromm, *Giovanni's Room* by James Baldwin, *Diamonds Are Forever* by Ian Fleming, *The Last Hurrah* by Edwin O'Connor, *A Devil In Paradise* by Henry Miller, *Seize the Day* by Saul Bellow, *Look Back in Anger* by John Osborne, *Bang the Drum Slowly* by Mark Harris, *The Outsider* by Colin Wilson, *Lady Sings the Blues* by Billie Holliday, *A History of the English Speaking Peoples* by Winston Churchill, *Old Yeller* by Fred Gipson, and *If I Ran the Circus* by Dr. Seuss.

Chapter 13. 1957: Sputnik I &II, the Rise of Dr. King, Desegregation Violence, Khrushchev on Television, and Ed Gein

January 1, France returned the industrial Saar Valley to Germany, twelve years after the war ended.

Also on this day the Irish republican Army, IRA, attacked the British Brookeburough military barracks. The attack was unsuccessful and resulted in the death of the two IRA leaders that lead the attack.

January 3, the first electric watch went on sale.

January 5, President Eisenhower proposed the Eisenhower Doctrine. Congress approved it in March. Under the Eisenhower Doctrine, a country could request American economic assistance and/or aid from U.S. military forces if it was being threatened by armed aggression from another state. The doctrine was motivated in part by an increase in Arab hostility toward the West, and growing Soviet influence in Egypt and Syria following the Suez Crisis and the British, French and Israeli invasion of Egypt. It would be used later in Vietnam.

January 9, British Prime Minister Anthony Eden resigned over the mishandling of the Suez Crisis.

January 10, the Southern Christian Leadership Conference was formed. Following their success in the Montgomery Bus Boycott Dr. Martin Luther King Jr. consulting with Bayard Rustin and Ella Baker invited about 60 Black ministers and other Black leaders to the Ebenezer Baptist Church in Atlanta. Their goal was to form an organization to coordinate and support non-violent direct action to promote desegregation in the South.

Also on January 10, four Black churches and two pastors' homes were bombed in Montgomery, Alabama, three days later the congregations held their Sunday services amidst the debris. Two white men affiliated with the Ku Klux Klan, Raymond Britt and Sonny Livingston, were later indicted in February 1957 after confessing to all the bombings. An all-White jury acquitted them of all charges in May 1957, while the White spectators cheered.

January 11, the Convention Africaine, CA, was formed in Dakar Senegal. This West African political party would win the regional assembly elections in Senegal and seats in three other African assemblies, Upper Volta, Niger and Nigeria. In 1958 the CA would merge with the African Socialist Movement to form the African Regroupment Party, PRA.

January 13, the Wham-O Company produced the first Frisbee.

January 16, to prove that American air power can reach anywhere, three B-52 bombers took off from California on a non-stop around the world flight. They returned to California January 18, setting a new record for around the world flight at 45 hours and 19 minutes.

January 22, Israeli forces finally withdrew from the Sinai.

Also on this date George P. Metesky, known as "the Mad Bomber," was apprehended. Angry and resentful about events surrounding a workplace injury he suffered years earlier, Metesky planted at least 33 bombs, of which 22 exploded, injuring 15 people over a sixteen year period. The court found him legally insane and he was sent to a state mental institution.

January 23, 1957, four Klansmen forced Willie Edwards Jr. to jump to his death from the Tyler Goodwin Bridge near Montgomery, Alabama. Edwards, a Black resident of Montgomery, was driving back from his first assignment as a deliveryman for a Winn-Dixie grocery store when four armed White men approached the vehicle. They forced Edwards out of the truck at gunpoint, and ordered him to get into their car. While in the car they threatened to shoot or castrate him. When the men reached the bridge they ordered Edwards out of the car. He was then told to "hit the water" or be shot, Mr. Edwards climbed the railing of the bridge and fell 125 feet to his death. Edwards' pregnant twenty-three-year-old wife, Sarah, was left to raise their two young daughters. Not knowing what had happened to her husband, she learned three months later that her husband was dead when two fishermen found his decomposed body in April 1957. In 1993, one of the Klansmen, Henry Alexander, confessed to his wife on his deathbed that he and three other Klansmen were responsible for "the truck driver's" death and revealed the truth of Edwards' last moments.

January 25, Jack Soble and his brother Robert Soble and Soble's wife Myra were arrested by the FBI for espionage. Jack Soble and his brother Robert admitted to spying for many years for the USSR. Jack and his brother were sentenced to seven years and Myra to five and a half years which was later reduced to four years. It was never clear if Myra had actually engaged in espionage. On July 5, 1991, President George H.W. Bush pardoned her of the crime.

January 26, India annexed Kashmir. The event became an on-going hot political disagreement between India and Pakistan.

January 31, a Douglas DC-7 passenger plane on a test flight collided with a USFA F-86 fighter jet and crashed into a junior high school in Pacoima, California. Eight people died and about seventy-five were injured.

February 1, the first Black airline passenger pilot was hired.

February 4, the first portable electric typewriter went on sale.

February 14, the Georgia State Senate unanimously approved a bill barring Blacks from playing baseball with Whites.

February 17, a fire in a nursing home in Warren, Missouri killed 72 people.

February 18, Dedan Kimathi, a Mau Mau leader, was executed by the British Colonial government in Kenya.

February 25, the US Supreme Court decided that Major League Baseball was exempt from anti-trust laws.

March 4, the S&P 500 stock market index was introduced and replaced the S&P 90.

March 6, the former British colony of the Gold Coast, declared independence as Ghana.

Also on this date the hundred year anniversary of the Dred Scott Slavery decision was marked by the re-discovery of Dred Scott's grave in Missouri. Dred Scott had previously been commemorated with a headstone at Ft. Snelling, Minnesota where he had lived in freedom until ordered back into slavery by the courts.

March 8, Israeli troops left the Sinai and the Suez Canal was partially reopened for shipping.

March 9, an 8.1 earthquake shook the Aleutian Islands off Alaska.

March 12, the Soviets stationed 22 Army divisions in East Germany.

March 13, anti Batista demonstrations turned bloody in Havana Cuba.

March 17, Ramon Magsaysay, President of Philippines died in a plane crash.

March 20, Britain accepted NATO's offer to mediate in Cyprus, but Greece rejected it.

March 22, a 5.3 earthquake shook San Francisco causing widespread damage. It was the largest quake since the 1906 quake that destroyed much of San Francisco.

March 23, the U.S. Army retired the last of its messenger homing pigeons.

March 25, the European Economic Community, EEC, more commonly known as the Common Market was established to promote free trade in Europe. It would eventually be replaced with the European Union, EU, in 2009.

April 7, the last New York City electric trolley cars were taken out of service. Electric trolleys were replaced throughout most of the US in the mid 1950s by gasoline and diesel powered buses with the encouragement of the oil industry.

April 11, Britain agreed to self-rule for Singapore.

April 13, due to a lack of funds Saturday mail delivery was temporarily halted by the US Postal Service. However on April 15, the US Congress gave the Postal Service $41 million to continue Saturday service.

April 26, a festival commemorating the 350th anniversary of the founding of Jamestown, Virginia was held.

May 1, the US gave $95 million in credit to Poland in exchange for allowing CARE and the American Relief for Poland to send packages to

Poles from their families in America. The Catholic Church and Senator John F. Kennedy were instrumental in bargaining this agreement.

Also on May 1, the US tested a multi-stage Vanguard rocket. The US had announced to the world that it would put a satellite in orbit during the coming year. The US space program had become bogged down in a bureaucratic squabble by the military over the use of rockets. The first priority of the military was to perfect a continental ballistic missile capable of delivering a nuclear warhead and the space program was given a distant second billing. Although the US military had more advanced rockets than the Vanguard they were being used and tested exclusively for military purposes. At one point the rocket scientist Wernher von Braun angrily said, "Vanguard will never make it. We have the hardware on the shelf. We can put up a satellite in 60 days." Of the eleven Vanguard rockets which were launched only three successfully placed satellites into orbit.

May 2, during a Mafia war, Frank Costello, a Mafia crime boss, was shot in the head in New York City by a hit man working for Mafia boss Vito Genovese. Costello survived. The bullet had grazed Costello's head, but he fell to the ground and the shooter assumed he was dead. After recovering from the assassination attempt, Frank Costello and Vito Genovese made peace. Costello agreed to abdicate as family boss in favor of Genovese. In return, Genovese agreed that Costello would keep all of his gambling operations in Louisiana and Florida as well as his legitimate business interests.

May 15, a religious crusade organized by Billy Graham attracted 18,000 people in New York City.

Also on this day the British exploded their first hydrogen bomb over Christmas Island.

May 17, nearly 25,000 civil rights demonstrators gathered at the Lincoln Memorial in Washington, D.C., for a Prayer Pilgrimage for Freedom, featuring three hours of spirituals, songs, and speeches that urged the federal government to fulfill the three-year-old promise to desegregate all public schools. The event was organized by Dr. Martin Luther King Jr. who was the final speaker. After this event King became recognized by both Blacks and Whites as the national leader of the Civil Rights movement. It was also during this time that J. Edgar Hoover and the FBI began keeping a file on King. Hoover, a racist, was convinced King was a communist, and that the Civil Rights movement was a communist plot. He insisted this was true to his death although he never found any justification for this despite hundreds of investigations.

May 22, the South African government approved racial segregation of all South African Universities.

May 24, a riot erupted in Taipei, Taiwan. During the riot the American Embassy was stormed and badly damaged. Eleven Americans were wounded in the attack. The riot began had because a US Army sergeant was acquitted of shooting and killing a Chinese man because he been found window peeping at his unclothed wife and he said he killed the man in self-defense. The widow of the deceased Chinese man told the authorities that the

Sergeant and her husband had been involved in the black market and that her husband was killed over money.

Also on May 24, a large earthquake struck in Columbia.

May 28, the Brooklyn Dodgers received approval to move the club to Los Angeles.

May 29, Algerian rebels captured and killed 336 French collaborators.

Also on this day the Laos government of Prince Suvanna Phuma collapsed, leaving the country in turmoil. The CIA began their secret war in Laos.

June 2, Nikita Khrushchev was interviewed on US national television. After two years of dead-end negotiations, *Face the Nation* producers had managed to book the very first television interview with Soviet leader Nikita Khrushchev. Most of the interview was fairly tame, but toward the end of the interview Khrushchev said while wagging a finger, "I can prophesize that your grandchildren in America will live under socialism." With Cold War tensions running high, many conservative government officials accused CBS of putting out Communist propaganda. Secretary of State Dulles refused to watch the interview and President Eisenhower inferred that it was damaging to US interests.

In part Khrushchev had agreed to the interview with *Face the Nation* in an attempt to thaw relations with the West and to shore up support in the USSR. After denouncing Stalin in a speech in 1956 a number of pro-Stalinist hard line Soviet leaders, Molotov, Kaganovich and Malenkov attempted to oust Khrushchev. At an extraordinary session of the Central Committee held in late June 1957 he won a vote which reaffirmed his position as First Secretary. Then he expelled Molotov, Kaganovich and Malenkov from the Secretariat and ultimately from the Communist Party itself. Khrushchev then ordered the release of millions of political prisoners from the Gulag camps. Under Khrushchev's rule the number of political prisoners in the Soviet Union was decreased from 13 million to 5 million people.

June 5, Dr. Herbert Berger, a New York City narcotics investigator, urged the American Medical Association to investigate the widespread use of narcotic stimulants by professional athletes.

June 11, twelve people died in a train crash in Colorado.

June 13, the Mayflower II a replica of the seventeenth century ship that brought the Pilgrims to the US arrived in Plymouth, Massachusetts from Plymouth, England.

June 16, the French launched a major offensive in Algeria.

June 17, the Black citizens of Tuskegee, Alabama began a boycott of the White businesses in response to gerrymandering the city boundaries to disenfranchise all Black voters. In 1957, in an effort to frustrate increasing black voter registration and the threat of losing a white voter majority, Alabama state senator Sam Engelhardt sponsored Act 140, which proposed to transform the Tuskegee City boundaries from a square into a twenty-eight sided shape resembling a "seahorse" that included every single one of the 600 white voters and excluded all but 5 of the city's 400 Black voters. It was this method that Republicans would later use to gerrymander their districts for congressional seats after 1980.

June 24, the US Supreme Court ruled that obscenity is not protected under the First Amendment in *Roth v United States*.

June 26, Hurricane Audrey killed 526 people in Louisiana and Texas.

Also on this date the British Medical Research Council published a report suggesting a direct link between smoking and lung cancer.

July 2, the US launched Grayback, the first submarine capable of launching guided missiles.

July 6, the Harry S. Truman Library was dedicated in Independence, Missouri.

July 12, the US Surgeon General stated that there was a connection between smoking and lung cancer.

July 19, the first rocket with a nuclear warhead was fired from a Nevada test site.

July 21 Althea Gipson became the first Black to win a major US tennis tournament.

July 26 the USSR successfully tested the first multi-staged intercontinental ballistic missile.

Also on this day Carlos Castillo Armas, the CIA's and United Fruit Company's puppet dictator of Guatemala, was assassinated by one of his palace guards.

July 28, heavy rains caused a landslide in Japan that killed 992 people.

July 29, the UN formed the International Atomic Energy Commission to promote the peaceful use of atomic energy.

August 1, the US and Canada formed the North American Air Defense Command, NORAD to defend against Soviet air attack over the Arctic Ocean.

August 5, *American Bandstand* went national airing on ABC.

August 8, the USSR began its military and economic support of Syria.

August 25, Prince Suvanna Phuma formed a government in LAOS with communist Pathet Lao who were backed by North Vietnamese communists. The CIA began recruiting the Hmong as their fighting force against Laotian communists.

August 28, South Carolina Senator Strom Thurmond began a 24 hour filibuster against the Civil Rights Act of 1957. The goal of the 1957 Civil Rights Act was to ensure that all Americans could exercise their right to vote. On August 29, despite Thurmond's record filibuster the law passed. After passage of the Act, Dr. King sent a telegram to President Eisenhower asking him to make a speech to the South, asking him to use "the weight of your great office to point out to the people of the South the moral nature of the problem." Eisenhower responded, "I don't know what another speech would do about the thing right now." Dr. King attempted to meet with the President but Eisenhower refused to meet. The Act was weak and without Eisenhower's leadership and support it came to nothing. By 1960, Black voting had only increased by a meager 3%.

August 31, Malaysia formally gained independence from Britain.

September 1, an excursion train in Jamaica crashed killing about 200 and injuring another 400 people who were on a religious outing.

September 4, the Ford Motor Company introduced the Edsel, a quality car that was a dud with the public. Chevrolet also introduced a new car design in September of 1957, the Chevy Bel Air, which became the classic car of the 1950s.

Also on September 4, Governor Orval Faubus called out the Arkansas National Guard to keep nine Black children from attending Little Rock High School. This blatant act against the court decision forced President Eisenhower's hand. His advisors said that he had to enforce the law of the land or be seen as a segregationist. Eisenhower federalized the Arkansas National Guard and ordered them to return to their armories which effectively removed them from Faubus' control. Eisenhower then sent the 101st Airborne to Little Rock to protect the nine Black students from large angry White mobs trying to prevent the Black children from attending the school. In retaliation, Faubus shut down Little Rock high schools for the 1958-1959 school year. This is often referred to as "The Lost Year" in Little Rock. In 1958 Faubus was included among the "Ten Men in the World Most Admired by Americans" according to a Gallup poll.

September 5, Castro's revolution against Batista began making headway. The City of Cienfuegos began to rebel against Batista. In retaliation Batista ordered his air force to bomb the city's civilian population. The bombing of innocent Cubans was a turning point forcing many more Cubans to side with Castro's revolutionaries.

September 9, Hattie Cotton Elementary School in Nashville, Tennessee was dynamited because one little Black girl enrolled in the first grade. The entire front right corner of the school was damaged in this explosion. Through the tireless efforts of the staff the damage was cleared and school was able to be continued in the remainder of the building after just a few weeks.

September 14, in a hopelessly late effort the UN condemned the Soviet invasion of Hungary.

September 16, a military coup took place in Thailand.

September 17 the USAF X-15, the first space plane, made its first powered flight. The X-15 became the first plane to take men into space. The aircraft also holds the world's speed record for a manned aircraft at 4,520 miles per hour. It was the forerunner of the much bigger Space Shuttle.

September 25, the Soviet 7th Year Plan was unveiled. The American rightwing would later seek to associate this with the locally-created five-year economic, land use and transportation plans developed by US regional commissions. The conservative right would ironically argue that these local regional plans were Soviet communist plots to turn America to communism.

September 26, the popular Dag Hammarskjöld of Sweden was re-elected as UN Secretary General.

September 29, in West Pakistan more than 300 people died in a train collision.

September 30, the French government lost support of the French people and resigned due to the unpopular and costly war in Algeria.

October 1, the Strategic Air Command began a twenty-four hour, seven days a week air alert placing B-52 bombers in the air at all times to retaliate in case of a Soviet attack or a first strike if they were ordered to do so by the President.

October 4, the USSR launched Sputnik I, the first manmade object in earth orbit. The satellite travelled at about 29,000 miles at 18,000 mph taking 96.2 minutes to complete each orbit. It transmitted a beep on 20.005 and 40.002 MGZ which could be monitored by amateur radio operators around the world. It was in low earth orbit and could be seen by millions as it flew over at night. The radio signals continued for 22 days until the transmitter batteries ran out on October 26, 1957. Sputnik 1 burned up on January 4, 1958, when it fell from orbit and reentered the earth's atmosphere.

This was a Soviet propaganda coup that caught the Americans napping. The US had no idea that the USSR was close to this technology and the US rocket program priority was still military. President Eisenhower and the Congress were angry and demanded that the American space program to catch up posthaste. Space exploration was now an American priority. The military was told by Congress and the President that it should give the same attention to the space program that it was in developing intercontinental ballistic missiles. The Space Race began in earnest.

October 8, Turkish and Syrian troops exchanged fire along their common border.

October 10, President Eisenhower was forced to apologize to the Finance Minister of Ghana who as a Black man was refused service in a Dover, Delaware, "Whites only" restaurant.

Also on October 10, the first nuclear reactor accident occurred when a reactor used to make weapon grade plutonium in Windscale, West Cumberland (now Cumbria) in Britain caught on fire. The fire was eventually smothered but not before the release of substantial amounts of radioactive contamination into the surrounding area.

October 12, Canadian Prime Minister Lester Bowles Pearson was awarded the Nobel Peace Prize for organizing the United Nations Emergency Force to resolve the Suez Crisis.

October 16, Queen Elizabeth and Prince Phillip visited Williamsburg, Virginia in recognition of the English settlers coming to North America. The following day they visited the White House.

October 16, the USAF sent two aluminum bullet canisters into space to measure radiation.

October 23, the US test fired Vanguard satellite launch vehicle.

October 26, another shakeup in the Soviet leadership resulted in the firing of Defense Minister Marshal Georgi Zhukov.

October 29, a hand grenade placed by a terrorist exploded in the Israeli Knesset.

November 1, the world's longest suspension bridge was opened in Mackinac Straits, Michigan.

November 2, the Soviet Union launched, Sputnik II, carrying a dog named Laika. The US President and Congress demanded to know why the

US space program was still testing its space rockets. Because of this incident the first discussions began concerning the removal of the US space program from the military to a civilian organization.

November 10, a record crowd of 102,368 attended an NFL game between the Los Angeles Rams and the San Francisco 49ers in Los Angeles.

November 14, a national meeting of Mafia leaders in Binghamton, New York was raided by the FBI and many Mafia leaders were arrested.

November 15, the US sentenced Soviet spy Rudolf Ivanovich Abel to 30 years in prison.

November 21, Ed Gein, a 51-year-old Wisconsin man, was arraigned on one count of murder. Upon investigation it was found that Gein was both a mass murderer and a grave robber who made clothing and household articles from girl's and women's body parts. He also admitted to cannibalism. Gein was the inspiration for several movies including *Psycho*, *The Texas Chainsaw Massacre* and *Silence of the Lambs*.

November 22, the Miles Davis Quintet debuted at a jazz concert at Carnegie Hall.

November 25, President Eisenhower suffered a stroke, affecting his speech.

November 30, an assassination attempt was made against Indonesian President Sukarno. During the 1955 Indonesian elections, the CIA had given a million dollars to the Masjumi Party, an opposition party to both Sukarno's Nationalist party and the Communist party in Indonesia. Sukarno blamed the Dutch for the assassination attempt and ordered that all Dutch leave the country and also nationalized all Dutch properties. The US publicly blamed the assassination on the communists. The attempt is now widely known to be the work of the CIA as they had been planning to get rid of Sukarno since 1955. The CIA operation to get rid of Sukarno was code named Operation Hike.

December 1, Sam Cooke and Buddy Holly and the Crickets debuted on the Ed Sullivan Show.

December 2, the first large scale US nuclear power plant opened at Shippingport, Pennsylvania.

December 4, two commuter trains collided in heavy fog in England killing 92 people.

December 6, the first attempt to launch a US satellite failed as the Vanguard rocket blew up on the launch pad.

Also on December 6, New York City passed the Fair Housing Practices Law becoming the first to legislate against racial or religious discrimination in housing.

December 17, the US successfully test fired the Atlas intercontinental ballistic missile (ICBM). The rocketry of the ICBM was well ahead of the rocketry in the space program irritating the Congress and President.

December 20, Elvis Presley was given his draft notice by the US Army.

By 1957 an Asian flu pandemic killed approximately 1 million people worldwide. The pandemic began in China in 1956. It was a zoonosis which came from a mutated virus from wild ducks. It spread to the US in 1957 and killed about 70,000 people.

Inflation in 1957 rose up a bit to just over 3%. The average annual wage was $4,550. New housing prices averaged just over $12,000, but average rent was still low at $90 per month. New car prices rose to $2,749 and American cars were now bigger and faster. Gasoline was 24 cents per gallon. Food prices were still low: milk $1 per gallon, butter 75 cents per pound, bread 19 cents a loaf, eggs 55 cents a dozen, bacon 60 cents per pound, hamburger 30 cents per pound, Campbell's Tomato Soup was 10 cents per can and a Swanson's TV Dinner cost 75 cents.

The new television shows in 1957 included some classics: *American Bandstand* (national television debut), *Perry Mason. Maverick, Leave It to Beaver, Zorro, Divorce Court,* and *Wagon Train.* Jack Paar became the permanent host of the *Tonight Show* replacing Steve Allen who left to start his own television show. NBC introduced its animated peacock logo. The *Phil Silvers Show* and the *Caesar's Hour* won Emmys. *Playhouse 90* won the Best New Show and the *Playhouse 90* Episode: *Requiem for a Heavyweight* won for the Best Single program and is still considered an American television classic.

Hollywood was now suffering as movie theaters lost attendance to television by the tens of thousands. However it helped Hollywood that the drive-in movie theaters were also being built and attended by the thousands. The top movies of the year included: *The Bridge on the River Kwai* starring William Holden and Alec Guinness; *Peyton Place* with Lana Turner, *Sayonara* with Marlon Brando and Red Buttons, *Raintree County* with Montgomery Clift and Elizabeth Taylor; *Island In the Sun* with James Mason, Harry Belafonte, Joan Fontaine and Joan Collins, *A Farwell to Arms* starring Rock Hudson and Jennifer Jones, *Gunfight at the OK Corral* with Burt Lancaster and Kurt Douglas, *Pal Joey* with Frank Sinatra, Rita Hayworth and Kim Novak, *Funny Face* with Audrey Hepburn and Fred Astaire, *The Three faces of Eve* with Joann Woodward, the Disney film *Old Yeller,* and two Elvis Presley movies, *Jailhouse Rock* and *Loving You.*

The *Bridge on the River Kwai* won most the Oscars including Best Picture, David Lean for Best Director, and Alec Guinness for Best Actor. *Sayonara* won two, Red Buttons for Best Supporting Actor and Miyoshi Umeki for Best Supporting Actress. Joann Woodward won best Actress in *The Three faces of Eve.*

The music of 1957 was dominated by Rock & Roll. Elvis Presley had five of the top hits including the year's number one hit *All Shook Up,* along with *Too Much, Teddy Bear, Love Me Tender* and *Jailhouse Rock.* Other top songs included: *Love Letter in the Sand* and *Don't Forbid Me* by Pat Boone, *Little Darlin'* by the Diamonds, *Young Love* by Tab Hunter, *Bye Bye Love* and *Wakeup Little Susie* by the Everly Brothers, *Tammy* by Debbie Reynolds, *Young Love* by Sonny James, *Day-O* (the Banana Boat Song) by Harry Belafonte, *Come Go with Me* by the Del-Vikings, *You Send Me* by Sam Cooke, *Searchin'* by the Coasters, *Diana* by Paul Anka, *That'll Be the Day* by Buddy Holly and the Cricketts, *Whole Lotta Shakin' Goin' On* by Jerry Lee Lewis, and *Chances Are* and *It's not for Me to Say* by Jonny Mathis.

In May, John F. Kennedy was awarded the Pulitzer Prize for *Profiles in Courage*. The books of 1957 contain some classics. *Atlas Shrugged* was written by Ayn Rand, the quirky icon of the American rightwing, and the mentor to Alan Greenspan and his failed anti-regulation economics. On the other end of the political spectrum, *On the Road* by Jack Kerouac was also published in 1957. Other books included: *Franny and Zooey* by J.D. Salinger, *Dr. Zhivago* by Boris Pasternak, a nuclear war aftermath novel *On the Beach* by Nevil Shute, *The Way of Zen* by Allison Wilson Watts, *The Guns of Navarone* by Alistair MacLean, *Exile and the Kingdom* by Albert Camus, *The Undiscovered Self* by Carl Jung, *How to Develop Self-Confidence and Influence People by Public Speaking* by Dale Carnegie, *Please Don't Eat the Daisies* by Jean Kerr, *Gidget* by Frederick Kohner, *The Birds* by Tarjei Vessas, *The Bridge at Andau* by James Michener, *Mandingo* by Kyle Onstott, *The Untouchables* by Eliot Ness, *The Cat In the Hat* and *How the Grinch Stole Christmas* by Dr. Seuss, and *A Death in the Family* by James Agee which won the Pulitzer Prize in 1958 after his death.

Chapter 14. 1958: Natural Born Killers, the Fraud of Charles Van Doren, Castro's Cuba and Other Latin American Problems, and Independence in Africa

January 3, Edmund Hillary became the first to reach the South Pole over land.

Also on this day The West Indies Federation was formed.

January 6, Gibson patented The Flying V guitar. Although it was not initially popular with the public it was a staple of many Blues guitarists and became a classic over time.

January 10, Jerry Lee Lewis' song *Great Balls of Fire* reached number one on the British pop charts.

January 13, over 9,000 scientists from 43 nations petitioned the UN for a ban on nuclear weapons.

Also on this day the Moroccan Liberation Army ambushed and defeated the Spanish Army in the Battle of Edchera.

January 18, William O'Ree became the first Black player in the National Hockey league.

January 23, Venezuelan dictator Marcos Pérez Jiménez was forced to flee Venezuela to the US during a popular revolt. Pérez Jiménez had come to power in a military coup in 1952. He was favored by the US who had assisted his rise to power. The US awarded the Legion of Merit medal to Marcos Pérez Jiménez in 1954.

January 26, a ferry capsized off the coast of Japan killing 167 crew and passengers.

January 28, the Lego Company patented their product and began to produce their toy building bricks.

January 29, twenty-year-old Charles Starkweather and his fourteen-year-old girlfriend, Caril Ann Fugate, were arrested for eleven murders committed in a two month murder spree in Nebraska and Wyoming. Three of the victims were Fugate's mother, stepfather and two-year-old sister.

Starkweather was executed seventeen months later. Fugate was given a life sentence but served seventeen years in prison before her release from incarceration in 1976. The pair influenced American movies and literature. Seven movies were based upon the two, most notable *Natural Born Killers* in 1994. Several books were also based upon the pair. Stephen King was fascinated by the killings as a boy said they greatly influenced his writings.

January 30, the first two way moving sidewalk began operation in Dallas.

February 1, the US launched its first satellite Explorer I. The satellite allowed Dr. James Van Allen to confirm the existence of radiation belts around the earth, which have since been named the "Van Allen Radiation Belts" in his honor.

Also on February 1, Syria and Egypt announced they would merge their nations to create the United Arab Republic. Both Lebanon and Jordan felt that the union was a threat to their existence. Iraq was also interested in merging with the two and seriously considered a merger later in 1960. However the merger of the two was ill-fated and short-lived lasting only until 1961 when Syria withdrew. In 1963 Iraq proposed a new union of the three, but the proposal failed to gain enough momentum.

February 5, the US appointed Clifton R. Wharton as the first Black American Foreign Service officer. He was posted to Romania.

February 7, the Brooklyn Dodgers officially became the Los Angeles Dodgers.

February 8, in their war with Algeria the French went after weapons caches and rebels in neighboring Tunisia. On this day they bombed a Tunisian village Sakiet-Sidi-Youssef killing 86 and wounding 100 Tunisians. The incident was immediately condemned by the UN.

February 11, Ruth Carol Taylor became the first American Black woman hired as a flight attendant in Ithaca, New York.

March 2, General José Miguel Ramón Ydígoras Fuentes became President of Guatemala with help of the CIA. In response to Ydígoras' autocratic rule and his close ties to the United States, a group of junior army officers led a rebellion in 1960. Although unsuccessful, the surviving officers went on to create a revolutionary movement that would conduct guerilla warfare in Guatemala for the next 36 years.

February 20, the Los Angeles Coliseum approved the use of the stadium by the Los Angeles Dodgers for two years until their new stadium was built.

February 24, Radio Rebelde (Rebel Radio) began broadcasting Castro's revolutionary messages to the Cuban people. A large number of Cubans began to turn against Batista and became more sympathetic to the revolution.

March 5, US satellite Explorer II was launched but failed to achieve orbit.

March 8, in one of the most improbable comebacks in sports history, race horse Silky Sullivan was behind by 40 lengths but went into a running frenzy to win the race by 3 lengths at the Santa Anita race track. Silky Sullivan would repeat this erratic behavior over his up and down career.

March 11, Dr. Charles Van Doren, a Columbia University professor and writer, and the son of a Pulitzer Prize winning father and uncle and a novelist mother, finally lost on the very popular television game show *Twenty-one*. Van

Doren delighted audiences with his amazing knowledge on a wide variety of subjects and won $129,000 on the show. He was said to be the most knowledgeable man in America. He became a household name and appeared on the cover of *Time* magazine February 11, 1957. NBC gave the popular Van Doren a three year television contract and he ultimately became the Cultural Correspondent for the *Today Show.*

Van Doren's fame began to unravel as Herb Stempel the previous champion on *Twenty-one* and others began to suspect that Van Doren had been given the questions and answers in advance. Van Doren denied any wrongdoing, saying "It's silly and distressing to think that people don't have more faith in quiz shows." Both the New York District Attorney and the Congress began an inquiry into the scandal. Van Doren continued to deny the allegations until another former *Twenty-One* contestant, an artist named James Snodgrass, finally provided indisputable corroborating proof that the show had been rigged. Snodgrass had documented every answer he was coached on in a series of registered letters he mailed to himself prior to the show being taped. In the aftermath Van Doren lost his job with NBC and his assistant professorship at Columbia.

March 14, the Recording Industry Association of America, RIAA, was founded. Before the RIAA, Gold Records were given to performers by record companies for records that sold over a million copies. On this date the RIAA gave the first Industry Gold Record to Perry Como for *Catch a Rising Star.*

Also on March 14, fearing that any arms sent to Cuba would end up in Castro's and the Cuban rebels' hands, the US government began an arms embargo against Cuba. However, this also served to further weaken the Batista regime. The CIA, US business interests, and the Mafia were still firmly on the side of Batista and still confident of a Batista victory.

March 17, the US successfully launched the Vanguard I satellite. The satellite was used to accurately measure the size of the Earth for the first time and to study the wear and tear on space vehicles in the harsh environment of space. It was also the first solar powered satellite. Although communication with it was lost in May of 1964 when its solar powered batteries wore out, it remains the oldest manmade satellite still in orbit and it is projected to stay in its orbit until the year 2208.

Also beginning March 19 and lasting into the following day a record setting snowfall fell on the East Coast. Morgantown, Pennsylvania recorded 50 inches of snow. Stroudsburg, Pennsylvania recorded 35.4 inches and Mount Airy, Maryland recorded 33 inches of snow, and in New York City about 12 inches were recorded in Central Park.

March 22, King Faisal, a US ally, became King of Saudi Arabia.

Also on March 22, the Havana Hilton opened. It was the largest and tallest hotel in Latin America designed by the well-known Los Angeles architect Welton Becket who had previously designed the Beverly Hills Hilton. Conrad Hilton personally attended the grand opening. US business interests were still very confident in Batista. Their confidence was misplaced as the Havana Hilton would later become the temporary headquarters of the victorious Fidel Castro on January 6, 1959.

March 24, Elvis Presley began US Army basic training.

March 25, the West German Parliament announced their desire to obtain nuclear weapons.

March 26, the US space program was finally up to speed as the US Army launched the Explorer III satellite aboard an Army Jupiter C rocket. The Jupiter C was a rocket the US Army was testing as an intercontinental ballistic rocket. After the US was embarrassed by Sputnik and after the explosion of the inferior Navy Vanguard rocket in February the Army's Jupiter C was pressed into service at the insistence of the President and Congress. The Explorer III continued mapping the Van Allen Radiation Belts.

March 27, CBS Laboratories announced a new stereophonic record that was still playable on ordinary LP phonographs. Now records could be recorded once in stereophonic format and still be played on every phonograph.

March 27, Nikita Khrushchev consolidated his power and became Chairman of the Council of Ministers and the Premier of the USSR. He began cutting the Soviet Army to 300,000 and built a defense plan based upon ballistic missiles. Part of this plan would later lead to conflict with the US during the Cuban Missile Crisis in October of 1962.

March 31, Khrushchev suspended Soviet nuclear tests and asked the US and Britain to do the same. The US and Britain refused and continued testing, forcing the USSR to follow suit.

April 4, the first protest march against nuclear weapons was held in Aldermaston, England where Britain's atomic weapons program was located. It was a member of this group, an artist Gerald Holtom, created the worldwide symbol for peace, a stick frame of a bomber surrounded by a circle.

April 10, Spain ceded part of Spanish Sahara to Morocco.

April 13, the Cold War competition began affecting music. Van Cliburn became a folk hero by being the first American to win the Chaikovsky Competition in Moscow.

April 14, Sputnik II with the space dog Laika fell out of orbit and burned up upon re-entry.

April 15, the first Major League Baseball game in California saw the San Francisco Giants beat the Los Angeles Dodgers 8-0. On April 18, a record single game crowd of 78,682 saw the Dodgers win the rematch against the Giants 6-5 in Los Angeles.

April 16, the French government of Gaillard fell due to a crisis caused by the bombing of Tunisia.

April 18 Ezra Pound was ordered released from a mental hospital by a US federal Court. Pound was an American who during WWII had embraced Fascism, Mussolini and Hitler. He became a paid propagandist for Mussolini and spent the war criticizing the American government and Roosevelt on Italian radio and writing anti-Semitic literature. In 1945 he was arrested in Italy as a traitor. It can be fairly argued that Pound was unstable to begin with, but his incarceration in Italy caused a complete mental breakdown. He was judged unfit to stand trial and was then incarcerated at St.

Elizabeth's psychiatric hospital in Washington, DC. When he was released he spent the remainder of his life in Italy.

Pound was something of a literary savant. He discovered and had several notable writers published including Ernest Hemingway, T.S. Elliot, James Joyce and Robert Frost. In 1933 *Time* magazine said of him "a cat that walks by himself, tenaciously unhousebroken and very unsafe for children."

April 20, Morocco demanded the removal of all Spanish troops in Spanish Sahara.

April 28, the failing Navy Vanguard rocket program tried another attempt at launching a satellite. It failed.

April 28, Vice President Richard Nixon and his wife Pat began a goodwill tour of Latin America where US interference and the US support of rightwing dictators had caused severe problems. The trip was controversial from the beginning and Nixon was confronted by angry demonstrations of students in both Peru and Uruguay. The arrogant and unapologetic Nixon had several hotly contested exchanges with the students which were widely publicized in the Latin American and the world press. This further angered many in Latin America.

By the time Nixon had arrived in Venezuela on May 13, the good will part of the trip had ended. He faced a large and very angry crowd. Venezuelans remembered the US support of the Venezuelan dictator Peréz Jimenéz and how the US awarded him the Legion of Merit medal in 1954 after the Venezuelans had finally ousted Peréz Jimenéz earlier that year.

As Nixon's car traveled through Caracas the crowd grew larger and angrier. They began to attack the car with rocks as the Venezuelan police stood by helplessly outnumbered. The car windows were smashed. The Secret Service Agents covered the President and Mrs. Nixon and the car drove recklessly through the crowd at high speed until it reached the American Embassy where a Marine Detail stood by. US troops were dispatched to the Caribbean to rescue the Vice president if need be. Nixon cut his goodwill tour short and the Venezuelan Army cordoned off the path to the airport for his early return.

May 3, Alan Freed, the creator of the term "Rock and Roll" and the new music's biggest on-air radio supporter, faced controversy again in Boston when he told an audience, "The police don't want you to have fun." As a result, Freed was arrested and charged with inciting to riot and was suspended by his radio station WINS in New York. Freed became angry about the suspension and quit the station and went to work at WABC in New York.

May 13, the French settlers in Algeria joined the Algerians and also began rioting against the French Army.

Also on May 13, the trademark for Velcro was filed and the product was introduced later this year.

May 15, the USSR successfully launched Sputnik III.

May 17, the dissatisfaction with the war in Algeria caused a military putsch to take place in France. It was caused by the increased misgivings of the French Army and of the French colonists that the war in Algeria was being undermined by party politics in France. Army commanders were angered at what they took to be inadequate and incompetent government support of the military effort. The putsch resulted in the return of Charles De Gaulle.

May 23, Mao Zedong began the Great Leap Forward in China. The Great Leap was supposed to rapidly transform China from a rural agrarian country to an industrialized nation. The rural farms were also collectivized during this time. The Great Leap Forward was an economic disaster. It resulted in famine with somewhere between 18 and 32 million Chinese people dying of starvation. The result of this famine led to the marginalization of Mao Zedong with the more moderate Deng Xaioping coming to power.

May 24, Cuban President Batista decided he would send the Cuban Army into the Sierra Maestra Mountains to destroy Castor's headquarters and his force of 300 rebel fighters. Under General Eulogio Cantillo and Alberto Del Rio Chaviano they surrounded the mountains with 14 battalions, about 12,000 men, to prevent the rebels from receiving new arms and men, and to prevent their escape. Then they attacked.

It took a while to find Castro and the actual first combat took place on June 28, and it lasted until August 8, when the Batista's Army disengaged with Castro's Army. The Army suffered 126 killed, with 30 seriously wounded. They also had 240 men and a huge supply of arms captured by the rebels. The 300 man rebel force lost about 76 men who were killed in the action, but the meager numbers of Castro's rebel force was still unknown to the Army. The two Generals squabbled about whose fault it was and had refused to coordinate during the attacks leading to the rebel advantage. The failure of the Cuban Army to defeat Castro's 300 man army made the Batista government and military look weak and vulnerable which then encouraged Cuban men to join the rebels by the thousands.

Also on May 24, the United Press merged with the International News Service to form the United Press International, UPI.

May 27, Ernest Green one of the nine Black students whose attendance had triggered the racial hatred and riots in Little Rock, graduated from Little Rock Central High School paving the way for more Black children to follow.

The Arkansas Gazette won the Pulitzer Prize for Journalism in 1958 "for demonstrating the highest qualities of civic leadership, journalistic responsibility and moral courage in the face of great public tension during the school integration crisis of 1957. The newspaper's fearless and completely objective news coverage, plus it's reasoned and moderate policy, did much to restore calmness and order to an overwrought community, reflecting great credit on its editors and its management." The pictures taken by photographer Will Counts, who was also nominated for a Pulitzer but didn't win, were an important reason for this award.

Also on May 27, the US launched the Vanguard SLV-1 satellite for Earth orbit. It failed.

May 28, the caskets for two unidentified WWII soldiers and an unidentified Korean War soldier lay in the Capitol Rotunda until May 30, when President Eisenhower decorated each with the Medal of Honor before they were buried at the Tomb of the Unknown Soldier at Arlington Cemetery.

May 31, Dick Dale created "Surf Music" with the song *Let's Go Trippin'*. This musical style would later be copied by such musical groups as the *Beach Boys, The Trashmen, The Surfaris, The Bel-Airs* and *Jan and Dean*. Later "Hot Rod Rock" would spin off of this genre.

June 1, Charles de Gaulle was elected the President of France.

June 4, on a trip to Algiers, the newly elected French President de Gaulle told the Algerians that Algeria would always be French.

June 7, battles between the Greek and Turkish Cypriots began with each side insisting that Cyprus be annexed to their home country.

June 9, Sheb Wooley had a number one hit with his song, *Purple People Eater*.

Also on June 9, Queen Elizabeth II formally opened Gatwick Airport in England.

June 14, the British sent paratroops to Cyprus to restore order between the Greeks and Turks.

June 17, Radio Moscow reported the execution of Hungarian Premier Imre Nagy for treason for his role in the Hungarian freedom uprising.

June 23, the Dutch Reformed Church announced that they would allow women ministers.

June 26, the Vanguard SLV2 satellite was launched and it too failed.

June 30, the Dutch government announced that it would no longer require married female teachers to resign.

July 1, the Canadian Broadcast System linked Canadian broadcast television across the whole country by microwave.

July 7, President Eisenhower signed the bill granting Alaskan Statehood on January 3, 1959.

July 9, a landslide of 90 million tons of rock and ice in Lituya Bay, Alaska caused a tidal wave to wash 1800 feet up the adjacent mountain.

July 10, former King Norodam Sihanoek became the premier of Cambodia.

July 14, General Abdul Kassem overthrew the monarchy and formed a military government in Iraq.

July 15, a civil war broke out between the Maronite Christian government of Lebanon and the Lebanese Muslims. There was a possibility of invasion from Egypt and other Muslim countries to side with the Muslims. President Eisenhower, at the Lebanese Christian government's request, sent approximately 14,000 US Army and Marines into Lebanon. They were supported by 70 US Navy Ships. This was the first use of the Eisenhower Doctrine. The Christian government was able to repel attacks from the Lebanese Muslims and Egypt backed off. The US troops left on October 25, 1958, but their invasion would long be remembered by the Muslim world.

July 20, worried that Egypt and their United Arab Republic, UAR, would try to annex all Muslim nations in the region, King Hussein of Jordan broke off diplomatic relations with Nasser and the UAR. Jordan relied on support from the US as the US-Jordanian relations had been good since the US began giving economic aid to Jordan in 1952. The break-off of relations with the

UAR helped to forge an even closer relationship between the US and Jordan, which have to this day remained close.

July 26, the US launched its fourth successful satellite on an Army Jupiter C rocket.

July 29, President Eisenhower signed the National Aeronautics and Space Act of 1958 to create NASA to focus the US space program which until now had been operated by separate US Army, Navy and Air Force programs. The Navy produced the troublesome Vanguard program, the Army produced the more successful Explorer program using their superior Jupiter C rockets, and the Air Force — with their space planes like the Bell X-1 and the X-15 — also had the Pioneer program. It would all now be under a civilian authority.

July 31, large anti-Chinese riots occurred in Tibet.

August 1, the US regular mail postage stamp was increased from three cents to four cents, the first increase in 26 years.

Also on this date the USS Nautilus nuclear submarine began its trip under the Arctic sea ice to the North Pole. On August 3, they reached the North Pole.

August 4, the original pioneer television network, the DuMont Network ceased operation due to lack of revenues and from inadequate broadcast time allotted from the FCC.

August 17, the first Pioneer Satellite, created by the Air Force to probe the moon, was launched. It is called "Pioneer 0" it failed after 77 seconds from liftoff.

August 18, Fidel Castro addressed the Cuban nation from a pirate radio station announcing that the end was near for Batista and his government.

April 18, in Omaha, Verne Gagne of Minnesota beat Edouard Carpentier of Montreal Canada to become National Wrestling Association World Champion.

April 19, Clara Luper the advisor to the Oklahoma City NAACP Youth Council, at the urging of her eight-year-old daughter, decided to conduct a sit-in at a segregated lunch counter at a Katz drug store in downtown Oklahoma City. Luper and the children then sat-in the Drugstore for two days until the Katz corporate management in Kansas City agreed to desegregate their lunch counters in three states. Clara Luper went on to be one of the most prominent figures in the Civil Rights movement.

Also on August 19, the luxury car makers, the Packard Automobile Company, ceased production. Packard cars had been in production since 1899.

August 23, the Second Taiwan Strait crisis began with the People's Republic bombarding of the island of Quemoy held by Chiang Kai-shek's Nationalists. The Nationalist troops began firing back. It appeared that the People's Republic was determined to take the islands of Quemoy and the nearby Matsu Archipelago. The Nationalist Chinese requested military aid and President Eisenhower sent the US 7th Fleet. The conflict went until September 22, when Eisenhower told the People's Republic he was prepared to use nuclear weapons on the Chinese mainland, a tactic later to become known as "brinkmanship," to force the People's Republic to a ceasefire. In the conflict about 2,500 Nationalist Chinese died and about 200 men from the People's Republic.

August 22, the US Senators Major League Baseball team announced that they would relocate to Minnesota. On September 2, Minnesota announced $9 million in improvements would be made at the Metropolitan Stadium in Bloomington, Minnesota for the new MLB team that would be called the Minnesota Twins.

August 27, the USSR launched Sputnik three with two dogs aboard.

September 2, a US Air Force C-130-A was shot down by two Soviet fighter jets when it strayed into Soviet airspace above Armenia, all crew members were killed.

September 9, race riots erupted in Notting Hill London. The riots were brought on by White working class "Teddy Boys" who began harassing Blacks and beating Black people. It was part of a White racist campaign to "keep Britain White." The riots lasted for several days. The riots started when a gang of White youths attacked a White woman who was living with a Black man.

September 14, two German rockets were launched and reached the upper atmosphere and the edge of space. These were the first German rockets launched since WWII.

September 15, a train crash in New Jersey killed 48 people.

September 22, the US nuclear submarine Skate remained under the ice of the North Pole for a record 31 days. America was perfecting its navy to attack the Soviets from the Arctic Ocean.

September 28, Guinea voted for independence from France. On October 2, they became a republic.

October 1, the new US space agency, NASA, began consolidating all the military space programs and also incorporated the civilian National Advisory Council on Aeronautics into their organization.

October 4, the Fifth French Republic was formed.

October 6, the US nuclear submarine Seawolf remained under the pole for a record 60 days.

October 7, Potter Stuart was appointed to the US Supreme Court.

Also on October 7, NASA announced that the US manned space flights would be named Project Mercury.

October 8, the first heart pacemaker was installed in Stockholm, Sweden.

October 11, Pioneer 1, the second US moon probe was launched. Due to a launch vehicle malfunction, the spacecraft attained only a ballistic trajectory and never reached the moon. However, it did return 43 hours of data on the near-Earth space environment.

October 14 the Malagasy Republic became an independent nation.

Also on October 14, the District of Columbia Bar Association voted to accept Black Americans as members.

October 15, Tunisia broke off diplomatic relations with Egypt.

October 21, the first women were seated in the British House of Lords.

October 23, the Springhill Mine, North America's deepest coal mine, in Springhill, Nova Scotia, suffered an earthquake and a cave-in trapping 174 miners. The rescue took many days and in the end 75 of the 174 miners died and 99 were rescued.

October 24, the USSR lent Egypt 400 million Rubles to build the Aswan Dam.

October 26, Pan Am flew the first trans-Atlantic jet flight New York to Paris.

October 28, Angelo Giuseppe Roncalli, was elected Pope, and took name Pope John the XXIII.

October 29, Boris Pasternak refused the Nobel Prize for Literature. Boris Pasternak first accepted the award, but was later forced by the Soviet authorities to decline the prize.

October 30, the first coronary angioplasty was performed at the Cleveland Clinic by Dr F. Mason Sones.

November 4, the Democrats won the Congressional elections.

November 24, Mali became an independent nation.

November 25, Senegal became an independent nation.

November 28, Chad, the Congo, and Mauritania became independent nations.

Also on November 28, the US reported the successful full range test of an ICBM missile.

November 30, the first guided missile destroyer, the USS Dewey was launched.

December 1, the Central African Republic became an independent nation.

Also on December 1, in Chicago, a fire at Our Lady of Angels Catholic School killed 92 children and three nuns.

December 4, the Ivory Coast (now Benin) achieved independence.

December 6, Pioneer III was launched and failed on a Vanguard rocket.

December 9, rightwing anti-communist Robert Welch and Fred C. Koch, father to the two rightwing Koch brothers, formed the John Birch Society. The organization was primarily anti-government insisting that all federal social and educational programs would lead to communism. Conservative leaders like William F. Buckley Jr. labeled the John Birch Society as the ultra-rightwing fringe of the conservative movement. It would become the main stream by 2016.

December 11, Upper Volta (now Burkina Faso) achieved independence.

December 18, the US launched the first communications satellite. It was called Operation SCORE. It captured world attention by broadcasting a tape recorded Christmas message from President Eisenhower on December 19, via short wave radio from the satellite. The president wished, "To all mankind, America's wish for Peace on Earth & Good Will to Men Everywhere."

December 21, Charles de Gaulle won an election for a seven year term as the President of France.

December 22, "the Chipmunk Song" reached number 1 on the Billboard Hot 100 Hits. Incredibly the song also won three Grammys in 1958 for Best Comedy Performance, Best Children's Recording, and Best Engineered Record.

December 28, "The Greatest Game Ever Played," resulted in the Baltimore Colts beating the New York Giants for the NFL Championship in the first sudden death overtime game in NFL history. Seventeen of the players in this game would eventually be in the NFL Hall of fame.

Also on December 28, Ché Guevara led the Cuban rebels in a successful attack to take the City of Santa Clara, Cuba.

December 31, Camilo Cienfuegos led the Cuban rebels to take the City of Yaguajay.

December 31, Cuban dictator Fulgencio Batista told his cabinet that he was fleeing the country.

In 1958 the three nuclear powers filled the Earth's air, waters and land with nuclear fallout as the US conducted 21 nuclear test explosions, the USSR conducted 11 nuclear explosions and the British conducted four nuclear explosions.

Although a couple of pizza chain restaurants had previously opened, the years 1958 through 1960 saw a flourish of pizza restaurants and chains open, making the food a staple of the American diet. These chains included: Pizza Hut, Pizza Inn, Little Caesars' in 1958, and later Aurillios, and Dominos, along with the earlier established Uno, Shakey's and Sbarro. About this time the first frozen pizzas went on sale in grocery stores across the nation including the first two Celentano and Totino's. Today Americans eat about 3 billion pizzas a year which is about 350 slices per second according to the website https://wonderopolis.org/wonder/who-created-frozen-pizza.

In 1958 the US went into recession and unemployment affected about five million workers. Inflation was 2.73% and thanks to the unions the average annual wage rose to $4,600. The average price of a new car was about $2,200 and gasoline was 25 cents per gallon. Sales of imported cars, particularly Volkswagen, Toyota and Datsun began to grow. The average new house price was $12,750 and monthly rent was still cheap at $92.

In 1958 in addition to making Frisbees, the Wham-O Company began manufacturing and selling the Hula Hoop which began a craze that swept the nation.

In television the fall scandal around Charles Van Doren and the quiz show *Twenty-One* spread to other quiz shows and brought down *The $64,000 Dollar Question* and the new quiz show *Dotto*. The scandal made Americans more skeptical about television, but television was still America's most popular entertainment. Television was also made less diverse with the fall of the DuMont Network due to the unfair practices of the FCC conspiring with the former radion networks CBS, NBC, and ABC.

New television shows debuting in 1958 included: *Sea Hunt* with Lloyd Bridges, the quiz show *Concentration*, the "hip" new detective show *Peter Gun* with its classic jazz music by Henry Mancini, *The Donna Reed Show*, three new cowboy shows *The Rifleman*, *The Lawman*, and *Bat Masterson*, a quirky popular detective show *77 Sunset Strip*, and Hanna Barbera's second hit cartoon show, *The Huckleberry Hound Show* with Yogi Bear which won an Emmy for Outstanding Achievement in Children's Programming. Previously Hanna

Barbera had created the Saturday morning cartoon show *Ruff & Ready*. Another show premiering in 1958 *An Evening with Fred Astaire* won nine Emmys.

In the movies of 1958, *South Pacific*, based off the book by James Michener *Tales of the South Pacific*, was the big winner at the box office. *Gigi* won the Oscar for Best Picture and Best Director. *Separate Tables* with David Niven, Rita Hayworth, Burt Lancaster, Deborah Kerr and Wendy Hiller won Oscars for Best Actor for David Niven and Best Supporting Actress for Wendy Hiller. *The Big Country* with Gregory Peck, Jean Simmons, Charlton Heston, and Carol Baker, and Burl Ives who won the Oscar for Best Supporting Actor. Susan Heyward won the Oscar for Best Actress in a film noir, *I Want to Live!* Other 1958 movies included: *Auntie Mame* with Rosalind Russell; *Cat on a Hot Tin Roof* with Paul Newman and Elizabeth Taylor; a quirky comedy *No Time for Sergeants* which made Andy Griffith at star; *Vertigo* with Jimmie Stewart and Kim Novak; *The Young Lions* with Marlon Brando, Montgomery Clift and Dean Martin, *Some Came Running* with Frank Sinatra, Dean Martin and Shirley MacLaine, and *The Defiant Ones* with Tony Curtis and Sidney Portier.

In August the Billboard Hot 100 was created. Elvis Presley's music career was hampered by his service in the Army and he had only two hits in the top twenty-five with *Don't* at number three and *Wear My Ring Around Your Neck* at twenty-two. An Italian, Domencio Modugno, had the number one hit with *Volaré*. Most of the hits were rock tunes called "Doo-wop" with classics like: *All I have to Do is Dream* and *Bird Dog* by the Everly Brothers, *Get a Job* by the Silhouettes, *Little Star* by the Elegants, *Twilight Time* the Platters, *At the Hop* and *Rock and Roll is Here to Stay* by Danny and the Juniors, *Yakety Yak* by the Coasters, *Poor Little Fool* by Ricky Nelson, *Sweet Little Sixteen* and *Johnny B Goode* by Chuck Berry, *The Book of Love* by the Monotones, *Tears on My Pillow* by Little Anthony and the Imperials, *Great Balls of Fire* by Jerry Lee Lewis, *Lollipop* by the Chordettes, *Who's Sorry Now* by Connie Francis, *Do You Want to Dance* by Bobby Freeman, *The Stroll* by the Diamonds, *Chantilly Lace* by the Big Bopper, *Come On Let's Go* by Richie Valens, *Peggy Sue* and *Oh Boy* by Buddy Holley and the Crickets, *Summertime Blues* by Eddie Cochran, *Born Too Late* by the Poni-Tails, and *To Know Him is to Love Him* by the Teddy Bears. Duane Eddy's guitar classic *Rebel Rouser* was also a 1958 hit. A few folk tunes also were also hits as folk music was again becoming popular particularly on college campuses. *Tom Dooley* and *Scarlett Ribbons* by the Kingston Trio were hits.

In January E.E. Cummings won the Bollinger Prize for Poetry. The books of 1958 included: *Exodus* by Leon Uris, *Breakfast at Tiffany's* by Truman Capote, *Doctor No* by Ian Fleming, *Ordeal by Innocence* by Agatha Christie, *Once There was a War* by John Steinbeck, *From the Terrace* by John O'Hara, *The Agony and the Ecstasy* by Irving Stone, *Our Man in Havana* by Graham Greene, *Cape Fear* by John D. MacDonald, *Dear and Glorious Physician* by Taylor Caldwell, *The Ugly American* by William J. Lederer, and two books by Jack Kerouac *The Subterraneans* and the book that started the Beatnik and Hippy movements *Dharma Bums*. The Pulitzer Prizes for fiction went posthumously to James Agee for *A Death in the Family*, and the Poetry Prize went to *Promises: Poems 1954-1956* by Robert Penn Warren.

Chapter 15. 1959: Castro's Cuba, the Dawn of Electronics, the Day the Music Died, Barbie, Astronauts, and the Ho Chi Minh Trail

January 1, Fulgencio Batista fled as Castro's rebels took Cuba. During his first decade in power, Castro began a wide range of progressive social reforms. Laws were passed to provide equality for Black Cubans and greater rights for women. Communications, medical facilities, housing, and schools were all improved. Cultural venues were an important part of Castro's Cuba and there were touring cinemas, art exhibitions, concerts, and theatres. By the end of the 1960s all Cuban children were receiving basic education, compared with less than half before 1959. Unemployment and corruption were greatly reduced. Organized crime was gone. And there were great improvements in diet, hygiene and sanitation. But despite all these improvements to Cuba, the one-time American territory, it infuriated the Americans because Castro was also a socialist.

Also on January 1, Chad became independent.

January 2, the USSR launched Luna 1 the first satellite to pass by the moon. Three days after launch it became the first man-made vehicle to leave Earth's gravity.

January 3, Alaska officially became the 49th state.

January 6, Caroline County Virginia police arrested a mixed race couple, Richard and Mildred Loving in their home in an early morning raid and took them to jail. They were charged with "Miscegenation," a felony crime for marrying outside your race, with a penalty of up to five years in prison. After marrying in Washington, D.C., in 1958, Richard and Mildred Loving returned to their native Caroline County, Virginia, to build a home and start a family. Their union was a criminal act in Virginia because Richard was White, Mildred was Black, and the state's Racial Integrity Act, passed in 1924, criminalized interracial marriage. The judge agreed to impose a suspended one-year prison sentence, so long as the couple left the state of

Virginia for 25 years. Before entering judgment, Judge Leon Bazile condemned their marriage and declared that it was God's decision to place the races on different continents that demonstrated a divine intent against intermarriage. They fought the law in court and after about nine years on June 12, 1967, they won a US Supreme Court decision which found that all laws banning interracial marriage were unconstitutional. At this time 16 states enforced miscegenation laws.

January 7, the US begrudgingly recognized Castro's Cuban government.

Also on this date Mafia boss Meyer Lansky and other Mafiosi fled Cuba.

January 9, the Tera River Dam collapsed in Montenegro during heavy winter rains and killed 135 people.

January 13, President De Gaulle granted amnesty to 130 Algerian independence fighters who had been sentenced to death.

Also on this day King Baudouin of Belgium promised future independence to the Belgian Congo.

January 25, the first transcontinental jet air service from Los Angeles to New York began. The cost of a round-trip ticket was $238.80, an incredibly high price for the time, about $1,700 dollars in today's money.

January 28, the American Olympic amateurs lost their first international basketball game when the USSR humiliated the Americans with a 62-37 win.

February 1, Swiss men again voted to reject voting rights for women.

Also on February 1, Texas Instruments patented the integrated circuit and the age of modern electronics began.

February 2, Coach Vince Lombardi signed a five year contract with the Green Bay Packers. He would later lead them to victory in the first two Super Bowls.

February 3, will always be known in Rock and Roll history as "The Day the Music Died." On their way to a winter concert in Moorhead, Minnesota, a small plane carrying rock stars Buddy Holly, Richie Valens and J.P. Richardson who was known as the Big Bopper crashed in a corn field near Clear Lake, Iowa. The three singers and the pilot died. Many teens at the time thought that with the death of these three stars and with Elvis Presley in the Army that Rock and Roll would die. The music survived and thrived, and this would be the first of many tragic young deaths in Rock and Roll history.

Also on February 3, an American Airlines flight crashed in New York and killed 65 passengers.

February 6, the US successfully test fired a Titan ICBM missile.

Also on February 6, Fidel Castro was interviewed by Edward R. Murrow for American television. The next day Castro declared a new Cuban constitution.

February 10, an early freak tornado injured 265 and killed 19 people in St. Louis, Missouri.

February 14, $3.6 million worth of heroine was seized in New York City. It was the largest drug bust in US history at that time.

February 16, Fidel Castro was named Premier of Cuba.

February 17, after the previous failures in the Vanguard program, Vanguard II, the first weather satellite, was successfully launched. The satellite transmitted data for 19 days as planned. The satellite still remains in earth orbit.

February 19, Britain, Greece and Turkey signed an agreement to make Cyprus independent.

February 22, the first Daytona 500 auto race was held.

February 28, Discoverer I, the first American reconnaissance satellite, was launched in a secret attempt to make it the first satellite with a polar orbit. The satellite failed. A much later declassified CIA assessment said it likely crashed near the South Pole.

March 3, Pioneer 4, a second lunar probe, was launched successfully becoming the first US satellite to leave Earth's gravity. The satellite was mostly successful and it transmitted data for 82 hours, but its orbit was too far from the Moon's surface to use some equipment. On March 6, the satellite's radio transmitted from 600,000 miles at the time, the furthest radio transmission ever received.

March 5, Iran and the US signed an economic and military treaty.

March 8, a pro-Egyptian coup in Iraq failed to take down the government.

March 9, the first Barbie doll went on sale manufactured by the Mattel Toy Company.

March 10, Tibetan government officials feared that plans were being laid for a Chinese abduction of the Dalai Lama, and spread word to the inhabitants of Lhasa, Tibet. The crowd became unruly and during the protest Chinese soldiers killed a senior Lama, Pagbalha Soinam Gyamco. The soldiers then infuriated the Tibetans by dragging his dead body by a horse in front of the crowd. The Tibetans armed themselves and began to fight the Chinese soldiers. The revolt lasted until March 22, and a reported 85,000 to 87,000 deaths resulted from the conflict. In its aftermath the Chinese dissolved the Tibetan government and the Dali Lama fled into exile.

March 12, the Congress approved Hawaii for statehood which was signed by the President on March 15.

March 17, the USSR and Australia resumed diplomatic relations.

April 7, Oklahoma ended prohibition after 51 years.

April 9, NASA named seven astronauts for Project Mercury. These would be the first Americans to go into space. They were John Glenn, Wally Schirra, Alan Sheppard, Gordon Cooper, Gus Grissom, Deke Slayton and Scott Carpenter.

April 12, reports begin to emerge about French troops using torture in Algeria.

April 13, the Discoverer 2 was successfully launched. The satellite successfully gathered data on propulsion, communications, orbital performance, and stabilization. All equipment functioned as programmed except a timing device. The satellite functioned until April 21, 1959. Discoverer 2 was the first satellite to be stabilized in orbit, to be maneuvered on command from the earth, to separate a reentry vehicle on command, and to send its reentry vehicle back to earth.

Also on this date the Vanguard 5 satellite was launched, but failed because of damages that occurred during the separation stage and the spacecraft did not achieve orbit.

On the same date, a Vatican edict was issued forbidding Catholics from voting for communists.

Also on April 13, the US and Britain asked the USSR for a joint moratorium on above ground nuclear testing.

April 14, the Atlas D rocket was tested at Cape Canaveral. It exploded several minutes after liftoff.

April 15, Fidel Castro began an eleven day goodwill tour of the US.

John Foster Dulles resigned as Secretary of State. Dulles was diagnosed with colon cancer the previous November. After two surgeries his health continued to decline. Dulles died shortly afterward in May of 1959. "The United States of America does not have friends; it has interests," is a quote sometimes attributed to Dulles, but the words were actually spoken by Charles De Gaulle about Dulles' State Department. When Dulles traveled to Mexico in 1958, hundreds of anti-American protesters held up signs reading "The U.S. has no friends, only interests." And the quote has since been attributed to Dulles after his death because it summarized his Cold War and State Department philosophy.

April 16, the US deployed Thor nuclear missiles in Britain.

April 18, the iconic Corvette Stingray was introduced by General Motors.

April 19, Fidel Castro appeared on *Meet the Press.*

April 23, Panama charged that the American actor John Wayne and the CIA were financing a coup by Roberto Arias to overthrow the government of Panama. Wayne denied his involvement.

April 25, Mack Charles Parker, a Black man from Mississippi, was murdered by a mob in Louisiana. Parker was dubiously accused of raping a White woman. When the police came to arrest him they beat and tortured him and his screams could be heard throughout the neighborhood. He was incarcerated in Poplarville, Mississippi. Parker denied the charges despite brutal attempts to force a confession. He passed several lie detector tests and a gun that was supposed to be used in the rape was never found. A White man who said he had personal knowledge of the alleged victim suggested that her rape accusation was fabricated as a means of concealing an ongoing consensual affair with a local White man.

According to the FBI report on the case, sometime around 12:15 a.m. on April 25, a vigilante mob of eight to ten hooded and masked men, wearing gloves, were let into the jail by a deputy sheriff who joined them. They kidnapped Parker and took him twenty miles away to Louisiana where he was beaten, shot and lynched. His body was weighted with chains and he was tossed in the Pearl River where his swollen body was found nine days later.

When the alleged victim was told about Parker's murder she fainted and when she was revived she said that Parker should have had a fair trial. Despite confessions to the FBI by the men involved in the kidnapping and murder of

Parker, a White grand jury failed to indict any of the men. Historian Howard Smead later called the Parker killing "the last classic lynching in America."

April 25, the St. Lawrence Seaway connecting the Atlantic Ocean and the Great Lakes was opened for traffic.

Also on April 25, a force of about 80 rebels invaded Panama from the Caribbean to overthrow the government. Despite denials by Castro and the OAS, the US claimed it was Cuban revolutionaries sent by Castro. Others thought the force had been sent by the CIA and financed by John Wayne.

April 27, Liu Shao-chi was named the President of the People's Republic of China replacing Mao Zedong. Mao was blamed for the mass starvation because of his "Great Leap Forward." Publicly it was said that Mao decided to step down to concentrate on communist party business.

April 28, former President Truman addressed the students at Columbia University. When asked about his decision to use the atom bomb on Japan, Truman said that as horrific as the decision was to drop the two bombs that it saved millions of Japanese and American lives that would have been lost in the invasion. The assertion that the atomic bombs dropped on Japan "saved millions of lives" was actually invented as a justification by the military after the fact. A later review of the military estimates made at the time showed many fewer deaths would have been caused in the projected invasion.

May 1, W.E.B. Du Bois, the co-founder of the NAACP, was awarded the Lenin Peace Prize by the USSR. The FBI and J. Edgar Hoover had accused Du Bois of being a communist and he was tried and acquitted as a communist traitor in 1951. He disavowed communism and called Stalin a tyrant, but he also blamed capitalism for poverty, classism and racism. Although he was acquitted of any crime in 1951 the US government refused to issue him a passport to go overseas. In 1958 they finally issued him a passport and he was able to go to Moscow to accept his prize.

May 2, a nineteen-year-old Black college girl while on a double date was kidnapped and raped seven times by four White men near the campus of Florida A & M University in Tallahassee, Florida. The men threatened to kill her several times with a knife and a shotgun. The horrific crime attracted nationwide attention including *Time* magazine when an all-White jury found the four men guilty and Judge W. May Walker sentenced all four to life in prison.

May 5, the US signed an agreement with West Germany to share nuclear weapons secrets and to train Germans in their operation and use.

May 6, South Vietnam passed a law allowing traveling military tribunals to issue the death penalty for anyone found to be Viet Cong or anyone assisting the Viet Cong.

Also on this day an F-84 jet fighter crashed in a backyard in Northville, Michigan injuring two children. The pilot had safely ejected before the crash.

May 11, representatives from the US, Great Britain, France and the USSR met in Geneva, Switzerland to discuss the reunification of Germany. They met for 17 days without reaching an agreement.

May 12, just hours after his divorce from Debbie Reynolds, Eddie Fisher married Elizabeth Taylor. Fisher and Taylor would divorce five years later in 1964.

May 14, President Eisenhower and a crowd of 12,000 attended the ground-breaking for Lincoln Center in New York.

May 15, General Edward G. Lansdale of the CIA delivered what was later described as "one of the most influential military documents of the past half century" to President Eisenhower. The report *Training Under the Mutual Security Program (With Emphasis on Development of Leaders)* proposed using the American military to further "political stability, economic growth, and social change" in developing nations, It was the start of America's failed counter-insurgency efforts in Vietnam and elsewhere.

May 19, Ho Chi Minh and his military leaders implemented plans to slowly conquer and capture the South and reunite Vietnam. Colonel Vo Bam was assigned the task of overseeing a program of transporting soldiers, weapons and equipment to the South, and General Nguyen Giap created Special Group 559 to construct a series of roads and tunnels and provide protection. This would become known as the Ho Chi Minh trail.

Also on May 19, the City of Atlanta desegregated their public libraries.

May 20, a group of 4,978 Japanese-Americans who had renounced their U.S. citizenship during their forced internment during World War II had their citizenship restored by the U.S. Justice Department.

May 21 the bathyscaphe Trieste made its first test dive of 700 feet taking over two and a half hours for the dive.

May 27, National Semiconductor was started by eight engineers from the Sperry Rand Corporation to produce semiconductors for electronic goods.

May 28, aboard a Jupiter rocket, Able and Baker, two rhesus monkeys, went into space and returned home successfully. This mission was criticized widely when the Russians put a man in space before the Americans. Many in Congress later said that the US should have sent up a man rather than monkeys in this mission.

Also on this day a passenger train in Indonesia crashed into a ravine killing 85 people.

May 30, an invasion of Nicaragua was made when two planes with rebel soldiers, under the direction of Nicaraguan exile Enrique Lacayo Farfan, landed and began a battle with government troops. The rebellion was put down by June 12 by students and unionist supporters of President Villeda Morales. The invasion was likely supported by the CIA on behalf of the United Fruit Company who were unhappy with the agrarian reforms instituted by Morales to benefit the Nicaraguan people.

June 1, in an ironic twist of fate Sax Rhomer, the creator of Fu Manchu, died from complications of Asian flu.

June 3, calling it a communist uprising, the army of Ecuador brutally murdered more than 500 people protesting the government in Guayaquil.

Also on June 3, Discoverer III was launched with plans to send two mice into space and return them to earth. The rocket misfired upon re-entry and burned up in the atmosphere.

June 5, Nikolay Artamonov a commander of a Soviet destroyer defected to the US. He then worked for the US Defense Intelligence Agency until he was recaptured by the Soviets in 1975.

Also on June 5, Singapore became a self-governing independent state within the British Empire.

June 8, in an odd experiment the US Post Office and the Navy sent a missile with 3,000 letters from a ship a hundred miles offshore in Virginia to Mayport, Florida. The flight took twenty-two minutes. An overly optimistic Post Master General, Arthur E. Summerfield, predicted that mail delivery by missile could become a regular postal service.

June 9, the first nuclear missile submarine, the George Washington, was launched. In June of 1960 the sub was fitted with two nuclear missiles.

Also on this day American spy planes intercepted the transmissions to a Soviet ICBM missile from its ground station. It was a step toward the US intercepting, reading and interrupting Soviet missile commands.

June 11, the Post Master General banned the book *Lady Chatterley's Lover* by D.H. Lawrence as "obscene and un-mailable." On July 21, a federal judge enjoined the Post Master General and allowed for US postal delivery of the novel.

June 13, a riot protesting the election of communists to the local state government took place in Angamaly, India. Seven people were killed by police in the riots, and in the aftermath the Indian government replaced the elected communist state government.

June 15, a Navy patrol plane was attacked by two Soviet MIG fighters in the Sea of Japan off the coast of North Korea. The tail gunner was severely wounded, but the pilot was able to fly his badly damaged plane back to his base in Japan. An inquiry afterward determined that the Navy plane could not properly defend itself because two of its guns were inoperable because they were awaiting spare parts.

June 16, President Eisenhower expressed his strong reservations about the placement of American medium range nuclear missiles in Turkey, and said. "If Mexico or Cuba had been penetrated by the Communists, and then began getting arms and missiles from them ... it would be imperative for us to take positive action, even offensive military action." The Jupiter missiles in Turkey were later believed to be one of the reasons for the placement of Soviet missiles in Cuba in 1962.

Also on June 16, actor George Reeves who played Superman on the television series *The Adventures of Superman*, was found dead from a single gunshot to his head. It was ruled a suicide. However the gun was wiped clean of fingerprints and there were no powder traces on his hand which would have been present if he had shot himself. These factors led many to conclude that Reeves was murdered.

June 17, a London jury awarded Liberace $22,400 in a libel suit against the *London Daily Mirror* and its reporter who had described the entertainer as a homosexual.

June 18, Queen Elizabeth began a 45 day tour of Canada.

June 20, the Soviet Union notified China that it was cancelling its agreement to give technical aid to the People's Republic of China to build nuclear weapons. Khrushchev later noted in his memoirs that a working bomb and blueprints to construct bombs were ready for shipment to China when he cancelled the agreement.

June 26, Ingemar Johansson of Sweden became the World Heavy Weight Boxing Champion by knocking out Floyd Patterson at Yankee Stadium.

June 27, voters in Hawaii overwhelming approved Hawaiian statehood.

June 28, two railroad tanker cars exploded on a railroad bridge over a beach on the Ogeechee River in Meldrim, Georgia sending down a shower of flames that killed 175 people.

June 30, a US Air Force plane crashed into an elementary school in Okinawa killing 21 children and injuring over a hundred.

July 2, a fire at the Pentagon forced the evacuation of 30,000 employees and destroyed over $30 million in computers. Twenty-five firefighters were treated for injuries in fighting the blaze.

July 4, the Cayman Islands became a Crown Colony of the British Empire.

July 6, a US Air Force C-124 cargo plane carrying nuclear weapons crashed in Louisiana. No weapons exploded, but one was destroyed in the fire from the crash. All seven crew members survived.

July 8, Major Dale Buis and Master Sergeant Chester Ovnand of the US Army were the first two official American casualties of the Vietnam War. They were killed in a Viet Cong attack at the South Vietnamese Army headquarters in Biên Hòa. There were at the time 700 US Army advisors in Vietnam.

July 11, the crew of a Pan American flight from Honolulu to San Francisco sighted a UFO at 21,000 feet over the Pacific. The sighting was confirmed by pilots on two other airlines. Captain George Wilson told reporters "There was an extremely bright light surrounded by small lights. The object traveled at inconceivable speed. I'm a believer now."

July 13, a nuclear accident in a reactor in Simi Valley about 30 miles northwest of Los Angeles partially melted down releasing radioactive gasses into the air for over two weeks.

July 14, in Kirkuk, Iraq, the Kurds clashed with the ethnic Turks. Over 30 Turks were killed and over a hundred were wounded. In Turkey the event became known as the "Kirkuk Massacre."

July 15, was the largest strike in US history as over 500,000 steelworkers walked off the job. The strike ended 116 days later with the intervention by the President and the US Supreme Court.

July 16, the satellite Explorer S-1 was launched. It was blown up shortly after liftoff when the rocket veered off course.

July 17, anthropologist Mary Leakey unearthed a 1.75 million-year-old skull fragment of Homo habilis in Tanzania. The find filled in the gaps of human evolution.

July 24, "the Kitchen Debate" between Vice president Nixon and Nikita Khrushchev took place at the American National Exhibition in Moscow. In front of an American modern kitchen display the two men debated over the merits of communism versus capitalism. *Time* magazine later described their meeting as "what may be remembered as peacetime diplomacy's most amazing 24 hours."

July 26, Fidel Castro rallied a half million Cuban people in support of his intention of running as Premier of Cuba.

August 3, an independence riot broke out in Portuguese Guinea (now Guinea-Bissau) Portuguese soldiers killed more than 50 and wounded more than 100 people. It was the start of a 13 year revolution which would ultimately lead to independence.

August 5, President Eisenhower supported a change in US National Security Policy to allow US military forces to use chemical and biological warfare.

August 7, a typhoon caused floods in Taiwan which killed over a thousand people.

Also on this day a dynamite truck exploded in downtown Roseburg, Oregon killing 14 people and leaving a fifty foot wide crater.

And also on this date Explorer 6 was successfully launched. The satellite took pictures of Earth from space.

August 9, after a successful test the Atlas ICBM missile with a range of 2,700 miles was declared operational.

August 13, the Philippines declared that the local language of Tagalog would replace English in Philippine grammar schools.

August 14, a typhoon struck Japan and killed 137 people.

August 17, a 7.1 earthquake struck Madison River, Montana and killed 28 people and caused the formation of a new lake.

Also on August 17, the US Chief of Naval Operations announced that the Soviet Union had the ability to launch missiles from submarines.

August 18, while fighting an oil storage tank fire at the Continental Oil Company in Kansas City, six firefighters died and 54 were injured.

August 21, Hawaii was officially granted statehood.

August 25, Indian and Chinese troops opened fire along the Indian-Tibet border.

August 28, Buddhist demonstrations against the Catholic government of South Vietnam began. It was eventually put down by South Vietnamese soldiers.

Also on this date India announced that it would defend and protect the mountain nation of Bhutan from Chinese aggression.

August 31, South Vietnamese intelligence agents attempted to assassinate the King and Queen of Cambodia by placing a bomb in a gift.

September 1, food shortages brought riots in India. In an attempt to stop the riots the police and Indian Army fired into a crowd at the University of Calcutta and killed 7 people wounding 30 others. In a second day of riots another 27 were killed. In the aftermath the Indian Defense Minister and his chiefs were all forced to resign.

September 2, at a Conference in Edmonton, Canada American bio-chemist Dr. Linus Pauling warned that over 290,000 people would die from cancer and other ailments caused by nuclear radiation from the atomic test blasts since 1945. He also warned that an additional 30,000 to 60,000 people would die of cancer for each additional nuclear test.

September 5, the Kingdom of Laos declared a state of emergency and asked for UN protection from the North Vietnamese.

September 9, an Atlas rocket with an empty one-man Mercury capsule was sent into space and the capsule returned in a test to see if the capsule could survive re-entry. The test was successful.

September 10, a school bus in Maryland with 26 elementary children aboard stalled on the railroad tracks and was hit by a freight train killing 7 of the children.

September 13, the Soviet satellite Lunik II crashed on the moon. The following day the Soviets declared the crash a success stating, "Today, the 14th of September, at 00:02:24 Moscow time, a Soviet cosmic rocket reached the surface of the moon. It is the first time in history that a cosmic flight has been made from the earth to another celestial body."

September 15, at a Houston elementary school a man set off a suitcase bomb killing himself, his son, a teacher, a custodian and two other children. Nineteen children and the principal were hospitalized with injuries. Two of the injured children each lost a leg. The bomber was angry because on the previous day the school would not enroll his son without his birth and health certificates.

Also on September 15, Soviet Premier Khrushchev arrived for an eleven day goodwill visit to the US.

September 16, after five years of war, five billion dollars spent and more than 21,000 French soldiers lost, French President Charles de Gaulle went on television in France and Algeria to announce that France would give independence to Algeria within four years.

Also on September 16, the first paper copying machine, the Xerox 914, made its debut.

September 17, the US Space program saw success with the first flight of the X-15 space plane at Edwards Air Force base in California. They also had a setback on this date when the satellite Transit 1A, the first navigational satellite launched from Cape Canaveral and failed.

On September 18, jetways became common when passengers in Atlanta boarded a Delta Airlines flight directly from the terminal by way of a jetway. A later that afternoon a United Airlines flight also used the same jetway. Until this date airplane passengers had to leave the terminal and walk out on the tarmac and up some portable stairs to get on a plane.

Also on September 18, Memphis State University, now the University of Memphis, allowed eight Black students to enroll, but they were restricted from many "White public areas."

September 19, Premier Khrushchev became annoyed and publicly proclaimed his displeasure that he would not be allowed to visit Disneyland while he was in California. The US government cited personal security reasons for the denial, saying they could not guarantee his protection in such large crowds.

September 21, two popular American cars made their debuts, the Ford Falcon and the Plymouth Valiant.

September 24, in the race to be the first to photograph the far side of the Moon, the United States suffered a setback when an Atlas-Able rocket exploded on the launch pad. On October 4, the Soviets launched Lunik III and two days later photographed the far side of the moon.

September 26, Typhoon Vera, the strongest typhoon ever to hit Japan, came ashore with a seventeen foot wave and 160 miles per hour winds. The storm killed over 5,000 people, injured over 32,000 and left 1.5 million people homeless.

September 29, a Braniff flight of a Lockheed Electra from Houston to Washington, DC, broke apart in midair, killing 33 people.

October 1, the Soviets began a series of high level meetings with Cuba. On October 15, they met with Fidel Castro. Castro was finally swayed to enter into an alliance with the Soviets. One of the reasons for this decision was that Major Pedro Diaz Lanz, the former head of Cuba's Air Force, defected to the US in July and returned October 21, to bomb Havana from Florida with US propaganda leaflets. Panic and a stampede caused two people to die and 45 to be injured when the Cubans thought they were being invaded by the US. Castro accused the US of bombing a neutral nation. During this time the Allen Dulles of the CIA and the US Military had begun their Cuban invasion planning. This included reaching out to the Mafia for their assistance. It was later learned that the CIA had also contracted with the Mafia to kill Castro.

Also October 1, the People's Republic of China celebrated the 10th Anniversary of the Republic at events across the country.

October 2, a total eclipse of the sun was visible from the eastern US to Northern Africa.

October 5, the IBM 1401 computer was introduced. It was the first fully transistorized computer with a memory of 16K. It was rented to businesses at $2,500 per month and more than 14,000 computers were leased.

October 7, the Iraqi president was ambushed on his way to the airport in Bagdad. The five man assassin team was led by Iraq's future president Saddam Hussein who killed the president's driver and body guard and wounded the president. Saddam Hussein was also injured in the attack.

Also on October 7, a Nationalist Chinese plane flying over Beijing was shot down by two surface-to-air missiles. It was the first time a plane had been brought down by a surface-to-air missile.

October 8, the Los Angeles Dodgers beat the Chicago White Sox in Game 6 to win the World Series.

October 10, Yasser Arafat created the nationalist Palestinian Liberation Party, Fatah, to fight for Arab control of Palestine.

Also on October 10, an unsuccessful petty thief, James Earl Ray, who was later the accused assassin of Dr. Martin Luther King, attempted to rob a grocery store of a couple hundred dollars. He was caught and given twenty years in prison.

October 11, Bert Bell the Commissioner of the NFL, the man credited with building the sport into America's favorite, died of a heart attack while attending a game between the Philadelphia Eagles and the Pittsburg Steelers.

October 12, the US successfully tested an anti-satellite missile. Also on this date Yuri Gagarin and Georgi Shonin were selected as the Soviet Union's first cosmonauts. Gagarin would later become the first man in space.

October 13, Explorer 7 satellite was successfully launched. Its mission was to study radiation and climatology. It continued to transmit data until late August of 1961 and is still in orbit.

October 14, a Pennsylvania widow killed her five children with overdoses of barbiturates and then attempted to commit suicide, but was found and revived. She later pleaded guilty to murder charges and was given life in prison.

October 15, Ukrainian nationalist leader, Stepan Bandera was murdered by a KGB assassin in West Germany.

October 16, Lee Harvey Oswald a US Marine who was given a "hardship" discharge as the sole support of his mother, defected to the USSR. Oswald gave the Soviets classified data on US radar operations and highly classified information about the American U2 spy flights over the Soviet Union in an attempt to join Soviet Intelligence. Oswald was likely a CIA spy and had received his training in the Russian language and intelligence operations as a Marine before his discharge. He and his Russian bride and child were later welcomed back into the US without courts martial or jail time as per the law. Although Oswald would later be blamed for killing President Kennedy, it remains a dubious claim as many documents and books, including *Hard Right Turn, The History and Assassination of the American Left*, have shown him to be a dupe.

Also on October 16, General George C. Marshall, the hero of WWII, the Secretary of State, and the Nobel Peace Prize winner, died at Walter Reed Hospital. His accomplishments were widely acclaimed by all but the Republican Party. While running for president in 1952, Eisenhower campaigned alongside McCarthy, and refused to defend Marshall's policies or the accusations by McCarthy that Marshall was a communist and a traitor. This was particularly cowardly of Eisenhower since it was Marshall who recommended and awarded Eisenhower for many of his promotions. Marshall had also effectively stood aside for the position of supreme commander, allowing his friend Eisenhower to be chosen for that role. Marshall was surprised and dismayed at the lack of loyalty and support from Eisenhower during the McCarthy hearings.

October 17, Belgian troops under the UN Trust Authority put down the Rwandan Revolt which saw the Hutu Tribe commit widespread killing, rapes and other crimes against the Tutsi tribe. The revolt forced about 100,000 Tutsi to flee to neighboring countries to avoid the Hutu violence. This would be the first major clash of many between the Hutu and Tutsi.

October 21, the Guggenheim Art Museum opened in New York City.

Also on October 21, Werner von Braun and his team of former Nazi scientists were transferred from the US Army to NASA. Von Braun publicly stated his motto had always been, "Shoot for the moon." To which Winston Churchill in reference to the former Nazi scientist's rocket attacks on civilians in London during the war quipped, "Unfortunately he kept hitting London."

Also on October 21, Chinese soldiers killed 10 Indian police officers and took 21 others prisoner in a border clash between Chinese soldiers and Indian police. The day is now observed as Police Commemoration Day in India.

October 22, riots broke out in a poor section of Tokyo and several hundred people attacked the local police station.

October 24, Cuba nationalized 150 American owned properties. Most of these were Mafia owned. The nationalized properties included hotels, casinos, and a race track.

October 27, a hurricane struck Mexico killing over a thousand people.

October 28, DuPont introduced a new manmade fabric which they trademarked as "Lycra."

Also on this day Senator John F. Kennedy and his brother Bobby began planning his run for the US presidency in 1960.

October 30, thirty independence protestors were killed by Belgian troops in the Belgian Congo. The Belgian Army also arrested Patrice Lumumba the head of the protest march. Lumumba would go on to be the first Premier of the independent Congo. He would later be assassinated in a CIA assisted coup.

Also on October 30, the Alabama Polytechnic Institute was formally renamed Auburn University.

October 31, the first ICBM fitted with a nuclear warhead was at Vandenberg Air Force Base. It went immediately on alert.

November 3, France announced its intention of building a nuclear strike force.

Also on November 3, after student demonstrators clashed with the police in the US Canal Zone, Panama erupted in riots.

November 4, over 6,700 people were paralyzed and another 10,000 became ill after using contaminated cooking oil in Morocco. Cooking oil was mixed with surplus jet fuel purchased at a US airbase. Five manufacturers of the cooking oil were sentenced to death because of the incident.

November 6, the heart defibrillator was created in Boston by Dr. Bernard Lown.

November 19, just 17 days before Thanksgiving the US issued a health warning that much of the US cranberry crop had been tainted by the carcinogen aminotriazole which was sometimes used as a herbicide.

November 11, Dr. Werner Heyde the Nazi doctor who oversaw the deaths of over 100,000 handicapped people in Germany was caught after having changed his name and was practicing medicine in Germany as Dr. Fritz Sawade. He later hung himself five days before his trial was to start.

November 15, Herbert and Connie Clutter and their three children were killed in their home near Holcomb, Kansas. These murders became the basis for Truman Capote's book *In Cold Blood*. The killers, Dick Hitchcock and Perry Smith, would be caught and hanged in 1965.

November 16, National Airlines Flight 967 from Tampa to New Orleans exploded over the Gulf of Mexico and killed 42 people. A bomb was suspected but was never proved because the wreckage was lost in the Gulf waters.

November 19, the last Ford Edsel was produced. The well made auto was cancelled because it failed to catch on with the American public, costing Ford over $350 million. Only 116, 000 were sold. The US was in the middle of the 1957 recession when the Edsel debuted, and most car makers saw their sales fall starting in 1957. Ford said later that the Edsel was "the wrong car for the wrong time."

November 21, the radio payola scandal reached its peak. The creator of Rock and Roll, Alan Freed, was fired from WABC for refusing to sign a statement saying he had not played music for record company kickbacks. *American Bandstand* host Dick Clark was also accused but survived. After a Congressional investigation, radio DJs were stripped of the authority to make programming decisions, and payola became a misdemeanor offense.

November 22, the *Minneapolis Star Journal* reported that Minnesota would receive an NFL team. Minnesota was to receive an AFL team but had turned it down in preference for an NFL team. As a result Minnesota got an NFL franchise, the Minnesota Vikings. The AFL franchise then went to another city, Oakland, California which became the Oakland Raiders. Minnesota had two previous NFL teams, the Minneapolis Marines and the once famous Duluth Eskimos which after bankruptcy moved on to eventually become the Washington Redskins.

November 24, a TWA cargo plane crashed in Chicago and killed the three crew members and eight people on the ground. Thirteen others were injured.

November 26, the Pioneer V satellite was launched on the maiden flight of an Atlas-Able rocket. The launch failed after forty seconds.

November 27, "the Angel of Death," Nazi war criminal Dr. Josef Mengele, was granted Paraguayan citizenship. It was believed that Mengele who performed some of the most atrocious acts at the Auschwitz and Birkenau concentration camps had used the Ratline through the Catholic Church to escape prosecution in Germany. He died in Paraguay as a fugitive from justice in 1979.

November 28, sit-ins at "Whites only" lunch counters in Nashville began at a department store and lasted until May 10, 1960. During this time the participants were verbally and sometimes physically abused, and over 150 Black students were arrested for refusing to vacate store lunch counters. The attorney representing the Black students had his home bombed. On May 10, Nashville lunch counters began serving Black customers. However it wasn't until the passage of the Civil Rights Act of 1964 that all public facilities in Nashville ceased being for "Whites only."

November 30, fearing another independence uprising, János Kádár, the Communist leader of Hungary, announced that the 60,000 Soviet troops that had invaded Hungary during the revolt would remain "as long as the international situation demands it." The troops stayed in Hungary until the USSR began their collapse.

December 1, the Antarctica Treaty was agreed to by all twelve nations with an interest in the continent. The treaty provides that the continent is open to all scientific expeditions and bans all military activities on the continent. Currently 50 nations have agreed to the treaty. The twelve original were Argentina, Australia, Belgium, Chile, France Japan, New Zealand, Norway, South Africa, the United Kingdom, the USSR and the US.

Also on December 1, an Allegheny Airlines plane traveling from Philadelphia to Cleveland crashed killing 24 of 25 people aboard.

December 2, Nazi Kurt Franz the Deputy Commander of the Treblinka concentration camp was arrested. Franz had taken another identity and had been working as a cook in Germany.

Also on this day a dam collapsed in France and killed 433 people in the flooding.

December 4, in a successful flight another rhesus monkey, Sam, was put into space to test an emergency escape mechanism for a future human flight.

December 7, the US naval base at Subic Bay was turned over to the Philippines.

December 8, Premier Khrushchev sent a secret memo to the Soviet Politburo to change the Soviet defense strategy by building up the nuclear arsenal to prevent invasion from the west on any Soviet territory or ally. On December 14, the Politburo approved the proposal.

December 9, at the end of a five day storm that claimed more than a hundred lives across Europe, a Norwegian freighter was swamped and sank killing the crew of twenty people.

December 10, the People's Republic of China began a campaign urging the Chinese people around the world to come back to their "mother land." The Chinese provided transportation for approximately 100,000 Chinese scattered throughout the world to come back.

Also on December 10, the 5,200 US military personnel who were based in Iceland since WWII were withdrawn. However a small post of 30 men remained until 2006.

December 11, Allen Dulles, the Director of the CIA began planning the many assassination attempts on Fidel Castro. He involved Castro's former mistress Marita Lorenz, who went to work for the CIA, and the Mafia among others. Although many attempts were made they all failed and would later only serve to embarrass the US government and the CIA when they came to light.

Also on December 11, Minnesota Governor Orville Freeman declared martial law in Albert Lea, Minnesota because of a strike against the Wilson Meat Packing Company. He then ordered the National Guard to impose order. A federal court later overruled his decision stating that "military rule cannot be imposed upon a community simply because it may seem to be more expedient than to enforce the law."

December 12, in another dismal failure in the US space program a Titan rocket failed after four seconds after launch and collapsed into and exploding the launch pad.

December 14, Gus Hall was elected Secretary General of the Communist Party USA and led the party until 2000.

December 16, the comedy troupe Second City was founded in Chicago. Many of its cast would go on to successful careers in American movies and television including: Ed Asner, John Candy, Bill Murray, Harold Ramis, George Wendt, Julia Louis-Dreyfus, Dan Aykroyd, Bonnie Hunt, Chris Farley, Mike Meyers, Dave Thomas, Rick Moranis, Tina Fey, Stephen Colbert, Steve Carell and many others.

December 20, nine people were killed and twenty-one injured when a cattle truck hit a Greyhound Bus in Arizona.

December 22, Rock singer Chuck Berry was arrested for having sex with and transporting a fourteen-year-old girl across state lines under the Mann Act. In January he was sentenced to three years in prison.

On December 22, it was also announced that the 10,000 US military personnel in Morocco would be withdrawn by 1963.

December 24, a wave of anti-Semitism swept Europe. A Swastika was painted in red on a synagogue in Cologne, Germany and over the next nine days 600 cases of anti-Semitic vandalism were reported in Western Europe.

December 29, is known as the birth of nanotechnology when Professor Richard Feynman presented his lecture to the annual meeting of the American Physical Society, "There's Plenty of Room at the Bottom."

December 30, Senator Hubert Humphrey of Minnesota announced he would seek the Democratic nomination for President.

In 1959 unemployment receded to about 5.5%. Inflation was about 1%. Average yearly wages rose to $5,010 and a new three bedroom house averaged about $12,400 with rents remaining low. A new car averaged $2,200 and gas was 25 cents per gallon. The Barbie doll cost $1.29.

Also in 1959 the first human died from HIV in the Congo. The disease is a zoonosis, like rabies, influenza or more recently Ebola and is caused by an animal virus morphing and transferring from an animal disease to humans. An HIV virus similar to the human strain was found in apes and may have been transmitted when the animals were eaten by humans.

May 4, the first Grammy Awards were held at the Beverly Hilton Hotel in Beverly Hills, California. Henry Mancini's *The Music from Peter Gun* won the Grammy for Best Album and Doenico Modugno's *Volare* was song of the year. Rock and Roll music was hit hard in 1959. Elvis was in the Army; Buddy Holly, Ritchie Valens, and the Big Bopper were killed in the plane crash; Chuck Berry went to prison for a consensual affair with a 14-year-old girl, and Jerry Lee Lewis' career nose-dived after his marriage to his 13-year-old cousin. And then the Payola Scandal hit which made it seem that everyone in the industry was corrupt. But the music played on. *The Battle of New Orleans* by Johnny Horton was a top hit. Bobby Darin had two in the top ten with *Mack the Knife* and *Dream Lover*. The Fleetwoods had two hits in the top ten with *Come Softly to Me* and *Mr. Blue*. Santo and Johnny had a hit with *Sleep Walk.* Richie Valens had two posthumous hits with *Donna* and *La Bamba.* Lloyd Price had two hits with *Personality* and *Stagger Lee.* Elvis still had a few hits with *A Big Hunk O' Love, I Need Your Love Tonight* and *A Fool Such as I.* Other hits included: *Poison Ivy* and *Charlie Brown* by the Coasters, *Sea of Love* by Phil Phillips, *16 Candles* by the Crests, *I Ran All the Way Home* by the Impalas, *A Teenager in Love* by Dion and the Belmonts, *Lipstick on Your Collar* by Connie Francis, *There Goes My Baby* by the Drifters, *Never Be Anyone Else But You* by Ricky Nelson, *Venus* by Frankie Avalon, and *Lonely Boy* by Paul Anka. *The Theme Song for Peter Gun* was also in the top 100.

Television was now by far America's favorite past time. In October former President Truman made a guest appearance on the *Jack Benny Show* while pundits debated if his appearance took some dignity away from the presidency. *The Wizard of OZ* was played for only the second time on television and was such a success that CBS made it an annual springtime event. The new shows making their debuts included plenty of Westerns with: *Rawhide, Bonanza, Laramie,* and *The Rebel. The Twilight Zone, Hawaiian Eye, Dennis the Menace* and *The Untouchables* also debuted.

On June 4, 1959 the last Three Stooges film, *Sappy Bullfighters* was released. It was the 190th short film made by the comedy team. The movie studios had decided to compete with television with "blockbuster" hits "with a cast of thousands" and *Ben-Hur* was the top grossing film of 1959 with almost $37 million. It also won the Oscar for Best Picture, Best Director, Charlton Heston for Best Actor, and Hugh Griffith for Best Supporting Actor. Walt Disney's *Sleeping Beauty* was the second highest grossing film with about $22 million. The Golden Globe Awards favored *Some Like It Hot* giving the it the Best Picture, the Best Actor for Jack Lemon and the Best Actress for Marilyn Monroe. *Room at the Top* won Oscars for Best Actress for Simone Signoret and for Best Screen Play. It also won the Golden Globe for Best Screen Play. Shelley Winters won the Oscar Best Supporting Actress in *The Diary of Anne Frank.*

Other movies of 1959 included: *North by Northwest* starring Cary Grant and Eva Marie Saint, *Pillow Talk* with Doris Day, Rock Hudson and Tony Randall, *Rio Bravo* with John Wayne, Dean Martin and Angie Dickenson, *Anatomy of a Murder* starring Jimmy Stewart and Lee Remick, *Operation Petticoat* with Cary Grant and Tony Curtis, and the movie about nuclear holocaust *On the Beach* with Gregory Peck, Ava Gardner and Fred Astaire.

The books and literature of 1959 was particularly good. *The Rise and Fall of the Third Reich* by William L. Shirer is a classic history. *Flowers for Algernon* by Daniel Keyes is a sci-fi classic. *Naked Lunch* by William S. Burroughs was a premonition of the 1960s. *The Sirens of Titan* by Kurt Vonnegut is an odd and interesting tale. *Hawaii* by James Michener is one of the best of the historical novel genre. *The Manchurian Candidate* is apolitical thriller. And *Goldfinger* by Ian Fleming is considered by some his best work. Other books of 1959 include: *The Longest Day* by Cornelius Ryan, *Goodbye Columbus and Five Short Stories* by Phillip Roth, *Advise and Consent* by Allen Drury, *To Sir, with Love* by E.R. Braithwaite, *Maggie Cassidy* by Jack Kerouac, *Emmanuelle* by Emmanuelle Arsan, and *The Zoo Story* by Edward Albee.

Chapter 16. 1960: Birth Control, US Troops in Vietnam, the Founding of the Viet Cong, the US Plans to Destroy Cuba, Sit-Ins and Kennedy Elected

January 1, the West African Republic of Cameroun became independent. UN Secretary Dag Hammarskjöld, US Ambassador to the UN Henry Cabot Lodge, and Soviet First Deputy Premier Frol Kozlov were present for the ceremony.

January 2, Senator John Kennedy formally announced his candidacy for President of the US. He was asked if his Catholicism would hamper his chance for winning he replied, "I would think that there is really only one issue involved in the whole question of a candidate's religion, that is, does a candidate believe in the separation of church and state?"

January 4, the US steel strike of 1959 was finally settled.

Also on this date Nobel Prize winning author Albert Camus was killed in a car accident in France.

January 5, the French newspaper *Le Monde*, revealed a confidential report from the International Red Cross to the French government revealing the French Army's systemic use of torture in Algeria.

January 6, Cardiopulmonary resuscitation (CPR) was used successfully for the first time by Dr. Henry Thomas. On July 9, the Journal of the American Medical Association introduced CPR to the rest of the world saving countless lives.

Also on January 6, a National Airlines flight from Miami to New York exploded and killed 34 people. On the plane was Julian Frank who unknowingly carried a bomb in his luggage that had been planted by Dr. Robert Spears who had taken out a life insurance policy on Frank. Dr. Spears was later arrested for the crime.

January 7, a Polaris missile hit a long range target using an internal guidance system. Previous to this missiles were guided from the ground. Also on this day the USSR announced it was testing a long range missile in the North Pacific. The soviet test rocket was launched on January 20, and successfully proved the Soviet rocket had a range of 7,760 miles making any target in the US within its range.

January 9, on his 47th birthday Vice President Nixon became a candidate for president when he placed his name on the ballot in the Oregon, New Hampshire and Ohio Republican primaries.

January 10, US Secretary of the Army Wilber Brucker announced in Taipei that the US would now defend Quemoy and Matsu from attacks by the People's Republic. The issue of whether the United States should go to war with China over the two islands would become a hot debate topic in the 1960 presidential campaign.

January 12, the seven-year-long State of Emergency that was declared because of the Mau Mau uprising in Kenya was finally lifted by the British government.

January 13, President Eisenhower and the National Security Council met and approved NSC special order #5412, Operation Zapata, to overthrow the government of Fidel Castro. The order would eventually bring about the disastrous Bay of Pigs Invasion for which Kennedy would later be blamed.

January 15, an early morning raid on the homes of eight Chicago police officers found "several carloads" of stolen merchandise. By the end of the month 15 police officers were indicted for operating a burglary ring in Chicago.

January 18, a Capitol Airlines flight from Washington, DC to Norfolk crashed and killed 50 people.

January 21, the worst mine disaster in history occurred in South Africa when a coal mine collapsed and killed 437 miners.

Also on this date an Avianca Flight from New York to Jamaica crashed when the landing gear collapsed and killed 36 of the 47 people on board.

January 23, Navy Lt. Don Walsh and Jacques Piccard descended in the US Navy bathyscaphe *Trieste* in the Mariana Trench, the deepest part of the ocean, to a depth of over seven miles.

January 24, over 5,000 French Algerian residents and some French soldiers barricaded themselves in Algiers demanding that France keep Algeria. In the clashes between the French residents and local police 24 were killed and 136 were seriously wounded.

January 27, the Kilauela Volcano in Hawaii erupted and the lava flow wiped out the village Kopoho. Fortunately all 300 residents were evacuated.

Also on this date a crowd surged forward in panic at the train depot in Seoul, Korea killing 31 people.

January 28, the NFL formally announced that it would add two new teams, the Dallas Cowboys and the Minnesota Vikings. Two days previous to this announcement the NFL appointed Pete Rozelle, the former General Manager of the Los Angeles Rams, as the new NFL Commissioner.

January 29, French President Charles de Gaulle appeared on French and Algerian television in his Army uniform stating that he was speaking as General de Gaulle former commander of the Army as well as the head of state in France. He said that the destiny of Algeria would be given to the Arab majority and not the French residents of Algeria. He ordered that all Army units obey this command. The French Army had been siding with the French Algerian residents against the French government, but with de Gaulle's order as a General and former commander of French forces the majority of the Army complied and put down the French Algerian rebellion.

January 31, a seventeen-year-old Black college freshman was turned away from an all-White lunch counter at a Woolworth's Department Store in Greensboro, North Carolina. When he told three college friends what happened they went back to the lunch counter and began a sit-in. They stayed until the store closed. On the following day 20 Black students came for the daylong sit-in and were heckled by a White mob. On the third day 60 Blacks came to sit-in and the national press began to cover the story and Woolworth's released a statement saying they would abide by their "Whites only" policy in the South. On the fourth day 300 Blacks came to the sit-in and also began a sit-in at the Kress Department Store. The sit-ins spread to other North Carolina cities like Winston-Salem, Raleigh, Durham, and Charlotte and even spread to other out-of-state lunch counters in Richmond, Virginia, in Nashville, Tennessee and Lexington, Kentucky. On Monday July 25, 1960 the lunch counter at the Greensboro Woolworth's was desegregated and the first lunches served were to the store's Black employees. Other lunch counters in the South including other Woolworth's remained segregated until the Civil Rights Act of 1964. The Greensboro Woolworth's lunch counter is now on display at the Smithsonian in Washington, DC as attribute to those who fought for civil rights. The Woolworth's Department Store in Greensboro is now the International Civil Rights Museum.

Also on January 31, Israeli and Syrian soldiers opened fire on each other killing 12 Syrians and 7 Israelis.

February 3, President Eisenhower recommended at a news conference that the United States should make nuclear weapons available to its allies. Eisenhower urged that the Atomic Energy Act be amended in order to permit the U.S. to transfer weapons to the arsenals of other allied nations. Nationalist China was high on his list.

February 4, Jordan announced that it would give citizenship to any Palestinians who were citizens of Palestine prior to 1948. The announcement excluded Jews.

Also on this date Soviet Deputy Premier Anastas Mikoyan visited Cuba.

February 8, the Hollywood Walk of Fame was dedicated with 1,558 names placed on stars along Hollywood Boulevard. The construction was done as part of an urban renewal project.

February 9, Adolph Coors III of the Coors Brewing Company was kidnapped and held for $500,000 ransom. The kidnapper later killed Coors. The killer was later caught and sent to prison.

February 11, the US Army revealed at a press conference that an atom bomb explosion could neutralize a larger hydrogen bomb and that the US could use this as a defense against a Soviet attack. General Arthur Trudeau stated it would be better to have "a small explosion a hundred miles over Hartford, Connecticut, than a large explosion in New York City."

February 13, France became the fourth nuclear power joining the US, Soviets and Britain when it successfully exploded a nuclear weapon in the desert of Algeria.

Also on February 13, because the US cancelled trade and economic exchanges with Cuba, Fidel Castro signed an agreement with the Soviets which gave Cuba a $100 million line of credit and a promise that the Soviets would buy one million tons of sugar per year for 5 years.

February 15, in a miscommunication President Nasser of the United Arab Republic received word that Israel was massing troops on the Syrian border. He responded by massing troops in Syria. In response Israel began to fortify the border and the two were poised for war. On March 1, Nasser realized it had been a mistake and the two sides de-escalated.

February 17, the US and Britain announced the construction of a Ballistic Missile Early Warning System from Britain to Alaska, including Greenland and Canada. It would become known as the DEW Line (Distant Early Warning Line.)

February 18, Vice President Nixon opened the Winter Olympic Games in Squaw Valley, California. The winter games along with the Summer Olympics would be shown almost in their entirety on television for the first time.

February 19, the People's Republic of China began their space program by successfully launching a T-7 rocket into sub-orbit. However the first Chinese satellite would not go into space until 1970 and they would not put a man in space until 2003.

February 22, an explosion at the Karl Marx coal mine in East Germany killed 49 miners.

February 24, a disgruntled man turned assassin and began to fire a rifle and randomly shoot people from his rooftop in Pennsylvania. His first shots killed two county maintenance workers repairing a road. He then began shooting at passing cars. He continued for nine hours until he was killed by police.

February 25, Saddam Hussein, who had fled to Syria after attempting to assassinate the Iraqi president, was found guilty and sentenced to death in absentia. He would not return to Iraq until 1963 after the Iraqi President was assassinated.

Also on February 25, a US Naval plane carrying a US Navy Band who was to perform during President Eisenhower's visit to Brazil collided midair with a Brazilian passenger plane killing 61 of 64 people aboard both aircraft.

February 29, an earthquake in Morocco killed an estimated 12,000 people.

March 2, in Montevideo, Uruguay President Eisenhower was accidently tear gassed in a motorcade when police used it to control protesting students.

March 4, a French cargo ship *La Coubre* carrying 70 tons of ammunition from Belgium to Cuba was blown up by a bomb in Havana harbor. A second explosion happened while the crew was being rescued. Seventy-six people were killed and over 200 were wounded. The Cubans and others blamed the CIA for the explosion and deaths.

March 5, 1960 Sergeant Elvis Presley was honorably discharged from the US Army.

March 6, President Eisenhower announced that an additional 3,500 American troops would be sent to Vietnam as "advisors" to supplement the 700 troops already stationed there.

March 7, the 14,000 member Screen Actors guild went on strike and brought the eight major US film studios to a halt.

March 8, in the New Hampshire Presidential Primaries Senator Kennedy won the Democratic primary and Vice president Nixon won the Republican.

March 11, the Pioneer V satellite was successfully launched. It was the first interplanetary satellite orbiting between the Earth and Venus. It was the most successful satellite launched by the US to date.

March 14, West German Chancellor Konrad Adenauer met with Israeli Prime Minister David Ben-Gurion secretly in New York. The meeting resulted in Germany giving financial and military support to Israel.

March 15, in Orangeburg, South Carolina, 389 Black sit-in protestors were arrested. In Atlanta 77 Black college students protesting segregation were arrested for protests at government offices.

March 17, at a White House Meeting between President Eisenhower, Allen Dulles and Richard Bissell of the CIA, the President authorized the final details for the covert operation which would overthrow Castro in Cuba. He gave the green light for the Bay of Pigs invasion.

Also on March 17, a Northwest flight from Chicago to Miami crashed and killed 63 people.

March 20, Florida Governor LeRoy Collins shocked his state and the South when he endorsed the goals of the sit-ins and came out for desegregating public places like lunch counters. In his speech he concluded with, "We can never stop Americans from struggling to be free." He was later that year appointed as the Chairman of the Democratic Convention that nominated President John Kennedy and Vice president Lyndon Johnson. He would later be appointed by Johnson as the Director of Community Relations for the 1964 Civil Rights Act, a job that would later cost him his election to the US Senate from Florida in 1968.

March 21, in what became known as the Sharpeville Massacre, over 5,000 South African Blacks protested the government's racial policies and were then machine-gunned by the police and soldiers. They killed 69 people and wounded many others.

Also on March 21, Israeli Mossad agents found Adolph Eichmann the architect of the Holocaust hiding in Argentina. He had been smuggled out of Germany by Bishop Hudal and the Catholic Church through their "Ratline." He was abducted by the Mossad and brought to Israel to stand trial. In Argentina Eichmann's abduction was met with a violent wave of anti-Semitism. On December 15, 1961 Eichmann was found guilty for crimes against humanity and sentenced to death. He was hung on May 31, 1962. His last words were, "Long live Germany. Long live Argentina. Long live Austria. These are the three countries with which I have been most connected and which I will not forget. I greet my wife, my family, and my friends. I am ready. We'll meet again soon, as is the fate of all men. I die believing in God."

March 22, the laser was patented by Bell Laboratories.

March 26, the Minneapolis Lakers played their last game in Minneapolis losing the last game of the Western Conference Championships. During the offseason the team would be sold and relocated to Los Angeles.

Also on March 26, the Ku Klux Klan burned crosses along highways in Alabama and South Carolina protesting the lunch counter desegregation protests.

March 27, the last passenger train pulled by a steam locomotive traveled from Detroit to Durand, Michigan.

March 29, the *New York Times* ran an ad *Heed Their Rising Voices* about Black protests in Montgomery, Alabama and described the horrific actions by the City's police department. Three Montgomery City Commissioners sued the *New York Times* for libel and the newspaper was found guilty by an all-White Alabama jury. They were ordered to pay $500,000. The verdict was later appealed to the US Supreme Court, *Sullivan v. New York Times*, which found that it was an infringement of the First Amendment to limit political free speech by threat of a libel suit. This verdict set legal precedent and has protected the press and others for speaking out on political issues.

March 30, in response to the Sharpeville Massacre in South Africa over 30,000 Blacks marched through the streets of Cape Town in protest. The South African government declared a state of emergency.

Also on this day over 5,000 Blacks marched through Baton Rouge, Louisiana to protest state segregation laws and the arrests and harassment of sit-in protestors.

April 1, the US launched the TIROS I the first true weather satellite. The TIROS used infra-red television images to send back video of cloud patterns and formations taken from an altitude of 450 miles.

April 2, a French treaty assuring independence for Madagascar was signed allowing the Malagasy Republic to be formed in June.

Also on April 2, the South African police confronted and broke up a march of several thousand Black protestors in Cape Town.

April 4, Sweden began the ordinations for women priests.

April 5, Senator John Kennedy surprised and beat Senator Hubert Humphrey in the Wisconsin Democratic Presidential Primary. The loss by Humphrey, a Minnesota Senator, in his own home territory, was a serious blow to his presidential ambitions. In the Wisconsin Republican Primary Vice President Richard Nixon won unopposed.

April 7, South Africa banned the African Nationalist Congress in South Africa, ANC. The ban caused Nelson Mandela and others to create an underground guerilla wing of the ANC.

April 9, Prime Minister Erik Verwoerd, "the architect of Apartheid" was wounded in an assassination attempt by David Pratt, a White businessman and farmer. Pratt said he was shooting "the epitome of Apartheid." Pratt managed to fire two pistol shots at Verwoerd before he was subdued, one striking Verwoerd in the right cheek and the other his right ear.

April 10, an American U 2 spy plane flew over and filmed the Soviet missile range at Tyruatam, Kazakhstan. After the event several Soviet commanders were relieved of command for not firing and brining the plane down.

April 11, a Korean fisherman found the mutilated body of a missing high school student who had disappeared during a protest of the dubious outcome of the South Korean presidential elections. The discovery of the boy led to widespread riots throughout South Korea.

April 12, the International Court of Justice ruled in favor of Portugal over India to allow Portugal to travel unobstructed through India to their Indian colonies in Goa, Daman, and Diu. The victory was short-lived as India annexed all three Portuguese colonies the following year.

Also on April 12, Vice President Nixon opened Candlestick Park, the San Francisco stadium, by throwing out the first pitch at a Giants game.

April 13, the Transit 1B satellite was successfully launched by the US. It was the first navigation satellite. It would eventually be replaced by Global Positioning Satellites (GPS).

April 15, the Student Nonviolent Coordinating Committee, SNCC, was organized at the nation's oldest Black college, Shaw University in Raleigh, North Carolina. The Committee was organized by 300 students from 58 colleges with the purpose to end segregation.

April 16, the uncomfortable alliance between the Chinese communists and the Soviets ended with the widespread publication of a Chinese editorial, *Long Live Leninism,* which severely criticized the Soviets for their desire of a peaceful coexistence with the West. The Chinese promoted Lenin's statement that "so long as imperialism exists, war is inevitable." They condemned the Soviets for their failure to follow their own founder.

The split between the USSR and China was much deeper and dated back to 1945 when the Soviet Union signed a Treaty of Friendship and Alliance with Chiang Kai-shek's Chinese Nationals. Stalin had at the time advised Mao and the Chinese Communists against seizing power in China. The Soviets didn't want to see a powerful Chinese communist state on their border and wanted to keep China weak and divided.

In 1960 the People's Republic felt powerful enough to confront the Soviets. This Sino-Soviet Split, as it became to be known, would see a cold war develop between China and the Soviet Union where the two competed for the allegiance of countries in the third world. It would be one of the primary reasons the Soviets would support North Vietnam against the US in the up-coming war in Vietnam. Contrary to the American Domino Theory the Vietnamese communists had their own suspicions and troubles with the Chinese as China didn't want to see a strong united Vietnam on its southern border. However the USSR wanted to see a strong Vietnam in Southeast Asia to check the Chinese communists. The conflict between China and Vietnam would also eventually lead to a war between the two socialist nations in 1979.

April 17, rock star Eddie Cochran was killed in an auto accident while touring Great Britain.

April 19, in another large protest against the fraudulent presidential elections in South Korea more than 100,000 college and high school students marched in protest in Seoul. The police opened fire into the crowd and killed 180 students and wounded thousands. The protests grew because of the killings and the South Korean Army and police began to side with the protestors. On April 25, President Syngman Rhee and his Interior Minister in charge of the police resigned. The vice president was blamed for the violence and committed suicide along with his entire family.

Also on April 19, the People's Republic of China struck oil in Daqing in northeast China.

April 20, now out of the Army, Elvis Presley returned to Hollywood and began filming the movie *G.I. Blues*.

April 24, in what would become known as 'Bloody Sunday," a group of 100 Black beachgoers attempted to desegregate a public beach in Biloxi, Mississippi with what they called a "wade-in." The local White police organized a local White mob and the police stood by and watched as the White mob attacked the Black beachgoers. Shots were fired and rocks were thrown at the Blacks which broke up the demonstration. It triggered violence between Blacks and Whites in Biloxi for several days and ten people were shot and many more injured during the riots. The office of Dr. Gilbert Mason, the organizer of the wade-in, was also bombed that night.

April 27, the former French colony of Togo was declared an independent republic.

May 1, a US U2 spy plane piloted by Francis Gary Powers was shot down by the Soviet Union. His plane was hit by a Soviet SA-2 missile at 70,000 feet. Powers ejected and parachuted to the ground where he was arrested by the Soviets. Powers would later blame Lee Harvey Oswald for giving secret information to the Soviets that allowed his U2 plane to be shot down.

The Eisenhower Administration and the CIA had assumed that Powers had been killed when his plane went down and they concocted a story that an American plane on a routine weather gathering mission in Turkey had gone missing after the pilot apparently lost consciousness due to a faulty oxygen system and accidently flew over Soviet air space. Khrushchev released a statement saying an American spy plane had been shot down over the Soviet Union, never mentioning Powers capture and allowing Eisenhower to continue to promote his cover up lie. It worked and Eisenhower lied and said he knew nothing of any spy missions and continued to lie about the event calling it a weather plane. He was greatly embarrassed when on May 7, Khrushchev said on television, "I must tell you a secret. When I made my first report I deliberately did not say that the pilot was alive and well... and now just look how many silly things the Americans have said." He then produced the U2 wreckage and Powers who admitted to spying on behalf of the US.

May 2, Caryl Chessman, "the Red Light bandit," was executed in the gas chamber at San Quinton Prison. Chessman posed as a police officer and would follow or find young couples in remote locations and then rob the men and kidnap and rape the young women. He was convicted of seventeen counts of robbery, kidnapping and rape.

May 3, in the first test of the CONELRAD system, later the Emergency Broadcast System, all the television and radio stations in the US were taken over for thirty minutes with viewers and listeners being directed to go to their closest fallout shelter. In New York City a demonstration of over 500 people protesting nuclear arms refused police orders to go to shelters resulting in arrests.

May 4, the US agreed to sell India 17 million metric tons of surplus grain for about $1.3 billion because of a food shortage in India.

May 6, after it was passed by both houses of Congress, the Civil Rights Act of 1960 was signed into law by the President. The law prohibited poll taxes and other methods used to keep Black Americans from voting or registering to vote. Three days later the US Attorney General began looking at the voting records of four southern counties in Alabama, Georgia, Louisiana, and South Carolina where each county had very large majority Black population, but had no registered Black voters.

Also on May 6, tornadoes went through Oklahoma and Arkansas killing 27 and injuring over 250 people and destroyed the town of Wilburton, Oklahoma.

May 9, the US Food and Drug Administration approved Envoid, the first birth control pill, which began America's sexual revolution.

May 10, Senator John Kennedy won his seventh Presidential primary in West Virginia. The following day Senator Hubert Humphrey, his main rival, announced "I am no longer a candidate for the Democratic Presidential nomination."

May 12, after Eisenhower admitted that the US had been spying on the USSR with the U2 over flights, Khrushchev announced that any further over flights would be considered an act of war and any US aggression would be met "with atomic bombs within minutes."

May 13, about 200 students from Berkeley and Stanford Universities copying the Black civil rights sit-ins, staged a sit-in at the San Francisco City where the House Committee on Un-American Activities was holding their communist witch-hunt hearings. Another 3,500 student demonstrators protested outside. It was the first time the public had brazenly protested the committee. The police used nightsticks and fire hoses to violently disperse the crowd. The event was shown on television and began to inspire other student protests around the country.

May 15, while arriving at the Four Power Summit meeting in Paris with Britain, France and the USSR, President Eisenhower and the Secretary of Defense Thomas Gates Jr. ordered a test of the military alert system. Their orders were misunderstood and the Joint Chiefs of Staff ordered American forces world-wide to a DEFCON 3 status scrambling combat fighters and bombers into the air awaiting the final attack orders to strike the USSR. At Lowry Air Force Base in Colorado the base commanders asked the local television and radio stations to order all key personnel and fighter pilots to return to base to prepare for the attack, and this news spread throughout the US that America was about to go to war with the USSR. Declassified documents later showed that the Secretary of Defense Gates had sent the wrong command when he ordered the test.

Also on May 15, the USSR launched Sputnik IV, a five ton space capsule with a test dummy in preparation for launching the first man in space. The launch failed when the rocket went off course. Most of the capsule also burned up on re-entry and the remaining 20 pound fragment crashed into a street intersection in Manitowoc, Wisconsin.

May 16, the Four Power Summit opened officially in Paris and Premier Khrushchev asked to speak first. He delivered an angry statement about the U2 flights and how the US was flirting with nuclear danger and cancelled the summit and withdrew an invitation for Eisenhower to visit Moscow that had been planned for mid June.

May 17, the CIA began transmitting over "Radio Swan," a supposed Cuban rebel radio station delivering anti-Castro propaganda to the Cuban people supposedly from Cuba. The radio station was actually transmitting from Swan Island off the coast of Honduras.

May 19, a large anti-nuclear arms rally was held in New York City attracting 17,000 people to hear speeches by Eleanor Roosevelt, former democratic presidential candidate Alf Landon, socialist Norman Thomas, and labor leader Walter Reuther.

May 20, despite large protests and a petition of over 1.9 million people objecting, the Japanese Diet passed a new mutual defense and security treaty with the US.

May 21 and 23, two Japanese soldiers who were still hiding in the jungles since WWII were captured in Guam and were told of the Japanese surrender and peace with the US. Both were returned to Japan the end of May.

May 22, one of the most violent earthquakes ever recorded, 9.5 on the Richter scale, struck Chile. Between five and six thousand people died and two million were homeless. The quake sent Tsunamis all the way to Japan and killed countless more people including 61 people in Hawaii and injuring 282 others, and killed 119 in Japan and destroyed more than 2,800 homes.

May 24, the US successfully launched the MIDAS II satellite, capable of detecting Soviet missile launches and giving the US immediate notice. Also on this date the earthquake in Chile and its aftershocks triggered an eruption of the Cordón Caulle Volcano.

May 26, at a press conference UN Ambassador Henry Cabot Lodge displayed a hand carved replica of the Great Seal of the United States presented as a gift to the American Ambassador in Moscow and showed how the Soviets had implanted a listening device in the gift.

May 30, part of the grandstand at the Indianapolis 500 collapsed and killed two people and injured another 70 people.

June 2, at a concert in a civic center in Britain, John Lennon, Paul McCartney and George Harrison and two others performed as the Beatles for the first time.

Also on this date all the Broadway theaters closed in a labor dispute which lasted eleven days.

June 6, an eighteen-year-old Barbara Streisand won the talent contest at a Greenwich Village nightclub, the Lion, and launched her professional singing career.

Also on June 6, the American Heart Association announced a connection between cigarette smoking and coronary heart disease.

June 7, a fire at McGuire Air Force base in New Jersey burned a nuclear missile causing a plutonium leak. The spillage had to be permanently encased in asphalt and concrete.

June 10, the Ambassador to Japan, Douglas MacArthur II, and two of President Eisenhower's aides who were preparing for a trip by the President to Japan, had their car surrounded by an angry mob in Tokyo. They were trapped in the car for over 90 minutes until they were rescued by the US Marines. The protest was about the US-Japan mutual defense treaty.

June 15, thousands of Japanese protesting the US-Japan defense treaty stormed the Japanese parliament building and clashed with the police. One female protestor was killed and over 600 were wounded. On this same day about 5.8 million people protested the treaty nationwide. President Eisenhower cancelled his planned trip to Japan at the request of the Japanese Prime Minister who then was forced to resign in disgrace.

June 16, in Portuguese East Africa (now Mozambique) Portuguese colonial troops fired into a crowd of Black independence protestors and killed more than 600 people.

Also on June 16, the 23rd Amendment to the Constitution was passed by Congress and sent for ratification to the states. The Amendment provided for three electoral votes for the District of Columbia allowing District residents to vote for president.

June 19, President Eisenhower began a Far East tour. At a stop in Okinawa he was greeted by 1,500 protestors who wanted their island returned to Japan.

June 20, the Mali Federation was given independence from France. Two months later it would split into two independent nations, Mali and Senegal.

June 22, the US successfully launched two satellites from the same rocket sending them into two separate orbits.

June 26, Somaliland gained independence from Britain and it would unite with the former Italian Somaliland and create the Somali Republic. The Malagasy Republic also gained their independence from France.

June 27, a typhoon struck the Philippines and killed 104 people with more than 500 people missing.

June 28, lightning strikes in Arizona and New Mexico started 143 fires.

June 29, the Texaco Oil refinery in Cuba refused to process Cuban oil that would be sold to Cubans. In response to their refusal Cuba nationalized the refinery. Two days later Cuba also nationalized the ESSO and Shell Oil refineries in Cuba for the same reason. In Washington, DC CIA Director Allen Dulles reaffirmed his plans with President Eisenhower to both assassinate Castro and to invade Cuba. It was called Operation Zapata because the Zapata Oil Company — owned by George Herbert Walker Bush — agreed to be a silent partner with the CIA and provide three ships for the Cuban invasion plans.

June 30 the Belgian Congo gained independence. Two days later the country dissolved into civil war. Western nations and their intelligence agents encouraged the violence. Many in the West accused Prime Minister Patrice Lumumba, the leader of the independence movement, of being a communist sympathizer. The CIA, the United Kingdom's MI6 and Belgian intelligence backed the anti-Lumumba faction and planned and executed Lumumba's capture and assassination, according to John Prados in his book *Unsafe for Democracy: The Secret Wars of the CIA.*

July 1, a US B-47 reconnaissance flight over the Soviet Union was shot down with four of the crew killed and two captured in the Soviet Union.

July 2, a riot broke out at the Newport Jazz festival when 3,000 mostly White middleclass patrons became angry over the lack of seating. Three companies of National Guard were required to subdue the riot.

Also on July 2, in an interview former President Truman, a supporter of Lyndon Johnson, said that Senator Kennedy lacked the maturity to be president.

July 5, saying that Kennedy lacked enough delegates to be nominated, Senator Lyndon Johnson said that he would contest and win the Presidential nomination at the upcoming Democratic National Convention.

July 6, President Eisenhower ordered that the US would cease buying Cuban sugar thereby cutting Cuba's primary trade with the US and damaging the Cuban economy.

July 8, the US minor league baseball team the Havana Sugar Kings, were relocated to New Jersey.

July 9, in the on-going crisis in the Congo, the Belgian airlines, Sabena, began airlifting White Belgian residents out of the former colony. In three weeks well over 25,000 returned to Belgium.

July 11, Congo Prime Minister Patrice Lumumba asked the UN to intervene as rebels protected by Belgian troops were attacking the country.

July 12, the first Etch A Sketch toy was sold.

July 13, in Los Angeles John Kennedy defeated Lyndon Johnson, Stuart Symington and Adlai Stevenson on the first ballot to win the Democratic nomination for president. In a surprising move Kennedy then asked Lyndon Johnson to be his running mate. Kennedy who was extremely weak in the South felt he needed Johnson on the ticket to carry Texas and the South in what would be a close election with Nixon.

July 14, by a unanimous vote the UN Security Council recognized Prime Minister Lumumba's request and agreed to send UN peacekeeping forces to the Congo. They also ordered all Belgian troops out of the Congo. UN troops from Tunisia arrived the following day.

July 16, the Sino-Soviet split worsened as the USSR withdrew 1,390 Soviet technical experts from China and cancelled 12 economic agreements and also cancelled 200 jointly funded projects.

July 17, the UN peacekeeping forces were unable to expel the Belgian troops from the Congo. Lumumba was frustrated with the response to the crisis in the Congo. He became angry at the US and the Belgians and he threatened to invite Soviet troops into the Congo to protect his nation. The Belgian security forces and the CIA then implemented plans to capture and assassinate Lumumba according to John Prados in *Unsafe for Democracy: The Secret Wars of the CIA.*

July 19, two US Navy destroyers, the *Ammen* and the *Collett*, collided off the coast of California killing ten sailors.

July 23, the USSR launched a space capsule with two dogs as passengers. This was a final test flight before sending a man into space. The launch was unsuccessful as the capsule burned up in re-entry.

July 7, in Chicago the Republican National Convention nominated Richard Nixon for President and UN Ambassador Henry Cabot Lodge Jr. as his Vice Presidential running mate.

July 29, the US launched an unmanned capsule into space as a test toward putting a man in space. The launch failed after a minute in flight.

July 30, North and South Korea fought a naval battle, the first since the Korean War Truce. A North Korean gunboat was sunk.

Also on July 30, the new American Football League (AFL) played its first game between the Buffalo Bills and the New England Patriots.

August 1, Premier Zhou Enlai proposed a peace treaty with the US to make East Asia and the Western Pacific a nuclear free zone. The US rejected the idea as "another meaningless propaganda gesture."

Also on August 1, a typhoon struck Taiwan killing 126 people.

Also on this day the Republic of Dahomey (now Benin) received independence from the French.

August 3, the Republic of Niger received independence from France.

Also on this day a fire at a Soviet weather station in Antarctica killed 8 meteorologists.

August 5, the Republic of Upper Volta (now Burkina Faso) gained independence from France.

August 6, in response to the sugar and trade embargo by the US, Fidel Castro nationalized all United Fruit Company and other US corporate holdings in Cuba.

August 7, the Ivory Coast gained independence from France. It would later change its name back to the French version, Côte d'Ivoire.

August 9, the government of Laos was overthrown by an Army coup.

August 12, Echo 1 the first communications satellite was successfully launched.

August 13, the Central African Republic gained independence from France.

August 14, the French Congo gained independence and was also called the Republic of the Congo, which was confusing as it was also the name of the newly freed former Belgian Congo.

August 16, the British colony of Cyprus gained independence from Britain.

August 17, Gabon gained independence from France.

August 18, the first spy satellite photos were taken by Discoverer 14, over the USSR. The photos showed 64 airfields and 26 missile bases previously unknown to the US.

Also on August 18, CIA Director Allen Dulles told President Eisenhower that Patrice Lumumba of the Congo should be assassinated to avoid another Cuba according to John Prado.

August 19, the Soviets launched Sputnik 5 into orbit containing two dogs, 40 mice, two rats, and a variety of plants. It re-entered and was successfully recovered.

Also on this day the Soviets convicted US pilot Francis Gary Powers of espionage and sentenced him to ten years of hard labor in prison. He would be traded to the US for the Soviet spy, Rudolf Abel, after two years.

August 23, lyricist Oscar Hammerstein died and a week later the lights of Times Square in New York were turned off for one minute in recognition of his contributions.

August 24, in a controversial interview in *Time* magazine President Eisenhower was asked about Republican nominee Nixon's eight years of experience as Vice President. Charles Mohr of *Time* specifically asked if Eisenhower could "give an example of a major idea of his [Nixon's] tha you [Eisenhower] had adopted." Eisenhower replied, "If you give me a week, I might think of one." The episode hurt Nixon and their already rocky relationship.

Also on this day the coldest temperature on Earth ever recorded sank to minus 126.9 degrees Fahrenheit at a Soviet weather station in Antarctica. This record would be broken on July 21, 1983 when the same station reported minus 129 degrees Fahrenheit.

August 25, the Summer Olympics opened in Rome.

August 28, the UN demanded that all Belgian forces leave the Congo.

August 29, the Prime Minister of Jordan was killed when a bomb went off in his office. The bomb killed eleven and wounded 65 others.

September 3, over 300 people were killed and more than 700 were wounded in the fight between rebels and government troops in the Congo.

September 4, Hurricane Donna killed 107 people in Puerto Rico before it moved north and killed another 22 in the continental US. The hurricane sustained winds of over 100 miles per hour for nine days.

September 5, in the Summer Olympics America won a Gold Medal in boxing when a young Cassius Clay, later known as Muhammad Ali, beat his Polish rival.

September 6, it was announced in Moscow that two US National Security Agency cryptologists that had gone missing from the US had defected to the USSR.

September 8, the Richardson-Merrell pharmaceutical company submitted an application to the FDA for approval of selling the drug thalidomide in the US as a sedative. It went on sale in the US in March of 1961. The drug caused birth defects in more than 10,000 babies world-wide who had been exposed to the drug when their mothers had taken thalidomide during their pregnancies. Many babies were born with stumps for limbs, were born blind or deaf or had heart defects. This pharmaceutical disaster caused more rigid drug reviews and testing.

September 9, the first Hardees restaurant opened in as a drive-in in Greenville, North Carolina. Fast food was becoming an American staple.

September 12, Senator Kennedy was asked to speak before an assembly of Protestant ministers to answer the question, "Could a Catholic operate independently from the Vatican?" Kennedy won over the ministers by assuring them that he believed in the separation of church and state.

September 13, Lee Harvey Oswald had received a dishonorable discharge because of his defection and giving highly classified information to the USSR; however on this day this was changed to an undesirable discharge. This meant Oswald would not face a mandatory court martial and imprisonment upon his return to the US. It is unknown who initiated this action but was thought to be done at the request of the CIA. In fact upon his return Oswald was not even questioned by the FBI as was standard practice for any American returning from the USSR. These inexplicable incidents and the rapid approval of his Russian bride and child to be brought to the US — with all their travel expenses paid by the US State Department — are some of the many incidents that were seen as proof that Oswald was actually a CIA agent.

September 14, the Organization for Petroleum Exporting Countries, OPEC, was created at a conference in Bagdad by the oil-rich countries of Iraq, Iran, Saudi Arabia, Kuwait, and Venezuela. OPEC was created to give these nations more say and fair prices in their dealings with the US, Britain and their powerful oil companies.

Also on February 14, a military coup in the Congo led by the Army Chief of Staff, Joseph Mobutu, and backed by the CIA and Belgian security, was successful.

September 15, in further response to the US economic embargo on Cuba, Castro nationalized the cigar and cigarette industry.

September 19, a World Airways flight that was returning 94 US Air Force personnel from the Philippines to the US crashed just after takeoff killing 80 people.

September 20, the opening of the UN General Assembly attracted most of the world's leaders. This meeting gave membership to fifteen new nations, mostly in Africa. Khrushchev and Fidel Castro met for the first time at a hotel in New York.

September 24, the aircraft carrier the USS Enterprise, the largest ship ever built at the time, was launched from Newport News, Virginia. It was also the first atomic powered aircraft carrier.

September 25, Pacific Gas and Electric became the first American company to use geothermal heat to generate electricity.

September 26, in Chicago in the first televised presidential debates John Kennedy and Richard Nixon faced off. The young Kennedy appeared tan and calm while Nixon appeared unkempt and tense. Nixon also sweated profusely which also made him appear nervous and some said dishonest. Nixon also refused make-up and appeared old. Most historians give the edge to Kennedy in this debate, which helped overcome the notion that he was too young and inexperienced to be president.

September 27, Mexico nationalized their entire electric industry buying out the private utilities.

October 1, the former British colony of Nigeria became an independent nation.

October 4, in Boston an Eastern Airlines flight struck a flock of birds just after takeoff, stopping three of the plane's four engines. The plane crashed and killed 62 of the 72 people on board.

Also on this date an explosion at the Eastman Chemical Company in Kingsport, Tennessee, killed fifteen workers and injured over 200 others.

October 4, the US launched the Courier 1B communications satellite. It failed after seventeen days.

October 7, the second televised debate between Nixon and Kennedy was held in Washington, DC. It was felt among the pundits that Nixon slightly edged Kennedy in this debate, but 20 million fewer viewers watched the second debate which gave Kennedy the overall edge in the debates. On this night, rather than watching the debate, many Americans were tuned into the debut of a new television show, *Route 66.*

Also on October 7, a typhoon struck the Philippines and killed 51 people.

And also this day, the CIA prepared a box of poison cigars in an attempt to kill Fidel Castro. It was the first of many failed assassination attempts on Castro.

October 10, the USSR launched the first Mars probe. It failed after the first five minutes. The Soviets launched another four days later, but that probe also failed.

October 12, Khrushchev became angry about remarks made by the Philippine delegation at the UN and removed his shoe to pound on the table in protest.

Also on October 12, Madalyn Murray (O'Hare), an atheist, withdrew her fourteen-year-old son from public junior high school because the city school district had required Bible reading and a prayer to open each school day. She took her complaint to court, *Murray v. Curlett*, and it was later consolidated with a similar case *Abington School District v. Schempp.* The Supreme Court would rule in her favor in 1963 stating that mandatory prayers and religious instruction in public schools were a violation of the Constitution. Conservatives protesting at the time decried that the Supreme Court had "taken God out of the schools and let the negroes in."

October 13, the third Kennedy–Nixon debate took place on television with each man in separate location, Kennedy in New York and Nixon in Los Angeles. This debate was close, however, like the second debate, the audience was half the size of the first debate and even smaller than the second. This time Nixon had air conditioning installed and running very cold to prevent his sweating. He also wore makeup to appear younger.

Also on October 13, NASA successfully launched three mice 700 miles into space and then recovered them.

October 14, in a short speech at the University of Michigan John Kennedy first proposed the Peace Corps.

October 15, Félix-Roland Moumié the leader of the French Cameroon independence movement was poisoned with thallium by the French secret service, the SDECE, in Geneva. On November 2, he died.

October 16, the Algerian rebellion erupted again and 277 Algerian fighters were killed along with 40 French soldiers in two days of battle.

October 17, more than 3,000 people were killed by a Tsunami in East Pakistan (now Bangladesh).

October 19, Dr. Martin Luther King Jr. was arrested along with 280 students who held a sit-in at a Rich's Department Store lunch counter in Atlanta. King was sentenced to four months hard labor, but was released after two days when Robert Kennedy made a special appeal to the Georgia governor.

Also on October 19, the US announced a complete embargo on all exports to Cuba except food and medicine.

October 22, a passenger ship, Alcoa Corsair, collided with the freighter near Louisiana and killed nine people and injured 25 others.

October 23, a woman in Milwaukee rushed from a crowd of on-lookers and dumped a glass of whiskey over Senator Kennedy as he rode in an open convertible. She then threw the whiskey glass at Kennedy, who caught the glass and handed it back to her, saying calmly, "Here's your glass." She did this to protest that his being Irish Catholic. Kennedy requested that the local authorities and the Secret Service ignore the incident and not arrest the woman.

October 24, a Soviet space rocket exploded on the launch pad at Baikonur Cosmodrome killing over a hundred and twenty people including Field Marshal Nedelin. The accident was kept secret by the USSR and not revealed until the mid 1990s.

Also on October 24, in response to the new American embargo Fidel Castro ordered the confiscation of all American businesses in Cuba.

October 27, eggs and tomatoes were thrown at Vice President Richard Nixon while he campaigned in Michigan. These incidents occurred in Muskegon, Grand Rapids, and Jackson.

October 29, a plane carrying the Cal Poly football team crashed in Toledo killing 26 people.

Also on this day Cassius Clay (Muhammad Ali) made his professional boxing debut and won against an experienced professional fighter in six rounds.

October 30, at lunch at the White House President Eisenhower offered to make campaign speeches for Nixon during the week leading up to the election. Nixon, still angry over Eisenhower's critical remarks in his television interview, declined the offer, offending the President who then told Republican National Committee Chairman Len Hall, "God damn it. He looks like a loser to me!"

November 1, President Eisenhower reacted to the Cuban confiscation of businesses by threatening that he would take whatever actions necessary to keep and defend the Guantanamo Naval Base in Cuba.

Also on this day British Prime Minister Harold Macmillan announced that US nuclear submarines would be allowed to be based in Scotland.

November 3, Explorer 8 was launched and successfully explored the ionosphere confirming a layer of helium in the upper atmosphere.

November 4, a rumor spread rapidly through Western news services that Khrushchev had been ousted in a coup in the Soviet Union. The Soviet news service TASS later debunked the rumors.

November 5, the People's Republic of China successfully launched their first ballistic missile, the Silkworm missile. However this missile only had a range of 350 miles.

November 6, a person called "the Sunday Bomber" in the New York media exploded his fifth bomb in the New York subway, killing his first victim. The bombings had injured 51 other commuters. The bombings mysteriously stopped and the bomber was never caught.

November 8, John Kennedy won the election for the presidency by a margin of 112,827 votes out of about 68 million votes cast. Kennedy carried 22 states, Nixon carried 26, and two states, Alabama and Mississippi, went to Harry F. Byrd, a segregationist. In California, Kennedy appeared to have won Nixon's home state by 37,000 votes. However, when the absentee votes were counted a week later, Nixon had won by a very small margin. Nixon would not concede the election until the following afternoon. The Republicans charged voter fraud against Kennedy and the Democrats. However, in the 11 states where they challenged, the subsequent recount only made a difference in one, Hawaii, which went from Nixon to Kennedy after the challenge and recount. A Young Republican, Hillary Rodham (later Clinton), volunteered with her parents to help find Kennedy voter fraud in Illinois.

November 10, it was alleged that on this day a Russian cosmonaut named Byelokonyev, who may have been the first man in space, may have died on board a Soviet spaceship in orbit according to a Russian journalist. Although this story has never been fully corroborated, this and other rumors persist that the USSR covered up the deaths of cosmonauts in a number of unsuccessful space missions.

November 11, two Colonels attempted a coup to overthrow Ngo Dinh Diem in South Vietnam. The coup was put down by army units loyal to President Diem. Over 400 people were killed after the coup attempt. In the American press Diem berated the United States for a perceived lack of support during the crisis. In private Diem accused the CIA of sponsoring the coup attempt which was likely true as they had grown weary of Diem's unpopular government.

November 12, a large solar flare, described as one of the largest recorded, disrupted communications worldwide. The aurora borealis was seen as a result of this flare as far south as Washington, DC.

November 13, popular actor and singer Sammy Davis Jr. married Swedish actress May Britt. The marriage caused controversy. Miscegenation (interracial marriage) was still highly unpopular with a majority of White Americans. Many Black Americans disapproved as well. Britt's acting career was destroyed as a result of the marriage.

November 14, four six-year-old Black girls were the first Black children to attend two public elementary schools in New Orleans. Ruby Bridges was the lone little girl who had enrolled at the William Frantz Elementary School; she was escorted by US marshals. This scene was the subject of Norman Rockwell's iconic civil rights painting *The Problem We All Live With*, which originally appeared as the centerfold of *Look* magazine in 1964.

November 18, President Eisenhower in a major shift in US policy said that the US would use force to deter communism in any Latin American nation. He ordered an aircraft carrier and four other warships to patrol off Guatemala and Nicaragua where the US claimed socialists were attempting to take control of the governments.

November 22, the United Nations, at the urging of the US and Belgium, voted in favor of the Western supported rebels and to end Patrice Lumumba's rule in the Congo.

November 23, the US successfully launched the TIROS 2, the second weather satellite which was positioned in an orbit directly above the continental US to track storms and monitor other weather phenomenon.

November 28, Mauritania gained independence from France.

November 29, presenting it as a fait d' accompli, CIA Director Allen Dulles briefed President-elect Kennedy on Eisenhower's approved plans to invade Cuba in what would become the ill-fated Bay of Pigs Invasion. Kennedy expressed his concerns.

Also on November 30, in one of the closest college football championship decisions, the University of Minnesota edged out both Mississippi and Iowa to be declared the number one college football team of the 1960 season by the votes of 48 sportswriters.

November 31, the last De Soto automobile rolled of the assembly line in Detroit. Over two million had been made and sold since 1928.

December 1, at the direction of the CIA, Patrice Lumumba, the deposed former head of the Congo, was detained by the Congolese Army while on his way to meet with his political supporters. December 7, the USSR called the UN Security Council into emergency session to ask for the release of Lumumba. The Army moved him from location to location hiding Lumumba before assassinating him on January 17, 1961. The assassination was at the direction of the CIA and Belgian security according to John Prados.

December 2, President Eisenhower authorized a relief fund to assist and encourage Cuban refugees to come to Florida from Cuba. On December 7, the US opened a Cuban refugee center in Miami with a staff of 14, but by the end of the following year the staff would increase to 300 employees to accommodate the wave of Cuban refugees. It would also become one of the locations used by the CIA to obtain current information about Cuba and to plan Operation JMWAVE to invade Cuba.

December 5, the US Supreme Court in *Boynton v. Virginia* decided that segregation on public transit was unconstitutional.

December 7, the US successfully tested the first drone, a pilotless remote controlled helicopter used to hunt submarines.

December 9, French President De Gaulle's visit to Algeria triggered country-wide protests in which 127 people were killed.

December 11, Richard Pavlick, a retired postal employee from Maine, loaded a car full of dynamite and went to the Kennedy family estate in Palm Beach Florida with the intention of assassinating President-elect Kennedy. He changed his mind when he saw that Kennedy had his wife and children with him and decided to wait for a better opportunity. He was arrested by the Palm Beach police two days later. Pavlick was known for his anti-Catholic and anti-government rants. He was sent to a mental hospital where it was later determined that he lacked the ability to tell right from wrong and was committed to a mental institution.

December 16, a United Airlines plane and a TWA plane collided over New York, crashing into Brooklyn. The crash killed all 128 crew and passengers on both planes and killed 8 others on the ground.

December 17, a US military plane with crew and passengers crashed in Munich, Germany killing all 20 on board and also killed an additional 32 people on the ground.

December 19, a fire swept through the aircraft carrier USS Constellation that was under construction in the Brooklyn Naval Yard killing 50 and injuring another 150.

December 20, the National Liberation Front, a communist political organization in South Vietnam, was created. South Vietnamese President Diem would call this group, "the Viet Cong" a name which was soon adopted by the Americans.

December 22, the Soviets launched the first Vostok-K rocket with a capsule and two dogs aboard. The rocket failed seven minutes after the launch, but the two dogs survived the crash.

December 23, news of Israel's attempt to build a nuclear bomb with the help of France was leaked to the press. President Nasser of Egypt threatened to attack Israel to prevent their development of the atomic bomb. According to the US Congressional Office of Technology Assessment, Israel had operational atomic weaponry at least as early as 1967, but Israel has never admitted to having nuclear weapons.

December 28, a train carrying mostly women and children refugees, which was protected by UN troops, was attacked in the Congo. At least 20 passengers were killed and many others were wounded, raped and kidnapped.

In 1960 the US Bureau for Economic Analysis reported that the average wage in 1960 was $4,817. The average price of a new house was $12,700 but the average cost of rent was still just $98 per month. The average cost of a new car was $2,600, and a new fad, the Vespa motor scooter was sold for $319.95. Gasoline was just 25 cents per gallon. Danish Modern furniture became very popular and a new Danish Modern living room set could be bought for $350.

A new 23 inch television could be bought for $219.95 and about 90% of US homes had televisions and those that didn't were mostly in very rural areas. In February Jack Paar threw a fit, quit and walked off the *Tonight Show* because his monologue had been edited the night before. Paar returned a month later. To the shock of most Americans Lucille Ball and Desi Arnaz filed for divorce on March 3, with their last show filmed three weeks earlier. In September the last *Howdy Doody Show* aired. It had been on the air since 1947. Clarabell the Clown, who communicated by honking a horn and never spoke on the show, looked into the camera and delivered the show's final words by saying, "Goodbye, kids."

Television shows making their debuts included; *Checkmate*, *My Three Sons*, *The Andy Griffith Show*, *Route 66*, and the prime cartoon hit *The Flintstones* by Hanna Barberra. The Emmys were awarded to *Playhouse 90*, *The Art Carney Comedy Special*, and Hanna Barberra's *Huckleberry Hound Show*. Robert Stack won the Emmy for Best Actor for his role as Elliot Ness in the *Untouchables* and Jane Wyatt for Best Actress for her role as the mom in *Father Knows Best*.

In April Motown Records were incorporated in Detroit, Michigan. Chubby Checker's *The Twist* was in the top ten hits, but it made more impact than any other song because of the dance craze of the same name. Percy Faith's *Theme from a Summer Place* was number one. Roy Orbison had his first hit with *Only the Lonely*. Brenda Lee had a several hits with *I'm Sorry*, *Sweet Nothin's* and *I Want to Be Wanted*. Elvis Presley had two with *It's Now or Never* and *Stuck on You*. The Everly Brothers had three with *Cathy's Clown*, *When Will I Be Loved?* and *Let It Be Me*. Connie Francis had several with *Everybody's Somebody's Fool*, *My Heart Has a Mind of Its Own*, and *Sixteen Reasons*. Other popular songs included: *Stay* by Maurice Williams and the Zodiacs, *Georgia on My Mind* by Ray Charles, *Tell Laura I Love Her* by Ray Peterson, *Let the Little Girl Dance* by Billy Bland, *You've Got What It Takes* by Marv Johnson, *Chain Gang* by Sam Cooke, and *Save the Last Dance for Me* by the Drifters. But perhaps some of the best remembered hits of 1960 were the comedy songs: *Alley Oop* by the Hollywood Argyles, *Itsy Bitsy Tennie Weeinie Yellow Polka Dot Bikini* by Brian Hyland, and *Mr. Custer* by Larry Verne.

The movies of 1960 contained some classics like: *Psycho* with Anthony Perkins; *Exodus* with Paul Newman, Eva Marie Saint, Sal Mineo and Lee J. Cobb; *Elmer Gantry* with Burt Lancaster and Shirley Jones; *The Apartment* with Jack Lemmon, Shirley MacLaine, Fred MacMurray and Edie Adams; *Spartacus* with Kirk Douglas and Peter Ustinov; *The Alamo* with John Wayne, and *Ocean's Eleven* with Frank Sinatra, Dean Martin, Peter Lawford, Sammy Davis Jr., and Joey Bishop. In the Oscars the Best Picture and Director went to *The Apartment*, which also won Golden Globes for Best Picture, Best Actor for Jack Lemmon and Best Actress for Shirley MacLaine. *Elmer Gantry* won the Best Actor for Burt Lancaster and Best Supporting Actress for Shirley Jones. It also won the Best Dramatic Actor Golden Globe for Burt Lancaster. *BUtterfield 8* won the Oscar for best Actress for Elizabeth Taylor. *Exodus* won the Oscar for Best Musical Score and Sal Mineo won a Golden Globe for Best Supporting Actor. *Exodus* also won two Grammys the following year for Best Song of the Year, *The Theme Song for Exodus*, and for Best Soundtrack Album.

The literature of 1960 was particularly good and included: *To Kill a Mockingbird* by Harper Lee, *Rabbit, Run* by John Updike, *Black Like Me* by John Howard Griffin, *Portnoy's Complaint* by Phillip Roth, *A Man for All Seasons* by

Robert Bolt, *The Making of the President 1960* by Theodore H. White, *Guerilla Warfare* by Ernesto "Ché," Guevara, *The Autobiography of Eleanor Roosevelt,* by Eleanor Roosevelt, *Conscience of a Conservative,* by Barry Goldwater, *What Ever Happened to Baby Jane?* By Henry Farrell, *The Dangerous Summer* by Ernest Hemingway, *The Book of Dreams* by Jack Kerouac, *Welcome to Hard Times* by E.L. Doctorow, *The Civil War* by Bruce Canton, *The Organization Man* by William H. Whyte, and *Green Eggs and Ham* and *One Fish, Two Fish, Red Fish, Blue Fish* by Dr. Seuss.

CHAPTER 17 1961: JFK, THE BERLIN WALL, THE BAY OF PIGS INVASION, AND CIVIL RIGHTS AND MORE RACIAL STRIFE

January 2, with the US imposing economic sanctions on Cuba, and with the CIA beginning the work of undermining the Castro government, Castro asked the US to reduce the US Embassy staff in Havana from 87 to 11. In response President Eisenhower cut off all diplomatic relations with Cuba.

January 3, a US Army atomic reactor, SL-1, 40 miles west of Idaho Falls, Idaho, melted down and exploded killing 3 people. The three victims were two US Army Specialists aged 22 and 27 and a 26-year-old Navy Seabee Construction Specialist. The accident released radioactive gasses into the air. The US Army claimed that this release probably wasn't dangerous because of the remote location of the reactor. The building and the contaminated radioactive soils around the building were buried nearby and sealed under concrete. The victims were placed in lead caskets and buried under a concrete cap.

January 6, a person smoking in bed was suspected to have caused a San Francisco flop house fire that killed 20 people. The suspected elderly smoker was arrested for manslaughter but released for lack of evidence. The suspect died of cirrhosis four months later.

January 7, the North Carolina State basketball team led Duke 36-33 at halftime. The NC State then seemed to collapse in the second half losing to Duke 81-67. On February 15, NC State, the favored team, suffered another loss to North Carolina 62-56. It was later learned that two star NC State players had accepted bribes of $2500 each to throw the two games.

January 9, the British announced that they had uncovered a five-person Soviet spy ring of three men and two women in London. The spy ring had successfully sent classified documents to the Soviets about the British nuclear submarine force over a period of seven years. They were all given sentences of 15 to 25 years. Three were later exchanged for captured British spies in the USSR. Two were released from prison after eight years, in 1970; they married and continued to live in Britain.

January 11, five days after a federal judge ordered the University of Georgia to integrate, two Black students were allowed to enroll.

January 16, President Eisenhower banned all travel to Cuba by US residents.

Also on January 16, a bank teller, Bernice Geiger, was arrested at the Sheldon National Bank in Sheldon, Iowa. After her arrest and an investigation it was determined that over time she had stolen $2,126, 859.10, a record for employee bank theft at that time.

January 17, on this day former Congo leader Patrice Lumumba was executed at the urging of the CIA. Ironically it is also the same day that President Eisenhower gave his farewell address warning of the "military industrial complex."

Janary 20, John F. Kennedy took the oath of office and became the 35th President of the US. The complete inauguration event was shown on color television for the first time.

January 24, a B-52 bomber with two hydrogen bombs crashed near Goldsboro, North Carolina. The five of the six safety switches failed on one bomb which almost exploded. The 24 megaton bomb would have killed hundreds of thousands.

January 28, in an odd meeting the Ku Klux Klan met with Malcolm X and the Nation of Islam to discuss their mutual agreement to prevent the integration and the mixing of races.

January 29, Minnesota folk singer/guitarist Robert Zimmerman, arrived in New York City and began introducing himself as "Bob Dylan."

January 30, on his fifth day in office President Kennedy met with CIA General Ed Lansdale to review a counterinsurgency plan for Vietnam that had been approved by President Eisenhower. The plan called for US military personnel as military advisors to support the Army and government of South Vietnam. Like the Bay of Pigs Invasion that Lansdale had presented to Kennedy a few weeks before, it too was presented as a fait accompli. Kennedy disliked both plans but Lansdale claimed both were already well underway.

Also on January 30, Lee Harvey Oswald contacted the US government asking to come back to the US. The US government agreed and quietly paid for his and his Russian wife and child's trip to the US which was slipped by the press. He was not arrested for his treason, nor was he even questioned by either the FBI which was the requirement of all returning Americans after travel to the USSR. He moved to Texas and he and his wife were befriended by an anti-communist White Russian-American oil executive, George de Mohrenschildt, who was a CIA operative and a personal friend of George Herbert Walker Bush. After the Kennedy assassination de Mohrenschildt protested and wrote a book strongly arguing that Lee Harvey Oswald did not kill Kennedy. It has been speculated by many that de Mohrenschildt was Oswald's CIA handler after Oswald's return to the US.

January 31, in a very successful flight a Mercury capsule was launched into space carrying a chimpanzee. The capsule returned safely to Earth proving that the US was ready to send a man into space.

February 1, the US successfully tested the Minuteman I ICBM missile. The missile flew 4,000 miles in less than 15 minutes, hitting its target.

February 2, after ten days, a 600 passenger cruise ship was hijacked in the Caribbean by Spanish and Portuguese separatists. It was released at Recife, Brazil.

February 3, a Boeing EC-135 jet took off on the orders of the Strategic Air Command. It was capable of launching an all-out nuclear attack on the USSR should the SAC Headquarters in Omaha be destroyed. For the next 30 years the EC-135s would be somewhere in the air at all times ready to attack the Soviet Union.

February 4, Angola began its war for liberation against the Portuguese.

Also on February 4, the USSR launched Sputnik 7 into earth orbit. Although hailed by the USSR as a success. It was learned later that the craft was supposed to be the first vessel to visit Venus, but it failed and was instead locked in earth orbit.

February 9, a plane with USSR President Brezhnev on its way to the Guinea Republic for a state visit was fired upon by French fighter jets near Algeria, but not hit. The French later claimed the Soviet plane had been in French air space.

February 10, what was then the largest hydroelectric power plant in the world, the Robert Moses power station at Niagara Falls, went online.

February 11, the first Black American to head a federal agency was appointed on this date as President Kennedy approved Robert C. Weaver as the Administrator of the Housing and Home Finance Agency. The position was later upgraded to a cabinet level position and re-named Secretary of Housing and Urban Development (HUD) with Weaver as the Department's first Secretary.

February 13, the assassination of Lumumba was confirmed publicly and sparked widespread riots in the Congo and protests around the world. The following day riots and protests occurred at the Belgian embassies in Moscow, Belgrade and New Delhi, and African students protested around the world. Many other Belgian embassies were attacked or saw protests.

February 15, a flight from New York to Brussels crashed and killed all 72 people aboard including the entire US Figure Skating Team.

February 18, Bertrand Russell led a crowd of 5,000 people to sit-in at the Ministry of Defense in London to protest an agreement to allow the US to base nuclear missiles in Britain.

February 19, a seven-year-old boy fell 275 feet into a well breaking both legs and his pelvis. He was rescued by ranch hands who tied lengths of rope together to rescue the boy.

February 21, the UN passed Resolution 161 providing for all necessary force to prevent a civil war in the Congo.

February 22, fans of the daytime soap opera *The Edge of Night* were horrified when the leading female character died in an episode. Many fans, some thinking that her soap opera death was real, inundated CBS with telephone calls. The actress, Teal Ames, appeared the next day on television to say she was alive and had requested to leave the show.

February 26, the Tyazhely Sputnik, "heavy Sputnik," was launched but crashed in re-entry over Siberia.

February 28, would later be acknowledged by US law 38 USC 101 (29) (a) as the start date of the "Vietnam era." Although there was never a legal declaration of war by the US Congress, all US military personnel serving in the Vietnam conflict from this date until May 7, 1975, would be officially considered Vietnam war veterans.

March 1, by Executive Order 10924 President Kennedy established the Peace Corps.

March 2, after seven years of war the Algerians and the French agreed to peace talks toward Algerian independence.

Also on this date Congolese soldiers massacred 44 people in Katanga.

Also on March 2, twenty-two miners were killed in a coal mine explosion near Terre Haute, Indiana.

March 4, the US Congress restored President Eisenhower to his former rank of Five Star General and Commander of the Army.

On this same day the USSR successfully tested their anti-ballistic missile, the SS-4 capable of shooting down incoming ICBM missiles.

March 5, the US Air Force announced they had developed an atomic clock that was so accurate that it would be off by "no more than one second in 1,271 years."

March 6, President Kennedy singed Executive Order 10925 insuring "affirmative action" would be used in all federal employment and federal contracts to assure racial equality in employment. It was the first use of the phrase "affirmative action" and the order also created the President's Commission on Equal on Equal Opportunity and the Equal Opportunity Commission (EEOC) to assure compliance.

March 9, the USSR launched Sputnik 9, with a test dummy, a dog, mice and a guinea pig. The launch was a successful test of their future manned flight.

March 10, the Port Authority of New York and New Jersey presented a feasibility study to build a World's Trade Center in New York City consisting of two twin towers and five other buildings.

March 11, after just two months in office the CIA and the Joint Chiefs of Staff (JCS) presented to President Kennedy a plan, Operation Trinidad, to invade Cuba. Although he was told Eisenhower had approved the plan Kennedy rejected it saying he would not authorize US military forces in an attack on Cuba. The CIA and JCS told Kennedy that it had widespread Cuban support, which turned out to be untrue. Kennedy said the he was prepared to covertly support rebel Cuban forces with materials and supplies but that any invasion would need to be by Cuban fighters and not US forces.

Four days later the CIA delivered plans to Kennedy for the Bay of Pigs Invasion involving what they said would be just Cuban rebel forces. They assured the new president that this invasion force would not require

US forces. They also claimed that the invasion forces would be joined by thousands of rebel fighters already in Cuba. They told President Kennedy that a rebel victory was a very high probability. The lied and knew they were lying to the President.

Kennedy reluctantly approved their plan. CIA Director Allen Dulles and the JCS felt that if the Cuban invasion began to fail that President Kennedy would be forced to use US military forces or look politically weak. They believed he would give in and use US forces when the invaders began to fail, just as Eisenhower had been forced to use US forces in Guatemala after the CIA-backed local invasion failed there. It was a mistake Dulles and the CIA would live to regret.

March 12, as part of their Cuba strategy the CIA and Miami Mafioso John "Handsome Johnny" Roselli met in Miami. They plotted to assassinate Fidel Castro. The CIA gave the Roselli money and poison pills to put in Castro's food which would kill him instantly. The CIA acknowledged these events in 2007. The assassination was unsuccessful.

March 13, a dam burst in the Ukraine killing 145 people.

March 15, Angolan rebel forces from the Congo came across the border and killed some Portuguese residents of Angola. In retaliation the Portuguese Army killed tens of thousands of Black Africans starting a bloody war that would last for 14 years.

May 16, in Yuba City, California, a B-52 bomber crashed carrying two nuclear weapons. The two bombs were thrown from the aircraft upon impact but didn't ignite.

March 21, the Beatles began the first of 300 performances at the Cavern Club in Liverpool.

March 23, a US Force transport plane crashed in Laos. The lone survivor, Major Lawrence Bailey Jr. was captured by the Viet Minh and became the first Vietnam Era POW.

March 24, a Mercury-Redstone Rocket was launched. Ironically Astronaut Alan Sheppard had volunteered for the March 24 flight and would have been the first man in space but his request was turned down at the last moment by Werner Von Braun who headed the program and it became another unmanned flight which allowed the Soviets to put the first man in space.

March 25, the Soviets launched Sputnik 10 as a final test before a manned space flight.

March 27, nine Black college students from Tugaloo College sat-in at the Whites only Jackson, Mississippi library. After refusing to leave they were arrested. The following day Black students from Tugaloo College began a protest outside the jail to free the nine students. The Mississippi Sovereignty Commission, which was a state police force created to prevent segregation, demanded that the White President of the all Black Tugaloo College expel the nine students and any others that demonstrated. When he refused they had him removed under Mississippi law for violating state orders.

March 31, the death of the Grand Ayatollah Seyyed Hossein Borujerdi in Iran led to the ascension of the more radical Ayatollah Khomeini to become the new leader of Iran's Shiite Muslims.

April 3, the National Education Network, which would later become National Public Radio, NPR, began broadcasting on six stations with a Ford Foundation Grant.

Also on April 3, country music star and innovator of the famous Bakersfield sound, Spade Cooley, "the King of Western Swing," murdered his wife after she admitted to having an affair.

April 4, Carlos Marcello the Mafia chief of New Orleans was deported by Robert Kennedy as an undesirable. He snuck back into the country two months later. Marcello would later brag that he got his revenge by participating in the plot that killed President Kennedy in 1963.

Also on April 4, CIA Director Allen Dulles updated President Kennedy on the Bay of Pigs Invasion Plans in the Office of Secretary of State Dean Rusk. Much to Dulles' irritation Kennedy had invited Senator William Fulbright who had also opposed the operation. Secretary of Defense Robert McNamara and the Joint Chiefs of Staff were in favor of moving ahead. Dulles lied again and assured the President that the CIA's official assessment was that operation would be a success without US military force. The President reluctantly approved their plan, but again emphasized that no US forces would be allowed to be part of the invasion.

April 8, the British passenger ship the MV Dara exploded near Dubai. The explosion and fire killed 238 passengers and crew, and another 565 were rescued. It was later determined that someone had deliberately exploded the ship with an anti-tank mine. The culprits were never caught.

April 9, the CIA learned that the USSR and Cuba knew of the Bay of Pigs Invasion which was about to occur. The CIA did not share this with the President or the Executive Branch as they were sure that if the invasion failed, that they could talk Kennedy into using US military in the invasion because the young president wouldn't want to suffer such a huge and embarrassing political loss. These facts were later uncovered in 1966 by the *New York Times.* One of their reporters, Tad Szulc, had uncovered the plot and wrote an article about the plot but his editor cancelled the story. This story was not revealed to the public until 2000 by the *Washington Post.*

Also on April 9, the last street car in Los Angeles made its final run.

April 10, President Kennedy threw out the first pitch of the 1961 Major League Baseball season.

April 12, the USSR launched the Vostok 1 into space and Yuri Gagarin became the first man in space. The Americans were caught off guard. They had assumed the US was well ahead of the USSR in manned flight. They planned to launch their man into space within a matter of weeks. President Kennedy was unhappy with both the space program and American intelligence which had assured him that the Soviets were not ready to launch a man into space. Gagarin made one orbit and landed safely. The following day the world watched on television the celebration and hero's welcome given to Gagarin in Moscow.

April 14, the Bay of Pigs invasion was given the green light by the CIA and Brigade 2506, a group of about 1,400 Cuban exiles, left Nicaragua on four CIA leased freighters for their three day trip to invade Cuba.

April 15, eight B-26 bombers piloted by US Air Force personnel temporarily assigned to the CIA, flew from a secret base in Nicaragua to destroy Castro's small air force in anticipation of the Bay of Pigs Invasion. A Cuban exile then flew one of the B-26 bombers to Miami claiming to the press that the attacks were part of a Cuban rebel air force. At the UN the Cuban Minister accused the US of these air attacks against Cuba. The US Ambassador Adlai Stevenson vehemently denied this was true and was later embarrassed with the truth when four of the American airmen were shot down and captured. The CIA had not told the President the truth about the attack because of Kennedy's orders barring the use of US forces.

April 17, before the invasion the CIA knew that the air attacks had not managed to destroy the entire Cuban Air Force, but they still gave the green light for the invasion knowing that the invading army was defenseless to air attacks. They still counted on persuading Kennedy to use the US Air Force to protect the invasion and to save his presidency from political embarrassment.

The Cuban Air Force attacked and two of the three freighters were sunk in Cuban waters and the Cuban air force slaughtered the troops arriving on the beach. Castro had known in advance and had prepared. The CIAs claim that thousands of Cubans would join the invaders proved grossly and blatantly false. Dulles and the CIA had known all along that the invasion would likely fail and they had assumed that like Eisenhower in the 1954 invasion of Guatemala, that when the rebel invasion failed that Kennedy, like Eisenhower, would also send in US Forces. They assumed the young new President would bow to their wishes rather than accept such a hard political defeat in front of the world. In fact the Joint Chiefs of Staff had pre-planned for this and the US Navy, Air Force and Marines were on standby alert. To their shock Kennedy still refused and said that he had warned them from the beginning that no US forces would be used in an invasion of Cuba. The Invasion was a fiasco. After several days of fighting, the Cuban Army had only 176 men killed and about 500 wounded. However the invading rebel force had 118 killed, 360 wounded and 1,202 were captured. About 30 of the attackers were eventually rescued in the waters off Cuba by the US Navy.

President Kennedy went on television and accepted the blame for the failure and suffered a huge political setback. After commissioning an investigation and receiving a report on the failed invasion he fired CIA Director Allen Dulles, Deputy CIA Director Charles Cabell, and Deputy Director for Plans Richard Bissell for their deceit. Kennedy then said that he wanted to "splinter the CIA into a thousand pieces and scatter it into the winds." He also told his friend journalist Ben Bradlee that the first advice he would give his successor "is to watch the generals and to avoid feeling that because they were military men their opinions on military matters were worth a damn." On December 21, 1962, Castro agreed to release all the Bay of Pigs prisoners to the US in exchange for $53 million in food and medicine.

April 20, President Kennedy was determined to beat the Soviets in space and was now uncertain about the CIA's assessments, so he asked Vice President Johnson, who he had appointed as the Chairman of the National Aeronautics and Space Council to assess if the US "had any chance of beating the Soviets to go to the moon and back with a man."

April 22, four French generals and two other high ranking French military officers tried to seize Algeria in a coup attempt to keep it a French territory. General de Gaulle ordered the French Army to put down the coup.

April 25, Robert Noyce, who would become the founder of the Intel Corporation, was awarded the patent on the integrated circuit or semiconductor.

April 27, Sierra Leone obtained independence from Britain.

May 1, a Miami Cuban-American electrician hijacked a plane flying from Miami to Key West and forced it to fly to Havana, Cuba. Castro allowed the plane and its passengers to depart for the US the following day. The hijacking set off a wave of copycat hijackings to Cuba.

May 3, the US federal minimum wage was set at $1.25 per hour.

May 4, thirteen "freedom riders" began a Southern bus trip to test if the new law to desegregate interstate bus travel would be enforced.

May 5, three weeks after the Soviets put the first man in space Alan Sheppard became the second man in space when Freedom 7 was launched from Cape Canaveral, Florida. It was a brief 19 minute ride and the capsule was recovered in the Atlantic Ocean.

May 9, Federal Communications Commission Chairman Newton H. Minow addressed the National broadcasters in Washington, DC. He described television as "a vast wasteland." He implied that in the future some licenses may not be renewed unless the quality of their product was significantly upgraded.

May 14, a Freedom Rider bus was fire-bombed in Anniston, Alabama. The Freedom Riders were then beaten by a White mob as they fled the bus. The Freedom Riders were then arrested and jailed for inciting a riot.

May 16, a military coup took over the government in South Korea. General Park Chung Hee took over as the new President of the nation. Park would rule South Korea with an iron fist for 18 years until his assassination in 1979.

May 19, the Soviet Venera 1 became the first man-made object to fly-by another planet when it passed Venus. However the probe's communications had failed a month earlier and it failed to send back any data.

May 21, with tensions already high from the Freedom Rider incidents, race riots began in Montgomery, Alabama and the Governor declared martial law. The trouble began when a White mob began hurling stones through the windows of a Black church where Dr. Martin Luther King Jr. was speaking. Later at the Greyhound Bus Depot a White mob with clubs attacked Freedom Riders. A US Justice Department official was beaten unconscious by the mob as he tried to prevent the violence. Between 20 and 75 people were injured in the violence while the police stood by. Attorney General Robert Kennedy dispatched US Marshals to Montgomery to Protect the Freedom Riders. Alabama Governor John Patterson threatened to arrest the

US Marshals. He told Kennedy to "take the US Marshals out of Alabama and to take Dr. King with them."

May 24, Freedom Riders were arrested in Jackson, Mississippi for "disturbing the peace."

May 25, President Kennedy addressed a joint session of Congress and said that before the decade was over that the US would put a man on the moon and bring him home safely. He asked Congress for increased funding for the space program.

May 28, an article by British journalist Peter Benenson, *The Forgotten Prisoners*, was published inspiring the founding of Amnesty International.

Also on this day the famed Orient Express, traveling from Paris to Bucharest, Romania, made its last trip.

May 29, President Kennedy instructed the Interstate Commerce Commission to immediately adopt "stringent regulations" prohibiting segregation on all interstate bus travel. His order was implemented on November 1, ending segregation on buses and in bus depots and enforced if necessary by US Federal Marshals.

Also on May 29, Rafael Trujillo the dictator of the Dominican Republic was assassinated.

Also on this day the first official US food stamps were issued in West Virginia.

May 31, President Kennedy and Charles de Gaulle met in Paris for talks. Both men were overshadowed in the press by Jackie Kennedy who captured the heart of the people of Paris and the French press. President Kennedy joked that he would now be known as the man who accompanied Jackie Kennedy to Paris.

June 1, United Airlines became the largest in the world by acquiring the fifth largest Capital Airlines.

June 3, President Kennedy and Soviet Premier Khrushchev met in Vienna, Austria. In what Kennedy described later as "the worst thing in my life," Khrushchev berated Kennedy and demanded the US withdraw from Berlin. The next day on June 4, the Berlin Crisis began. The Soviets announced a peace treaty with East Germany to begin in December that would nullify the WWII agreement that allowed US forces in Berlin. It was also announced that the East Germans would then close all the rail and road corridors from the West to Berlin. Khrushchev then told Kennedy, "It is up to the U.S. to decide whether there will be war or peace."

June 5, in separate rulings the US Supreme Court upheld the constitutionality of the McCarran Act and the Smith Act making communism illegal and requiring all communists to register with the US Department of Justice. However the Court reversed itself in 1965 and 1967.

June 8, Spanish communist Jaime Ramón Mercader del Río who was released earlier from prison in Mexico having served 20 years for the murder of Leon Trotsky in 1940, was awarded the Hero of the Soviet Union and The Oder of Lenin in Moscow by Soviet President Leonid Brezhnev.

June 10, the Soviet news agency TASS and the East German Press published notices from the Soviet Union demanding that all US troops be withdrawn from Berlin.

Also on June 10, two US Army deserters from Ft. Hood, Texas went on a killing spree strangling two women, shooting two men and a woman to death and beating two other men to death. They were caught in Colorado. The two were later hung for their crimes in 1965 in Kansas.

June 15, forty-five Freedom Riders were arrested in Mississippi for "disturbing the peace." They were transferred to the infamous Mississippi State Penitentiary where they were tortured and mistreated by guards. Two White Freedom Riders had an electric cattle prod with 10,000 volts applied repeatedly to sexual and sensitive body parts for the amusement of the guards.

June 17, President Kennedy's dissatisfaction with the CIA led to his decision to seek regular intelligence briefings from all intelligence sources rather than just the CIA as was the custom. The first *Presidents Daily Brief*, a confidential intelligence memo from all agencies began on this day and has continued since.

June 19, Kuwait gained independence from Britain.

June 24, *Tropic of Cancer*, a novel by Henry Miller that had been published in Europe 27 years earlier, was finally cleared by the US Justice Department and the US Post Office and was distributed by Grove Press. However, the novel contained graphic descriptions of sex and was declared "pornographic" by many local authorities and booksellers were threatened with jail for selling the novel. The issue was not resolved until the US Supreme Court heard the issue in 1964 making the novel legal.

June 25, Iraq announced its intention of a military invasion to annex the newly independent nation of Kuwait. The British responded that they would defend the new nation and sent troops and Iraq then rescinded its announcement in early July.

June 28, President Kennedy issued National Security Memorandum 55 transferring all peace paramilitary operations from the CIA to the Joint Chiefs of Staff infuriating both the Joint Chiefs and the CIA. The order would be later rescinded after Kennedy's assassination by President Johnson.

July 2, Soviet Premier Khrushchev warned the British Ambassador that Britain and France should avoid supporting the US in Berlin saying that "Six hydrogen bombs would be quite enough to annihilate the British Isles, and nine would take care of France."

July 4, a Soviet nuclear submarine the K-19 developed a leak in its nuclear reactor in the North Atlantic. Eight crew members were killed by radiation poisoning and the others were treated and survived.

July 5, Israel successfully launched its first rocket Shavit 2.

July 6, North Korea signed a mutual defense treaty with the USSR. They would sign a similar treaty with the People's Republic of China five days later.

July 7, a coal mine explosion in Czechoslovakia killed 108 miners.

July 8, Robert Sheldon united the divided faction of the KKK with several other national racist groups to form the United Klans of America with himself as the Grand Wizard.

July 10, in a secret meeting the Soviets decided to end their agreed to moratorium with the US on testing nuclear weapons. They began building and testing a 100 megaton hydrogen bomb.

July 16, a total of about 200 hundred Vietnamese were killed in one of the largest battles in Vietnam on the Plain of Reeds between the Viet Cong and the South Vietnamese Army, the ARVN.

July 21, astronaut Gus Grissom in the Liberty Bell 7, became the third man in space. The mission went well until splash down and he had to be rescued as his Mercury capsule sank in the ocean during recovery.

July 24, another Cuban-American hijacked a flight from Miami to Tampa diverting it to Havana Cuba. Again the crew and passengers were allowed to return to the US the following day.

July 25, in response to the USSR, President Kennedy went on national television stating that the US was prepared to go to war with the Soviet Union if the Soviets tried to take West Berlin.

July 26, the East German government asked Soviets permission to begin the construction of the Berlin Wall.

July 31, the most popular typewriter to ever be produced, the IBM Selectric went on sale for $395. It remained the most popular writing instrument until being replaced by computer word processors.

August 1, in keeping with President Kennedy's wishes to broaden the US intelligence apparatus and not just rely on the CIA, Secretary of Defense Robert McNamara issued a directive ordering the creation of the Defense Intelligence Agency.

August 2, a holiday tour bus carrying American teachers was side-swiped by another vehicle and plunged off a cliff into Lake Lucerne in Switzerland. Sixteen female teachers died and twenty-two others were rescued.

August 4, despite later claims by Donald Trump and other right-wing conspiracy theorists, Barak Obama was born on this day in Honolulu, Hawaii. His birth was reported in the next issue of the *Honolulu Advertiser*.

August 5, at the close of a Warsaw Pact meeting it was announced that a peace treaty would be signed with East Germany ending the agreement for Western forces in Berlin. After the announcement more than 1,500 East Germans began to flee to West Berlin, a rate of one per minute. The Soviets gave the East Germans their approval to begin building the Berlin Wall to stop the defections.

August 6, Gherman Titov became the fourth man and the second Soviet in space when Vostok 2 was launched. He stayed a day in space becoming the first person to sleep in space. He was also the first person to experience space sickness.

August 7, as Titov returned from space the US Congress approved the President's request to give $1.6 billion to the US space program, with about $472 million for a specific manned moon landing.

August 9, at the reception for Titov in Moscow Khrushchev announced to the foreign press that the USSR now had the capability to produce 100 megaton nuclear weapons.

Also on August 9, James Benton Parsons became the first Black American to be nominated and confirmed as a US District Judge.

August 12, the East Germans sealed off West Berlin with barbed wire and guards while the wall was being constructed. On this last day before the city was sealed off 2,662 East Germans fled to the West and another 1,200 who had been shopping in West Berlin refused to return.

August 14, Jomo Kenyatta the leader of the Kenya African Union, an independence group, was allowed to return from exile to Kenya. He had been sent to prison in 1952 after he was falsely accused of masterminding the Mau Mau rebellion. He was released from prison 7 years later in 1959, but immediately sent into exile. Thousands of supports greeted Kenyatta as he returned to Nairobi.

August 16, the Bell UH 1D helicopter (Huey) which would become the primary troop transport and medivac helicopter during the Vietnam War was successfully tested.

August 18 the East German government gave the border guards the order to "shoot to kill" any persons attempting to flee to West Berlin.

August 19, Dr, Timothy Leary one of the University researchers in the CIA's MK Ultra program delivered his paper, "How to Change behavior" at an international conference in Copenhagen. The paper described the use of the drug LSD to expand consciousness and to change the mind.

August 20, in a show of support for West Berlin the US sent a truck convoy of 1,500 additional troops, weapons, supplies and three additional tanks to augment the 11,000 US troops stationed in West Berlin.

August 24, a young 24-year-old tailor's assistant became the first person shot by East German border guards as he attempted to swim across the Humboldt Harbor to West Berlin. About 5,000 people successfully escaped over, under or through the Berlin Wall until it was opened in 1989. The number killed in trying to escape is widely disputed and may never be known. The Center for Historical research in Potsdam lists 136 deaths, but the Director of the Checkpoint Charlie Museum lists over 200 killed.

August 26, the US Supreme Court in *Reynolds v. Sims* found that legislative districts that became unequally divided by population overtime were unconstitutional. The ruling led the way to redistricting based upon population growth and shifts. The ruling also had the unforeseen effect of allowing parties (particularly the Republican Party) to gerrymander districts to assure the election of their candidates.

August 28, the UN peace keeping forces in the Congo struck at dawn rounding up and defeating the White Belgian officers and mercenaries in the Congo. They captured and arrested 79 and another 350 surrendered.

August 29, the first Peace Corps volunteers left Washington, DC to serve for two years in Ghana.

August 30, Atlanta High Schools became integrated without incident as nine Black children enrolled at White schools. The Atlanta elementary schools however remained segregated.

August 31, the USSR announced it was cancelling the Nuclear Test Ban Treaty and stated they would test a large weapon the following day. They would explode 45 bombs over the next 65 days.

September 1, the Eritrean War for independence from Ethiopia began.

Also on this date a TWA flight crashed shortly after takeoff from Chicago's Midway Airport killing all 79 people aboard.

September 3, British Prime Minister Harold Macmillan and President Kennedy attempted to renegotiate the Nuclear Test Ban treaty but were rejected by the USSR.

September 4, the United States Agency for International Development, USAID, was created with the passing of the Foreign Assistance Act of 1961.

September 5, President Kennedy announced that the US would begin nuclear testing in response to the third Soviet nuclear test.

September 6, the top secret National Reconnaissance Office, a joint project of the US Air Force and the CIA, began. The project coordinated secret satellite reconnaissance around the world. These satellites and the National Reconnaissance Office were not revealed to the public until after the Cold War in 1992.

Also on September 6, a secret secure telephone line (a hot line) between the President and the British Prime Minister became operational.

September 7, *The Tonight Show* host Jack Paar filmed part of his show in front of the Berlin Wall. He was accompanied by seven US Army officers, 50 US soldiers with jeeps and weapons. The program which could have caused an international incident enraged the US Congress who removed a Lt. Colonel and another Colonel for their participation. They were later re-instated after it was determined they had violated no laws or orders.

September 8, an assassination attempt on President Charles de Gaulle of France failed. It was likely an attempt by members of the French Army who were dissatisfied over Algeria.

September 9, the Arab Iraqi government began bombing Kurdish cities in northern Iraq.

September 10, a chartered plane with 83 people, mostly the wives and children of US military personnel returning the US, crashed just after takeoff from Shannon Airport in Ireland.

Also on September 10, a driver at the Italian Grand Prix crashed into the crowd, the driver and 17 spectators died and another 19 were severely injured. The bodies of the dead were unceremoniously covered with newspapers and not moved until the race concluded two hours later.

September 11, Hurricane Carla a category V hurricane struck Texas with winds of 175 MPH. Fortunately between 300,000 and 500,000 people had been evacuated, which was at the time "the largest evacuation in American history." However 31 people died and the storm caused $325 million in damages.

September 12, twelve women who had been selected as US Astronauts received telegrams five days before they were to report for training saying the woman's astronaut program had been cancelled. It would take another twenty-two years before the first American woman, Sally Ride, would go into space.

September 13, the Joint Chiefs of Staff delivered to President Kennedy their Operational Plan for Nuclear War. The plan had 13 options most requiring the US to completely annihilate the USSR, the People's Republic of China and all the Warsaw Pact countries and accepting that most of the US would be destroyed. The President was reportedly furious that the plan lacked any other options.

September 15, the US resumed nuclear testing detonating a bomb in Nevada.

On September 16, a typhoon struck Japan and killed 203 people and did a half billion dollars in damage.

The same day, UN Secretary General Dag Hammarskjöld of Sweden was killed in the Congo when his plane crashed. All on board were killed. Although the plane crashed only a very short distance from the airport, the wreckage was supposedly not found for fifteen hours, leading many to believe that a cover-up took place. Witnesses on the ground at the time stated that they saw a bright flash like a rocket fired at the plane and then sparks and flames as it hit. According to these witnesses this happened immediately after they saw that a second smaller aircraft was following Hammarskjöld's plane. Despite these witnesses, the crash was still ruled an accident. Many suspected the CIA.

On September 9, 2013, the Associated Press article *U.N. Chief's '61 Death: A Cold War Mystery*, by Ralph Slater reported evidence that may solve the mystery. It appears that the US National Security Agency, NSA, was monitoring radio transmissions of Hammarskjöld's plane and the radio transmissions of another plane that was following it. Cmdr. Charles Southhall who was stationed at an NSA listening post at that time said that he heard an intercepted message from the plane that was pursuing Hammarskjöld's. The message was spoken in American English and said, "I have hit it. There are flames. It's going down. It's crashing."

The U.N. has continued looking into the mystery. In October 2017 the *New York Times* reported, "The finding by Judge Mohamed Chande Othman, a senior Tanzanian jurist who was asked by the United Nations to review both old and newly uncovered evidence, gave weight to a longstanding suspicion that Mr. Hammarskjold may have been assassinated."

Hammarskjöld was a fierce critic of the CIA and their clandestine wars for corporate colonization in other people's countries. He had made an enemy in the CIA by publicly chastising them for the coup in Guatemala and other actions. The US, Belgium and the United Kingdom had a vested interest in maintaining control over the Congo's copper industry. They worried that the Congolese transition from Belgian colonialism to independence would cause the new country to nationalize their most profitable resource. They were also worried that these resources would be exploited by the Soviets.

Hammarskjöld won the Nobel Peace Prize for his efforts in Africa after his death.

September 18, Georgia Tech was integrated peacefully when three Black students were admitted.

Also on September 18, a South Vietnam provincial capital only 55 miles from Saigon, Phuoc Vinh, was captured by the Viet Cong. The ARVN took back the capital in heavy fighting the following day, but not until the Viet Cong had killed the governor and many of the top military officers in the city.

September 19, NASA Administrator James Webb announced that a new Space Center would be built near Houston, Texas on land donated by Rice University. It would serve as Mission Control for the Apollo Program.

September 20, in a small sign of cooperation the US and Soviets released a "Joint Statement of Agreed Principles for Disarmament Negotiations." This agreement of principles was to be the start of future disarmament negotiations.

Also on September 20, the CIA began their move into their new headquarters at Langley, Virginia.

September 21, French dissidents protesting the proposed Algerian independence blew up a television tower just before General de Gaulle was to speak to the Algerian people. The dissidents then went on the air on a pirate station and mocked President de Gaulle and calling for French demonstrations against an independent Algeria.

September 22, the Interstate Commerce Commission ruled that, effective November 1, all interstate buses in the United States were required to display signs that said "Seating aboard this vehicle is without regard to race, color, creed, or national origin, by order of the Interstate Commerce Commission." All bus terminals were also instructed to follow the order. It was a victory for the Freedom Riders.

September 25, US Department of the Army Message 578636 designated the "Green Beret" as the official uniform cap of the US Army Special Forces.

Also on September 25, Wisconsin became the first state to require that all motor vehicles come equipped with seat belts for safety.

And on this date President Kennedy addressed the UN about the perils of nuclear war saying, "Today, every inhabitant of this planet must contemplate that day when this planet may no longer be inhabitable. Every man, woman and child lives under a nuclear Sword of Damocles hanging by the slenderest of threads, capable of being cut at any moment by accident or miscalculation or madness. The weapons of war must be abolished before they abolish us."

September 27, former Vice president Richard Nixon announced that he would not seek the presidency in 1964, but would instead run for Governor of California in 1962.

September 29, in response to Kennedy's address to the UN, Khrushchev sent a highly secret and personal letter to President Kennedy. Khrushchev apologized for his previous harsh treatment of Kennedy at their summit meeting. He said that although he and Kennedy had irreconcilable differences that he believed they also shared the belief that nuclear weapons should never be used.

Also on September 29, the last casino in Havana was closed as part of Castro's promise to the Cuban people to clean up Havana and rid it of crime, prostitution and corruption.

September 30, the Sports Broadcasting Law of 1961 was signed into law allowing a minor exemption from anti-trust regulations to allow American sport leagues to negotiate exclusive television contracts to support their leagues.

October 1, evangelist Pat Robertson began broadcasting his conservative Christian message on television in Portsmouth, Virginia.

October 2, President Charles de Gaulle went on television simultaneously in France and Algeria to outline his plans to allow the Algerians to determine their own future and said he would work with the Algerians to form their own security forces to replace the French military.

October 3, the Motion Picture Association of America declared that "homosexuality and other sexual aberrations" could be shown "with care, discretion and restraint providing that they could be suggested but not actually spelled out."

October 4, at the request of the local White authorities a Black high school student in McComb, Mississippi was expelled from school for having participated in an earlier sit-in. In response 116 Black high school and junior high school students walked out of school and marched to City Hall. They were all arrested and jailed for their protest. An adult from the Student Non-violent Coordinating Committee, SNCC, accompanied the marching children was beaten by a White mob as the police watched without intervening. The students refused to return to their high school and SNCC then organized an alternative school called "the Freedom School." Shortly after it opened the SNCC teachers at the Freedom School were all arrested and charged with "contributing to the delinquency of minors."

October 8-12, over four nights, 134 East German residents escaped to the West through an underground sewer line that they had accessed through a manhole cover.

Also on October 8, a group of conservative Republicans met in Chicago to organize "The Draft Goldwater Committee" to secure the Republican nomination for Senator Barry Goldwater at the 1964 Republican Convention.

October 10, all 260 residents of the tiny remote British island of Tristan de Cunha in the South Atlantic were evacuated when the volcano on the tiny island erupted. They were brought to South Africa before permanently being resettled in Britain.

October 11, at the recommendation of the Joint Chiefs of Staff, President Kennedy sent the US Air Force 4400th Combat Crew Training Squadron to Vietnam to begin flying combat missions and training the Vietnamese Air Force at the Ben Hoa Air Base. The unit was renamed the 1st Air Commando Wing. The Operation was code-named "Jungle Jim."

October 13, after three years as part of United Arab Republic with Egypt, Syria became independent and became a member of the UN as the Syrian Arab Republic.

October 14, all commercial air traffic in the US and Canada was halted for 12 hours so the US and Canadian military could conduct war games and a simulated attack on North American targets called Operation Sky Shield II. This unprecedented halt of air traffic was only exceeded by the halt in air traffic in the aftermath of the 2001 terrorist attacks.

October 15, it was reported that a B-52 bomber, "Pogo 22" and its crew of 8 disappeared during Operation Sky Shield II. The bomber was one of 2,250 that flew missions that day. It was lost off the coast of Newfoundland and never found.

October 17, the French government imposed a night time curfew on all Muslims in France because of the situation in Algeria. About 30,000 Muslims protested the curfew in Paris. The resulting conflict with police became known as "The Paris Massacre of 1961." The police arrested 11, 938 people and held them in soccer stadiums at the outskirts of the city. The confrontations with police were violent and at least 142 Muslims died. Their bodies were thrown into the Seine River where 74 later washed up on the shores. The other 68 victims disappeared. The death toll was suppressed for several decades until the Paris Police Chief Maurice Papon was put on trial in 1988 for his cooperation with the Nazis in WWII for arresting and sending 1,600 French Jews to their deaths in the concentration camps. It then became known that Papon was also responsible for the Paris Massacre as well as for torture and murder of Muslim prisoners while serving in Algeria.

October 17, Premier Khrushchev delivered a six and a half hour speech to the 22nd Congress of the Communist Party of the Soviet Union. He denounced many former leaders of the Soviet Union for contributing and continuing the dictatorship of Joseph Stalin. He also announced that he would refuse to sign the peace treaty with East Germany which would question the legality of US troops in Berlin. Khrushchev also boasted that the USSR now had a vast superiority over the US in numbers and quality of nuclear missiles which later proved to be untrue.

October 19, the Arab League pledged to protect Kuwait from Iraq as the last British troops left.

October 21, the Assistant Secretary of Defense, Roswell Gilpatric, on instructions from President Kennedy, gave a speech stating that there was no missile gap with the USSR and that the US second strike missile force was larger and more deadly than the Soviets. Gilpatric provided some proof of this from US intelligence agencies embarrassing Khrushchev.

October 22, the American Deputy Chief in Berlin Allen Lightner Jr. was stopped by East German police and refused entrance at Check point Charlie to East Berlin in violation of previous agreements. The incident escalated over the next three days. General Lucius Clay dispatched troops and tanks and the East Germans then allowed Lightner to continue into East Berlin accompanied by 8 US military policemen.

October 23, China's Prime Minister Chou En Lai who had been invited to the Soviet Communist Party summit angrily left over a dispute concerning Albania. The departure was seen as a further rift in Sino-Soviet relations. The Soviets cancelled all delivery of exports to China shortly afterward.

Also on October 23, Thurgood Marshall, the chief legal counsel to the NAACP was appointed by President Kennedy as a judge on the federal Court of Appeals for the Second Circuit.

October 26, Grégoire Kayibanda became the President of Rwanda. His Hutu Party then replaced all officials of the previous Tutsi monarchy. His presidency caused gross repression of the Tutsi under Hutu rule.

October 27, the Berlin crisis elevated when 33 Soviet tanks arrived at the Brandenburg Gate to confront American tanks that had been placed there by General Clay. The tanks from both sides drew closer together in a standoff which lasted for 16 hours when both sides withdrew their tanks.

Also on October 27, the Saturn 1 Rocket was successfully launched. The Saturn 1 would be the vehicle launching the Apollo missions to the moon.

October 30, the Soviets exploded a 58 megaton hydrogen bomb in over the island of Novaya Zemlya in the Arctic Ocean. It is still the largest made-made explosion.

October 31, a Hurricane Hattie struck British Honduras (now Belize) killing 307 people. The city of Belize was devastated. In 1970 because of Hattie and the dangers of future hurricanes the government moved the capital from Belize inland to Belmopan.

November 1, the Women's Strike for Peace founded by Bella Abzug and Dagmar Wilson brought together about 50,000 American women who marched in 60 cities protesting the nuclear testing by the US and USSR that was producing radioactive fallout in the atmosphere.

November 2, Col. Oleg Penkovsky of the Soviet Military Intelligence Service (GRU) passed secret Soviet information to the US. He was caught on this day after a Soviet double agent Jack Dunlap, US Army Sergeant and an NSA employee, discovered his identity and passed it to the Soviets. He was not arrested until 1962 to protect Dunlap. He was executed May 17, 1963. Dunlap was never caught and his treason was only discovered after he had committed suicide when he mistakenly believed he was under investigation in 1963.

November 3, U Thant from Burma (now Myanmar) was elected as the UN Secretary General to replace Dag Hammarskjöld.

Also on November 3, the ultra-conservative and racist Army Major General Edwin "Ted" Walker resigned after he was chastised by President Kennedy for alleging to the press that Eleanor Roosevelt and President Truman were communists and for attempting to sway the votes of his men during elections. Kennedy accepted his resignation.

General Walker had also been previously admonished by President Eisenhower for promoting his far right political views while in uniform. Walker would later run as for Governor of Texas in 1962 losing in the Democratic primary to John Connolly. Walker was also arrested in October of 1962 for leading the race riots at the University of Mississippi' after the enrollment of its first Black student, James Meredith. During the riots two people were killed and hundreds were wounded, including six US Marshals who were shot by rioters. Walker was sent to a mental asylum for a mental evaluation after his arrest, but released five days later.

Someone later attempted to assassinate Walker in April of 1963 when a bullet was fired through his dining room window just missing Walker. The assassination was much later blamed on Lee Harvey Oswald by a German CIA funded newspaper, Die Deutsche Soldaten-Zeitung, which provided questionable documents showing Oswald as the shooter. However Walker publicly refuted that Oswald was the shooter later claiming it was two people, one of whom he said "had killed Kennedy." US authorities and the Warren Commission found the story about Oswald as Walker's assassin very questionable. In 1976 Walker was arrested in a restroom at a Dallas public park for "public lewdness" for fondling an undercover police officer. He pled no contest and received a 30 day suspended jail sentence and was fined $1,000 and then faded from public view.

Also on November 3, General Maxwell Taylor returned from a fact finding mission in Vietnam and strongly recommended that President Kennedy immediately send 10,000 combat troops to Vietnam to fight the Viet Cong.

November 6, Heinz Felfe, West Germany's Chief of Counterintelligence of the Bundesnachrichtendienst, BND, was arrested by his own agents as a Soviet spy who had over the years had identified for the USSR over 100 US spies and CIA agents in the Soviet Union, many of whom had been executed. Felfe was a former Nazi SS Officer. The Americans had hid his Nazi past and sanitized his war records and recruited him with General Reinhard Gehlen under Operation Paperclip.

November 7, a large brush fire in the Hollywood hills of California destroyed many homes including those of Burt Lancaster, Zsa Zsa Gabor and Joe E. Brown.

Also on November 7, France secretly tested a nuclear weapon with an underground explosion.

November 8, a charter flight taking new US Army recruits from Baltimore to basic training in Ft. Jackson, South Carolina crashed during an emergency landing near Richmond Virginia and killed 77 of the 79 people on board.

November 9, the Professional Golfers Association, PGA, amended its rules to allow non-Whites to be members.

Also on November 9, Brian Epstein saw the Beatles perform at the Cavern Club. He began discussions with the group that lead to them signing a contract with him in December.

November 10, the city of Stalingrad was re-named Volgograd as the Soviets continued to disavow their former leader.

November 13, "the world's biggest fire" began as the pressure blew the cap off a natural gas well in Algeria and a spark caused it to explode sending flames 600 feet into the air. The fire raged for months until April 29, 1962 when Texas oil well firefighter Red Adair extinguished the fire with an explosion using 660 pounds of dynamite.

November 14, a UN resolution to expel the Union of South Africa from membership for their apartheid policies failed.

November 17, Portuguese troops from Goa fired upon without provocation on an Indian passenger ship killing one person and wounding another. The incident caused the Indian government to begin planning to oust the

Portuguese from their Indian Colony. On December 8, the Indians responded. The Portuguese Ambassador to the UN appealed for help as 30,000 Indian troops massed at the borders of Goa and seven Indian naval vessels appeared off the Goa coast. December 18, India invaded Goa. By evening all but the capital had been secured. A Portuguese naval ship exchanged fire with the Indian Navy and was sunk. That evening the Portuguese Governor-General received a cable from the Portuguese government in Lisbon saying that they were not to surrender, but that the Governor-General and all Portuguese troops should fight to the death. Upon reviewing his hopeless situation, the Portuguese Governor-General defied his orders and surrendered his forces to India rather than watch them be slaughtered. The Indian victory ended 451 years of Portuguese colonial rule in Goa.

November 18, Senator Barry Goldwater delivered a speech in Atlanta chastising President Kennedy on civil rights issues saying "I wouldn't like to see my party assume that it is the role of the federal government to enforce integration of schools."

November 24, the UN General Assembly passed a resolution prohibiting the use of nuclear and thermonuclear weapons.

November 28, nuclear test ban talks resumed at Geneva, Switzerland between the US, USSR and Britain.

November 29, in another test of the Mercury space capsule a chimpanzee was sent into space and recovered after two earth orbits.

November 30, General Lansdale of the CIA and the Joint Chiefs of Staff convinced President Kennedy that there were strong elements inside Cuba that wanted to overthrow Castro. Lansdale claimed it was possible to achieve this by October of 1962. They asked the President to approve covert support for these Cubans. President Kennedy then tentatively approved the continuation of Operation Mongoose, to covertly overthrow the Cuban government by Cuban forces. The Plan had been previously approved by Eisenhower in 1960.

Later the Joint Chiefs of Staff also proposed Operation Northwoods as part of Operation Mongoose. They proposed carrying out horrific terrorist attacks on US civilian targets like shopping centers,passenger aircraft and military bases, etc. which would then be blamed on Cuba as a pretext for a US invasion. President Kennedy said he was revolted by the idea and immediately rejected it.

December 2, in a midnight speech Fidel Castro declared that he was now a Marxist and confirmed that he would guide Cuba to becoming a Communist state, but added, "I'm saying this for any anti-communists left out there. There won't be any Communism for at least thirty years."

December 4, the Armed Forces Expeditionary Medal was created by Executive Order of the President Kennedy to honor US Forces deployed in combat in undeclared wars. Retroactive awards were given for service in the Quemoy and Matsu Islands, Lebanon in 1958 and for service during the Berlin Crisis. It was later given for service in Laos during the Vietnam War and for service in Korea during 1968-69 for what has become known as the

Second Korean War. It was later given to US forces in undeclared combat in Africa and the Middle East.

December 5, an East Berlin train engineer found a little used railroad line between East and West Berlin that was set to be demolished by the authorities the next day. He loaded his train with his wife, mother and four children and seventeen friends and switched his train to the track running his train to West Berlin as the stunned border guards watched. The tracks were destroyed the next day. The conductor and a half dozen other passengers on the train who were not part of the escape returned to East Berlin the next day.

December 7, NASA announced the next phase of the space program would be a two man capsule which was later named "the Gemini Program."

December 9, the British colony of Tanganyika gained its independence. In 1962 it would merge with Zanzibar to become Tanzania.

December 10, the USSR broke of diplomatic relations with the communist country of Albania. They also cancelled a significant aid package. In response the People Republic of China signed an aid treaty with Albania which then allied itself with China against the USSR.

Also on December 10, an atomic explosion 1200 feet underground in a salt cavern in New Mexico vaporized the water in the salt crystals, sending a radioactive geyser to the surface and 300 feet into the air.

December 11, a combat force of 33 helicopters and 400 US Army troops arrived in Vietnam to begin operations against the Viet Cong.

December 12, the police in Tokyo uncovered and arrested 13 men involved in an assassination attempt against the Japanese Prime Minister and his cabinet. The plot was financed by a wealthy Japanese industrialist and a former army general.

December 13, the US and USSR announced that they had reached an agreement to form a commission to reduce nuclear weapons.

Also on December 13, Grandma Moses the American folk painter died at the age of 101.

December 14, a Union Pacific train traveling at 80 MPH struck a school bus at an unlighted crossing in Colorado killing 20 children and severely injuring 13 others.

Also on December 14, by Executive Order President Kennedy created the Presidential Commission on the Status of Women. Their report which came out in 1965 described the unfair and unequal treatment women received in American society.

December 15, a UN resolution admitting the People's Republic of China as a member of the UN failed.

Also on December 15, Anatoliy Golitsyn a Soviet KGB officer defected to the West. Golitsyn provided some valuable information to the US and British intelligence. However his paranoid conspiracy theories also caused many problems including his false accusation that British Prime Minister Harold Macmillan was a Soviet agent.

December 16, Nelson Mandela's Spear of the Nation organization exploded bombs on this Saturday in three empty government buildings in

Johannesburg, Durban and Port Elizabeth to protest apartheid. Later at his trial when Mandela was accused of attempted murder he would explain, "If we intended to attack life we would have selected targets where people congregated, and not empty buildings and power stations."

December 17, a fire at a circus in Rio de Janeiro, Brazil killed 323 people, mostly children. Three men later admitted setting fire to the tent because they did not receive their promised free tickets to the circus for helping to erect the tent.

December 19, former British Ambassador Joseph Kennedy, the father of President Kennedy suffered a massive stroke. Although he lived until 1969, he never recovered his ability to speak.

December 25, the Soviet passport office notified Lee Harvey and Marina Oswald that they and their child would be allowed to leave for the US.

December 31, the Green Bay Packers defeated the New York Giants 37-0 to win the NFL Championship.

The inflation rate in 1961 was about 1%. The average income was $5,315. The average cost of a new house was $12,500 and rent about $110 per month. The average price of new cars was about $3,850 and they were advertised as "bigger and better." Gasoline was at 25 cents per gallon. You could buy a Brownie Camera for $10.19 or a Kodak 8mm movie camera for $29.99. A console stereo was $128.88 and record albums sold between $1.99 to $3.98 each. An RCA color television was expensive at $495.00, but a new black and white 19 inch Westinghouse television was only $158.88.

The new shows debuting in 1961 included the new sitcoms: *The Dick Van Dyke Show, Car 54 Where Are You?* and *Mr. Ed.* Two medical dramas, *Ben Casey*, and *Dr. Kildare* a radio, show which made its television debut. The popular game show *Password* also made its debut. The show was created by Bob Stewart who wanted Betty White to host the show, but television was still male dominated in 1961 and she lost the job to Allen Ludden because the producers didn't think a female host was suitable. Ludden became her husband in 1963 and White would later guest host on the show many times. *The Mike Douglas Show* and *Wide World of Sports* also premiered.

January 15, Motown Records signed a young trio called the Supremes. In December a group called the Pendeltones released their first single record, called "Surfin'." However the record producer was unhappy with the group's name, so he released it under the name "The Beach Boys." The single became a hit and their name was officially changed. The hit music of 1961 included two for Roy Orbison, *Crying* and *Running Scared.* Bobby Lewis had the top hit with *Tossin' and Turnin'.* Patsy Cline had the number two hit with *I Fall to Pieces.* Del Shannon hit with *Runaway* and *Hats Off to Larry,* Bobby Vee with *Take Good Care of My baby,* the Shirelles had three with *Dedicated to the One I Love, Mama Said* and *Will You Still Love Me Tomorrow? The Theme Song to Exodus* was still a hit for Ferrante and Teicher. Connie Francis had *Where the Boys Are,* and Ray Charles had *Hit the Road Jack.* Ernie K-Doe hit with *Mother-in-Law;* Dick and Dee Dee had *The Mountains High.* Shep and the Limelites hit with *Daddy's Home* and Chris Kenner with *I Like It Like That.* Dion had *Run Around Sue,* Neil Sedaka had *Calendar Girl* and Ricky Nelson hit with *Hello Mary Lou.* Ben E. King had

Stand by Me and *Spanish Harlem*. Dave Brubeck's album *Take Five* was a jazz sensation.

At the movies in 1961 *West Side Story* with Natalie Wood was the top grossing picture and also won the Oscars for Best Picture, Best Director, Best Supporting Actress for Rita Moreno, and Best Supporting Actor for George Chakiris. The Classic *Judgment at Nuremburg* premiered with Spencer Tracy and Burt Lancaster and Maxmillian Schell who won the Oscar for Best Actor. Schell also won Best Actor and Stanley Kramer the Best Director award at the Golden Globes. Another 1961 classic was *Breakfast at Tiffany's* with Audrey Hepburn and George Peppard. Three Walt Disney films were also hits: *The Parent Trap* with Haley Mills, *The Absent Minded Professor* with Fred MacMurray and the animated feature *101 Dalmatians*. Elvis Presley's picture *Blue Hawaii* also did well at the box office.

The literature of 1961 included: *Catch 22* by Joseph Heller, *The Winter of Our Discontent* by John Steinbeck, *Franny and Zooey* by J.D. Salinger, *Mila 18* by Leon Uris, *Valley of the Dolls* by Jacqueline Susann, *The Prime of Miss Jean Brodie* by Muriel Spark, *The Agony and the Ecstasy* by Irving Stone, *Where the Red Fern Grows* by Wilson Rawls, *The Making of the President 1960* by Theodore White, *The Night of the Iguana* by Tennessee Williams, *Mastering the Art of French Cooking* by Julia Child, *James and the Giant Peach* by Ronald Dahl, and another children's classic *Go, Dog. Go!* by P.D. Eastman.

CHAPTER 18. 1962: NUCLEAR TESTING, THE SPACE RACE, AND THE CUBAN MISSILE CRISIS

January 1, Western Samoa (now Samoa) received its independence from New Zealand.

Also on this day the communist People's Revolutionary Party was formed in South Vietnam.

January 2, Executive Secretary Roy Wilkins praised President Kennedy for his personal involvement in the Civil Rights Movement and but said he was disappointed that racial discrimination in federal housing was still prevalent.

January 3, Pope John the XXIII publicly revealed that he had excommunicated Fidel Castro from the Catholic Church the prior September for being a communist.

January 5, Clarence Gideon sent a letter to the U.S. Supreme Court he had written in pencil from his jail cell in Florida. Gideon claimed he had been wrongly accused and of theft and convicted without a lawyer. He allegedly stole $5 dollars in change, two bottles of beer and a soda from a pool hall and was given five years in prison by a Florida judge. In 1963 the US Supreme Court found in *Gideon* v. *Wainwright* that the right to counsel is a fundamental right. Gideon was re-tried in 1963 and found not guilty.

January 8, the first two Navy SEAL (Sea, Air and Land) teams were commissioned. SEAL Team One was based in California and SEAL Team Two in Virginia. Each team had 50 men and ten officers.

Also on January 8, Soviet Premier Nikita Khrushchev in a secret speech at the Presidium told the Soviet leaders that the USSR was much weaker militarily than the US. He said that the only way the Soviet Union could compete with the US was by maintaining its nuclear force and the threat of nuclear war.

January 9, the USSR and Cuba signed a trade pact.

January 10, an avalanche in Peru killed over 4,000 people and wiped out the city of Ranrahirca on the slopes of Huascarán, Peru's tallest mountain. The city was rebuilt only to be destroyed by an earthquake and an avalanche in 1970.

January 12, Operation Chopper began. It was the first American helicopter combat assaults in Vietnam. US Army helicopters crews ferried South Vietnamese Army troops into battle against the Viet Cong near Saigon.

January 13, the U2 spy flights began over China. Officially they were nationalist Chinese flights from Taiwan; however all the planes and their crews were Americans. They were nick-named the Black Cat Squadron.

January 14, an Indonesian torpedo boat was sunk by a Dutch warship near to what was then, West Iran which was claimed by both Indonesia and the Netherlands. Indonesia and the Dutch would later go to war over this area which is now called New Guinea.

January 15, Portugal quit the UN when the General Assembly began a debate over the independence of the Portuguese colony of Angola.

January 16, a leftist military coup took over the government of the Dominican Republic. Two days later a right-wing military coup backed by the CIA took the government from them.

January 17, ten former television game show contestants who had all previously testified under oath that they had not received answers in advance of their appearances on several television game shows pled guilty to perjury, finally ending the game show scandal.

January 18, the US began to use a defoliant called Agent Orange in Vietnam. The campaign to use it was called Operation Ranch Hand and its use was approved the previous November. The chemical was manufactured by Monsanto and Dow Chemical. It came in orange colored barrels which is how it got its common name. Agent Orange was actually one of six powerful herbicides used in Vietnam. Most were used at strengths many times more concentrated than agricultural uses, sometimes 50 times more concentrated. They would be responsible for devastating the Vietnamese countryside and attacking the health and well-being hundreds of thousands of Vietnamese and US troops. The side effects include cancer, neuropathy, skin disease and infertility in the many civilians and military personnel who were exposed. It also caused miscarriages and birth defects such as spina bifida in the offspring of those exposed. The US Army also used these herbicides to spray around military bases in Vietnam and Korea. It was an eco-disaster that still has on-going consequences affecting many US veterans, including the author and his son.

January 21, at a meeting of the Organization of American States (OAS) the US agreed to give aid to a desperate Haiti in exchange for all the member Latin American countries support of a trade sanctions against Cuba. Two days later at the request of the US the OAS also suspended Cuba from membership and on January 30, Cuba was formally expelled.

January 23, Kim Philby, a British intelligence officer turned Soviet Spy, defected to the Soviet Union.

Also on January 23, Jackie Robinson was elected as the first Black member of the Baseball Hall of Fame.

January 25, Governor Donald Nutter of Montana on his way to a speaking engagement from Helena to Cut Bank was killed in a plane crash along with five other people.

January 26, the US attempted to launch the Ranger 3 spacecraft to land on the Moon. The mission failed as the rocket fired too quickly missing Moon orbit and sending the craft into an orbit around the sun.

Also on January 26, the Catholic Bishop of Buffalo declared Chubby Checker's dance "the Twist" as impure and obscene. Both the song and dance were banned in all Catholic schools.

January 27, the space mission of John Glenn, who would become the first American in earth orbit, the flight was cancelled at the last minute because of weather conditions, disappointing millions watching on television.

January 28, the last street car made its final run in Washington, DC. Only ten US cities still had an electrical street car systems remaining at this time. Most cities had changed to gasoline powered buses because of the oil lobby.

January 30, the children's Laughing Epidemic erupted in what is now Tanzania. It began in a school and soon spread to other schools. Children burst into uncontrollable fits laughter, some fainted, some had rashes and others screamed. These laughter episodes would last for short periods and then start up again. The epidemic spread to other schools and throughout Tanzania. Although the episodes have been greatly exaggerated over time, they were serious. This phenomenon was a joyless laughter and has since been diagnosed as Mass Psychogenic Illness (MPI) which is caused by children under extreme stress and fear who feel helpless. It affected about a dozen schools in Tanzania some of which were closed. Some reports said it affected over a thousand students. A similar MPI epidemic occurred on the West Bank in 1983 among Palestinian children that became known as the West Bank Fainting Epidemic.

Also on January 30, two of the Flying Wallendas, the famous family tightrope walking group, were killed when their "Seven Person Pyramid" failed in front of a large crowd at the Shrine Circus in Detroit.

January 31, an unusually thick fog covered the San Joaquin and Sacramento Valleys of California. It didn't lift for four days. Twenty-eight people were killed in traffic accidents during that time because of visibility issues.

February, the US conducted a series of atomic tests to perfect its nuclear arsenal during the month in Nevada.

February 2, for the first time in 400 years eight of the nine planets in our solar system came into alignment.

February 4, in Cold War propaganda one-upmanship the Soviet newspaper *Izvestia* claimed that it was the Russians and not the Americans who invented baseball.

February 5, despite strong disapproval from the military and many in France, French President Charles De Gaulle called for Algerian independence. Three days later in Paris violent protests erupted against Algerian independence and eight people died.

February 5, a lawsuit was filed in Englewood, New Jersey to end racial segregation in their public schools.

February 7, the US began a trade blockade against Cuba. The blockade forced Cuba to up its trade with the USSR. The Soviets in a secret agreement promised to buy most Cuban sugar which had been banned in the West in exchange for locating nuclear missiles in Cuba. The agreement also included a provision that the USSR would defend Cuba if the Americans invaded.

February 10, the US traded the Soviet spy Rudolph Abel for the captured U2 pilot Francis Gary Powers.

February 12, a bus boycott against racial discrimination began in Macon, Georgia.

February 14, in an event watched by many Americans, Jackie Kennedy conducted a televised White House tour.

February 20, John Glenn became the first American to orbit the Earth in Friendship 7. He was the third American and the fifth man in space.

February 26, the US Supreme Court ruled against segregation in all public transportation.

February 27, two South Vietnamese air force pilots attempted to assassinate President Ngô Đình Diệm by bombing the presidential palace. Diệm was not injured in the attack.

March 1, the dime store S.S. Kresge opened the first Kmart with its "blue light specials" in Garden City, Michigan. It became the second largest discount chain behind Sears, but would later fall behind Walmart and Target to become the third largest. Kmart bought Sears in 2004 for $11 billion. Kmart reached its peak in 2000 and declined rapidly thereafter.

March 2, the US announced that it would again begin testing nuclear weapons above ground.

March 8, the Beatles performed for the first time on television on the BBC.

March 9, the first American ground troops deliberately engaged in combat in Vietnam when US military advisors were ordered to join the South Vietnamese Army in a combat mission.

March 15, five different scientific research groups simultaneously announced the discovery of anti-matter.

March 27, the Catholic Church ended racial discrimination in New Orleans Catholic Schools.

March 29, Jack Paar made his final appearance on the *Tonight Show*.

April 20, a NASA civilian pilot, Neil Armstrong, flew the first plane into space when his X-15 aircraft achieved an altitude of 39.2 miles. On July 17, NASA pilot Robert White achieved an altitude of 59.6 miles a record for the X-15 plane. These flights were important in establishing the Space Shuttle program.

April 24, the US satellite Ranger 4 became the first US satellite to reach the moon. It crashed two days later on the dark side of the moon. Also on April 24, MIT successfully sent the first television signal from Massachusetts to California via satellite and satellite television transmission was born.

April 27, the US conducted an atmospheric nuclear test at Christmas Island in the South Pacific. They would continue many atmospheric nuclear tests throughout the year at both Christmas and Johnson Islands in the South Pacific and in Nevada.

May 1, France performed an underground nuclear test in the Sahara desert in Algeria and officially became a nuclear power.

May 6, the US fired the first nuclear warhead from a Polaris submarine.

May 9, a laser beam was successfully bounced off the moon by US scientists.

May 11, the US sent troops to be stationed in Thailand to protect the country from China.

May 23, Scott Carpenter went into space and orbited the Earth three times on the Aurora 7 spacecraft.

May 25, US labor unions began a coordinated campaign for a 35 hour work week. The campaign failed as the unions had begun their decline.

May 28, a lawsuit was filed in Rochester, New York alleging "de facto racial segregation" in Rochester public schools, as schools were predominantly White or Black according to their geography within the city.

Also on May 28, the stock market declined dramatically losing almost $21 billon in one day.

June 16, two US Army officers were killed by the Viet Cong in Saigon.

June 25, the US Supreme Court ruled that school prayer and religious instruction in public schools was unconstitutional.

In June the USSR resumed above ground nuclear testing. They too would conduct multiple nuclear tests throughout the year.

July 1, Rwanda and Burundi became independent African nations.

July 2, Fidel Castro visited Moscow.

Also on July 2, the first Walmart discount store was opened in Rogers, Arkansas.

July 5, after 132 years of French rule Algeria became an independent nation.

July 6, the largest test of Operation Plowshare was conducted in Sedan, Nevada. Operation Plowshare was the US government's attempt to use nuclear explosions for peaceful construction purposes. The Sedan test was 104 kilo tons. The tests were conducted from 1962 to 1973. The Sedan test was the second test. The first was a very small test of three kilo tons at Carlsbad, New Mexico which occurred in December of 1961. The list of proposed peaceful uses included an explosion to create the Pan-Atomic Canal through Nicaragua to replace the Panama Canal, another to create a deep water harbor in Alaska, and a series of 22 nuclear explosions to create a highway and a Santa Fe Railroad passage through the Bristol Mountains on the Mojave Desert in California. Operation Plowshare was cancelled when the testing revealed that there were severe long term health effects to humans caused from the radiation involved in the potential explosions. The tests involved twenty seven explosions from 1961 through 1973. Most were in Nevada. However, New Mexico and Colorado each had two test explosions.

July 10, Dr. Martin Luther King Jr. was arrested at a peaceful demonstration in Georgia. Following his lead on July 21, another 160 civil rights activists would be arrested in Albany, Georgia. After his release, Dr. King was arrested again on July 27, in Albany, Georgia.

Also on this day Telstar the first geosynchronous communication satellite was successfully launched. On July 11, the first transatlantic television transmission was made through Telstar. An instrumental song by the rock group the Tornadoes called *Telstar* in the satellite's honor went to number one on Billboard's Hot 100 by the end of the year.

July 11, Soviet Cosmonaut Micolaev was launched into orbit and set a record of four days in space.

Also on July 21, conflicts between the Chinese and Indian armies erupted along their border.

July 22, Mariner 1, the first US probe of Venus failed.

July 26, the first secret shipment of Soviet nuclear missiles arrived in Cuba.

July 27, Mariner 2 was launched and later successfully made a fly-by of Venus.

August 4, Nelson Mandela was captured and imprisoned by the South African police.

August 6, actress Marilyn Monroe was found dead, apparently having taken or, as some have alleged, having been forced to take an overdose of drugs.

Also on July 6, Jamaica became an independent nation after 300 years of British rule.

August 11, Cosmonaut Andrian G Nikolayev became the third Russian in space aboard the Vostok 3. On August 12, the Soviets launched Vostok 4, with Cosmonaut Pavel Popovich making this the first time that two men were in space simultaneously.

August 17, East German border guards shot and killed an eighteen-year-old boy attempting to escape to West Berlin.

August 22, rogue members of the French military failed in their attempt to assassinate Charles De Gaulle.

August 23, the first live television show was broadcast from the US to Europe via the Telstar satellite.

August 29, a U2 flight over Cuba discovered the Soviet SAM missile sites being built in Cuba.

August 31, Trinidad and Tobago became independent from Britain.

September 1, over 12,000 people were killed in an earthquake in western Iran.

September 8, Chinese troops crossed over the Indian border in their ongoing dispute with India.

September 17, NASA announced the selection of 17 new astronauts.

September 20, Governor Barnett of Mississippi refused to allow the admission of a Black student, James Meredith, to the University of Mississippi. On September 24, the US Circuit Court of Appeals ordered Meredith admitted to the University. September 9, President Kennedy ordered the US Army to prevent riots by those attempting to stop integration at the

University of Mississippi. The next day 3,000 troops were sent to Oxford Mississippi. Meredith was allowed to register for classes on September 30.

September 27, Rachel Carlson published *Silent Spring* about the disastrous effects of pesticides on the environment.

September 30, César Chávez founded the United Farm Workers.

October 3, Wally Schirra was launched into Earth orbit.

October 9, Uganda became independent from Britain.

October 10, India counterattacked Chinese troops along the border.

October 14, U2 spy planes located and positively identified Soviet missile launch sites in Cuba. According to Robert Kennedy in his memoir, *Thirteen Days*, the Joint Chiefs of Staff and the CIA unanimously agreed that a full-scale attack and invasion of Cuba was the only solution and immediately and strongly advised President Kennedy to do so. They also told Kennedy that the Soviets would back down and would not attempt to stop the US from conquering Cuba. After the Bay of Pigs Kennedy was very skeptical of their advice and said, "They, no more than we, can let these things go by without doing something. They can't, after all their statements, permit us to take out their missiles, kill a lot of Russians, and then do nothing. If they don't take action in Cuba, they certainly will in Berlin."

Kennedy met with his top advisers throughout October 21, and considered two options: an air strike primarily against the Cuban missile bases, or a naval blockade of Cuba. General Curtis Le May the Chief of Staff of the US Air Force was strongly advocating for a total knock out first strike against the USSR. The rest of the Joint Chiefs and the CIA were strongly advocating for a full Cuban invasion. Against all their advice Kennedy chose the blockade.

Even after the decision was made Le May continued to argue with Kennedy that he was ignoring sound and experienced military advice and insisted that the President authorize an immediate air strike to remove the threat. He would later call Kennedy's decision "the worst defeat in American history."

Kennedy held his ground and at 3:00 pm EDT on October 22, President Kennedy formally established his command, the Executive Committee (EXCOMM) with National Security Action Memorandum (NSAM) 196. At 5:00 pm he met with Congressional leaders who had also been lobbied by Le May and the Joint Chiefs and they too contentiously opposed Kennedy's blockade. They forcefully demanded a full invasion of Cuba. Kennedy cautioned them that such an action could lead to a nuclear war. They were opposed to Kennedy's blockade, but Kennedy again stood his ground.

The crisis deepened when the Soviets threatened to run through the American blockade. The USSR had shown no indication that they would back down and they made strong comments to the contrary. Despite the President's wishes the US military began preparing for an invasion of Cuba as well as a possible nuclear first strike on the Soviet Union if the Soviets attempted to run through the blockade. Both the American military and the Soviet military were now advising Kennedy and Khrushchev respectively that military action was the only solution. Fortunately neither Kennedy nor Khrushchev wanted war and both realized this was a potential nuclear catastrophe that could end humanity and they began very secret negotiations.

In the end the USSR agreed to remove their missiles from Cuba if the US removed their missiles from Turkey. Khrushchev also told Kennedy of the Soviet's promise to Castro that the USSR would come to their aid in the event of a US invasion. He appealed to Kennedy and received a pledge from Kennedy that the US would not invade Cuba. It was a pledge that infuriated both the US military and the CIA.

October 18, the US launched Ranger 5 to land on the moon. It missed the moon and went into orbit around the sun.

October 20, the Chinese Army responded to the Indian counterattack and struck deeper into India starting the Sino-Indian War that would last until November 21 when a ceasefire was agreed and the mountain borders were permanently set for the two nations.

November 1, the USSR launched Mars 1 which failed when it lost radio contact.

November 6, in the fall elections Edward Kennedy was elected Senator from Massachusetts. The following day Richard Nixon who had lost the Governor's race in California to the Democrat Pat Brown, threw a fit in front of the press and told them, "You won't have Richard Nixon to kick around anymore." It was at the time said to be "Nixon's political obituary."

November 27, the first test flight of the Boeing 727 was completed successfully.

December 9, Tanganyika (Tanzania) officially obtained independence from Britain and became a republic.

December 14, Mariner 2 made a successful fly-by of Venus.

December 23, with the Cuban Missile crisis over, Cuba released the Bay of Pigs invasion prisoners to the US in exchange for food and medicine for Cuba's poor.

In 1962 the average income was $5,556.00. A factory worker's average take home pay was about $95 per week, just under $5,000 annually. The average cost of a new home was $12,500.00. The monthly payment for this home on an 8% thirty year mortgage was $88.06 with a $500.00 down payment making hone buying very affordable. The average cost of a new car was $3,195.00 which a five year loan at 8% was at a monthly payment of $64.89 making a new car very affordable. The payment on a new house and car would only be about a third of the average worker's monthly wages leaving the worker and his family two thirds of their income for other things.

In 1962 over 90% of all homes had at least one television. September 23, ABCs fist color series the *Jetsons*, a prime time cartoon aired on television for the first time. In addition to the *Jetsons*, the other new shows of 1962 included: *The Beverly Hillbillies, The Virginian, The Lucy Show, Combat!, The Saint, McHale's Navy, The Match Game. The Tonight Show Starring Jonny Carson* also made its debut with the departure of Jack Paar. Walter Cronkite became the news anchor for CBS and continued in this capacity for 19 years. NBC aired the first live color broadcast of a football game with the Rose Bowl in January. *The Bob Newhart Show* won the Emmy for Best Comedy, *The Defenders* for the Best Drama, and

The Garry Moore Show as the Best Variety Show. E.G. Marshall won the Emmy for Best Actor in the *Defenders* and Shirley Booth as Best Actress in *Hazel*. Don Knotts won Best Supporting Actor for his role as Barney Fife in *The Andy Griffith Show*, and Pamela Brown as Best Supporting Actress for her portrayal of the Duchess of Kent in the *Hallmark Hall of Fame* episode *Victoria Regina*.

The movie crop of 1962 was excellent with the top grossing film *Lawrence of Arabia* leading the pack. Other notable movies include: *The Longest Day, Mutiny On the Bounty, To Kill A Mockingbird, Music Man, Gypsy, The Manchurian Candidate, Lolita, The Days of Wine and Roses, The Man Who Shot Liberty Valance, State Fair* and *The Miracle Worker*. The Oscars went to *Lawrence of Arabia* for Best Picture and to David Lean for Best Director. The Best Actor went to Gregory Peck in *To Kill A Mockingbird*, Best Actress to Anne Bancroft in *The Miracle Worker*, Best Supporting Actor to Ed Begley for a Tennessee Williams script *Sweet Bird of Youth*, and Best Supporting Actress to Patty Duke for her role as Helen Keller in *The Miracle Worker*.

On March 24, 1962 Mick Jagger and Keith Richards performed for the first time as the Blue Boys. In April they would form the Rolling Stones with three others and perform their first paid gig at the Marquee Club in London in July. The music of 1962 was an eclectic mixture. Acker Bilk, an English clarinetist's instrumental *Stranger on the Shore* was atop Billboard's Hot 100. Other hits included: the folk songs *If I Had A Hammer* by Peter Paul and Mary, and *Where Have All the Flowers Gone* by the Kingston Trio. Other top songs included: *Ramblin' Rose* by Nat King Cole, *Moon River* by Henry Mancini, *Green Onions* by Booker T. and the MGs, *I Can't Stop loving You* by Ray Charles, *Roses Are Red (My Love)* by Bobby Vinton, *Johnny Angel* by Shelley Fabares, *The Loco-Motion* by Little Eva, *The Twist* by Chubby Checker, *Let Me In* by the Sensations, *Soldier Boy* and *Baby Its You* by the Shirelles, *Breaking Up is Hard To Do* by Neil Sedaka, *Sherry* by the Four Seasons, *I Can't Help Falling In Love* by Elvis Presley, *Let's Dance* by Chris Montez, *Surfin Safari* by the Beach Boys.

The Beach Boys began their meteoric rise in 1962 along with the surfer music that would be emulated by other American rock groups. Folk Music was at its peak with groups like Peter Paul and Mary, the Kingston Trio, the Brothers Four, the Chad Mitchell Trio and the New Christy Minstrels. Unknown to Americans, the Rolling Stones and The Beatles were just beginning their rise to fame in Britain.

The literature of 1962 produced some classics including: *A Clockwork Orange* by Anthony Burgess, *One Flew over The Cuckoo's Nest* by Ken Kesey, *Mother Night* by Kurt Vonnegut, *Something Wicked This Way Comes* by Ray Bradbury, *One Day In The Life of Ivan Denisovitch* by Aleksandr Solzhenitsyn, *Who's Afraid of Virginia Woolf* by Edward Albee, *King Rat* by James Clavell, *Travels with Charlie* by John Steinbeck, *Seven Days In May* by Fletcher Knebel, *Ship of Fools* by Katherine Anne Porter, *Another Country* by James Baldwin, as well as *The Structure of Scientific Revolutions* by Thomas Kuhn and *Silent Spring* by Rachel Carlson.

CHAPTER 19. 1963: THE TURNING POINT OF THE CIVIL RIGHTS MOVEMENT AND THE KENNEDY ASSASSINATION

January 4, the Soviet satellite Luna 4 reached Earth orbit but failed in its mission to reach the moon.

January 8, the Mona Lisa, on loan from France, was displayed at the National Gallery of Art.

January 11, the first discotheque, Whisky-A-Go-Go, opened in Los Angeles.

January 14, George Wallace was sworn in as Governor of Alabama. In his inauguration speech he made his infamous vow, "Segregation now: segregation tomorrow; segregation forever!"

January 22, the Elysée Treaty was signed by France and Germany in the hope of uniting Western Europe and minimizing conflicts. The US was initially unhappy with the treaty as it was an attempt by France to reduce US influence in Europe.

February 1, Nyasaland (now Malawi) became self-governing after breaking away from Rhodesia. They would also break away from British rule in 1964 to become the independent nation of Malawi.

February 9, New York City recorded a record breaking 16.7" snowfall.

February 14, the US launched the Syncom 1 communications satellite.

February 20, baseball great Willie Mays signed a record $100,000 contract with the San Francisco Giants. This began a trend where sports heroes became some of the highest paid people in America. On February 27, Mickey Mantle also signed a $100,000 contract with the New York Yankees.

February 21, the US continued with its nuclear testing in Nevada.

March 1, in France 200,000 miners struck. The strike raised fears in the US of growing socialism in France.

March 13, the Soviets sent two reconnaissance flights over Alaska.

March 17, a volcanic eruption in Bali killed over 1,900 people.

March 18, France resumed nuclear testing in Algeria.

March 20, the first Pop Art exhibition was held in New York City.

March 21, Alcatraz Penitentiary in San Francisco Bay closed. It would become a tourist attraction.

March 22, British Secretary of War John Profumo denied rumors of an affair with a nineteen-year-old girl Christine Keeler. However he would be forced to admit to the affair several weeks later. The British teen was also having a concurrent affair with a Soviet naval attaché raising the fear of Soviet blackmail. It brought the end of the Conservative government of Harold Macmillan. He would resign in October.

March 31, Los Angeles ended their streetcars after 90 years of service and went to gasoline powered buses.

April 1, a 114 day newspaper strike in New York City ended.

April 2, the US Launched Explorer 17 into Earth orbit.

April 7, Yugoslavia declared that it was an independent socialist republic.

April 9, the US Congress proclaimed Winston Churchill as an honorary US citizen. Churchill's mother Jeanette Jerome was an American who was born and raised in New York City who moved to Britain and married Lord Randolph Churchill.

April 10, the nuclear submarine the USS Thresher was lost during deep diving tests in the Atlantic Ocean about 220 miles from Boston. All 129 crewmen were lost making this the worst American submarine disaster. The Thresher likely imploded at a depth of 1,300 to 2,000 feet after a short in the electrical system caused her reactor to shut down.

April 11, the US conducted another nuclear test in Nevada.

April 12, police dogs were used to terrify peaceful civil rights demonstrators in Birmingham, Alabama. Pictures of the assault later appeared in the press horrifying many.

May 1, James Whittaker became the first American to climb Mt. Everest.

Also on this day Indonesia finally took control of western New Guinea from the Netherlands.

May 7, the communications satellite Telstar 2 was launched.

May 9, more nuclear testing was conducted in Nevada.

May 11, Dr. Martin Luther King Jr. addressed a crowd from the Gaston Motel in Birmingham where he announced the successful negotiation that would desegregate fitting rooms, lunch counters and water fountains in the city. That evening Imperial Wizard Bobby Shelton addressed a KKK rally in Birmingham urging rejection of "any concessions or demands from any of the atheist so-called ministers of the nigger race or any other group here in Birmingham." That night Dr. King received a death threat and White racists bombed the Gaston Motel and his brother's house in Birmingham. A.D. King and his wife Naomi and their five children were not severely hurt but their home was badly damaged. A witness, Roosevelt Tatum, saw the bombing of the King home and said they were carried out by uniformed Birmingham Police in patrol cars. It was reported that immediately after the bombings that at the Birmingham jail the police began singing *Dixie* over the jail's loudspeakers.

A.D. King called the FBI and reported that the bombers were by the Birmingham Police and demanded an investigation. That night a Black rally and protest took place and about 2,500 took to the streets. It was a Saturday night and a few Blacks who had been drinking at a local club were confronted by a Birmingham police officer and he was stabbed by one of the men in a scuffle. They police sprayed the crowd with tear gas. The police charged into the crowd with a battalion of State Troopers, with about 100 of them on horseback and began to commit violence on the demonstrators. White journalists were also beaten in the violence by the police and State troopers and were then imprisoned in the bombed motel overnight. In the aftermath fifty Blacks were treated for serious wounds.

The confrontation ended the following day when President Kennedy assembled 18,000 US Army personnel and threatened to put Birmingham under martial law. Governor Wallace complained to the US Supreme Court about the President's actions which he claimed were usurping his and the local police department's authority. They responded by stating that the President was acting on proper authority to protect the peace and lives of the citizens of Alabama.

May 15, Faith 7 the last of NASA's Mercury program was launched with L. Gordon Cooper as the last single Astronaut to go into space. He completed 22 orbits before returning to Earth.

May 17, another nuclear test took place in Nevada.

May 20, Sukarno was appointed the President of Indonesia.

May 27, Jomo Kenyatta was elected the first Prime minister of Kenya. On June 1, he was formally installed.

May 28, over 22,000 people were killed and a million houses were destroyed in Bangladesh by a cyclone.

June 3, a Northwest Airlines DC-7 crashed into the Pacific Ocean killing all 101 people aboard.

Also on June 3, Pope John XXIII died and was succeeded on June 30, by Pope Paul VI.

June 7, the Rolling Stones made their first English television appearance on the BBC.

June 8, the American Heart Association began the first campaign against smoking and cigarettes.

June 9, Barbara Streisand appeared on the *Ed Sullivan Show*.

June 10, President Kennedy singed the Equal Pay for Equal Work Act to give women equal rights in the workplace.

June 11, Governor Wallace made national headlines when he stood in the registration doorway at the University of Alabama in an attempt to prevent Blacks from registering. That same day President Kennedy told the press that all "segregation is morally wrong and that it is time to act."

June 13-June 19, in a joint effort to allow two spacecraft to communicate with each other in space Vostok 5 and 6 were launched by the Soviets and Valentina Tereshkova in Vostok 6 became the first woman in space. Vostok 5 was manned by Valeriy Bykovskiy who made 81 orbits over five days setting a space endurance record.

June 15, the Japanese song *Sukiyaki* by Kyu Sakamoto — which is the only Japanese language song ever to make Billboard's Hot 100 — went to number one on this date. The song was ironically popular with Americans. It was written as a protest song against the continued US military presence in Japan. Americans thought it was a love song. In the US the song was titled *Sukiyaki*, after the popular Japanese beef dish with soy sauce and bean curd. The Japanese were dumbfounded as the American title and popularity had no relevance to the Japanese lyrics or meaning. The Japanese title is *Ue o Muite Arukō* meaning "I Look Up As I Walk," signifying Japanese pride.

June 18, over 3,000 Blacks boycotted the Boston public schools claiming de facto segregation.

June 23, President Kennedy toured Western Europe. On June 26, Kennedy gave his famous "Ich bin ein Berliner" (I am a Berliner) speech in West Berlin.

June 24, the first demonstration of a home video recorder was made in London by the BBC.

June 28, in a tit for tat with Kennedy, Khrushchev visited East Berlin.

June 30, a car bomb meant to assassinate Mafia boss Salvatore Greco killed seven police and military officers near Palermo, Sicily.

July 1, the US Postal Service implemented its Zone Improvement Plan (Zip Codes).

July 5, the fist Beatle's song to hit the Billboard Hot 100 was *From Me To You* however it was sung by the American singer, Del Shannon.

July 13, the government of India cut all ties with South Africa over its apartheid policies.

July 18, the United Nations urged economic and military sanctions against South Africa until apartheid is ended.

July 25, the US, USSR, and Britain agreed in principle to a nuclear test ban treaty bringing an end to the proliferation of radiation, water contamination and other hazards from nuclear tests. It would be ratified by Congress and signed into law by Kennedy on October 7, 1963.

July 26, the US launched Syncom 2 the second geosynchronous communications satellite.

August 7, Jackie Kennedy gave birth to a son. It was the first birth to a president in the White House since the Cleveland administration. The baby had Infant Respiratory Distress Syndrome (IRDS) and died two days later. John Jr. was born seventeen days after President Kennedy was elected, but before he was sworn into office.

August 21, martial law was declared in South Vietnam and the Catholic government used this as an excuse to raid Buddhist temples and monasteries.

August 28, over 200,000 civil rights demonstrators marched on Washington, DC where Dr. King delivered his "I have a dream" speech at the Lincoln Memorial.

September 2, Governor Wallace prevented the integration of Tuskegee High School by delaying the opening and enforcing his orders against integration with Alabama State Troopers. He took similar actions in Huntsville, Birmingham and Mobile. On September 9, Wallace received a federal injunction prohibiting him from interfering with the integration of Alabama schools.

Also on September 2, CBS and NBC expanded the national nightly news from fifteen minutes to thirty minutes.

September 7, *American Bandstand* moved to California and began broadcasting nationally every Saturday.

Also on September 7, The Pro Football Hall of Fame was dedicated in Canton, Ohio.

Sunday September 15, four Klansmen bombed the 16th Street Baptist Church in Birmingham killing four little girls and injuring 22 others. Dr King called the act "one of the most vicious and tragic crimes ever perpetrated against humanity." This vicious act became the turning point in the Civil Rights movement as a growing majority of Whites began to sympathize with the movement.

September 20, President Kennedy in a speech before the United Nations General Assembly proposed a joint US-Soviet manned mission to the moon. The proposal was never taken seriously by the Soviets who had concerns about the technical viability of a manned moon mission. The scientists from the two space programs also reasoned that their equipment and methods were so vastly different that a joint effort would be too difficult.

September 27, the US Census announced that the US population had reached 190,000,000.

September 28, New York disc jockey Murray the K played the first Beatles song. *She Loves You,* on American radio.

September 29, the Rolling Stones began their first US tour as the opening act for The Everly Brothers. Bo Diddley was also on this tour and Little Richard joined after the tour was in progress.

October 2, according to Secretary of Defense Robert McNamara in his 1995 autobiography *In Retrospect,* said that President Kennedy ordered him to begin the withdrawal of all US forces from Vietnam.

October 3-9, hurricane Flora struck Haiti and Cuba killing over 6,000 and injuring over 100,000.

October 7, Senate Democratic Secretary, Bobby Baker, a former adviser and aide to Lyndon Johnson, resigned during a scandal where he was accused of bribing and providing sexual favors in exchange for congressional votes. In the Democratically controlled Senate both Baker and Vice President Johnson came under Senate investigation for bribery. However the senate stopped their investigation of Johnson after Baker's resignation.

October 9, a dam burst in Italy killing about 3,000 people.

October 20, South Africa put Nelson Mandela and eight others on trial for conspiracy.

October 22, about 225,000 students boycotted the Chicago Public Schools as part the Chicago Freedom movement's attempt to end de facto segregation in Chicago Public Schools.

October 31, a propane gas leak caused an explosion that killed 64 people at the *Holliday on Ice* tour in Indiana.

November 1, a military coup backed by the CIA over threw President Diệm in South Vietnam. Diệm and his brother were assassinated the following day by South Vietnamese troops.

November 11, Ed Sullivan and Brian Epstein signed an agreement for the Beatles to appear three times on the *Ed Sullivan Show*.

November 12, a train crash in Japan killed 164 people.

November 16, the touchtone phone was introduced.

November 22, President Kennedy was assassinated in Dallas, Texas. Lyndon Johnson was sworn in as the President of the United States. During the assassination Governor Connolly of Texas was also wounded, along with an observer on the sidewalk, James Tague, who was hit with fragments when a bullet hit the cement curb in front of him. Tague told the Warren Commission that the bullet that caused his injury came from the grassy knoll contributing to the growing evidence that Kennedy's assassination was a conspiracy. In 1979 the House Select Committee on Assassinations reviewed all the evidence overlooked by the Warren Commission and found that Kennedy had been killed in a conspiracy. According to the UPI on November 23, when Nikita Khrushchev was told of Kennedy's death, he broke down and cried. He had become close to Kennedy during the Cuban Missile Crisis and credited Kennedy with preventing nuclear war. He sent a cable to Johnson stating the "indignation of Soviet people against the culprits of this base crime." He also delivered a private message to Jackie Kennedy. In their book *The Sword and the Shield, the History of the KGB*, Christopher Andrew and Vasili Mitrokhin said that they found in the KGB records (released after the collapse of the USSR) that Soviet intelligence decisively believed Kennedy was killed by a rightwing conspiracy.

November 24, Jack "Ruby" Rubenstein killed Lee Harvey Oswald on national television in what was thought a tightly secured basement of the Dallas Police Department. It was later learned that Ruby had Mafia connections and managed Mafia bribes to the Dallas police, and therefore he had access. Ruby also later told his attorney and others, before he died from cancer, that he was forced by the Mafia to kill Oswald to coverup the real assassins.

November 25, President Kennedy was buried at Arlington Cemetery in Washington, DC.

November 26, Explorer 18 was launched.

December 7, instant replay was used for the first time on television during the Army-Navy football game.

December 9, nineteen-year-old Frank Sinatra Jr. was kidnapped and held for ransom. The kidnappers demanded $240,000, which was paid by his father, and on December 11, and he was released. The FBI later caught three men and recovered the ransom money.

December 20 a trial against twenty one Auschwitz camp guards began.

Also on December 20, Studebaker produced its last car in the US. The company would move to Canada and struggle to make a profit until finally closing their doors in 1966.

December 23, the Beach Boys made their first television appearance on *Shindig.*

December 24, violence between the Greeks and Turks erupted in Cyprus.

December 30, Congress approved the Kennedy half dollar.

In 1963 inflation rate was still very low at about 1.24%. The average cost of a new home rose slightly from $12,500 in 1962 to $12,650 in 1963. The average wage also rose slightly to $5,807. The price of the average new car rose to $3,233.00. Window air conditioners which were now becoming more common cost on average $149.95. The Sabin oral polio vaccine was also distributed nationwide and given to children as a drop on a sugar cube. The first silicone breast implants went on the market. Saline solution implants would be available the following year.

In addition to instant replay and more color broadcasts the FCC authorized the remote control for televisions in 1963. For the first time Americans surveyed said that more of their news came from television rather than their newspapers. In February Julia Child's show *The French Chef* made its debut. Other new shows debuting in 1963 included: *Shindig, Mutual of Omaha's Wild Kingdom, The Outer Limits, The Fugitive, The Patty Duke Show, Burke's Law, Petticoat Junction, My Favorite Martian, The Judy Garland Show* and two new soaps *General Hospital* and *The Doctors.* On the BBC *Doctor Who* began and eventually become a cult classic in the US.

Some favorite shows also ended included: *Leave It to Beaver, The Real McCoys, Laramie* and *Hawaiian Eye.* Once again *The Defenders* won the Emmy for Best Drama. The Best Comedy was won by *The Dick Van Dyke Show.* The Best Variety Show was won by *The Andy Williams Show.* The Best Dramatic Actor Emmys went again to E.G. Marshall in *The Defenders* and Glenda Ferrell in *Ben Casey.* The Best Comedy Actress and Actor were Shirley Booth in *Hazel* and again by Don Knotts in *The Andy Griffith Show.*

American movies were making a comeback. *Cleopatra* was the largest at the box office but *Tom Jones* won Best Picture and Best Director for Tony Richardson. *Hud* won the Best Actress for Patricia Neal and Best Supporting Actor for Melvyn Douglas. *Lilies of the Field* won the Best Actor for Sydney Poitier. Other notable films of 1963 include: Alfred Hitchcock's *The Birds,* the multi-starred comedy *It's a Mad, Mad, Mad World, How the West Was Won, Charade, Bye Bye Birdie, The V.I.Ps, Irma La Douce,* and the World War II prisoner of war drama *The Great Escape.*

In February the Beatles reached the top of the British pop charts with *Please, Please Me.* On February 25 the song was the first Beatles tune released in the US. The schools in 1963 may have not been integrated, but the music of the young was and included many Black performers. In addition to the ironically popular song *Sukiyaki* the songs of 1963 included: the number one hit *Sugar Shack* by The Fireballs, *Surfin' USA* and *Surfer Girl* by the Beach Boys, *Rhythm of the Rain* by the Cascades, *He's So Fine* and *One Fine Day* by The Chiffons, *Blue Velvet* and *Blue On Blue* by Bobby Vinton, *Hey Paula* by Paul and Paula, *My Boy Friend's Back* by The Angels, *Puff the Magic Dragon* and *Blowin' In the Wind* by Peter Paul and Mary, *Deep Purple* by Nino Tempo and April Stevens, *Wipe Out* by the Surfaris, *Walk Like A Man* and *Candy Girl* by the Four Seasons, *Be My*

Baby by the Ronettes, *Da Do Ron Ron* and *Then He Kissed Me* by the Crystals, *Devil in Disguise* by Elvis Presley, *Another Saturday Night* by Sam Cooke, and the party song *Louie Louie* by the Kingsmen —ironically, since no one could understand the lyrics, it was called obscene by conservative critics. Allan Sherman also had a comedy song reach the Hot 100 with *Hello Muddah, Hello Fadduh (A Letter From Camp)*.

On May 6, historian Barbara Tuchman won the Pulitzer Prize for *The Guns of August*. In February poet Robert Frost won the Bollingen Poetry Prize. The crop of books from 1963 was excellent for children's literature. Some classic 1963 children's books included: *Where the Wild Things Are* by Maurice Sendak, *Clifford the Big Red Dog* by Norman Bridwell, *Amelia Bedelia,* by Peggy Parrish, *Hop On Pop* by Dr, Seuss, and *Encyclopedia Brown, Boy Detective* by Donald J. Sobol. Some of the more popular adult books included: *Cat's Cradle* by Kurt Vonnegut, *The Bell Jar* by Sylvia Path, *The Feminine Mystique* by Betty Friedan, *Planet of the Apes* by Pierre Boulle, *The Collected Poems1909-1962* by T.S, Elliott, *The Fire Next Time* by James Baldwin, *The Grifters* by Jim Thompson, *Ice Station Zebra* by Alistair MacLean, *The Graduate* by Charles Webb, and *Armageddon* by Leon Uris.

CHAPTER 20. 1964: VIETNAM, THE CIVIL RIGHTS ACT, THE BEATLES, MUHAMMAD ALI, AND TOPLESS SWIM SUITS

January 3, a film clip of the Beatles was shown on the Jack Paar Show making it their first appearance on American television.

January 5, Pope Paul VI visited Israel and Jordan.

January 6, the Rolling Stones toured Britain as headliners with The Ronettes.

January 7, the Bahamas became independent from Britain.

January 8, President Johnson declared the "War on Poverty."

January 9, Anti-US riots erupted in Panama. The Panamanian government severed ties with the US the following day.

January 10, the first Beatles album, *Meet the Beatles*, was released in the US.

January 11, the US Surgeon General reported that smoking may be hazardous to your health.

January 13, Hindu-Muslim riots broke out in Calcutta. Over a hundred people were killed.

January 16, *Hello Dolly* began showing at the St. James Theater in New York City. The musical was performed 2,844 times before closing. *Hello Dolly* won ten Tony Awards, a record for its time and the album later went to number one on Billboard's album chart in June.

January 18, Beatlemania began in the US when the Beatles song, *I Want to Hold Your Hand*, became their first song to appear in Billboard's Hot 100. The song appeared at number 35.

Also on January 18, final plans to build the New York Trade Center were announced.

January 23, the Twenty-Third Amendment to the Constitution went into effect barring poll taxes.

January 24, CBS purchased the television rights for NFL football for 1964 and 1965 for an astounding $24.2 million. On January 29, NBC purchased the television rights for AFL football for five years for $36 million.

January 25, the Echo 2 communications satellite was launched.

January 29, the unmanned Apollo 1, the program that would bring men to the moon, was launched as a test.

January 30, Ranger 6 was launched and made a successful trip to the moon. However the cameras that were to send back the first pictures failed.

Also on January 30, another military coup led by South Vietnamese General Nguyễn Khánh took the government of South Vietnam. This was not a CIA inspired coup and the US was caught by surprise.

January 31, a US medical report firmly linked smoking with lung cancer.

February 1, the Beatles song *I want to Hold Your Hand* went to number one on Billboard's Hot 100. Also on February 1, Governor Mathew Walsh of Indiana attempted to ban the song *Louie Louie* by The Kingsmen for obscenity.

February 2, the first GI Joe toy soldier went on sale.

February 3, the album *Meet the Beatles* went Gold.

Also on February 3, Black and Puerto Rican children boycotted New York City schools for discrimination.

February 6, France and Britain agreed to build a tunnel under the English Channel.

February 7, the Beatles landed in New York City and began their first US tour.

Also on February 7, boxer Cassius Clay converted to Islam and became Muhammad Ali.

February 9, the Beatles appeared on the *Ed Sullivan Show* and about 74 million US viewers watched their performance.

February 11, Greeks and Turks began fighting for the control of Cyprus. The United Nations sent a peace keeping force within the month.

February 16, the Beatles appeared for the second time on *The Ed Sullivan Show*. They performed six songs and were seen by a television audience of about 70 million.

February 25, Muhammad Ali knocked out Sonny Liston in the seventh round to win the heavyweight championship.

March 2, the Beatles announced they had begun filming a movie, *Hard Day's Night*.

March 4, Teamster boss Jimmy Hoffa was convicted of jury tampering. He was later sentenced to eight years in prison.

March, 8 Malcolm X resigned from the Nation of Islam.

March 9, the first Ford Mustang rolled off the assembly line. Ford formally introduced the Mustang in April with a base price of $2,368.

March 10, a US reconnaissance plane was shot down over East Germany.

March 16, President Johnson asked Congress to pass the Economic Opportunity Act as part of his War on Poverty creating local Community Action Agencies, Partnerships and Councils (Sometimes referred to as CAP Agencies) whose nonprofit boards were made up of local disadvantaged people. These agencies were given federal funds to solve their own local poverty issues. Out of these local nonprofits came the innovative programs of Head Start, Legal Aid, energy and weatherization assistance, tax preparation assistance, housing rehab programs, food pantries, job training, and meals on wheels and other senior programs.

March 20, the European Space Research Organization was established.

March 28, an 8.4 Earthquake killed 118 in Alaska.

April 2, the USSR launched Zond 1 to Venus. The craft did a fly-by but failed to transmit any data back to Earth.

April 3, Panama agreed to resume diplomatic relations with the US.

April 7, IBM began marketing the 360 Main Frame computer for commercial customers.

April 8, the unmanned Gemini 1 was launched as a test.

April 15, the world's longest bridge, Chesapeake Bay Bridge, opened for traffic.

April 19, the CIA initiated and backed a rightwing coup in Laos to replace the socialist government.

April 20, over 80% of the Black students of the Cleveland Public Schools boycotted protesting discrimination.

April 22, the World's Fair opened in Flushing Meadows, New York.

May 5, French separatists rioted in Quebec.

May 19, over forty microphones planted by the USSR were found in the US Embassy in Moscow.

May 21, the US began intelligence flights over Laos.

May 22, President Johnson presented his "Great Society."

May 24, the Beatles appeared for the third time on *The Ed Sullivan Show*. It was a taped performance, not live. They played three songs.

May 25, the US Supreme Court ruled it was unconstitutional to close schools to avoid desegregation.

May 28, the second unmanned Apollo 2 test was launched.

Also on this day the Palestine Liberation Movement (PLO) was formed.

June 1, the Rolling Stones arrived in New York City and began their first US concert tour.

June 3, designer Rudi Gernreich introduced the topless bathing suit, the monokini, to the public with a controversial picture of model Peggy Moffitt in *Women's Wear Daily*. Moffitt modeled it for free with the condition that it didn't appear in *Playboy* or other men's magazines. The photograph was republished in *Look* and several other mainstream magazines. Both Gernreich and Moffitt believed that the topless bathing suit was liberating for women. The suit and the picture received instant condemnation from many including the Catholic Church. Republicans blamed the monokini as an example of moral decline under the Democrats. The USSR said it was an example of American "capitalist decay." The suit was banned in many cities and a Chicago woman was fined $100 for indecent exposure for wearing it at a public beach.

The suit was first sold in San Francisco. On June 22, at the Condor Club in San Francisco's North Beach district a women dancer was featured in a monokini which started the wave of topless dancers in bars and men's clubs across the United States.

While topless suits never became everyday beach wear in the US, in Europe and the Riviera in particular they were embraced and women sunbathing topless is common.

June 12, Nelson Mandela was sentenced to life in prison for conspiracy in South Africa.

June 21, three civil rights workers registering Black voters in Mississippi, Michael Schwerner, Andrew Goodman and James Chaney, disappeared after they were released from a Mississippi jail where they had been jailed for allegedly speeding. They were caught by Klansmen, tortured and murdered upon their release. Seven men with Klan ties were later convicted for the murders, but three others including the Sheriff were acquitted by a hung jury.

June 23, General Maxwell Taylor was appointed the US Ambassador to South Vietnam.

June 24, the Federal trade Commission ruled that health warnings must be put on all cigarette packages.

June 26, Blacks and Whites rioted over desegregation in St. Augustine, Florida.

July 2, President Johnson signed the Civil Rights Act of 1964 into law. The Act outlawed discrimination based on race, color, religion, sex, or national origin. The bill had been promoted by President Kennedy in a speech in June of 1963. Despite turmoil in the House and a filibuster in the Senate the bill passed. President Johnson told Bill Moyers, his press secretary, that its passage would cost the Democratic Party the Southern vote "for a hundred years."

July 6, a small US Army Special Forces base on the border between South Vietnam and Laos was attacked by two Battalions of Viet Cong. The Special Forces unit defeated the attack after about five hours. The commander of the camp, US Army Captain Roger Donlan, was awarded the first Congressional Medal of Honor in Vietnam for his actions under fire at a White House ceremony in December.

July 13-16, at the Republican National Convention Senator Barry Goldwater from Arizona was nominated as the Republican candidate for President of the United States.

July 21, ethnic riots between Chinese and Malay erupted in Singapore resulting in 23 deaths and 454 injured.

July 24-27 a race riot erupted in Rochester, New York and four people were killed.

July 28, the Ranger 7 was launched to the moon. It sent back the first television footage of the moon from a satellite in close moon orbit.

August 2, the USS Maddox, while gathering intelligence data, claimed it was attacked by North Vietnamese torpedo boats. In the aftermath it was learned the Maddox had fired on the boats rather than the North Vietnamese attacking the Maddox as the US claimed. The Maddox hit three North Vietnamese torpedo boats killing four North Vietnamese sailors and wounding six others. On August 4, the US Navy again claimed that they were attacked on the open seas by the North Vietnamese Navy. It was a phony battle as there were no North Vietnamese ships in the vicinity. These two events were called "the Gulf of Tonkin Incident." Johnson then used the phony incident to get a declaration of war from Congress against North Vietnam.

Also on August 2, a race riot occurred in Jersey City, New Jersey.

August 5, the US began bombing North Vietnam.

August 6, Prometheus, the world's oldest living tree, estimated between 4,800 and 5,000 years old, was cut down by mistake by a graduate student for research. The bristle cone pine tree was located in the Great Basin National Park near Baker, Nevada.

August 7, Turkey attacked Greek forces on Cyprus.

August 11, the Beatles movie *A Hard Day's Night* premiered in New York City.

Also on August 11, a race riot occurred in Patterson, New Jersey.

August 12, a race riot erupted in Elizabeth, New Jersey.

August 15, a race riot began in the Chicago suburb of Dixmoor when a Black woman was allegedly beaten for shoplifting a bottle of gin from a liquor store. It was dubbed the "Gin Bottle Riot."

August 15, the Beatles began their second US tour playing in nine US cities and one in Toronto, Canada. The tour set records for attendance and revenue.

August 18, the USSR launched three Cosmos satellites.

August 19, the US launched the Syncom 3 communications satellite.

August 20, President Johnson signed the Economic Opportunity Act pledging a billion dollars to anti-poverty programs.

August 24-27, Lyndon Johnson was nominated for president at the Democratic Convention in Atlantic City, New Jersey.

August 28, a race riot occurred in Philadelphia, Pennsylvania.

On the same date, August 28, the Nimbus 1 weather satellite was launched.

September 3, because of his growing discomfort with Johnson, Attorney General Robert Kennedy resigned. Kennedy had been the choice of most democrats to be Vice President but he and Johnson loathed each other. At the convention Johnson had Senator Hubert Humphrey elected as the vice presidential candidate on a voice vote fearing that the usual roll call vote would give the vice presidential nomination to the popular Kennedy.

Also on September 3, more ethnic riots occurred in Singapore and 13 people were killed and over one hundred were injured.

September 4, NASA launched the first Orbital Geophysical Laboratory.

September 17, the Supremes released their hit song *Baby Love*.

September 18, monster shows became television fun as *The Addams Family* premiered on ABC and *The Munsters* premiered on September 24, on CBS.

September 27, the Warren Commission using only evidence from the CIA and FBI found that Lee Harvey Oswald acted alone in assassinating Kennedy. Rather than settling the issue as President Johnson had hoped, many doubted the Commission's findings. Robert Kennedy later said privately that the Commission's report was "a shoddy piece of craftsmanship" and didn't believe their findings. The day after his brother's death he privately asked the CIA if they had killed his brother. He believed there was a conspiracy to kill his brother which was also the conclusion of the House Assassinations Committee in 1978. In the years following a number of Warren Commission members admitted to mistakes and expressed doubts about their own conclusions. Some have said they were misled by Allen Dulles and the CIA and FBI who lead the Commission investigations. (Dulles was fired by Kennedy the previous year as CIA Director and was mysteriously appointed to the Warren Commission by Johnson.)

October 1, the Free Speech Movement was launched at the University of California at Berkley when students protested over their right to political free speech on campus. The primary goal was to promote other ideas in opposition to the American Cold War mentality. Some see this as the start of the Vietnam anti-war movement. On December 3, the police arrested over 800 student sit-in protesters at the University. But as the demonstrations only worsened the University eventually gave into the students and allowed free political speech.

Also on this date across the Bay in San Francisco cable cars were declared a National Landmark assuring their continued use.

October 4-7, Hurricane Hilda with winds up to 150 MPH struck Louisiana, and killed 38 people and did $126 million in property damage.

October 10, the Olympic Games opened in Tokyo.

October 12-13, the USSR launched Voskhod 1 with a crew of three it became the first space flight to carry more than one person. It was also the first flight without space suits.

October 14, Dr. Martin Luther King Jr. was awarded the Nobel Peace Prize. J Edgar Hoover threw a fit, telling his surrogates that "I am the one that deserves the Peace Prize." Hoover greatly disliked King before the incident and became obsessed with him afterward. He began launching investigations to find anything against King and the civil rights leaders. He claimed the civil rights movent was Soviet inspired.

Also on October 14, Nikita Khrushchev was replaced by Leonid Brezhnev as the head of the USSR.

October 16, China became the fifth nuclear power after the US, USSR, Britain and France.

October 20, a riot began at a Rolling Stones concert in Paris causing the arrest of 150 people.

October 22, French philosopher and writer Jean-Paul Sartre refused the Nobel Prize for Literature saying that, "a writer should not allow himself to be turned into an institution."

October 24, the US Air Force and Belgian paratroopers liberated about 300 White hostages from the Victoria Hotel in Stanleyville in the Congo. The Simba rebels seeking freedom for the Congo from European influence had taken the prisoners. The Belgian Paratroopers and US Air Force also evacuated about 1800 other Whites from the area. In the process about 200 Whites including 24 hostages and many Blacks were killed. On December 11, representatives from Belgium were called before the United Nations to answer charges that Belgium with US assistance was trying to force the Congo back to colonial status.

Also on October 24, Zambia gained independence from Britain.

October 25, the Rolling Stones appeared on *The Ed Sullivan Show*.

October 27, Albert DeSalvo was arrested. He would later confess to being the Boston Strangler.

October 31, Barbara Streisand's album, *People*, climbed to number one on Billboard's album chart.

November 1, showing surprising strength the Viet Cong attacked the airport at Ben Hoa near Saigon. The airport was the primary base for the US and South Vietnamese air forces. Twenty-seven US Air force planes were badly damaged or destroyed.

November 3, Johnson won the presidential election in a rout and received over 43 million votes to Goldwater's 27 million votes. Goldwater carried only the five Southern states of Louisiana, Mississippi, Alabama, Georgia and South Carolina, along with barely winning his home state of Arizona. The five Southern States voted against Johnson primarily due to his signing of the Civil Rights Act. For the first time the District of Columbia was allowed to vote in the presidential election.

November 5, Mariner 3 was launched toward Mars but the craft failed to send back any data.

November 18, FBI Director J. Edgar Hoover, according to his aides and others, was still fuming over Dr. King's award of the Nobel Peace Prize and Hoover publicly described Dr, King as the "most notorious liar." He ordered his agents to get recorded evidence of King's infidelity with the intention of blackmailing King about an extramarital affair.

November 21, the world's longest suspension bridge, the Verrazano Narrows, opened for traffic in New York City.

November 23, the Catholic Church abolished Latin as the official language the Catholic liturgy.

November 28, Mariner 4 was launched toward Mars. In 1965 it would send back the first close pictures of another planet.

November 30 the USSR launched Zond 2 toward mars but it failed to send back any data.

December 1, Dr. King angrily confronted J. Edgar Hoover about his slander campaign.

December 6, the North Vietnamese Army defeated the South Vietnamese Army at An Lao and captured the South Vietnamese Army Regional Headquarters. They held the area for some time despite several large South Vietnamese attacks.

December 11, Ché Guevara spoke at the United Nations in New York City. A woman jumped over a security fence in an attempt to kill Guevara with a knife. Two men from the Cuban Nationalist Movement attempted to strike the UN during his speech with a bazooka but it misfired into the river. There was also a bomb threat and the caller ended his threat with, "Long Live Cuba."

December 14, the US began Operation Barrel Roll, the secret and illegal US Air Force bombing of Laos.

December 15, Canada adopted the maple leaf flag.

December 20, another military coup lead by General Khanh took control of the South Vietnamese government. He was berated by Ambassador Maxwell Taylor who said, he had acted "without consulting with U.S. representatives and in disregarding our advice on important matters." Khanh responded to an American journalist two days later that if Ambassador Taylor "did not act more intelligently, Southeast Asia would be lost."

December 23, a cyclone hit struck Ceylon (now Sri Lanka) and India killing over 1800 people and causing $150 million in damage.

December 24, the Brinks Hotel in Saigon, which housed American Army officers was bombed by the Viet Cong killing two and wounding sixty others.

December 30, President Johnson cabled Ambassador Taylor and criticized his inability to control the South Vietnamese government.

By the end of 1964 there were 23, 210 American military in South Vietnam and 216 had been killed. The South Vietnamese forces had 7,457 killed in 1964. The Viet Cong and North Vietnamese forces in the country were estimated to be about 100,000.

In 1964 prices rose moderately. The average cost of a new house rose to just a little over 13,000 with the average monthly rent at $115. The cost of the average new car was $3,500. Average wages also rose to about $6,000.

Sony introduced the first the home video recorder, the VCR. In addition to *The Munsters* and *The Addams Family*, the 1964 television debuts included: *Bewitched, Gomer Pyle, Gilligan's Island, Daniel Boone, Flipper, Voyage to the Bottom of the Sea, Peyton Place, The Man from U.N.C.L.E., Underdog, Jeopardy, Another World,* and *That Was The Week That Was.* At the 1964 Emmys the winners included: *The Dick Van Dyke Show* for Best Comedy with Dick Van Dyke for Best Comedy Actor, Mary Tyler Moore as Best Comedy Actress, and Jerry Paris for Best Director of a Comedy. *The Defenders* once again won for Best Drama. *The Danny Kaye Show* won for Best Variety or Music Show and Robert Scheerer won as its Best Director.

The music of 1964 was captured by the Beatles and the British Invasion with *I Want to Hold Your Hand* and *She Loves You* which were the number one and two hits of 1964 on Billboard's Hot 100. They also had *A Hard Day's Night, Love Me Do, Please, Please, Please Me, Twist and Shout, Can't Buy Me Love, I Saw Her Standing There* and *Do You Want to Know A Secret.* Some other British invaders in the Hot 100 included: The Dave Clark Five with *Glad All Over, Bits and Pieces, Because,* and *Can't You See That She is Mine.* The British blues group, *The Animals,* also hit with *The House of the Rising Sun.*

American artists with hits in 1964 included: Roy Orbison with *Pretty Woman* and *Its Over;* The Kingsmen with *Louie, Louie* and *Money (That's What I Want),* The Four Seasons had three hits with *Rag Doll, Dawn* and *Ronnie.* Other performers who appealed to older listeners had hits which included: Dean Martin with *Everybody Loves Somebody Sometime* and *People* by Barbara Streisand.

Black artists began to be appreciated more by White audiences and appeared regularly on the Hot 100 including: The Supremes, with *Baby Love* and *Where Did Our Love Go;* Mary Wells with *My Guy, Dancing In the Street* by Martha and the Vandellas, *Under the Boardwalk* by the Drifters, and *Baby I Need Your Loving* by the Four Tops. The genres of Surf Music and Hot Rod Rock were still popular with primarily White teens with songs like *I get Around* by the Beach Boys, *Dead Man's Curve* and *The Little old Lady From Pasadena* by Jan and Dean, *G.T.O.* by Ronny and the Daytonas, and *Surfin' Bird* by the Trashmen.

At the movies in 1964 *My Fair Lady* took most of the awards as well as being number three at the box office. It won the Oscar for Best Picture, Best Director for George Cukor, and Best Actor for Rex Harrison. *Mary Poppins* was number two at the box office and won the best Actress Award for Julie Andrews. The James Bond movies *Goldfinger* and *From Russia with Love* were number one and five at the box office respectively. Some other significant films included: Several movies featuring the comedic talents of Peter Sellers including: *A Shot In the Dark, Dr. Strangelove* and *The Pink Panther. A Fist Full Of Dollars* the first of Clint Eastwood's so-called spaghetti westerns (because they were filmed in Italy) made its debut along with the Beatles' movie *A Hard Day's Night*, Richard Burton appeared in *Night of the Iguana* and *Beckett*, and the movie *Zorba the Greek* also made its debut.

Some of the most popular books of 1964 included: *I Never Promised You a Rose Garden* by Joanne Greenberg, *Games People Play* by Eric Berne, *Herzog* by Saul Bellow, *Sometimes A Great Notion* by Ken Kesey, *The Feynman Lectures on Physics* and *The Character of Physical Law* by Richard Feynman, *Trout Fishing In America* by Richard Brautigan, *Nigger* by Dick Gregory, *Up the Down Staircase* by Bel Kaufman, *Little Big Man* by Thomas Berger, *My Autobiography* by Charles Chaplin, *Understanding the Media: The Extension of Man* by Marshall McLuhan, *After the Fall* by Arthur Miller, *Is Paris Burning?* by Larry Collins, *Funeral in Berlin* by Len Deighton, and the so called "Little Red Book," *The Quotations From Chairman Mao Tse-tung.* Some popular children's books were: *The Giving Tree* by Shel Silverstein, *Charlie and the Chocolate Factory* by Roald Dahl, *Harriet the Spy* by Louise Fitzhugh, *Chitty Chitty Bang Bang* by Ian Flemming, and *Flat Stanley* by Jeff Brown.

CHAPTER 21. 1965. VIETNAM BECAME AMERICA'S WAR

January 2, Dr. King organized a large protest meeting to register Black voters in Selma, Alabama. The voter registration office in the city was open only two days per month and could only process fifteen registrations per day preventing the Student Non-violent Coordinating Committee from expediently registering over 15,000 qualified Black voters in Selma. King again risked jail as this meeting was in violation of a local Alabama judge's orders against mass meetings to prevent large civil rights demonstrations.

Also on January 2, in Vietnam the Battle of Binh Gia which had begun on December 28, came to an end. In the six days of fighting the Viet Cong killed 201 of South Vietnam's most elite soldiers along with their five American advisors. Another 192 were wounded and 68 were missing presumed dead. The Viet Cong losses were estimated at 32 killed. The Viet Cong proved that they could fight a prolonged large battle against superior air, armor and artillery and still inflict heavy damage.

January 4, President Johnson gave the first televised and evening State of the Union Address to congress. Johnson changed the traditional daytime address to evening to get a national audience. He spoke of his support for civil rights and his Great Society and said, "A President's hardest task is not to do what is right, but to know what is right."

January 6, Ambassador Maxwell Taylor summed up the situation in Vietnam for President Johnson, "We are faced here with a seriously deteriorating situation characterized by continued political turmoil, irresponsibility and division within the [South Vietnamese] armed forces, lethargy in the pacification program, some anti-US feeling which could grow, signs of mounting terrorism by the VC (Viet Cong) directly at US personnel and deepening discouragement and loss of morale throughout South Vietnam. Unless these conditions are somehow changed and trends reversed, we are likely soon to face a number of unpleasant developments ranging from anti-American demonstrations, further civil disorders, and even political assassinations to the ultimate installation of a hostile government which will ask us to leave while it seeks accommodation with the National Liberation Front and Hanoi." He concluded by advising Johnson to send more US combat forces to fight the war.

January 15, the USSR, mirroring the US program, began experimenting with using nuclear explosions for construction and peaceful uses. A 41-kiloton blast created Lake Chagan, which is a round 8,100 acre lake that is 328 feet deep. The water remains very radioactive today. The blast caused Japan to complain that the USSR had broken the Limited Test Ban Treaty when a cloud of radiation blew over Japan from the explosion.

January 22, the US launched the TIROS 9 weather satellite. It was the first satellite in a near polar orbit.

January 24, Sir Winston Churchill died. On January 30, the largest state funeral in British history was held at St. Paul's Cathedral. Official representatives from 112 countries attended and over 350 million Europeans watched the funeral live on television.

January 27, General Nguyễn Khánh overthrew the Vietnamese civilian government in a bloodless coup. Ambassador Taylor told Johnson he feared that Khánh was a Buddhist and that he could eventually displace the Catholics leading to a negotiated peace with the Viet Cong. Johnson sent a telegram to Ambassador Taylor in Saigon saying that this must not be allowed and that "the U.S. will spare no effort and no sacrifice in doing its full part to turn back the Communists in Vietnam." He then ordered more US combat units to Vietnam.

February 1, Dr. King and over 700 voting rights demonstrators were arrested in Selma for violating a local judges' order against demonstrations.

February 3, 105 US Air Force Cadets were forced to resign for cheating on their exams.

February 7, the Viet Cong attacked the airbase at Pleiku. They killed 8 Americans and wounded 128 others and destroyed or damaged 24 US aircraft. In retaliation Johnson ordered the bombing of Hanoi. Unfortunately Prime Minister Alexei Kosygin was in Hanoi at the time and he accused the US of an act of war. The Soviets began sending North Vietnam military assistance including weapons, ammunition and surface to air missiles.

February 10, the Viet Cong attacked Qui Nhon killing 23 American soldiers. In response Johnson ordered a second bombing of North Vietnam.

February 13, Johnson approved Operation Rolling Thunder an on-going air campaign to continuously bomb North Vietnam.

Also on this day Peggy Fleming and Gary Visconti won the women's and men's US Figure Skating Championship.

February 17, disagreeing with the Johnson administration, Democratic Senator Mike Mansfield said on the Senate floor that, "The Saigon government is losing its war, not for lack of equipment, but for lack of internal cohesion." He advocated that the US negotiate a solution with the North rather than expand the war. Several other Democratic Senators including George McGovern and newly elected Senator Robert Kennedy along with French President Charles De Gaulle and the Secretary General of the United Nations agreed with Mansfield. Influential columnist Walter Lippmann wrote on February 18, "For this country to involve itself in such a war in Asia would be an act of supreme folly."

However Johnson, a Democrat, also received plaudits from the Republicans, including former President Eisenhower who fully supported Johnson's policy of widening the war.

Also on February 17, the US launched Ranger 8 a very successful space mission. It landed on the moon and sent 7,137 lunar pictures back to earth.

February 18, the tiny West African nation of The Gambia became independent from Britain.

February 19, South Vietnamese Colonel Phạm Ngọc Thảo attempted a coup against General Khánh but it failed. It was later learned that Thảo was a communist agent and planned on expediting the unification with the North.

February 21, Malcolm X was assassinated by the Nation of Islam agents in New York City.

February 22, General Westmorland, the commander of US forces in Vietnam, requested two battalions of US Marines to protect the US airbase at Da Nang from Viet Cong attacks.

February 25, the US forced General Khánh, a Buddhist, to resign and replaced him temporarily with Air Marshal Nguyễn Cao Kỳ, a Catholic) pending an election of a civil government.

February 26, the Republic of Korea began sending troops to Vietnam. At their peak in 1969 South Korean forces would total just over 50,000. The ROK (pronounced "rock") Marines were one of the most feared fighting forces in Vietnam and were later accused of many atrocities.

March 2, Rolling Thunder was launched which began the regular bombing of North Vietnam. It lasted for three years. During the operation the US killed over 52,000 North Vietnamese military and 182,000 civilians and wounded hundreds of thousands. The US lost 938 aircraft and had 1,084 airmen killed or captured. As a result of the bombing the North Vietnamese shut down the diplomatic channels it had with Canada and France for exploring peace negotiations with the US and Ho Chi Minh vowed that he would push the US out of Vietnam even if it took twenty years.

March 5, a protest by high school students in Bahrain was put down harshly by the British using infantry troops. The protest began because of layoffs of Bahraini at the British controlled Bahrain Petroleum Company. As the word of British oppression spread, the country began massive civil demonstrations against British presence in Bahrain. It became known as the March Intifada. Six Bahraini were killed in the civil resistance and hundreds injured. The Intifada eventually resulted in Bahrain's independence from Britain in 1971.

March 7, Alabama State troopers some on horseback, local police and militia attacked about 600 civil rights marchers walking from Selma to Montgomery for voters rights. It became known as "Bloody Sunday." The peaceful marchers were crossing the Edmund Pettis Bridge in Selma when the police and troopers attacked with tear gas and used clubs on the marchers. Many were injured including one of the organizers of the march, Amelia Boynton, who was beaten unconscious by a state trooper. That night a White mob caught beat to death James Reeb a White Unitarian minister from Boston who had joined the march.

March 8, large units of US combat troops began arriving in Vietnam. The two battalions of US Marines landed at Da Nang and by the end of the month about 5,000 US marines were based in the city.

March 12, Vice President Hubert Humphrey had dinner with Soviet Ambassador Anatoly Dobrynin, who demanded to know why the US had bombed Hanoi when it knew that Prime Minister Alexei Kosygin was there. He angrily told Humphrey that the event could have brought war between the US and the USSR. He also formally informed Humphrey that the USSR would now supply North Vietnam in their war against the South.

March 14, Israel approved diplomatic relations with West Germany.

March 18, the USSR launched Voskhod 2 and Cosmonaut Alexei Leonov became the first person to walk in space.

March 19, Indonesia nationalized all foreign petroleum companies. The CIA began to explore the overthrow of the Indonesian government. They backed Indonesian General Suharto in a military coup and forced President Sukarno to reverse course and eventually had him replaced with a more American friendly regime.

March 21, protected by federal troops Dr. King continued the historic Selma to Montgomery voting rights march.

Also on March 21, the Ranger 9 was launched and took over 5,000 pictures of the moon in preparation of a manned flight.

March 22, the US admitted that it was using chemical weapons (Agent Orange) in Vietnam.

March 23, Gemini 3 was launched. It was the first two man fight by the US in preparation of a manned mission to the moon.

March 24-25, the first teach-in to protest the Vietnam War was held at the University of Michigan where over 3,500 students and faculty participated.

March 25, fearing a Soviet puppet state, the People's Republic of China offered military assistance to North Vietnam. Ho Chi Minh was able to play the rivalry between China and the USSR to gain maximum assistance from the two countries.

March 29, Johnson ordered two army combat brigades to Vietnam.

March 30, the Viet Cong exploded a car bomb in front of the US Embassy killing 22 people including 2 Americans.

April 7, in a television address Johnson proposed peace negotiations in Vietnam.

April 8, North Vietnam responded to the US peace proposal and said that all US troops must leave Vietnam before negotiations begin.

April 11, forty tornados struck the Midwest killing 272 people and injuring over 5,000.

April 16-18, the Mississippi, Minnesota and St. Croix rivers in Minnesota crested at record flood stages killing 14 people, destroying over 14,000 homes and causing $125 million in damages.

April 17, over 20,000 people gathered in Washington, DC to protest the US sending combat troops to Vietnam.

April 19, the first all-news radio station, WINS in New York City, began operating.

April 28, the US invaded the Dominican Republic. The Dominicans were attempting to restore democratically elected President Juan Bosch who had been overthrown by a CIA supported military junta two years before. When it appeared that the Dominicans would restore Bosch to the presidency the US sent in the Marines. Over 3,000 Dominicans were killed in the invasion and 31 US military personnel. The Marines occupied the country until October of 1966 supporting the CIA's handpicked military junta.

April 28, Richard Helms became the head of the CIA.

May 1, a Nationalist Chinese destroyer sunk four small gun boats from the People's Republic of China and damaged two others in disputed waters.

May 3, in the first regular use of satellite television the *Today Show* was broadcast via satellite.

Also on May 3, Cambodia severed diplomatic ties with the US.

May 5, the 173rd Airborne Brigade, the first large US Army combat unit, arrived in Vietnam.

May 9, the USSR attempted a soft landing on the moon with Luna 9, but it failed and crashed.

May 10-15, in the Battle of Song Be the Viet Cong overran a provincial capital about 60 miles north of Saigon. Under heavy bombing and air cover by the US the South Vietnamese Army, ARVN, was able to take it back.

May 11, the first of two cyclones in the month struck India and Bangladesh. The two cyclones killed over 35,000 people.

May 13, several Arabic nations severed diplomatic ties with West Germany over their new diplomatic relations with Israel.

May 14, China detonated their second atomic bomb as a test and a show of strength.

May 16, Ho Chi Minh accepted military aid from the People's Republic of China but refused to accept any Chinese troops in the war with the Americans and the South. He agreed that if the US attempted to invade North Vietnam then he would allow Chinese forces to be used. Ho let the US know of this arrangement to deter any US invasion.

Also on May 16, an American bomb accidently exploded at Bien Hoa airbase and killed twenty-seven Americans and four Vietnamese and destroyed about forty aircraft.

Also on this date the Campbell's Soup Company introduced Spaghetti-Os.

May 19, Patricia Harris was named Ambassador to Luxembourg. She was the first Black woman to be appointed as a US ambassador.

May 25, Muhammad Ali knocked out Sonny Liston in the first round for the Heavyweight Championship.

May 26, Australia sent 800 combat troops to Vietnam. New Zealand announced it would also send a battalion.

May 28-June 1, in the Battle of Ba Gia the Viet Cong killed or wounded 915 ARVN, took 270 prisoners, and captured 370 weapons. The ARVN claimed to have killed about 500 Viet Cong, but this appeared to be false since only 20 weapons were captured. It was a victory for the Viet Cong who then gained control of the Quang Ngai Province. The defeat caused Johnson and his advisers to realize that the Vietnam War could not be won by the ARVN and that a large US force would be necessary.

May 30, Vivian Malone became the first Black graduate from the University of Alabama.

June 3, Gemini 4 was launched with another two man crew.

June 6, the Rolling Stones released *Satisfaction*. In July the song rose to number one on the pop charts.

June 7, General Westmorland advised the Joint Chiefs of Staff that the ARVN were quickly losing the country and recommended 44 US combat battalions be sent to Vietnam to stop the Viet Cong.

Also on this day the Sony Corporation introduced their home video recorder, VCR, with a price tag of $995.

June 9-13, in the Battle of Dong Xoai the Viet Cong overran the provincial capital 60 miles northeast of Saigon. However the Viet Cong withdrew after the US began heavily bombing the city and then sent in the ARVN en masse via US helicopters. The ARVN suffered over 800 casualties. The US had 7 killed, 12 missing and 15 wounded. It was estimated that about 350 Viet Cong were killed.

June 11, Air Marshal Nguyễn Cao Kỳ took complete control of the South Vietnamese government deposing the civilian government becoming Prime Minister. General Nguyễn Văn Thiệu was appointed president by Cao Kỳ.

June 12, the Big Bang Theory on the creation of the universe became widely supported with the discovery of new celestial bodies known as blue galaxies.

June 16, Senator J. William Fulbright Chairman of the Senate Committee on Foreign Relations said in a national television address that the US should cease hostilities and negotiate directly with North Vietnam for a peaceful solution. Republicans led by Richard Nixon criticized Fulbright saying that his proposed negotiations "would be surrender on the installment plan."

June 18, the US began bombing Vietnam with B-52 bombers.

June 26, the Maldives gained independence from Britain.

June 28, Johnson ordered an additional 50,000 US Army troops to Vietnam.

June 28-30, the 173rd Airborne conducted the first search and destroy mission about 40 miles north of Saigon. No Viet Cong were found.

July 6-9 the 173rd Airborne performed another sweep about forty miles north of Saigon. They reported killing over 100 Viet Cong. A news story from the New York Times reported on July 10, that the Americans suffered 10 killed and 42 wounded and that the reports that they killed over 100 Viet Cong were greatly exaggerated.

July 16-20, Secretary of Defense Robert McNamara visited Vietnam. Upon his return he recommended that the US troop levels be increased to 175,000 and also recommended that the airstrikes on North Vietnam be increased from 2,500 per month to 4,000.

July 24, the first Russian supplied surface-to-air missile, SAM, was fired by North Vietnam and shot down a US F-4c Phantom Jet.

July 28 Johnson ordered the US military draft expanded from 17,000 to 35,000 per month.

July 29, the 101st Airborne arrived in Vietnam at Cam Rahn Bay.

July 30, Johnson signed the Medicare Bill providing health care to senior citizens. The Act went into effect in 1966.

In August the Gallup Poll conducted a survey asking, "Do you think the US made a mistake sending troops to fight in Vietnam?" and 61% answered no.

August 2, CBS television newsman Morley Safer sent his first report from Vietnam saying the Viet Cong were winning the war.

August 5, what started as minor skirmishes over disputed lands on the Pakistan-India border in April escalated to war. By the time a ceasefire was declared in September about 3,000 Indian military personnel and 3,800 Pakistani military personnel were killed. India lost 128 tanks, but captured or destroyed 302 Pakistani tanks. India won and took most of the disputed territory.

Also on August 5, the Viet Cong attacked and destroyed a US petroleum storage facility at Da Nang and over two million gallons of fuel was set ablaze.

August 6, Johnson signed the Voting Rights Act prohibiting racial discrimination in voting.

August 9, a fire began in a Titan II nuclear missile silo in Arkansas and killed 53 people. From 1962 to 1987, Arkansas hosted 18 Titan II missile sites. There were similar Titan II sites in California, Arizona and Kansas. The missiles stood 110 feet tall and each could travel some 6,000 miles at a speed of 18,000 mph. Each Titan contained nine separately targeted nuclear warheads with a destination in the Soviet Union. They were on alert 24 hours a day, 365 days a year until 1987.

August 10-17, a US Special Forces camp at Duc Co about 28 miles southwest of Pleiku came under siege by the Viet Cong. The ARVN couldn't open a highway to the base which was held by the Viet Cong. The 173rd Airborne Brigade was sent in to clear the road.

August 11, a race riot began in the Watts neighborhood of Los Angeles. What started as a traffic stop by Los Angeles Police of a Black motorist escalated into a full blown six day riot by Blacks and Latinos. In the aftermath 34 were dead, 1,032 were injured, 200 buildings were destroyed and more than 600 were damaged by fire and looting. The McCone Commission later found the causes of the riot were severe police discrimination, hopeless poverty and inequality.

August 12, a race riot erupted on Chicago's West Side in twenty-eight blocks of the Austin neighborhood.

August 15, the Beatles played before 55,000 fans at Shea Stadium.

August 17-24, Operation Starlite, the first exclusive US military attack on the Viet Cong, began when 5,500 Marines attacked the Viet Cong held territory near Chu Lai. The Marines claimed to have killed 600 Viet Cong while losing 50 Americans. The numbers of Viet Cong dead were greatly exaggerated. The Commanding General William DePuy said of the Viet Cong after the battle, "(they) did a first class job. We'd be proud of American troops...who did as well."

August 21, the Gemini 5 was launched with two astronauts.

August 31, the US Department of Housing and Urban Development was created by Congress.

September 6-13, Hurricane Betsy struck Florida and then the Gulf Coast killing 74 people in three states.

September 7, because of the Indo-Pakistani War, China announced it was reinforcing its military along the Indian border.

September 9, China declared Tibet an autonomous region of China.

September 11, the 1st CAV Air Mobile was the first complete US Army Division to arrive in Vietnam. The Division was the first to use helicopters as their main transport in and out of battle. Soon the sound of "choppers" became synonymous with the Vietnam War.

September 13, the Beatles won their first Grammy as the Best Group of 1964.

Also on September 13, conservative columnist Joseph Alsop said in the Washington Post that with the US military buildup that there was finally "a light at the end of the tunnel." This phrase would be used by both the Johnson and Nixon administrations in Vietnam even as the situation became more hopeless.

September 20, seven US warplanes were shot down over Vietnam.

September 22, General Westmorland requested 35,000 additional combat troops in Vietnam.

October 4, the USSR launched Luna 7 which crashed on the moon trying to make a soft landing.

October 15, David Miller became the first American draft resister to burn his draft card refusing to serve in Vietnam. He was arrested by the FBI and later served 22 months in prison for his actions.

October 16, widespread protests against the US involvement in Vietnam took place in forty US cities as well as some European cities.

October 28, Pope Paul VI proclaimed that Jews were not collectively guilty for the crucifixion. It was a statement that many thought that the Catholic Church should have made at the time of the Holocaust.

November 2, Norman Morrison a Quaker protested the Vietnam War by dousing himself with kerosene and burning himself to death in front of the Pentagon.

November 8, a Republic of Korea Army division landed in Vietnam and set up their base at Qui Nhon in the Binh Dinh Province on the south central coast of South Vietnam.

Also on November 8, the Australian Army saw their first action in the Ben Hoa Province.

November 9, an electrical blackout occurred in the Northeastern US and Ontario, Canada. It affected over 30 million people and lasted for thirteen hours. Human error was later blamed for the blackout. New York City had an unexpected large jump in childbirths nine months after the blackout.

November 14-18, in the first large confrontation between the US and the North Vietnamese Army began in the Ia Drang valley. About 450 men of the 1st Battalion of the 7th Infantry sent on a search and destroy mission were surrounded immediately by over 2,500 North Vietnamese from the 33rd Regiment. The US sent in reinforcements. During the battle the 305 US soldiers were killed and 524 were wounded. The North Vietnamese had 559 soldiers killed and 669 wounded. The book, We Were Soldiers Once...And Young and a later a movie was made about the battle. According to American journalist Joe Galloway who won a Bronze Star for his coverage during the battle, "the Ia Drang was the battle that convinced Ho Chi Minh he could win." He said the Vietnamese would do as they had done to the French, "they would grind down the Americans until they give up and leave."

November 16, Venera 3 was launched by the USSR. It later crashed into Venus.

November 19, the Kellogg Company introduced Pop Tarts, the toaster pastry.

November 22, Muhammad Ali beat Floyd Patterson in twelve rounds for the Heavyweight Title.

November 27, France launched its first satellite into space and became the third nation in space.

Also on November 27, about 20,000 anti-war demonstrators protested in Washington, DC.

November 30 in the aftermath of the Battle of Ia Drang Defense Secretary McNamara advised Johnson to increase American troops to 400,000 with an additional 200,000 to be added by 1967 if needed.

December 4, Gemini 7 was launched.

December 15, another cyclone struck and killed over 15,000 in Bangladesh.

Also on December 15, Gemini 6 was launched and made a space rendezvous with Gemini 7, a task that would later be needed for the manned moon flights.

December 18, Marine Corps General Victor Krulak wrote a stinging report to the Joint Chiefs of Staff saying American war policy in Vietnam has "small likelihood of a successful outcome."

In the results of the US build up in 1965 saw American troops grow from 23,310 mostly advisors at the beginning of the year to 184,314 combat troops by the end of the year. In 1964 the US had suffered 214 killed compared to 1,928 in 1965. The ARVN suffered 11,242 killed, and over 93,000 deserted. Vietnam became America's war.

In the US women's skirts became much shorter especially with the new mini skirt and men's hair much longer. The super ball and the skate board were the latest children's fads. Smoking was becoming socially stigmatized largely because of the new health warnings. The Gateway Arch in St. Louis was completed.

Prices rose; the cost of the average new house went to $13,600 and average monthly rents were $118. The average price of a new car was $2,650 and gasoline sold for 31 cents per gallon. The average annual income was $6,450.

In January the television music variety show *Hullabaloo* premiered on NBC and the Beatles appeared on *Shindig*. On April 28, *My Name is Barbara*, the Barbara Streisand television special premiered on CBS. On *October 10, the Supremes appeared on the Ed Sullivan Show. The Jack Benny Show which had been televised since 1950 and was also broadcast on the radio from 1932 to 1955 ended. Shows that made their debuts included: My Mother the Car, Lost In Space, The Big Valley, Green Acres, Gidget, I Spy, Please Don't Eat the Daisies, Hogan's Heroes, The Wild Wild West, I Dream of Jeannie, Get Smart, The Dating Game, and the day time soap, Days of Our Lives. The Dick Van Dyke Show was still the most popular show and won another Emmy as did Dick Van Dyke for Best Actor. The Defenders was still the most popular drama and won Emmys for director and writing.*

On March 2, one of the most popular and most successful films of all time *The Sound of Music* was released. Another blockbuster of 1965 was *Doctor Zhivago*. Both made well over a hundred million dollars at the box office. Although *Thunderball* was another major hit it fell considerably short of this mark at about sixty-three million dollars. Other major box office hits included: *Those Magnificent Men in Their Flying Machines, The Great Race, Shenandoah, Von Ryan's Express* and three comedies *Cat Ballou, How to Murder Your Wife* and *What's New Pussy Cat*. The Oscars went to *The Sound of Music* for Best Picture and Best Director. The Best Actor went to Lee Marvin in *Cat Ballou.*

In music no one artist topped the charts. *Wooly Bully* by Sam the Sham and the Pharaohs, *I Can't Help Myself (Sugar Pie Honey Bunch)* by the Four Tops and *Satisfaction* by the Rolling Stones were Billboard's top three songs of 1965. Other top tunes included: The Supremes with *Stop In the Name Of Love* and *Back in My Arms Again*, The Rolling Stones also had another hit *The Last Time*, The Four Tops also had *It's the Same Old Song*, The Righteous Brothers hit with *You've Lost That Loving Feeling* and *Unchained Melody*, the Beatles continued with *Help* and *Ticket to Ride*, The Beach Boys had *Help Me Rhonda* and *California Girls*, Herman's Hermits had three hits *Can't You Hear My Heart Beat, I'm Henry the Eighth I Am*, and *Mrs Brown You've Got a Lovely Daughter*. Other hits were *My Girl* by the Temptations, *Mr. Tambourine Man* by the Byrds, and *We Gotta Get Out of This Place* by The Animals. *What's New Pussy Cat* and *It's Not Unusual* were hits for Tom Jones. Elvis Presley made the top ten once again with *Crying in the Chapel.*

In the 1965 the new books included the sci-fi classic *Dune* by Frank Herbert, *God Bless You Mr. Rosewater* by Kurt Vonnegut, *Hotel* by Arthur Hailey, *The Looking Glass War* by John Le Carrié, *Flight of the Falcon* by Daphne Du Maurier, *In the Heat of the Night* by John Dudley Ball, *Cool Hand Luke* by Don Pearce, and *The Autobiography of Malcolm X*. Children's books included: *Fox in Socks* by Dr, Seuss and *A Charlie Brown Christmas* by Charles Schultz. *A Thousand Days: John Kennedy in the White House* by Arthur Schlesinger Jr. was released in 1965 and won the Pulitzer Prize in 1966.

CHAPTER 22. 1966: VIETNAM ESCALATION, CIVIL RIGHTS AND RIOTS, AND THE BEATLES VS. JESUS

January 1, the transit workers in New York City went on strike shutting down the subways for twelve days.

Also starting on January 1, it was ruled that all cigarette packs must be labeled with the warning, "Caution : cigarette smoking may be hazardous to your health."

January 3, the US Marine base at Khe Sanh near the DMZ between the two Vietnams came under heavy fire. It would largely remain under fire for the rest of the entire war.

January 7, Dr. King announced start of the Chicago Freedom Movement to bring the civil rights movement to northern states.

January 8, The Beatles' Rubber Soul Album became number one on the Billboard album chart and their song We Can Work It Out went to number one on the pop charts. Also on this day, the Who and the Kinks performed on the last television broadcast of Shindig.

January 10, India and Pakistan signed a peace accord.

Also on this day Representative Julian Bond was denied his seat in the Georgia legislature for his opposition to the Vietnam War.

January 11, over 550 people were killed in mudslides during heavy rains in Rio de Janeiro.

January 12, President Johnson said in a news briefing that the US military will stay in South Vietnam until communist aggression is ended.

January 17, two US planes, a B-52 bomber and a refueling tanker collided over the Mediterranean, near Spain, causing the bomber to lose three hydrogen bombs. Two bombs dropped near Palomares, Spain. The bombs' safety mechanisms prevented explosions but there was still a significant problem from the radioactive active wreckage. It took over 2,000 US troops to clean up the radioactive soils with 1,400 tons shipped to the US for disposal. The third bomb fell into the sea and was later recovered intact. The

US later settled over 500 health claims with Spanish residents whose health was damaged by radiation.

This story attracted a lot of media attention. Similar incidents occurred in the US but were hushed up. Two hydrogen bombs and a highly radioactive core lie in undetermined locations in the Warsaw Sound off the Georgia coast, in Puget Sound in Washington and in the Swamplands near Goldsboro, North Carolina. Many Americans have suffered unreported health problems and cancer from these accidents.

January 29, "the storm of the century" a blizzard with heavy snowfall up to 100 inches in some places lasted for four and a half days in the northeast. Winds were over 60 miles per hour with gusts up to 100 mph. Some drifts completely covered two story houses. The arctic blast that caused the storm also brought record low temperatures in the South the following day and Mississippi saw a state record of minus 19 degrees. Another record was set in Alabama of minus 27 degrees Fahrenheit.

January 31, the USSR launched Luna 9 and on February 3, it made a soft landing on the moon after so many failed previous attempts.

February 9, the Dow Jones Index hit a record just short of 1,000 at 995 points. The American economy was doing well.

February 17, the French launched a second satellite into earth orbit.

February 22, the USSR launched Kosmos 110 with two dogs.

February 23-25 military coups took over the governments Uganda, and Ghana. There was also a coup in Syria.

March 3, a large tornado in Jackson, Mississippi killed 57 people.

March 4, Beatle John Lennon infamously said, "Christianity will go. It will vanish and shrink. I needn't argue about that; I'm right and I'll be proved right. We're [the Beatles] more popular than Jesus now; I don't know which will go first—rock and roll or Christianity. Jesus was all right but his disciples were thick and ordinary. It's them twisting it that ruins it for me." His narcissist statement enraged the American Christian community. Many others thought he and the Beatles had become too self-important. The statement would haunt the band as their appearances drew less people, causing them to give up touring in the US.

March 6, Barry Sadler's jingoistic music attempt at putting a heroic spin on the war in Vietnam, *The Ballad of the Green Berets*, seemed to work as it became the number one hit on the charts.

March 9-10, the US and the South Vietnamese lost the Battle of the A Shau Valley. The North Vietnamese overran an American Special Forces base and took the A Shau Valley as their territory. The US suffered 100% casualties with five killed and twelve seriously wounded. The South Vietnamese force also stationed at the base was also devastated with only 122 of 410 surviving. The A Shau Valley was fortified by the North Vietnamese and later became a sanctuary for their troops and served as a staging area for the massive TET Offensive in 1968. Sergeant Major Bennie Adkins was years later awarded the Congressional Medal of Honor by President Obama in 2014 for his heroic defense of the base.

March 10, General Nguyễn Chánh Thi was relieved by Premier Nguyễn Cao Kỳ as the Division I Commander of the ARVN forces in Hue. He was accused of "siding with the Buddhists against the [Catholic] government." South Vietnam was about 80% Buddhist but the South Vietnamese government and the ARVN officer corps was predominately Catholic. The Buddhists began several weeks of anti-American and anti-government demonstrations. It was dubbed by the Americans as the "Buddhist Uprising" and the US Ambassador and General Westmorland strongly advised the South Vietnamese to end it with brute force, which they did. The Americans had now turned the large Buddhist majority against them. The US also intervened in the Buddhist Uprising with the CIA and some Special Forces. On April 9, the US Marines blocked a Buddhist ARVN force from entering Hue, a large Buddhist center. The Buddhist ARVN force was attempting to protect the Buddhists and the temples from the five Divisions of ARVN Rangers sent to Hue by Cao Kỳ to forcibly put an end to the Buddhist influence in the city.

March 11, in a military coup backed by the CIA General Suharto took over the government of Indonesia.

March 16, Gemini 8 with two astronauts was launched.

March 25, the Beatles posed with mutilated dolls and butchered meat for the cover of their album *Yesterday and Today*. The album caused more negative publicity for the group which was still suffering from Lennon's "more popular than Jesus" remarks. The cover was called gratuitously violent and tasteless by most critics. The initial reaction to its release was harsh and the album covers were then pulled from stores.

March 27, anti-war demonstrations were held in the US, Europe and Australia.

March 31, over 25,000 anti-war demonstrators marched in New York City.

Also on March 31, the USSR launched Luna 10 which on April 3 became the first spacecraft to orbit around the moon.

April 11-12, the Battle of Xa Cam My about 42 miles east of Saigon took place. The 134 men of A Company from the 1st Infantry Division were sent on a search and destroy mission and were ambushed and surrounded by about 400 Viet Cong. The Company took 80% casualties with 36 killed and 76 wounded. Those that survived were extracted when the US Army began an artillery barrage firing at a rate of five to six rounds per minute. The Viet Cong left the area after losing 41 men. The US Army claimed more Viet Cong were likely killed but stated that their bodies were extracted when they left the area. Two posthumous Congressional Medals of Honor were given and a Silver Star was given to one of the survivors.

Also on April 11, Frank Sinatra recorded his biggest hit *Strangers in the Night* which would go to number one on Billboard's Hot 100.

April 26, a 7.5 earthquake struck Tashkent Uzbekistan in the USSR. It destroyed most of the town killing about 200 and leaving 300,000 people homeless.

April 24-May 17, a large infantry action called Operation Birmingham, involving the US 1st Infantry Division and the ARVN 5th Division successfully cleared a wide area North of Saigon opening highway 13 to the north which had been under control of the Viet Cong.

May 6, Premier Cao Kỳ told General Westmorland that the Northern Provinces of South Vietnam were under the control of Buddhists who he claimed were working with the Viet Cong and North Vietnamese. He sought more US help against the Buddhists.

May 13, US education funding was denied to 12 Southern school districts for violations of the 1964 Civil Rights Act.

Also on this day the Rolling Stones released *Paint it Black* a song that would become synonymous with Vietnam. It went to number one on Billboard's Hot 100 in June.

May 17, responding to Premier Cao Kỳ's request, an American helicopter gunship opened fired on a civilian Buddhist demonstration near the airport at Hue. The Buddhists retaliated by burning down the US Information Service Library in Hue.

May 16, Chairman Mao released the infamous *May 16 Notification* that launched the Cultural Revolution in China. The revolution set goals to destroy what they called the "four olds" meaning China's old customs, culture, habits and ideas. China suffered a cultural and economic setback as its leaders, intellectuals, institutions, temples, and culture were destroyed or replaced. The revolution formally ended with the death of Mao in 1976.

May 18, the US Marines fired on a Buddhist friendly ARVN unit near Hue. The ARVN unit then attempted to blow up a bridge leading into the city to keep anti-Buddhist ARVN forces from entering the city to attack the Buddhist civilians but they were attacked by the US Marines. Many of these troops then switched sides and joined the Viet Cong.

May 26 to June 1, several Buddhist monks immolated themselves to protest the South Vietnamese government, the ARVN and their US protectors. The US Consulate in Hue was set on fire by Buddhist demonstrators. The ARVN killed over 150 Buddhist civilians and wounded over 700 more. The ARVN also lost about 150 men almost all of these were Buddhists killed by other ARVN forces. The Americans had 23 Marines wounded while fighting the Buddhist ARVN troops.

On May 26, the South American country of Guyana, formerly British Guiana, declared its independence from Britain.

June 1, Surveyor 1, the first of seven US spacecraft to make soft landings on the moon was launched. All of the seven are still on the moon. However two of the seven failed to make a soft landing and crashed failing to complete their mission. The Surveyor Program was an important step toward the first manned moon landing.

June 3, Gemini 9 was launched with its two man crew.

June 6, Stokely Carmichael began the Black Power Movement.

June 8, a large F5 tornado struck Topeka, Kansas, and killed sixteen people and injured hundreds of others. It became the first tornado to cause over $100 million in damages.

June 13, the US Supreme Court delivered the Miranda decision making it law that a police suspect must be given their rights before questioning.

June 25, the USSR launched Kosmos 122 the first Soviet weather satellite.

July 1, Medicare went into effect giving American seniors affordable medical care for the first time.

July 4, the Beatles and particularly John Lennon's arrogance was on display on a trip to the Philippines. The Beatles were attacked by a crowd after Lennon insulted the Filipino first lady Imelda Marcos.

July 3-7, after a day of 103° temperatures in Omaha a large crowd of African-Americans gathered in the streets to enjoy the cooler evening. They were ordered to disperse and go indoors by the Omaha police, and a riot began which lasted three days. Many stores and businesses in Omaha were looted and burned. The National Guard was mobilized to put down the riot. The rioting resumed on August 1, when a Black teenage boy was shot and killed by an off-duty White policeman while looting.

July 4, President Johnson signed the Freedom of Information Act into law which would become effective the following year.

July 8, a strike by 35,000 airline workers from five airlines crippled the nation's air travel by shutting down about 60% of the industry. The strike lasted until August 19, when their wage demands were granted.

July 10, the US Lunar Orbiter 1 was launched to find and map safe places for a landing in a manned trip to the moon.

July 12, the first Puerto Rican parade was held in Chicago. On that day a young Puerto Rican man was shot by the Chicago police. The crowd attending the parade erupted into began to riot which lasted for seven days. In the aftermath the City met with representatives of Chicago's Puerto Rican community to hear their grievances concerning police discrimination and brutality, discrimination in housing and hiring, and bias in the Chicago schools.

July 14, Richard Speck broke into a house that functioned as a dormitory for eight student nurses. He spent the night torturing, raping and killing eight young women. A ninth had hidden and then escaped through a window.

July 15-August 3, the US conducted Operation Hastings to take back the northern part of South Vietnam from the North Vietnamese Army which had infiltrated and controlled much of the area. US intelligence estimated the number of North Vietnamese troops in the area at about 8,000. Under air cover about 8,000 US marines with 3,000 troops from the ARVN 1st Division attacked the area. In the two weeks of fighting more than 10,000 helicopter and 1,677 bomber sorties were flown. The US secured the area from the North Vietnamese with 126 killed and 448 wounded. The ARVN lost 21 and had 40 wounded. The US claimed it killed over 700 of the North Vietnamese Army (NVA) and captured 17 NVA.

July 18, Gemini 10 was launched with two astronauts.

July 18-23, a riot occurred in the Hough neighborhood of Cleveland. It began when a bar owned by a White man posted a sign that said "No water for niggers." When a Black woman and a Black customer were denied a drink of water an angry crowd gathered outside the bar. The Cleveland police attempted to disperse the crowd and made things worse and a riot began. The Ohio Governor called out the National Guard and in the aftermath four Blacks were killed, over 30 people were critically injured and 275 were arrested. The area which had been red-lined by the banks and had suffered disinvestment for years suffered even worse economic hardship after the riots.

July 31, a Christian group in Alabama burned Beatles products in a protest against John Lennon's remarks that The Beatles were more popular than Jesus.

August 1, a Marine Corps sharpshooter murdered his wife and mother in Austin, Texas. He then went to the University of Texas and from the observation deck of a building called "the Tower" he proceeded to kill 16 people and wounded 32 others during a 90 minute killing spree before being killed by the police.

August 3, the South African government banned Beatles records because of Lennon's remarks. They also banned television performances and interviews of the group.

August 5, Dr. King led a peaceful march for housing equality in Chicago. As the marchers went through a White neighborhood they were attacked with bricks, stones and bottles. Dr. King was struck and felled by a rock. He rose and continued the march. Afterward he noted, "I have seen many demonstrations in the South but I have never seen anything so hostile and so hateful as I've seen here today." However the marches were successful and by the end of August, Mayor Daley agreed to new policies to assure non-discrimination against Blacks in public housing and the Chicago banks agreed to stop red-lining neighborhoods and discriminating against non-Whites in mortgage and small business lending.

August 12 to 29, The Beatles began their third US tour. It was the last tour of the US by the group. They gave seventeen US shows and two in Toronto, Canada. The tour was plagued with controversy and what many called a disrespectful superior attitude by the group. They received some threats and at a press event in Memphis, Tennessee, and were pelted with rotten fruit and vegetables. More Christian groups burned Beatles records. Later that night, someone threw a fire cracker on stage and the band members all thought they were being shot at. Although the tour was profitable, the numbers of tickets had declined very dramatically from their previous tours. In San Francisco, after much publicity for their final live concert, they sold less than 25,000 tickets at Candlestick Park — which can hold 42,500. The group decided to give up touring and became a studio band focusing on record production.

August 24, the USSR launched Luna 11 to orbit the moon.

August 27, a race riot began in Waukegan, Illinois.

September 5, Jerry Lewis began his first annual television program to raise funds for children with muscular dystrophy.

September 6, a race riot began in the Summerhill neighborhood of Atlanta following an incident of police brutality. In the aftermath Stokely Carmichael and other Black Power advocates were accused by the Atlanta police of inciting the riot. The four day riot ended with one death and twenty serious injuries.

September 8, *Star Trek* premiered on television which rapidly developed a cult-like following.

September 11, the Rolling Stones performed for the third time on the *Ed Sullivan Show*. The band was beginning to eclipse the Beatles in popularity.

Also on this day Gemini 11 was also launched for a seventy-one hour flight.

September 14-November 24, in an attempt to remove the Viet Cong from control of Tay Ninh Province the 197th Light Infantry Brigade launched Operation Attleboro. In a month and one half of fighting the Brigade managed to gain control over the Province. However it was a tactical retreat by the Viet Cong to Cambodia and they returned as soon as the 197th retreated back to their bases. In the operation 155 US soldiers were killed and 494 were seriously wounded. The US claimed that they killed over 2,000 Viet Cong but it was unconfirmed. They did capture 44 Viet Cong during the fighting.

September 21-October 11 hurricane Inez struck the Caribbean and Florida Keys killing more than a thousand people and caused over $226 million in damages. More than 84,000 were left homeless.

September 30, the former British colony of Bechuanaland received its independence and became Botswana.

October 4, the former British colony of Basutoland gained independence and became Lesotho.

October 15, the Black Panther Party was created by Bobby Seale and Huey Newton.

October 16, Joan Baez and 123 others were arrested for protesting the military draft in Oakland, California.

October 21, in the village of Aberfan in South Wales a mountain of mining debris caused a landslide smashing twenty houses and a school killing 144, people mostly children between the ages of 7 to 10.

October 26, the US aircraft carrier *Oriskany* in the Gulf of Tonkin caught fire when a flare accidently went off in a locker. The fire killed 44 air crewmen and injured 156 others on the ship.

October 29, the National Organization of Women was founded to promote women's rights.

November 2, the Cuban Adjustment Act passed which allowed 123,000 pro-American Cuban refugees living in the US to become permanent residents.

November 4, flooding on the Arno River in Florence, Italy, killed 101 people and damaged or destroyed millions of dollars of art works in the city.

November 8, with anti-war demonstrations and Black riots happening across the US, Johnson's democrats lost 47 seats in the House and 3 in the Senate during the midterm elections. The former McCarthy era Hollywood informer and B grade movie actor, Ronald Reagan, was also elected as Governor in California.

November 11, Gemini 12 was launched for a four day flight.

November 12, eighteen-year-old Robert Smith entered a beauty college in Mesa, Arizona, with a gun and forced five women and two children into a back room where he proceeded to shoot them one at a time in the head killing five. The victims were a twenty-seven-year-old woman, three teenage girls and a three-year-old child. Smith later told police he did it to become famous and make a name for himself.

November 16, Dr. Sam Sheppard who was jailed for murdering his wife was given a new trial and found not guilty. Sheppard had served nine years in prison for the murder. The television show and subsequent movie *The Fugitive* was based upon his story.

November 18, the Roman Catholic Church ended their rules against eating meat on Fridays.

November 24, "a killer smog" blanketed New York City and was blamed for 169 deaths; it brought about stronger air pollution laws.

November 30, Barbados gained independence from Britain.

December 8, the US and Soviet Union signed a treaty banning nuclear weapons in space.

December 18, *How the Grinch Stole Christmas* by Dr. Seuss aired for the first time on CBS.

December 19, the CIA wrote a classified memo to the Joint Chiefs of Staff putting the number of Viet Cong in South Vietnam at 600,000 or more. This estimate greatly contradicted the Military's estimate of 282,000 that had been given to the President. It was Johnson's first inkling that the military was not being honest with him about Vietnam.

December 21, the USSR launched Luna 13 which successfully soft landed on the moon three days later.

In 1966 the US troop levels in Vietnam increased to 385,300. There were about 25,000 Korean troops in Vietnam and small numbers of troops from Thailand, Australia, New Zealand and the Philippines as Johnson attempted to make the war appear to be an international effort. The US Selective Service drafted more men, 382,010, compared to a little over 230,000 in 1965 with just a little over 112,000 in 1964. The Gallup Poll showed that a majority of Americans still supported the war at 52% but it was a significant drop from the 61% who had supported it the year before. Anti-war sentiments were rising.

In 1966 inflation rose over 3% and began to grow as the war expenditures took their toll. The average price of a new house rose to $14,200 and the average cost of a new car to $2,650 with gas at 32 cents per gallon. The average annual income rose to $6,900. Clothes were now "Mod" with the new styles originating from Carnaby Street in London. The mini skirt became popular for young women.

Color televisions were in more homes as they became more affordable. *In January the premiere of Batman with Adam West premiered on ABC.* The television show *Amos and Andy* was pulled from syndication after charges of racism were brought by civil rights groups. A number of other popular shows ended this year including *The Dick Van Dyke Show*. In addition to *Star Trek* and *Batman* other debuts in 1966 included: *The Monkees, That Girl, Family Affair, Rat Patrol,*

Mission Impossible, and the two game shows, *Hollywood Squares* and *The Dating Game*. *The Dick Van Dyke Show* went out on a high note winning the Emmys for Best Comedy and Best Actor and Actress for Dick Van Dyke and Mary Tyler Moore. *The Fugitive* won as the Best Drama.

None of the movies of 1966 touched the box office success of the previous year which saw two movies gross over $100 million. *The Bible* was the top grossing film at just under $35 million. *Hawaii, Who's Afraid of Virginia Wolf*, and *The Sand Pebbles* also grossed over $30 million. Other popular films of 1966 included: *Blow Up, The Good the Bad and the Ugly, The Russians Are Coming the Russians Are Coming, Georgy Girl, Alfie, The Blue Max* and *The Professionals*.

1966 was a good year in music. On September 12, the popular television rock music show, *The Monkees*, made their debut on NBC. The most popular song of 1966 was *The Ballad of the Green Berets*. The Mamas and Papas had *Monday, Monday* and *California Dreamin'* in the top ten. The Righteous Brothers again had one of the year's top hits with *Soul and Inspiration*. Other top 100 tunes included: The Monkees with *The Last Train to Clarksville*, The Supremes with *You Can't Hurry Love* and *You Keep Me Hangin' On*, the Beach boys with *Good Vibrations, the Sloop John B.* and *Barbara Ann*, the Four Tops *I'll Be There*, the Temptations *Ain't to Proud to Beg* and *Beauty is Only Skin Deep*, Johnny Rivers *Poor Side of Town* and *Secret Agent Man*, Simon and Garfunkel had three *I am a Rock, Homeward Bound* and *Sounds of Silence*, the Rolling Stones had *Paint It Black* and *19th Nervous Breakdown*, the Sinatra family had two hits with *Strangers In the Night* by Frank and *These Boots Are Made for Walking* by his daughter Nancy. The Beatles still had four hits with *We Can Work It Out, Paperback Writer, Nowhere Man*, and *Yellow Submarine*.

Some of the most popular books of 1966 included: *Flowers for Algernon* by Daniel Keyes, *In Cold Blood* by Truman Capote, *The Last Picture Show* by Larry McMurtry, *Tai Pan* by James Clavell, *The Confessions of Nat Turner* by William Styron, *Valley of the Dolls* by Jacqueline Susann, *Fantastic Voyage* by Isaac Asimov, *The Moon is a Harsh Mistress* by Robert Heinlein, and *The Proud Tower* by Barbara W. Tuchman.

CHAPTER 23. 1967: HIPPIES, THE SUMMER OF LOVE, THE SUMMER OF RACE RIOTS, AND VIETNAM PROTESTS

January 3, Carl Wilson of the Beach Boys was indicted for draft evasion.

January 6-15, in Operation Deckhouse Five the US Marines and ARVN attacked the Mekong River region in amphibious assaults to clear the area of Viet Cong. It was mostly show and accomplished little. The US lost seven troops the ARVN one and the US claimed to have killed 21 Viet Cong. Most of the Viet Cong had left the area prior to the attack.

January 8-26, the US Army began Operation Cedar Falls to clear a Viet Cong stronghold near Saigon known as the Iron Triangle. Over 30,000 US and ARVN troops were involved. Most of the Viet Cong retreated from the area but some were entrenched in vast tunnel systems. The US Army attacked these tunnel systems with some success. During the operation the US had 72 killed and 337 seriously wounded. The ARVN had 11 killed and 8 wounded. The US claimed to have killed 750 Viet Cong and captured 280. The US then defoliated much of the area with Agent Orange and destroyed the Vietnamese villages in the area which were deemed friendly to the Viet Cong and placed the residents of these destroyed villages in harsh relocation camps. The operation made even more enemies for the US among the civilian population. Two days after the US Army left the area the Viet Cong returned and within a week a US intelligence report claimed the area was again "crawling with VC."

January 13, the Rolling Stones appeared for the fourth time on the *Ed Sullivan Show* becoming the most popular British band and eclipsing the Beatles.

January 14, in an event that launched the counterculture and the Hippie movement, the Human Be-In occurred at San Francisco's Golden Gate Park. On October 6, 1966 the State of California passed a law banning the sale or use of LSD and the Human Be-In was in opposition to this along with a rejection of war and racism and "middle class morality." Dr. Timothy Leary set the tone with his speech to the crowd which told them to "Turn on, tune in and drop out." The beat generation poets Alan Ginsberg and Gary Snider were also speakers. The music was provided by the Jefferson Airplane, the Grateful Dead and by Janis Joplin with Big Brother and the Holding Company. About 20,000 mostly young people attended the event.

On this same day the *New York Times* reported that the US Army was conducting secret germ warfare experiments.

January 15, in the first Super Bowl Green Bay defeated the Kansas City Chiefs. The Super Bowl became the most important US sports event of the year eclipsing the World Series.

January 26, a blizzard in Chicago dropped 23 inches of snow on the city. Over 800 buses and 50,000 automobiles had to be abandoned as the roads became impassable.

January 27, a fire in the Apollo I command module killed astronauts, Grissom, White and Chaffee during a launch rehearsal.

February 7, a fire in a Montgomery, Alabama restaurant killed 25 people.

February 12, in a sex and drug scandal singer Marianne Faithful was found nude and wrapped in a fur rug in a police raid of Keith Richard's house. Faithful, Richards and Mick Jagger were all arrested on drug possession charges. Faithful's career was wrecked by the incident while the public was much more forgiving of Jagger and Richards.

February 22-May 14, the US launched the largest offensive of the war so far with Operation Junction City. It was also the largest airborne operation since Operation Market Garden in WWII. The purpose of the operation was to capture what American intelligence thought was the fortified operational headquarters for all Viet Cong and North Vietnamese Army (NVA) in South Vietnam. Although the exact location was unknown the Army planned to drop in 30,000 men in a surprise attack to surround the area just northeast of what was labeled the as the Parrot's Beak near the Cambodian border. After the war it was learned that a woman agent had infiltrated the social circles of both Premier Cao Ky and General Westmorland and had tipped off the Viet Cong and NVA before the operation and most escaped into Cambodia. It was also learned after the war that the real operational HQ was kept small and very mobile to assure that it would not be captured or destroyed. The operation was largely a failure but the US did manage to kill about 2,728 NVA who did not have time to escape to Cambodia before the operation. The Army used this to claim a "significant victory." The US forces had 282 killed and over 1,500 wounded. The North Vietnamese re-entered the area after the US troops left.

March 1, the House voted 307 to 116 to exclude Congressman Adam Clayton Powell Jr. from the House of Representatives. In January the House had stripped him of his Committee Chairmanships when he had come under scrutiny for misuse of public funds including lavish trips abroad and unjustified and large congressional staff salaries which included his ex-wife while she was living in Puerto Rico. Despite this Powell was later re-elected. The Supreme Court later ruled against the exclusion saying that Powel could not be excluded by Congress because he had been legally re-elected.

March 6, Muhammad Ali was inducted into the US Armed Forces. Ali refused military service claiming that he was a conscientious objector citing his Muslim religious beliefs saying that he could not kill unless commanded by Allah. He also said at the time, "No Vietcong ever called me nigger." On March 22, Ali's boxing title was stripped from him. On June 20, he was convicted by an all-White jury and given five years in prison and a $10,000 fine. He appealed and was allowed to go free pending the appeal process. However he was denied a boxing license in every state and also denied his passport so he could not box overseas. As a result Ali lost his prime years as a boxer from 1967 to 1971 waiting for his appeal. In 1971 the US Supreme Court overturned his conviction.

Also on March 6, Svetlana Allilujeva, the daughter and youngest child of Joseph Stalin, stated her desire to defect to the United States while in India. It became official on March 9, 1967.

March 14, the first player draft of the newly combined NFL/AFL football league was held.

March 24, a "teach-in" was held at the University of Michigan to protest the war in Vietnam.

March 28, UN Secretary General U Thant made a public proposal for peace in Vietnam. It was ignored by the US.

April 1, the newly created US Department of Transportation began operations.

April 3, 113 eastern Europeans attending the World Amateur Hockey Championship in Vienna asked for asylum.

April 7, conflict erupted between Israel and Syria. The USSR had given false intelligence to Syria that Israel was massing troops to attack. This prompted Syria to strike Israel in a border clash. Syria then asked Egypt for assistance. The conflict escalated. On June 5, the Israelis attacked the Syrian and Egyptian air forces in a pre-emptive strike. The attack effectively destroyed their two air forces and the subsequent war lasted only six days. It resulted in a decisive victory for Israel with the capture of the Old City of Jerusalem, the Sinai Peninsula, the Gaza Strip, West Bank, and the Golan Heights.

April 9, the first Boeing 737 made its first flight.

April 15, in Central Park in New York City 158 young men burned their draft cards to protest the war, including Gary Rader a US Army Green Beret.

April 17, Surveyor 3 was launched and on April 20, made a successful soft landing on the moon.

April 20, the US bombed Haiphong Harbor in North Vietnam.

April 21, the US Marines launched Operation Union attacking the North Vietnamese 2nd NVA Regiment in the Que Son Valley. The fighting lasted until May 16, with 110 Marines killed, 2 missing and 473 wounded. It was reported that the NVA lost 865 men. President Johnson awarded the 5th Marines the Presidential Unit Citation for their actions.

Also on April 21, a CIA backed military junta succeeded in taking control of the government in Greece.

April 24, at a news conference General Westmoreland chided US anti-war demonstrators saying that the enemy had "gained support in the United States that gives him hope that he can win politically that which he cannot win militarily."

April 25, abortion was legalized in Colorado.

May 1, Elvis Presley and Priscilla Beaulieu were married.

May 3, African-American students protesting discrimination seized the finance building at Northwestern University in Evanston, Illinois.

May 4, Lunar Orbiter 4 was launched by the US. On May 7, it began orbiting the Moon.

May 6, a group of 400 protesting students took over the administration building at Cheney State College in Pennsylvania, a historic Black university. (Now Cheney University)

May 10, the Stockholm Vietnam Tribunal declared that the US was the aggressor in Vietnam.

May 11, the 101st Airborne division launched Operation Malheur search and destroy missions in the Quang Ngai Province. The operation was divided into two parts and lasted until August 2, 1967. It resulted in 81 US paratroopers killed and claimed that 868 Viet Cong and NVA were killed. USAID also said over 6,400 civilians were killed in these conflicts.

May 19, the US heavily bombed Hanoi.

May 22, a fire in a department store in Brussels killed 323 people and injured more than 150.

May 30, Biafra declared its independence from Nigeria. The move started a civil war beginning in July which lasted until January 1970. It resulted in more 725,000 military casualties on both sides and over 3 million civilian deaths. Biafra lost and remained part of Nigeria.

June 2, a race riot began in the Roxbury section of Boston. Racial riots would occur across the US in the summer of 1967. In June riots broke out in Atlanta, Boston, Buffalo, Cincinnati, and Tampa. In July they occurred in Baltimore, Cairo, Cambridge, Chicago, New York, Milwaukee, Minneapolis, New Britain, and Rochester, with the largest occurring in Detroit and Newark. In August a riot occurred in Washington, DC. FBI Director J. Edgar Hoover told Johnson that the riots and anti-war demonstrations were communist inspired and controlled, a claim without any proof or merit. The US began training US Army personnel in riot control. President Johnson doubted Hoover and the FBI's conclusions and created the Kerner Commission to investigate why the riots were occurring.

June 8, during the Six Day War, Israel attacked the USS Liberty, a US intelligence ship, in international waters. The attack resulted in the deaths of 34 Americans and wounded 171 others and severely damaged the ship. Israel claimed their attack was an error. Documents have come to light proving that Israel knew it was attacking an American inteligence ship and did so to prevent the US from gaining intelligence on them. The US also knew it was a deliberate attack. The Americans and Israel both suppressed the story in the media, claiming it was an unfortunate accident.

June 10, the USSR broke off diplomatic relations with Israel over the Six Day War.

June 12, the US Supreme Court struck down all state laws against interracial marriage.

Also on this date the USSR launched Venera 4 to explore Venus.

June 14, the US launched Mariner 5 to explore Venus.

June 15, California Governor Ronald Reagan signed a bill making abortions legal in California. He would later campaign against abortions when he ran for president endearing himself to the religious right.

June 18, over 50,000 attended the International Monterey Pop Festival.

June 19, Paul McCarthy admitted that he and the three other Beatles took LSD.

June 23, in Los Angeles 10,000 peace marchers demonstrated against the war in front of the Century Plaza Hotel where Johnson was attending $1,000 per plate Democratic fundraising dinner. The LAPD sent 1,300 officers to forcefully break up the demonstration with night sticks. Hundreds of demonstrators were injured and 51 were arrested. The LAPD Chief Tom Reddin admitted later that the department indirectly worked with four private security agents who infiltrated the march-planning group. The agents were hired by a security company that was retained by the Century Plaza Hotel. The peace protest organizers said that one of those spies was an agent provocateur, who constantly suggested such acts as breaking into the hotel and attacking President Johnson. Chief Reddin also later admitted that the police singled out and purposefully beat the women demonstrators with night sticks. Despite strong protests by its reporters on the scene, the *Los Angeles Times* reported in favor of the police and covered up their brutality.

June 23-25, President Johnson and Soviet Premier Alexei Kosygin met in Glassboro, New Jersey. They met to discuss problems in the Mideast and Vietnam. Although no agreement was made in this meeting, Kosygin assured the US that North Vietnam would be willing to discuss peace, which eventually led to the Paris Peace Talks.

June 25, over 400 million watched the first global satellite program, the British pop rockers concert *Our World Television Special*.

June 27, the first ATM machine began operation in England.

July 1, American Samoa's constitution became effective allowing self-governance for the American territory.

July 2-14, the US marines launched Operation Buffalo south of the Vietnamese DMZ. During the operation 159 Marines were killed, 845 were wounded and one was taken prisoner. The Marines reported that they killed 1,290 NVA and took one NVA prisoner.

July 4, Britain's Parliament decriminalized homosexuality.

July 16, many were injured and 34 inmates were killed in a prison riot in Florida.

July 24, the Beatles caused another controversy by signing a petition to legalize marijuana.

July 29, an accidental explosion on the US Navy aircraft carrier Forrestal in the Gulf of Tonkin killed 134 sailors and did over $100 million in damage.

August 2, Lunar Orbiter 5 was launched by the US.

August 3, an additional 45,000 soldiers were sent by President Johnson to Vietnam.

August 7, the People's Republic of China agreed to give North Vietnam an undisclosed amount of military equipment as a grant.

August 21, the People's Republic of China announced that it shot down two US bombers over its territory.

August 22 and 29, the final episode of the television show *The Fugitive* attracted 78 million viewers and had a Nielsen Rating of 72% which is still the third highest in US television history.

August 27, Naomi Sims became the first Black model on a US magazine cover.

August 30, the US Senate confirmed Thurgood Marshall as the first Black US Supreme Court Justice.

September 1, General Nguyễn Văn Thiệu who had led the military junta which took control of the civilian government was elected the president of South Vietnam. He remained in control of Vietnam until the fall of Saigon in 1975.

September 4-15, the Marines began Operation Swift another search and destroy mission in the Que Son Valley. In conclusion the marines lost 127 men and had 362 wounded. They claimed to have killed over 600 NVA.

September 5-22, Hurricane Beulah struck Haiti, Mexico and Texas killing 688 people and destroying over a billion dollars in property.

September 8, Surveyor 5 was launched by the US and on September 10, it made a successful landing on the Moon.

September 11, small military confrontations occurred on the India/China border.

October 6, the Haight-Ashbury Hippies had large community a funeral to mark the death of the Hippies.

October 8, Ché Guevara was killed in Bolivia.

October 16, large anti-war protests occurred in 30 US cities.

October 17, the Battle of Ong Thanh in Bin Doung Province was a defeat for the US Army 1st Cavalry to the Viet Cong. In a search and destroy mission 144 US soldiers were surrounded by about 1400 Viet Cong. They suffered 98% casualties with 64 killed, 2 missing, and 75 wounded.

Also on October 17, the musical *Hair*, made its debut off-Broadway. It would move to Broadway the following April. It was immediately controversial for its nudity, profanity, anti-war opinions and drug references.

October 18, students at the University of Wisconsin, Madison protested Dow Chemical Company's recruitment at the University. Dow and Monsanto were the makers of Agent Orange and Napalm for the Vietnam War. During the protest 76 students were injured by police.

October 21-23, over 100,000 people protested the war in Washington, DC. Norman Mailer later wrote *Armies of the Night* about the event.

October 26, Navy pilot and future senator and presidential candidate John McCain was shot down over Vietnam and taken prisoner.

October 27, a Catholic priest, Fr. Phillip Berrigan, a WWII veteran, went into a Baltimore Draft Board and drenched the draft records in blood.

November 2, President Johnson held a secret meeting of "the Wise Men," a group of senior American leaders to ask their advice on how to get the American people to support the Vietnam War. Their advice was to give more optimistic reports about the war. This started an era of false enemy body counts, dubiously claimed victories and overly optimistic progress reports, along with the prodigious granting of medals to US military personnel in Vietnam for heroism.

November 3, the NVA attacked Dak To in the Kon Tum Province. The battle lasted until November 22, and while the Americans secured the area temporarily it was a costly victory. In 19 days of fighting the US suffered 1,441 wounded, 351 killed, 15 missing, 40 helicopters lost, and three USAF planes downed. The ARVN also suffered heavy casualties with 73 killed, 18 missing and several hundred wounded. The US claimed it killed 1,400 NVA but this figure is largely disputed.

November 7, President Johnson signed a bill establishing the Corporation for Public Broadcasting System (PBS). It would begin operations on October 5, 1970.

November 9, the Apollo Program was successfully launched with an unmanned Apollo capsule on a Saturn V rocket into Earth orbit.

November 13, Carl Stokes was elected as Mayor of Cleveland becoming the first Black mayor of a major US city.

November 17, Surveyor 6 became the first manmade object to take off from the Moon. The US was quickly perfecting their technology to make a manned mission to the Moon.

November 20, the US Census reported that the US population had reached 200 million.

November 21, the US commander in Vietnam, General Westmorland said in a press conference, "I am absolutely certain that whereas in 1965 the enemy was winning, today he is certainly losing."

November 22, the British government banned the Beatles song, I am the Walrus for drug references.

November 30, Julie Nixon the daughter of Richard Nixon announced her engagement to David Eisenhower, the grandson of President Eisenhower.

Also on November 30, Senator Eugene McCarthy of Minnesota announced he would run for the Democratic nomination for president against Johnson as an anti-war candidate.

December 3, Dr. Christian Barnard made the first successful heart transplant in South Africa.

December 5, pediatrician Dr. Benjamin Spock was arrested with poet Allan Ginsberg and others for demonstrating against the Vietnam War.

December 13, the temperature plunged to a record 19 degrees Fahrenheit in San Diego which then saw its first snowfall.

December 28, Muriel Siebert became the first woman to own a seat on the New York Stock Exchange.

In 1967 the US troop levels were at 485,600 by the end of the year. During the year 11,153 Americans had been killed. It was reported that North Vietnam had lost 140,000 people both civilian and military.

The inflation rate in 1967 reached was about 3%. The average new home cost $14,250 and the average rent was $125. The average new car cost $2,750 with gasoline at 33 cents per gallon. The average income was $7,300. *Rolling Stone* magazine made its debut in November. The war in Vietnam overshadowed everything.

On May 22, Mr. *Roger's Neighborhood* made its debut on NET (NET was the forerunner to PBS). Television in 1967 was particularly interesting with the first Super Bowl, the final episode of *The Fugitive* and the British Pop Rockers concert *Our World* becoming the first live via satellite world transmissions. A new soap opera, *Love Is a Many Splendored Thing* made its debut on CBS but was censored because it showed interracial couples. CBS soap operas also made the switch from live to taped performances. *Gunsmoke* was cancelled but brought back by public protest causing the popular *Gilligan's Island* to be bumped off the air.

Television debuts included: *The Newly Wed Game, The Smothers' Brothers Comedy Hour, The Carol Burnett Show, The Flying Nun, Spider-Man, Ironside,* and *Mannix.* The game show *What's My Line?* that had been on the air since 1950 made its last broadcast. The Emmy for the Best Comedy went to *The Monkees,* the Best Drama to *Mission Impossible,* and the Best Variety Show to *The Andy Williams Show.* The Emmys for Best Comedy Actors went to Don Adams of *Get Smart* and Lucille Ball for *The Lucy Show.* The Best Dramatic Actors were Bill Cosby in *I Spy* and Barbara Bain in *Mission Impossible.* Don Knotts and Frances Bavier won as the Best Supporting Comedy Actors for their roles as Barney Fife and Aunt Bee on *The Andy Griffith Show.*

The movies of 1967 were particularly good with a number of classics. The top picture at the box office was *The Graduate.* The other important films included: *Cool Hand Luke, Guess Who's Coming to Dinner, Bonnie and Clyde, The Dirty Dozen, Valley of the Dolls, To Sir with Love, In the Heat of the Night, Casino Royale, In Cold Blood, Wait Until Dark, Barefoot In the Park,* and the first X rated hit *I am Curious Yellow.* The Academy had a difficult selecting with the quality of the films in 1967 and their selections reflected this. The Oscars went to *In the heat of the Night* for Best Picture and Best Actor for Rod Steiger. Mike Nichols won Best Director for *The Graduate.* Katharine Hepburn won best Actress for *Guess Who's Coming to Dinner,* and Best Supporting Actor went to George Kennedy for *Cool Hand Luke,* with Best Supporting Actress to Estelle Parsons for *Bonnie and Clyde.*

In March the British rock groups The Who and The Cream made their US debut on Murray the K's Easter Show. The top tunes in Billboard's Hot 100 of 1967 included four by the Monkees: *I'm a Believer, A little Bit Me a Little Bit You, Day Dream Believer* and *Pleasant Valley Sunday.* The Beatles had just two with *All You Need is love,* and *Penny Lane.* The Supremes had three hits with *Love is Here and Now You're Gone, The Happening* and *Reflections.* The top three songs of the year were *To Sir with Love* by Lulu, *The Letter* by the Box Tops and *Ode to Billie Joe* by Bobbie Gentry. Other significant hits were *Gimme Some Lovin'* by the Spencer Davis Group, *Whiter Shade of Pale* by Procol Harem, *Brown Eyed Girl* by Van Morrison, *Ruby Tuesday* by the Rolling Stones, *Light My Fire* by the Doors and the Jefferson Airplane hits *Somebody to Love* and *White Rabbit*.

In February the Bollingen Prize for Poetry was awarded to Robert Penn Warren. The favorite books of 1967 included: *The Outsiders* by S.E. Hinton, *Rosemary's Baby* by Ira Levin, *The Chosen* by Chaim Potok, *Nicholas and Alexandra* by Robert K. Massie, *Where Eagles Dare* by Alistair Mclean, *I'm Okay, You're Okay* by Thomas A. Harris, *Logan's Run* by William F. Nolan, *The Medium is the Message* by Marshall McLuhan, *The Naked Ape* by Desmond Morris, *House Made of Dawn* by N. Scott Momaday, *Topaz* by Leon Uris, *Death of a President* by William Manchester, *A Garden of Earthly Delights* by Joyce Carol Oates, *Black Power: the Politics of Liberation* by Stokely Carmichael, and *Coffee, Tea or Me* by Trudy Baker.

CHAPTER 24. 1968: THE VIOLENT YEAR: THE ASSASSINATIONS OF KING AND KENNEDY, RIOTS, NIXON COMMITTED TREASON AND THE TET OFFENSIVE

January 1, despite a truce agreement negotiated by the Pope for New Year's Day the US Army moved to set up a new camp near the Cambodian border in Tay Ninh Province. The Viet Cong in the area saw this as a provocation and attacked. The US had 23 killed and 153 wounded. The US claimed to have killed over 300 which were unconfirmed. A later movie about the Vietnam War, *Platoon* by Oliver Stone, who was a soldier in the battle, was made about this battle. Author Larry Heinemann, who also was a soldier in the battle, wrote a book about it, *Black Virgin Mountain: A Return to Vietnam.*

January 5, Anti-war protester Dr. Benjamin Spock, America's baby doctor, was indicted for conspiring to violate the draft law.

January 14, Super Bowl II saw the Green Bay Packers defeat the Oakland Raiders. The game became a fixture in American culture surpassing the World Series as the premier sporting event in the US.

January 21-July 9, the US Marine base at Khe Sahn came under siege by the NVA. The aftermath of these battles saw 1,520 American Marines, Army and Air Force personnel killed over 7,600 wounded. The ARVN and other South Vietnamese forces lost between 1,500 and 2,000 men and over 250 captured. The US publicly claimed to have killed between 10,000 and 15,000 NVA however the secret official report stated that only 1,602 enemy bodies had been counted and estimated about 5,500 killed. The NVA official history lists 2,469 NVA killed by the Americans and ARVN. The US abandoned the base July 9, and the official NVA history said that the Khe Sahn area came under complete control of the NVA by July 15, 1968.

Also on January 21, a B-52 bomber with a nuclear bomb crashed in Greenland.

January 22, Apollo 5 was launched. It was the first unmanned test of the lunar module that would land men on the Moon.

January 23, the US spy ship the USS Pueblo was captured by North Korea in international waters. It is believed that the North Koreans were testing the US to see if they would respond to a possible North Korean attack of the South. The North Koreans believed that the US was overwhelmed with Vietnam and would possibly not defend the South. The US responded with Operation Combat Fox, putting a large naval force in the seas around the Korean peninsula and about 33,000 additional troops into South Korea. The Pueblo and its crew were held for a year in North Korea before their release in early December.

Earlier the North Koreans sent a commando team to assassinate South Korean President Park, called the Blue House Raid, which was unsuccessful, but 25 South Korean soldiers, one policeman and four US soldiers were killed. The North Koreans also attempted to create revolutionary cells (like the Viet Cong in Vietnam) in South Korea which were operated by about 2,500 North Korean agents who were eventually killed or captured during the following year. These events have become known as the Second Korean War which saw 299 South Koreans killed, 550 wounded and 43 Americans killed and 111 wounded during the conflict. The US Congress authorized awarding the Armed Forces Expeditionary Medal for US troops serving during in this undeclared conflict (including the author).

January 30, the Viet Cong and the NVA launched the Tet Offensive, the largest offensive of the Vietnam War at the time. More than 80,000 Viet Cong and NVA troops attacked over 100 cities including 36 of the 44 provincial capitals. The US and ARVN lost control of many cities including the key City of Hue. It would take the US a month to recapture Hue which was almost completely destroyed it in the battle. A commander was heard to remark, "We had to destroy it to save it."

The Viet Cong also targeted Saigon, attacking the downtown commercial area, the Palace, Tan Son Nhut airbase, and the most devastating to the Americans, the US Embassy. A Viet Cong sapper team held part of the embassy grounds for six hours.

The Tet offensive lasted until late September. Although the US was able to regain all the lost ground, the Battle for Khe Sahn and Tet were the turning points in the war. The battles destroyed American morale in Vietnam and encouraged the growing anti-war movement back home. It became clear that South Vietnam would only continue to exist if a large and permanent US combat force was kept in the country.

February 1, photojournalist Eddie Adams photographed the Saigon Police Chief executing a Viet Cong officer by shooting him in the head on a public street. The gruesome photograph won the 1969 Pulitzer Prize and turned more Americans against the war.

Also on February 1, the Pennsylvania Railroad and the New York Central railroad merged which at this time was the largest corporate merger in US history.

And also on February 1, Richard Nixon announced his candidacy to be President.

February 8, a college sit-in protest in a South Carolina Whites only bowling alley was raided by Highway Patrolman and three Black college students were killed.

February 12, In the American friendly village of Phong Ni, the Republic of Korea (ROK) Marines got into a dispute with local elders and massacred about 79 people, mostly women and children. Some of the women had been raped and sexually mutilated, including a woman survivor who had both breasts cut off. The US Army arrived, provided first aid and took some surviving victims to hospitals. The Korean commanders lied and claimed it was the Viet Cong in Korean uniforms that had caused the incident. The US Army covered up the massacre, but years later the Korean commander admitted to the atrocities. Two weeks later on February 25, the ROK Marines massacred the village of Hà My. They killed 135 women children and old men and buried them in a shallow ditch. This too was covered up by the US Army.

February 13, civil rights demonstrations were held at the University of Wisconsin at Madison and the University of North Carolina at Chapel Hill.

Also on February 13, in answer to the Tet Offensive the US sent an additional 10,500 soldiers to Vietnam.

February 15, Former Congresswoman Jeannette Rankin led over a thousand women who protested the Vietnam War in Washington, DC.

February 16, the first 911 emergency phone services went into operation in Haleyville, Alabama.

February 18, over 10,000 people protested the Vietnam War in West Berlin.

February 19, Florida teachers went on strike. It was the first statewide teachers strike.

February 29, the *Kerner Report*, commissioned by President Johnson to find the causes of racial riots was released. The report warned, "Our nation is moving toward two societies, one black and one white, separate and unequal." It blamed racism, police violence and brutality, economic injustice and poverty, and lack of decent housing as causes for the riots.

March 4, stating that poverty is a problem for all races Dr. King announced plans for a US Poor People's Campaign. Dr. King pledged to fight against economic injustice for all races.

March 9, Lima Site 85 was a secret remote mountain top US Air Force facility in Laos. It was manned by 19 USAF personnel and protected by the Hmong Army. It was part of the US secret war in Laos. The site was a radar base used in USAF air attacks on North Vietnam and Laos. It came under artillery attack the day before and was then surrounded by NVA Special Forces. The site was captured by the NVA with 12 of the 19 USAF personnel killed. It was the largest one day loss of USAF personnel in the Vietnam War. The Hmong Army also lost 42 men.

March 12, President Johnson barely edged out anti-war Senator Gene McCarthy in the New Hampshire Primary with 49% of the vote to 42% for McCarthy. Although he won, the closeness of the primary began to raise doubts about Johnson's ability to be re-elected.

March 13, the US Army conducted nerve gas tests at the Dugway Proving Ground in Utah. Over 3,000 sheep in nearby fields were accidently killed. The US Army denied their culpability in the incident until a US Army report blaming the sheep deaths on nerve gas was discovered and reported by reporter Jim Woolf the Salt Lake Tribune in 1998.

March 16, US Army soldiers massacred the villages of My Lai and My Khe. In total 504 old men, women and children, including infants, were tortured, raped and killed. Like the ROK massacres some of the women were gang raped and sexually mutilated. The US Army managed to cover up the incident for a year. Three US soldiers were shunned and even denounced by Congress for trying to save the Vietnamese civilians and halt the massacres. Later twenty-six soldiers were charged with war crimes but never convicted. Their platoon leader Lt. William Calley Jr. was found guilty of 22 murders and was given a life sentence. However he only served three and a half years under House Arrest and was then pardoned by President Nixon.

Also on March 16, Robert Kennedy announced his candidacy for President in opposition to the war and Lyndon Johnson.

Also on March 16, General Motors produced their 100 millionth automobile.

March 18, the Congress repealed the gold standard which required a gold reserve to back US currency.

March 19-23, students at the historically Black Howard University in Washington, DC staged a five day sit-in closing down the University to protest the war and demanding a more culturally appropriate Black curriculum.

March 31, the Vietnam War was now haunting Johnson and he was demoralized by the military's lies and poor assessments. Johnson felt he was in a hole he couldn't get out of and on this date he shocked the nation when he announced he would not seek another term as president.

April 4, Dr. King was shot and killed at a motel in Memphis, Tennessee. James Earl Ray was blamed for the assassination. Ray briefly confessed but later said that his confession was forced by the FBI who threatened him with the death penalty and also told him that if he didn't confess that they would convict his father and brother as accessories. The King family believe that Ray was not the killer and a subsequent civil trial also proved that the police and others were involved in a conspiracy to kill King.

After King was assassinated riots broke out across the United States and also in some overseas military units. The largest riots took place in Washington, DC, Baltimore, Louisville, Kansas City and Chicago. President Johnson sent in US Army units and many state governors mobilized their national guards to quell the riots. The FBI and the US Army also sent in undercover agents to infiltrate radical and civil rights groups who they believed were encouraging the riots. Some of these undercover agents were provocateurs and encouraged violence by the groups so that the government could declare martial law and use more physical methods. Richard Nixon and the Republican Party then used the riots and White racism to foment a

White backlash and then successfully campaigned on bringing about "law and order" in the 1968 elections.

April 6, the assassination of King led to an ambush of two Oakland police officers by the Black Panthers in revenge for the murder of King. The officers were seriously wounded. Afterward the police surrounded the Black Panthers in a house and a shoot-out began. Two Black Panthers surrendered. One, a sixteen-year-old boy Bobby Hutton, was killed by police while unarmed and in police custody after his surrender.

The Academy Awards and the opening of the professional baseball season were postponed on April 8, due to King's assassination.

April 11, President Johnson signed the 1968 Civil Rights Act.

April 18, London Bridge was sold to an American company to be disassembled and re-assembled in Arizona.

Also on April 18, 178,000 employees of the Bell telephone company went on strike.

April 24, students protesting the war took over Columbia University in a sit-in and shut it down for a week.

April 26, Box Car, the largest nuclear test of Operation Crosstie, a series of 48 underground nuclear tests in Nevada during 1967-1968, was detonated. During the Cold War between 1945 and 1992 the US detonated 1,054 nuclear explosions. Most were underground but above ground, midair, and underwater tests were also conducted. Nevada was the primary site of these tests, but there were also tests in Alaska, Colorado, Mississippi, New Mexico, and in the South Pacific. The Soviets conducted about as many at their site Eastern Kazakh/Semipalatinsk.

Also on April 26, a student anti-war sit-in seized the administration building at Ohio State University.

May 2, gold reached a record all time high of $39.35 per ounce.

May 6, a wave of civil disobedience and riots hit France and lasted through the month. It began with a protest by French university students and spread to factories bringing 11 million workers out on strike. The French government and police attempted to quell the protests with force which made matters worse. The events polarized French politics into two camps.

May 10, the US and North Vietnamese envoys began secret discussions in Paris about an eventual peace. This was the result of a previous meeting in Glassboro, New Jersey when Soviet Premier Kosygin suggested to Johnson that the North Vietnamese may be willing to talk.

May 12, the Reverend Ralph Abernathy and Coretta Scott King carried on Dr. King's Poor People Campaign. They brought 3,000 people to Washington, DC to set up a tent city for six weeks. They presented five demands to the US government including: Living wage jobs, a secure income or safety net for the under employed and unemployed, fair access to land by small farmers, access to capital for small businesses, women and minorities, and a greater role for poor people in the decisions of government. It ended in shambles. President Johnson and the Congress refused to hear their concerns and treated them as an insurrection. Without King the group's leadership was divided. The FBI's secret and illegal COINTELPRO program used FBI and police agents to infiltrate the group with provocateurs. They caused disorder, destroyed their leadership and encouraged violence. At one point a group of escaped mental patients caused havoc and some crime in the tent city. When a White man was shot and robbed near tent city the Campaign was blamed. On June 20, the police fired tear gas into the tent city claiming someone had thrown rocks at them. On June 24, over one thousand police officers forcefully cleared the camp and arrested 288 people including Reverend Abernathy.

May 15, severe thunderstorms caused F5 tornadoes to strike Jonesboro, Arkansas killing 36 people. Tornadoes struck in Charles City and Oelwein, Iowa killing 18 people and injuring 619 others. It was the most deadly one day of tornadoes in US history.

May 21, the USS Scorpion a nuclear powered submarine went missing. The wreckage was found later on the ocean bottom near the Azores Islands. All 99 crewmen perished in the accident. A US Navy investigation released years later suspected that one of the sub's torpedoes may have malfunctioned and exploded.

May 25, the Gateway Arch in St. Louis was dedicated.

June 1, at the age of 87 years Helen Keller died.

June 5, Robert Kennedy was shot and killed in Los Angeles, California after his victory in the California Democratic Primary. The contest was hotly contested between Kennedy and McCarthy. The win by Kennedy in California and his expected win in New York where he was the US Senator would have given Kennedy the Democratic nomination for President. He was assassinated by Sirhan Sirhan in a hotel after his victory speech. Many continue to believe that it was a conspiracy as multiple witnesses, including Kennedy's staff reported that there was more than one shooter and that more bullets were fired than Sirhan's pistol could fire. A subsequent audio tape has also proven this. The Los Angeles Police department inexplicably destroyed all evidence from the scene that could have proven the exact amount of bullets fired and coerced and altered witness' statements. It has also been alleged by Sirhan's psychiatrist and his attorneys that Sirhan was a victim of the CIA's MK-ULTRA mind control program. Sirhan was in a trance the day of the assassination and still has no memory of the assassination even under deep hypnosis. Sirhan also had no animosity toward Kennedy nor did he have any motive.

June 18, the US Supreme Court ruled that all racial discrimination in housing for sale or rent was illegal.

June 21, Supreme Court Chief Justice Earl Warren resigned.

June 26 The Bonin Islands, including Iwo Jima, were given back to Japan after 23 years of occupation by the US Navy.

July 1, the CIA's Operation Phoenix officially went into effect in Vietnam. The program had been active as a covert operation since 1965, but was sanctioned openly on this date. Operation Phoenix was a program that sought to destroy the Viet Cong by any means necessary. The Operation was a US and South Vietnamese terrorist campaign that used sexual humiliation, torture, assassination, and murder of Vietnamese men, women, and children who they suspected of being communists or sympathizers.

In the Operation's interrogation centers CIA and US Army Special Forces interrogators used gang rape, rape by eels, snakes, and dogs. They often raped their victims in front of their spouses or children. They attached electrical devices to vaginas and testicles to shock prisoners into submission. They sadistically called this "the Bell Telephone Hour" and frequently used US Army field telephones to deliver the electrical shocks. They used dogs to bite and mutilate prisoners. They beat prisoners with iron bars to break bones. They had men, women, and children prisoners fight each other to death with the promise the winner would be set free and then bet on the results. The CIA conducted medical, torture and mind control experiments on the prisoners. US Army personnel committed random acts of murder and collected the ears of their victims as trophies. The torture techniques learned in Operation Phoenix were later used by the CIA and US military elsewhere especially in Iraq and Afghanistan and in the war against terror.

Many of the victims were innocent civilians and had nothing to do with the Viet Cong. Frequently Operation Phoenix personnel used the program to have sex with innocent Vietnamese women they desired. They also chose random men, women and children, sometimes whole families to kill and torture just to make an example of them to their village. Frequently villagers with grudges against a person or family would report them as Viet Cong to Operation Phoenix personnel. During the torture program victims were forced to name others who were Viet Cong and many lied and named other innocent people to stop their torture or to save their own lives.

In 1971 a Congressional Hearing uncovered these horrors. Several former soldiers testified to the torture used. In response to an inquiry from Congress the CIA and military command in Vietnam issued a directive that reiterated that they had based the anti-Viet Cong Phoenix Program on South Vietnamese laws. They lied and said that the program was in compliance with international law and the laws of land warfare. CIA Director William Colby insisted that the program was effective, but admitted that some field commanders had "committed some abuses." He then destroyed almost all of the CIA files on Operation Phoenix before Congress could investigate the program. It was later learned that the destruction of Operation Phoenix files was ordered by Henry Kissinger. The operation was supposedly ended at this time but it continued as F6, a highly secret program until the war's end. The US officially lists about 82,000 torture victims of Operation Phoenix with over 40,000 killed, but the Vietnamese give a numbers almost double this.

July 18, the Intel Corporation, a pioneer in computers, was founded by physicist Robert Noyce, the co-inventor of the integrated circuit, and chemist Gordon Moore. In 2014 Intel had total assets of about $92 billion.

July 20, the first international Special Olympics were held in Chicago.

July 23, in a race riot in Cleveland 11 people were killed.

July 25, Pope Paul VI issued his encyclical Humanae Vitae making birth control and abortion a sin. The publication of the encyclical marked the first time in the twentieth century that open dissent from the laity about teachings of the Church was voiced widely and publicly. American and

Canadian Catholic leaders openly disagreed and advised their followers to "decide according to their conscience." In its history the Catholic Church had previously approved abortion as a way for poor women to limit the size of their families, but prior to this decision the Church had said it was a woman's choice and took no position. The decision would lead to a contentious divide in US politics.

August 4, over 100,000 attended the Newport Pop Festival in California.

August 5-8, the Republican National Convention in Miami, Florida nominated Richard Nixon for President and Spiro Agnew as Vice President. Nixon edged out Governor Ronald Reagan of California with more delegates despite the fact that Reagan had slightly more votes in the primaries than Nixon. Nelson Rockefeller was a distant third in the vote but actually had more delegates than Reagan. One of the Rockefeller supporters at the convention was a Young Republican, Hillary Rodham (not yet Clinton), who had worked in Rockefeller's campaign.

Also on August 8, while Nixon was being nominated in Miami, a race riot erupted in the city.

August 20-21 the USSR invaded Czechoslovakia with 750,000 troops, 6,500 tanks and 800 planes to shut down "Prague Spring" which had sought greater freedoms for Czechoslovakians from the USSR.

August 21, Marine Private First Class James Anderson Jr. became the first African-American to receive the Congressional Medal of Honor. He was awarded it posthumously for jumping on a grenade to save his fellow Marines.

August 22-30, the Democratic National Convention in Chicago nominated Hubert Humphrey for President and Senator Edmund Muskie as Vice President. Although Senator McCarthy had many more votes in the primaries than Humphrey, the delegates won by Robert Kennedy split between McCarthy and George McGovern which gave President Johnson and the party bosses' the opportunity to force Humphrey's nomination to the dismay of the anti-war movement. During the convention anti-war demonstrators in Chicago were beaten by police on orders of Chicago Mayor Richard Dailey a Humphrey supporter. Television news scenes of the police beating anti-war protestors, convention delegates and members of the press repulsed many and scarred Humphrey's nomination.

August 28, US Ambassador John Gordon Mein of Guatemala was killed in an attempted kidnapping by rebels. He was the first US Ambassador killed in the line of duty.

September 6, led by writer/poet Robin Morgan about 150 women's liberation advocates protested the Miss America Pageant in Atlantic City, New Jersey.

September 16, on the advice of his aides Richard Nixon to appear more friendly and approachable, Nixon appeared on the comedy show *Laugh-in*.

September 23, the Tet Offensive finally ended in Vietnam.

September 30, the Boeing Corporation publicly unveiled their new jumbo jet, the 747, to the public and media.

October 2, just ten days before the opening of the 1968 Summer Olympics in Mexico City the police and the military fired on student demonstrators killing more than 300 people. The demonstrators were protesting Mexican government oppression.

October 6, the US began Operation Sealord to use Swift Boats and other means to control the Mekong Delta region.

October 11, Apollo 7 was launched. The mission produced the first live television broadcast from space and tested docking with the lunar module.

October 12, the 1968 Sumer Olympic Games in Mexico City began.

October 14, the US Army and Marines announced they would send about 24,000 troops back to Vietnam for a second tour.

October 16, two Black athletes Tommy Smith and John Carlos caused a controversy at the Olympics when they bowed their heads raised their hands in a black power salute when the US National Anthem played just after they were awarded their Gold and Bronze medals in the men's 200 meter race.

October 20, Jacqueline Kennedy married Greek shipping tycoon Aristotle Onassis in Greece.

October 31, citing progress at the peace talks in Paris President Johnson told the American people he will stop the bombing of North Vietnam. The news was a blow to Nixon who feared that a peace agreement would aid Humphrey's election. Humphrey surged in the polls.

On the secret advice of Henry Kissinger who was at the Paris Peace talks, Nixon through the American diplomat Anna Chennault committed treason by persuading the South Vietnamese President Nguyễn Văn Thiệu to boycott and kill the peace talks. He persuaded Thiệu by bribing him saying that when he (Nixon) was elected President that Thiệu would be given a much better deal.

Johnson had illegally and secretly bugged the Nixon campaign and knew about Nixon's treasonous act and told Republican Senator Everett Dirksen that he would have Nixon tried for treason for bribing Thiệu to kill the peace deal. Dirksen told Nixon. Not knowing that Johnson had bugged his conversations Nixon then called Johnson and lied to him saying that he hadn't talked to Thiệu. Johnson taped this phone call as well and threatened to publicly expose Nixon as a traitor and liar but was counseled by Humphrey and others not to do so because the public would also find out that Johnson had bugged Nixon's campaign. As a reward for his leaking information to Nixon and his advice about stopping the peace talks, on December 2, President-Elect Nixon named Kissinger his National Security Advisor. He would also later be named Secretary of State.

November 5, the traitorous Richard Nixon barely edged out Humphrey in the election 43.4% to 42.7%. Alabama Governor George Wallace of the American Independent Party had 13.5% of the vote and won the five states of Alabama, Arkansas, Georgia, Louisiana, and Mississippi.

November 11, Operation Commando Hunt began and widened the secret war in Laos. It was a covert USAF and Naval air operation that lasted until March 29, 1972 which saw millions of tons of bombs dropped on Laos in an attempt to stop supplies and men from North Vietnam going south. Despite self-proclaimed success the fierce bombing actually stopped less than 3% of the men and materials flowing south. The operation was a failure.

November 11, John Lennon and his then mistress, Yoko Ono, appeared nude on their 2 Virgins album cover. The cover was filmed at Lennon's home studio after an all-night session with Yoko Ono while Lennon's wife Cynthia was on vacation with her friends.

November 14, the anti-war movement promoted National Turn in Your Draft Card Day.

Also on November 14, Yale University announced it would admit women.

November 20, in a mine disaster 78 men were killed in Farmington, West Virginia.

November 22, the television show *Star Trek* became controversial as the first television inter-racial kiss between a White actor William Shatner as Captain Kirk and Black actress Nichelle Nichols as Lt. Uhura was aired. The scene caused protests.

November 27-30, the first National Women's Liberation Conference was held at Lake Villa, Illinois.

December 3, Elvis Presley's comeback special aired on television.

December 21-27, the first men to orbit the moon, the three Apollo 8 astronauts, became the first people to see the dark side of the moon and the entire earth from space.

December 23, the crew of the USS Pueblo was released from North Korea.

December 28, over 100,000 attended the Miami Pop Festival.

In 1968 the US had 549,500 troops in Vietnam and 16,592 US men were killed in action and 87,388 wounded. The Khmer Rouge was officially formed in Cambodia as the war spread to other nations. The Koreans had 50,000 men in Vietnam, Australia 7,660, Thailand 6,000, and there were a small number of troops from the Philippines and New Zealand. The ARVN had about 820,000 in uniform but these forces were less reliable after the Tet Offensive and the Buddhist uprising.

In 1968 inflation went to 4.27%. The average cost of a new house was $14,950 and average rent rose to $130 per month. The average price of a new car was $2,822 with gasoline at 34 cents per gallon. The average income was $7,850. Federal minimum wage was a $1.60 per hour. The Mc Donald's Big Mac went on sale for the first time with a price of 49 cents. The Hong Kong Flu also struck the US.

In 1968 there were 78 million television sets. The Lennon Sisters made their final appearance on *The Lawrence Welk Show* in January. In April 2, English singer Petula Clark appeared in a television special with African-American Harry Bellefonte and caused controversy because she affectionately touched him on the arm during a duet which caused protests and threats of cancellation from the Chrysler Corporation, the show's sponsor.

On November 17, NBC broke away from the final moments of a football game between the New York Jets and the Oakland Raiders to show a Shirley Temple movie *Heidi*. The Raiders which had been losing at the time then scored two touchdowns in the final minute to win. So many angry fans called NBC that their switchboard shutdown. NBC apologized. The game is now referred to as "the Heidi Game."

Some of the television debuts included: *Rowan and Martin's Laugh-in, 60 Minutes, Julia, Adam 12, The Mod Squad, Hawaii Five-0, One Life to Live, the GE College Bowl* and the first appearance on US television of the British show *The Prisoner*. Jacques Cousteau's first undersea special also debuted. Shows ending included: *The Man from U.N.C.L.E, The Monkees, Lost in Space, The Lucy Show*, and *Batman*.

On October 7, the Motion Picture Rating System went into effect with G for general audiences, M for mature audiences, R restricted to adults and under 16 years old accompanied by an adult, and X with no one under 16 allowed. Later the 16 year age limit would be changed to 18 for R and 21 for X. 1968 produced some notable movies including: *2001: A Space Odyssey, Funny Girl, The Odd Couple, Bullitt, Oliver, Rosemary's Baby. Planet of the Apes, The Lion in Winter, The Green Berets, Charly*, and *The Thomas Crown Affair*. The Oscar for Best Picture went to *Oliver*, Cliff Robertson in *Charly* won for Best Actor, Best Actress was a tie between Katharine Hepburn in *The Lion in Winter*, and Barbara Streisand for *Funny Girl*, the Best Director went to Carol Reed for *Oliver*.

The Billboard's top songs of 1968 included some rock classics like the Beatles' *Hey Jude* and *Lady Madonna*, Simon and Garfunkel's *Mrs. Robinson* and *Scarborough Fair*, the Rolling Stones' *Jumpin' Jack Flash*, Otis Redding's *The Dock of the Bay, Love is Blue* by Paul Mauriat, *Mony Mony* by Tommy James and the Shondells, *Woman, Woman (Have You Got Cheating on Your Mind?) Young Girl, Lady Willpower* and *Over You* by Gary Puckett and the Union Gap, *Angel of the Morning* by Merrilee Rush, *Classical Gas* by Mason Williams, *McArthur Park* by Richard Harris, *Dance to the Music* by Sly and the Family Stones, *I wish it Would Rain* by the Temptations, *Ain't Nothing Like the Real Thing* and *You're All I Need to Get By* by Marvin Gaye and Tammi Terrell, and *Tighten Up* by Archie Bell and the Drells.

The Books of 1968 featured *Slaughterhouse-Five* and *Welcome to the Monkey House* by Kurt Vonnegut Jr., *2001: A Space Odyssey* by Arthur C. Clarke, *The Electric Kool-Aid Acid Test* by Tom Wolf, *The Teachings of Don Juan* by Carlos Castaneda, *True Grit* by Charles Portis, *Airport* by Arthur Hailey, *Stand on Zanzibar* by John Brunner, *Cancer Ward* and *The First Circle* by Aleksandr Solzhenitzen, *Chariots of the Gods* by Erich von Däniken, *Soul on Ice* by Eldridge Cleaver, *Couples* by John Updike, *M*A*S*H* by Richard Hooker, *Myra Breckenridge* by Gore Vidal, *Iberia* by James Michener, *Red Sky at Morning* by Richard Bradford, *A History of the Vikings* by Gwyn Jones, *The Arms of Krupp* by William Manchester, *Coming of Age in Mississippi* by Anne Moody, and *Armies of the Night* by Norman Mailer which would win a Pulitzer Prize in 1969.

CHAPTER 25. 1969: MEN ON THE MOON, WOODSTOCK, THE
MEGA CONCERTS, THE INTERNET, ENVIRONMENTAL AND GAY
RIGHTS MOVEMENTS, AND HAMBURGER HILL

January 2, Emil Zátopek, a Czech hero who won three Gold medals at the
1952 Helsinki Summer Olympics, was declared a public enemy by the USSR
for his support of the democratic reforms of Prague Spring. He was stripped
of his communist party and military rank and forced to work in the mines
and as a garbage collector.

January 3, John Lennon and Yoko Ono's 2 *Virgins* album was declared
pornographic in New Jersey. Most outlets in the UK, US, and elsewhere
refused to sell the album with their nude picture on the cover.

January 5, the USSR launched Venera 5 toward Venus. On May 16, it
became the first human craft to land on another planet.

January 10, Sweden became the first western government to recognize
the government of North Vietnam.

January 14, an accidental explosion aboard the USS Enterprise near
Hawaii killed 27 and injured 314 sailors.

January 14-17, the USSR launched Soyuz 4 and 5 the two ships met and
docked in space and exchanged crews, a maneuver necessary for the eventual
space station.

January 16, a Czech student, Jan Palach, became a martyr when he
immolated himself in Prague to protest the Soviet invasion. Although
onlookers put the fire out and attempted to rescue the young man, he died
three days later.

January 18, the Paris peace talks to end the Vietnam War were expanded.
On January 25, the talks began with South Vietnam finally agreeing to
participate.

January 20, Richard Nixon became President.

January 28, a blow out on a Union Oil Platform off the California coast
spilled 100,000 barrels of crude oil onto the Beaches of Santa Barbara. The

accident inspired Senator Gaylord Nelson of Wisconsin to organize the first Earth Day in 1970 beginning the modern environmental movement.

January 30, the Beatles performed their last live concert on the roof of the Apple Records headquarters.

February 4, the Palestine National Congress elected Yasser Arafat as the head of the Palestinian Liberation Organization (PLO).

February 8, the last issue of Benjamin Franklin's magazine, *The Saturday Evening Post* went on sale.

February 17, Golda Meir, the daughter of a Milwaukee grocer, was named as the Prime Minister of Israel. Meir went to grade school, high school and college and taught school in Milwaukee, Wisconsin before emigrating to Palestine (now Israel) in 1921.

February 18, the PLO attacked an Israeli passenger plane in Zurich, Switzerland.

February 27, in Cold War posturing newly elected President Nixon visited West Berlin. In an attempt to copy JFK's popular Ich Bin Ein Berliner speech a long-winded Nixon said to Berlin, "Sometimes you must feel that you are very much alone, but always remember we are with you, and always remember that people who are free and who want to be free around the world are with you. In the sense that the people of Berlin stand for freedom and peace, all the people of the world are truly Berliners."

March 2, to September 11, disproving the dogmatic US belief that communism was a united front with a singular world plot, the USSR and the People's Republic of China began a series of border skirmishes. In these attacks the USSR had 59 killed and 94 wounded. The USSR claimed, but has never confirmed, that it killed between 300 and 600 Chinese troops. China has never revealed their casualties. The skirmishes were a standoff although the Chinese captured the T-62 Soviet tank with its secret new equipment and weaponry. The Sino-Soviet battles raised the fear of an all-out nuclear war between the two countries.

March 3-13, Apollo 9 was the first test flight of the Command/Service Module and the Lunar Module in space. The ten day mission was a success.

Also on March 3, the US Navy established the Navy Fighter Weapons School at Miramar Naval Air Station in California which has become known as "Top Gun" training.

March 15, Supreme Court Justice Abe Fortas resigned amid scandal. Fortas was a close friend and appointee to the Court by President Johnson. In 1968 Johnson had attempted to elevate Fortas to Chief Justice with the resignation of Earl Warren. However issues began to arise about payments Fortas received from businesses which had issues before the court. It was discovered that he had also accepted a deal for $20,000 a year for life ($121,681 in 2015 dollars) from a Wall Street financier who was under investigation for securities fraud.

March 18-May 26, the US began Operation Menu, the secret bombing of Cambodia. During the Vietnam War between 40,000 and 150,000 Cambodians, mostly civilians, died from the US bombing campaigns.

March 19, the Chicago 8 were indicted for their roles during the protests at the 1968 Democratic Convention.

March 20, with a majority of Americans now against the war, President Nixon publicly announced that the Vietnam War would be over in 1970.

March 23, in reaction to the allegations that Jim Morrison of the Doors had publicly exposed himself in Miami, a conservative group organized a "Rally for Decency" against the youth counter-cultural movement. It was supposedly American teenagers who were outraged by the youth Hippie culture. However the leaders, organizers and speakers were Jackie Gleason, Kate Smith and Anita Bryant. Bryant would later be fired as a spokesperson for the citrus industry for her anti-gay remarks. President Nixon cheered the event and wrote to an organizer, "I was extremely interested to learn about the admirable initiative undertaken by you and 30,000 other young people at the Miami Teen-age Rally for Decency held last Sunday."

March 25, John Lennon and Yoko Ono began a public bed-in for peace at the Hilton Hotel in Amsterdam. They held a second bed-in later in May at the Queen Elizabeth Hotel in Montreal.

March 28, President Eisenhower died at the age of 79 years. He was brought to the Capital to lie in state in the Rotunda. He was buried on the grounds of his presidential library in Abilene, Kansas.

April 3, US Secretary of Defense Melvin Laird announced the US plans to "Vietnamize" the war with the ARVN playing a greater role and US forces a supporting role.

April 5, massive anti-war demonstrations occurred in most major US cities. J. Edgar Hoover told Nixon that it was communist inspired. Over 100,000 demonstrated in New York. Other cities with very large protests included: San Francisco, Los Angeles and Washington, DC.

April 7, a networking group at UCLA developed host software and sent a group request for comment. This event is the official start of the internet.

April 9, students protesting the war took over the administration building at Harvard University. The police ended the sit-in injuring 34 students and arrested 184 others.

April 15, North Korea fired at a US aircraft over the Sea of Japan.

April 24, amid rumors that Paul McCarthy of the Beatles was dead, McCarthy was forced to proclaim publicly that he was still alive.

May 1, in New York City 43 couples were wed by Reverend Sun Myung Moon's Unification Church. The followers of Moon soon became known as "the Moonies." The couples had never met as the marriages were arranged by Moon. By 1973 there were about 3,000 Moonies in the US who were known for their vigorous fundraising and begging, particularly at airports.

May 9, a rock concert, Zip to Zap was organized by students from the University of North Dakota and North Dakota State University as a spring break destination. The little town of Zap, North Dakota was overwhelmed by 3,000 rowdy students seeking a spring break experience. The National Guard was ordered in by the Governor when the students began fighting and committing vandalism. The town suffered $25,000 in damages which the student governments of the two schools had to pay.

May 10-20, Hill 937 in the Thua Thien Province had no strategic value, but the US Command ordered it be taken by an infantry assault rather than by artillery or airstrikes. The Viet Cong had heavily fortified the Hill and waited for the Americans. The Battle became known as Hamburger Hill. The US lost 72 killed and had 372 wounded. The US claimed it had killed 630 and captured 3, but this was unsubstantiated. ARVN losses were heavy but unknown and several of their helicopters were shot down during the battle. The Hill was abandoned by US troops after it was taken which allowed the Viet Cong to reclaim it. Hamburger Hill became a watershed event as a majority of the American public saw the gruesome pictures of US casualties on Hamburger Hill in *Life* magazine and turned against the war.

May 15, a St. Louis teenager died of a then unknown medical condition. In 1984 it was confirmed as the first case of HIV/Aids in North America.

May 18-26, Apollo 10 was the final dress rehearsal for the moon landing. The lunar module came within 8 miles of the Moon's surface. The mission also set a speed record as the Apollo 10 attained a speed of 39,897 miles per hour returning from the Moon.

May 20, the California National Guard used a helicopter in a chemical attack to spray stinging powder on anti-war demonstrators.

June 2, a naval accident occurred when the Australian aircraft carrier the MHAS Melbourne turned the wrong direction and sliced the American destroyer the USS Frank E. Evans in half killing 74 US sailors in waters near Vietnam.

June 5, a race riot occurred in Hartford, Connecticut.

June 8, Nixon met Vietnamese President Thiệu at Midway Island and announced that 25,000 troops would leave Vietnam by August. The US would begin to steadily reduce the number of troops in Vietnam as "Vietnamization" took place.

June 9, Warren Berger was confirmed as the US Supreme Court Chief Justice.

June 17, *Oh! Calcutta* debuted in New York City. The controversial show featured six sketches on sexual topics which were mostly performed by nude actors.

June 19, racial riots erupted in Cairo, Illinois.

June 20, over 150,000 attended the Newport Jazz Festival.

June 22, the Cuyahoga River which flows through Cleveland was so polluted it caught fire. The 1969 fire caused approximately $50,000 in damage, mostly to an adjacent railroad bridge. A fire on the river in 1952 actually caused more damage, but this time it was captured by *Time* magazine which said the river "oozes rather than flows" and that a person swimming in it "does not drown but decays." The outrage over the heavily polluted river eventually resulted in the passage of The Clean Water Act.

Also on June 22, Judy Garland died of a drug overdose at her home in London.

June 27, over 50,000 attended the Denver Pop Festival.

June 28-July 3, a brutal raid by police of Stonewall, a gay bar in Greenwich Village in New York City, caused a gay riots and protests over several nights. This was considered the incident gave rise to the modern gay rights movement. One year later on July 28, 1970 large Gay Pride parades were held in New York, Chicago, San Francisco, and Los Angeles to commemorate the incident.

June 29, the first Jewish worship service was held at the White House.

July 3, after being forced to quit the Rolling Stones in June because of mood swings brought on by his increasing drug and alcohol problems, Brian Jones was found dead in his swimming pool. Jones was the original founder and the first leader of the Rolling Stones. He was replaced in the band by guitarist Mick Taylor. Bill Wyman the bassist of the band later said, "He formed the band. He chose the members. He named the band. He chose the music we played. He got us gigs. Very influential, very important, and then slowly lost it – highly intelligent – and he just kind of wasted it and blew it all away."

July 4, the Atlanta Pop Festival drew over 140,000 to hear Janis Joplin, and Lead Zeppelin.

Also on July 4, a straight-line thunderstorm and wind storm, called a derecho, killed 18 and destroyed over a 100 boats on Lake Erie.

July 16-July 24, Apollo 11 was launched from Cape Kennedy. On July 20, the Lunar Module landed on the Moon. On June 21, Neal Armstrong became the first man to walk on another celestial body. The event was televised to an audience of about 600 million people. The astronauts landed back on Earth on June 24, in the Pacific Ocean.

July 18, late in the evening Senator Edward Kennedy left a party with a young woman, Mary Jo Kopechne, on Chappaquiddick Island in Massachusetts. He accidently drove his car off a bridge but managed to escape. It was revealed later that Kopechne was alive after the crash but suffocated inside the car. Kennedy went home and did not report the crash and was later charged with leaving the scene of an accident after causing injury. He tried but failed to persuade his cousin to claim he was the driver. Later he addressed the press and said there was "no truth whatever to the widely circulated suspicions of immoral conduct" between himself and Kopechne. The Senator's wife, Joan Kennedy, accompanied him to the press briefing and the funeral. She was pregnant at the time but suffered a later miscarriage. She blamed her miscarriage on the incident. The Chappaquiddick incident permanently damaged his career, reputation and marriage.

July 25, over 70,000 attended the Seattle Pop Festival.

July 30, Nixon made an unscheduled visit to South Vietnam to meet with US military commanders.

July 31, the National Guard was mobilized to stop a race riot in Baton Rouge.

August 1, over 110,000 attended the Atlantic City Pop Festival.

August 9, Charles Manson and his followers (called the "Manson Family" in the press) killed five people at the home of actress Sharon Tate and Director Roman Polanski. Tate, three friends, and a person visiting her caretaker were murdered. Tate was eight months pregnant at the time. The victims had more than a hundred stab wounds. The next day the Manson family killed Leno and Rosemary La Bianca in a similar fashion. They left evidence suggesting it was done for racial reasons and believed the murders would be blamed on Blacks and would start a race war in the US.

August 14-22, Hurricane Camille struck Alabama, Louisiana, and Mississippi killing 259 people and caused about $1.5 billion in damages.

August 15-18, the Woodstock Festival began. An audience of 200,000 was expected but over 400,000 came. The event was captured in a documentary film called *Woodstock*. The festival was considered one of the pivotal events of rock and roll and the 1960s counterculture. The festival was remarkably peaceful but two accidental deaths occurred. One was a drug overdose and the second came when a young man fell asleep in a nearby hay field and was accidentally run over by a tractor. There were also two births at the festival.

Also on August 30, a race riot occurred in Ft. Lauderdale.

August 31, about 25,000 attended the New Orleans Pop Festival.

September 1, over 120,000 attended the Texas International Pop Festival in Lewisville, Texas.

September 2, Ho Chi Minh died of heart failure at the age of 79 in Hanoi.

September 2, the first US ATM was installed in Rockville Center, New York.

September 24, the trial of the Chicago 8 began. The trial resulted in acquittals and some convictions, which were followed by appeals, reversals, and retrials. There were some final convictions but none of the defendants were ultimately sentenced to jail or given fines. However Bobby Seale was sentenced to four years for contempt of court. His trial was severed from the others which then became the Chicago 7 trial. The government eventually suspended his convictions and Seale was released from prison in 1972.

October 5, *Monty Python's Flying Circus* made its debut in Britain on the BBC.

October 8-11, the Days of Rage anti-war protests were held in Chicago. The National Guard was called out and 287 people were arrested.

October 11-16, the USSR launched Soyuz 6, 7, and 8 into space for a coordinated mission of the three craft and seven crew members.

October 14, a race riot struck Springfield, Massachusetts.

October 15, the Moratorium to End the War in Vietnam was held in cities and colleges across the US. Boston had the largest demonstration at well over 100,000, but many other cities like Minneapolis also saw large turnouts. The Moratorium was followed by a large national demonstration one month later in Washington, DC. Future President Bill Clinton participated in an anti-war demonstration at Oxford University in Britain which would be a contested subject during the presidential debate between Clinton and George H.W. Bush in 1992.

October 22, Paul McCarthy was again forced to deny rumors of his death.

October 27, consumer advocate Ralph Nader set up a consumer group known as Nader's Raiders.

October 29, the US Supreme Court ordered all public schools to desegregate "at once."

Also on October 29, the first message was sent over the ARPANET the forerunner of the internet.

October 31, a race riot struck Jacksonville, Florida.

November 3, President Nixon appeared on national television and asked "the silent majority" to continue supporting him and the war in Vietnam. That day Vice President Agnew called Nixon's critics "an effete corps of impudent snobs and nattering nabobs of negativism."

November 9, a group of Native Americans inspired by the American Indian Movement (AIM) seized Alcatraz Island in San Francisco Bay and the home to the recently closed Alcatraz Federal Prison. They occupied the site for 19 months claiming the land was rightfully theirs. AIM had started in Minneapolis in 1968 because of discriminatory treatment of the city's large Native population by the Minneapolis Police Department. The police had a reputation of harsh treatment toward the large Native community which included reports of intoxicated Natives being arrested and transported in the trunks of patrol cars to jail. In October 1969 AIM also made national news by taking over the Bureau of Indian Affairs offices in Minneapolis to protest Bureau their policies.

November 10, *Sesame Street* made its debut on NET, the forerunner to PBS. It is one of the longest running shows in television history. It is also one of the most influential. In 2009 on its 40th anniversary it was calculated that over 77 million children had grown up watching the show. As of 2018 the program had won hundreds of awards including 180 Emmy Awards and 8 Grammy Awards.

November 12, investigative reporter Seymour Hersh broke the My Lai massacre story to the American public.

November 13, Vice President Agnew accused the three television networks of distorted news coverage about the Vietnam War.

November 14-24, Apollo 12 became the second manned mission to the Moon. Although not as dramatic as the first it was heavily followed by the American public.

November 15, over 500,000 anti-war demonstrators arrived in Washington, DC to protest the Vietnam War. It was the largest anti-war demonstration in the nation's history. It was also one of the most peaceful. In response to the demonstration President Nixon responded, "Now, I understand that there has been, and continues to be, opposition to the war in Vietnam on the campuses and also in the nation. As far as this kind of activity is concerned, we expect it; however under no circumstances will I be affected whatever by it."

Also on November 15, the USSR submarine K-19 collided with the US nuclear submarine USS Gato in the Barents Sea. Both submarines survived the collision but were damaged.

November 17, the Strategic Arms Limitation Talks (SALT) between the USSR and the US began in Helsinki, Finland. The talks would lead to a treaty in 1972.

November 21, the US Senate rejected the nomination of Clement Haynsworth Jr. to the US Supreme Court. It was alleged that Haynsworth had ruled in previous cases where he had a financial interests. It was the first rejection of a President's appointment to the court since 1930.

November 24, Lt. William Calley Jr. was formally charged with murder in the My Lai massacre.

November 26, a bill authorizing a lottery to choose draftees for the Selective Service was signed by President Nixon.

December 1, the first random draft lottery was held since WWII. In January the *New York Times* ran an article claiming the lottery was not random as claimed by the Nixon Administration and the Selective Service.

December 4, Black Panther leaders Fred Hampton and Mark Clark were killed by 14 Chicago police officers in their apartment. Hampton was killed as he lay sleeping in his bed. FBI Special Agent Gregg York later said, "We expected about twenty Panthers to be in the apartment when the police raided the place. Only two of those black niggers were killed, Fred Hampton and Mark Clark." Despite all evidence to the contrary, Hampton's death was ruled as a justifiable homicide. FBI documents later revealed that the assassinations were part of the FBI's secret illegal operation COINTELPRO.

December 6, over 300,000 attended the Altamont Rock Concert in California to see the Rolling Stones and other bands. The concert promoters used the motorcycle gang the Hell's Angels to provide security. The Angels got drunk and began to fight with the crowd and one man was stabbed and killed by one of the gang. *Rolling Stone* magazine called it "rock and roll's worst day." In 2008 a former FBI agent revealed that the Hell's Angels later tried to assassinate Mick Jagger for blaming the violence on them.

December 8, the Los Angeles Police Department (LAPD) at the direction of the FBI, planned a massive raid involving more than 350 officers on the Black Panthers in Los Angeles. The Black Panthers were surrounded and fired upon by the police. The Panthers returned fire, resulting in a four-hour gun battle. Before the shoot-out, the LAPD and SWAT maneuvered themselves into surrounding the Panthers' headquarters and then fired over 5,000 rounds of ammunition. Three Panthers were wounded. The Panthers fired back and wounded three SWAT officers. As the battle continued, the Black Panthers realized they were surrounded; there were eleven Panthers and hundreds of gunmen outside. They surrendered. The Panthers later claimed they only returned fire because they thought they would be executed like Fred Hampton.

December 17, the USAF Project Bluebook closed its UFO investigations and concluded that there was no proof of visits from aliens. During Project Bluebook over 12,000 cases were investigated between 1952 and 1969.

The year of 1969 ended with 549,500 US troops in Vietnam of which 11,616 were killed. The HIV/Aids virus arrived in the US by way of Haiti. Bell bottom jeans and tie-dyed shirts became fashionable. Some Americans believed in rumors circulating that the moon landings were staged by Nixon and were a fake.

The inflation rate jumped to 5.46 per cent. Average income was $8,550. The average cost of a new house rose to $15,550 and average rent to $135.00 per month. The average car rose to $3,270 but you could buy a new Japanese

Toyota for $1,950. Gasoline sold at 35 cents per gallon. The first battery-powered smoke detectors came on the market.

In television the debuts included: *Hee Haw*, *The Johnny Cash Show*, *Scooby-doo Where Are You*, *Room 222*, *The Courtship of Eddie's Father*, *Marcus Welby MD*, *Medical Center*, *The Brady Bunch*, *Love American Style* and *Sesame Street*. Shows ending included: *Star Trek*, *Gomer Pyle USMC*, *Peyton Place* and *The Smothers' Brothers Comedy Hour* which was dropped because the network and sensors felt that the show with its anti-war bias was too politically controversial.

The movies of 1969 included *Butch Cassidy and the Sundance Kid* which grossed over $102 million. Other top films included: *Midnight Cowboy*, *Easy Rider*, *Hello Dolly*, *Bob & Carol & Ted & Alice*, *Paint Your Wagon*, *True Grit*, *Cactus Flower*, *Goodbye Columbus*, *Z*, *They Shoot Horses Don't They?*, *The Wild Bunch*, *Sweet Charity*, *Where Eagles Dare*, *Alice's Restaurant*, and *The Prime of Miss Jean Brodie*. At the Oscars *Midnight Cowboy* won Best Picture and Best Director. John Wayne won Best Actor in *True Grit*. Maggie Smith for Best Actress in *The Prime of Miss Jean Brodie*. The Best Supporting Actors were Gig Young and Goldie Hawn in *They Shoot Horses Don't They?* and *Cactus Flower* respectively.

In music *Sugar Sugar* by the Archies was number one on Billboard's Hot 100. The Rolling Stones had a top hit with *Honky Tonk Woman*. Sly and the Family Stone had two top hits with *Everyday People* and *Hot Fun in the Summertime*. Tommy James and the Shondells had a couple with *Crimson and Clover* and *Crystal Blue Persuasion*. The 5th Dimension had the number two hit with *Aquarius*. Elvis Presley came back with two hits, *Suspicious Minds* and *In the Ghetto*. The Beatles barely cracked the top twenty-five with *Get Back*. Creedence Clearwater Revival had three hits, *Proud Mary, Bad Moon Rising* and *Green River*. The Temptations (with Diana Ross) and the Supremes had *I Can't Get Next to You Now*, *Run Away Child Running Wild* and *I'm Going to Make You Love Me*.

The popular literature of 1969 included: *I Know Why the Caged Bird Sings* by Maya Angelou, *The Godfather* by Mario Puzo, *The Andromeda Strain* by Michael Crichton, *Portnoy's Complaint* by Phillip Roth, *Papillion* by Henri Cherriére, *The French Lieutenant's Woman* by John Fowles, *Betty Crocker's Cookbook* by Betty Crocker, *The Economy of Cities* by Jane Jacobs, *The Peter Principle* by Laurence J. Peter, *Rich Man Poor Man* by Irwin Shaw, *Inside the Third Reich* by Albert Speer, *The Best and the Brightest* by David Halberstam, *The Poseidon Adventure* by Paul Gallico, *The Love Machine* by Jacqueline Susann, *The Wild Boys* by William S. Burroughs, *Memoirs of a Beatnik* by Diane Di Prima, *Thirteen Days: A Memoir of the Cuban Missile Crisis* by Robert Kennedy was published this year after his death.

CHAPTER 26. 1970: A YEAR OF VIOLENCE, KENT STATE, THE WEATHERMEN, MORE BLACK PANTHERS, POLICE BRUTALITY, RACIAL UNREST, AND THE INVASION OF CAMBODIA

January 2, the US Census reported a population of over 203 million and stated that the African-American population was about 11%.

January 4, an earthquake in China killed over 15,000 people.

January 11, the Kansas City Chiefs beat the Minnesota Vikings in Super Bowl IV.

January 12, Biafra surrendered in its war of secession with Nigeria.

January 15, the Philippines withdrew their token force from Vietnam.

January 16, Muammar Gaddafi came to power in Libya in a military coup.

January 19, President Nixon named G. Harold Carswell as his appointment to the Supreme Court. Nixon's previous appointment of Clement Haynsworth was rejected for ruling on cases where he had a financial interest and because had accepted money from questionable sources. Carswell was also rejected by the Senate. The NAACP and others campaigned against Carswell because of his poor civil rights record and his past racists remarks. It was also revealed that he was a poor judge and that 58% of his judicial decisions had been reversed on appeal. The Senate refused to confirm Carswell.

Also on January 19, under pressure from California Governor Ronald Reagan, the Board of Regents of the University of California fired Black activist Angela Davis for being a member of the Communist Party USA. Davis had turned down offers from Princeton and Swarthmore in 1969 to join the Philosophy Department at UCLA. The Board of Regents were then censured by the American Association of University Professors for their action. A judge ruled against the Board of Regents saying they could not fire Davis solely for being a communist. She was reinstated but the Regents continued to look for ways to fire Davis and did on June 20, saying she had made speeches using inflammatory language.

January 21, the first Boeing 747 commercial flight flew from New York to London.

January 31, nineteen members of the Grateful Dead touring group were busted on LSD charges in New Orleans. Most of the charges were eventually dropped and the band later wrote the song *Truckin* about this incident.

In the January edition of the *Washington Monthly*, Christopher Pyle a former US intelligence officer reported that "For the past four years, the U.S. Army has been closely watching civilian political activity within the United States." Public alarm and outrage prompted the Senate Subcommittee on Constitutional Rights, chaired by Senator Sam Ervin of North Carolina, to investigate. For more than a year, Senator Ervin struggled against a coverup to get to the bottom of the US Army domestic surveillance system. He was constantly frustrated by the Nixon Administration's lies and misleading statements, claims of inherent executive powers, and their refusal to disclose information on the basis of national security. Senator Ervin called for public hearings in 1971 to examine "the dangers the Army's program presents to the principles of the Constitution."

February 1, in a thaw of Cold war tensions, West Germany signed a natural gas contract with the USSR.

February 11, Japan launched Osumi, their first satellite into space.

February 13, Black Sabbath released their debut album which was regarded by many as the first heavy metal album.

February 17, in a bizarre Manson family copy-cat killing the pregnant wife and two young daughters of Jeffery MacDonald, a US Army Green Beret officer and medical doctor, were murdered at their home at Fort Bragg. Military Police responded to a call from MacDonald who reported the stabbings. They found the bodies of the murdered wife and two daughters and the word "pigs" written in blood on the headboard of the bed next to where his wife was found on the floor. All the victims were clubbed and stabbed multiple times. MacDonald was discovered with cuts and scrapes on his hands, face and chest. He also had one stab wound. He claimed that "a gang of drugged-out Hippies" were responsible. The American media initially believed his story of "Hippie killers" and MacDonald even appeared and told his story on the *Dick Cavett Show*. He remained free until 1975 when forensic evidence proved he was the killer and he was convicted of the murders.

February 16, a bomb went off in a San Francisco Police Department branch office killing one officer and wounding several others. It was later learned that this was the work of a terrorist group called the Weather Underground Organization. What had started as a student protest group eventually morphed into a small extremist anarchist gang. The Weathermen went on to commit bombings in federal buildings and banks usually warning those in the buildings in advance. In 1981 they robbed a Brinks truck. Their mayhem continued off and on until 1981. During that span several bomb factories in New York, Chicago and San Francisco were discovered and many of the Weathermen were caught and convicted. The majority of their damage was caused in 1970.

February 18, the Chicago 7 protestors on trial from the incidents at the 1968 Democratic Convention were found innocent of conspiring to incite a riot, but several were convicted of minor offenses.

February 23, the former South American British colony of British Guiana became the Republic of Guyana.

February 27, the *New York Times* falsely reported the US Army had stopped their domestic spy program on US civilians.

March 1, the US ended commercial whale hunting.

March 5, the Nuclear Non-Proliferation Treaty went into effect. It was signed by the US, the USSR and 41 other countries to stop the spread of nuclear weapons and to eventually achieve nuclear disarmament.

March 7, a solar eclipse occurred on the eastern coast of North America.

March 12, in recognition of the hundreds of thousands of US troops in combat between the ages of 18 and 21 the US Congress voted to lower the voting age from 21 to 18. The vote was to amend the constitution and the subsequent amendment was ratified the following year.

March 13, Digital Equipment Corporation introduced the first mini-computer.

March 17, fourteen US Army officers were charged in the cover-up of the My Lai massacre.

Also on March 17, the US cast their first UN Security Council veto to support the British who were under pressure by the UN to end the all-White government in Rhodesia.

March 18, one of the largest labor strikes in US history occurred when 210,000 of 750,000 US postal employees walked off the job. The strike lasted two weeks. President Nixon assigned US Army troops to some New York City post offices to assist during the strike.

March 28, over a thousand people died in an earthquake in Turkey.

March 31-April 3, after a large Protestant parade against the Catholics in Northern Ireland, riots erupted and were put down by British troops. The British Army warned that rioters would be "shot dead."

April 1, President Nixon signed the Public Health Cigarette Smoking Act banning cigarette ads on television beginning in 1971.

April 2, Qatar gained independence from Britain.

April 4, the KGB finally disposed of the remains of Adolf Hitler, Eva Braun, Joseph and Magda Goebbels and their children by crushing their remains and dumping the dust into the Biederitz River in Madgeburg, East Germany.

April 10, Paul McCarthy formally announced the split-up of the Beatles.

April 11-17, Apollo 13 was launched to the Moon. The jinxed mission never made a Moon landing and was lucky enough to return safely after an oxygen tank exploded. The mission made famous the phrase, "Houston we have a problem."

April 22, the first Earth Day founded by Senator Gaylord Nelson of Wisconsin was held. Hundreds of communities, schools and universities celebrated the event. Nelson later received a Presidential Medal of Freedom for his environmental work.

April 24, after a failure in late 1969, China successfully launched its first satellite into space.

April 29 to July 22, in an attempt to find NVA and Viet Cong forces and supply centers the US Army and the ARVN invaded the neutral country of Cambodia. In months of fighting the US lost 338, with 13 missing and 1,525 wounded. The ARVN lost 809 men with 3,486 wounded. The US claimed to have killed 12,354 NVA or Viet Cong but the CIA later admitted that these figures included many non-combatant Cambodian civilians. The Cambodian invasion set off large anti-war protests across the US along with calls to impeach President Nixon.

May 4, Ohio National Guardsmen shot and killed four students and wounded nine others (one who was permanently paralyzed from the chest down) who were peacefully protesting the war at Kent State University. The students were not violent or threatening the Guardsmen. Two of the four killed were 19 years old and the two others were 20. A Pulitzer prize winning photograph showed a fourteen-year-old girl crying as she knelt over the body of one of the victims. The shooting led to a nationwide student strike of over 4 million students that closed 450 colleges and universities with large and sometimes violent protests. In New York City an antiwar protest was met by a large construction worker protest which resulted in violence called the Hard Hat Riot where over 70 people were injured including four policemen. According to the *New York Times* October 4, 1996, the construction worker riot was organized by Peter Brennan who was later appointed as Nixon's Labor Secretary. Five days after the shootings on May 9, over 100,000 protested in Washington, DC. A Presidential Commission on Campus Violence appointed by Nixon called the Scranton Commission found in September that the shootings at Kent State were unjustified and said that the tragedies "must mark the last time that, as a matter of course, loaded rifles are issued to guardsmen confronting student demonstrators." The State of Ohio later settled with the Kent State Victims for $675,000.

May 8, eleven students were bayoneted at the University of New Mexico by the National Guard.

May 11, Henry "Dickie" Marrow Jr. a twenty-three-year-old Black man was beaten and killed by Whites in front of a White storefront in Oxford, Mississippi. The store owner and his son were charged but found not guilty by an all-White jury. As a result of the verdict the Blacks of Oxford began a boycott of all the White businesses. The year-long boycott eventually led to the end of segregation in all public facilities and businesses in Oxford.

May 12, Nixon's third attempt at appointing a US Supreme Court Justice finally met with success in the Senate with the confirmation of Harry A. Blackmun.

Also on May 12, in racial unrest at Jackson State University in Mississippi police opened fired and killed two students and wounded 12 others. As with the Kent State killings the Scranton Commission later found "that the 28-second fusillade from police officers was an unreasonable, unjustified overreaction."

May 15, Elizabeth Hoisington and Anna Mae Mays were named to be the first female US generals. On June 11, they received their formal promotion.

May 17, Thor Heyerdahl set sail on the Ra II from Morocco to sail the Atlantic. Having sailed in a similar raft, the Kon-Tiki in 1947 to prove that Polynesians could have sailed the Pacific to South America, he attempted to show that Egyptians could have sailed from Africa to the New World. He successfully completed the crossing.

May 31, an estimated 65,000 to 70,000 people were killed or severely injured in the Ancash earthquake and landslide in Peru.

June 1-19, Soyuz 9 was launched. The mission set a record for manned days in space testing human endurance in space. The information was another step in the development of the international space station.

June 2, Norway announced that it would develop the newly discovered oil rich deposits just offshore in the North Sea.

June 4, the tiny island nation of Tonga in the South Pacific achieved independence from Britain.

June 16, race riots in Miami brought the city to a standstill.

June 22, in Northern Ireland police arrested Bernadette Devlin, a Member of Parliament, a Catholic and Irish Republican accused of rioting. Northern Ireland erupted in violence. Intense riots took place in Derry and Belfast which led to prolonged gun battles between Protestant British Loyalists and Catholic Irish Republicans.

June 24, the US Senate voted overwhelmingly to repeal the Gulf of Tonkin Resolution authorizing military action in Vietnam. However the vote to repeal failed in the US House.

June 28, in Northern Ireland over 500 Catholic employees of the shipyards were forced out of their jobs by the Protestants as rioting continued.

June 29, the US Army and ARVN left Cambodia.

July 1-23, the Battle of Fire Support Base Ripcord took place in the A Shau Valley. The remote artillery outpost came under heavy attack by the NVA. The battle lasted three weeks with 75 Americans killed, 463 wounded, 6 aircraft destroyed and 36 badly damaged. The US claimed 422 NVA were killed.

Also on July 1, the British Home Secretary Reginald Maulding visited Northern Ireland amidst the rioting and exclaimed, "What a bloody awful country."

July 3, over 200,000 attended the Atlanta Pop Festival.

July 4, the radio music countdown show, *American Top 40*, with Casey Kasem made its debut on five radio stations.

Also on July 4, over 100 people were injured in a race riot in Asbury Park, New Jersey.

July 6, California enacted the first no fault divorce law.

July 12, Tanzania signed a contract with China to build a railway infuriating the West.

July 17, the Randall's Island Rock Festival in New York City was attended by over 30,000.

July 21, Libya ordered the confiscation of all property owned by Jews.

July 23, Northern Ireland banned all parades and demonstrations for the remainder of the year.

July 29 to August 3, there was six days of race riots in Hartford, Connecticut.

July 31 to August 3, the NFL players went on strike. This strike began the rapid rise of inflated salaries for professional athletes.

July 31-August 5, Hurricane Celia struck Western Cuba and Texas. It was one of the costliest storms in US history. The storm killed 28 people and caused $930 million in damages in Texas.

August 7, the Soledad Brothers, three inmates of Soledad Prison, went on trial for allegedly killing a prison guard in retaliation for the shooting and killing three Black inmates by prison guards during a disturbance. During the trial one of the defendants, George Jackson a Black Panther, had his seventeen-year-old brother, Jonathan Jackson, smuggle weapons under a raincoat into the courtroom during the trial. The three defendants and Jonathan then took the Judge and three female jurors hostage in an attempt to escape. During the melee that followed the Judge, two defendants and the seventeen-year-old were killed. The third defendant was wounded but survived. A prosecutor was left paralyzed from his wounds and one of the female jurors also suffered a bullet wound to the arm. After the incident it was discovered that the weapons were registered to the Black Activist Angela Davis, who had bought them and donated them to the Black Panthers to use for their self-defense. She claimed no knowledge of the incident. Davis fled saying she could not receive a fair trial. After a manhunt she was caught and was later tried as an accomplice to the kidnappings and murder of the Judge. She was found not guilty.

August 15, Patricia Palinkas became the first woman to play professional football. She was a kicker for a minor league team the Orlando panthers of the Atlantic Coast Football League. She remained the only professional woman football player until 2010 when Katie Hnida, also a kicker, played for the Fort Wayne Fire Hawks in the Continental Football League.

August 17 to December 15, the USSR launched Venera 7 to Venus which became the first man made craft to land on another planet and send data back to earth. It recorded the surface temperature on Venus at 887 degrees Fahrenheit.

August 17-18, the US disposed of 3,000 tons of nerve gas in the Atlantic Ocean. This incident lead to the public's discovery of US Army Operation Chase, which had dumped highly deadly nerve gas in containers into the ocean since 1964. All three television networks ran news stories about Operation Chase. The coverage led to the passage of a law banning the disposal of toxic waste into the oceans in 1972.

August 24, a bomb by an anti-war activist went off at the University of Wisconsin in Madison killing one student.

August 26, the National Organization for Women sponsored the Women's Strike for Equality. Different events were held across the country. Over 20,000 women demonstrated in New York City for equal pay, equal opportunity, the right to birth control, abortion and child care. In Detroit women demanded equality by staging sit-ins in men's rest rooms. A march was held in Washington, DC, demanding equality. In Los Angeles silent vigils were held. In Minneapolis women staged guerilla theaters mocking traditional women's roles while fawning over men. In Pittsburgh a local radio disc jockey dared the city's women to show their liberation and the station was pelted with eggs by many women. Conservatives in opposition to women's liberation and this event organized a counter demonstration the "National Celebration of Womanhood," a day which they asked women to dress in "frilly," feminine clothing, sing while doing the laundry, and provide breakfast in bed for their husbands.

Also on August 26, the largest rock concert was held at the Isle of Wight Festival 1970 in Britain. About 600,000 people came to hear Jimi Hendrix, The Doors, The Who, Chicago, The Moody Blues and other artists.

August 29, the Chicano Moratorium against the Vietnam War was held in East Los Angeles and drew about 30,000 marchers. The event was organized by the Brown Berets, a Chicano civil rights group. The march was broken up by the Los Angeles Police Department (LAPD) who claimed that a liquor store had been robbed during the march. The brutal police tactics caused a riot. During the riot the police killed four and arrested 150 Latinos. One of those killed was Ruben Salazar a reporter for the *Los Angeles Times* and the news director of a Los Angeles Spanish language television station. The Latino community believed his death to be police murder as Salazar was a civil rights reporter and had previously written numerous stories critical of the LAPD.

August 31, After a Philadelphia police officer was shot and killed on duty, the police used it as motive to raid Black Panther headquarters although the police knew the killing was not by the Black Panthers. They lined the men up, handcuffed them and put a gun to the back of the neck of each and ordered them to walk backward telling them that if they stumbled they would be killed. Then they lined them up against a wall stripped them and photographed them. They stripped and photographed the women Panthers too. They fired a machine gun above their heads when their faces were turned to the wall to make them think they were being executed. Then they took all of them to the police station for interrogation. They raided and physically destroyed their headquarters and two other buildings. They even demolished the plumbing in one of the bathrooms to make the building unusable.

The raid was designed by Police Commissioner Frank Rizzo who in one of his first acts as commissioner in 1967 was to stop a demonstration by 3,500 Black high school students asking for a Black studies program in the schools. He started the event by shouting to his men, "Get their black asses." A witness from the American Civil Liberties Union later said, "I myself was there and saw children who were fleeing from the police lying on the ground, each with three patrolmen beating them unmercifully with clubs." President Nixon said of Rizzo, "As I see it, other cities could use Rizzo's ideas."

September 4, while on tour in London with the Kirov Ballet from Leningrad, Russian prima ballerina Natalia Romanovna Makarova defected to the West and asked for asylum in the US.

September 5, to October 6, 1971 the US launched operation Jefferson Glenn with the 101st Airborne and the 5th infantry Division to secure Areas around Hue and Da Nang to be turned over to the ARVN. The US did not reveal US casualties for the 13 month operation but claimed to have killed over 2,000 NVA.

September 12, the PLO hijacked three passenger planes and destroyed them. The passengers were later released. It was the beginning of Black September, a terrorist Palestinian movement started in reaction to King Hussein of Jordan who declared a military emergency when the Fedayeen Palestinians attempted to seize the country. On September 15, PLO Chairman Yassir Arafat said he would make Jordan a graveyard. The fight between the Fedayeen and Fatah against the Jordanian Army lasted until July of 1971. Black September continued to make terrorist attacks around the world until 1975.

Also on September 12-24, the USSR launched their unmanned Luna 16 which brought Moon samples back to Earth.

September 21, *Monday Night Football* made its debut on ABC with the Cleveland Browns defeating the New York Jets. The announcers were "Dandy" Don Meredith, Howard Cosell and the play-by-play announcer was Keith Jackson. Jackson was replaced by Frank Gifford the following season. Gifford was not available the first season because he still had a contract with CBS. ABC had also tried to get Vin Scully "the Voice of the Dodgers" but he too was under contract.

September 22, President Nixon proposed the hiring of an additional 1,000 FBI agents for the purpose of monitoring the nation's college campuses and students.

September 26, one of the largest fires in California, the Laguna Fire, started in San Diego County California. The fire burned 175,425 acres. It is the third largest wildfire in California history. It was the largest of many wildfires that burned in the state during September and October of 1969.

September 28, President Nasser of Egypt died and Anwar Sadat was named the new president.

September 29, Congress gave Nixon the authority to sell arms to Israel.

October 2, one of two planes carrying the Wichita State University football team crashed killing 31 of 40 passengers and crew.

Also on October 3-4, the National Oceanic and Atmospheric Administration (NOAA) was formed. The Weather Bureau under NOAA was reorganized as the National Weather Service.

October 5, the National Education Television (NET) was formally reorganized as the Public Broadcasting System (PBS).

October 10, the south Pacific island nation of Fiji achieved independence from Britain.

October 12, Nixon announced that he would withdraw 40,000 troops from Vietnam before Christmas.

October 21, Norman Borlaug, the father of the Green Revolution, was awarded the Nobel Peace Prize for his vital contributions to the world's food supply. Borlaug, a University of Minnesota scientist, developed more efficient and high-yielding strains of wheat in Mexico which allowed a large expansion of the world's food supplies, particularly in third world countries. He also received the Presidential Medal of Freedom from Jimmy Carter in 1977 for his work feeding the hungry in Africa and Asia.

October 26, the counter-culture comic strip *Doonesbury*, which became instantly popular on college campuses made its debut.

October 28, the US and USSR signed an agreement to discuss joint space efforts. This would ultimately result in the International Space Station.

October 30 the worst monsoon to hit Vietnam in many years and all but stopped the Vietnam War as flooding killed 293 people and left over 200,000 homeless.

Also on October 30, rioting continued to erupt in Northern Ireland.

November 3, on the morning of the 1970 Congressional elections President Nixon promised to begin a complete gradual withdrawal from Vietnam. The Democrats lost three seats in the Senate but still held a majority, while the Republicans lost 12 seats in the House expanding the Democratic majority. However many of the Democratic seats in Congress were held by conservative Southern Democrats. These conservatives would began switching to the Republican Party because of Nixon's Southern Strategy of promoting state's rights to slow segregation and his law and order campaigns against Black civil rights and anti-war protesters.

Also on this date State Senator Jimmy Carter won the election for Georgia Governor campaigning against segregation and for affirmative action. Carter beat the segregationist former Governor Carl Sanders in the Democratic primary and then beat Republican candidate Hal Suit in the general election. Carter had previously lost the gubernatorial race in 1966 to the once popular segregationist Governor Lester Maddox in the Democratic primary. In his January inaugural address he made national headlines by stating "the time of racial segregation is over."

On November 4, socialist Salvador Allende became the President in Chile. The Allende government nationalized the copper industry, the most valuable resource in Chile which was then wholly owned by two US corporations, Anaconda Copper and Kennecott. The American company International Telephone and Telegraph Corporation (ITT) also owned the Chilean telephone system which was also nationalized. According to the *New York Times* March 6, 2001 the CIA at the direction of Nixon and his National Security Advisor Henry Kissinger began to undermine Allende by destroying the Chilean economy and eventually overthrew the Allende government in a military coup. Tim Weiner in his book *Legacy of Ashes* has since documented that the American companies paid the CIA to work in Chile on their behalf. The CIA sponsored a kidnapping of the Commander in Chief of the Chilean Army who was killed resisting the kidnappers. In 1973 a CIA sponsored a military coup that surrounded the palace and assassinated President Allende.

November 5, the Nixon Administration widely reported the lowest weekly death toll in five years, with 24 killed in the Vietnam. However much of this was weather related due to the monsoon and the flooding. There were also 431 reported wounded that week that the Administration didn't report. November 10, the Administration reported there were no fatalities in Vietnam. This was also mostly due to the monsoons and flooding.

November 7, racial riots broke out in Daytona Beach, Florida.

November 12, tropical cyclone Bhola struck Eastern Pakistan (now Bangladesh) killing between 300,000 and 500,000 people. The storm killed about half the population of the city of Tazumuddin, a town of about 167,000. The storm surge was estimated to be between 20 to 30 feet high.

November 13, General Hafez al-Assad came to power in a military coup in Syria. He would rule Syria as a dictator until his death in 2000. He would be replaced by his son, Bashar Hafez al-Assad.

Also on November 13, Vice President Spiro Agnew called television news executives "impudent snobs" for their coverage of the Nixon Administration.

November 14, the entire Marshall University football team in West Virginia was killed in a plane crash, a 2006 movie, *We Are Marshall* was later made about the incident.

November 16, South Vietnamese Vice President Nguyen Cao Ky defended US and ARVN operations in Cambodia by overstating the danger saying communist forces there could have overrun South Vietnam "within 24 hours."

November 17, the USSR landed Lunokhod 1 a remote controlled explorer on the Moon.

Also on November 17, the computer mouse was patented.

November 18, Nixon asked the Congress for $155 million for military aid to Cambodia.

November 21, the US Army attempted a raid into North Vietnam in Operation Ivory Coast to rescue their POWs at Son Tay Prison. However due to monsoon flooding the prisoners were moved and the Army mission failed.

November 25, a rightwing military coup failed to take over the government of Japan.

November 27, a Bolivian painter named Mendoza, disguised as a priest, attacked and wounded Pope Paul VI with a dagger on a visit to the Philippines. The pope was not seriously injured and Mendoza spent about three years in prison before he was sent back to Bolivia. In a bizarre related story President Ferdinand Marcos lied and claimed in the Filippine press that he had blocked the assassin with a single blow saving the Pope's life. His claim was also widely reported to the world press at the time. Marcos was not near the Pope during the incident. The Pope was saved by security people and police who had wrestled Mendoza to the ground.

December 2, the Environmental Protection Agency was established.

December 9, at a meeting of the Organization of the Petroleum Exporting Countries (OPEC) met in Venezuela and declared a 55% tax on oil with prices set immediately to reflect the new tax.

December 13-22, the government increased food prices in Poland setting off food riots. Soldiers fired on protestors striking at the Gdansk Shipyards killing dozens and Martial law was imposed. On December 23, the Polish government announced they would freeze food prices for three years.

December 22, Franz Stangl the Nazi commander of the Sobibór and Treblinka concentration camps was found guilty of crimes against humanity and sentenced to life imprisonment. Stangl had escaped through the Catholic Church's Ratline and was discovered in Brazil in 1967 and was extradited to Germany for the murders of 900,000.

December 23, the North Tower of the World's Trade Center in New York City was constructed to 1,368 feet making it the tallest building in the world.

December 30 the final cost of the riots in Northern Ireland were given at five and a half million pounds (approximately $10 million dollars.)

December 31, Paul McCartney went to court to dissolve the Beatles partnership.

At the end of 1970 there were still 335,750 US troops in Vietnam despite troop withdrawals. The US lost 6,081 men in Vietnam in 1970. Korea still had about 49,000 troops in Vietnam, Thailand about 12,000 troops, and Australia had 6,800 troops. The US built up the ARVN to a troop level of about 968,000 as Nixon's "Vietnamization" program was well underway.

In 1970 the inflation rate grew to almost 6%. as war debts mounted. The Average price of a house went to $23,450 and the average monthly rent rose to $140. The average income was $9,400 a year. A Chrysler Newport cost $3,861, but the new inexpensive AMC Gremlin was $1, 879 and a new car 8 track stereo tape player cost $38.99.

A new 28 inch color television was still expensive at $739.95. In addition to *Monday Night Football* the new television shows of 1970 included: *The Mary Tyler Moore Show*, *McCloud*, *The Flip Wilson Show*, *The Odd Couple*, *The Partridge Family*, and the soap operas: *All My Children*, *Somerset*, *A World Apart*, and *The Best of Everything*. Shows ending included: *The Flying Nun*, *Here Comes the Brides*, *Petticoat Junction*, *Daniel Boone*, *Get Smart*, *I Dream of Jeannie* and *Spiderman*. The Emmys went to *My World and Welcome to It* for Most Outstanding Comedy, *Marcus Welby MD* for Most Outstanding Drama, *The David Frost Show* for the Most Outstanding Variety Show, and *Sesame Street* for the Most Outstanding Children's Show. Outstanding Comedy Performances went to William Windom and Hope Lange for *My World and Welcome to It* and *The Ghost and Mrs. Muir* respectively. Outstanding Drama Performances went to Robert Young in *Marcus Welby MD* and Susan Hampshire in *The Forsythe Saga* the British mini-series which inspired American television's production of the mini-series.

In the movie rating system the M for mature rating was changed to PG for Parental Guidance. The movies of 1970 included two pictures that grossed over $100 million, *Love Story* and *Airport*. Other big hits included: *M*A*S*H*, *Patton*, *Woodstock*, *Little Big Man*, *Ryan's Daughter*, *Tora! Tora! Tora!*, *Catch-22*, *Women in Love*, *The Cheyenne Social Club*, *Five easy Pieces*, *There's a Girl in My Soup*, *Diary of a Mad Housewife* and *Chariots of the Gods*. At the Oscars *Patton* won Best Picture, Best Director and Best Actor, which was turned down by George C. Scott. Glenda Jackson won Best Actress for *Women in Love*.

The songs of 1970 were an eclectic and interesting mix. Simon and Garfunkel had the top tune with *Bridge Over Troubled Water* and another hit *Cecelia*. The Jackson 5 had four hits with *I'll Be There*, *ABC*, *The Love You Save*, and *I Want You Back*. The Guess Who hit with *American Woman*, B.J. Thomas had a hit with *Raindrops Keep Fallin' on My Head*, Edwin Starr with *War*, Diana Ross with *Ain't No mountain High Enough*, the Beatles with *Let it Be*, Freda Payne with *Band of Gold*, Ray Stevens with *Everything Is Beautiful*, Five Stairsteps with *O-o-h Child*, *Rainy Night in Georgia* by Brooke Benton, *Give Me Just a Little More Time* by the Chairmen of the Board, *Snowbird* by Anne Murray, *Hey There Lonely Girl* by Eddie Holman, *Lola* by the Kinks, *In the Summertime* by Mongo Jerry, *Indiana Wants Me* by R. Dean Taylor, *Fire and Rain* by James Taylor, *The Wonder of You* by Elvis Presley, and *Close to You* and *We've Only Just Begun* by the Carpenters.

The Nobel Prize for Literature in 1970 went to Aleksandr Solzhenitsyn. Some of the most popular books included: *Bury My Heart at Wounded Knee* by Dee Brown, *Jonathan Livingston Seagull* by Richard Bach, *QB VII* by Leon Uris, *The Bluest Eye* by Toni Morrison, *84 Charing Cross Road* by Helene Hanff, *The Driver's Seat* by Muriel Spark, *Time and Again* by Jack Finney, *The Female Eunuch* by Germaine Greer, *Love Story* by Erich Segal, *Frederick the Great* by Nancy Mitford, *A Pagan Place* by Edna O'Brien, *Bomber* by Len Deighton, *The Blessing Way* by Tony Hillerman, *Are You There God? It's Me, Margaret* by Judy Blume and *Islands in the Stream* by Ernest Hemingway which was published nine years after his death.

CHAPTER 27. 1971: THE DAWN OF THE DIGITAL AGE, MORE
VIETNAMIZATION, CO-INTELPRO EXPOSED, THE TROUBLES IN
NORTHERN IRELAND, AND THE INDO-PAKISTANI WAR

January 1, cigarette ads were banned from television.

January 4, the Congressional Black Caucus began organizing and adopted their name in February. All the founding members eventually found themselves on Nixon's political secret "enemies list."

January 8, Voyageurs National Park was established in northern Minnesota. The park contains the only genuine forest wilderness left in the contiguous 48 states.

Also on this same date 29 pilot whales mysteriously beached themselves and died on San Clemente Island in California beginning a continuous and unexplained phenomenon.

January 12, anti-war priest, Father Phillip Berrigan, and six others including two other priests and a nun, were accused of plotting to kidnap Henry Kissinger. A trial in 1972 found all six innocent. It was the first defeat by government prosecutors against anti-war demonstrators.

Also on January 12, a meeting in Tehran by 23 oil companies and six Persian Gulf members of OPEC came to set world's oil prices. They came to agreement in February.

January 23, a US record low temperature was recorded at minus 80 degrees Fahrenheit in Prospect Creek Camp, Alaska.

January 25, Charles Manson and three female members of his "family" were found guilty for the Tate-LaBianca murders.

January 31, to February 2, the Winter Soldier Investigation was a media event held in Detroit to give former American servicemen an opportunity to speak out about atrocities and crimes committed by the US military and CIA in Vietnam.

January 31to February 9, Apollo 14 the third successful Moon landing made its journey from Earth to the Moon and back.

January-April, called "The Troubles," riots and violence continued in Northern Ireland between Catholics and Protestants.

February 4, Rolls Royce declared bankruptcy and was nationalized by the British government.

Also on February 4, the National Guard was mobilized in Delaware to quell a racial riot in Wilmington.

February 8, a new stock market index, the NASDAQ Composite made its debut.

February 9, the Sylmar Earthquake stuck California with a magnitude of 6.7 on the Richter scale. Communities north of Los Angeles suffered heavy damage. About 68 people died. Four major hospitals in the San Fernando Valley suffered heavy damage and two collapsed.

February 11, the US, USSR and the UK signed the Seabed treaty barring nuclear weapon testing and detonations in the oceans.

February 13 to March 25, Operation Lam Son 719 saw the ARVN invade Laos with US helicopters and air cover and logistical support to shut down the Ho Chi Minh Trail. The NVA massed 36,000 troops against the invasion. The ARVN planned to keep troops in Laos until the rainy season thus setting back the NVA re-supply of troops in the south. However the NVA forced the ARVN out of the area with heavy losses. On April 7, Nixon went on television and lied, saying that the operation was a large success, proving that his plan for Vietnamization was working. However the US Army report contradicted Nixon's public statements to the American people. The Army report said that the operation "went in favor of the enemy." They further said that US "Airpower played an important, but not decisive role, in that it prevented a defeat from becoming a disaster that might have been so complete as to encourage the North Vietnamese Army to keep moving right into Quang Tri Province."

The 101st Airborne which had supplied the helicopters for the Operation had 84 destroyed and another 430 damaged. The US had 19 pilots killed, 11 missing and another 59 were badly wounded. The US Air Force flew 8,000 sorties and dropped 20,000 tons of bombs and napalm on the NVA during the ARVN attack and their retreat. The ARVN had 2,154 men killed or missing and 5,483 wounded. During their retreat the ARVN lost or abandoned 60% of their tanks and armored personnel carriers and 54 artillery pieces which then had to be destroyed by the US Air Force to prevent the NVA from capturing and using them on the retreating ARVN forces. It was a complete disaster. The US Army report also stated the operation had exposed grave deficiencies in ARVN "planning, organization, leadership, motivation, and operational expertise."

February 14, Nixon installed a secret voice recording system in the White House. The system would greatly assist in his eventual downfall.

February 20, an error at the National Emergency Center ordered all US television and radio stations to go off the air. The mistake caused the stations to be off the air for 30 minutes.

February 21, fifty tornados hit Mississippi and Louisiana causing widespread damage and killing 117 people.

February 28, Evil Knievel set a world record and became famous by jumping over 19 cars on a motorcycle.

March 8, a Citizens Commission to Investigate the FBI, broke into a small FBI office in Media, Pennsylvania and removed all their records. Among the files were records on the ultra-secret and illegal Operation COINTELPRO. The group mailed these documents to US newspapers which ended with the media and Congress investigating the FBI about their domestic spying, break-ins, drugging, framing and abusing anti-war protestors, Black, Latino and Native civil rights activists, leftists, and women's groups. The documents showed that well over half of the FBI's time and resources were spent on these political issues rather than on criminal activities.

Also on March 8, Muhammad Ali fought Joe Frazier, the World heavyweight champion, for the title. The Fight was dubbed by the media as "The fight of the century." Both boxers were undefeated. Ali had 31 straight victories, 25 by knockout before he was stripped of his title and lost his license to box in 1967 for refusing to serve as a conscientious objector. Frazier had 26 wins with 23 by knockouts. The fight showed that Ali was rusty and he lost to Frazier in a 15 round unanimous decision. Ali would eventually beat Frazier in two additional fights and win back his title in 1974 against George Foreman.

March 15, "chat rooms" begin on the internet.

March 26, the British television comedy program, The Benny Hill Show, went to the top of the US television ratings.

March 29, Lt. William L Calley Jr. was found guilty in the My Lai massacre.

April 5, the long sleeping volcano, Mt. Etna, suddenly erupted in Italy.

April 7, Nixon pardoned Lt. William Calley Jr. from his life sentence in the My Lai massacre.

April 10, in a rare US-China collaboration the US Table Tennis Team arrived in China for matches with Chinese teams.

April 19, the USSR launched Salyut 1 the first operational space station.

April 20, the US Supreme Court unanimously held that busing to achieve racial integration in schools may be implemented by school districts, state and local governments.

April 23, a student anti-war strike shut down Columbia University.

April 25, about 200,000 anti-war protestors marched in Washington, DC.

April 28, Admiral Samuel Lee Gravely Jr. became the first Black US Navy Admiral.

May 1, AMTRAK began passenger rail service taking over the service which was abandoned by the US railroads.

May 3, All Things Considered the long-running classic public radio show made its debut on the first day of broadcasting by National Public Radio.

Also on May 3, the Harris Poll showed that 60% of Americans were against the war in Vietnam.

May 3-6, Nixon ordered a crack-down on anti-war protestors. Within the next few days over 13,000 protestors were arrested on various charges in Washington, DC.

May 5, a race riot struck Brooklyn.

May 18, the US Congress denied funding to and killed the US Supersonic Transport program. The program was to provide government subsidies to private air carriers to operate supersonic air passenger service.

May 28, the USSR Mars 2 spacecraft became the first space craft to make a soft landing on Mars. The previous Mars 1 had crash landed.

June 1, Chuck Colson, a top White House aide who ran Nixon's infamous dirty tricks division, recruited John O'Neill, a Navy veteran who served on a minesweeper in the coastal waters off of Vietnam. Colson and O'Neil covertly organized the Vietnam Veterans for a Just Peace as an independent political group. It was supposed to be a counterweight to the growing anti-war Vietnam Veterans for Peace. O'Neill would later work for George W. Bush in a similar secret capacity to organize the Swift Boat Veterans for Truth who smeared John Kerry's Vietnam service record with lies and innuendo during the 2004 election.

June 6-30, Soyuz 11 was launched. It was the second attempt to put men in the Soviet Space Station. Upon re-entry the three man crew was killed in an accident when their capsule depressurized.

June 10, the US ended their trade embargo with China. Sino-US relations warmed up especially after the Chinese stopped supporting North Vietnam.

June 13, the *New York Times* began publishing the "Pentagon Papers." It is a history of the US conflict in Vietnam that showed that the Joint Chiefs of Staff, the CIA, the military and Presidents Johnson and Nixon had lied to the American people and to Congress about Vietnam and kept US troops there long after they realized it was a lost cause.

June 16, a race riot erupted in Jacksonville, Florida.

June 17, Nixon declared war on drugs. The US began incarcerating low level drug offenders contributing to an explosion in the US prison population.

June 19, the Mayor declared a state of emergency in Columbus, Georgia, home to Ft. Benning, one of the US Army's largest bases after race riots broke out in the city.

June 21, over 50,000 attended the Celebration of Life rock concert in McCrea, Louisiana.

June 30 the Nixon Administration went to court to try and stop the publication of the classified *Pentagon Papers*. The US Supreme Court ruled that the *Pentagon Papers* may be published.

July 1, Washington became the first state to ban sex discrimination.

July 3, Jim Morrison of the Doors was found dead in a bathtub in his Paris apartment.

July 5, the 28th Amendment was ratified lowering the voting age to 18.

July 6, the Nixon White House began a political unit called "the Plumbers" to stop leaks and to undertake secret political assignments. The Plumbers were mostly ex-CIA and intelligence personnel.

July 9, Henry Kissinger visited China.

July 11, the UK increased troop levels to 11,000 in Northern Ireland because of "the Troubles."

July 12, Juan Corona, a migrant farm worker, was indicted for the murder of 25 farm workers over a four month span. His victims, all men believed to be gay, were hacked to death with a machete and buried. In January 1973, Corona was convicted of first degree murder on all twenty five counts. He is serving twenty-five life sentences in California.

July 15, Nixon announced he would visit China.

July 19, the South Tower of the World trade center was "topped out" making it the second tallest building in the world.

July 26 to August 7, Apollo 15 was the fourth manned US Moon mission. It brought the Lunar Roving Vehicle, the first extraterrestrial manned vehicle.

July 29, citing economic reasons, the UK cancelled its Black Arrow launch vehicle killing the British space program.

August 1, riots erupted in Camden, New Jersey after the police killed a Puerto Rican man.

Also on August 1, over 40,000 attended The Concert for Bangladesh.

August 9, India signed a 20 year friendship agreement with the USSR.

August 14, Bahrain declared independence from Britain.

August 15, unemployment rose to 6.1% and an inflation rate rose to 5.84%. The president's advisors stated that drastic measures were needed to prevent further inflation and worse economic decline. Nixon declared that the US dollar would no longer be backed by gold. He also declared a 90 day price and wage freeze to combat growing inflation. It was the first time since WWII that the US government enacted a price and wage freeze.

Also on August 15, Britain raised the number of troops in Northern Ireland to 12,500.

August 18, Australia announced the decision to withdraw its 6,000 troops from Vietnam.

August 20, a US Navy oiler, the USS Manatee, spilled over 1,000 of fuel oil off the California coast which washed up on the beach at San Clemente and Nixon's "Western White House."

August 22, J. Edgar Hoover and Attorney General Mitchell announced the arrest of the Camden 28, a group of anti-war protestors lead by four Catholic priests and a Protestant minister who had allegedly raided and destroyed records in a Camden, New Jersey draft office. In May of 1973 all 28 were found not guilty by a jury. It was discovered during the trial that the FBI, through an informant had incited and assisted in the plot to destroy draft records in order to achieve the convictions of the protestors.

September 3, a burglary took place in the offices of Daniel Ellsberg's psychiatrist. It would later be revealed that this was the work of Richard Nixon's covert team, the Plumbers.

Also on September 3, John Lennon announced he was leaving Britain to live permanently in New York City.

September 8, the John F. Kennedy Center for the Performing Arts opened in Washington, DC.

September 9-13, over 1,000 convicts rioted at Attica State Prison in New York. In the aftermath 43 people were dead including 10 prison employees who the prisoners held hostage to negotiate better treatment. The conflict began after continued harassment and mistreatment of Black inmates by the all-White prison guards. Governor Rockefeller refused to negotiate and sent in the police and National Guard in force resulting in the deaths. In the aftermath, lawsuits filed by the families of the slain inmates against the State of New York resulted in a settlement paying $12 million in compensation for their wrongful deaths. New York also paid $12 million to the families of the slain hostages.

September 13, former Soviet Premiere, Nikita Khrushchev died and was buried in Moscow.

September 16, six Ku Klux Klansmen were arrested for bombing 10 school buses.

September 24, in the largest expulsion of the Cold War, 90 Soviet diplomats were expelled from Britain for spying.

September 27, the British, Northern Ireland and Irish Prime Ministers met to discuss the continued violence in Northern Ireland.

September 29, a tropical cyclone and tidal wave in the Bay of Bengal killed over 10,000 people in India.

October 1, Walt Disney World opened near Orlando, Florida.

October 12, the musical *Jesus Christ Superstar* opened.

October 14, two people were killed in race riots in Memphis.

Also on October 14, the environmental activist group, Greenpeace, was founded.

October 19, the last issue of *Look* magazine was published.

October 20, US Senator Edward Kennedy called for the withdrawal of British troops from Northern Ireland and negotiations to reunite Northern Ireland with Ireland.

October 21, Nixon nominated Lewis Franklin Powell Jr. and William Rehnquist to the Supreme Court. Both were later confirmed.

October 25, the United Nation voted to admit the People's Republic of China into membership and expelled Nationalist China.

October 28, Great Britain became the sixth nation to launch a satellite into space.

November 10, the US Table Tennis Team arrived in China, The trip greatly renewed American's interest in the game of ping pong.

November 13, Mariner 9 began its orbit around Mars and became the first manmade satellite to orbit another planet.

November 15, the first commercial micro-processor, the Intel 4004, was advertised.

November 24, a man calling himself D.B. Cooper hijacked a Northwest Orient Airlines flight in the state of Washington. After receiving $200,000 in cash he parachuted from the plane. He was never found and the case remains open.

December 2, six Persian Gulf sheikdoms merged and formed the United Arab Emirates.

December 3-16, Pakistan launched strikes on nine Indian airbases beginning the Indo-Pakistani War of 1971. The war came to an end when Indian forces captured the entire Eastern Command of the Pakistani Forces in East Pakistan, now Bangladesh. Their surrender began the new nation of Bangladesh and ended the war. India had about 8,000 killed and 9,581 wounded. Pakistan had about 9,000 killed, about 4,500 wounded and 97,386 taken prisoner. Pakistan lost 14 naval vessels to only one for India. During the war Nixon ordered the US 7th Fleet to the Bay of Bengal.

In Vietnam the US troop level fell to 158,120 as the US financed and built the ARVN forces up to more than 1 million men. There were also about 54,000 other allied troops, mostly Koreans still in South Vietnam. The US had 2,357 men killed in Vietnam in 1971.

1971 may be seen as the dawning of the digital age with commercial micro-processors and hand held calculators. National Public Radio began broadcasting. The DOW closed at 890 and the inflation rate was 4.3% but rising. Nixon declared a freeze on wages and prices to prevent it from rising further. The price of the average new house was $25,250, with average monthly rent rose to $150. The average income was $10,600 per year. The average price of a new car was $2,700 and gasoline rose to 40 cents per gallon.

In January the highly controversial television show *All in the Family* made its debut on television. The show brought previous taboo subjects like race, homosexuality, women's issues and politics to prime time television. In addition to *All in the Family* other television shows making their debuts in 1971 included: *Masterpiece Theater* and *The Electric Company* on PBS, *The Sonny and Cher Comedy Hour, McMillan and Wife, The New Dick Van Dyke Show,* and *Soul Train.* On the BBC the mini-series *Upstairs, Downstairs* also made its debut in Britain and would later become popular with Americans on PBS.

Shows ending included: *The Beverly Hillbillies, Green Acres, Julia, Mayberry R.F.D., The Ed Sullivan Show, Hogan's Heroes, Family Affair* and *That Girl.* At the Emmys *All in the Family, The Bold Ones, The Flip Wilson Show* and *Sesame Street* were the big winners.

The most popular movies of 1971 included: *Fiddler on the Roof, The French Connection, Diamonds Are forever, Dirty Harry, Billy Jack, Summer of '42, The Last Picture Show, Klute, Carnal Knowledge, Shaft, Vanishing Point,* and *A Clockwork Orange.* At the Oscars *The French Connection* swept with Best Picture, Best Director, Best Actor, Best Editing and Best Screenplay. Jane Fonda won best Actress in *Klute. The Last Picture Show* won two with Cloris Leachman and Ben Johnson for Best Supporting Actress and Actor. *Fiddler on the Roof* was nominated for six but won only two for Cinematography and Best Sound Mixing.

The top three on Billboard's Hot 100 for 1971 included: *Joy to the World* by Three Dog Night, *Maggie May* by Rod Stewart, and Carol King's *It's Too Late.* The Stones had *Brown Sugar,* Janis Joplin had *Me and Bobby McGee,* Paul Revere and the Raiders hit with *Indian Reservation,* the Bee Gees with *How Can You Mend a Broken Heart,* John Denver had *Take Me Home Country Roads,* The Temptations hit with *Just My Imagination,* Cornelius Brothers and Sister Rose sang *Treat Her Like a Lady,* James Taylor had *You've Got a Friend,* Marvin Gaye had two hits *What's Going On* and *Mercy Mercy Me,* Tom Jones sang *She's a Lady,* The Jackson Five had *Never Can Say Goodbye,* Ike and Tina Turner with *Proud Mary,* and the Carpenters with two *Rainy Days and Monday* and *For All We Know.*

The best books of 1971 included: *Fear and Loathing in Las Vegas* by Hunter S, Thompson, *Go Ask Alice* by Beatrice Sparks, *The Hiding Place* by Corrie ten Boom, *The Exorcist* by Peter Blatty, *The Day of the Jackal* by Frederick Forsythe, *Post Office* by Charles Bukowski, *The Winds of War* by Herman Wouk, *Hell House* by Richard Matheson, *Another Roadside Attraction* by Tom Robbins, *That Was Then, This Is Now* by S.E. Hinton, *The Other* by Thomas Tyron, *Rabbit Redux* by John Updyke, *Lives of Girls and Women* by Alice Munro, *The Book of Daniel* by E.L. Doctorow, *The Autobiography of Miss Jane Pittman* by Ernest J. Gaines, *Steal This Book* by Abbie Hoffman, *Eleanor and Franklin* by Joseph P. Lash and *The Drifters* by James Michener.

CHAPTER 28. 1972: WATERGATE, PARIS PEACE TALKS, THE BIRTH OF FINANCIAL DERIVATIVES AND RECOMBINANT DNA

January, "the Troubles" continued in Northern Ireland.

January 2, Mariner 9 began mapping Mars.

January 4, the first hand-held scientific calculator the HP35 went on sale for $395. The prices would come down quickly with mass production.

January 5, the development of the US Space Shuttle program began.

January 9, the reclusive Howard Hughes said the biography about him by Irving Wallace was a fake. Wallace would later admit in court that he had fabricated the biography.

January 11, the former state of East Pakistan formally became the independent state of Bangladesh.

January 20, unemployment in Great Britain exceeded a million.

Also on January 20, Pakistan began a program to develop nuclear weapons.

January 24, a WWII Japanese Army soldier was found hiding in the jungles of Guam. He believed the war was still on-going.

January 25, Congresswoman Shirley Chisholm announced her candidacy for President and became the first Black woman to run.

Also on January 25, Nixon announced that Kissinger had been secretly meeting with North Vietnam in Paris to negotiate a peace agreement. The North Vietnamese criticized Nixon for revealing the secret negotiations.

January 30, in "the Troubles" British soldiers shot 27 unarmed demonstrators in Northern Ireland and 14 died. The incident became known as "Bloody Sunday."

February 2, angry protestors burned the British Embassy to the ground in Dublin over the killings on Bloody Sunday.

February 3-13, the Winter Olympics were held in Sapporo, Japan.

February 9-13, the US conducted the heaviest bombing of the Vietnam War on North Vietnam and along the Ho Chi Minh trail.

February 11, the Ambassador to Laos, G. McMurtrie Godley, criticized Nixon's plan to abandon the US secret CIA base in Laos at Long Tieng. He said it would plunge the country into the abyss. Nixon relented and allowed Godley to take charge of the base. It remained in operation for three more years until it was overrun by the NVA and Laotian communists.

February 16, three US aircraft were shot down over North Vietnam.

February 21, the unmanned Soviet spaceship Luna 20 landed on the moon.

February 22, the Irish Republican Army (IRA) exploded a car bomb at Aldershot Barracks in Britain killing 7 paratroopers. It was in retaliation for Bloody Sunday.

February 21- 28, Nixon visited China with strong approval from the international community.

February 25, Paul McCartney released his single, *Give Ireland Back to the Irish* which was banned by the BBC.

February 26, a coal sludge heap began to slide and killed 125 people in Buffalo Creek, West Virginia.

March 2, Pioneer 10 was launched and would much later become the first spacecraft to leave the solar system.

March 3, the carvings of three Southern Civil War figures were completed at Stone mountain, Georgia the birthplace of the modern Ku Klux Klan. Today it is operated as a historic state park and Civil War memorial in Georgia masking its Klan origins.

March 7, it was announced that the air raids conducted against North Vietnam in the first two months of 1972 exceed all of the raids in 1971. The US ground battles had been greatly reduced but the US air war was expanding. At the end of February the North Vietnamese walked out of the peace negotiations because of the increased heavy bombing.

March 8, the Goodyear Blimp made its first flight.

March 10, the 101st Airborne left Vietnam. It was the last official US combat division in Vietnam, however US air power and support troops remained engaged in the war. Also on this date General Lon Nol became the president of Cambodia with US backing.

March 13, China and Great Britain normalized diplomatic relations.

March 22, the Equal Rights Amendment to the Constitution which proposed equal rights for women was ratified by Congress and sent to the states for ratification. In the time allotted for adoption by the states only 35 of the necessary 38 states approved and the Amendment failed. Since that time five states have rescinded their approval.

Also on March 22, the US Supreme Court ruled that single people have the same right to contraception as married people.

March 23, the US boycotted the Paris Peace Talks saying the North Vietnamese were not negotiating in good faith.

Also on March 23, after successfully jumping over 35 cars on his motorcycle Evel Knievel crashed and was severely injured.

March 30 to October 22, the NVA attacked in what became known as the Easter Offensive. They launched a three prong invasion of South Vietnam. They captured the provincial capital at Quảng Trị and the important city of Lộc Ninh. They also threatened Hue and the provincial capital at An Lộc. However the ARVN kept control of both cities and launched a counter offensive in September re-capturing Quảng Trị. During the attacks the US launched massive airstrikes against the invaders and against North Vietnam. Nixon infamously stated at the time. "These bastards have never been bombed like they're going to be bombed this time." Because of the air strikes in North Vietnam the peace talks stopped.

Although the ARVN did better than expected they had still lost the northern part of South Vietnam to the NVA. The NVA claimed it had killed 213,307 ARVN. The US claimed that between 40,000 and 75,000 NVA were killed. The ARVN also lost over 1,000 tanks and APCs. During all of 1972 there were 300 US troops killed, almost all in this offensive. In these battles over 25,000 South Vietnamese civilians were killed and there were about 1 million refugees, about 600,000 began living in temporary government camps.

Also on March 30, as "the Troubles" in Northern Ireland continued Great Britain dissolved the Northern Ireland government and imposed direct rule. A general strike was held in protest.

April 7, Richard McCoy Jr., a Vietnam veteran attempted to copy the hijacking of D.B. Cooper, by hijacking a United Airlines jet and demanding $500,000. He was later captured.

April 10, the US, USSR and 70 other nations entered in to a treaty banning biological weapons. Since that time a total of 173 nations have become parties to the agreement.

April 15-20, anti-war protests flared across the US with the new bombing campaign against North Vietnam. Hundreds of demonstrators were arrested.

April 16-27, Apollo 16 was launched. It was the fifth Apollo crew to land on the Moon. They brought back 211 pounds of rock samples.

Also on April 16, a gift from China of two giant pandas, Ling Ling and Hsing Hsing arrived at the National Zoo in Washington. DC.

April 25, George McGovern won the Massachusetts Democratic Presidential Primary. Immediately after the primary conservative columnist Robert Novak quoted a US Senator saying that McGovern was for amnesty for draft dodgers, abortion and the legalization of pot. Hubert Humphrey running against McGovern then actively campaigned calling McGovern the candidate for "amnesty, abortion and acid." It was a theme Nixon later used in the general election.

April 27, the Tutsi in Burundi began mass genocide against the Hutu. The 2002 *International Commission of Inquiry for Burundi* estimates that over 100,000 were killed and 300,000 fled the country.

April 28, Senator Edmond Muskie, the Democrat's most likely candidate ended his campaign for president. Muskie had lost the important New Hampshire Primary and the Massachusetts Primary after a letter to the *Manchester Union Leader* claimed he wrote disparaging remarks in a letter about the large French-American population in New England. It was learned later that the letter was a forgery made by Nixon's "dirty tricks unit." It was also in *Manchester Union Leader* that Nixon's dirty tricks unit also spread rumors that Muskie's wife was a drunk and used un-lady-like foul language, which triggered a very emotional response from Muskie which was then also used against him.

April 30, the popular radio show, *Arthur Godfrey Time* ended its 27 year run.

May 2, in Kellogg, Idaho, 126 miners died in a fire in silver mine.

May 8, with the loss of the northern areas of South Vietnam to the NVA, Nixon ordered the mining of Haiphong Harbor in North Vietnam. Anti-war protests erupted across the US. Nixon also secretly told North Vietnam that he would drop his demand for the withdrawal of all NVA troops from South Vietnam as a condition of peace. Instead he offered to withdraw all US forces in exchange for the US prisoners of War and a six month cease fire. The North Vietnamese responded favorably and secret negotiations began.

May 11, on the *Dick Cavett Show* John Lennon revealed that the FBI was tapping his home phone.

May 15, Governor George Wallace running for President in the Democratic primaries was shot in an assassination attempt in Laurel, Maryland. The attempt left Wallace paralyzed and in a wheelchair and destroyed any chance at being president. Wallace would however later run and win two more terms as Governor of Alabama. His assassin Arthur Bremer had wanted to assassinate either Nixon or George McGovern to prove his manhood and to become famous, but he settled for assassinating Wallace after the other two proved too difficult.

Also on May 15, the United States formally returned Okinawa back to Japan after 27 years of occupation. The islands of Ryukyu and Daito are also returned to Japan.

May 16, the first financial derivatives exchange, the International Monetary Market, was opened on the Chicago Mercantile Exchange. Derivatives were meant as a way for financial institutions to hedge their bets and help mitigate risk. Unfortunately they also led to rampant speculation in the financial markets. By the 1990s rapid electronic trading of derivatives became the norm and set off a massive wave of speculation in the financial markets. In the mid 1990s Brooksley Born, the Chair of the Commodities Future Trading Commission (CFTC), warned that unregulated derivatives could potentially bring down the US economy and proposed regulating the industry. She was opposed by the Chairman of the Federal Reserve System Alan Greenspan and Treasury Secretaries Robert Rubin and Lawrence Summers. President Clinton and the Congress sided against her and the derivative market remained unregulated. In 1998 a derivative hedge fund called Long Term Capital Management failed and the US economy hung in the balance. The US bailed out the fund. However, on the advice of Greenspan, they still refused to regulate the derivative market. In 2007-8 financial and housing bubble the derivative market collapsed causing several large financial institutions to collapse, and with it the US economy. Once again the financial institutions were bailed out by the US government.

May 22, President Nixon began an official visit to Moscow. On May 26, the visit would result in the signing of the Strategic Arms Limitation Treaty (SALT) which limited the number of nuclear weapons held by both nations.

Also on this day Ceylon became the Republic of Sri Lanka.

May 24, the German Red Army Faction exploded a bomb at a US base in West Germany killing three American soldiers. The culprits were arrested by the German police on June 2, after a shoot-out in Frankfurt.

May 28, four men, dubbed "the Plumbers" by the Nixon White House, broke into the Democratic Party campaign headquarters in the Watergate complex which began the scandal called Watergate. This event would ultimately lead to the resignation of President Richard Nixon and the conviction of his closest aides for numerous crimes and misdemeanors.

June 1, Iraq nationalized the Iraq Petroleum Company that was owned by American and Western European oil companies.

June 4, Angela Davis was found not guilty by an all-White jury in her murder trial. The jury stated that the fact she donated weapons to the Black Panthers to defend themselves which were then later used in a courtroom shoot-out did not make her guilty of murder.

June 6, the US bombed Haiphong, North Vietnam, killing thousands.

June 7, in a historic move to make amends West German Chancellor Willie Brandt visited Israel.

June 8, Vietnam War photographer Nick Ut took a photo of a naked nine-year-old girl crying and running down a road in Vietnam after being burned by an American napalm bomb. The photo became one of the iconic pictures of the war and Ut later won the Pulitzer Prize for this photo.

June 9, a flood in the Black Hills of South Dakota burst a dam and killed 237 people.

June 14-23, Hurricane Agnes stuck the East Coast of the US killing 128 people and causing over $3 billion in damages.

June 17, five Nixon White House employees are arrested for the burglary and the electronic bugging of the Democratic Party headquarters at the Watergate complex.

Also on June 17, Salvador Allende a socialist was elected and formed a new government in Chile. He nationalized Chile's copper and banking industries infuriating American business interests in Chile. According to Tim Weiner in his book *Legacy of Ashes*, Nixon, Henry Kissinger and the CIA began their plans for the overthrow of Allende and a military government that would be more suitable to American business interests.

June 23, President Nixon and his Chief of Staff H.R. Haldeman constructed a plan using the CIA to cover up the Watergate Burglary. The CIA refused to cooperate.

June 25, Bernice Gera became the first female umpire in professional baseball.

June 28, trying to quell the anti-war movement President Nixon announced that no new draftees would be sent to Vietnam.

July 1, anti-war actress Jane Fonda toured North Vietnam during which she was filmed posing on a North Vietnamese anti-aircraft gun. She was roundly criticized and years later she apologized for this act.

Also on this day the first copy of Ms. Magazine went on sale and the musical *Hair* closed after 1,750 performances.

June 7, the first two women FBI agents were sworn to duty.

July 8, the US sold $750 million in grain to the USSR.

June 10-14, The Democratic Convention was held in Miami. George McGovern was nominated for President with Senator Thomas Eagleton of Missouri as his running mate.

June 18, the Pocono Rock Festival in Pennsylvania drew about 200,000 people.

Also on June 18, in an on-going dispute with the USSR, Egyptian President Anwar Sadat ordered 20,000 USSR military aides to leave the country.

July 21, fifty-seven murders occurred in a twenty-four hour period in New York City giving the impression that the city was becoming the crime capitol of the nation.

July 25, after a whistleblower leaked the story to the press, US government health officials disclosed the Tuskegee Experiment where the US government had conducted inhumane medical experiments on Black males for over 40 years under the guise of free medical care. Officials confirmed that Black male patients diagnosed with syphilis were not told of their disease and deliberately went untreated so that doctors could study their progressive deterioration from the untreated disease. The 399 men were given free medical care, free meals and burial insurance for their participation in this group. Later 128 died of syphilis or from complications due to the disease. Other Black males with syphilis were later added to the study and an exact number is unknown. A later lawsuit against the government brought a $10 million dollar settlement to the victims or their surviving families. Some survivors were given life time health care as a result of the settlement including wives who were infected by syphilis by husbands who didn't know they had the disease and passed it on. Forty of their wives were infected and nineteen of their children were born with the disease.

July 26, Rockwell received a contract to build the first NASA Space Shuttle.

July 31, it had been previously disclosed that Senator Eagleton, McGovern's running mate, had been treated for depression. Critics claimed that because of this he was unfit to serve. McGovern initially stood by his running mate but by this date McGovern was under such pressure that he asked for a voluntary resignation from Eagleton and he complied. The Kennedy brother-in-law Sergeant Shriver was then added to the Democratic ticket as the Vice Presidential candidate.

August 4, Arthur Bremer was sentenced to 63 years in prison for shooting George Wallace.

August 12, the last "official" American ground combat troops left Vietnam, but advisors, support personnel and air units continued their work.

Also on August 12, *Oh! Calcutta!* Closed after 1, 316 performances.

August 21, the Republican Convention Opened in Miami. Nixon and Agnew were nominated for a second term.

August 26 to September 11, the Summer Olympics were held in Munich, Germany. On September 4, Mark Spitz an American Swimmer became the first athlete to win seven Olympic gold medals. During September 5 and 6, an Arab terrorist group, Black September, invaded the Olympic Village to take hostages and murdered 11 Israeli athletes. Five of the eight terrorists and one policeman were also killed in the attack.

August 27, the US again heavily bombed North Vietnam.

August 29, President Nixon was asked a question about Watergate at a news conference and falsely stated, "I can say categorically that no one in the White House staff, no one in this administration, presently employed, was involved in this very bizarre incident."

September 1, Bobby Fischer became the first American world chess champion by defeating the Russian Boris Spassky in Reykjavik, Iceland.

September 15, a rare 4.5 Midwest earthquake shook northern Illinois.

September 24, an F-86 Sabrejet performing at an air show killed 23, including 12 children, when it crashed into an ice cream parlor in Sacramento.

September 28, Japan and the People's Republic of China re-established diplomatic relations.

September 29, *The Washington Post* revealed that Attorney General John Mitchell controlled a secret fund for the Nixon campaign which was used to spy on the Democrats.

October 8, during the final election campaigning there was widespread speculation, most likely leaked from the Nixon Administration that claimed that a major breakthrough had been reached between Henry Kissinger and Le Duc Tho at the Paris Peace Talks.

October 10, *The Washington Post* revealed that Watergate was part of a massive spying and mischief operation on behalf of Nixon Administration officials.

October 11, 50 inmates rioted at a DC jail, captured 11 prison officials and held them hostage. The riot was over harsh conditions in the DC jail. The DC Corrections Director went into the jail in an attempt to negotiate but was captured and subjected to abuse and threatened with death. During the prison standoff the inmates requested that Congresswoman Shirley Chisholm come to the jail. Chisholm negotiated a deal whereby six of the inmates along with the Corrections Director who was still their hostage would be allowed to speak to a judge about their grievances. The crisis was then ended with promises of better conditions and immunity from prosecution of the inmates involved. Despite an agreement to not prosecute the inmates, a Grand Jury found them all guilty of multiple crimes and found that the judge and Corrections Director who had been under physical threats could not grant immunity under the law.

October 12, according to Franklin H. Bruce in his book *Vietnam and Other American Fantasies* while en route to the Gulf of Tonkin off Vietnam a 200 person anti-war and race riot erupted among the crew on the Aircraft Carrier USS Kitty Hawk and over 46 sailors were injured. The Kitty Hawk had been ordered to return to Vietnam after the air craft carriers USS Ranger and USS Forrestal had been disabled by their crew's deliberate sabotage.

October 16, Congressman Hale Boggs and Alaskan Congressman Nick Begich along with the pilot and a Begich aide died in a plane crash on a flight from Anchorage to Juneau. Despite a massive search the wreckage was never found. Boggs was one of the Warren Commission members who had stated that the Commission had been "hoodwinked." He was a severe critic of the CIA. He also had begun to criticize the FBI and J Edgar Hoover for illegal activities abuses of power just prior to the crash. These statements and Boggs' on-going inquiries have led some to believe that Boggs was assassinated.

October 26, returning from South Vietnam Henry Kissinger announced that "peace is at hand."

October 30 in one of the worst rail accidents in US history 45 passengers were killed and 332 were injured when two commuter trains collided in Chicago.

November 3-9, the American Indian Movement occupied the Bureau of Indian Affairs Offices to negotiate better housing and living conditions on reservations and the restoration of their rights under previously granted treaties. They protestors left after a week.

November 7, in the 1972 presidential election President Nixon was re-elected with 47 million votes to Senator George McGovern's 29 million votes. McGovern won only Massachusetts and DC giving Nixon the fourth largest landslide in US history.

November 11, the DOW Jones Index rose above 1000 for the first time.

Also on this day the US Army base at Long Bihn in South Vietnam was turned over to the South Vietnamese Army.

November 22, the US ended a twenty-two year travel ban for Americans visiting China.

November 29, the first video game, Pong, was released and became a commercial success.

November 30, Nixon's press secretary Ron Zeigler stated that there would be no more announcements of US troop withdrawals from Vietnam. The US troop levels stood at 24,200 at the end of the year and 641 Americans lost their lives in the war during 1972.

December 4, with the election in the rearview mirror Henry Kissinger's pre election statement that "peace is at hand" looked to be an election ploy. He returned to Paris where Tho had accused him of deception. The negotiations went nowhere and on December 13, Kissinger returned to Washington.

December 7-19, the final manned lunar mission Apollo 17 was launched.

December 8, an American Airlines plane crashed in Chicago killing 45 people.

December 12, President Thieu of South Vietnam announced that he opposed a peace agreement. On December 16, in referring to a peace agreement Kissinger warned the South Vietnamese that "no other party will have a veto over our actions."

December 14, Nixon, Kissinger and General Alexander Haig planned and agreed to an intensive bombing campaign on the cities of Hanoi and Haiphong and to keep bombing "until the enemy's will is broken." They called the new offensive Operation Linebacker II.

December 22, an American peace delegation led by folk singer Joan Baez brought mail and gifts to the American POWs in North Vietnam. They were caught in Nixon's Christmas bombing of North Vietnam. Swedish Prime Minister Olof Palme compared Nixon's bombing campaign of civilians in North Vietnam to the massacres of the Nazis and the Nixon White House severed diplomatic relations with Sweden.

December 25, Nixon was widely criticized at home and abroad for the bombing campaign. Although most civilians had been evacuated from Hanoi and Haiphong 1,623 Vietnamese civilians were still killed.

December 26, former President Harry Truman died in Kansas City.

December 28, Kim Il Sung succeeded his father and became the President of North Korea.

December 29, an Eastern Airlines flight crashed in Florida killing 101 people.

December 31-January 7, Mark Essex was a mentally disturbed man who had been discharged from the Navy for "behavior disorders" joined the Black Panthers. On December 31 in New Orleans he went on a killing spree. He started by killing a Black police cadet. By the time he was killed in a shoot-out with police he had shot and killed 9 people and injured 13 others including 10 police officers. Two of the dead were a couple on their honeymoon. He sent a note to a New Orleans television station claiming that he attacked police for many reasons but particularly in revenge for the deaths of two Black men.

Also during the year scientists presented the concept of recombinant DNA changing the fields of biology and genetics and making available genetically modified organisms. And in 1972 digital watches were introduced.

Inflation subsided a little with the wage and price freeze at 3.27%. The cost of a new house rose to $27,550 and the average rent was $165 per month and the average price of a new car was $3,853 gasoline rose to 55 cents per gallon. A college education was still cheap. The annual tuition at Harvard University was $2,800. The average income was $11,800.

In television half of the nation's households now had color television sets. The *Tonight Show* with Johnny Carson moved from New York to Burbank, California. The first Star Trek convention was held in January. The game show *The Price is Right* made its debut and would become the longest running game show in television history. In November HBO was launched in Wilkes-Barre, Pennsylvania. Captain Kangaroo made his 5,000th show. Other television debuts included: *M*A*S*H, The Bob Newhart Show, Bridget Loves Bernie, Sanford and Son, Emergency, Fat Albert, Maude, The Waltons, The Streets of San Francisco, The Rookies, Kung Fu.* Shows in their final season included: *The Courtship of Eddie's Father, Bewitched,* and *My Three Sons.* In the Emmys *All in the Family* won Best Comedy and Carroll O'Connor for Best Comedy Actor and Jean Stapleton for Best Comedy Actress. *The Carol Burnett Show* and *The Dick Cavett Show* won for Best Variety and Talk Show. *Sesame Street* won for Best Children's Program. Peter Falk in *Columbo* and Glenda Jackson in the PBS show *Elizabeth R.* won as the Best Dramatic Actors. Ed Asner and Valarie Harper won Best Comedy Supporting Actors both in *The Mary Tyler Moore Show.*

At the movies the runaway top film was *The Godfather* which grossed almost $134 million. The film won Oscars for Best Picture and the Best Actor for Marlon Brando. It also won the Golden Globes for Best Picture, Best Actor and the Best Director for Francis Ford Coppola. *Cabaret* was notable and won Oscars for Best Director, Bob Fosse, Best Actress Liza Minnelli, and Best Supporting Actor Joel Gray. Other notable movies included: *Deliverance, The Poseidon Adventure, What's Up Doc, Jeremiah Johnson, The Getaway* and WoodyAllen's *Everything You Always Wanted to Know About Sex.* Two X rated movies were in the top ten grossing films of 1972, *Behind the Green Door* and the first animated X rated movie, *Fritz the Cat.* Another X rated movie was poplar, *The Last Tango In Paris* starring Marlon Brando, its rating was later changed to NC-17.

The music of 1972 included a variety of top songs. Billboard's Hot 100 had rock and rollers, crooners, country, old and new groups. Roberta Flack had the top hit with *The First Time Ever I Saw Your Face* which won a Grammy and had a second top 100 hit in *Where is the Love?* Gilbert O'Sullivan had the number two hit *Alone Again (Naturally).* Don McLean hit at number three with *American Pie* and had another top 100 hit in *Vincent.* Harry Nilsson hit at number four with *Without You. The Candy Man* by Sammy Davis Jr. was number five in the Hot 100. Other top songs of the year included: *Lean on Me* by Bill Withers, *Baby, Don't Get Hooked On Me* by Mac Davis, *Brand New Key* by Melanie, *Brandy (You're a Fine Girl)* by the Looking Glass, *Oh Girl* by the Chi-Lites, *Song Sung Blue* by Neil Diamond, *Knights in White Satin* by the Moody Blues, *Everybody Plays the Fool* by the Main Ingredient, *To Late to Turn Back Now* by Brother Cornelius and Sister Rose, *Rocket Man* by Elton John, *Morning Has Broken* by Cat Stevens, *Burning Love* by Elvis, *Garden Party* by Ricky Nelson, *Layla* by Derek and the Dominoes, *You Don't mess Around with Jim* by Jim Croce, *School's Out* by Alice Cooper, *Family Affair* by Sly and the Family Stone, *Sealed with a Kiss* by Bobby Vinton, *Doctor My Eyes* by Jackson Browne and *I Would Like to Teach the World to Sing* by the New Seekers.

In 1972 the book *Fire in the Lake: the Vietnamese and the Americans in Vietnam* by Francis Fitzgerald was published and went on to win the Pulitzer Prize. *The Optimist's Daughter* by Eudora Welty also won a Pulitzer Prize. Other popular books of 1972 included *The Joy of Sex* by Alex Comfort, *Watership Down* by Richard Adams, *The Stepford Wives* by Ira Levin, *All Creatures Great and Small* by James Herriot, *The Gods Themselves* by Isaac Asimov, *My Name is Asher Lev* by Chaim Potok, *The Odessa File* by Frederick Forsyth, *Virginia Wolf: A Biography* by Quentin Bell, *Which Tribe Do You Belong to?* By Alberto Moravia, *Rise to Globalism: American Foreign Policy Since 1938* by Stephen Ambrose, *The Social Animal* by Elliott Aronson, and *No Name in the Street* by James Bladwin.

Chapter 29. 1973: The End of the US Involvement in the Vietnam War, Cell Phones, More Watergate and The Energy Crisis

January 8, secret talks between the US and North Vietnam resumed near Paris.

January 14, Elvis Presley's concert in Hawaii was the first worldwide ever broadcast by an entertainer. His audience was larger than those that watched the Apollo moon landings.

January 15, Richard Nixon announced he would suspend hostile actions (bombing) against North Vietnam citing progress in peace negotiations.

Also on this day the four Watergate burglars pled guilty in Federal Court.

January 20, Richard Nixon was inaugurated for a second term.

January 22, the Supreme Court decision on Roe v. Wade overturned state bans on abortions.

Also on January 22, former President Lyndon Johnson died at his home in Texas.

January 23, Nixon announced a peace agreement had been reached to end the Vietnam War.

January 27, the US and North Vietnam signed a peace agreement ending the longest war in US history.

January 30, a jury found the Nixon "Plumbers" G. Gordon Liddy and James McCord guilty on all counts for their burglary of the Democratic Party Headquarters in the Watergate Complex.

February 5, the funeral for Lt. Colonel William Nolde, the last American soldier killed in Vietnam, was held.

February 8, the Senate appointed 7 members to investigate the Watergate Scandal.

February 10, a gas tank exploded on Staten Island killing 40 people.

February 12, the first American POWs, 116 of 456 held were released and flown to the Philippines.

February 13, the US dollar was devalued by 10 per cent.

February 18, a giant octopus was captured in the Hood Canal in the state of Washington.

February 25, mass murderer Juan Corona was sentenced to twenty-five consecutive life terms for killing 25 migrant farm workers.

February 27 to May 8, Members of the American Indian Movement and members of the Oglala Sioux met at the town of Wounded Knee to discuss their grievances about the poverty and government corruption on the Pine Ridge Indian Reservation in South Dakota. The FBI had previously infiltrated the group and within hours the US Marshals had surrounded the tiny reservation town with fifteen armored personnel carriers, and a military force equipped with automatic rifles, grenade launchers, .50 caliber machine guns and 130,000 rounds of ammunition. They also had helicopters and snipers. It was a horrible overreaction. The Natives took defensive positions only to protect their lives. The US government cutoff the electricity and food supplies to the town. The standoff lasted 71 days. The first casualty was Native man who was shot in the head by a federal sniper from a helicopter through a window as he slept in bed. In all two Natives were killed and 13 were wounded. The Natives fired back in self-defense and 2 federal agents were wounded.

The Natives later told an Assistant Attorney General who entered the town under a white flag that they feared for their lives and took defensive positions. They believed that like the Black Panthers, the agents had come to kill all of them. His negotiations led to the end of the siege. Two AIM members, Dennis Banks and Russell Means, were tried for conspiracy and assault. A twelve-person jury found that the government agents and provocateurs had caused the problem and acquitted both on the conspiracy charge, but before they could rule on the assault charge one juror suffered a stroke and the government refused to accept the verdict of the remaining eleven. During the trial, the federal judge became aware of misdeeds by the FBI and the government prosecutors not only during the siege, but during the trial, including hiding evidence and infiltrating and spying on the defense counsel. The judge dismissed all charges, saying that the defendants could no longer have a fair trial. The judge's ruling was upheld on an appeal.

The Wounded Knee incident was ruled to have been caused by the government and not by the Natives. Judge Fred Nichol said in part "the misconduct by the government in this case is so egregious that a dismissal must be entered in the interests of justice." He castigated the FBI for their role in these unlawful misdeeds.

March 2, Black September terrorists occupied the Saudi Arabian Embassy in Khartoum.

March 8, "The Troubles" between Britain and the IRA continued and spread to England. The IRA planted four car bombs in London.

March 19, Presidential Counsel John Dean warned Nixon about Watergate and the Administration's cover-up telling him "There is a cancer growing on the presidency."

March 23, in a letter to Judge John Sirica, Watergate Burglar James McCord admitted that he and the other Watergate defendants were pressured by the White House to remain silent about the crimes. He named Attorney General John Mitchell as the instigator and leader of the Watergate break-in.

March 29, the last US combat troops left Vietnam. The US left about 7,000 Department of Defense advisors to work with the South Vietnamese military.

March 30, Ellsworth Bunker resigned as the Ambassador to South Vietnam.

April 2, CBS Radio began the first 24 hour day news coverage.

April 3, Martin Cooper of Motorola made the first handheld cell phone call in New York City.

April 6, Pioneer 11 was launched to explore Jupiter and the outer solar system. It would provide the first exploration of Saturn.

April 9, Governor Otto Kerner of Illinois was convicted of accepting bribes. Kerner had previously received national recognition as chair of the Kerner Commission that investigated the Los Angeles Riots in 1967.

April 12, France recognized North Vietnam.

April 14, acting FBI director L. Patrick Gray resigned after admitting he destroyed evidence in the growing Watergate scandal at the request of the White House.

April 26, Judge William Byrne was given a government memo disclosing a White House ordered break-in into the offices of Daniel Ellsberg's psychiatrist's office and illegal wire-tapping. Judge Byrne ordered that it be revealed to Ellsberg's defense counsel. Ellsberg had been charged under the Espionage Act of 1917 with treason for leaking the secret Pentagon papers about the Vietnam War to the press.

April 28, a fire in a railway boxcar in Roseville, California, set off bombs that were being transported for the US Navy. Over the next 32 hours 18 boxcars loaded with bombs exploded. Forty-eight people were injured and over $24 million dollars of damage was done to the railroad yard and surrounding community.

April 30, in an attempt to save his presidency from the growing Watergate scandal Nixon accepted the resignations of Attorney General Richard Kleindienst, and his two top aides, H.R. Haldeman, John D. Ehrlichman. He also stated that he was requesting the resignation of White House Counsel John Dean. Nixon stated that these resignations were not an admission of any guilt.

May 3, The Chicago Sears Tower officially became the world's tallest building at 1,451 feet surpassing the New York Trade Center.

May 4, PBS aired the play *Steambath*. It was controversial for its satire on religion, strong language and particularly because it contained the first television female nudity. Only 24 PBS affiliates dared to show the play.

May 11, Judge William Byrne dismissed all charges against Daniel Ellsberg in the release of the Pentagon Papers citing the burglary of Ellsberg's psychiatrist's office, illegal wiretapping and other government misconduct in the case.

May 14, the US Supreme Court decided in *Frontiero v. Richardson* that the US military cannot provide different benefits to women and that all service members are entitled to equal benefits. It was a landmark case in equal rights for women in the military. Prior to this ruling, only men were allowed housing benefits and other provisions for spouses and children.

Also on May 14, Skylab the first semi-permanent space station was launched. Skylab would be successfully used for experiments until 1979 when its orbit decayed and it burned up on re-entry. It was a precursor of the International Space Station.

May 17, the Senate Watergate Committee began their hearings. The hearings were televised live by the three commercial networks and re-broadcast in the evenings by PBS. Over 85% of all US households watched at least a portion of the hearings on their televisions daily. They were also aired live on public radio.

May 18, in a spirit of new Cold War realities the leader of the USSR, Leonid Brezhnev, visited West Germany.

May 22, Nixon confessed to some guilt in a Watergate cover-up. He said, "With hindsight, it is apparent that I should have given more heed to the warning signals I received along the way about a Watergate cover-up." However he continued to lie about his own role and stated categorically that he had no role in the break-ins or their subsequent cover-up.

May 29, Thomas Bradley was elected the first and only Black mayor of Los Angeles.

June 14, with inflation concerns rising again President Nixon ordered another price freeze. Wages were not included in this freeze.

June 18-24, in an attempt to redirect public attention from Watergate Nixon began a series of meetings with the Soviet leader Brezhnev in the US. The White House tapes show a distracted and quiet Nixon and a warm understanding Brezhnev. During their meetings Nixon surprised Brezhnev with a gift of a dark blue Lincoln Continental at Camp David and the two of them took off speeding down the road with Brezhnev behind the wheel. It happened before the Secret Service could react and caused a panic. The two men developed a friendship and Brezhnev went with Nixon to his house in San Clemente, California and stayed in his daughter Tricia's room. Brezhnev said he couldn't understand how Americans could be so upset over a few trivial broken laws by their President. The meetings paved the way for the SALT II agreement under President Ford.

June 25, John Dean began his testimony before the Senate Watergate Committee. During his testimony on June 27, he revealed the existence of Nixon's Enemies List.

July 1, the US Drug Enforcement Administration was founded.

July 2, Congress passed the Education of the Handicapped Act mandating Special Education and provided for Individual Education Programs (IEPs) for each child.

July 10, the 16-year-old grandson of oil baron J. Paul Getty was kidnapped in Rome. The kidnappers cut off the boy's ear and a lock of his hair and sent it to Getty who then paid $2.2 million to have him freed. Several kidnappers were later arrested but most of the money was never recovered.

July 12, the National Record Center in St. Louis caught fire and between 16 – 18 million military personnel records were destroyed.

July 16, White House Technical Aide Alexander Butterfield revealed in testimony before the Senate Committee revealed that Nixon had a secret White House tapping system that recorded all White House conversations.

July 18-20, the US Congress passed The War Powers Act limiting the President's ability to commit US troops in conflicts without the consent of Congress. The Act was vetoed by President Nixon, but the veto was overridden by Congress November 7, 1973.

July 23, citing Executive Privilege Nixon refused to turn over the White House tapes to the Watergate investigators.

July 28, about 600,000 rock fans attended the Summer Jam at Watkins Glen, New York.

July 31, a Delta passenger plane crashed in Boston killing 89 people.

August 5, the Arab terrorist group Black September killed 3 and wound 55 at the airport in Athens.

August 8, Vice President Agnew answered calls for his resignation by stating that rumors that he took kickbacks and bribes were "damned lies." He vowed he would never resign.

Also on August 8, Kim Dae-jung a political opponent of South Korean President Park Chung-hee was kidnapped by the Korean CIA and was to be executed. He was released when the Pope, the US and other governments put pressure on the South Korean dictator to free him. Kim had nearly beat Park Chung-hee in the 1971 Presidential election despite election rigging by Park's government. Despite another imprisonment by the government in 1976 and another arrest and a sentence to death for sedition in 1981 which was commuted at the request again at the request of the Pope and the US government, Kim eventually became President of South Korea in 1998. He was awarded the Nobel Peace prize in 2000 for his work to bring peace and democracy to the Korean peninsula.

August 14, after discovering the secret bombing of Cambodia, Congress ordered that it stop on this day. It was revealed that the US had dropped more tons of bombs on Cambodia, 2.7 million tons, than on Japan during WWII, including the tonnage of the two nuclear bombs. It is estimated that approximately 500,000 civilians died from the bombings and another 200,000 from displacement and starvation. The CIA has stated that the bombing led to the popularity of the previously marginalized Khmer Rouge and greatly aided in their coming to power and the consequent killing of perhaps another 2 million people. There were calls of impeachment over these secret bombings.

August 28 an earthquake measuring 6.8 stuck Mexico killing 527 people.

September 4, William Colby became the Director of the CIA.

September 11, Nixon and Kissinger and the CIA's plans to overthrow Salvador Allende in Chile came to fruition. It was alleged that Allende had committed suicide during the coup, but according to the *Washington Post* on May 31, 2011 newly discovered top-secret military documents showed that he had been assassinated in the coup. A US backed dictatorship of General Augusto Pinochet ruled for the next 16 years.

September 18, the two German Republics, East and West, were admitted to the United Nations.

September 20, in a tennis match titled "The Battle of the Sexes" Billy Jean King Defeated Bobby Riggs in three sets. During the match Riggs set out to prove that male athletes were always superior to female athletes. It is still the largest attendance for a tennis match with 30,492 attending. It was also viewed on television by 90 million people in 36 countries.

Also on September 20, singer-songwriter Jim Croce and five others were killed in a small charter plane crash in Louisiana.

September 21, Jackson Pollock's painting *Blue Poles* sold for $2 million.

September 22, Nixon named Henry Kissinger Secretary of State.

September 26, the supersonic passenger jet the Concorde flew from Washington, DC to Paris in a record 3 hours and 33 minutes.

September 28, the ITT building in New York City was bombed in protest over ITT's role in the US backed military coup in Chile.

Also on September 28, Palestinian terrorists hijacked an Austrian train.

October 6, the Yom Kippur War began as Syria attacked Israel from the Golan Heights and Egypt attacked from the Sinai Peninsula. Israel took the Golan Heights and though it lost some ground to the Egyptian Army in the Sinai it had crossed the Suez Canal and occupied a portion of Egypt and cutoff the Egyptian 3rd Army. The USSR threatened to get involved on behalf of Egypt and Syria while the US sided with and supplied Israel. Nixon was so embattled and preoccupied with Watergate that Kissinger and Chief of Staff General Alexander Haig made the decision to not involve Nixon in these issues believing Nixon to be too mentally fragile to handle the conflict. Vice President Agnew was still under investigation for corruption. On October 22, the US and USSR negotiated a ceasefire. However battles continually erupted after the ceasefire. Syria and Egypt suffered more losses of men and equipment, but Israel also sustained heavy losses of men and equipment. A final agreement was negotiated between Egypt and Israel on January 18, 1974 with Syria and Israel coming to an agreement May 31, 1974.

October 10, Vice President Agnew resigned and pled "no contest" to charges of accepting bribes and kickbacks while he had been governor of Maryland.

October 12, Congressman Gerald Ford was nominated by Nixon to be Vice President replacing Agnew. The Senate voted to confirm Ford on November 27, and the House confirmed him on December 10, and Ford was sworn into office an hour afterward.

October 15, in Thailand a student demonstration of over 100,000 protesting the military government was put down by the army using tanks. About 77 students were killed and over 800 wounded.

October 16, in a twist of irony Henry Kissinger and Le Duc Tho were jointly awarded the Nobel peace Prize. In 1968 Kissinger helped Nixon commit treason to scuttle a very similar deal proposed by Johnson to get Nixon elected. It was almost the same, except many years and many deaths later.

Also on this day Maynard Jackson was elected the first Black mayor of Atlanta.

Also on October 16, the six Gulf oil nations unilaterally raised the price of oil by 17%. The next day OPEC agreed to cutoff of oil for anyone supporting Israel. On the 19th OPEC began an oil embargo on all exports to the US triggering an energy crisis and gasoline shortages resulted. Many gas stations were closed and long lines appeared at many others.

October 20, as all signs pointed to Nixon's guilt in Watergate. Archibald Cox the Special Prosecutor subpoenaed Nixon to testify in the matter. Nixon ordered him to drop the subpoena and when he refused he ordered Deputy Attorney General William Ruckelshaus to fire Cox. Ruckelshaus and Attorney general Elliot Richardson both resigned rather than firing Cox saying it was an illegal order from the president. Nixon then ordered the Solicitor General Robert Bork to fire Cox and he did. The event became known as "the Saturday night massacre."

October 23, with mounting pressure from Congress and the court Nixon finally agreed to turn over the White house tapes to Judge Sirica.

October 24, a heavy fog on the Jersey Turnpike caused a 65 car collision and killed nine people.

Also on this day John Lennon sued the US government for the FBI illegally tapping his phone.

November 1, Acting Attorney General Robert Bork appointed Leon Jaworski as the new special Watergate prosecutor.

November 3, Mariner 10 was launched to study Venus and Mercury.

November 5, amidst the oil crisis the Arab producers announced a 25% production cut.

November 7, the US and Egypt announced a resumption of diplomatic relations that had been halted because of the Yom Kippur War.

November 15, Israel and Egypt exchanged prisoners of war.

November 16, Nixon authorized the construction of the Alaskan Oil Pipeline.

November 17, in Orlando, Florida, Nixon addressed 400 Associated Press editors about Watergate and said, "People have got to know if their president is a crook. Well I am not a crook."

Also on November 17, hundreds of students in Greece protested the military junta. At least 24 students were killed during the protest.

November 19, amid the continued energy crisis the stock market had the largest drop in 19 years.

November 21, Nixon's personal attorney revealed to the court that there was an unexplained 18 and a half minute gap in the White House tapes dealing with Watergate.

November 25, the federal government reduced the highway speed limit to 55 miles per hour to reduce gasoline consumption during the energy crisis.

November 26, Nixon's secretary Rosemary Woods told the court that she accidently erased the 18 and a half minutes of White House tapes concerning Watergate.

November 27, Nixon signed the Emergency Petroleum Allocation Act to allow the federal government to control pricing and allocation of petroleum products.

December 3, Pioneer 10 came within 82,179 miles of Jupiter. The first pictures were transmitted beginning in November. Incredibly Pioneer 10 would continue on exploring the far reaches of the solar system sending back data until January 23, 2003 when its radio transmitter finally ran out of power.

December 6, Gerald Ford was sworn in as Vice President.

December 9, Arab oil producers announced a further 5% production cut in oil in January.

Also on December 9, in response to the continued "Troubles" in Northern Ireland, Britain negotiated the Sunningdale Agreement. The agreement called for power sharing the executive in Northern Ireland and a cross-border Council of Ireland. The attempt failed in May of 1974 because of Protestant opposition that led to a general strike.

December 11, in continuing the Cold War thaw West Germany normalized trade with the Czech Republic.

December 15, The American Psychiatric Association declared that homosexuality was not a mental illness.

December 22-23, OPEC agreed to more than double the price of oil from $5.12 to $11.65 starting January 1, 1974.

December 24, the District of Columbia Home Rule Act was passed allowing the residents of DC to elect their own local government officials. Previously they had been appointed by Congress.

December 25, the ARPANET, the precursor of the internet, developed a software bug causing all ARPANET traffic to be routed through a server at Harvard University causing the server to freeze.

December 28, the Endangered Species Act was signed into law.

Between March and May the Mississippi River flooded for 77 days. This flood caused 33 deaths and over $252 million in damages. Beginning in the summer of 1973 the US suffered a beef shortage which lasted into 1975. During the shortage Americans ate more pork and lamb and even buffalo and horse meat. The consumption of horse meat declined after the beef shortage ended but the consumption of buffalo continued. Also in 1973 the Miller Brewing Company introduced Lite Beer for the first time. Other new items included introduced during the year were the product bar code, jet skis, and optical fiber.

Inflation rose to 6.16%. The average cost of a new house was $32,500 and average monthly rent rose to $175. The average price of a new car was about $3,200 and gas rose to 40 cents per gallon, but there were shortages throughout the year. The average income was $9,572. The crock pot cooker became popular and sold for $17.79.

The longest running television comedy, *The Last of the Summer Wine*, a British television show later shown by PBS in the US, began on November 12, and continued until August 29, 2010. Beginning on May 17, daytime television was interrupted while Americans watched the Watergate hearings. *A Charlie Brown Thanksgiving* made its debut and won an Emmy. On December 19, Johnny Carson on *The Tonight Show* inadvertently started a rumor when he joked about a toilet paper shortage which set off a three week panic by American consumers and a toilet paper buying spree in the US.

Some shows making their debuts included: *Barnaby Jones, Police Story, The Young and the Restless, The Tomorrow Show, The Six Million Dollar Man*, and *Kojack*. Shows ending in 1973 included: *Bonanza, Mission Impossible, Laugh-In, The Mod Squad*, and *The Doris Day Show*. During 1973 *All In the Family, The Waltons*, and *The Julie Andrews Show* won Emmys. Jack Klugman won in *The Odd Couple*, Mary Tyler Moore, Ted Knight and Valarie Harper won for their roles in *The Mary Tyler Moore Show*, and Richard Thomas, Michael Learned and Ellen Corby all won for their roles in *The Waltons*.

At the movies *The Sting* was the top box office draw and won 7 Oscars including: Best Picture and Best Director for George Roy Hill. *The Exorcist* was the next highest box office draw and won the Golden Globe Awards for Best Picture and Director for William Friedkin. *American Graffiti* was third at the box office and won the Golden Globe for Best Comedy Picture. *A Touch of Class* won the Oscar for Best Actress for Glenda Jackson and a Golden Globe for Best Actor for George Segal. *Save the Tiger* won the Oscar for Best Actor for Jack Lemmon, *Serpico* won a Golden Globe for Best Actor for Al Pacino and *Cinderella Liberty* won the Golden Globe Best Actress Award for Marsha Mason. Other notable films included: *Paper Moon, Papillon, The Way We Were, Magnum Force, Live and Let Die, The Paper Chase, Bang the Drum Slowly, Charlotte's Web, High Plains Drifter, Soylent Green, Westworld* and Woody Allen's *Sleeper*.

The Literature of 1973 included: *Gravity's Rainbow* by Thomas Pynchon which won a Pulitzer Prize, *Breakfast of Champions* by Kurt Vonnegut, *Burr* by Gore Vidal, *The Honorary Consul* by Graham Green, *Small is Beautiful* by E.F. Schumacher, *The Princess Bride* by William Goldman, *Fear and Loathing on the Campaign Trail* by Hunter S. Thompson, *If I Die in a Combat Zone* by Tim O'Brien, *Evening in Byzantium* by Irwin Shaw, *The Gulag Archipelago* by Aleksandr Solzhenitsyn, *Sybil* by Flora Rheta Schreiber, *The Onion Field* by Joseph Wambaugh, *Fear of Flying* by Erica Jong, *Enemy at the Gates: The Battle for Stalingrad* by William Craig, and *The Ascent of Man* by Jacob Bronowski.

CHAPTER 30. 1974: NIXON RESIGNED, THE ENERGY CRISIS, RECESSION AND INFLATION

January 1, NBC Radio followed CBS and started twenty-four hour news coverage.

January 2, a large wild fire destroyed 1.2 million acres in Argentina.

January 3, as the European recession deepened due to the energy crisis. Gold hit a record $121.25 per ounce in London.

January 4, Nixon refused to hand over the Watergate tapes to the Senate Watergate Committee.

January 6, in response to the energy crisis the US started daylight savings four months early to save electricity. The United Kingdom went to a three day work week. The Dutch began to ration gasoline.

January 8, gold hit another record at $126.50 per ounce and silver hit a record $3.40 per ounce.

January 12, Libya and Tunisia announced a merger of the two countries into the Arab Islamic Republic.

January 15, experts determined that Nixon's eighteen and a half minute gap in the Watergate tapes was not an accident and that there were at least 5 separate and deliberate erasures.

January 16, a landslide in Oregon killed 9 people.

January 21, gold and silver hit record highs again.

January 25, Dr. Christian Barnard completed the first human heart transplant.

February 4, Patty Hearst, the daughter of publisher Randolph Hearst was kidnapped by the Symbionese Liberation Army an American radical militant group.

On February 5 and 6, the Germans and the Dutch reduced roadway speeds to save gasoline.

February 6, the US House of Representatives began their consideration for the impeachment of President Nixon.

February 10, Iraq and Iran began fighting along their border.

Also on this date Silver hit another record high in London.

February 11, Henry Kissinger announced Nixon's "Seven Point Project Independence" to make the US energy independent as the new Arab Islamic State (Libya) announced the nationalization of three American oil companies.

February 13, dissident writer Aleksandr Solzhenitsyn was expelled from the USSR.

February 21, silver hit another record at $5.96 for a half an ounce.

February 26, gold hit a record $188 an ounce in Paris.

March 1, the Watergate grand jury indicted seven of Nixon's presidential aides.

March 2, the Watergate grand jury concluded that President Nixon was involved in the Watergate cover-up.

March 10, another Japanese Army holdout from WWII surrendered in the Philippines.

March 18, the Arab oil producing states lifted the oil embargo on the US and Europe.

March 28, Chinese farmers discovered the 8,000 terracotta clay warriors buried near Xi'an, China. It was determined that they were buried to protect China's first emperor in the afterlife.

March 29, Mariner 10 photographed the planet Mercury in a flyby.

April 1, the US Census Bureau estimated the world population at 4 billion.

Also on April 1, the Ayatollah Khomeini called for an Islamic state in Iran.

April 3, large storms produced 148 tornadoes over a dozen states that killed 315 people and injured about 5,500 others.

April 5, the 110 story twin towers of the World Trade Center opened.

April 6, the California Jam concert attracted over 250,000 fans in Ontario, California.

April 11, a PLO terrorist attack killed 18 people and wounded another 16 at an Israeli school.

April 15, the kidnapped teenager, Patty Hearst was photographed holding an M-1 carbine during a robbery of the Sunset Branch of the Hibernia Bank in San Francisco. She was 19 at the time and was kept blindfolded in a closet for weeks. She was raped by two men and told she would be killed numerous times. She was then told she had a choice of being killed or joining the group. She later said she made the decision to join to save her life. She made a video tape that was given to news outlets on April 3, 1973, announcing she had joined the group. She was captured in 1975 and convicted of this bank robbery in 1976 and sentenced to seven years in prison. Despite psychiatric testimony that she had experienced severe trauma that negated any free choice, the court ruled that brainwashing was not a defense. She lost an appeal and the US Supreme Court refused to hear her case. She had served 22 months in prison before President Carter commuted her sentence to time served. President Clinton later gave her a full pardon. After her release from prison she married a police officer who had been hired by her father to protect her. They have two children and Hearst has spent her time involved in children's charities.

April 20, "The Troubles" in Northern Ireland claimed its 1,000th victim.

April 24, the revelation of an East German communist spy ring operating in the West German government of Willie Brandt forced the Chancellor's resignation later in May.

April 29, Nixon announced that he would release edited White House tapes.

May 2, former Vice President Agnew was disbarred and not allowed to practice law.

May 8 the government of Canadian Prime Minister Pierre Trudeau fell.

May 9, the House Judiciary Committee formally began their hearings on the impeachment of President Nixon.

May 17, the Protestant Ulster Volunteer Force killed 33 Catholics and wounded over 300 with four bombs. It was the largest highest number of casualties during "the Troubles" in Northern Ireland.

Also on May 17, in a shoot-out the Los Angeles Police killed 6 members of the Symbionese Liberation Army.

May 18, India exploded a nuclear weapon becoming the 6th country with nuclear weapons.

May 31, Israel and Syria signed an agreement regarding the Golan Heights.

June 1, the Heimlich maneuver, a method of rescuing choking victims was published in the journal *Emergency Medicine*.

June 3, Yitzhak Rabin formed a new government in Israel.

June 8, the US and Saudi Arabia signed a military and economic treaty.

June 17, the IRA bombed the Houses of Parliament in London injuring 11 people in revenge for the 33 Catholics killed and over 300 wounded on May 17.

June 26, the Universal Product Code (UPC) was scanned for the first time at a supermarket in Troy, Ohio.

June 27, in an attempt to draw attention away from his growing Watergate problems Nixon visited the USSR.

June 30, Soviet ballet dancer Mikhail Baryshnikov defected to the US.

July 9, Pierre Trudeau's Liberal Party won Canada's elections putting Trudeau back in power.

July 11, the House Judiciary Committee publicly released its evidence against Nixon.

July 12, former Nixon staffer John Ehrlichman was convicted of violating Daniel Ellsberg's rights for his role in the break-in at his psychiatrist's office.

July 15, news anchor Christine Chubbuck committed suicide on a live broadcast in Sarasota, Florida.

July 19, a rail car explosion in Decatur, Illinois killed seven people, injured another 349 and caused over $18 million in property damages.

July 21, the House Judiciary Committee approved two articles of impeachment against President Nixon.

July 24, the Supreme Court unanimously ruled that Nixon must turn over the Watergate Tapes.

July 27, the House Judiciary Committee voted 27-11 to recommend the impeachment of Nixon.

July 29, the Episcopal Church began to ordain female ministers.

August 4, the passage of the Crawford-Butler Act allowed Puerto Rico to elect a governor.

August 5, Nixon admitted he withheld information about the Watergate break-in.

August 8, on the advice of Republican leaders, particularly Senator Barry Goldwater, Nixon announced on national television that he would resign as President the following day.

August 9, Nixon resigned and Gerald Ford was sworn in as the new president.

August 20, Nelson Rockefeller was selected by Ford to be the Vice President.

September 3, the US formally recognized the GDR, East Germany.

September 8, President Ford pardoned Richard Nixon of all crimes and misdemeanors.

September 16, President Ford announced amnesty for Vietnam War deserters.

September 21, Mariner 10 made a second flyby of Mercury.

September 25, scientists reported that Freon gas from aerosol spray cans was destroying the ozone layer which protects the earth from harmful ultraviolet radiation.

September 28, First Lady Betty Ford underwent a radical mastectomy.

October 1, the Watergate Cover-up trial began in Washington, DC.

October 8, the Franklin National Bank on Long Island in New York collapsed due to money laundering, fraud and mismanagement. At the time it was the largest bank failure in US history. Michele Sindona had strong ties to the Mafia and their drug money laundering operations. He also had close ties to the Nixon administration which kept his fraud and mismanagement from being discovered.

Also on October 8, President Ford declared inflation the number one threat to America. He began the "WIN" campaign to "Whip Inflation Now." WIN buttons and posters were mass produced and disseminated.

October 9, a race riot occurred in Boston over school busing for integration.

October 15, the National Guard was called out to restore order in Boston.

October 29, federal financial regulations were enacted banning discrimination on the basis of sex in credit applications.

October 30, Mohammad Ali defeated George Forman in the Rumble in the Jungle. Ali regained the heavyweight title that he was stripped of seven years earlier.

November 5, Walter Washington became the first elected Mayor of Washington, DC.

November 15, the International Energy Agency was formed in Paris in the wake of the energy crisis.

November 20, the US filed an anti-trust suit to breakup AT&T breaking up "Ma Bell" into the "Baby Bells."

November 21, the Congress overrode President Ford's veto of the Freedom of Information Act making it law. The federal government would now have to reveal its innermost works to the public.

November 21, in Birmingham, England pub bombs killed 21 making it the deadliest attack in England during "the Troubles."

November 24, the US and USSR signed the SALT II nuclear treaty limiting nuclear weapons.

November 25, the Irish Republican Army was outlawed in Britain.

November 30, "Lucy" the most complete early human skeleton was found in Ethiopia. It has been tested and dated at over 3 million years old.

December 1, a Boeing 727 crashed in Virginia killing 92.

December 10, the European Economic Community called for a European Parliament.

December 19, Nelson Rockefeller was sworn in as the Vice President.

December 22, a cease fire between Britain and the IRA began and lasted until April 1975.

December 25, cyclone Tracy destroyed most of the city of Darwin, Australia.

December 30, another Japanese army holdout from WWII surrendered on the Indonesian Island of Morota.

Also in December the *New York Times* began to report domestic abuses and violations of laws by the CIA, including conducting drug experiments on unknowing US citizens. These reports would later lead to President Ford to form a commission to look into these abuses. It was the first time most Americans had heard of Project MK-ULTRA.

During 1974 the Rubik's cube puzzle was invented by a Hungarian professor Erno Rubik and the fantasy game *Dungeons and Dragons* was also released. The first medical MRI scanners came into use. PepsiCo became the first American company to sell a commercial product in the USSR. Pocket calculators became common. The first word processors were produced for common office use and resembled typewriters with a limited computer memory.

During 1974 the inflation rate jumped to 11.3%. The average price of a new house was $34,900 and the average price of a new car was $3,750 and at the end of the gasoline shortage gas rose to 55 cents per gallon. Average monthly rent rose to $185. The average household income was $13,900.

1974 television highlights included the live resignation President Nixon in August and the end of a 23 year long television reign for Lucille Ball when her show *Here's Lucy* was cancelled. The new shows of 1974 included: *Happy Days, Good Times, Land of the Lost, Valley of the Dinosaurs, Shazam!, Rhoda, Little House on the Prairie, Chico and the Man, The Rockford Files, Police Woman, Kolchak: The Night Stalker, Dinah!* And the PBS show *Nova*.

In addition to *Here's Lucy*, other shows ending in 1974 included: *Love American Style, Room 222, The Brady Bunch, The Partridge Family, The Dean Martin Show, The Sonny and Cher Comedy Hour, The FBI, The Flip Wilson Show, The Newlywed Game*, and the BBCs *Monty Python's Flying Circus*.

M*A*S*H and Alan Alda won Emmys for Best Comedy and Actor. Mary Tyler Moore also won comedy Best Actress. PBS won for the British Drama *Upstairs, Downstairs*. *The Carol Burnett Show* won for the Best Variety Show. Telly Savalas won Best dramatic Actor in his show *Kojack* and Michael Learned for Best Actress in *The Waltons*. The drama *The Autobiography of Miss Jane Pittman* won five Emmys including best Actress for Cicely Tyson.

At the movies three disaster films were in the top seven biggest box office hits. They were *The Towering Inferno, Earthquake*, and *Airport1975*. The biggest box office draw was the western comedy spoof *Blazing Saddles*. *The Godfather Part II* won the Oscar for Best Picture, Best Director for Francis Ford Coppola, Best Supporting Actor for Robert Di Nero and Best Adapted Screen Play for Coppola and Mario Puza. *Chinatown* was also heavily nominated and won the Oscar for Best Original Screenplay for Robert Towne. It also won the Golden Globes for Best Picture, Best Director Roman Polanski, Actor Jack Nicholson, and Original Screenplay.

Other films of 1974 included: *The Longest Yard, The Trial of Billy Jack, Young Frankenstein, The Life and Times of Grizzly Adams, Harry and Tonto, Alice Doesn't Live Here Anymore, The Great Gatsby, Murder on the Orient Express, The Texas Chain Saw Massacre, The Taking of Pelham One Two Three, The Lords of Flat Bush, Benji, The Man with the Golden Gun, Death Wish*, and the documentary of the Vietnam War *Hearts and Minds* which won the Oscar for Best Documentary.

In music Barbara Streisand had the top hit for 1974 with *The Way We Were*. *Seasons in the Sun* by Terry Jack was second. Other hits of 1974 included: *Dancing Machine* by the Jackson Five, *The Loco-Motion* by Grand Funk Railroad, *The Streak* and *Spiders and Snakes* by Ray Stevens, *Bennie and the Jets* by Elton John, *Jungle Boogie* by Kool and the Gang, *Midnight at the Oasis* by Maria Muldaur, *Hooked on a Feeling* by Blue Suede, *Band on the Run* by Wings, *Time In a Bottle* by Jim Croce after his death, *Annie's Song* by John Denver, *Rock Me Gently* by Andy Kim, *Rock the Boat* by the Hughes Corporation, *The Night Chicago Died* by Paper Lace, *Having My Baby* by Paul Anka, and ABBA's first hit *Waterloo*.

The books of 1974 included the book about Watergate, *All the Presidents Men* by the Pulitzer Prize winning journalists Carl Bernstein and Bob Woodward. Their book also won the Pulitzer Prize. *The Power Broker* by Robert Caro also won a Pulitzer Prize. Other 1974 books included: *Tinker Tailor Soldier Spy* by John le Clare, *Zen ad the Art of Motorcycle Maintenance* by Robert Persig, *Helter Skelter* about the Manson Family by Vincent Bugliosi and Curt Gentry, *Centennial* by James Michener, *Working* by Studs Terkel, *Pilgrim at Tinker Creek* by Annie Dillard, *The Dogs of War* by Frederick Forsyth, *Jaws* by Peter Benchley, *Gather Together in My Name* by Maya Angelou, *Something Happened* by Joseph Heller, *A Bridge Too Far* by Cornelius Ryan, and Steven King's first novel *Carrie*.

Chapter 31. 1975: The Church Committee, the Collapse of South Vietnam, and the Near Bankruptcy of NYC

January 2, Nixon's senior aides H.R. Haldeman, John Ehrlichman, and Robert Mardian were all convicted of crimes in the Watergate trial.

January 4, amid growing CIA scandal President Ford issued an Executive Order banning all CIA activities in the United States.

January 7, OPEC raised oil prices by 10%.

January 8, amid a continuing and growing CIA scandal President Ford appointed Vice President Rockefeller to look into illegal domestic abuses by the CIA. It is an interesting choice as it was Rockefeller's industrial spies and saboteurs that originally formed the OSS the forerunner to the CIA. During WWII Rockefeller Center was called the "House of Spies." Some were concerned that this was a cover-up and wanted the Congress to undertake its own investigation.

January 13, Secretary of State Kissinger hinted that a war with the oil producing countries was possible because of "actual strangulation of the industrialized world."

January 14, the USSR cancelled their trade agreements with the US.

January 20, in Hanoi the Politburo approved the final plans for the final campaign to unite Vietnam.

January 27, the Senate formed the Church Committee to look into the reported illegal activities of the CIA that had been reported by the *New York Times*, including drug experiments upon unwitting American citizens. The House also formed the Pike Committee for their investigations. The committees uncovered a long list of illegal CIA activities which became known in the CIA and later by the American public as "the Family Jewels."

Included in these crimes were the assassinations of Patrice Lumumba of the Congo, Rafael Trujillo of the Dominican Republic, the Diem brothers of Vietnam, and using the Mafia and others in attempts to kill Fidel Castro of Cuba. According to Tim Weiner in *Legacy of Ashes* the Lumumba assassination and Castro attempted assassinations were also approved secretly by Eisenhower. Some in the CIA had tried to claim that Kennedy had authorized the assassination of the Diem brothers in Vietnam but this has been disproven. The Committee also discussed the likelihood that President Kennedy was a victim of a CIA assassination as well, and the House Committee on Assassinations was formed the following year to investigate this as well as the assassinations of Robert Kennedy and Dr. Martin Luther King Jr.

The Church Committee also found that the CIA had spent a considerable amount of resources on illegally spying on Americans domestically by opening mail and tapping American domestic phone conversations. They found that the CIA had also conducted illegal mind control, drug and torture tests on unsuspecting Americans and Canadians in mental hospitals and at universities on people treated for minor depression in a large on-going project called MK-ULTRA. Jack Kerouac, Charles Manson, Ted Kaczynski the Unabomber, and the Reverend Jim Jones were later said to be among some of these human experiments, along with Robert Kennedy's killer Sirhan Sirhan. The CIA also set up whorehouses in San Francisco to test LSD on unsuspecting male customers who would then be blackmailed into further mind control tests. Drugs were also tested on US military personnel and CIA agents with and without consent and with coerced consent.

It was also discovered that through another illegal operation, Operation Mockingbird, the CIA had bought, bribed, frightened, blackmailed, intimidated and otherwise controlled the American press and media into publishing CIA favorable and false stories, suppressing any stories about their illegal activities and any bad press for the agency or its plans, operations or goals. They had also destroyed the careers of people in the media who were unsympathetic or resisted their controls.

It was also learned by the Church Committee that the FBI had also operated many similar illegal programs under a covert program called COINTELPRO which sought to spy on, discredit, harass, imprison for false crimes by planting false evidence, beat and intimidate leaders of the anti-war movement, civil rights leaders, the American Indian Movement, the United Farm Workers and Latino Rights advocates, women's liberation leaders, and gay rights activists as well as anyone they considered to be a socialist or leftist. The Committee found that the FBI, the nation's top law enforcement agency, had habitually broken the law and committed crimes against many innocent Americans.

During the hearings President Ford and Vice President Rockefeller and the CIA became concerned that CIA Director William Colby was too cooperative and was not strong enough to protect the CIA from the inquiries of the Church Committee. Colby was replaced as Director by George H.W. Bush in January of 1976.

At the conclusion of the committee's work George H.W. Bush on behalf of the CIA apologized and assured Congress that these activities had stopped. He claimed these crimes had been done by a few rogue elements of the agency. It was a false statement as the crimes and illegal activities had been approved by all CIA Directors since Allan Dulles. It has since been learned that most of these secret operations also continued under new code names after this time, according to Tim Weiner in *Legacy of Ashes* (Tim Weiner) including Operation Mockingbird which still controls the US press. Bush said of Operation Mockingbird that the agency would no longer pay news sources, editors or reporters, but may seek their voluntary help.

January 29, the radical student group, the Weather Underground, exploded a bomb at the US State Department. It was done before the offices opened and there were no fatalities. The Weather Underground was a radical group of students against the Vietnam War and racism, with a goal to "destroy fascism in America." They set off about 25 more bombs over the next several years.

February 1, the US Defense Department allowed the first security clearance for an openly gay man, Otis Francis Tabler. Previous to this gays and lesbians were considered untrustworthy and a security risk.

February 8, the Unification Church of the Reverend Sun Myung Moon, a radical Christian movement that began in Korea, married 1,800 couples in a mass wedding ceremony. The couples had been chosen by the church and most had not met their intended spouses until the ceremony. The religion spread to the US. The Unification Church would be accused of brainwashing their followers who became known as the "Moonies." The Moonies were seen in many public places such as airports seeking donations for their church.

February 10, the Irish Republican Army agreed to a truce with Britain.

February 20, Margaret Thatcher, the Iron Lady, became head of the British conservative party "The Tories."

February 21, former Nixon aides H.R. Haldeman, John Ehrlichman, and former Attorney General John Mitchell were sentenced between 30 months and 8 years in prison for their crimes in the Watergate Scandal.

February 23, daylight savings time was again implemented early to save electricity during the energy crisis.

February 26, a kidney transplant was televised on *The Today Show.*

February 27, the US House of Representatives passed an anti-recession tax cut of $21.3 billion.

March 4, the actor/comedian and a pioneer filmmaker, Charlie Chaplin was knighted by Queen Elizabeth II for his contributions to the Arts. Chaplin, an Englishman, who came to the US as a teenager became one of the first American filmmakers. Back in the 1940s he'd been accused by J. Edgar Hoover of being "a communist," which Chaplin denied. In 1944 Hoover tried to prosecute Chaplin for an affair with a young actress under the Mann Act. This was quickly decided in Chaplin's favor by the court, further infuriating Hoover. In the 1950s Chaplin was again accused of being a communist and again he denied it. In 1952 Chaplin left with his family on a business trip to London. The next day the US Attorney General at the request of Hoover and the FBI disallowed his re-entry to the US unless he agreed to be interviewed by the FBI as a communist. He refused, stating that he was not a communist. Chaplin only returned once to the US after this. In 1972 the Academy of Motion Picture Arts and Sciences offered Chaplin an Honorary Life Time

Achievement Award at the Oscars. He returned to the US to accept the award. He was given an emotional 12 minute standing ovation by his peers, which remains the longest in Oscar history.

March 6, Iran and Iraq settled their frequently bloody border dispute in Algiers, Algeria which became known as the Algiers Accord.

March 8, the United Nations declared International Women's Day.

March 9, the construction of the Alaskan Pipeline began.

March 16, Mariner 10 made the final flyby of Mercury.

March 13, in South Vietnam President Thieu ordered the Central Highlands evacuated as the North Vietnamese Army advanced. The order triggered a panic and full blown retreat and mass exodus. South Vietnam and its Army began to collapse.

March 25, King Faisal of Saudi Arabia was assassinated by his nephew.

April 1, Prime minister Lon Nol the military dictator backed by the US fled from Cambodia to the United States as the Khmer Rouge threatened the capital, Phnom Penh.

April 3, Bobby Fisher refused to defend his world chess championship and was stripped of the title.

April 4, Microsoft was founded by Bill Gates and Paul Allen in Albuquerque, New Mexico.

April 12, in "the Troubles" six Catholic civilians were killed by Protestant militia in Northern Ireland.

April 13, a bus massacre by Christians killing 27 Palestinians triggered a civil war in Lebanon which lasted until 1990.

April 18, the Khmer Rouge captured Phnom Penh ending the Cambodian civil war. The US evacuated all Americans. The Khmer Rouge began huge relocations and mass genocide. Ultimately between 2 million and 2.5 million Cambodians were butchered and killed in what were called "the Killing Fields."

April 19, India launched its first satellite.

April 21, President Thieu of South Vietnam resigned as the country collapsed.

April 28, General Minh was sworn in as President in what remained of South Vietnam.

April 29-30, Saigon fell to the North Vietnamese and the Viet Cong and the US Embassy was evacuated. Charles McMahon and Darwin Judge were the last two servicemen killed in Vietnam. Thousands of Americans and Vietnamese loyal to the United States fled. Many more were left stranded on the ground as the last helicopters left the embassy.

May 1, a border war between Vietnam and Cambodia began which eventually led to the Vietnamese invading Cambodia in December of 1978 and the capture of Phnom Penh and the removal of the Khmer Rouge. The Vietnamese occupied Cambodia for ten years. The Chinese had backed the Khmer Rouge and this war also led to China invading Vietnam on February 17, 1979 and lasted until the Chinese began to withdraw on March 5, after taking heavy casualties. It is estimated the Chinese lost about 50,000 men while the Vietnamese lost just 10,000.

May 6, three people died when a tornado struck Omaha, Nebraska.

May 7, President Ford declared an end to the "Vietnam Era."

May 12, the Khmer Rouge captured the US merchant ship the Mayaguez in international waters. It was disclosed later that the ship was within two miles of the coast within the US recognized three mile limit and not in international waters. On May 15, the Americans sent the US Marines to take back the ship. Unknown to the US the American crew had already been released by the Khmer Rouge. The marines encountered about 100 Khmer Rouge dug in and fortified on the island where the ship was taken. The Marines took back the Mayaguez but 15 were killed in action, two were captured and later killed. An additional 23 were killed and 50 wounded when a helicopter failed en-route to the rescue. The Mayaguez incident is officially listed as the last battle of the Vietnam War and its casualties are listed on the Vietnam War Memorial Wall in Washington, DC.

May 17, NBC paid $5 million for the one time rights to show *Gone with the Wind* on television.

May 30, the European Space Agency was formed.

June 5, the Suez Canal re-opened for the first time since the start of the Six day War in 1967.

Also on June 5, the United Kingdom voted to become a member in the European Common Market.

June 7, the Sony Corporation introduced the Betamax videocassette recorder for sale to the public.

June 8, the USSR's Venera 9 was launched. Its orbiter became the first spacecraft to orbit Venus. Its landing craft sent back the first pictures from another planet in October.

June 10, after a press leak, the Rockefeller Commission revealed that the CIA was keeping over 300,000 illegal files on individual Americans.

June 11, the first oil was pumped from the North Sea.

June 16, Italy's Communist Party won the elections.

June 17, the Mariana Islands in the Pacific voted to become a US Commonwealth.

June 24, an Eastern airlines flight crashed at JFK Airport in New York and killed 113.

June 25, Mozambique gained independence from Portugal.

Also on June 25, Indira Gandhi declared a state of emergency in India and suspended civil liberties and elections.

June 26, two FBI agents were killed in a shoot-out at the Pine Ridge Indian Reservation. An American Indian Movement leader, Leonard Peltier was sought for the murders and fled to Canada saying that he wouldn't get a fair trial. He was later extradited and tried and convicted of the murders. His trial, like the previous Wounded Knee trial was controversial with numerous accusations of FBI malfeasance. Three witnesses who testified against Peltier later voluntarily recanted their testimony and stated they had been tied to chairs, threatened and coerced into giving false testimony by the FBI. It was discovered after the trial that the FBI had performed ballistic tests on Peltier's rifle which showed that the cartridge that was used in evidence to convict Peltier did not come from his rifle. However the FBI withheld this evidence. Amnesty International listed his conviction as an "Unfair Trial." In addition to Amnesty International Peltier is listed as a political prisoner by many US and international organizations. Peltier's supporters had thought President Obama would grant a pardon but he left office without doing so and Peltier remains in prison as of this writing.

July 5, Cape Verde gained independence after 500 years of Portuguese rule.

July 6, the Comoros received their independence from France.

June 8, President Gerald Ford announced he would seek the Republican nomination for president.

Also on June 8, Israeli Premier Yitzhak Rabin visited West Germany.

July 12, Sao Tome and Principe declared their independence from Portugal.

July 17, a joint US/USSR space mission took place as Soyuz 19 linked up with an Apollo Command Module. The two crews conducted scientific experiments. The mission was a precursor to the International Space station and was the last US manned space flight until the first Space Shuttle flight in 1981.

July 22, amidst controversy the US House of Representatives voted to restore the citizenship to the Confederate General Robert E. Lee.

July 27, the British consulate in Angola was closed as the civil war between the Popular Movement for the Liberation of Angola and South African Troops began to accelerate.

July 29 President Ford became the first American President to visit the Auschwitz Concentration Camp.

July 30, in suburban Detroit the Teamsters Union President Jimmy Hoffa disappeared. In 1982 he was declared legally dead. His disappearance, death and the location of his remains are still a mystery.

August 1, the Helsinki Accords on Security and Cooperation were signed in Helsinki, Finland. The US, Canada, and all of Europe except Albania signed the Accords which attempted to promote peace between the West and communist countries.

August 2, a heat wave struck New England. State high temperature records were set in Rhode Island at 104 degrees and 107 degrees in Massachusetts.

August 3, the Superdome in New Orleans was opened.

August 5, amidst more controversy President Ford signed the bill restoring the US citizenship of Confederate General Robert E. Lee.

August 10, British journalist David Frost purchased the exclusive rights to interview Richard Nixon for $600,000 with Nixon receiving 20% of any profits. The four part interview was aired in 1977.

August 11, the US vetoed Vietnam's membership in the United Nations.

August 20, the US launched Viking 1 the first mission to Mars. It successfully landed on Mars on July 26, 1976.

August 21, the US tightened the trade embargo with Cuba.

August 23, the communists came to power in Laos.

September 1, the US removed the price controls from oil.

September 5, 1975 Lynette "Squeaky" Fromme, a member of the Charles Manson Family cult attempted to kill President Ford in Sacramento, California. She was able to get within an a few feet from the president and pulled her pistol which failed to fire. She was arrested and later convicted and spent 34 years in prison.

September 6, Czech tennis star Martina Navratilova defected and asked for political asylum in the US during the US Open.

September 8, after continued violence Boston began court ordered bussing for school integration.

September 9, the Viking 2 Mars probe was launched and later successfully landed on mars.

Also on September 9, Riverfront Coliseum opened in Cincinnati.

September 13-24, hurricane Eloise killed 80 people in the Caribbean and Florida and caused $560 million in damages.

September 16, Papua New Guinea received independence from Australia.

September 18, kidnapped victim Patty Hearst was found by the FBI.

September 22, Sara Jane Moore, a radical and FBI informant, attempted to assassinate President Ford. She fired one shot and missed and as she fired the second she was taken down by an ex-Marine. The second shot missed and hit a cab driver who survived. Moore was convicted and sentenced to life in prison. She escaped from prison in 1979 but was caught the next day. At the age of 77 she paroled in 2007.

September 24, OPEC announced a 15% increase in oil prices.

September 28, Congress passed a law allowing women to be admitted to US military academies.

September 29, Sharon Bush became the first African-American television weathercaster.

October 1, Muhammad Ali beat Joe Frazier in the "Thrilla in Manila" to win the heavyweight championship.

October 7, the US decided to not deport John Lennon.

October 9, Soviet dissident and nuclear physicist Andrei Sakharov was awarded the Nobel Peace Prize.

October 14, in a traffic accident President Ford's limousine was struck broadside but he was unhurt.

October 17, NASA tested the engines for the new Space Shuttle program.

October 21, the US Coast Guard Academy allowed women to enroll.

October 23, Cuban and South African forces battled in Angola for the first time.

October 26, Anwar Sadat became the first Egyptian president to visit the US.

October 27, the covers of both *Time* magazine and *Newsweek* had Bruce Springsteen on the cover.

October 28, Venezuela nationalized the oil companies.

October 30 the health of Spanish dictator Francisco Franco rapidly declined and King Juan Carlos assumed power in Spain. Franco died shortly after and democracy finally came to Spain.

November 3, an independent audit of the giant toy manufacturer Mattel showed that the corporation had been producing false documents and press releases to give the appearance of financial health. The corporation was in serious financial crisis and Elliott and Ruth Handler who had cofounded the company with Harold Matson were forced to relinquish control.

November 5, with Guatemala making border claims on the western border of Belize and threatening invasion, Britain sent troops along with a flight of fighter aircraft to protect Belize. The Guatemalan threats halted Belize independence until 1981 when Britain agreed to protect Belize even after independence.

November 10, a violent storm on Lake Superior caused the iron ore freighter, the Edmund Fitzgerald, to sink killing the 29 crew members. A later popular ballad, *The Wreck of the Edmund Fitzgerald* by Canadian folksinger Gordon Lightfoot memorialized the catastrophe.

Also on November 10, Palestinian leader Yasser Arafat addressed the UN in New York. The United Nations passed a resolution proclaiming that Zionism was a form of racism. The proclamation was repealed by the UN in 1991.

November 11, Angola gained independence from Portugal.

November 12, the longest serving Supreme Court Justice in American history, William O. Douglas, retired from the Supreme Court after serving for over 36 years.

November 18, Black Panther leader Eldridge Cleaver who had jumped bail on an attempted murder charge and been in exile in Cuba, Algeria and France, returned to the US. Because of the discovery of the illegal operations of COINTELPRO by the FBI against Cleaver and the Black Panthers a federal judge reduced the charges and convicted Cleaver on three counts of assault on the Oakland police. He then gave him community service with no jail time. Cleaver renounced his radical past and became a born again Christian.

November 20, former California Governor Ronald Reagan announced that he would run for the Republican nomination for President against Gerald Ford.

November 22, in "the Troubles" in a response to the attacks and killings by the Protestants, the IRA attacked a British Army watchtower in Northern Ireland killing three British soldiers and capturing one.

November 25, Suriname, formerly Dutch Guiana, was granted independence from the Netherlands.

November 29, under a new law all US states were required to provide appropriate and free education to handicapped children.

November 30, the African nation of Dahomey became Benin.

December 1, President Ford visited China.

December 9, at the last minute, with lawyers representing New York City at the New York Supreme Court prepared to file bankruptcy papers, President Ford signed a $2.3 billion loan to bail out the city. The US would loan NYC a total of $6.9 billion over the next several years to resolve its financial difficulties.

December 17, John Paul Stevens was appointed to the Supreme Court replacing William O. Douglas. On December 19, he was sworn to office.

December 23, the Metric Conversion Act was signed into law mandating that the US convert to the metric system. The US began the "Think Metric" campaign to educate Americans. It was later abandoned halted by the Reagan Administration in 1981 making the US one of only three countries not on the metric system. The other two are Myanmar and Liberia.

December 28, an earthquake in Pakistan killed over 4,000.

December 29, a bomb set off at La Guardia Airport in New York City killed 11 and wounded another 74. Although the bomb was most likely the work of Croatian terrorists, the crime remains unsolved.

Also during 1975 Lyme disease was first diagnosed in Lyme, Connecticut. The first monster truck "Bigfoot" was created by Bob Chandler. The Jehovah's Witnesses predicted that Armageddon was upon us and some members sold houses, businesses and quit jobs in preparation. When the event failed to materialize many Jehovah's Witnesses quit the faith.

Unemployment reached 9.2% and inflation was also at 9.2%, in Britain inflation rose to 24.2%. The average cost of a new house was $39,300 and the average rent rose to $200 per month. The average cost of a new car was $4,250 with the price of a new Ford Mustang II at $4,105. Gas fluctuated and averaged about 44 cents per gallon.

Shortly after Sony began marketing the Betamax video cassette recorder, JVC introduced the VHS video cassette recorder which would come dominate the VCR market until 2016 when the last VCR was made. In 1975 a VCR cost on average $1,280.

In November two long running soap operas, *As the World Turns* and *The Edge of Night*, ended their live broadcasts in favor of pre-taped broadcasts, ending the era of regular live broadcast television programs. The new television shows of 1975 included *Fawlty Towers* on BBC2 and *The Good Life* (re-titled *Good Neighbors* in the US), both British shows which would later become popular in the US through PBS. *Saturday Night Live* aired for the first time with guest host George Carlin. *Good Morning America* also premiered. Other television debuts included: *Wheel of Fortune, Baretta, Barney Miller, The Jeffersons, S.W.A.T., Ryan's Hope, The Grape Ape Show, Phyllis, Welcome Back Kotter, McCoy* and *One Day at a Time.*

Television shows that came to a close included two long running westerns, *Death Valley Days* and *Gunsmoke,* as well as the game show *What's My Line* which had been on television since 1950. Others ending in 1975: *Jeopardy* (which returned in 1984), *Password, Ironside, The Odd Couple, Mannix, Kung Fu,* and *Adam 12.*

The Carol Burnett Show, The Mary Tyler Moore Show and the British Drama Series *Upstairs, Downstairs* on PBS won the Emmys for Best Variety, Comedy and Drama shows. Tony Randall in *The Odd Couple* and Valarie Harper in *Rhoda* won the Emmys for Best Comedy Actors. Robert Blake in *Baretta* and Jean Marsh in *Upstairs, Downstairs* won Best Dramatic Actors. *The Mary Tyler Moore Show* won Best Supporting Comedy Actors for Ed Asner and Betty White. *The Waltons* won Best Supporting Dramatic Actors for Will Geer and Ellen Corby.

A Long Cold War

The films of 1975 included the blockbuster *Jaws* that took in over $260 million at the box office. *Rocky Horror Picture Show* was second in the box office draw and *One Flew Over the Cuckoo's Nest* was third and won the Oscars for Best Picture, Best Director for Milos Forman, Best Actor Jack Nicholson and Best Actress, Louise Fletcher. The film also won in the same categories for the Golden Globe Awards. Other notable movies included: *Dog Day Afternoon, Shampoo, Funny Lady, The Return of the Pink Panther, The Sunshine Boys, The Other Side of the Mountain, The Stepford Wives, The Prisoner of Second Avenue, Rollerball, Brannigan, Monty Python and the Holy Grail, The Happy Hooker, The French Connection II, The Drowning Pool, The Great Waldo Pepper, Three Days of the Condor, The Wind and the Lion,* and *Moonrunners* the movie that later inspired the popular television show *The Dukes of Hazard.*

In music Ron Wood became a guitarist with The Rolling Stones. The Sex Pistols made their first appearance. Elton John had three number one hits in 1975 including *Lucy In the Sky with Diamonds, Philadelphia Freedom* and *Island Girl.* The Eagles had two with *Best of My Love* and *One of These Nights.* The Captain and Tennille had Billboard's top hit with *Love Will Keep Us Together.* Other significant songs were: *Bohemian Rhapsody* by Queen, *Thank God I am a Country Boy* by John Denver, *Rhinestone Cowboy* by Glenn Campbell, *My Eyes Adored You* by Frankie Valli, *Jive Talkin'* the Bee Gees, *Lovin' You* by Minnie Riperton, *Kung Fu Fighting* by Carl Douglas, *At Seventeen* Janis Ian, *The Hustle* Van McCoy, *Wasted Days and Wasted Nights* Freddie Fender, *Sister Golden Hair* by America, *Mandy* Barry Manilow, *Cat's in the Cradle* Harry Chapin, *When Will I Be Loved* and *You're No Good* by Linda Ronstadt, *You Are So Beautiful* Joe Cocker, *How Sweet It Is* James Taylor, and *The Theme Song for the Rockford Files* by Mike Post.

The books of 1975 included: The Pulitzer Prize winning book *Humboldt's Gift* by Saul Bellows, *Shogun* by James Clavell, *The Great Train Robbery* by Michael Crichton, *Ragtime* by E.L. Doctorow, *Looking for Mr. Goodbar* by Judith Perelman Rossner, *Factotum* by Charles Bukowski, *The Eagle Has Landed* by Jack Higgins, *Salem's Lot* by Stephen King, *The Road to Gandolfo* by Robert Ludlum, *Terra Nostra* by Carlos Fuentes, *The Money Changers* by Arthur Haley, *Terms of Endearment* by Larry Mc Murtry, *High-Rise* by J.G. Ballard, *Rumble Fish* by S.E. Hinton, *Somewhere In Time* by Robert Matheson, Joseph Wambaugh's *The Choirboys* and *The Age of Capital 1848-1875* by Eric Hobsbawm.

Chapter 32. 1976: The Bicentennial, Tiananmen Square, Legionnaires Disease, and the 1976 Election

January, the Cray-1, the first commercial supercomputer, went on sale.

January 5, Pol Pot declared a new constitution in Cambodia and renamed the nation Kampuchea.

January 6, with the US, USSR, France and India performing on-going nuclear tests, China performed another nuclear test at Lop Nor.

January 11, a CIA backed military coup took over the government of Ecuador.

January 12, the UN Security Council voted 11-1 to seat the Palestinian Liberation Organization. It was vetoed by the US.

January 17, the European Space Agency successfully launched a Hermes rocket.

January 19, in an upset Georgia Governor Jimmy Carter won the Iowa Democratic Caucus for president running as a Washington outsider. The Democratic Party regulars called him "Jimmy Who?" implying that he was a "nobody." Carter remained unpopular with many Democratic Party insiders who would support Ted Kennedy against him in the 1980 primaries. Carter was running against a large Democratic field that sensed a victory after Nixon and the Republican's scandal filled years. The field included Governors Jerry Brown and George Wallace, Senators Henry Jackson, Frank Church, Robert Byrd, Congressman Mo Udall and others. In February Carter also won the New Hampshire primary. In March he won Vermont, Florida, Illinois, and North Carolina while losing only Massachusetts to Jackson. He would go on to win most of the other states with only three states going to Brown, three to Church and one each to Udall and Byrd. In the Democratic primaries Carter had almost 7 million votes compared to 2.4 for Brown, 2.2 for Wallace, 1.6 for Udall, 1.1 for Jackson and only 800,000 for Church.

Also on January 19, President Ford squeaked out a victory in Iowa beating Ronald Reagan by only 2.7 per cent. The New Hampshire primary was also a very close win for Ford. By the end of the Republican primaries Ford won the popular vote 5.5 million to Reagan's 4.8 million and won the nomination. Ford blamed Reagan's acrimonious campaign against him for his eventual loss to Carter.

January 21, the Concorde began the first supersonic flights between Britain and France.

January 23, in response to an Ann Landers column question, "If they could do it over again would parents still be parents?" over 10,000 responded and 70% said no.

January 27, the UN approved a resolution to create an independent Palestinian state.

Also on January 27, Morocco and Algeria battled over Western Sahara.

January 30, amid the Church Committee inquiry into illegal activities by the CIA, George H.W. Bush was appointed by Ford to replace William Colby, whom Kissinger and Rockefeller thought was too cooperative with the investigating committee. They believed that Bush would be more protective of the agency.

February 4, an earthquake killed almost 23,000 in Guatemala and Honduras.

Also on February 4, the Winter Olympics began at Innsbruck, Austria.

February 5, a race riot involving 2,000 occurred at a high school in Pensacola, Florida. About 30 students were injured during a four hour riot.

February 6, at a Senate Sub-committee hearing lead by Senator Frank Church, it was discovered that the Lockheed Corporation was bribing foreign government officials into buying their aircraft. On February 13, the Chairman of the Board and the President of Lockheed were forced to resign. During the rest of the year foreign officials taking these bribes were uncovered in Japan, Germany, Italy, the Netherlands, and Saudi Arabia. The Lockheed Scandal played a key role in the development of the Foreign Corrupt Practices Act which was later signed into law by President Carter in 1977, making it a crime for an US citizen to bribe a foreign official.

February 7, the world's largest telescope, 600 cm, began operation in the USSR.

February 13, Dorothy Hamill won the Gold Medal for figure skating at the Winter Olympics.

February 20, the Southeast Asian Treaty Organization which the US used to defend its policies in Southeast Asia disbanded.

February 27, Richard Nixon greatly angered President Ford when he visited China acting as if Nixon was still playing a major role in US foreign policy. Nixon was well received in China. A Ford campaign aide stated that Nixon's untimely visit would only remind primary voters that Ford had pardoned Nixon.

Also on February 27, Spanish Sahara declared itself independent from Spain, forming a new Arab republic.

March 1, in the continued "Troubles" in Northern Ireland, the British Home Secretary ended the "Special Category Status" which treated those convicted of crimes as prisoners of war. The British began to treat those involved as terrorists.

March 4, Home Rule ended in Northern Ireland. Northern Ireland became directly ruled by the British in London.

March 5, the British pound fell below $2 for the first time.

March 9, the first female cadets were allowed entrance to West Point.

March 9-11, two explosions in a coal mine in Letcher, Kentucky, killed 26 miners.

March 12, South African troops left Angola.

March 20, Patty Hearst was convicted of bank robbery.

March 24, Argentine President Isabel Parón was overthrown by a CIA backed military junta. The junta banned all leftist parties.

March 27, the first 4.6 miles of the Washington, DC Metro opened.

March 31, the parents of long term coma patient Karen Ann Quinlan won their court battle to allow their daughter to be taken off a respirator to die. It marked the beginning of the Right to Die Movement and for Living Will orders.

April 1, Conrail took over six bankrupt railroads, including the Penn Central and Erie Lackawanna Railroads, in the US northeast. Conrail, which was short for the Consolidated Rail Corporation, was organized by the federal government to take over the profitable lines of the bankrupt carriers. It turned a profit in 1980 and was turned over to private investors in 1987.

April, 5, the Tiananmen Square incident made world-wide news. Large crowds lay wreaths to mourn the death of Zhou Enlai and read poems against the Cultural Revolution which sparked a confrontation between the crowd and the Chinese military who roughly dispersed the crowd.

April 7, in an unexpected move China removed Deng Xiaoping as the Communist Party Leader. He was accused of being responsible for planning the Tiananmen Square incident.

April 9, the US and USSR agreed to limit the size of their nuclear tests.

April 11, the first Apple I computer went on sale.

April 13, the $2 bill was reintroduced into US currency as part of the US Bi-Centennial celebration.

April 21, the Swine Flu vaccine underwent human testing.

April 22, Barbara Walters became the first woman prime time television newscaster.

April 25, the first nationwide elections were held in the newly unified Vietnam.

May 4, LAGEOS, the first geo satellite, was launched.

May 6, an earthquake in Northern Italy killed 989 and wiped out whole villages and made about 100,000 homeless.

May 19, citing the need for oversight over the CIA and the National Security Agency (NSA) because of on-going abuses, the senate established the permanent Select Committee on Intelligence.

May 21, a school bus transporting the Yuba City high school choir, a driver and 52 passengers, crashed when the brakes on their bus failed. One teacher and 28 students were killed. The driver and remaining 24 other passengers were all seriously injured.

May 24, the Concorde began the first commercial supersonic trans-Atlantic flights to Washington, DC.

May 24, in The Judgment of Paris wine tasters judged California wines to be superior to their French counterparts. This was the first time the conventional bias was challenged that French wines were always the most superior. California wine domestic sales and exports rose.

May 31, Syria intervened in the Lebanese civil war.

June 2, the Philippines began normal relations with the USSR.

June 3, in honor of the Bi-Centennial the Britain gave the US the second oldest copy of the Magna Carta.

June 5, the Teton Dam in Idaho burst killing 14 and causing over $1 billion in damages.

June 17, Indonesia annexed Portuguese East Timor.

June 18, in Britain a Joseph William watercolor painting sold for a record £340,000.

June 19, after a ten month flight Viking I entered into an orbit around Mars.

June 20, following the murder of the US Ambassador in Lebanon, the US military evacuated all Americans out of Lebanon.

June 23, the world's tallest structure, 553m, the CN Communications Tower in Toronto began operations.

June 23, the US vetoed Angola's membership in the UN.

June 25, the Soweto Uprising against apartheid in South Africa erupted. Following 10 days of riots 174 Blacks and two Whites were dead.

June 27, an Air France plane carrying 12 crew and 248 passengers, mostly Jewish, was high-jacked by the Palestinian Liberation Movement in Athens and was flown to Entebbe, Uganda. The Palestinian high-jackers demanded $5 million and the release of 53 terrorists from prison. They said if these demands were not met they would begin to kill the passengers. The terrorists separated the Jews from the non-Jewish passengers and released the non-Jewish elderly and children. When Israel agreed to negotiate the terrorists released the remaining other non-Jews. On July 4, Israeli commandos struck. They rescued 102 of 105 passengers. Only three were killed. All seven terrorists and 45 of 100 Ugandan soldiers supporting the terrorists were killed by the commandos. One commando, Yonatan Netanyahu the commander of the raid was killed and 5 were wounded. Netanyahu's brother Benjamin would later become Prime Minister of Israel. The raid on Entebbe is now used as a model for long-range hostage rescue operations.

June 27, the G-6 was created informally at a 1973 meeting of the world's industrial nation's economic ministers to meet and discuss the energy crisis. The first summit was held in 1975 and included the finance ministers of France, Britain, Germany, Japan, Great Britain and the Treasury Secretary of the United States. On this date Canada joined and it became known as the G-7. Later Russia joined in 1997 and it became the G-8, however Russia was suspended from the group in 2014 for their annexation of the Crimea.

June 28, the first woman was admitted to the Air Force Academy in Colorado Springs.

June 29, the Conference of Communist and Workers Parties of Europe began in East Berlin.

July 1, Kenneth Gibson became the Mayor of Newark, New Jersey. He was the first Black mayor of a major Northeastern city and became the first president of the US Conference of Mayors.

July 2, the Socialist Republic of Vietnam was created formally uniting North and South Vietnam into one nation.

July 3, the US Supreme Court in *Gregg v. Georgia* ruled that the death penalty was not cruel or unusual punishment.

July 3-4, the American Bicentennial Celebration began on July 3, with a 12 hour television show *The Great American Celebration* hosted by Ed McMahon on NBC and *The Inventing of America* a two hour show hosted by Raymond Burr and James Burke was shown on both NBC and BBC. On July 4, Walter Cronkite hosted a 16 hour show *In Celebration of US* on CBS, John Chancellor and David Brinkley hosted a 10 hour celebration *The Glorious Fourth*, and a second show *Best of the Fourth* on NBC, and ABC celebrated with the *Great American Birthday Party* hosted by Harry Reasoner. Bob Hope and Paul Anka each had special Bicentennial shows on NBC, and PBS celebrated the event with a mock-newscast of a re-enactment of the debate in the British House of Commons concerning the future of the American colonies.

July 6, the first women were allowed into the US Naval Academy.

Also on July 6, Soyuz 21 carried two cosmonauts to the Salyut 5 Space Station.

July 10, one American and three British soldiers of fortune were executed after a trial in Angola.

July 12, at the Democratic National Convention Congresswoman Barbara Jordan became the first African-American to give the keynote address at an American political convention.

July 14, at the Democratic Convention in New York City Jimmy Carter won the nomination for President. Senator Walter Mondale of Minnesota was nominated as the Vice President.

July 15, three armed men stopped a school bus of 26 students aged 5-14 and kidnapped them and their bus driver Ed Ray in Chowchilla, California and held them for ransom. The children were in a voluntary summer school program and on their way to a nearby pool. The kidnappers forced the children and their driver into a moving van and buried it in an abandoned quarry with a little food and water and left. After about 16 hours of digging the bus driver with help from the children were able to dig their way out and fled to safety. The three kidnapers were caught and sentenced to life in prison. Ed Ray Day is still celebrated in Chowchilla in honor of the bus driver.

July 17, the Summer Olympic Games began in Montreal. On July 18, Nadia Comaneci, a Romanian, became the first gymnast to achieve a perfect score.

July 20, Viking I became the first spacecraft to land on Mars.

Also on July, 20 the US withdrew its final troops left over from the Vietnam War from Thailand.

July 21, a mysterious "Legionnaires Disease" began to sicken people at an American Legion Convention at a hotel in Philadelphia. Within a week 130 were hospitalized and 25 died. It was later discovered that a bacterium in the air-conditioning system of the hotel was to blame.

July 21, in retaliation to continued killing of Catholics by the Protestant Ulster Force, the British Ambassador to Ireland and his secretary were killed in Dublin by a bomb planted in his car by the IRA.

July 26, trying to attract moderate Republicans in a last ditch effort to defeat Ford, Ronald Reagan named Senator Richard Schwieker as his running mate.

July 27, former Japanese Premier Tanaka was arrested for taking bribes in the Lockheed scandal.

July 28, an earthquake in China killed over 242,000.

July 31, a flood on the Big Thompson River in Colorado killed 143 and destroyed over 400 cars, 418 homes and 52 businesses.

August 1, Trinidad and Tobago became a Republic.

August 7, Viking 2 entered mars Orbit.

August 9, the USSR launched unmanned Luna 24, the last moon flight. On August 18, it landed on the moon. On August 21 it returned to earth.

August 11, a sniper went on a rampage in a Wichita, Kansas Holiday Inn killing 3 and wounding 6 before he was wounded by police and arrested.

August 14, in the "Troubles" ten thousand Catholic and Protestant women marched for peace in Northern Ireland.

August 18, two US soldiers on a work detail to cut down a tree and then were hacked to death with an axe by North Korean soldiers in the DMZ between South and North Korea. Three days later in Operation Paul Bunyan the US and South Koreans occupied the DMZ in force and cut down the tree as a symbol to the North Koreans who then backed down and accepted blame for the American deaths.

August 19, at the Republican convention in Kansas City, President Ford edged out Ronald Reagan for the Republican nomination for President. Senator Bob Dole was nominated as his running mate. Ford won with 1,121 delegate votes to Reagan's 1,078. Ford had won 27 contests to Reagan's 24 with the final primary vote totals of 5.3 million for Ford, to 4.7 million for Reagan.

August 26, the first known outbreak of the Ebola virus occurred in Zaire.

Also on August 26, Queen Juliana and Prince Bernard of the Netherlands were forced to resign for taking bribes in the Lockheed scandal.

August 27, transsexual Rene Richards was barred from competing in the US Tennis Open.

September 1, Congressman Wayne Hayes a Democrat from Ohio resigned following discovery that he had hired Elizabeth Ray, Miss Virginia 1975, to have sex with him on a regular basis in exchange for a salary as a congressional staffer. During a closed session House inquiry Ray admitted, "I can't type, I can't file, I can't even answer the phone." Ray also admitted she was paid by a lobbyist to have sex with Senator Mike Gravel of Alaska in exchange for his vote on a bill.

September 3, Viking 2 landed on Mars and sent back the first colored photos of the planet.

September 6, Soviet Air Force pilot Lt. Viktor Belenko landed a MIG-25 in Japan and asked for political asylum in the US.

September 9, at 82 and in declining health Mao Zedong died of a heart attack just after midnight. On September 18, the funeral was held.

September 10, five Croatian terrorists captured a TWA fight at La Guardia Airport in New York.

September 16, the American Episcopal Church approved the ordination of women as priests and bishops.

September 17, the first space shuttle Enterprise was unveiled to the public.

September 21, Chilean economist and diplomat Orlando Letelier was assassinated by a bomb in his car in Washington, DC after CIA Director Vernon Walters notified the Chilean Military Dictator Augusto Pinochet that Letelier was a threat and was organizing a democratic government in exile. At the assassin's trail it was learned that the murder was directly ordered by the Chilean Military Dictator Augusto Pinochet. According to now declassified documents published by the National Security Archive, the assassination was part of Operation Condor a South American operation of political suppression and assassinations of Latin American "leftists" which was sponsored by the CIA. CIA agents along with Anti-Castro agents worked with an American CIA asset, Michael Townley, who worked with both the CIA and the DINA, the Chilean secret police, to murder Letelier. Townley was convicted and sentenced to 62 months in prison and given immunity for other crimes and assassinations for his testimony. Townley had traveled with a false passport provided by the CIA under the name of Kenneth Enyart and had also murdered another member of Allende's government General Carlos Prats and his wife living in exile in Argentina. He was also convicted in absentia in Italy for an assassination attempt on an Italian. The US refused to extradite Townley to either Italy or Argentina. He was also suspected in the death of the Chilean poet Pablo Neruda, who opposed Pinochet. He was also alleged to be involved in Chile's chemical weapons program under Pinochet. He was living in the US in the Federal Witness Protection Program according to the *Washington Post* in a July 26, 1983 article, *Diplomat's Assassin to Be Freed.*

September 23, President Ford and Jimmy Carter debated on television.

September 29, Syria drove the Palestinian rebels out of Lebanon.

October 4, Agricultural Secretary Earl Butz was forced to resign for publicly telling a racist joke, giving the Ford more election baggage.

October 6, during the second television debate between President Ford and Jimmy Carter, Ford stumbled badly when he declared that "There is no Soviet domination of Eastern Europe." Instead of admitting he had misspoken, Ford repeated his remark, a mistake that cost him the votes of many independent voters.

Also on October 6, two anti-Castro Cubans associated with the CIA placed two bombs on a Cuban flight from Barbados killing all 73 on board.

October 11, Mao's widow along with the other "The Gang of Four" members who led the Chinese Cultural Revolution were arrested in Beijing.

October 13, the United States Commission on Civil Rights released a report showing that Puerto Ricans in the Continental US were the most impoverished group with over a third living in dire poverty.

October 14, the Nobel Prize for Economics was awarded to Milton Friedman for his consumption analysis.

October 15, the first televised debate of the Vice Presidential nominees was held between Senator Dole and Senator Mondale.

October 19, Chimpanzees (Pan Troglodytes) were placed on the list of endangered species.

October 20, a Mississippi River ferry in Louisiana was struck by a ship killing 78 passengers and crew.

October 22, Red Dye No. 4 was banned by the US Food and Drug Administration because it was found to cause tumors.

November 1, two West German Generals admitted that they were past members of the German Nazi Party.

November 2, in a close election Jimmy Carter defeated Gerald Ford for President. Carter managed to take the South and most of the large Eastern states, while Ford carried the West, and much of New England. The two split the Midwest. The final vote was about 41 million for Carter and 39 million for Ford. However Ford carried more states 27, to Carter's 23 plus DC. Carter was the last Democratic nominee for President to win Texas and the South. Carter was the first president elected from the Deep South since Zachary Taylor in 1848.

November 9, the UN condemned South Africa for apartheid.

November 15, the Syrian Army took control of Beirut.

November 24, over 3,800 people were killed in an earthquake in Turkey.

November 25, the Viking 1 radio signals from Mars helped to prove the Theory of Relativity.

December 1, Angola was admitted to the UN.

December 3, during a Jamaican election leftist Bob Marley and his manager were shot in an attempted assassination. Many in Jamaica believe it was at the behest of US agents.

December 8, the Congressional Hispanic Caucus was formed.

December 15, the oil tanker Argo Merchant ran aground on Nantucket Shoals spilling 7.6 million gallons of fuel oil.

December 16, the government halted the vaccinations for Swine Flu amid some reports of paralysis.

December 21, the notorious Mayor of Chicago Richard Daily died.

December 22, another thirty-five couples from the Reverend Moon's Unification Church were married in a mass wedding ceremony in New York.

December 28, Winnie Mandela was banned from South Africa.

The inflation rate in 1976 was 5.75%. The average cost of a new home rose to $43,400 and monthly rent went to $220. The average price of a new car was $4,100 and gas rose to 59 cents per gallon. The average income was about $16,000. Microwave ovens were popular and cost about $169 and CB radios became a fad and cost $147. In 1976 the first laser printer was introduced by IBM. Gambling was approved by the New Jersey Legislature in Atlantic City.

The cost of a new Zenith 25 inch color television was $599. The Superstation WTBS Atlanta went national. And on November 7, *Gone with the Wind* premiered on television and to the largest audience at that time. Although Sonny and Cher had divorced, they continued to do their television show. The dramatic series *Rich Man Poor Man* based upon the book was a hit. *The McNeil-Lehrer Report* and *Live From Lincoln Center* aired for their first time on PBS. Jackie Gleason and cast re-united in their show *The Honeymooners* in an ABC special. *The Blues Brothers* made their first appearance on *Saturday Night Live*.

Television debuts included: *The Bionic Woman, Laverne & Shirley, Family, The Gong Show, Family Feud, What's Happening?, Alice, Delvecchio, The Scooby Doo Hour, Baa Baa Black Sheep, Charlie's Angels, Serpico, The Muppet Show,* and *Quincy M.E.*. Shows ending their run in 1976 were: *Marcus Welby MD, Cannon, The Rookies, and Medical Center.* At the Emmys *The Mary Tyler Moore Show, Police Story, Upstairs Downstairs, and Saturday Night Live* won in their categories. Mary Tyler Moore in her show and Jack Albertson in *Chico and the Man* were the best comedy actors. Peter Faulk in *Columbo* and Michael Learned in *The Waltons* were the best dramatic actors. Ted Knight and Betty White also won best Supporting Comedy Actors once again in *The Mary Tyler Moore Show*.

The movies of 1976 were well attended. They included: *Rocky, Network, A Star is Born, All the President's Men, The Omen, King Kong, Silver Streak, Midway, Taxi Driver, The Bad News Bears, Logan's Run, The Outlaw Josie Wales, The Pink Panther Strikes Again, The Shootist,* and *The Eagle Has Landed. Rocky* won the Oscars for Best Picture and Best Director. *Network* won Oscars for Best Actor for Peter Finch, Best Actress for Faye Dunaway and Best Supporting Actress for Beatrice Straight. Jason Robards won the Best Supporting Actor in *All the President's Men. Taxi Driver* won at the Cannes Film Festival.

In music the band U2 began and the Cars also played their first gig, the Ramones recorded their first album and George Harrison was convicted of plagiarizing his music. Punk Rock made its debut. Billboards number one on the yearend Hot 100 was *Silly Love Songs* by Wings. *Don't Go Breakin' My Heart* by Elton John and Kiki Dee was number two. Other Billboard 1976 hits included: *December 1963 (Oh What a Night)* by The Four Seasons, *Play That Funky Music* by Wild Cherries, *50 Ways to Leave Your Lover* by Paul Simon, *Sara Smile* by Hall & Oates, *Afternoon Delight* by The Starland Vocal Band, *I Write the Songs* by Barry Manilow, *Bohemian Rhapsody* by Queen, *I'd Really Love to See You Tonight* by England Dan and John Ford Coley, *You Sexy thing* by Hot Chocolate, *Take it to the Limit* by The Eagles, *Shake Your Booty* and *That's the Way I Like It* by KC and the Sunshine Band, *Moonlight Feels Right* by Starbuck, *Let Your Love Flow* by the Bellamy Brothers, *Dream Weaver* by Gary Wright, *Love to Love You Baby* by Donna Summer, *If You Leave Me Now* by Chicago, *Dream On* by Aerosmith, *Convoy* by C.W. McCall, *Welcome Back* by John Sebastian, *Still the*

One by Orleans, *Take the Money and Run* by the Steve Miller Band, *Slow Ride* by Foghat and *Breaking Up is Hard to Do* by Neil Sedaka.

In 1976 literature some of the most popular books were as follows: *Roots* by Alex Haley which won the Pulitzer Prize, *Slapstick* by Kurt Vonnegut Jr., *The Boys from Brazil* by Ira Levin, *Trinity* by Leon Uris, *Kiss of the Spider Woman* by Manuel Puig, *1876* by Gore Vidal, *Interview with the Vampire* by Anne Rice, *The Final Days* by Carl Bernstein and Bob Woodward, *A River Runs Through It* by Norman Maclean, *Even Cowgirls Get the Blues* by Tom Robbins and *The Grass is Always Greener Over the Septic Tank* by Erma Bombeck.

CHAPTER 33. 1977: JIMMY CARTER TOOK OFFICE, CIA'S MIND CONTROL PROGRAM REVEALED, AND ELVIS DIED

January, the first all-in-one CPU, screen and keyboard, the Commodore PET went on sale.

January 3, Apple Computer was formally incorporated.

January 6, Andrew Lee, an American cocaine dealer, was arrested in Mexico for killing a police officer. In his possession was a top secret microfilm that he was planning to sell to the Soviet Embassy in Mexico City. He admitted to being a spy and implicated his friend Christopher Boyce a TRW employee with a top secret security clearance. Boyce was convicted on May 14 and sentenced to 40 years as a spy. Lee was nicknamed the Snowman because of his cocaine dealing and Boyce was known as the Falcon because of his hobby in Falconry. The story was later told in a book and a movie called *The Snowman and the Falcon*. In January 1980 Boyce escaped from prison and had a life as a bank robber. He committed 17 robberies until he was caught in August 1981. In September 2002 he was paroled from prison in part for assisting the government on how to prevent future insider spy threats.

January 8, an Armenian separatist group set off three bombs in Moscow killing seven.

January 17, a landing craft used to shuttle marines and sailors on the USS Trenton and USS Guam from ship to shore in Barcelona, Spain was run over by a tanker killing 49 sailors and marines.

January 19, snow fell in Miami. It is the only snowfall ever recorded in the city.

January 20, President Carter was sworn into office.

January 20, with the Church Committee no longer looking at the illegal activities of the CIA, George H.W. Bush resigned as Director.

January 21, President Cater pardoned the Vietnam draft evaders.

January 23-30, the eight part series *Roots* premiered and became the most watched entertainment event with over 100 million watching the television series.

February 1, the Great Lakes Blizzard of 1977 struck and claimed over 100 lives.

February 2, the Tandy Corporation through their Radio Shack stores developed the TRS 80 computer. Radio Shack began selling the micro computers in August.

February 4, an elevated train in Chicago jumped the tracks killing 11 and injuring over 200.

February 8, *Hustler* magazine publisher Larry Flint was sentenced on obscenity charges for 7 to 25 years in prison. He served only six days as the sentence was overturned on appeal.

February 11, Clifford Alexander Jr. was appointed by President Carter as the first African-American Secretary of the Army.

February 18, the Space Shuttle Enterprise's first transfer test flight moving the shuttle across the country in preparation to lift off was successful.

February 21, another 74 couples of Reverend Moon's Unification Church were wed in a mass ceremony in New York.

February 24, President Carter announced that all US foreign policy and foreign aid would consider human rights in the decision making.

February 25, an oil tanker exploded off Honolulu, Hawaii spilling 31 million gallons of oil.

March 1, the US extended their territorial waters to 200 miles.

March 1, Bank of America decided to use Visa for the name their credit cards.

March 4, the first Cray 1 super computer was bought by Los Alamos Laboratories.

March 4, an earthquake in Romania killed over 1500.

March 7, Israeli Prime Minister Yitzhak Rabin met with President Carter.

March 9-11, the Hanafi Siege took place. The City Hall, the Islamic Center and the headquarters of B'nai B'rith in Washington, DC, were seized by twelve radical Black Muslim gunmen who had split from the Nation of Islam to form their own group, "the Hanafi Movement." They took 149 hostages and killed a news reporter and police officer. Councilmember Marion Barry, who would later become mayor, was also hit by a bullet. The ambassadors from Egypt, Pakistan and Iran talked the gunmen into releasing their hostages and surrendering after 139 hours.

March 9, Admiral Stansfield Turner was appointed Director of the CIA.

March 10, rings were discovered around Uranus.

March 15, the US House of Representatives began televising their sessions.

March 16, in a town meeting in Massachusetts, President Carter said that a Palestinian homeland would be a key to peace in the Mideast. Israeli reaction was immediate and negative. Many in Congress condemned Carter's statement.

March 18, the US State Department restricted US citizens from visiting Cuba, Vietnam North Korea, and Cambodia as hostile governments.

March 18, Vietnam returned some remains of American MIAs to the US.

March 20, the communists and socialists won the French municipal elections.

March 22, after her party suffered severe election losses Indira Gandhi resigned as Prime Minister in India.

March 27, the worst accident in aviation history occurred when Pan AM and KLM planes collided, killing 583 over Tenerife, in the Canary Islands.

April 3, President Carter met with Egyptian President Anwar Sadat.

April 4, a flood in Grundy, Virginia, damaged 228 homes and businesses causing over $15 million in damages. Much of the town was then relocated to higher ground.

April 4, a Southern Airlines plane crashed on a highway in New Hope, Georgia killing 72 passengers and crew.

April 6, the Kingdome was opened in Seattle and the new Seattle Mariners baseball team lost to the Los Angeles Angels.

April 8, Yitzhak Rabin resigned as Israeli Premier.

April 22, Simon Peres became the Israeli Premier.

April 22, Optical fiber was used for telephone traffic for the first time.

April 26, Studio 54 was opened in New York City.

April 30, Vietnam invaded Cambodia.

May 1, a labor demonstration at Taksim Square in Istanbul, Turkey involving 500,000 people was broke up by the Turkish Army with armored vehicles and high pressure water hoses. Officially 34 were killed and about 220 injured but popular estimates are higher. The casualties were the result of gunshot wounds, being crushed to death by the armored vehicles, and being trampled by the panicked crowd. Over 500 demonstrators were arrested and 98 were indicted for rioting. Despite many claims of abuse against the Army and police none were ever tried for these crimes.

May 16, an NI Airway helicopter crashed and killed 5 on the Pan Am building in New York.

May 17, the conservative Likud Party won the Israeli elections led by Menachem Begin. He became Prime Minister the following day.

May 23, South Moluccan extremists hijacked a train in the Netherlands holding 105 school children and 50 others hostage. The children were released on May 27, and on June 11, the Dutch Royal Marines stormed the train. Six terrorists and two hostages were killed.

May 28, the Beverly Hills Supper Club in Southgate, Kentucky, just across the river from Cincinnati, caught fire killing 165 and injuring another 200. The club could safely hold 600 but had approximately 1,300 guests on the holiday weekend to see singer John Davidson.

June 4-6, during Puerto Rican Day in Chicago, police harassment and abuse of the Puerto Rican community triggered a riot. Two people were killed and more than 80 were arrested.

June 6-9, Britain held the Jubilee celebrations to celebrate the 25-year reign of Queen Elizabeth II.

June 7, singer/spokesperson Anita Bryant began a campaign, "Save Our Children" to overturn Dade County Florida laws prohibiting discrimination against gays. She went on to become a national spokesperson against gay rights. Bryant claimed that gays recruited children into their gay lifestyle and that most were child molesters. Her name became synonymous with homophobia.

June 10, the first Apple II computers went on sale.

June 20, the US Supreme Court ruled that states were not required to spend Medicaid funds on elective abortions.

June 20, the first oil began flowing through the Alaskan pipeline.

June 26, 200,000 gay rights protesters marched in San Francisco to protest Anita Bryant's Save Our Children campaign.

June 30, the Women Marines were disbanded as women were allowed to be Marines.

June 30, the Southeast Asian Treaty Organizations was formally disbanded.

June 30 the US Railway Post Office made its final run. The last trip was from New York to DC.

July 5, a military coup overthrew the democratically elected Premier Zulfikar Ali Bhutto in Pakistan.

July 11, Martin Luther King Jr. was awarded the US Medal of Freedom posthumously by President Carter.

July 13, New York City lost power and was blacked out for 25 hours. Crime and looting commenced and 1,616 of stores were looted and 1,037 set ablaze. Over 550 police were injured during the looting and 4,500 looters were arrested. Damages were estimated at over $300 million.

July 13, Somalia declared war on Ethiopia.

July 14, North Korea shot down a US helicopter and killed 3 Americans.

Also on July 14, due to on-going abuses the US House also established a permanent Select Committee on Intelligence to oversee the NSA and CIA.

July 19-20, massive flooding in Johnstown, Pennsylvania, killed 75 people and caused billions in damages.

July 20, under the Freedom of Information Act the CIA was forced to reveal documents showing that it had conducted mind control experiments on knowing and unknowing Americans and Canadians in an operation called MK-ULTRA. The CIA thought it had destroyed all documents for the operation but 20,000 records had been misfiled in a little used facility and were found. Although most project details were destroyed in 1973 and these newly found records lacked details, they did show the enormous reach of this large project. The goal of the project was to make "Manchurian Candidates" human robots capable of having orders placed unknown to them in their unconscious brain for actions such as assassinations, espionage, bombings, etc. to be carried out at a later date when given external commands. Improved torture methods and information gathering from unwilling captives were other secondary goals.

July 21-24, border clashes erupted into war between Egypt and Libya.

August 3, the United States Senate began hearings on MK-ULTRA. They would learn that Project MK-ULTRA used drugs, torture, sexual humiliation and other methods to erase memories and build human robots in many experiments at many facilities including: universities, medical centers and the military bases on thousands of subjects. The final numbers will never be known as all those records were destroyed by the CIA in 1973.

August 4, President Carter created the US Department of Energy. One of the goals of the department was to find and expand alternative energy sources including solar, wind, wave and hydrogen.

August 10, David Berkowitz was arrested for the Son of Sam Murders. Berkowitz was a New York City serial killer who killed six and wounded seven others while leaving clues and mocking the police in the press. After his arrest it was discovered that he had also been the culprit in numerous unsolved arsons. He was convicted and is serving six life sentences.

August 16, Elvis Presley died at the age of 42 of a drug overdose at his home in Memphis, Tennessee. Over 75,000 fans lined the streets in Memphis for his funeral.

August 17 the Soviet submarine *Arktika* became the first surface ship to reach the North Pole.

August 19, at the age of 86 Groucho Marx died in Los Angeles.

August 20, Voyager 2 was launched to explore Jupiter, Saturn, Uranus and Neptune. As of this writing it is still functioning and it has left the solar system and now explores deep space. It is expected to function and send back data until 2025.

August 26, French became the official language of Quebec.

September 4, the Golden Dragon Restaurant Massacre killed 5 and wounded 11 in San Francisco. Members of a Chinese youth gang were attempting to kill members of a rival gang. None of those killed or wounded were rival gang members. The gang members hid under tables before escaping. The killers were caught and prosecuted.

September 5, Voyager 1 was finally launched after a delay. It was the first craft to leave the solar system and explore interstellar space. As of this writing it continues to function and like its sister ship Voyager 2 and it will also likely continue until about 2025.

September 7, President Carter and Panama executed the Panama Canal Treaties giving control of the canal to Panama in 2000. The exchange infuriated conservatives and some independents. Although Carter was blamed, the transfer was negotiated by the Ford Administration.

September 11, Atari's video game system went on sale beginning a wave of electronic gaming.

September 12, South African freedom activist Steve Bilko was killed in police custody.

September 18, the yacht Courageous, skippered by Ted Turner, won the 24th American Cup race.

September 19, the North Koreans made the first of many kidnappings of Japanese citizens.

September 21, fifteen nations including the US and the USSR signed a nuclear proliferation agreement.

September 29, the Food Stamp Act of 1977 was passed. The Supplemental Nutrition Assistance Program, SNAP, went into effect providing food to low income people, mostly children.

October 2, the Pakistan military junta banned all political opposition.

October 12, the US Supreme Court heard University of California v. Bakke the so called "reverse discrimination" case which challenged affirmative action for college acceptance. In June of 1978 the court ruled and upheld affirmative action, but struck down provisions citing specific quotas.

October 13, a German Lufthansa plane was hijacked in Somalia. The hijackers demand the release of 11 Red Army terrorists from prison. On October 18, German Special Forces stormed the airliner killing three of the four hijackers and freed all 86 hostages.

October 21, President Carter recalled the ambassador to South Africa in protest of Apartheid and other human rights abuses.

October 26, the last case of small pox was recorded in Somalia. The World health Organization lists this date as the date small pox was eradicated due to the vaccine.

November 1, President Carter raised the minimum wage from $2.30 per hour to $3.35 per hour effective January 1981.

November 1, American astronomer Charles Kowal discovered 2060 Chiron, the first Centaur, a group of planetoids between Jupiter and Neptune.

November 4, the United Nations Security Council began a weapons embargo against South Africa.

November 6, the Kelly Barnes Dam in Toccoa, Georgia, failed and 39 were killed in the flooding.

November 8, in the elections Ed Koch was elected Mayor of New York and Harvey Milk, the first openly gay politician to hold a significant office, was elected a San Francisco City Supervisor.

November 12, Ernest Morial was elected the first Black mayor of New Orleans.

November 13, the last *Lil' Abner* comic strip was published. The iconic and popular comic strip began in 1937. At its peak the comic strip had 60 million readers in over 900 American newspapers and 100 foreign papers in 28 countries.

November 15, the Shah of Iran visited the United States.

November 19-21 Egyptian President Anwar Sadat visited Israel.

November 22, the first three nodes of the ARPANET were linked in what would become the internet.

December 1, the first top-secret stealth aircraft, created by Lockheed, made its first flight.

Also on December 1, the first cable children's television channel The Pinwheel Network, which later became known as Nickelodeon made its debut.

December 13, a charter plane carrying the University of Evansville Basketball team to a game in Nashville crashed killing 29 including 14 team members and their head coach.

December 20, Vietnam and Djibouti join the United Nations.

December 22, a grain elevator exploded in Westwego, Louisiana killing 36.

In 1977 the Defense Department began using a GPS system that is the precursor to the GPS system used today. Computers started to come into common use in small businesses. The inflation rate was still high at 6.5% and the average household income hit $15,000. The price of the average new home was $49,300 and rent rose to $240 per month. The average new car cost $4,317 with 65 cents for a gallon of gas. At an average cost of $9 the Bikini was very popular with young women.

In television Jay Leno made his first appearance on the *Tonight Show* with Johnny Carson in March. Many years later Leno would replace Carson on the show. September marked the first use of the "Viewer discretion is advised" warning. It first appeared on the comedy spoof *Soap*. *The Match Game* was the number one game show for the fifth year in a row. After 48 years of service to CBS news on both radio and television Eric Severeid bade his farewell in November. The new shows in 1977 included: *The Hardy Boys/Nancy Drew Mysteries, Carter Country, Hunter, Eight is Enough, Three's Company, The Amazing Spiderman, The Betty White Show, Soap, Inside the NFL, CHIPs, Logan's Run, Lou Grant, The Love Boat*, and returning after being off the air since 1959 *The Mickey Mouse Club*.

Shows ending in 1977 included: *Sanford & Son, The Mary Tyler Moore Show, The Streets of San Francisco, McCloud, McMillan & Wife, Emergency*, and *Let's Make a Deal* which would later come back.

The *Mary Tyler More Show* won the Emmy for Best Comedy. The Best Actors were Carroll O'Connor for *All in the Family*, Bea Arthur in *Maude*, James Gardner in *The Rockford Files*, and Lindsay Wagner as *The Bionic Woman*. *Roots* won for Most Outstanding Series and was nominated for 21 and won 6 Emmys.

At the movies George Lucas' *Star Wars* was the most successful while Woody Allen's *Annie Hall* was the most recognized at the Oscars with Best Picture, Director Woody Allen, and Actress Diane Keaton. *The Goodbye Girl* also won recognition with Best Actor Richard Dreyfuss and Best Picture Actor and Actress Marsha Mason in the Golden Globes. Other notable films of 1977: *The Turning Point, Smokey and the Bandit, Julia, Saturday Night Fever, Close Encounters of a Third Kind, A Bridge Too Far, Oh God!, The Deep, The Spy Who Loved Me. 3 Women, Airport 1977, Fun with Dick and Jane, Looking for Mr. Goodbar, Semi-Tough*, and one of the best sport/comedy movies of all time, *Slap Shot* with Paul Newman.

In February, Fleetwood Mac released their record breaking Grammy winning album, *Rumors*. Kiss also played their first concert in February. The Clash released their first album in April. In June the Supremes and Elvis Presley each played their last concerts. At the end of the year the Sex Pistols released an album that went to number one in the UK despite most retail outlets refusing to sell it.

Andy Gibb and the Bee Gees were propelled to the top of American music with the hit film *Saturday Night Fever*. Their hits included: *Tonight's the Night, Love So Right,* and *How Deep is Your Love.* Rod Stewart had the number one with *Tonight's the Night.* Fleetwood Mac had *Dreams, Don't Stop* and *Go Your Own Way.* ABBA had *Dancing Queen* and *Knowing Me Knowing You.* Leo Sayer had *You Make Me Feel Like Dancing* and *How Much Love.* The Eagles had *Hotel California* and *New Kid in Town.* Other hits included: *Margaritaville* by Jimmy Buffet, *Rich Girl* Hall & Oates, *Fly Like and Eagle* by the Steve Miller Band, *Easy* by the Commodores, *Swayin' to the Music* by Johnny Rivers, *Night Moves* by Bob Seger and the Silver Bullet Band, *Smoke from a Distant Fire* by the Sanford-Townsend Band, *Lido Shuffle* by Bozz Skaggs, and *Walk This Way* by Aerosmith.

The Pulitzer Prize for fiction was not given in 1977. The books of 1977 include: *The Thorn Birds* by Colleen McCullough, *The Shining* by Stephen King, *The Amityville Horror* by Jay Anson, *Song of Solomon* by Toni Morrison, *Master of the Game* by Sidney Sheldon, *Coma* by Robin Cook, *Love is a Dog From Hell* by Charles Bukowski, *Suffer the Children* by John Saul, *Delta of Venus* by Anaïs Nin, *In Patagonia* by Bruce Chatwin, *A Rumor of War* by Philip Caputo, *The Plague Dogs* by Richard Adams and *The Women's Room* by Marilyn French.

Chapter 34. 1978: The Camp David Accords, Jonestown, Serial Killers and The First Test Tube Baby

January 3, China and the European Market signed a trade deal.

January 6, the USA returned the Holy Crown of Hungary which it had been holding since WWII.

January 7, the rarest book, a complete Gutenberg Bible, the first major mass printed book, was sold at auction in New York City for $2.2 million. It was the last sale of a complete copy. These books are currently estimated to be worth between $25 and $35 million. There are 49 remaining but only 21 are complete.

January 13, former 1968 Democratic candidate for president, and the Vice President under Lyndon Johnson and Minnesota Senator, Hubert Humphrey, died of cancer at his home in Waverly, Minnesota. After his failed presidential bid in 1968 he returned to Minnesota and was again elected to the Senate. On January 14-15, his body lay in state in both the Minnesota State Capitol Rotunda and the US Capitol Rotunda before his funeral and burial in Minnesota. His wife Muriel was appointed by the Minnesota Governor to serve in his Senate seat until an election could be held. In 1980 President Carter awarded Humphrey the Medal of Freedom.

January 18, the European Court of Human Rights found the British government guilty of mistreating prisoners in Northern Ireland.

January 24, a Soviet satellite, Kosmos 954, lost orbit and partially burned and broke up on re-entry scattering debris over Canada's Northwest Territory.

January 25-27 The Great Blizzard of 1978, also known as the White Hurricane, struck the Great Lakes and Ohio Valley killing 70. South Bend, Indiana received 36 inches of snow over several days. In southeast Michigan over 100,000 cars were abandoned on highways during the storm.

January 28, Richard Chase, "the Vampire of Sacramento" was arrested for six murders where he drank the victim's blood and cannibalized their remains. Chase was insane and blamed Nazis and UFOs for the killings. In 1980 he committed suicide in prison by hoarding and hiding prescribed antidepressants and taking them all at once.

February 1, Hollywood film director Roman Polanski skipped bail and fled to France. Polanski had pled guilty to having sex with a thirteen-year-old girl. He continued to make films in Europe. It was Polanski's pregnant wife, Sharon Tate, who was murdered in 1969 by the Manson family.

February 3, President Carter and Egyptian President Anwar Sadat began talking about a Mideast peace process in Washington, DC.

February 6-7, the Northeastern Blizzard of 1978 dumped record amounts of snow on New England, New York and New Jersey and killed about 100, severely injured over 4,500 and caused over $520 million in damages. Boston and Providence both received over 27 inches of snow. Some places reported up 40 inches of snow. At Boston Garden over 11,000 college hockey fans were stranded and many spent the next several days living at Boston Garden eating hot dogs and sleeping in the bleachers.

February 8, the US Senate proceedings were broadcast on the radio for the first time.

February 11, sixteen couples from the Unification Church, "the Moonies," wed in a mass ceremony in New York.

February 15, serial killer Ted Bundy was arrested. Bundy had raped and killed well over 30 young women. He was particularly cruel and sadistic. He also kept the women's bodies and continued having sex with them after their deaths. He cut off some heads and kept them as trophies. His defense attorney later described him as "the very definition of heartless evil." He was executed in January of 1989.

February 17, a bomb placed by the IRA exploded near Belfast killed 12 and injured 30.

February 21, electrical workers digging in Mexico City discovered the remains of the Great Pyramid of Tenochtitlan in the middle of the city.

February 22, two propane tankers exploded killing 15 people in Waverly, Tennessee.

March 1, Charlie Chaplin's remains were stolen by grave robbers who held them for ransom. The robbers were later caught in May. Chaplin was re-buried in a concrete tomb by his family to prevent further incidents.

March 2, Soyuz 28 was launched with two Soviet and one Czech cosmonaut, Vladimir Remek, who became the first person in space who was neither American or Soviet.

March 3, David Rorvik, a Pulitzer Prize-winning American journalist, wrote the book, *In his Image: The Cloning of Man,* which was published by *The New York Post.* In it he claimed to be part of a scientific team that had cloned the first human. Rorvik made many appearances talking about the book and the cloning, including on *The Today Show* where he was interviewed by Tom Brokaw. The book was controversial and raised concerns about the ethics of cloning. The book was later subject of a legal settlement with his publisher after it was proven to be a hoax.

March 6, controversial publisher Larry Flynt of *Hustler* magazine was shot and paralyzed in Lawrenceville, Georgia. Flynt and his lawyer were returning to a courthouse where he was facing obscenity charges related to his publications when a sniper shot him. Years later a White supremacist, Joseph Paul Franklin, admitted that he was the shooter. He said he tried to kill Flynt because he had published photos of a Blacks and Whites having sex.

March 11, the Coastal Road Massacre, one of the worst terrorist acts in Israeli history occurred when a bus on the Coastal Highway was attacked by the Fatah faction of the Palestine Liberation Organization who killed 38 civilians including 13 children. They wounded 71 others. The attack was a warning trying to scuttle the Israeli-Egyptian peace negotiations advocated by President Carter. In response Israel invaded Lebanon in Operation Litani forcing the PLO North of the Litani river away from Israel's border.

March 16, Italian Premier Aldo Moro's five body guards were killed and he was captured by the Italian Red Brigade a terrorist communist group. Moro was put on trial by the Red Brigade and sentenced to death. The Pope offered to exchange himself for Moro after the Italian government refused to release three terrorists in exchange for Moro. The terrorists killed him firing ten times into his body. Moro's kidnappers and the killers were never caught.

March 18, California Jam II drew over 300,000 rock fans to Ontario, California.

March 19, over 50,000 demonstrated against the neutron bomb in Amsterdam. The neutron bomb kills humans with massive radiation while leaving buildings and other infrastructure intact.

March 28, the San Francisco City Council signed a comprehensive gay civil rights bill into law.

April 7, President Carter cancelled the US production of the neutron bomb. President Reagan later began producing the bomb, but it was met with such international protest that the US stopped production and the last neutron bomb was deactivated in 2011.

April 10, Volkswagen became the second non-American car company to open a plant in the US, Rolls Royce was the first. The Volkswagen plant produced the Rabbit at a facility near New Stanton, Pennsylvania. The plant closed in 1992.

April 14, over 20,000 demonstrators took to the streets in Tbilisi, Georgia in the USSR to protest a Soviet attempt to make Russian the official language along with Georgian. The Soviets reconsidered and Georgian remained as the only official language.

April 20, a navigation error caused a South Korean passenger jet flying from Paris to Seoul to veer off course and fly over Soviet air space. The Soviets misidentified the plane as an American spy plane and ordered it to be fired upon. The plane was hit and made an emergency landing on a frozen lake. Two passengers were killed. The surviving 97 passengers were held for several days and then released to the US Consulate in Leningrad. The Soviets charged Korea $100,000 for their care. The flight crew was detained and imprisoned. They were released after making a public apology.

April 25, the city of St. Paul, Minnesota followed Dade County Florida and repealed their gay rights ordinance because of Anita Bryant's Save the Children Campaign.

April 27, President Daoud Khan was assassinated in a military coup which began the Afghan civil war which still rages as of this writing in 2016.

April 27, a cooling tower under construction collapsed at a Willow Island power plant in West Virginia killing 51.

May 3, President Carter proclaimed Sun Day as day to make the public aware of solar energy. Events and demonstrations of solar power were held in the US and 21 other countries. President Carter flew to Denver, Colorado to participate in events at a solar power research institute.

May 4, to improve relations Soviet leader Brezhnev visited West Germany.

May 11, Margaret Brewer became the first woman Marine Corps General.

May 12, the US Department of Commerce announced that hurricanes would also have male as well as female names.

May 15, students at the University of Tehran rioted and the Army was called in to put down the riot. It was a precursor of things to come.

May 18, Italy legalized abortions.

May 20, the Pioneer Venus 1 orbiter was launched and reached Venus in December. The orbiter made the first topographic map of Venus using radar to penetrate the thick cloud covered planet.

May 20 Mavis Hutchinson at 53 became the first woman to run coast to coast across the US. Her run took 69 days.

May 21, the mass wedding of 118 couples of the Unification Church took place in England.

May 26, the first Atlantic City casino, Resorts International, opened.

June 6, California passed Proposition 13 which slashed property taxes to their 1975 level cutting taxes by about 57%. It also restricted property tax raises to the inflation rate but not to exceed 2% unless the property was sold. Within a decade California schools which had been ranked as the best in the nation fell to 48th according to the Rand Institute. Public libraries and other municipal services greatly declined. The tax payer revolt that Proposition 13 started was one of the things that solidified Ronald Reagan as a leader of the Republican Party and assured his nomination to be president in 1980.

June 13 Israeli forces withdrew from Lebanon after clearing the PLO from the borders.

June 15, Lisa Halaby, a 26-year-old Syrian-American, married King Hussein of Jordan to become Queen Noor. Her father was the CEO of Pan American Airways and the head of the Federal Aviation Administration under President Kennedy. Halaby had been one of the first women admitted to Princeton University where she graduated in 1973 with a degree in Urban Planning.

June 19, the comic strip *Garfield* about a fat lazy orange cat made its debut and would soon become the world's most widely syndicated comic strip.

June 22, James Christy at the US Naval Observatory discovered Charon the largest of the five moons orbiting the dwarf planet Pluto.

June 25, the American Nazis threatened to parade through the principally Jewish community of Skokie, Illinois, where at the time one of six were Holocaust survivors. Although the City of Skokie had refused a parade permit, the courts intervened, stating that the Nazis had the right to free speech and assembly, but they also ruled that they were not allowed to display the Swastika because it was a symbol of murder and hate. President Carter issued a statement, saying: "I must respect the decision of the Supreme Court allowing this group [the Nazis] to express their views, even when those views are despicable and ugly as they are in this case. But if such views must be expressed, I am pleased they will not go unanswered. That is why I want to voice my complete solidarity with those citizens of Skokie and Chicago who will gather Sunday in a peaceful demonstration of their abhorrence of Nazism." Several large Jewish and anti-Nazi demonstrations developed and forced them to cancel.

June 29, Vice President Walter Mondale made a visit to the Mideast as part of the on-going peace negotiations.

July 1, in a small town in Kentucky former President Nixon made his first public speech since resigning in disgrace. His criticized President Carter for his Mideast peace initiative. Nixon also criticized Carter's human rights initiatives. Nixon had asked that *God Bless America* be played as he left, but in an ironic dig at the former president the local band played *The Washington Post March* in reference to the newspaper that had broken the Watergate scandal leading to his resignation.

July 3, in a close vote the Supreme Court ruled 5-4 that the FCC had the right to reprimand New York radio station WBAI for allowing George Carlin to use four letter words on the air.

July 9, over 100,000 women marched in Washington, DC to ask for an extension of the Equal Rights Amendment (ERA). Thirty-five states passed the act out of the necessary thirty-eight required to change the Constitution before the 1979 deadline. Congress did approve an extension to 1982 but no further states approved the ERA and the amendment failed.

July 15, a march which began in San Francisco in February ended when 2,000 Native Americans came to their destination on the Mall in Washington, DC. They protested 11 bills that were being considered by Congress to limit Native rights to land, hunting and fishing, to close native schools and hospitals on reservations, and limit federal poverty support to Natives. After two weeks of demonstrations and lobbying, the marchers returned home. Congress did not pass any of the 11 bills.

July 18, Egypt and Israel began two days of peace talks.

July 25, the Cerro Maravilla Murders or Massacre occurred when Puerto Rican police shot and killed two men, a 25-year-old and a 19-year-old, who were pro-independence Puerto Rican activists. The two were beaten and killed in a police ambush. The police claimed they were responding to terrorist violence and this fabrication was originally supported by the FBI. After a public outcry more investigations were conducted which showed that the police murdered the two young men. In the end, ten police officers were convicted of various crimes and the FBI and the government were found culpable in the cover-up.

July 25, Bob Dylan was booed off the stage at the Newport Folk Festival for attempting to use an electric guitar.

July 25, Louise Brown — the first "test tube" baby (in vitro fertilization) — was born in Oldham, England.

August 6, Pope Paul VI died. On August 11, the funeral was held.

August 8, Pioneer Venus 2 was launched. The mission was to launch three probes to explore the heavy atmosphere of Venus. The probes were launched in November into the Venusian atmosphere. They were successful. Although they were not designed to survive the fall one probe landed intact on the surface and continued to send back information.

August 12, the Treaty of Peace and Friendship between Japan and China was signed ending decades of animosity. It was strongly opposed by the USSR.

August 13, a bomb killed 175 and injured another 80 at the PLO headquarters in Beirut, Lebanon. A rival Palestinian group, the Popular Front for the Liberation of Palestine-General Command, was likely responsible.

August 17, three Americans became the first to cross the Atlantic in a balloon when the Double Eagle II traveled from Maine to France.

August 19, four Islamic fundamentalists barred the doors of a cinema in Abadan, Iran and set it on fire killing between 400-800 people. It was one of the events that began the Iranian Revolution.

August 22, the Sandinistas an anti-American group seeking to free Nicaragua from American influence took power in Nicaragua by seizing the National Palace in Managua.

August 26, Pope John Paul I became the 263rd Pope.

August 31, Emily and William Harris of the Symbionese Liberation Army pled guilty to kidnapping Patty Hearst.

September 5, secret negotiations between Egypt and Israel urged and hosted by President Carter began at the presidential retreat at Camp David, Maryland. The talks went on until September 11, when the Camp David Accords were signed by the two parties. Negotiations broke down several times and nearly ended, but at President Carter's strong insistence the two men stayed and continued their talks. Carter's insistence eventually forced the two reluctant leaders to reach an agreement. Carter and his administration had worked for months to get the two parties to come to Camp David for discussions. The Accord led to the 1979 Egypt-Israel Peace Agreement.

September 8, in an event in Iran known as Black Friday, the Iranian Army fired on rioters and killed 84 or 85 people, according to the current Iranian government which compensated the victim's families. Many more were wounded. Most of the victims were Islamic followers of the Ayatollah Khomeini. Initial rumors of thousands shot and killed swept the nation and caused a country-wide outrage. The next day the Ayatollah Khomeini called for the men of faith in the Iranian Army to revolt. Black Friday was another key event which began the Iranian revolution.

September 11, Georgi Markov, a Bulgarian writer and broadcast journalist who had defected to Britain in 1969, was assassinated on a London street by a poison pellet that was fired into him by the Bulgarian secret police with help from the KGB according to *The Umbrella Assassin* on the November 20, 2009 PBS television show *Secrets of the Dead*. Ten days before the assassination another Bulgarian defector living in Paris was also attacked in the same manner but survived the attack when the pellet failed to emit the poison.

September 14-18, in the "Troubles," the IRA exploded over 50 bombs across Northern Ireland injuring 37 people.

September 16, a violent earthquake at Tabas, Iran, killed between 15,000 and 25,000 people and destroyed much of the city and damaged 85 other towns.

September 26 the Brotherhood of Railway and Airline Clerks went on strike against 72 railroads shutting down rail way traffic and idling factories and mines across the US. At the time railroads carried 47% of the nation's freight. President Carter appointed a mediation board and ordered the workers to end the strike. The Union initially refused until a federal judge signed an order prohibiting the railroads from retaliating against the striking workers.

September 28, heavy fighting began between the Syrians and Lebanese. Also on this day Pope John Paul I died, after only 33 days of papacy.

October 1, Vietnam attacked the Khmer Rouge in Cambodia.

October 4, Pier 39 opened in San Francisco on the edge of the Fisherman's Wharf District. The Pier became a tourist Mecca with its shopping center and the ever present sea lions.

October 6, Hannah Holborn Gray became the first woman president of a major American university when she accepted the post as President of the University of Chicago. Gray had been the acting President of Yale after their president had been appointed as an ambassador.

October 6, Iran declared Ayatollah Khomeini an undesirable person.

October 10, President Carter signed a bill authorizing the Susan B. Anthony dollar coin.

October 13, in an attempt to provide more interaction between the president and the American people, President Carter went live on National Public Radio and answered unscripted questions from callers.

October 16, Pope John Paul II was elected Pope. He was the first Polish Pope and the first non-Italian Pope in over 400 years.

October 27, Egypt's Anwar Sadat and Israel's Menachem Begin were named the joint winners of the Nobel Peace Prize for the Camp David Accords. Many felt that President Carter deserved the award for his insistence that the two men reach an agreement.

October 27, President Carter signed the Humphrey-Hawkins Full Employment Act to enact goals to provide full employment, stable prices and growth in production in the United States.

November 3, the USSR and Vietnam signed a peace and friendship treaty.

November 5, Iranian protestors attacked the British Embassy in Tehran. The following day the Shah of Iran placed the country under martial law.

November 7, in the elections California voters rejected the Briggs Initiative that would have prohibited gay school teachers. Marion Berry was elected the first Black mayor of Washington, DC.

November 17-18, after many complaints of abuse in his Congregation and a media article about the abuses in the "Peoples Temple," the cult leader, the Reverend Jim Jones, began the mass exodus of about a thousand of his followers from California to Guyana to live in a commune that he named Jonestown after himself. After receiving petitions and letters from former temple members and their relatives accusing Jones of many abuses including: mind manipulation and intimidation, physical beatings and torture, the forced separation of children and parents, drug sedation of offenders and the forced detainment by armed guards who prevented anyone from leaving, Congressman Jim Ryan of California and an 18 person delegation decided to go to Jonestown and investigate. The delegation included a reporter from the San Francisco Examiner and a television crew from NBC and eight concerned relatives of family members in Jonestown.

Ryan's visit to Jonestown was unwelcome and he was initially turned away. However, Jones changed his mind and became determined to convince Ryan that everything in Jonestown was legitimate and even conducted mass rehearsals with his followers on what to do and say to the Congressman and his delegation. During a musical reception to greet Ryan and his delegation, two members of the cult passed a note to them expressing a desire to leave, and Ryan and his party took the two out of the compound. Ryan was then told that no accommodations could be made for them that night in the compound, so they left for a nearby café to find accommodations with a promise to return the following day. In the meantime eleven cult members fled into the jungle and escaped.

Ryan and the delegation returned the following day and 14 more defectors asked to go with him. As the delegation and defectors left for the airfield, Jones became despondent and said all had been lost. At the airport, Congressman Ryan and five others were killed; eleven others were wounded by Jones' men. Jones then ordered his flock to commit "revolutionary suicide." The members, including the children, were asked to line up and were forced to drink a cyanide poisoned grape drink, while the youngest children and infants were killed by a cyanide syringe. In the end over 918 people died, including 270 children. The later discovery of still classified CIA documents about the event have led some to believe that Jonestown and the People's Temple were a CIA mind control experiment gone awry. Columnist Jack Anderson was the first to allege this in 1980. In 1989 the investigative journalist Michael Meiers wrote the book: *Was Jonestown A CIA Medical Experiment? A Review of the Evidence.* It has also been alleged that the Reverend Jim Jones was a victim of the CIA MK-ULTRA mind control experiments.

November 19, the first anti-crime "Take Back the Night" event was held in San Francisco.

November 27, San Francisco Mayor George Moscone and City Supervisor Harvey Milk were shot and killed by former City Supervisor Dan White. A week later Diane Feinstein became the first woman Mayor of San Francisco.

November 29, the United Nations observed a Palestinian Solidarity Day which was boycotted by the US.

December 2, chanting "Allah is great" masses of Islamic fundamentalist protestors marched through the streets of Tehran.

December 11, six men from the Lucchese Mafia crime family robbed $5.857 million from Lufthansa Airlines at JFK Airport in New York City. The money was from monetary exchanges on US bases in Germany.

December 15, Cleveland became the first American city to go into default since the great depression.

December 17, OPEC announced a raise in oil prices of 18% and agreed to a further price increase of 14.5% to be implemented in the following year.

December 22, the 11th Congress of the Chinese Communist Party was held and reversed the Maoist economic policies to allow China to modernize and reform its economy.

December 22, serial killer and rapist John Wayne Gacy was arrested in Chicago. He was subsequently convicted of 33 murders of young men and boys from 1972 to 1978. Police found 29 of his victims buried on his property and he admitted to throwing the others in the Des Plaines River. He was executed in 1994 for his crimes.

December 27, the Spanish Constitution was approved and marked the return of democracy to Spain.

In 1978, the Soviet nuclear weapons stockpile exceeded that of the US for the first time. Milton Bradley made a new board game, Fat Chance, to teach kids to eat right and prevent obesity. During a *Monday Night Football* Howard Cosell was asked to fill some dead air during a time out and began talking about how much he liked a new stadium snack, and overnight Nachos went mainstream and became a favorite American snack. Sweden became the first country to ban aerosol cans to protect the ozone layer.

Inflation rose to 7.62%, largely because of energy prices and the Vietnam War debt, and interest rates rose to 11.75%. The cost of the average new home rose to $54,800, which wasn't very affordable with the high interest rates. The average monthly rent rose to $260 as there were more renters since home-buying had become prohibitive. The average cost of a new car was $4,645 and gas went to 63 cents per gallon forcing Americans to buy more fuel efficient Japanese cars. Half of all newly purchased American cars were Japanese. The average income was about $17,000. Gold reached $200 per ounce. A Radio Shack TRS80 Tandy computer sold for $399.

Televisions were now in 98% of American homes. During March 26-April 1, CBS commemorated 50 years of radio and television service with a nine and a half hour retrospective which aired over the seven nights. The television new shows included: *Fantasy Island, How the West was Won, The Incredible Hulk, Dallas, The Ted Knight Show, Vega$, 20/20, The Paper Chase, Taxi, Battle Star Galactica, WKRP in Cincinnati,* and *Diff'rent Strokes.*

The shows making their final appearances were: *The Carol Burnett Show, The Bob Newhart Show, The Six Million Dollar Man, The Bionic Woman, Police Woman, Maude, Rhoda, Columbo, Baretta,* and *Chico and the Man.*

In the Emmys *All in the Family* won Best Comedy and Carroll O'Connor and Jean Stapleton Best Comedy Actors and Rob Reiner as Best Supporting Comedy Actor. *The Rockford Files* won Best Drama and the Best Dramatic Actors were Ed Asner in *Lou Grant* and Sada Thompson in *Family*.

Twelve-year-old Brooke Shields starred in an R rated movie, *Pretty Baby*, that she wasn't old enough to legally watch. At the movies *Grease, Superman*, and *National Lampoon's Animal House* were the top box office draws. *The Deer Hunter* won the Oscars for Best Picture, Best Director and Best Supporting Actor for Christopher Walken. John Voight and Jane Fonda won the Oscars for Best Actor and Actress in *Coming Home*. Some of the other significant pictures of 1978 included: *Midnight Express, Halloween, Hooper, Every Which Way but Loose, Heaven Can Wait, Jaws II, Revenge of the Pink Panther, California Suite, Same Time Next Year, Convoy, The Boys in Company C, An Unmarried Woman, Gray Lady Down, The Buddy Holly Story, Ice Castles, the Eyes of Laura Mars, Watership Down, Lord of the Rings, Force 10 from Navarone, Dawn of the Dead, Invasion of the Body Snatchers*, and the Cheech and Chong comedy *Up in Smoke*.

The Bee Gees and Andy Gibb topped the music scene with their hit singles: *Shadow Dancing, Night Fever, Stayin' Alive, How Deep is Your Love, An Everlasting Love* and *Thicker than Water*. Debbie Boone had a top hit with *You Light Up My Life*. Other top singles were: *Don't it Make My Brown Eyes Blue* by Crystal Gayle *Three Times a Lady* by the Commodores, *Grease* by Frankie Valli, *You're the One that I Want* and *Summer Nights* by John Travolta and Olivia Newton-John, *Hopelessly Devoted to You* also by Olivia Newton-John, *Lay Down Sally* by Eric Clapton, *Miss You* by the Rolling Stones, *It's a Heartache* by Bonnie Tyler, *We Will Rock You/We are the Champions* by Queen, *Too Much, Too Little, Too Late* by Johnny Mathis and Denise Williams, *Copacabana* by Barry Manilow, *Two Out of Three Ain't Bad* by Meatloaf, *Last Dance* by Donna Summer, *Still the Same* and *Hollywood Nights* by Bob Seeger and the Silver Bullet Band, *Blue Bayou* and *It's so Easy* by Linda Ronstadt, *Running on Empty* by Jackson Browne, *Bluer than Blue* by Michael Johnson, *Name of the Game* by ABBA, and *Short People* by Randy Newman.

In books Carl Sagan won the Pulitzer Prize for *The Dragons of Eden*. In addition to David Rorvik's book *In his Image: The Cloning of Man* which turned out to be a hoax, the other significant books of 1978 included: *Mommy Dearest* by Christina Crawford, *The World According to Garp* by John Irving, *Chesapeake* by James Michener, *The Stand* and *Night Shift* by Stephen King, *War and Remembrance* by Herman Wouk, *The Far Pavilions* by M.M. Kaye, *And Still I Rise* by Maya Angelou, *Scruples* by Judith Kranz, *Requiem for a Dream* by Herbert Selby Jr., *Eye of the Needle* by Ken Follett, *The Year of Living Dangerously* by Christopher Koch, *Women* by Charles Bukowski, *Bloodline* by Sidney Sheldon, *American Caesar* by William Manchester, and *A Distant Mirror* by Barbara Tuchman.

CHAPTER 35. 1979: THREE MILE ISLAND, THE HOSTAGE CRISIS, THE SINO-VIETNAMESE WAR AND HAPPY MEALS

January 1, the US and China established full diplomatic relations.

Also January 1, the United Nations proclaimed the Year of the Child.

January 4, the State of Ohio agreed to pay $675,000 to the families of the dead and wounded students shot by the National Guard in the Kent State shootings.

January 7, Vietnam announced the fall of Phnom Penh, Cambodia, and the collapse of Pol Pot and the murderous Khmer Rouge regime.

January 13-15, Chicago was hit with a blizzard which dumped 21 inches of snow in two days. O'Hare Airport was closed for three days delaying air traffic across the country. The city's poor response to the blizzard cost Mayor Michael Bilandic his job. He was defeated in a February primary by Jane Byrne who went on to become Chicago's first female mayor.

January 14, President Carter proposed that the Martin Luther King Jr. birthday become a national holiday.

January 16, after nationwide violent protests, the US-supported Shah of Iran fled Iran as his regime collapsed.

January 20, in Tehran, a massive demonstration shut down the streets in support of the exiled Ayatollah Khomeini.

January 29, a sixteen-year-old girl, Brenda Spencer, opened fire at an elementary school in San Diego killing the principal and custodian and wounded eight children and a police officer before she was taken into custody. When asked why she said, "I don't like Mondays." She was convicted and as of 2016 is still serving her life sentence.

January 29, with full diplomatic relations in place, Deng Xiaoping visited the US and met with President Carter in Washington, DC.

February 1, the Ayatollah Khomeini returned to Iran after fifteen years in exile. He formally took over the government of Iran on February 10, after creating the Council of the Islamic Revolution.

February 13, after sustained winds of 85 MPH the Hood Canal Bridge in the state of Washington collapsed and sunk. State Route 104 was closed causing a transportation nightmare. The bridge was rebuilt and opened in October of 1982 at a cost of $143 million.

February 14, the US Ambassador to Afghanistan Adolph Dubs was kidnapped in Kabul He was later killed in a gun battle between his kidnappers and the police.

February 17- March 16, China invaded Vietnam in response to Vietnam invading Cambodia. Both sides claimed victory after the month long war. It's estimated that China suffered about 62,000 casualties according to Vietnam, and the Vietnamese suffered between 30,000 and 57,000 according to China. Most analysts agree that the Vietnam outperformed the Chinese. However, the big loser may have been the USSR, because they had pledged to protect Vietnam against invasion and failed to do so. When Deng Xiaoping visited Carter at the end of January, Deng warned Carter about their frustration with Vietnam, saying, "The child [Vietnam] is getting naughty and needs to be spanked." He told Carter that the Chinese incursion into Vietnam would be a limited but costly war for the Vietnamese. The Chinese were taken aback by the fierce Vietnamese opposition.

February 26, a total solar eclipse was visible over the US.

February 27, Mardi Gras in New Orleans was cancelled due to a police strike.

March 1, the Dutch firm Phillips demonstrated the compact disc (CD) for the first time.

March 4, Voyager 1 sent back photographs revealing the rings around Jupiter.

March 13, Maurice Bishop led a successful coup in Grenada. He would remain in power until overthrown during the US in the invasion in 1983.

March 22, in the "Troubles" the IRA exploded 24 bombs across Northern Ireland.

March 25, the first fully functional Space Shuttle, the Columbia, arrived at the Kennedy Space Center to be prepared for launch.

March 26, the Egypt-Israeli Peace Treaty was formally signed at a formal ceremony hosted by President Carter at the White House.

Also on this date OPEC raised oil prices 14.5%.

March 27, the US Supreme Court ruled that police must have probable cause and cannot randomly stop cars.

March 28, the most significant nuclear power plant accident in US history occurred at the Three Mile Island Nuclear Electrical Generating Station in Pennsylvania when the reactor suffered a partial meltdown due to a stuck valve and human error. The accident released radioactive gases and iodine into the air. An evacuation zone of 20 miles was established around the site and about half the population was evacuated from the area, but most stayed. A later medical research study showed a significant increase in cancer patients from 1979-1985 within 10 miles of the accident. The clean-up started in August of 1979 and was completed in December of 1983 at a cost of about $1 billion. Ironically the Accident occurred just 12 days after the movie

The China Syndrome was released. The movie was a about a fictitious safety cover up and accident at a nuclear power plant. The movie along with the accident gave rise to more vigorous anti-nuclear power protests.

April 1, Iran officially became an Islamic Republic.

April 1, the Federal Emergency Management Agency, FEMA, was created by President Carter to coordinate the nation's disaster response.

April 2, a biological weapons center in Sverdlovsk (Yekaterinburg) Russia about 900 miles east of Moscow accidently released weaponized anthrax powder into the air when a filter was taken to be cleaned and not re-installed. All hospital and medical records were destroyed by the KGB and covered up by the Soviet government who claimed they had no biological weapons in violation to international treaties. Medical personnel investigating the incident after the fall of the USSR estimated that 105 people died from the accident along with a large number local livestock. After the accident the Soviets moved their biological weapons plants underground.

April 10-11, 26 tornados struck the Red River Valley in Texas. Three tornados from the same super cell struck Wichita Falls and Wilbarger killing 42 and 12 respectively and did over $400 million in damages.

April 11, Tanzania invaded Uganda and the corrupt and murderous dictator Idi Amin was forced to flee.

In the May 1979 issue of *Playboy* magazine composer and keyboardist Walter (Wendy) Carlos revealed that she had gender dysphoria and had undergone sex reassignment surgery in 1972 but had hid it from the public. Although the American Christine Jorgenson had broken this barrier in 1951 with the first sex reassignment surgery in Denmark, it was still considered an oddity until Carlos revealed her surgery. In 1985 when asked if the revelation of her sex change had affected her career in music Wendy Carlos said, "The American public turned out to be amazingly tolerant."

May 4, Margaret Thatcher became the first woman to be British Prime Minister.

May 21, former City Supervisor Dan White was convicted of manslaughter for assassinating Mayor Moscone and Supervisor Harvey Milk. He was sentenced to seven years in prison. The gay community in San Francisco rioted over the light sentence. White would commit suicide about a year after being released from prison in 1984.

May 25, the deadliest accident in US airliner history occurred when an American Airlines DC 10 crashed during takeoff at Chicago's O'Hare Airport killing 271 on board and 2 more on the ground.

June 1, MacDonald's introduced the Happy Meal to the delight of American children and their parents.

June 1, the first Black led government of Rhodesia took power.

June 2, Pope John Paul II visited his native Poland, and it was the first visit by a Pope to a communist country. His visit solidified the Polish people's resistance to the USSR which eventually led to the Solidarity Movement.

June 2, Los Angeles adopted a gay rights bill.

June 3, PEMEX, the Mexican oil company's exploratory well Ixtoc 1 in the Gulf of Mexico suffered a blowout resulting in 428 million gallons of oil spilling into the Gulf, polluting the waters and affecting over 168 miles of shoreline.

June 7, the first elections of the European Parliament took place.

June 18, President Carter and Premier Brezhnev signed the Salt II nuclear arms treaty in Vienna limiting nuclear arms.

June 20, a Nicaraguan soldier killed ABC TV news correspondent Bill Stewart and his interpreter. The news crew captured the killings on video tape.

June 25, NATO Commander General Alexander Haig escaped an assassination attempt by Baader-Meinhof terrorist organization.

July 1, the Sony Walkman went on sale for the first time.

July 2, on the advice of the NSA and CIA, President Carter agreed to secretly give aid to the rebel opponents of the pro-Soviet regime in Afghanistan. He would later regret their advice.

July 9, in an assassination attempt a car bomb destroyed the car of two Nazi hunters, Serge and Beate Klarsfeld. They were not hurt. The clandestine ODESSA network of former German SS Officers claimed credit. Many former SS Officers were working as intelligence agents for the American CIA after WWII. Many also turned out to be double agents selling their services to USSR as well.

July 11, Skylab began its descent back to Earth after 6 years and 2 months in orbit. The re-entry and disintegration of Skylab became a world-wide event with the *San Francisco Examiner* offering $10,000 reward for the first piece of Skylab delivered to their offices. Skylab pieces were scattered over an area just east of Perth, Australia. A 17-year-old Australian boy claimed the reward. The Miss Universe Pageant that was coincidently held on July 20 in Perth that year displayed a large piece of Skylab on the stage during the pageant.

July 16, Saddam Hussein seized power in Iraq. He would remain in power until the 2003 Iraq War.

July 17-21, the US and CIA backed dictator of Nicaragua, General Anastasio Somoza Debayle fled to Miami as the Sandinista Liberation Front won the revolution and came to power.

July 19, two super tankers collided off Tobago killing 27 crewmen and spilled 287,000 metric tons of oil into the Caribbean Sea. It is the fifth largest oil spill on record.

July 24, President Carter named Paul Volker as Chairman of the Federal Reserve Bank.

August 8, two American divers died in the North Sea when their diving bell became stranded at 520 feet. The accident permanently changed safety regulations in the diving industry.

August 8, Saddam Hussein of Iraq executed 22 political rivals cementing his control over the country.

August 9, Raymond Washington, the notorious founder of the Crips, a Los Angeles street gang, was shot with a sawed off shot gun in a drive-by shooting and died a short time later. Washington had reformed and was at the time no longer affiliated with the gang; he was attempting to bring peace between two warring gangs at the time. The killers were never caught.

August 11, a record low for the contiguous 48 states for August was recorded at 28°F in Embarrass, Minnesota.

August 12, Iranian fundamentalist Muslim demonstrators begin massive book burning demonstrations as part of a censorship campaign.

August 14, UN Ambassador Andrew Young, on his own initiative, met in secrecy with the Palestine Liberation Organization in violation of an agreement the US had with Israel to not meet with the PLO until they recognized Israel's right to exist. When the Israeli's discovered the meeting and protested to President Carter, it threatened to undermine Carter's successful Mideast peace process. Carter was forced to ask Young to resign. The resignation caused a rift between Carter and some Black leaders, 200 of whom protested Young's forced resignation.

August 18 the Ayatollah Khomeini declared war against the Kurds.

August 19, two Russian cosmonauts returned to Earth after a record 175 days in space.

August 25-September 8, Hurricane David struck the Caribbean and the US east coast killing 2,068 people (15 in the US) and did $1.54 billion in damages. The worst hit was the Dominican Republic which lost about 2,000 people and had about $1 billion in damages.

August 27, in the "Troubles" Lord Mountbatten, a member of the Royal Family, was assassinated by the IRA. That same day the IRA ambushed a British Army convoy killing 18 and wounding another 6 soldiers. The IRA stated that killings were in retaliation for the British Army previously killing 14 unarmed Catholic protesters on Bloody Sunday in 1972.

August 29-September 15, Hurricane Frederic hit the Gulf Coast states of Mississippi and Alabama. It killed 12 and did $2.3 million in damages. The US evacuated thousands before the hurricane struck or many more deaths would have resulted.

September 1, Pioneer 11 became the first spacecraft to visit Saturn it discovered a new moon.

September 7, the first cable sports channel ESPN began.

September 16, two families managed to flee from East Germany in a hot air balloon.

September 16, two Russian Bolshoi ballet dancers, Leonid Kozlov and Valentina Kozlova defected from the USSR and sought and received asylum in the US.

September 19-23, in reaction to the Three Mile Island disaster, five "No Nukes" rock concerts against nuclear power were held in New York City. Fourteen top acts performed and a No Nukes album and movie were also made. One of the concerts in Battery Park, New York City, attracted about 200,000 people.

September 20, Lee Iacocca became the president of the Chrysler Corporation.

September 22, an unidentified double flash characteristic of a nuclear explosion was detected by a US Vela satellite in the far South Atlantic between South Africa and Antarctica. The incident is still classified and controversial but most widely thought to be a joint nuclear weapons test by Israel and South Africa.

September 24, two Champion Russian ice skaters asked for and received asylum in Switzerland.

September 29, gold went prices over $400 dollars per once in Hong Kong.

September 29, amid the "Troubles" Pope John Paul II became the first Pope to visit Ireland. He prayed for peace.

October 1-8, Pope Paul II became the first Pope to visit the White House at the invitation of President Carter. He met privately with him in the Oval Office. He also addressed the United Nations. In addition to Washington, DC and New York he visited Boston, Philadelphia, Chicago and Des Moines.

October 14, between 75,000 and 125,000 marched in Washington, DC for gay rights and protective civil rights laws. The march was broadcast live on public radio.

October 14, over 100,000 demonstrated against nuclear energy in Bonn, Germany.

October 17, President Carter created the US Department of Education.

Also on October 17, Mother Teresa of India was awarded the Nobel Peace Prize.

October 20, the John F. Kennedy Library was dedicated in Boston.

October 22, the deposed Shah of Iran was allowed to come to the US for medical treatment for cancer. Iran was angry and protested, the Shah left the US in December and lived in asylum in Egypt until his death from cancer the following July.

October 26, President Park Chung-hee, the US supported South Korean dictator, was assassinated by the Korean CIA (KCIA).

October 27, the Voluntary Euthanasia Society published a how-to-do-it suicide guide.

October 30, Richard Arrington Jr. was elected the first Black mayor of Birmingham, Alabama.

November 1, the Ayatollah Khomeini urged Iranians to demonstrate and attack US and Israeli interests.

Also on November 1, the US government made a $15 billion loan to rescue the Chrysler Corporation.

November 3, during a "Death to the Klan" rally in Greensboro, North Carolina held by the Communist Workers Party, five were killed and seven wounded by the Klan and Neo-Nazis.

November 4, Khomeini called the US "the Great Satan" and said the Embassy was "an American spy den in Tehran" and he urged his militant protesters "to kick them out." After these words hundreds of protesters stormed the American embassy and took all the Americans present as hostages. Iranian police found embassy employees who had not been at the Embassy and a few who had escaped and brought them to the embassy as hostages totaling 66 that would be held. In mid November 13 hostages women and Blacks were released because the revolutionaries said that oppressed minorities were not culpable. A man was also released when he became seriously ill. The final 52 hostages received some brutal treatment including tying their hands and blindfolding them and parading them through the streets as people derided and spat on them and burned American flags. These humiliations were shown on television around the world. The hostages were also subjected to beatings and threats of death including being forced to play games of Russian roulette with a gun to their heads.

President Carter attempted to persuade Khomeini to return the hostages on humanitarian grounds, but after consideration Khomeini decided that the hostages had increased Iran's prestige and united the country behind him and he refused. The US froze Iranian assets and placed economic sanctions on Iran including the exportation of their oil.

November 4, sensing that the hostage crisis had weakened President Carter's popularity, Senator Ted Kennedy announced he was running for President in a television interview with Roger Mudd. When Mudd asked Kennedy why he wanted to be president, Kennedy was unprepared and stumbled, not being able to answer why. It was an awkward start but the Kennedy campaign kicked off three days later. Many "Eastern establishment" Democrats supported Kennedy. When he lost the nomination to Carter, ironically some then supported and voted for Republican Congressman John Anderson (running as an independent) and some voted for Reagan. Many in the Democratic Party disliked Carter as an "outsider."

November 13, also sensing Carter's vulnerability and a decline in his popularity because of events in Iran, Ronald Reagan also announced in New York that he would run for president.

November 15, ABC television began airing news segment every night on the Iranian hostages. It was expanded and became the first twenty-four hour news station, expanding the American television news cycle to twenty-four hours.

November 18, Khomeini charged that the US Ambassador and Embassy personnel were all spies.

November 20, the first blood transfusion using artificial blood took place at the University of Minnesota Hospital.

November 20, the Grand Mosque in Mecca, Saudi Arabia, Islam's holiest place, was initially taken by 200 Islamic militants, later attracting more, who demanded the end of the Al-Saud rule of Saudi Arabia, the abolition of television and all western influence and the expulsion of all non-Muslims. They were later expelled by French Special Forces brought in by Saudi Arabia. During the fighting about 250 were killed and 600 were wounded.

November 21, on a radio broadcast the Ayatollah Khomeini stated that the militants in the Grand Mosque were actually American infidels attacking holy Muslim shrines. His broadcast caused a riot among Muslims in Pakistan who stormed the American embassy set it ablaze and killed four Americans.

November 24, amid many complaints from veterans and military personnel the US government finally admitted that some US military personnel exposed to Agent Orange may develop medical problems. However the Veterans Administration would continue to deny veteran's claims and the military covered up where Agent Orange (AO) was used. It would be later learned that it was used in Vietnam, Laos, Cambodia, Korea and Thailand. The effects of AO are infertility, neuropathy, cancer, and birth defects such as spina bifida in the affected veteran's children. (The author was exposed to AO while in the US Army and has neuropathy and had a child born with spina bifida.)

November 26, the International Olympic Committee agreed to allow China to participate for the first time in 21 years.

December 2, anti-American crowds attacked the US Embassy in Tripoli, Libya.

December 3, eleven fans were crushed to death when the crowd rushed the stage at The Who rock concert in Cincinnati.

December 12, a military coup took place in South Korea.

December 13, general strikes were held in Gdansk, Poland against price increases. It was the beginning of Solidarity.

December 15, the World Court ruled that Iran should release all US hostages.

December 24, the USSR invaded Afghanistan. Soviet Special Forces took the presidential palace in Kabul.

Also in 1979: In recognition of their overpopulation problems China implemented their "One child" policy. In Russia the remains of Tsar Nicolas II and some of the Romanovs were discovered near Sverdlovsk. The precursor to the internet, USENET, the first worldwide discussion system for computers, began working. The first Sony Walkman went on sale for $200. The snowboard was invented. A gasoline shortage forced the US to implement a policy using alternating days to purchase gas based upon whether an automobile license plate ended in an odd or even number. The women's lingerie store, Victoria's Secret, opened for business.

Driven by rising oil prices inflation rate rose to 11.2% and interest rates jumped to 15.25%. The cost of a new house rose to $58,100 and rent to $280 per month. The average new car to $5,012 and a gallon of gas jumped to 86 cents. The average income went to $17,500.

In addition to ESPN, the USA cable television channel premiered along with the Movie Channel and C-SPAN. On February 11, over 43 million watched the television movie *Elvis* with Kurt Russell playing Elvis Presley. A 14-year-old Broke Shields made a controversial television commercial full of sexual innuendo for Calvin Klein jeans saying, "Nothing comes between me and my Calvins." Shows making their debuts were: *The Dukes of Hazard, Hello Larry, The Ropers, The Facts of Life, Hart to Hart, Sports Center, Benson, Buck Rogers in the 25th Century, Eischied, The New Adventures of Flash Gordon, Trapper John MD, This Old House, Knots Landing, House Calls,* and ABC's news show *Nightline* which began with the hostage crisis.

Shows ending included: *All in the Family, The Match Game, What's Happening, Welcome Back Kotter, Starsky & Hutch, Battlestar Galactica, Good Times* and *Wonder Woman,* unfortunately for the networks it also included many shows that premiered that season.

At the Emmys *Taxi, Lou Grant, Steve & Edie* were the Best Comedy, Drama and Variety shows. Carroll O'Connor won again as Best Comedy Actor and Sally Struthers, the only main caste member of *All in the Family* who had not won an Emmy finally won an Emmy for Best Supporting Actress. Ruth Gordon won Best Comedy Actress in an appearance on *Taxi*. The Best Dramatic actors were Ron Leibman in *Kaz* which lasted only one season and Mariette Hartley in *The Incredible Hulk*.

In 1979 at the movies *Kramer vs. Kramer* was number one at the box office and won the Oscars for Best Picture, Best Director, Best Actor for Dustin Hoffman and Best Supporting Actress for Meryl Streep. However *Kramer vs. Kramer* had some competition in a year of decent movies which included: *Alien, Apocalypse Now, Norma Rae, The Rose, The China Syndrome, Mad Max, All that Jazz, Star Trek the Motion Picture, Amityville Horrors, Rocky II, The Warriors, Being There, The Muppet Movie, Monty Python's The Life of Brian, Moonraker, Escape from Alcatraz, The Jerk, North Dallas Forty, The Onion Field, 10, The Electric Horseman,* and Woody Allen's *Manhattan*.

In music Sid Vicious died in January of a heroin overdose while out of jail while on bail. Pink Floyd premiered the live version of *The Wall* in Los Angeles. By the end of July seven of the top ten hits on Billboard's Hot 100 were disco tunes. *My Sharona* by The Knack was number one. *Bad Girls* by Donna Summer and *Le Freak* by Chic were the number 2 and all three were hits for the Year-end Hot 100. Other big hits included: *Do Ya Think I'm Sexy?* by Rod Stewart, *Hot Stuff* and *MacArthur Park* by Donna Summers, *Reunited* and *Shake Your Grove Thing* by Peaches and Herb, *I will Survive* by Gloria Gaynor, *YMCA* and *In the Navy* by the Village People, *Tragedy, Love You Inside Out* and *Too Much Heaven* by the Bee Gees, *Heart of Glass* by Blondie, *You Don't Bring Me Flowers* by Neil Diamond and Barbara Streisand, *The Gambler* by Kenny Rogers, *Music Box Dancer* by Frank Mills, *We are Family* by Sister Sledge, *The Devil Went Down to Georgia* by the Charlie Daniels Band, *Chuck E.'s in Love* by Rickie Lee Jones, *I Love the Nightlife* by Alicia Bridges, *Ooo Baby Baby* by Linda Ronstadt, *Bad Case of Loving You* by Robert Palmer, and *We Got Tonight* by Bob Seeger and the Silver Bullet Band.

The books of 1979 included: *Sophie's Choice* by Thomas Styron, *The Right Stuff* by Tom Wolfe, *The Executioner's Song* by Norman Mailer, *The Rise of Theodore Roosevelt* by Edmund Morris, *The Brethren* by Bob Woodward and Scott Armstrong, *Days with Frog and Toad* by Arnold Lobel, *Smiley's People* by John le Carré, *The Dead Zone* and *The Long Walk* by Stephen King, *Flowers in the Attic* by VC Andrews, *The Neverending Story* by Michael Endie, *Overload* by Arthur Haley, *Ghost Story* by Peter Staub, *Jailbird* by Kurt Vonnegut Jr. and *The Hitchhiker's Guide to the Galaxy* by Douglas Adams.

Chapter 36. 1980: the 1980 Election, Reagan and Bush Commit Treason, and the Beginning of the Iran–Iraq War

January 1, Islamic militants stormed the Russian Embassy in Tehran.

January 4, President Carter with the support of the European Commission placed a grain embargo on the USSR because of their invasion of Afghanistan.

January 9, Saudi Arabia beheaded 69 Islamic extremists for their role in the takeover of the Great Mosque.

January 21, the Iowa caucuses were held. Among the Democrats President Carter beat Ted Kennedy 59.1% to Kennedy's 32.2%, with 9.7% undecided. Among Republicans George H.W. Bush upset Ronald Reagan 31.6% to 29.5% with Senator Howard Baker taking 15.3% and four other candidates and the undecided splitting the remainder.

Also on January 21, the price of gold went to $850 per ounce in London.

January 24, the Rock Island Line, the Railroad that inspired the song, went bankrupt and was liquidated. The large Midwestern railroad had 10,669 miles of track serving 13 states with billions of tons of freight per year and had 118 million passenger miles in 1970. Through mergers and acquisitions the Union Pacific ended up with most of their service.

January 25, the Dutch called for a boycott of the Olympics to be held in Moscow because of the Soviet invasion of Afghanistan.

January 26, Israel and Egypt formally established diplomatic relations.

January 27, six American diplomats who were hidden in the Canadian embassy in Tehran managed to escape posing as Canadian citizens.

January 31, in a copycat effort of the Iranian militant's capture of the American Embassy, militants captured the Spanish Embassy in Guatemala killing 36 people and setting it ablaze. It became known as "The Spanish Tehran."

February, the public became aware of the ABSCAM FBI sting operation against Congress. The FBI sting operation was and still is very controversial. In the late 1970s with Congress investigating and criticizing the FBI for

COINTELPRO and other illegal acts, the FBI persuaded a con-man and convicted swindler, Melvin Weinberg and his girlfriend Evelyn Knight, that in exchange for voiding his pending three year prison sentence for fraud and $150,000 that they would help entrapment members of Congress in a bribery sting operation. The two posed as fronts for wealthy Arab businessmen who offered large sums of money to members of Congress in exchange for "private immigration bills" allowing foreign nationals into the US to work in New Jersey Casinos supposedly owned by the Arab sheiks. The money exchanges were then videotaped by the FBI as evidence against the senators and congressmen.

The FBI went after 31 officials, but most refused the bribes. One senator and six Congressmen accepted the bribes and were convicted in 1981. Five local officials including a mayor, three city council members and a state senator also accepted money and were also convicted. Although the convictions were upheld, the FBI was severely criticized for running a retaliatory entrapment scheme. The Department of Justice recommended changes and guidelines to prevent further FBI abuses which were enacted into law. The reputations of both the Congress and the FBI were damaged in the scandal.

February 2-3, a riot broke out in the New Mexico State Penitentiary. The prison was severely overcrowded and had poor sanitary facilities and poor food. Twelve prison guards were taken prisoner and the prisoners took over the prison and obtained keys and weapons. The National Guard was called out. The inmates also began to fight, torture and rape other inmates. Eighty prisoners fled the violence. The prison was set ablaze. The police stormed the prison and by the time control was established 33 inmates were dead 200 were wounded. None of the twelve prison officers were killed but seven were severely beaten and gang raped.

February 3, Muhammad Ali began a tour of Africa as President Carter's special envoy.

February 10, the Maine Caucuses were held. In a close race, Carter beat Kennedy 43.6% to 40.2% with Governor Jerry Brown taking 13.9%. Kennedy had expected to win this state, as he considered New England to be his "backyard."

February 13-24, the Winter Olympic were held in Lake Placid, New York. The USSR and East Germany both outperformed the Americans in the medal competition, so for US audiences the American Hockey Team was made the highlight of the Olympics. A group of underdogs comprised of college students, with 13 of the 20 players and their coach from Minnesota, beat the highly favored professional Soviet hockey team who had dominated the Olympics and had previously won four gold medals in a row. The young Americans then beat a very strong Finnish team for the Gold. It became known as the "Miracle on Ice." It remains as perhaps the greatest win in American Olympic history and the Soviets' greatest loss. A vote conducted by *Sports Illustrated* later called it "the greatest sport moment of the 20th century." As part of their 100 Year anniversary in 2008, the International Ice Hockey Federation chose it as "The number one Ice Hockey Story of the

Century." The Soviets won the medal round against Sweden for the silver medal, but the Soviet players were so disappointed in their loss to the US that they did not turn in their silver medals to have their names inscribed on them as is the custom.

February 17, in the Republican presidential primary in Puerto Rico, George H.W. Bush took 60% to Baker's 37%. Reagan was not on the ballot.

February 23, ignoring the directive of the World Court, the Ayatollah Khomeini announced that his parliament would decide the fate of the American hostages.

February 26, again in Kennedy's New England "backyard," in the New Hampshire Primary Carter took 47% to Kennedy's 37.3% and Brown took 9.6%. In the Republican primary Reagan took his first win with 50% to Bush's 23%, Baker's 13% and Congressman John Anderson's 10%.

February 27, another copycat group of militants seized the Dominican Embassy in Columbia and held 60 people hostage.

March 1, the Crude Oil Windfall Profit Act was signed into law. It was a compromise between Congress and the Carter Administration over oil deregulation and the large profits earned by oil companies during the energy crisis.

March 4, in his home state of Massachusetts Kennedy had his first win beating Carter with 65% to 28.7% with Brown taking only 3.5%. However in Vermont Carter beat Kennedy with 73% to 25%. The Republicans in Massachusetts chose Bush with Reagan winning Vermont.

March 8, the first rock festival in the Soviet Union was held.

March 8, Reagan beat Bush and John Connolly decisively in South Carolina.

March 11, Carter won decisive victories over Kennedy in Alabama, Florida, and won with almost 90% in his home state of Georgia. Reagan also beat Bush decisively in all three states.

March 14, a Polish airliner crashed near Warsaw killing 73 including 14 American boxers touring Eastern Europe.

March 16, Carter beat Kennedy in Puerto Rico.

March 18, at the Soviet spaceport, the Plesetsk Cosmodrome, 50 people were killed when a rocket exploded during fueling.

March 18, Carter beat Kennedy in Illinois. Reagan beat Bush and John Anderson in his home state came in second among the Republicans.

March 21, following the Dutch lead, President Carter announced the US would also boycott the Summer Olympics in Moscow because of the Soviet invasion of Afghanistan. Republicans charged that he was playing politics with the Olympics. The Australian Olympic Committee in defiance of their Prime Minister said they would not boycott the Olympics.

March 21, in a much talked about episode of the popular television show *Dallas* the main character J.R. was shot. It became a national pop culture media event to find out "Who shot J.R.?"

March 25, Bush beat Reagan in Connecticut and Kennedy eked out a win against Carter. Kennedy won also won a victory, in New York.

March 27, the billionaire Hunt brothers tried to corner the silver market in an event known as "Silver Thursday." As a result the price of silver plummeted. In the chaos the Hunt brothers lost a fortune and they had to put up all of their assets to cover their bailout. As a result their total worth declined from $5 billion in 1980 to $1 billion on 1988. In 1988 they were also found guilty of conspiracy to take over the silver market and were forced to pay out $134 million in damages and were then forced to file bankruptcy. This is still one of the largest bankruptcies in Texas history.

April 1, a New York transit strike crippled the city.

April 1, the 1980 US Census began with the Bureau declaring that there were now over 226 million people in the nation.

April 1 Reagan won in Wisconsin and Kansas. Carter also easily won both states, and Governor Brown dropped out of the Democratic race.

April 5, Carter and Reagan both won Louisiana.

April 12, the US Olympic Committee agreed to boycott the Moscow Olympics,

April 15, after many Cubans took refuge in the Peruvian Embassy in Cuba and asked for asylum, Cuban President Fidel Castro announced that anyone who wanted to leave Cuba could go. The Carter administration was pushed by the Cuban-American community and the Republican members of Congress to allow the Cuban refugees to come to the US on humanitarian grounds. It became known as "The Mariel Boatlift." It was organized by the Miami Cuban-American community and Castro, with over 125,000 Cubans coming to the US by October when President Carter shut it down. Castro deceived the Cuban-Americans and emptied his prisons and criminal mental asylums and placed them among the refugees seeking to go to America. Soon massive problems arose in the refugee settlements from these individuals. President Carter took the blame for this disaster which had been forced upon him.

April 18, Zimbabwe gained independence from Britain.

April 22, both frontrunners Carter and Reagan suffered setbacks as Kennedy won Pennsylvania and Bush beat Reagan in Pennsylvania.

April 24, the Pennsylvania Lottery was rigged by six men in a scandal called the "Triple Six Fix." However, the unusual betting patterns alerted officials and the six men were quickly caught, and most of the fraudulent winnings were never paid out.

April 24-25, the National Security Agency, NSA, persuaded President Carter that the Iranian hostages could be rescued by a military intervention. Operation Eagle, the rescue attempt by the US military, was very poorly planned by the NSA and uncoordinated by the military. The details of the raid were poorly communicated among the participating branches of service and this caused fatal flaws to the operation. For one, they omitted to install sand screens on the helicopters, causing three of eight to fail. With mounting technical and communication problems, the military advisorsadvised President Carter to abort the mission. However, even this recommendation is still heavily debated in military circles. In aborting the mission a helicopter crashed into a transport plane, causing a fire and killing eight servicemen. It also alerted the Iranians to the presence of an American military force in Iran. Carter was blamed by the media and the public for this failure and Iranians took to the streets to burn American flags and shout "Death to America."

April 26, in a very close race Kennedy managed to hold on, to barely beat Carter in the Michigan Caucuses.

April 30-May 5, armed Arab militants invaded the Iranian Embassy in London and took 26 embassy staff hostage. They demanded a separate Arab homeland in Iran. After their negotiations slowed they killed a hostage and threw his body out of the embassy. The British SAS were ordered to take the embassy and end the siege. They successfully took the embassy with only losing the life of one hostage saving the remaining 24 and killed 5 of the six terrorists. The lone survivor spent 27 years in prison.

May 3, Carter easily beat Kennedy and Reagan beat Bush in Bush's home state of Texas.

May 6, Carter and Reagan won Indiana, North Carolina and Tennessee. Kennedy and Bush both won DC.

May 7, Iran continued to refuse negotiations to the release of the hostages or to observe the ruling of the World Court and Carter formally severed diplomatic relations.

May 9, a freighter hit the Skyway Bridge in Tampa killing 35 when a 1,400 foot section of the bridge to collapsed. A design flaw was ruled to be the reason for the collapse.

May 11, the Equal Employment Opportunity Commission (EEOC) published guidelines making sexual harassment in the workplace illegal and punishable by federal law.

May 13, Carter won Nebraska and Maryland.

May 17-20, four Miami police officers were tried and acquitted for manslaughter and falsifying evidence in the killing of a Black insurance agent the previous December, despite a police officer testifying against them. Their acquittal triggered a race riot where 18 people were killed, over 350 were injured and 600 were arrested. Property damage exceeded $100 million. Dade County later settled with the insurance man's family for $1.1 million.

May 18, in Washington the long dormant volcano, Mt. St. Helens, erupted killing 57 and caused $1.1 billion in property damage. Ash covered 11 states and five Canadian provinces.

May 18-27, in Gwangju, Korea, university students were fired upon, killed and beaten by police for demonstrating for democracy. The populace then revolted. During a week-long revolt the government said the military and police killed over 144 civilians, wounded 127, with another 76 missing and presumed dead. However third party estimates later said between 2,000-3,000 civilians died. About 1400 civilians were arrested. During the uprising 14 troops and police were killed by the revolt and 13 police and troops were killed by friendly fire.

May 20, Bush won Michigan and Reagan won Oregon. Carter won Oregon and the undecided delegates won the Democratic Michigan caucus.

May 20, voters in French-speaking Quebec, Canada, voted against a proposal to separate from Canada to form their own country.

May 22, Pac-man the best selling arcade game of all time was released in Japan.

May 27, Carter swept four Democratic primaries winning Arkansas, Idaho, Kentucky and Nevada. Regan won Kentucky and Nevada.

May 29, civil rights advocate and attorney Vernon Jordan was shot in an assassination attempt in Fort Wayne, Indiana. President Carter's visited him in the hospital on June 1, and it became the first news story covered by the new news network CNN.

June 2, tornadoes hit Grand Island, Nebraska killing 5, injuring over 250.

June 3, Carter won Ohio, Montana and West Virginia. Kennedy won California, New Jersey, New Mexico, Rhode Island and South Dakota.

Carter was assured of the nomination. During the primaries Carter won over 10 million votes to Kennedy's 7 million. Carter went to the convention with 64% of the delegates more than enough to be nominated. However despite this decisive victory the bitter Kennedy and his supporters vowed to fight to the end.

Reagan won the final nine state primaries on this date and assuring his nomination. During the Republican primaries Reagan won 7 million votes to Bush's 3 million. Congressman John Anderson won over a million votes which inspired him to launch an independent campaign for president.

June 9, comedian Richard Pryor was badly burned in a fire attempting to freebase cocaine.

June 12, with some concerns about Reagan's age and fitness to serve as a president, Reagan offered to submit to regular medical tests.

June 13, the UN proclaimed that Nelson Mandela was a political prisoner and asked South Africa to release him.

June 19, police killed 34 Blacks in freedom demonstrations in Cape Town, South Africa.

June 23-September 6, a heat wave struck Midwest and southern plains. It brought unusually high temperatures and drought. The high temperatures were responsible for the loss of around 1,700 lives, mostly elderly people. The drought caused over $20 billion in damages, NOAA lists the 1980 heat wave as one of the nation's most costly weather related disasters in US history.

June 27, the draft registry requirements were reinstated and all US males between the ages of 18 and 25 were again required to register.

June 30, West German Chancellor Helmut Schmidt visited Moscow.

July 8, Polish workers went on strike against their socialist government for higher wages and lower prices.

July 15, a severe storm stuck western Wisconsin. In Eau Claire three people were killed and the strong straight-line winds ripped roofs from buildings and uprooted trees causing damage to hundreds of homes and businesses. The storm caused $240 million in damages. At the time it was the most costly storm in Wisconsin history.

July 14-17, at the Republican Convention in Detroit Ronald Reagan was nominated for President and George H.W. Bush was nominated for Vice President. The convention also marked a shift in Republican politics as the religious right, strong supporters of Reagan, became a majority at the convention. One of their first acts was to infuriate moderate Republicans, particularly women, by ending Republican support for the Equal Rights Amendment. In some convention drama Gerald Ford was initially asked to be the vice president but during the sometimes heated negotiations Ford insisted on concessions that some described as his wanting to be co-president. In the end he was rejected in favor of Bush.

July 19-August 3, the Summer Olympics in Moscow began. The Olympics were boycotted by 65 countries including the US due to the Soviet invasion of Afghanistan. The Soviets would later retaliate in 1984 when 14 nations led by the Soviet Union boycotted the games held in Los Angeles.

July 31-August 11, Hurricane Allen swept across the Caribbean and hit southern Texas and Mexico. In its wake it left 290 people dead and did over $1.24 billion on damages. Most of the damages were in Haiti and Texas.

August 7-31, Lech Walesa led the Solidarity strike in the shipyards in Gdansk, Poland, which many saw as the beginning of the Soviets losing control over their Eastern European satellites.

August 11-14, the Democratic Convention was held in New York City. President Carter and Vice president Mondale were nominated again by a large margin. Although Carter had two thirds of the delegates going into the convention, Kennedy became temperamental and he demanded that his supporters continue to attempt to derail Carter's nomination by trying to get the Carter delegates released from their voting obligations to vote for him. At a non-political event at Radio City Music Hall for the delegates, New York Governor Hugh Carey, a Kennedy supporter, in his welcome to New York speech attempted to persuade the delegates to abandon their commitments to Carter and vote for Kennedy. The delegates booed the governor for over twenty minutes and did not let him finish his remarks. He left the stage in frustration. After Carter won the nomination, Kennedy initially refused to endorse him. Speaker of the House Thomas "Tip" O'Neil told Kennedy that if he wanted a future in the Democratic Party, he should play by the rules and endorse Carter, which Kennedy petulantly did. (The author was a Carter delegate to the Democratic Convention and witnessed these events.)

August 15-November 4, the 1980 Presidential campaign began with the conclusion of the Democratic Convention. Carter made the fateful decision that he could not take time away from the presidency to campaign, particularly because of the hostages in Iran. He wanted the American people to know that he was spending full time on his presidential duties. He was also deeply in secret diplomatic negotiations with the Iranians to bring the hostages home. The election campaign was delegated to surrogates particularly Vice President Mondale and his wife Roselyn Carter who both crisscrossed the nation that fall and campaigned on his behalf.

The election was ill-fated for Carter from the start. The hostage crisis, the Mariel Boatlift, the bad economy due to oil prices and gas shortages, the Kennedy revolt within the Democratic Party, and Carter's refusal to campaign seemed to point to a defeat. Despite this, in late September the Gallup polls showed that Carter led with 39% to Reagan's 38%, with John Anderson at 13%. Anderson was the wildcard and despite the fact he was a Republican and had run in the GOP primaries for president, most of his support came from Democrats, at Carter's expense. Many Kennedy supporters switched to John Anderson and some to Reagan. They became known as the Reagan Democrats.

In October, Carter actually increased his lead in the Gallup poll, which showed 44% for Carter, 40% for Reagan and 9% for Anderson. Carter was now in serious negotiations with Iran, who had agreed to release the hostages. That would have likely assured Carter's re-election as it was the primary issue that voters held against him.

However, after being tipped off about the secret diplomatic negotiations by a member of Carter's National Security Team, Donald Gregg, who had worked directly for George Bush when he was Director of the CIA, Reagan and Bush decided to commit treason and scuttle Carter's settlement with the Iranians to insure their victory.

According to former Iranian President Abolhassan Banisadr in a letter to Congress in 1993, Reagan and Bush made an illegal deal with the Iranians to keep the hostages. "They made a deal with Reagan that the hostages should not be released until after Reagan became president. So, in return, Reagan would give them arms. We have published documents which show that US arms were shipped, via Israel, in March, about two months after Reagan became president."

Banisadr also stated that the Ayatollah Khomeini had agreed to release the hostages to Carter and to accept the directive from the World Court in October, with Carter's agreement to lift the embargo, but he stated that Khomeini decided he wanted the much needed weapons offered by Reagan for Iran's fight against the Kurds and their war against Iraq which started in September. These weapon sales were illegal by an act of Congress and by UN Security Council Resolution. Khomeini decided to take Reagan's illegal secret deal and accept the weapons in exchange for keep the hostages an extra three months. He also agreed to continue the television demonstrations against the Americans to make Carter look weak.

Former Reagan advisor Barbara Honegger and Gary Sick, a former Intelligence Officer and National Security Council Member under Reagan, became aware of these acts of treason and have talked publicly about them and each wrote a book about the Reagan/Bush treason, *October Surprise* by Honegger and *All Fall Down: America's Tragic Encounter with Iran* by Sick. Honegger was both a Reagan campaign adviser and then a White House policy analyst under Reagan. She resigned when she learned of and verified the incident. Several participants in the incident have also testified to its occurrence in court. In a deposition Richard Brenneke testified that he secretly flew William Casey on Reagan's behalf to Paris to negotiate the deal October 19-20, at the Crillon Hotel and that George Bush had also participated. It was also later revealed in 2001 by the PBS show *Frontline* that the eldest brother to Osama Bin Laden, Salem Bid Laden, a friend of both the Bush family and the Saudi royal family had been the negotiator between the Reagan-Bush people and the Iranians. It was later revealed that Reagan was so vain that he wanted the hostages held not just until after the election, but until he took office thereby denying Carter any credit, and so the hostages were held and tortured for three more months to assure Reagan's victory and to spite Carter. They were released twenty minutes after Reagan's inaugural address.

With the illegal deal in place and the hostages in limbo, Reagan and his surrogates made the hostages the main issue in the last weeks and continuously mocked Carter for his "incompetence." The election turned from a Carter lead of 45 to 39% to a Reagan landslide, with Reagan winning 51%, Carter with 41% and Anderson with just 7%. The "October Surprise" as it is called got Reagan the victory. In the exit polls the hostage situation was given as the number one reason for voters in making up their minds or switching to Reagan.

August 20, the UN Security Council voted to unanimously condemn Israel for proclaiming Jerusalem as its capital. The US abstained in the vote.

August 31, as a result of the strikes in Gdansk, Poland, Solidarity forced the government to grant democratic reforms and the Soviets began losing control over Poland.

September 2, Ford Motors unveiled the Escort, a new small front-wheel drive economy car which became one of the most popular vehicles ever made by Ford. Although Ford manufactured a car called the Escort in Europe, the actual predecessor for this model was the Ford Pinto. It was manufactured from 1980 to 2003. The Escort was succeeded by another small economy car, the Ford Focus.

September 22, the Iran-Iraq war began with Iraq invading the Iran. The war lasted six years.

October 9, the first home banking via computer was started by United American Bank in Knoxville, Tennessee.

October 14, in an effort to demonstrate that the Republicans are not anti-woman after their decision to stop supporting the Equal Rights Amendment Ronald Reagan promised he would name a woman to the Supreme Court if elected.

November 4, Ronald Reagan was elected President.

November 21, eighty-five people were killed in a fire at the MGM Grand Hotel and Casino in Las Vegas.

Also on November 21, in an international pop culture event a record number of people watched the premiere of the television show *Dallas* to find out "Who shot J.R.?"

December 2, an American missionary and three nuns who were working with the poor in El Salvador were gang raped and murdered by the El Salvador military. The CIA covered up these crimes in their support of the El Salvador military junta.

December 8, John Lennon was shot and killed in New York City. It was first announced by Howard Cosell at the end of *Monday Night Football*.

December 11, President Carter signed the law creating the Superfund to contain and clean up toxic waste. The fund also authorized the federal government to charge those responsible.

December 16, OPEC decided to raise oil prices another 10%.

In 1980 Japan surpassed the US for the first time to become the top auto-producing country. Electronic miniaturization allowed for the facsimile (fax) machine and the home camcorder become available. Post-It Notes arrived on the market. The Supreme Court allowed gene patenting to allow corporations like Monsanto and individuals to own genetically modified life and DNA. Whole Foods was founded in Austin, Texas. The computer modem was invented; however, it would take a while for it to be used by most as 1 GB of hard drive cost $40,000 and the hardware for it weighed over 500 pounds.

The inflation rate stood at 13.58%. Interest rates hit 21.5%. The average new home shot up to $68,700 and average rent went to $300 per month. The average new car went to $7,210 and gas went over a dollar to $1.19 per gallon. The average income was $19,500.

The Screen Actors Guild and the American Federation of television and Radio Artists struck in 1980 and negatively affected both movies and television. Black Entertainment Television premiered on Nickelodeon, but would later achieve its own cable channel in 1983 as BET. Walter Cronkite retired. The first use of closed captioning began. The NFL Draft was televised for the first time. Because of the strike fewer new shows premiered. Some of the new shows in 1980 included: *Flo, Mystery!, That's Incredible!, The Tim Conway Show, Solid Gold, Blockbusters, Too Close for Comfort, Bosom Buddies, Magnum P.I.* and Carl Sagan's PBS series *Cosmos*. The shows ending in 1980 included: the soap opera *Love of Life* which had aired since 1951. Other shows ending included: *Hawaii Five-O, Hello Larry, Hollywood Squares, The Rockford Files* and *Barnaby Jones*.

At the Emmys *Taxi* and *Lou Grant* were the best comedy and drama shows. Ed Asner in *Lou Grant* won for Best Dramatic Actor and Barbara Bel Geddes in *Dallas* for Best Dramatic Actress. The comedy *Soap* won the Best Actor and Actress in a comedy series for Richard Mulligan and Kathryn Damon. Harry Morgan and Loretta Swit won Best supporting Comedy Actors for their roles in *M*A*S*H*. The two shows *Lou Grant* and *M*A*S*H* were nominated for 14 and 10 Emmys respectively.

The movies of 1980 included: the highest grossing film at the box office *The Empire Strikes Back*. Other hits were: *Ordinary People, Raging Bull, The Blues Brothers, Stir Crazy, 9 to 5, Airplane!, Private Benjamin, Coal Miner's Daughter, Caddyshack, The Elephant Man, The Blue Lagoon, The Shining, The Jazz Singer, American Gigolo, The Big Red One, Brubaker, The Competition, The Dogs of War, Fame, Friday the 13th, The Gods Must Be Crazy, Heart Beat, Popeye, Stardust Memories, Urban Cowboy,* and one of the worst box office flops of all time *Heaven Can Wait*.

Ordinary People won the Oscars for Best Picture, Robert Redford for Best Director, and Tim Hutton as Best Supporting Actor. Robert Di Niro won Best Actor for *Raging Bull*. Sissy Spacek won Best Actress for *Coal Miner's Daughter*.

The hit songs of 1980 included: *Call Me* by Blondie, *Another Brick in the Wall Part II* by Pink Floyd, *Against the Wind* by Bob Seger and the Silver Bullet Band, *Magic* by Olivia Newton-John, *Do That to Me One More Time* by the Captain and Tennille, *Crazy Little Thing Called Love* by Queen, *Funkytown* by Lipps Inc., *Its Still Rock and Roll to Me* and *You May Be Right* by Billy Joel, *The Rose* by Bette Midler, *Upside Down* by Diana Ross, *Still* by the Commodores, *Sailing* by Christopher

Cross, *Coward of the County* by Kenny Rogers, *On the Radio* by Donna Summer, *Emotional Rescue* by the Rolling Stones, *Heart Ache Tonight* and *I Can't Tell You Why* by the Eagles, *Hurt So Bad* by Linda Ronstadt, *Sara* by Fleetwood Mac, and *Heartbreaker* by Pat Benatar.

The books of 1980 included: *Restaurant at the End of the Universe* by Douglas Adams, *Cosmos* by Carl Sagan, *A People's History of the United States* by Howard Zinn, *A Confederacy of Dunces* by John Kennedy Toole, *The Borne Identity* by Robert Ludlum, *The Clan of the Cave Bear* by Jean Auel, *The Third Wave* by Alvin Toffler, *The Covenant* by James Michener, *The Fire Starter* by Stephen King, *Maus* by Art Spiegelman, *Congo* by Michael Crichton, *The Six Wives of Henry VIII* by Allison Weir, *Catch Me If You Can: The True Story of a Real Fake* by Frank W. Abagnale, *Aztec* by Gary Jennings, *No One Gets Out of Here Alive* by Danny Sugarman, and *Side Effects* by Woody Allen.

CHAPTER 37. 1981: ASSASSINATION ATTEMPTS ON REAGAN, SADAT
AND THE POPE, THE SPACE SHUTTLE AND EL SALVADOR

January 10, during the previous October, five rebel groups united against the US backed military dictatorship in El Salvador and formed the Frente Farabundo Martí para La Liberación Nacional, FMLN. On this date the FLMN launched their first successful offensive and captured two areas Morazán and Chalatenango on the Honduran border. From these two areas they began launching attacks to conquer the rest of the country.

January 15, the Pope received a Polish delegation led by the Solidarity leader, Lech Walesa.

January 16, in the "Troubles" Bernadette Devlin, a Member of the UK Parliament and an Irish Republican activist was shot fourteen times in front of her children by three Protestant militants who broke into her home while she was under the protective guard of British paratroops. Her husband was also shot. The British paratroops allowed the militants to escape then entered the house and cut the phone lines and waited a half hour for the couple to die. Another military unit arrived on the scene and began to give Devlin and her husband emergency medical first aid and one medic went to a neighboring house and took a neighbors car and drove for help. The couple was then air-lifted to a hospital and survived.

January 20, Ronald Reagan was inaugurated as President. Twenty minutes after the finish of his inaugural address, as per the arms for hostages agreement with Iran, the 54 American hostages were released after fourteen months in captivity.

January 21, Northern Irish Protestants Norman and James Strong, father and son former Members of the UK Parliament were assassinated by the IRA at their home in retaliation for the shooting of Bernadette Devlin and her husband.

January 25, "Madame Mao," Jiang Qing, Mao's wife, was sentenced to death by China for her role in the violent Cultural Revolution. Two years later her sentence was commuted to life in prison. In 1991 she was diagnosed with throat cancer and was released on medical grounds. She committed suicide shortly after.

January 28, President Reagan named William Casey, his negotiator in the arms for hostages deal, as Director of the CIA; the illegal arms sales to Iran would continue in what later came to be known as the "Iran-Contra Scandal." Twelve of Reagan's advisers were indicted. Most would later be pardoned by George H.W. Bush, who was thought to have master-minded the illegal deal.

January 28, a chemical tanker struck the Olympic Glory, an oil tanker near Galveston, Texas, spilling 20,000 gallons of oil into the bay.

February 1, the French sold 60 mirage fighter jets to Iran.

February 5, Robert Garwood a US marine Private First Class was convicted of cooperating with the enemy and assaulting a US Prisoner of War in Vietnam. Garwood went missing in 1965 in Vietnam. At first it was believed he had been captured by the Viet Cong. However later propaganda notes signed by Garwood were found encouraging US soldiers to desert. Then several US soldier eyewitnesses reported an English speaking American fighting in battle with the Viet Cong against US soldiers and these witnesses later identified this soldier from photos as Garwood. The US then changed his status was changed from captured to deserter/collaborator. It is also alleged that he was a prison guard for the Vietnamese holding American POWs. Many US POWs saw Garwood collaborating with the enemy. Garwood stayed in Vietnam when the POWs left and did not return to the US until 1979. He was listed by the Pentagon as a voluntary "stay behind." When Garwood finally returned to the US he claimed he had been a prisoner the entire 14 years in Vietnam. Although he was tried for desertion he was acquitted for lack of evidence. His was convicted of cooperating with the enemy and assaulting a US Prisoner of War in Vietnam. He appealed and lost. He was dishonorably discharged and forfeited his POW pay and his veteran's benefits, but he was not sentenced to prison. Garwood claimed that he was held as a POW and that there were still living POWs in Vietnam. It was this story that fueled the theories of missing POWs in Vietnam. Although his claims were investigated the US never found any POWs held after 1973.

February 10, an arsonist Phillip Bruce Cline set fire to the Las Vegas Hilton Hotel. Eight were killed and 198 were injured. Cline was convicted in 1982 and sentenced to eight life sentences.

February 13, a Ralston Purina soy bean processing plant in Louisville, Kentucky began dumping hexane solvents into the municipal sewer system. The volatile vapors set off two miles of explosions in the sewer lines. Although there were no fatalities the explosions caused about $18 million in damages to the municipal sewer system which the company paid. They also settled a lawsuit for $8.9 million in damages to plaintiffs of private properties. In addition to destroying the sewer lines and damaging surrounding properties, the blast also severed water lines and parts of the city were without sewer or water for weeks.

February 17, the Chrysler Corporation reported that the company had lost $4.2 billion in 1980 the largest corporate loss in US history.

February 24, Britain's Prince Charles announced his engagement to Lady Diana Spencer. She was 19 and he was 32. When asked by a journalist if they were marrying for love Diana replied "Of course." Prince Charles added, "Whatever love means."

March 1, IRA prisoner Bobby Sands began a hunger protest against the British for taking away the Special Category Status (Prisoners of War) for IRA members held in British prisons. May 5, at the age of 27 he died of hunger. Prime Minister Margaret Thatcher said of his death, "Mr. Sands was a convicted criminal. He chose to take his own life. It was a choice that his organization did not allow to many of its victims." Nine other IRA prisoners followed Sands and died during their hunger strikes.

March 8, the Reagan Administration decided to give more support to the El Salvador military dictatorship. Despite growing evidence that human rights abuses by the military government were worsening and despite the Administration's knowledge that the El Salvador military had raped and murdered an American missionary and three nuns during the previous year, they put five US Military Training and War Strategy Groups in El Salvador each headed by a lt. colonel and placed 150 CIA operatives in the country to advise and assist the military government.

March 9, Dan Rather became the anchor man of CBS news.

March 19, after a successful test firing of the space shuttle Columbia's engines, five technicians were asphyxiated by nitrogen. One died en route to the hospital, another died two weeks later and the other three recovered.

March 30, John Hinckley Jr., a mentally disturbed man with a fixation on the actress Jodie Foster, attempted to assassinate President Reagan as the President left the Washington Hotel after a speech. Hinckley fired his .22 caliber pistol six times, hitting Reagan once in the chest and wounding three others including Press Secretary James Brady, a police officer, and a secret service agent protecting the President.

Shortly afterward a White House reporter asked who was in charge, and immediately Secretary of State General Alexander Haig pushed past the Deputy Press Secretary at the podium and made a statement, saying, "I am in control here." Haig was embarrassed and angry when the reporters laughed at him. They also reported it in the news and ridiculed him with commentary about the order of succession. Secretary of Defense Casper Weinberger and other cabinet members also angrily raised objections to Haig's shocking claim. An argument ensued amongst the Cabinet where an angry Haig told them to "go read a copy of the Constitution." Vice President Bush was in Texas when the assassination happened and was at this moment onboard a flight back.

Reagan stayed 13 days in the hospital and then returned to light duty working two hours a day in his living quarters, until April 25 when he began to work two-hour light days out of the Oval Office. However, his doctor did not rule him completely recovered and he didn't return to a more normal schedule until October. George Bush was by all accounts the acting president during this time.

James Brady was hit in the head and suffered the worst injury in the assassination attempt and was left permanently disabled. He died in 2014 from complications from these injuries. Brady and his wife Sara became gun control advocates after the shooting. The Handgun Violence Prevention Act is called "The Brady Bill" in his honor. Hinckley was found not guilty for reasons of insanity. He remained in a psychiatric facility until 2016.

April 4, Henry Cisneros became the Mayor of San Antonio. He was the first Mexican-American of a modern large city.

April 6, a democratic socialist, Bernie Sanders, was elected the Mayor of Burlington, Vermont. Sanders, a former civil rights activist, would have a long political career becoming a US Senator and running for president in 2016. As of this writing Sanders is still the Senator from Vermont.

April 9, IRA hunger striker Bobby Sands was elected as a Member of Parliament from his prison cell. The result caused Britain to change the law which disallowed prisoners to run for office.

April 11, violent race riots broke out in South London resulting in 85 arrests, 280 police injured, 45 citizens injured, over 100 vehicles burned and 150 buildings damaged. *Time* magazine called the incident "Bloody Saturday."

April 12-14, the first reusable space vehicle, the Space Shuttle Columbia, was launched from the Kennedy Space Center in Florida with two astronauts landing at Edwards Air Force Base in California after two days in space.

April 15, Coca-Cola opened its first bottling plant in China, marking a new era of trade with the US.

Also on April 13, Janet Cooke won the Pulitzer Prize for her horrific September 1980 article in the *Washington Post* "Jimmy's World," about an eight-year-old heroin addict. Two days after the award was given, the *Post* announced that they had discovered the article was a hoax. Cooke resigned and returned the prize.

April 21, the US agreed to sell $1 billion in arms to Saudi Arabia.

April 24, the Reagan Administration ended the grain embargo to the USSR,

May 6, Maya Lin's design for the Vietnam Veteran's Memorial was selected by a jury of architects over 1,421 others.

May 6, the Reagan administration instructed all Americans to leave Libya and expelled the Libyan diplomats from the US for terrorism. At the time 10% of all US oil came from Libya.

May 11, popular Jamaican singer Bob Marley died of cancer.

May 13, a Turkish assassin shot and wounded the Pope. Who hired him (and why) remains a subject of intense controversy.

May 19, in the "Troubles," five British soldiers were killed in an armored vehicle by a bomb from the IRA in Northern Ireland.

May 21, a socialist, François Mitterrand, was elected as the President of France.

May 26, the Italian Prime Minister Arnaldo Forlani and his cabinet were forced to resign when their membership in the fascist Masonic lodge Propaganda Due was discovered.

June 5, the Centers for Disease Control and Prevention reported that five homosexual men in Los Angeles had a rare form of pneumonia seen only in patients with weakened immune systems. These become the first recognized cases of AIDS.

June 7, the Israeli Air Force destroyed Iraq's Osirak nuclear reactor, killing ten Iraqis and a French nuclear technician.

June 13, in Germany, 39 Unification Church couples (Moonies) were wed in a mass ceremony.

June 14, a "NO Nukes" concert was held at the Hollywood Bowl.

June 21, Wayne Williams was arrested in Atlanta for the murder of Nathaniel Carter, whose strangled nude body was found in the Chattahoochee River. The cord marks on the neck were identical to marks found on previous victims of the "Atlanta child murders." Over a two-year period, 28 young Black male victims, most children, were strangled. Williams was tried and convicted of two. He was sentenced to two consecutive life sentences. Although he is considered guilty of the others, he was never tried for those. Later DNA evidence suggests that Williams was guilty of the other murders.

June 25, Microsoft became a corporation in the state of Washington.

June 30, the Chinese Communist Party formally condemned former Maoist policies that led to the Cultural Revolution.

July 1, four people were murdered in Laurel Canyon area of Los Angeles. The four were allegedly members of the Wonderland drug gang and had been involved in a violent robbery of a home belonging to Eddie Nash, a gangster and convicted drug dealer. The two men and two women were found to have been bludgeoned to death with a steel pipe and hammers. A fifth, a woman, survived the ordeal with severe brain damage; she had no recollection of the incident. It is still officially an unsolved crime although three men, including Eddie Nash, John Holmes, and Gregory Diles were tried and acquitted. In 2000, in his seventies and in ill health, Nash pled guilty to bribery of a judge and a jurist in his previous trial and to ordering his associates to retrieve stolen property from the Wonderland Gang, but he denied the murders. Because of his age and health, he was given a four and a half year prison sentence and a $250,000 fine.

July 7, Sandra Day O'Connor became the first woman nominee to the US Supreme Court. She was later confirmed by the Senate.

July 9, the arcade game Donkey Kong was released by Nintendo, in the game Mario, originally called Mr. Video.

July 10, Britain suffered more violent race riots in the cities of Birmingham, Liverpool and Leeds.

July 17, two walkways collapsed at the Hyatt regency in Kansas City killing 114 and injuring 216. At the time it was the deadliest structural collapse in US history.

July 17, the Israeli Air Force attacked the PLO offices in Beirut killing 300 civilians. The bombing brought world-wide condemnation and a US embargo on military aircraft to Israel.

July 29, a world-wide audience of 700 million watched the wedding of Prince Charles to Lady Diana Spencer at St. Paul's Cathedral in London.

August 1, the 24 hour music channel MTV began their operations. The music video became part of American culture.

August 3, the federal air traffic controllers went on strike for better conditions and higher wages. Reagan ordered them back to work under the Taft-Hartley Act citing air safety. Only 1,300 of the 13,000 returned to work. Reagan issued a warning stating that all striking air traffic controllers had to report for work in 48 hours or they would be fired. Several strikers were jailed for their refusal to work. On August 5, Reagan fired 11,345 air traffic controllers. Reagan then banned the strikers from any employment with the federal government for life, which was later lifted by Bill Clinton in 1993. Members of Congress objected saying that Reagan couldn't cite safety as his reason for declaring Taft-Hartley and then terminate the majority of controllers without negatively affecting air safety. Most of the controllers were veterans who had learned their jobs in the military. Ironically most of the controllers and their union had backed the election of Reagan.

August 10, Coca-Cola agreed to hire more African-Americans and to invest $34 million into Black businesses. This was in response to a Black boycott that was started against the company in July for corporate racism.

August 12, IBM introduced their first personal computer, the IBM PC, with an 8088 Intel processor which went on sale for $1,565.

August 19, two US Navy F-14 fighters shot down two Soviet-made Libyan fighters that fired at them off the coast of Libya over international waters.

August 26, Voyager 2 sent back photos of the Saturn moon Titan.

August 28, South African troops invaded Angola.

September 10, Picasso's painting Guernica was moved from the Metropolitan Museum of Art in New York to Madrid. The controversial painting of the fascist bombing of Guernica, Spain was taken to the US during WWII for safekeeping. It is a part of Spain's heritage and was to be returned to the Prado in Madrid, according to Picasso's will. Spain in recognition of the painting importance built a special place for it in the Museo Reina Sofia in Madrid. The American museum attempted to keep the painting arguing that this was not the Prado as per Picasso's wishes. They eventually bowed to world pressure and released it to Spain.

September 19, Simon & Garfunkel's free Concert in Central Park was performed before about 500,000. A subsequent album made of the event was critically acclaimed and did well commercially. Through donations the concert raised about $51,000 for Central Park.

September 21, Belize was granted independence from Britain.

October 1, the US national debt went past $1 trillion.

October 5, Raoul Wallenberg, a Swedish citizen was posthumously named an Honorary Citizen of the US by the Congress for his bravery in saving the lives of hundreds of Hungarian Jews in WWII. In 1945 he was detained by the Soviet SMERSH on espionage charges and disappeared and was presumed dead. US Congressman Tom Lantos who sponsored the bill was one of those saved by Wallenberg. Lantos was the only Holocaust survivor to serve in the US Congress.

October 6, Islamic militants in the Egyptian military assassinated Egyptian President Anwar Sadat. Former Presidents Nixon, Ford and Carter attended the funeral on October 10, along with Israeli Prime Minister Meacham Begin. October 13, Vice President Hosni Mubarak became president.

October 27, a Soviet submarine hung up on some rocks and became grounded in Sweden near a Swedish naval base. The Swedish government who had made complaints about soviet submarine espionage in their waters used this as proof certain. The sub was stuck for 10 days before a Swedish tug boat freed it from the rocks and towed it to international waters where the sub and crew were returned to the Soviets.

October 27, Andrew Young the former US Ambassador to the UN was elected Mayor of Atlanta.

November 12, the Space Shuttle Columbia was launched at the Kennedy Space center for its second space flight and landed November 14, at Edwards Air Force Base.

November 12, the Church of England voted to allow women to accept Holy Orders and to become vicars.

November 23, President Reagan signed the top secret National Security Decision Directive 17 authorizing the CIA to recruit, build and financially support the Contras in Nicaragua. It was the beginning of another phase in the Iran-Contra Scandal.

November 30, representatives of the US and USSR met to discuss reducing the number of nuclear weapons. The discussions ended December 17, with no progress.

December 4, Reagan signed a top secret illegal order allowing the CIA to once again engage in domestic counter-intelligence.

December 8, an explosion in a coal mine in Tennessee killed 13 miners. The US found the mine owners negligent. The owners eventually agreed to pay out $10 million the families of the miners killed.

December 11, soldiers of the US backed Junta in El Salvador massacred over 800 civilians in and around the village of El Mozote. After separating the men from the women and children, they tortured and killed all the men. Then they raped the women and girls, some as young as ten years old, and then killed them. They killed the small children by slitting their throats or hanging them in trees. They looted all the buildings including the church before setting them ablaze.

The Reagan administration covered up the incident saying initially that news reporters had fabricated the story. Assistant Secretary of State Thomas Enders lied to a Senate committee stating that *New York Times* reporter Raymond Bonner's reporting was false and that there was a small battle between guerrilas and the army but that "no evidence could be found that government forces had systematically massacred civilians." He also lied and claimed that only 300 people lived in the village. Proving that Operation Mockingbird was still in operation and that the CIA's program to control the press was still fully functional, the *Wall Street Journal* and *Time* magazine wrote articles favorable to the administration and questioned and criticized the *New York Times* and Bonner's claims of a massacre. The US Ambassador to El Salvador Deane Hinton criticized and discredited Bonner as an unreliable "activist journalist."

Bonner was recalled back to New York by the *New York Times* and he left the paper shortly afterward. Bonner's reports of the massacre were later all confirmed in subsequent investigations in 1990 and 1992. In December 2011 the government of El Salvador formally apologized for the massacre. Later he was awarded the Robert F. Kennedy Book Award in 1985 for his book *Weakness and Deceit: US Policy and El Salvador.* Years later after being exonerated Bonner went back to work for the *New York Times.* In 1999 he won and was nominated again in 2001 for a Pulitzer Prize while at the *New York Times.*

December 13, martial law was declared in Poland to prevent the communists from being swept from power by Solidarity. On December 19, the polish Ambassador defected to the US.

December 15, a car bomb destroyed the Iraqi embassy in Beirut, Lebanon killing 61 people.

December 17, General James L. Dozier, a Deputy Chief of Staff for NATO in Italy was kidnapped by the Red Brigade (radical Italian Communists). He was later freed by an Italian Swat team after 42 days in captivity.

December 28, the first American "test tube baby" (in-vitro fertilization) was born in Virginia.

December 31, CNN Headline News (HLN) made its debut.

In 1981 the world's population went over five billion. The Dengue fever struck Cuba infecting 344,203 people. A Harvard professor advocated that the nuclear codes be placed in a living man so that if the president wanted to launch a nuclear war he would have to kill a man to get the codes, thereby insuring the president understood the seriousness of the act. It was quickly rejected by the US government. In addition to Coca-Cola, Pepsi also entered the market in China.

According to Alexander Cockburn and Jeffrey St. Clair in their book *Whiteout,* in 1981 highly addictive crack cocaine began to make its way into the US from Central America. It was particularly marketed to urban Blacks and Los Angeles was particularly hit hard. It would be revealed much later that the sale of these drugs was part of the illegal financing for the CIA supported military juntas in Central America particularly the Contras. This drug trade was started, aided and covered up by the CIA.

In 1981 inflation was still high at 10.35% and the interest rates were at 15.75%. Average cost of a new house shot up to $78,200. Average monthly rent rose to $315. The average new car cost $5,743 and gas was now over a dollar per gallon at $1.25. The average wage was $20,050. The cost of personal computers went down, a Tandy TRS 80 PC-1 sold for $149.95. MS-DOS was released by Microsoft.

The cost of a 19 inch color television came down in price to $399.95 and found its way into more homes. In December HBO began broadcasting 24 hours per day. Some of the television debuts included: *Hill Street Blues, Dynasty, SCTV Network 90, Private Benjamin, The Smurfs, Entertainment Tonight, Gimme a Break!, The Fall Guy, Simon & Simon, Falcon Crest, Harper Valley PTA* and *Love Sidney* the first show to feature a gay character. Shows ending included: *SOAP, FLO, Charlie's Angels, The Waltons, Eight is Enough* and *The Mike Douglas Show.*

Taxi and *Hill Street Blues* won the Emmys for Best Comedy and Drama. Judd Hirsch for *Taxi* and Isabel Sanford for *The Jeffersons* won Best Comedy Actors with Danny De Vito as Best Supporting Comedy Actor also in *Taxi.* Daniel Travanti and Barbara Babcock won Best Dramatic Actors and Michael Conrad Best Supporting Dramatic Actor in *Hill Street Blues.*

At the movies *Raiders of the Lost Ark* was the top box office hit in 1981. Other movies included: *Ordinary People, Raging Bull, Coal Miner's Daughter, On Golden Pond, Chariots of Fire, Stripes, Arthur, The Cannonball Run, For Your Eyes Only, American Werewolf in London, Escape from New York, Gallipoli, Das Boot, The Postman Always Rings Twice, History of the World Part I, Fort Apache the Bronx, Reds, Ragtime, Mommie Dearest,* and Cheech and Chong's *Nice Dreams.*

The Oscars were delayed by a day due to the assassination attempt on President Reagan. *Ordinary People* won Best Picture, Best Director for Robert Redford and Best Supporting Actor for Timothy Hutton. Robert De Niro and Sissy Spacek won The Best Actor Awards for *Raging Bull* and *Coal Miner's Daughter* respectively.

In 1981 the Go-Go's became the first all female group to write, play and sing all their own music. Their album *Beauty and the Beat* reached number one on Billboard's album chart. The top tunes of 1981 included: *Bette Davis Eyes* by Kim Carnes, *Endless Love* by Diana Ross and Lionel Richie, *Angel of the Morning* by Juice Newton, *Lady* by Kenny Rogers, *Jessie's Girl* by Rick Springfield, *Celebration* by Kool and the Gang, *I Love a Rainy Night* by Eddie Money, *9 to 5* by Dolly Parton, *Rapture* and *The Tide is High* by Blondie, *Slow Hand* by the Pointer Sisters, *The Winner Takes It All* by ABBA, *Elvira* by the Oak Ridge Boys, *Hit Me with Your Best Shot* and *Treat Me Right* by Pat Benatar, *Hungry Heart* by Bruce Springsteen, *America* and *Hello Again* by Neil Diamond, *Another One Bites the Dust* by Queen, *Don't Stand so Close to Me* by the Police, and *Whip It* by Devo.

Konrad Kujau sold *Hitler Diaries* to a West German news magazine for $3.2 million dollars which turned out to be a fraud. The books of 1981 included: *Hotel New Hampshire* by John Irving, *Mornings on Horseback* by David McCullough, *Noble House* by James Clavell, *Jumanji* by Chris Van Allsburg, *The Heart of a Woman* by Maya Angelou, *Rabbit is Rich* by John Updike, *Cujo* and *Danse Macarbe* by Stephen King, *Tar Baby* by Toni Morrison, *The One Minute Manager* by Kenneth Blanchard, *Gorky Park* by Martin Cruz Smith, *When Bad Things Happen to Good People* by Harold S, Kushner, *Women, Race and Class* by Angela Davis, *The Comfort of Strangers* Ian Mc Ewan, and one of the best books on sports *The Breaks of the Game* by David Halberstam.

CHAPTER 38. 1982: THE TIME MAGAZINE MAN OF THE YEAR WAS A COMPUTER, THE VIETNAM VETERANS MEMORIAL, SOLIDARITY, NUCLEAR PROTESTS AND PLANS FOR A NUCLEAR WAR

January 4, the Golden Gate Bridge was closed for the third time because of a large storm.

January 5, an Arkansas judge ruled against the obligatory teaching of creationism in public schools.

January 7, the Commodore 64 home computer went on sale. It would become the all-time best selling personal computer.

January 8, AT&T was broken up under the monopoly laws into 22 "Baby Bells."

January 9, a 5.9 earthquake struck New England and Eastern Canada. It was the first major earthquake in the area since 1855.

January 11, a large cold snap swept across the US and Atlanta recorded below zero temperatures.

January 13, an Air Florida 737 crashed upon take off during a snow storm in Washington, DC. Seventy-eight people were killed.

January 17, the cold snap continued. "Cold Sunday" saw temperatures fall to their lowest in a hundred years in setting records in many US cities.

January 18, four of the US Air Force Thunderbirds crashed during training killing all four pilots.

January 20, rocker Ozzie Osborne bit the head off a bat on stage in Des Moines, Iowa.

January 22, as the cold snap continued, about 75% of the US was covered in snow.

January 26, for the first time since the Great Depression unemployment in Britain went over three million.

January 28, Brigadier General James Dozier the NATO commander in Italy was rescued from captivity by the Italian Red Brigades. He had been in captivity for 42 days.

January 30, the first PC computer virus was written. It was disguised as an Apple Computer boot program. It was written by a fifteen-year-old boy.

February 1, Syrian government troops battled Muslim fundamentalists.

February 2, the Syrian Army began a massacre in the town of Hama. In the aftermath the Syrian Army killed 30,000 to 40,000 civilians, with another 15,000 never accounted, for and over 100,000 displaced according to the Syrian Human Rights Commission.

February 15, the oil platform Ocean Ranger was hit by a storm and sunk off the coast of Newfoundland killing 84 workers.

February 28, the Puerto Rican Freedom Movement, FALN set off four bombs on Wall Street. They were deliberately set of in the early morning to avoid harm to workers and there were no casualties.

March 1, the USSR spacecraft Venera 14 was launched. It landed on Venus March 5, sending back data.

March 10, the US announced an embargo on Libyan oil to punish the country for terroristic activities.

Also on March 10, all nine planets aligned on the same side of the sun. A previously written popular book called the Jupiter Effect predicted that this alignment would cause calamities such as setting off a major earthquake along the San Andreas Fault line. No calamities occurred.

March 11, New Jersey Senator Harrison Williams resigned from the US Senate rather than being expelled. He was the only Senator convicted of taking bribes in the FBI ABSCAM Sting operation.

March 19, in the South Atlantic, Argentine military forces landed on South Georgia to claim the island from Britain. This event would result in the Falkland War between Britain and Argentina. The war would last until mid June with Argentina being defeated.

March 22, the third space shuttle mission was launched as Columbia 3 took off from Cape Kennedy. It would land March 30, in White Sands, New Mexico.

Also on March 22, Iran launched a major offensive against Iraq.

March 26, a ground-breaking ceremony for the Vietnam Veterans Memorial was held in Washington, DC.

March 31, an oil tanker spilled 1.47 million gallons of oil in the Mississippi River near Montz, Louisiana.

April 1, the US formally transferred the Panama Canal Zone to Panama.

April 2, the United Nations Security Council demanded that Argentina remove their forces from the British territory.

April 19, the US announced that Sally Ride would be the first American woman astronaut in space.

April 25, in accordance with the Camp David Accords, Israel withdrew from the Sinai Peninsula.

April 26, after a quick battle the Argentine military surrendered to the British who took back the South Georgia Island in Operation Paraquet.

April 27, John Hinckley Jr. went on trial for the attempted assassination of President Reagan.

May 1, the World's Fair opened in Knoxville, Tennessee.

May 2, a British submarine sunk an Argentine Cruiser killing about 350 sailors.

Also on May 2, the Weather *Channel* made its debut on cable television.

May 3, *The New York Times* reported that the US military was receiving 25% of NASA's total budget for their secret space program.

May 4, a British destroyer was struck by an Argentine missile killing about 20 sailors. The ship sank six days later.

May 5, the Unabomber set off a bomb in the computer science building at Vanderbilt University injuring a secretary.

May 13, the Soviet spacecraft Soyuz T-5 was launched and would spend 211 days in space.

May 18, the Unification Church founder, the Reverend Sun Myung Moon was convicted of tax evasion. He would be later sentenced to 18 months in prison.

May 19, actress Sophia Lauren was convicted of tax evasion in Italy.

May 21 British troops landed on the Falkland Islands.

May 24, Iran recaptured lost territory from Iraq.

May 26 two British ships were hit by Argentina killing about 39 crew members.

May 28-29, the British defeated a large Argentinean force to win the Battle of Goose Green in the Falklands about 45 Argentine troops were killed and 961 captured. The British lost 18 men and 64 were wounded.

May 29, the Pentagon held strategy planning sessions to fight a nuclear war.

Also on May 29, the Pope visited Britain, the first Papal visit since 1531.

May 30, Spain became a member of NATO.

June 4, Israel planes attacked southern Lebanon and they invaded with 30,000 troops on June 6 beginning the Lebanon War of 1982.

June 7, President Reagan met with Pope Paul II in Rome. They agreed to form a clandestine union between the US and the Catholic Church to free Poland from the Soviets. Doubts about Reagan's age and health were raised as Reagan fell asleep in his televised conversation with the Pope.

June 8, the United Nations Security Council voted to demand that Israel withdraw its forces from Lebanon.

Also on June 8, President Reagan became the first US President to address a joint session of the British Parliament.

June 12, estimated at over a million, anti-nuclear demonstrators protested in New York City while the UN discussed nuclear disarmament. It was thought to be the largest demonstration in the city's history.

June 14, Argentina surrendered to Britain in the Falklands War.

June 15, the US Supreme Court ruled that all children regardless of citizenship are entitled to public education.

June 18, the Voting Rights Act of 1965 was extended by a Senate Vote of 85-8.

June 21, John Hinckley Jr. was found not guilty by reason of insanity in the assassination attempt on President Reagan.

June 23, a minus 117 degrees Fahrenheit was recorded in Antarctica. It was the lowest temperature ever recorded. This record would later be shattered in 2010 when satellites measured a temperature of minus 135.8 in Antarctica.

June 25, Secretary of State Alexander Haig tendered his resignation. Haig had clashed with members of the Reagan Administration, particularly Secretary of Defense Casper Weinberger. When he suggested that a "nuclear warning shot" may be the best deterrent to the USSR, Vice President Bush and Reagan's staff and Cabinet members convinced Reagan that it was time for Haig to go. Haig was replaced by George Shultz.

June 30, the Equal Rights Amendment was defeated when enough states failed to ratify it. The Christian Right took credit for the defeat.

July 1, in response to reverend Moon's conviction of tax fraud, 2,100 Unification Church couples were wed in New York City.

July 2, Larry Walters, who became known as "Lawn Chair Larry," attached 42 weather balloons to a lawn chair and rose about 15,000 feet above San Pedro, California, where he began to shoot the balloons with a pellet gun to make his descent. However he dropped the pellet gun and had to drift slowly down. He drifted into controlled airspace over the Los Angeles International Airport, delaying flights, and eventually landed in power lines causing an electrical blackout in Long Beach. He was arrested and fined $4,500 but this was reduced to $1,500. He failed to become famous or make much money from his adventure, and later he committed suicide at the age of forty-four in 1993.

July 9, a Pan Am 727 crashed in Louisiana killing 153.

July 12, FEMA oddly announced that any survivors of nuclear war would be able to get their mail via FEMA.

Also on July 12, the Checkers Motor Company, the maker of the Checker Cab, closed its doors.

July 19, David Dodge the acting President of the American University of Beirut was kidnapped by Iranian terrorists and held hostage. A short time later he was flown to a prison in Iran. He was released one year later in exchange for more arms from the Reagan Administration.

July 23, the International Whaling Commission voted to ban all whaling to be effective in 1985.

August 12, Mexico announced that it couldn't repay its large foreign debt, setting off a debt crisis throughout Latin America.

August 14, the Ramadan Offensive was launched by Iran into Iraq.

August 17, the first compact discs (CDs) co-developed by Phillips and Sony were released to the public for the first time. They were originally designed to record and play sound recordings, but they were also later adapted for data storage (CD-ROM).

August 18, the NYSE set a record trading over 136 million shares.

August 20, the US Marines landed in Lebanon as a peacekeeping force.

August 19, the Soyuz T-7 was launched with the second woman in space. It would return August 27.

September 1, the USAF Space Command was founded.

September 15, the first issue of *USA Today* was published.

September 17, a 36 inch snow fell in Red Lodge Montana.

September 19, the first emoticons were posted.

September 29, cyanide-laced Tylenol killed seven people in Chicago. This caused the US to re-think packaged merchandise security to prevent product tampering.

October 1, Sony marketed the first CD players.

Also on October 1, Disney opened the EPCOT Center in Orlando, Florida.

October 8, Poland banned Solidarity and all labor unions.

October 10, the US imposed economic sanctions on Poland for outlawing labor unions.

October 14, Reagan declared the War on Drugs. President Reagan's refocus on drugs led to a significant increase in incarcerations for nonviolent drug crimes and overcrowded the nation's prisons. Many critics of Reagan's drug polices also point to data showing that people of color are targeted and arrested on suspicion of drug use at higher rates than whites, leading to disproportionate incarceration rates among communities of color.

Also on October 14, another 6,000 Unification couples wed in South Korea.

October 16, Secretary of State George Schultz warned that the US would withdraw from the UN if they voted to ban Israel.

October 21, a private funeral was held for former first lady Bess Truman.

October 26, the US budget deficit was reported at $110 trillion dollars.

October 27, China announced that its population had surpassed 1 billion.

November 1, Honda became the first Asian car company to produce automobiles in the US with their factory in Marysville, Ohio. They manufactured Honda Accords.

November 10, the Vietnam Veterans Memorial opened.

Also on November 10, the International Monetary Fund agreed to lend $3.8 billion to Mexico to avoid the county's bankruptcy.

November 11-16, the Columbia made the 5th space shuttle mission, the first fully operational mission.

November 12, KGB Chief Yuri Andropov succeeded Leonid Brezhnev upon his death as the leader of the Soviet Union.

November 14, Polish Solidarity Leader Lech Walesa was freed after eleven months in prison.

November 23, the FCC at the Reagan Administration's insistence dropped all regulations on the amount and duration of television ads leaving this decision to the networks.

November 25, on Thanksgiving Day an entire Minneapolis city block including the headquarters of Northwest Bank (Wells Fargo) and the Donaldson's Department Store burned to the ground.

December 1, the first artificial heart was implanted.

December 3, a soil sample in Times Beach, Missouri was found to have 300 times the safe level of dioxin a known carcinogen. On December 23, the US Environmental Protection Agency ordered the town evacuated.

December 8, Norman Mayer held the Washington Monument hostage demanding an end of nuclear weapons. He was killed after ten hours. He was found with no explosives or weapons.

December 10, Soyuz T-5 returned to earth after 211 days in space.

Also on December 10, the CDC reported that the AIDS virus had been transmitted through a blood transfusion. The announcement caused a panic about the nation's blood supply.

December 12, $9.8 million was stolen from an armored transport vehicle in New York City.

December 15, Teamster President Roy Williams and four others were convicted of bribery.

December 16, the Federal Reserve announced that American factory production capacity had been reduced to less than 68% of its peak capacity.

December 24, a Christmas Eve blizzard struck Denver.

December 26, the *Time* magazine's Man of the Year was the computer.

In 1982 the board game Trivial Pursuit was released and became immediately popular. General Motors introduced the Saturn.

The US went into recession in 1982 and inflation was troubling at 6.16%. Year-end interest rates were also still high at 11.5%. The cost of the average new house rose rapidly to $82,200 while the median price of an existing home rose to $67,800 and average monthly rent was $320. The average income was $21,050 and the price of the average new car was $7,983. Electronics were cheap and home computers, microwave ovens and color televisions became common.

In December Michael Jackson's album, *Thriller* was released. It would become the top selling album of all time. In the 1982 Billboard's the top tunes were: *Physical* by Olivia Newton John, *Eye of the Tiger* by Survivor, *I Love Rock 'n Roll* by Joan Jett and the Blackhearts, *Ebony and Ivory* by Paul McCartney and Stevie Wonder, *Centerfold* and *Freeze Frame* by the J. Geils Band, *Do You Want Me* by the Human League, *Jack & Diane* and *Hurts So Good* by John Cougar (Mellancamp), *Chariots of Fire* by Vangelis, *Harden My Heart* by Quarterflash, *Rosanna* by Toto, *Gloria* by Laura Brannigan, *Working for the Weekend* by Loverboy, *I can't Go for That* and *Private Eyes* by Hall and Oats, *Shake It Up* by the Cars, *867-5309/Jenny* by Tommy Tutone, *Waiting for a Girl Like You* by Foreigner, *Vacation, We Got the Beat* and *Our Lips Are Sealed* by the Go-Gos and *Always On My Mind* by Willie Nelson. Also in 1982 Elvis Presley's home, Graceland, was opened to the public as an Elvis Presley Museum.

In November, at age seven, Drew Barrymore hosted *Saturday Night Live*. She was the youngest person to host a prime time show. On 1982 television, in addition to the debut of the Weather Channel, CNN debuted CNN2 which would be renamed the following year as CNN Headline News (HLN). *Late Night with David Letterman* made its debut in January with guests Bill Murray and Mr. Wizard. Other 1982 television debuts: *Fame, T.J. Hooker, Joanie Loves Chachi, Cagney and Lacy, The Gary Coleman Show, Family Ties, Silver Spoons, Knight Rider, Square Pegs, Cheers, Remington Steele, It Takes Two, St. Elsewhere,* and *Newhart*.

Shows ending in 1982 included: *The Lawrence Welk Show, Late Night with Tom Snyder, WKRP in Cincinnati, The Incredible Hulk, Barney Miller, Mork and Mindy, Lou Grant, Bosom Buddies* and *The Doctors.*

In its eighth and final season *Barney Miller* finally won the Emmy for Best Comedy. *Hill Street Blues* won for Best Drama Series. Allan Alda won Best Comedy Actor as Hawkeye Pierce in *M*A*S*H*. Carol Kane won Best Comedy Actress as Simka in *Taxi.* Daniel J. Travanti won Best Dramatic Actor for his role in *Hill Street Blues,* and Michael Learned as Best Dramatic Actress for Her role in *Nurse. Hill Street Blues* was nominated for sixteen awards and won four. *M*A*S*H* was nominated for ten and won two. *Taxi* was nominated for three and won three.

In 1982 the price of a movie ticket was still only $3.00. The movie *E.T. the Extra-Terrestrial* was by far the top grossing film at about $360 million. Other popular films were: *Gandhi, Sophie's Choice, Tootsie, An Officer and A Gentleman. Rocky III, Porky's, Star Trek II: The Wrath of Khan, 48Hrs, Poltergeist, The Best Little Whorehouse in Texas, Annie, Blade Runner, Fast Times at Ridgemont High, The Verdict,* and *Victor/Victoria.*

The Oscars went to *Gandhi* for Best Picture, Director and Actor. Meryl Streep won Best Actress in *Sophie's Choice.* The Golden Globe for Best Drama Picture went to *E.T. the Extra-Terrestrial.* The Golden Globe for Best Comedy or Musical Picture went to *Tootsie* which also won Dustin Hoffman a Golden Globe for Best Actor in a Musical or Comedy.

In 1982 literature the most popular books included: *The Color Purple* by Alice Walker, *Life, the Universe and Everything* by Douglas Adams, *The Skull Beneath the Skin* by P.D. James, *Schindler's List* by Thomas Keneally, *Different Season* by Stephen King, *Ham on Rye* by Charles Bukowski, *The Running Man* by Richard Bachman, *Master of the Game* by Sydney Sheldon, *Deadeye Dick* by Kurt Vonnegut Jr., *Dinner at the Homesick Restaurant* by Anne Tyler and *The Path to Power: The Years of Lyndon Johnson* by Robert A. Caro. *Rabbit is Rich* by John Updike won the Pulitzer Prize for fiction and *Grant: A Biography* won the Pulitzer for William S, McFeely. *The Collected Poems of Sylvia Plath* won the poetry prize.

CHAPTER 39. 1983: A CLOSE CALL WITH NUCLEAR WAR, WAR IN GRENADA, TRUCK BOMBS IN THE MIDEAST, AND A TROUBLED ECONOMY

January 1, the transfer of the military ARPANET created by DARPA was completed to the public TCP/IP the Internet Protocol Suite which marked the beginning of the internet.

January 3, the Kilauea volcano erupted in Hawaii.

January 7, President Reagan ended the US arms embargo to Guatemala.

January 17, George Wallace became Governor of Alabama for a record fourth time.

January 19, Nazi SS chief Klaus Barbie was found and arrested for his WWII war crimes in Bolivia.

January 21, President Reagan lied and claimed that El Salvador's human rights abuses had stopped. He therefore made them eligible for US military aid.

January 23, a radioactive Soviet satellite fell into the Indian Ocean.

February 5, the Nazi Gestapo leader Klaus Barbie was brought to trial and officially charged with war crimes.

February 8, Ariel Sharon was forced to resign as Israeli Defense Minister for his involvement in the Sabra and Shatila massacre of about 3,500 Palestinian civilians.

February 11, New York City was hit with an eighteen inch snow storm.

February 23, the US EPA announced its intention of buying the property in Times Beach, Missouri due to the high Dioxin levels.

February 24, a Congressional Commission condemned the US Internment of Japanese-American citizens in WWII.

February 28, the final episode of M*A*S*H* was shown on television to a record 125 million viewers.

March 1, a rare tornado in Los Angeles injured thirty-three people.

March 4, the US Public Health Service published guidelines for blood donors and AIDS.

March 7, TNN the country cable television network began.

March 8, the House Foreign Affairs Committee endorsed a freeze of nuclear weapons with the USSR.

March 8, President Reagan used the term "Evil Empire" to describe the USSR in a speech in Florida.

March 14, OPEC cut oil prices for the first time in twenty-three years.

March 23, in a speech President Reagan introduced his Strategic Defense Initiative which became popularly known as "Star Wars."

April 1, anti-nuclear protestors in the United Kingdom linked arms in a fourteen mile long demonstration.

Also on April 1, Iraq began intensive missile attacks on Iran.

April 4-9, the Space Shuttle Challenger was launched on its first mission.

April 5, France expelled forty-seven Soviet diplomats for spying.

April 7, the oldest known completely intact human skeleton, 80,000 years old, was discovered in Egypt.

April 12, Harold Washington was elected as the first Black mayor of Chicago.

April 13, the Target Corporation expanded to California and opened eleven stores there. It would eventually become the largest discount retailer in California and second largest in the nation behind Walmart.

April 17, India joined the space race with the launch of their first satellite.

April 18, a lone suicide car bomber killed sixty-three at the American Embassy in Lebanon. Seventeen were Americans, mostly CIA and four were US military personnel. A court later found that Hezbollah were the perpetrators.

Also on April 18 the Disney Channel began on cable television.

April 20, President Reagan signed a $165 billion rescue of Social Security.

April 22, the West German magazine *Stern* publicly announced that it had found 60 volumes of Adolf Hitler's diaries. It was later discovered to be a hoax.

April 25, the NASA space probe Pioneer 10 traveled past Pluto's orbit. On June 13, Pioneer 10 became the first manmade object to leave the solar system.

May 2, a 6.2 earthquake injured 487 people in California.

May 3, a group of US bishops condemned nuclear weapons.

May 17, Lebanon and Israel signed a peace treaty and Israel agreed to withdraw its forces.

May 18, the US revised immigration laws giving millions of undocumented people legal status in an amnesty program.

May 24, the US Supreme Court ruled that the US could withhold tax exempt status to schools that racially discriminate.

May 25, the first National Missing Children's Day was proclaimed.

May 27, in Benton, Tennessee an unlicensed fireworks operation exploded killing eleven people and causing extensive damage as far as five miles away.

June, a drought began which lasted the summer and affected much of the Midwest causing water shortages.

June 2, an Air Canada DC-9 toilet caught on fire killing twenty-three in Cincinnati.

June 15, the US Supreme Court struck down all state and local restrictions on abortion.

June 16, Pope John Paul II visited Poland. On June 22, Lech Walesa the leader of Solidarity met with the Pope.

June 18-24, the Space Shuttle Challenger made its second voyage with America's first woman astronaut, Sally Ride, aboard. On June 22, the Challenger made the first recovery of a satellite from orbit.

June 20, in their on-going war Iranian forces moved into Northern Iraq.

June 29, the Soyuz T-9 carried two cosmonauts to the Salyut 7 Space Station.

July, Europe saw record high temperatures throughout the month.

July 1, a nuclear accident at a power plant in Phillipsburg, Germany caused the release of radioactive iodine 131.

July 14, a Republican Congressman Dan Crane and Democratic Congressman Gerry Studds admitted to having had sex with their 17-year-old congressional pages.

Also on this date Nintendo first released Mario Bros in Japan.

July 15, a bomb was set off at the Turkish check-in counter at Orly Airport in Paris, France. It killed eight people and caused another fifty-five casualties. An Armenian radical group was responsible.

July 22, the Polish government ended nineteen months of martial law.

July 23, an ambush killing thirteen Sri Lanka soldiers by the militant Tamil Tigers began the Sri Lankan Civil War which would last until 2009.

July 25, the Washington Public Supply Power System defaulted on their $2.25 billion debts.

July 26, the US threatened Iran with action to keep oil and other navigation open in the Persian Gulf.

August 7, about 675,000 AT&T employees went on strike.

August 12, with the assistance of the US CIA, General Manuel Noriega seized power in Panama.

August 15-20, hurricane Alicia struck in Texas with 115 mph winds. The storm caused 21 deaths and about $2.6 billion in damages.

August 25, the US agreed to sell $10 billion in grain to the USSR.

August 30-September 5, the Space Shuttle Challenger made its third mission with Guion Bluford, the first African-American in space.

September 1, Korean Air Lines 747, flight 007 from Seoul to Anchorage, strayed over Soviet airspace and was shot down by a Soviet jet, killing all 269 crew and passengers including a U.S. Congressman, Larry McDonald. The incident once again brought the US and USSR close to war and heightened Cold War tensions. The Soviets initially denied their actions, but later admitted the incident claiming that they shot down "an American spy plane." One of the results of the incident was that the US government began to allow civilian aircraft and others to use the then classified US Military DNSS satellite navigation system, which later became known as GPS.

September 9, Radio Shack introduced the Color Computer 2.

September 12, Wells Fargo security guard Víctor Manuel Gerena took the weapons of two other guards at gunpoint. He handcuffed and tied them up and escaped with over $7 million, which was the largest robbery in US history at that time. He fled to Mexico and then to Cuba where it is thought he lives today. He was put on the FBI's Ten Most Wanted List and is the fugitive that has spent the longest time on this list. A million dollar reward will be given to anyone leading to his capture.

September 17, Vanessa Williams became the first African-American to be crowned Miss America.

September 26, with heightened tensions from the shooting down of Korean Air Lines 007, on September 1, the Soviet Forces were on alert when their early warning system indicated that the US had launched five nuclear missiles in a first strike against the USSR. The Soviets had been preparing for this event since Reagan had said that a first strike was on the table. A nuclear was between the US and USSR nuclear war was only avoided when Lieutenant Colonel Stanislav Petrov who was in command of the satellite early warning center refused to give the order for a Soviet counter nuclear missile attack. He had correctly assessed that the Soviet warning system was flawed. He later justified his actions to his superiors by saying that if the US was to launch an attack it would likely be hundreds of missiles and not five. The incident was not known outside of the USSR until after the Soviet Union fell. Petrov ironically was punished for these actions as the incident had embarrassed his superiors who had implemented the faulty warning system. He left the Army. He was awarded the Dresden Prize "for avoiding nuclear war" in 2013. A 2014 a movie, *The Man Who Saved the World* was made about the incident.

September 29, the US Congress invoked the War Powers Act at President Reagan's request to allow the US to keep 1,600 US Marines in Lebanon as a peacekeeping force.

October 5, Solidarity leader Lech Walesa won the Nobel Peace Prize.

October 11, hand cranked telephones in the US went out of service as the last 440 users of hand cranked telephones in Maine had them replaced with direct dial phones.

October 13, the first cellular phone network, Ameritech, now Cingular, began operations in Chicago.

October 15, US Marine sharpshooters killed five snipers at the Beirut Airport.

October 22, two correctional officers were killed by inmates at a prison in Marion, Illinois. The incident inspired the Supermax model for prisons.

October 23, simultaneous suicide truck bombs at the American and French barracks in Beirut killed 241 US Marines, 58 French paratroopers, 6 civilians and the two bombers.

Also on October 23, about 400,000 demonstrated against the cruise missile.

October 25, the US invaded Grenada. After the island nation's rightwing dictator was thrown out of office by a socialist coup, the US under the guise of protecting 600 American medical students invaded the tiny Caribbean island nation of just 91,000 people. Several countries including Canada condemned the invasion. The UN also condemned the action.

In the conflict 19 Americans were killed and 116 wounded. The Grenada forces and a small Cuba contingency had 69 killed, 396 wounded and 638 captured. There were 24 civilian casualties most of which occurred when a mental hospital was mistakenly bombed by the US. The US gave their participating troops more than 5,000 medals for valor causing a humorous headline in the *New York Times* in their March 30, 1984 analysis of the invasion of "Medals Outnumber GIs in Grenada Assault."

October 29, about 550,000 Dutch protested the cruise missile.

November 2, in a White House Rose Garden Ceremony President Reagan signed the bill creating the Martin Luther King Jr. federal holiday. President Carter was the originator of the legislation during his presidency and Reagan failed to give Carter credit.

Also on November 2, NATO conducted a command post exercise code named Able Archer 83 which tested a coordinated nuclear attack against the Soviet Union. The Soviets thought it was a genuine first strike attack and put their military on the highest alert. A slight misstep of the US or NATO could have triggered a nuclear war.

November 3, Reverend Jesse Jackson announced that he was running for the Democratic nomination for president.

November 7, a bomb exploded in the Capitol late in the evening after a caller had notified the Capitol switchboard that it was about to detonate. There were no casualties and damage to the Capitol was not significant except for the loss of a Daniel Webster painting. The perpetrators who called themselves "The Armed Resistance Unit" cited US imperialism in Lebanon and Grenada as the reasons. Six people were later found and convicted.

November 8, in the elections Democrat Martha Collins was elected the first woman governor of Kentucky and Democrat Wilson Goode was elected the first African-American Mayor of Philadelphia.

November 13, the first cruise missiles arrived in Europe in the United Kingdom amid large protests.

November 18, Argentina announced that they had the ability to produce enriched uranium for nuclear weapons.

November 20, over a hundred million Americans watched an ABC movie, *The Day After*, about a nuclear war.

November 23, the Soviets left the nuclear disarmament talks.

November 24, the Israelis exchanged 4,500 Palestinian and Lebanese prisoners for six of their own.

November 28-December 8, the ninth Space Shuttle Mission Columbia 6 was launched.

December 1, Rita Lavelle the Assistant Administrator of the US EPA for Solid Waste and Emergency Response was convicted of lying about her misuse funds from the Superfund cleanup program. Previous to her

EPA position, Lavelle had been a Republican Party official and an aide to Ronald Reagan when he was the California governor. She later served three months of a six month sentence and was fined $10,000. In 2004 Lavelle was also found guilty of wire fraud in her business dealings and making false statements to the FBI. She was sentenced to 15 months in federal prison and paid a $3,000 fine.

December 4, US aircraft struck Syrian anti-aircraft positions in Lebanon. Two American pilots were shot down one died in the crash, the other was held in captivity for 30 days until the Reverend Jesse Jackson negotiated his release.

December 9, Edwin Meese, one of President Reagan's top advisors made headlines by disparaging the poor and homeless by saying that poor people go to soup kitchens "because food is free and it's easier than paying for it."

December 12, a truck bomb exploded at the US Embassy in Kuwait killing five people, two Palestinians, two Kuwaitis, and one Syrian. Five other targets in Kuwait were hit with bombs during the next hour with no fatalities.

December 15, the last of the US combat soldiers withdrew from Grenada.

December 17, in the "troubles" the Irish Republican Army set off a bomb at Harrods Department Store in London killing six and wounding ninety others.

December 23, the journal *Science* published the first report on Nuclear Winter in the event of atomic warfare.

December 27, a propane gas fire destroyed sixteen blocks of Buffalo. Five firefighters and two civilians were killed and about 150 others were injured.

December 31, Benjamin Ward was named the first African-American police commissioner in New York City.

In other 1983 news the Drug Abuse Resistance Education program, DARE, began, McDonalds introduced McNuggets, and Microsoft Word the most popular word processing program and Lotus 1-2-3 were also launched. US unemployment rose to 12 million the highest since 1941 as the US went into recession. The US and the world continued to feel the weather effects of an El Niño. Cabbage Patch dolls became a fad. The US was so occupied with potential nuclear war that the PBS children's show, *Mr. Rodgers Neighborhood*, aired five episodes that dealt with the subject to reassure children. In 1983 over 90% of the US media was controlled by 50 companies, by 2017 over 90% would be controlled by just six.

Inflation fell to 3.22% due to the recession, but interest rates were still high at 11%. The average income was $21,070. The average cost of a new home was $82,600 and an existing home averaged $70,300 and rents averaged $355 per month. A new Ford Mustang sold on average for $6,572 and gas was $1.25 per gallon.

In music Danny Wilson, songwriter, drummer, vocalist and was the co-founder of the Beach Boys with his two brothers drowned while intoxicated. He had suffered from drug and alcohol addiction and was no longer with the band. Karen Carpenter died from complications from anorexia nervosa. And the estranged Everly Brothers finally reunited again to perform at London's Royal Albert hall.

The songs of 1983 were dominated by Michael Jackson who hit with *Beat It*, *Billie Jean*, *Wanna Be Startin' Something*, *Human Nature* and *The Girl is Mine* with Paul McCartney. Other top tunes of 1983 included: *Every Breath You Take* by The Police, *Flashdance (What a Feeling)* by Irene Cara, *Maneater*, *One On One*, and *Family Man* by Hall & Oates, *I'm Still Standing*, by Elton John, *Sweet Dreams* the Eurythmics, *Come On Eileen* by Dexy's Midnight Runners, *She Works Hard for the Money* by Donna Summer, *Down Under*, *Overkill* and *It's a Mistake* by Men at Work, *Do You Really Want to Hurt me?* and *I'll Tumble 4 Ya* by Culture Club, *Solitare* and *How Am I Supposed to Live Without You* by Laura Branigan, *Up Where We Belong* by Joe Cocker and Jennifer Warnes, *Sexual Healing* by Marvin Gaye, *Little Red Corvette* and *1999* by Prince, *Allentown* and *Tell Her About It* by Billy Joel, *Let's Dance* and *China Girl* by David Bowie, *Our House* by Madness, *Rock the Casbah* by The Clash, *We've Got Tonight* by Kenny Rogers and Sheena Easton and *True* by Spandau Ballet.

In addition to the millions watching the final episode of *M*A*S*H** in February of 1983, in March, First Lady Nancy Reagan appeared on the sitcom Diff'rent Strokes to begin her "Just Say No" anti-drug campaign. On December 2, the fourteen minute music video for Michael Jackson's *Thriller* was broadcast on television for the first time.

The new television shows in 1983 included a lot of single season shows dubbed failures by their networks. Some of the more lasting shows of 1983 included: *AfterMASH*, *The A Team*, *Fraggle Rock*, *Mama's Family*, *Buffalo Bill*, *Star Search*, *Webster*, *Hotel*, *Goodnight Beantown*, *Hardcastle & McCormick*, *The Love Connection*, *Wheel of Fortune*, *Riptide* and *Scarecrow and Mrs. King*.

In addition to *M*A*S*H**, shows ending their runs in 1983 included: *Little House on the Prairie*, *Laverne & Shirley*, *SCTV*, *CHiPs*, *Taxi*, *Quincy M.E.*, *Square Pegs*, *Archie Bunker's Place*, and *The Incredible Hulk*.

At the Emmys *Cheers* won Best Comedy, *Hill Street Blues* won Best Drama. Judd Hirsch in *Taxi* and Shelley Long in *Cheers* won as Best Comedy Actors. Ed Flanders in *St. Elsewhere* and Tyne daily in *Cagney & Lacy* won as the Best Dramatic Actors. Christopher Lloyd and Carol Kane won as Best Comedy Supporting Actors for their roles in *Taxi*. James Coco and Doris Roberts won as Best Supporting Dramatic Actors for their roles in *St. Elsewhere*.

The Movies of 1983 were notable. They included *The Return of the Jedi* which was the highest grossing film at over $250 million. Other popular films included: *Terms of Endearment*, *Tender Mercies*, *Flashdance*, *Trading Places*, *War Games*, *Octopussy*, *Sudden Impact*, *Scarface*, *The Outsiders*, *National Lampoon's Vacation*, *Staying Alive*, *Mr. Mom*. *Risky Business*, *All the Right Moves*, *Bad Boys*, *Rumble Fish*, *The Year of Living Dangerously*, *Fanny and Alexander*, *The Right Stuff*, *Silkwood*, *Monty Python's The Meaning of Life*, *Yentl*, *Educating Rita*, *The Big Chill*, *Curse of the Pink Panther*, *D.C. Cab*, and *A Christmas Story*.

Terms of Endearment won most of the top Oscars including Best Picture, Best Director for James L. Brooks, Best Actress for Shirley MacLaine and Best Supporting Actor for Jack Nicholson. Robert Duvall was a surprise winner for Best Actor in *Tender Mercies*.

The popular books of 1983 included: *Space* and *Poland* by James Michener, *The Little Drummer Girl* by John le Carré, *The Name of the Rose* by Umberto Eco, *Pet Sematary* and *Christine* by Stephen King, *Frida, A Biography of Frida Kahlo* by Hayden Herrera, *Fatal Vision* by Joe McGinness, *Gorillas in the Mist* by Dian Fossey, *Ironweed* by William Kennedy, *The Last Lion: Winston Spencer Churchill: Visions of Glory 1874-1932* by William Manchester, *Shame* by Salman Rushdie, *Hot Water Music* by Charles Bukowski, *Glengary Glen Ross* by David Mamet, *First Among Equals* by Jeffery Archer, *In Search of Our Mother's Gardens: Womanist Prose* by Alice Walker, *Hollywood Wives* by Jackie Collins, *Waterland* by Graham Swift, *Prometheus Rising* by Robert Anton Wilson, *Vietnam: A History* by Stanley Karnow, *The Game* by Ken Dryden, *Frames of Mind: The Theory of Multiple Intelligences* by Howard Gardener, and *Organizational Behavior* by Stephen P. Robbins. *Night Mother* by Marsha Norman won a Pulitzer Prize as did *Selected Poems* by Galway Kinnell, along with *Is There No Place On Earth for Me?* by Susan Sheehan.

CHAPTER 40. 1984: THE ELECTION, THE BEGINNINGS OF THE
IRAN-CONTRA SCANDAL, THE BHOPAL DISASTER, ETHIOPIA
STARVES, AND THE SPACE SHUTTLES AND SOYUZ

January 1, the "Baby Bells," the regional telephone companies mandated in the breakup of AT&T in 1982, began their independent operations.

January 5, President Reagan nominated Elizabeth Dole, the wife of Senator Robert Dole as US Secretary of Transportation.

January 10, the Reagan Administration pushed for restored full diplomatic relations with the Vatican after 117 years. The administration had formed a partnership with the Catholic Church to fight communism in Eastern Europe. The restoration was protested by many groups as an act that violated the separation of church and state. The ban against diplomatic relations with religious organizations had been enacted by Congress in 1867 to assure the separation of church and state.

January 16, Paul and Linda McCartney were arrested in Barbados for the possession of marijuana.

January 17, the US Supreme Court ruled that the private use of VCRs in taping television shows and movies for later viewing did not violate copyright laws.

January 24, Apple Computer introduced the Macintosh personal computer.

January 29, with some concern about his age and mental acuity, President Ronald Reagan announced his intention of running for a second term for president.

February 1, China and the Netherlands restored diplomatic relations.

February 3-11, the tenth space shuttle mission, Challenger 4 was launched.

February 8-19, the Winter Olympic Games were held in Sarajevo, Yugoslavia.

Also on February 8, Soyuz T-10 was launched, with both the Challenger and Soyuz missions it was the first time eight people were in space at the same time.

February 13, Konstantin Chernenko succeeded Yuri Andropov as the head of the USSR,

February 15, in the Iran-Iraq War over 500,000 Iranian soldiers occupied northern Iraq.

February 20, former Vice President Walter Mondale won about half the votes in the Iowa Democratic Caucus. Among the other contenders Senator Gary Hart had 17%, George McGovern 10%, Alan Cranston 7%, Senator John Glenn 5%, former Governor Rueben Askew 3%, and Jesse Jackson 2%. President Reagan was unopposed among Republicans. The Iowa Caucus established Mondale as the front runner and McGovern, Cranston and Glenn soon dropped out.

February 25, a fire in Cubatao, Brazil killed 508 people, mostly children, when an oil pipeline exploded and caught fire.

February 26, with the country in chaos, the US Marines left Lebanon.

Also on February 26, during his campaign for the Democratic nomination for President the Reverend Jesse Jackson admitted to making anti-Semitic slurs by calling New York City "Hymietown."

February 29, Canadian Prime Minister Pierre Trudeau announced he was stepping down after 15 years.

March 2, the large Iranian offensive against Iraq failed. On March 5, the US accused Iraq of breaking the Geneva Convention rules for using poison gas.

March 7, the US attacked Nicaragua mining its harbors. They began arming and providing money, leadership, training and intelligence to a militia group known as the Contras whose membership had been part of the ruthless police and military of Somoza, the deposed Nicaraguan dictator. They acted as death squads to overthrow the democratic government of Nicaragua to restore its military dictatorship. This marked the beginning of the Reagan Administration covert involvement that would later become the Iran-Contra scandal which led to the indictment of twelve senior Reagan Administration officials including the Secretary of Defense, several National Security Advisors and the Assistant Secretary of State who oversaw the illegal sale of arms to Iran to finance the Contras after Congress cut off funds for this purpose. It has also been shown that the CIA was involved in the smuggling and sale of cocaine in the US to support these operations (Cockburn and St. Clair).

March 9, the Competitive Enterprise Institute (CEI), a rightwing think tank was formed in Washington. DC. Its policies were to deny global warming and climate change and oppose government health and safety regulations through legal advocacy and by supporting like-minded political candidates. CEI funding comes from oil and energy, automotive, alcohol, tobacco, chemical and related companies.

March 16, gunmen kidnapped William Buckley, the CIA Station Chief of Lebanon. He would be held captive by Hezbollah until he was killed in June of 1985.

March 19, a Mobil Oil tanker spilled 200,000 gallons of oil into the Columbia River.

March 20, the US Senate rejected an amendment to the Constitution to allow prayers in school.

March 21, a Soviet submarine and the US Air Craft Carrier Kitty Hawk collided off Japan.

March 22, teachers at a preschool in Manhattan Beach, California were charged with satanic ritual abuse of children at the school. After receiving national press attention the charges were proven to be false and unfounded.

March 27, began "the tanker war" where over the next nine months shipping in the Persian Gulf would be hampered as forty-four multinational ships were either fired upon by either Iran or Iraq or damaged by their mines.

March 29, in the middle of the night the NFL Baltimore Colts were moved to Indianapolis.

April-August, China invaded Vietnam again. Both sides claimed to inflict extensive casualties on the other side. Despite overwhelmingly larger forces China could not penetrate more than 5 km into Vietnam. These border wars would continue off and on until 1990.

April 1, singer Marvin Gaye was shot and killed by his father a day before his forty-fifth birthday.

April 2, the Soyuz T-11 carried the first Indian, Rakesh Sharma into space.

April 6-13, the eleventh shuttle mission Challenger 5 was launched and with Soyuz T-11 they set a new record of eleven people in space simultaneously.

April 10, the US Senate condemned the mining of Nicaraguan harbors by the Reagan Administration claiming Reagan was violating the War Powers Act.

April 16, over a million people demonstrated in Brazil against the CIA supported military government and demanded democratic elections.

April 20, the USSR began an offensive in Afghanistan.

April 23, the Centers for Disease Control announced that AIDS is caused by a virus.

April 26, amid their conflict in Vietnam, President Reagan visited China.

April 27, a record-setting seventy inches of snow fell in Red Lake Montana.

May 7, a $180 million settlement with Dow Chemical and six other makers of Agent Orange was made by attorneys representing Veterans of Vietnam (and later 1960s Korean veterans) who had been harmed by their exposure to the chemicals.

May 8, the USSR announced that it would not participate in the summer Olympic Games in Los Angeles. It was in retaliation for the US not participating in the 1980 Moscow Games because of the Soviet invasion of Afghanistan.

May 10, the International Court of Justice ruled against the US in the mining of Nicaraguan ports.

May 12, South African anti-Apartheid political prisoner Nelson Mandela was allowed to see his wife for the first time in twenty-two years.

Also on May 12-November 11, the 1984 World's Fair in New Orleans and the Louisiana World Exposition, was held.

May 13, an explosion at a Soviet Naval base destroyed two-thirds of the Soviet Navy missiles, destroyed the primary maintenance facility and killed their maintenance crews. It was called the Severomorsk Disaster and was the worst Soviet naval catastrophe since WWII.

May 26, President Reagan publicly ruled out US involvement in the Iran-Iraq War, while his administration was secretly and illegally selling weapons to Iran.

Also on May 26, flooding killed 14 people after heavy rains in Oklahoma.

May 31, six death row inmates escaped from the Mecklenburg Correctional Center in Virginia. They were all caught and returned to prison for their executions.

June 1, the bankruptcy of the Chicago, Rock Island and Pacific Railroad was finalized.

June 3, President Reagan visited Ireland.

June 4, at the University of California at Berkeley genes from an extinct animal were extracted and cloned in a laboratory. The DNA was from a Quagga, an animal that went extinct over a century ago. It was reported that the ability to reproduce the DNA would eventually allow for the cloning of a Quagga or other extinct animals animal.

June 8, a large F5 tornado struck in Barneveld, Wisconsin and killed nine, injured about 200 and caused over $25 million in damages.

June 14, the Southern Baptist Convention ruled against women as clergy members.

June 16, the Cirque de Soleil entertainment company was founded in Canada.

June 19, in a rare public appearance by a Supreme Court Justice, Chief Justice Warren Berger appeared on Nightline.

June 26, the flight of the space shuttle Discovery was cancelled due to a computer malfunction.

July 1, the PG-13 designation for movies was introduced by the Motion Picture Association of America.

July 3, the US Supreme Court ruled that the Jaycees must admit women members.

July 11, the US laws mandated that seatbelts would be required in all cars by 1989.

July 16-23 the Democratic Party held their National Convention. After Ted Kennedy decided not to run the Party leaders rallied around Vice President Walter Mondale. Despite this he initially faced some opposition from Colorado Senator Gary Hart and the Reverend Jesse Jackson. At the convention Mondale captured 2,191 delegates to Hart's 1,200 and Jackson's 465 delegates. He chose New York Congresswoman Geraldine Ferraro as his Vice Presidential running mate.

July 17, the US passed the national Minimum Drinking Age Act prohibiting anyone under the age of twenty-one from drinking as a condition to the states receiving highway funding. Previous to this states had lowered their drinking ages to 18 because of the large number of underage US servicemen during the Vietnam War.

July 18, a man opened fire in a San Ysidro, California McDonalds, killing twenty-one people and wounding nineteen others before being killed by police.

June 19, Lynn Ripplemeyer became the first woman captain to pilot a commercial passenger aircraft across the Atlantic.

July 23, Vanessa Williams was forced to resign as Miss America after nude photos of her were published in *Penthouse.*

July 25, Soviet Cosmonaut Svetlana Savitskaya became the first woman to walk in space.

July 28-August 12, the Summer Olympic Games were held in Los Angeles.

July 30 an oil tanker spilled 2.8 million gallons of oil near Cameron, Louisiana.

August 3, the New York Stock Exchange set a trading record of over 365 million shares.

August 11, during a radio address President Reagan said as a joke into a live microphone, "My fellow Americans I'm pleased to tell you that today that I have signed legislation that will outlaw Russia forever. We begin bombing in five minutes." Reagan was criticized widely for this provocative recklessness and some claimed the president was losing his faculties.

August 18, an above ground oil storage tank in Jacksonville, Florida leaked 2.5 million gallons of oil which was struck by lightning setting it ablaze.

August 20-23 the Republican National Convention re-nominated President Ronald Reagan and Vice President George H.W. Bush.

August 21, a half million protested the regime of Ferdinand Marcos in the Philippines.

August 30-September 5, the twelfth space shuttle mission Discovery 1 was launched.

September 6, the *Today Show* aired with a live broadcast from Moscow.

September 18, Joe Kittinger completed the first solo hot air balloon crossing of the Atlantic.

September 19-26, Britain and China agreed to transfer Hong Kong back to China by 1997.

September 20, a Hezbollah suicide car bomb attacked the Us Embassy Annex in Beirut and killed twenty-three.

September 26, President Reagan vetoed the sanctions imposed by Congress on the Apartheid government of South Africa.

September 29, Elizabeth Taylor was admitted for treatment at the Betty Ford Clinic.

October 2, Russian cosmonauts returned after a record 237 days in space.

October 3, Richard W. Miller became the first FBI Agent to be indicted for espionage. He was arrested with two Russian immigrants who were in reality KGB agents. Miller began an affair with the female KGB Agent and began to provide classified data to her and her partner for money. Miller was planning to travel to Vienna with the female KGB Agent to meet with the KGB officials. He was convicted of espionage but the conviction was thrown out on a technicality and he was then retried and convicted. He was sentenced to 20 years in prison, but was released after 13 years.

October 5-13, the thirteenth space shuttle mission, Challenger 6 was launched, which included the first space walk of an American woman, Dr. Kathryn Sullivan and the mission also included first Canadian in space, Marc Garneau.

October 7, in the first of two Presidential debates between Reagan and Mondale the President failed badly. He seemed mentally confused much of the time and admitted after to being tired. He didn't appear to know where he was and talked about "going to church here in Washington" with the debate in Louisville. He referred to military uniforms as "wardrobe." His performance gave doubt to his suitability to serve and gave a boost to Mondale's chances. It left his campaign advisers and surrogates struggling to answer questions about his age (73) and his confused mental state.

October 11, the Vice Presidential debate raised questions about Geraldine Ferraro's and her husband's finances. Bush suurogates made allegations of shady real estate investments, mob ties, and spread rumors that her husband had profited in the pornography trade. Ferraro became a liability for Mondale.

October 12, in the "troubles" the IRA set off a bomb intending to kill British Prime Minister Maggie Thatcher and her cabinet ministers at the Grand Brighton Hotel in Brighton England. The attack on Thatcher and her cabinet was unsuccessful but the bomb killed five others and wounded thirty-one.

October 16, Archbishop Desmond Tutu of South Africa won the Nobel Peace Prize.

Also on October 16, a baboon heart was successfully transferred to a baby girl, called "Baby Fae" in the press to protect her identity.

October 19, Polish Secret Police kidnapped a Catholic priest who openly supported Solidarity. He was found dead in a reservoir eleven days later.

October 21, after the disastrous first debate Reagan's team made sure the President was well rested and prepared. His speech writers prepared a joke to deflate the age issue which Reagan delivered perfectly during the debate. When asked about his age Reagan responded, "I will not make age an issue of this campaign. I am not going to exploit, for political purposes, my opponent's youth and inexperience." Mondale who also appeared to laugh later said that he knew when Reagan delivered the line that Reagan had erased voter's fears and he believed that the election was over. Mondale was at the time considerably behind in the polls.

October 23, BBC coverage of mass starvation in Ethiopia alerted the world to the crisis where 10 million lives were at risk. On October 25, the European Economic Community made £1.8 million available for famine relief in Ethiopia.

October 31, After Indira Gandhi ordered an attack on a Sikh religious holy site two Sikh security guards assassinated her. Anti-Sikh riots by the majority Hindu population killed about 20,000 Sikhs in retaliation.

November 4, Nicaragua held the first free elections in fifty-six years. The Sandinistas won with about two-thirds of the voters supporting them. The Reagan Administration and the CIA were already making secret plans to bring down the Sandinista government with a military coup by the Contras.

November 6, President Reagan easily won the presidential election against Walter Mondale. The former Vice President carried only his home state of Minnesota and the District of Columbia. Reagan took 54 million votes to Mondale's 37 million votes.

November 8-16, the fourteenth space shuttle flight Discovery 2, was launched. Anna Lee Fisher became the first mom in space.

November 9, Cesar Chavez delivered his speech "What the Future Holds for Farm Workers and Hispanics" in San Francisco.

November 18, the USSR helped deliver American wheat to the famine victims in Ethiopia.

November 20, McDonalds announced the sale of its 50 billionth hamburger.

Also on November 20, the SETI Intitute to look for alien intelligence was founded.

November 26, the US and Iraq reestablished diplomatic relations.

December 3, the Bhopal Disaster began as leaks from a Union Carbide pesticide plant in Bhopal, India exposed a half million people to toxic chemicals resulting in the eventual deaths of over 23,000.

Also on December 3, Band Aid, a group of international performers, recorded a Bob Geldof song "Do They Know It's Christmas?" to raise money for Ethiopian famine relief.

December 4, In the Sri Lankan civil war, government soldiers killed over 150 civilians thought to be sympathetic to the Tamil rebels.

Also on December 4-9, Hezbollah hijacked a Kuwait Airlines plane and killed four passengers. The highjackers were killed by commandos.

December 8, White supremacist leader Robert Jay Matthews was killed in a battle with the FBI on Whidbey Island, Washington

December 10, the first planet outside our solar system was discovered.

Also on December 10, the networking technology company Cisco Systems was founded.

December 19, a fire at the Wilberg Mine in Utah killed twenty-seven.

December 22, Bernhard Goetz, "the Subway Vigilante" shot four alleged Black muggers on a New York City subway train. He fired five times, seriously wounding all four. He was charged with attempted murder and several firearm offenses. He was found not guilty of the attempted murser charges but was found guilty of illegally owning a firearm and served eight months of a one year term. The incident sparked controversy over urban crime and race. The National Rifle Association used the incident to rally support against laws that made carrying concealed weapons illegal.

December 28, a Soviet cruise missile fell into a lake in Finland.

In 1984 the recession worsened. Seventy banks failed. The annual inflation rate was 4.1%. Interest rates were still high at 10.75%. The average annual income was $21,600. Prices for new and existing homes were $86,730 and $72,400 respectively with median monthly rent at $350. A new car averaged $6,294 and gasoline went to $1.13 per gallon. The McIntosh computer made its debut in 1984.

Howard Cosell retired from Monday Night Football in December. A Wendy's television commercial with an older woman, Lara Peller, shouting, "Where's the beef?" premiered in January and was used by Vice President Mondale in the Democratic primaries to belittle Senator Gary Hart's political track record. In October Farrah Fawcett appeared in a controversial television movie, *The Burning Bed*, about a woman who shot her physically abusive husband. Other than the Super Bowl it was the highest watched television event of the 1985-85 season. New television shows that made their debut in 1984 included: *Night Court, Airwolf, Kate & Allie, Lifestyles of the Rich and Famous, Double Trouble, Scrabble, Santa Barbara, E/R, Punky Brewster, Hunter, Highway to Heaven, The Cosby Show, Who's the Boss?, Threes a Crowd, Miami Vice, Charles in Charge, Murder She Wrote, V, Crazy Like a Fox* and *The Transformers*.

Some of the shows ending in 1984 included: *That's Incredible, Hart to Hart, One Day at a Time, Happy Days, Three's Company, Dean Martin Celebrity Roast, AfterMASH, The Edge of Night,* and *Captain Kangaroo*.

Cheers and *Hill Street Blues* won the Emmys for Best Comedy and Drama. John Ritter and Jane Curtain won for Best Comedy Actors in *Cheers* and *Kate & Allie* respectively. Tom Selleck in *Magnum P.I.* and Tyne Daily in *Cagney & Lacy* won Best Dramatic Actor and Actress.

In music Michael Jackson achieved a Platinum Record and won eight Grammys. September was the debut of the first MTV Awards. 1984 was a premier year for music. Some of the most popular songs included: *When the Doves Cry* and *Let's Go Crazy* by Prince, *Say, Say, Say* by Michael Jackson and Paul McCartney, *Thriller* by Michael Jackson, *Girls Just Want to Have Fun, Time After Time* and *She Bop* by Cyndi Lauper, *Footloose* by Kenny Logins, *Jump* by Van Halen, *Drive, You Might Think,* and *Magic* by The Cars, *Karma Chameleon* by Culture Club, *Let's Hear It for the Boy* by Denise Williams, *Dancing in the Dark* by Bruce Springsteen, *Jump* and *I'm So Excited* by the Pointer Sisters, *99 Luftballons* by Nena, *I can Dream About You* by Dan Hartman, *Oh Sherrie* by Steve Perry, *Here Comes the Rain Again* by the Eurythmics, *Eyes Without a Face* by Billy Idol, *Borderline* and *Lucky Star* by Madonna, *Legs* by ZZ Top, *Cruel Summer* by Bananarama, *The Heart of Rock & Roll, I Want a New Drug* and *If This Is It* by Huey Lewis and the News, *Love is a Battlefield* by Pat Benatar, *The Warrior* by Scandal, *Caribbean Queen* by Billy Ocean and *Head Over Heels* by the Go-Gos.

The top movies of 1984 included the top box office draws like: *Beverly Hills Cop, Ghostbusters, Indiana Jones and the Temple of Doom, Gremlins, The Karate Kid, Police Academy, Footloose, Romancing the Stone, Star Trek III: The Search for Spock,* and *Splash*. It also included some critically acclaimed pictures like: *Amadeus, Places in the Heart, The Killing Fields,* and *Passage to India*. Other significant films of 1984 were: *The Terminator, A Nightmare on Elm Street, Sixteen Candles, Red Dawn. Purple Rain, Dune, Repo Man, Streets of Fire, Blame It on Rio, The Woman in Red, Broadway*

Danny Rose, *Tightrope*, and the fake comedy documentary (mockumentry) *This is Spinal Tap*.

Amadeus won the Oscars for Best Picture, Best Actor and Best Director. It also won the Golden Globes for the same. Sally Field won the Oscar and Golden Globe Best Actress in *Places in the Heart*.

In literature Robert Penn Warren was named the American Poet Laureate. The books of 1984 include: *The Unbearable Lightness of Being* by Milan Kundera, *Neuromancer* by William Gibson, *The Hunt for Red October* by Tom Clancy, *So Long and Thanks for All the Fish* by Douglas Adams, *The House on Mango Street* by Sandra Cisneros, *The Talisman* by Stephen King, *The Wasp Factory* by Iain Banks, *Jitterbug Perfume* by Tim Robbins, *Bright Lights Big City* by Jay McInerney, *Money* by Martin Amis, *Love Medicine* by Louise Erdrich, *The Fourth Protocol* by Frederick Forsythe, *The Lives Of Poets* by E.L. Doctorow *The Quality of Mercy* by William Shawcross, and the winners of the Pulitzer Prize for Literature *Ironweed* by William Kennedy, and the poetry prize: *American Primitive* by Mary Oliver.

CHAPTER 41. 1985: THE YEAR OF THE SPY, A RECORD-SETTING COLD WINTER AND WINDOWS

January 1, the first mandatory seat belt law went into effect in New York. Also on January 1, the internet domain name system was created.

January 10, a committed socialist, Daniel Ortega, was elected the President of Nicaragua. The Reagan Administration stepped up its secret war in Nicaragua and its illegal covert support of the Contras.

January 20-22, a cold snap occurred and temperatures plunged across the US. In Chicago the temperature plunged to minus 27 Fahrenheit with a wind chill of minus 77 F, both were record lows. In the aftermath about 126 deaths were blamed on the bitter cold. Domesticated and wild animals died across the US and over 90% Florida's citrus crop worth $1.2 billion was destroyed.

January 21, President Reagan's second inauguration was held inside the Capitol Rotunda due to the cold and the Inauguration Parade was cancelled.

January 24-27, the fifteenth space shuttle mission Discovery 3 was launched.

January 28, copying the British Band Aid, the charity hit single *We are the World* was made by US performers to aid the famine in East Africa.

February 1, record cold temperatures were recorded across Colorado and Utah and set records lows for those states.

February 4, US Naval exercise in the South Pacific was cancelled when the US refused to tell New Zealand if nuclear weapons were aboard the ships.

February 5, Australia cancelled all involvement with the MX missile tests.

February 10, Nelson Mandela rejected an offer of freedom from South African government for his denouncement of the freedom movement.

February 14, Jerry Levin, a CNN reporter who was kidnapped and held prisoner by Hezbollah for eleven and a half months in Lebanon, escaped.

February 16, Israel began withdrawing troops from Lebanon.

February 19, the first bottles and cans of Cherry Coke went on sale.

February 27, the nation's struggling farmers converged on Washington to demand economic relief.

March 1, the Pentagon finally accepted the scientific evidence that a nuclear war would cause global nuclear winter.

March 3, a massive earthquake struck Santiago, Chile leaving about a million people homeless.

March 4, the US EPA banned the use of leaded gasoline.

March 11, Mikhail Gorbachev became head of the USSR.

March 16, Associated Press correspondent Terry Anderson was taken hostage in Lebanon. He was held until 1991.

March 24, during a military liaison mission to East Germany Arthur Nicholson a US Intelligence Specialist was shot and killed by an East German soldier. The US claimed the Soviets deliberately murdered Nicholson, but the Soviets claimed that he was in an unauthorized sensitive area and failed to follow the orders of a guard. The US cancelled joint celebrations with the USSR celebrating the 40th anniversary of the defeat of Nazi Germany. In 1988 the USSR formally apologized for Nicholson's death.

April 10, Madonna launched her Virgin Tour.

April 11, the aircraft carrier USS Coral Sea collided with an Ecuadorian tanker near Cuba. The Captain of the Coral Sea and four other officers were relieved of command.

April 12-19, the sixteenth space shuttle mission Discovery 4, was launched with US Senator Jake Garn aboard.

April 19, the FBI and ATF agents raided the compound of a radical and armed right-wing Christian group, The Covenant, The Sword and The Arm of the Lord, in northern Arkansas for weapons violations and acts of terrorism including the murder of a police officer. The group had links to other rightwing Christian and racist groups like Aryan Nation. In 1983 the group tried to dynamite a natural gas pipeline. The FBI obtained a search warrant to search the compound. When the group realized they were surrounded by 300 federal agents they surrendered. Seven members were charged with crimes and sent to prison, including one for the murder of a police officer and a pawn shop owner. He was later sentenced to death by lethal injection.

April 23, New Coke debuted with changes from the original recipe. It flopped with consumers and Coca-Cola was forced to return to the original recipe within three months.

April 29- May 6, the seventeenth shuttle mission Challenger 7 was launched.

May 5, in an odd and what many people thought inappropriate gesture President Reagan joined West German Chancellor Helmut Kohl for a controversial ceremony for German WWII dead in mourning the loss of fifty-nine elite Nazi SS officers in Bitburg, West Germany. Filmmaker Michael Moore and a Jewish friend were there in the crowd and held up a banner which read: "We came from Michigan, USA, to remind you: they killed my family."

May 11, the FBI brought multiple charges against five Mafia families in New York City.

May 12, Amy Eilberg of New York City was ordained as the first woman conservative rabbi.

May 13, the police raided a building in a Black neighborhood of Philadelphia that housed MOVE, a Black power group. The raid was made after the Mayor and police chief labeled MOVE as a terroristic group for using a bullhorn to deliver political messages to the neighborhood and other minor offenses. The raid became a standoff and the Police Commissioner ordered that the building be bombed. Two bombs were dropped from a helicopter starting a fire that burned the building and 65 nearby houses in the Black neighborhood as the fire department stood by and watched. Officials later tried to justify their actions saying that they feared the firefighters would be shot at and gave orders to let the fire burn. Eleven people including five children died in the fire and more than 250 people were left homeless. One of the MOVE survivors claimed that the police fired at those trying to escape the fire, trapping some in the buildings.

May 15, the Unabomber exploded a device at the University of California, Berkeley injuring one person.

May 16, British scientists in Antarctica announced the discovery of a large ozone hole in the atmosphere raising concerns about the disintegration of the ozone layer that protects earth from harmful x-rays.

May 19, Navy Chief Warrant Officer John Anthony Walker was arrested for espionage. Walker had spied for the Soviet Union starting in 1968, He did this for money. Walker recruited others to grow his spy ring including Walker's son Seaman Michael Walker and Chief Petty Officer Jerry Whitworth. He also recruited his brother Arthur who was a Lt. Commander. He attempted to recruit his daughter in the US Army, but she became pregnant and left the army. He was discovered when his wife reported him to the FBI to save her children. Walker, his brother and Whitworth all received life sentences. Walker's son received 25 years. Walker's wife was not charged.

May 23, Thomas Cavanaugh an aerospace engineer for Northrop was convicted of trying to sell stealth bomber secrets to the USSR for $25,000. Cavanaugh was caught in an FBI sting operation in December of 1984.

May 31, violent weather struck Ohio, Pennsylvania, New York and Ontario, Canada producing 41 tornados and killing 90 people, causing hundreds of injuries and resulting in hundreds of millions in damage.

June 4, the US Supreme Court struck down Alabama's "Moment of Silence Law" saying that it promoted religious prayer in schools.

June 6, the remains of Nazi war criminal Dr. Josef Mengele were discovered in a grave in Brazil and were exhumed.

Also on June 6, the Soyuz T-13 took two cosmonauts to the space station.

June 9, an American, Thomas Sutherland, was kidnapped by Hezbollah in Lebanon.

June 13, the Unabomber attempted to set a bomb off at the Boeing facility in Auburn, Washington. It was diffused by police.

June 14, a TWA flight from Athens to Rome was hijacked by Hezbollah and taken to Beirut. They tortured and killed one passenger, US Naval Petty Officer Robert Stethem, because their demands were not met. The remaining hostages were freed June 30 and the kidnappers escaped. One would later be brought to trial for the murder of Stethem and another would be later killed in an explosion.

June 15, the Soviet spacecraft Vega 2 dropped a landing craft on Venus.

Also on June 15, an insane man threw acid on Rembrandt's painting Danaë and slashed it with a knife at the Hermitage in St. Petersburg, Russia. The painting was horribly damaged but carefully restored over a twelve year period.

June 17-24, the eighteenth space shuttle mission Discovery-5 had French and Saudi astronauts as part of the crew.

June 25, a fireworks factory near Hallett, Oklahoma exploded killing twenty-one.

June 27, the iconic Route 66 Chicago to Santa Monica was officially decertified as a highway. The highway was known at its peak for its unique 1940s and 1950s highway architecture and was considered the national pathway to the west.

July 10, the Greenpeace vessel Rainbow Warrior was sunk by French agents near Auckland to prevent it from interfering in French atomic tests in the South Pacific. A Dutch journalist was killed.

Also July 10, *Playboy* and *Penthouse* magazines published nude photos of Madonna.

July 12, Ronald Reagan was diagnosed with colon cancer. Vice President George H. W. Bush served as President while Reagan underwent surgery. Reagan, whose mental health was suspect, began to decline more rapidly both mentally and physically after the operation.

July 13, Live Aid concerts were held at Wembley Stadium in London and JFK Stadium in Philadelphia and raised over $70 million for Ethiopian famine relief.

July 19, Vice President George Bush announced that schoolteacher Christa McAuliffe would be aboard a future Challenger Space Shuttle Mission.

July 20 South Africa declared a state of emergency due to a Black civil uprising throughout the nation.

July 23, Commodore launched the Amiga personal computer.

July 25, it was announced that film star Rock Hudson had AIDS.

July 29-August 6, the nineteenth space shuttle mission Challenger 8 was launched.

August 2, a Delta Airlines flight crashed near Dallas and killed 137.

August 5, the building of a future Rock & Roll Hall of Fame in Cleveland was announced.

August 10, Michael Jackson purchased ATV Music and the rights to all the Beatles songs.

August13-19, there were large protests and unrest in South Africa

August 17, over 1,500 meat packers struck at the George Hormel Plant in Austin, Minnesota. Worker's safety and wage cuts were the primary issues. The local union P-9 defied their international union to strike. The strike went on for six months and the local union collapsed after the Minnesota Governor sent in the National Guard to protect the company and their scab labor. The strike divided the community for years to come.

August 20, more of the Reagan Administration's illegal arms were sent through Israel to Iran in exchange for hostages held in Lebanon. Iran made illegal cash payments to the Reagan Administration which were then money-laundered and went to illegally support the Contras in Nicaragua. Congress had previously banned any US support to the Contras.

August 27-September 3, the twentieth space shuttle mission Discovery 6, was launched.

August 28, the first restaurant smoking ban in the US was enacted in Aspen, Colorado.

September 1, a US and French expedition located the wreckage of the Titanic off Newfoundland.

September 2, Hurricane Elena stuck the gulf region of the US doing damage from Florida to Louisiana. It killed nine and destroyed $1.3 billion worth of property.

September 6, a Midwest Express Airlines flight crashed taking off from Milwaukee killing thirty-one.

September 9, over the Reagan administration's objections the US Congress implemented sanctions against South Africa for apartheid.

September 13, the soon to be popular Super Mario Bros game went on sale in the US.

September 16-October 2, Hurricane Gloria struck the US east coast and the Maritime Provinces of Canada. Eight were killed and over $900 million in property was destroyed.

September 17, Soyuz T-14 carried three cosmonauts to the Salyut 7 space station.

September 19, an earthquake in Mexico City killed over 10,000 and left over 250,000 homeless.

September 22, Willie Nelson, Neil Young and John Mellencamp organized the first Farm Aid concert to benefit distressed US farmers.

September 29, the first of the five victims of cyanide-laced Tylenol died. The poison had been put into the Tylenol container on a drug store shelf. This incident led to anti-tampering devices for products. The culprits were never caught.

October 3-7, the twenty-first shuttle mission Atlantis 1 was launched. This shuttle was a classified military mission.

October 7, 1985 the cruise ship Achille Lauro was boarded by four armed members of the Palestinian Liberation Front who took control of the ship near Egypt. They sailed the ship to Tartus, Syria and demanded the release of fifty Palestinians in Israeli prisons. When this was refused and they were denied permission to dock, they killed a disabled Jewish-American passenger and threw his body overboard. The ship headed back to Port Said where the hijackers agreed to abandon their control of the ship for safe passage to Tunisia in an Egyptian airliner. However, the airliner was intercepted by American jets who took it to Sicily where the Americans attempted to extradite the hijackers to the US to stand trial for murder. Italy refused to extradite the men and they were later were given safe passage to Yugoslavia after the Italians paroled them and they escaped. The incident damaged US-Italian relations.

October 12, the group, International Physicians for the Prevention of Nuclear War, received the Noble Peace Prize.

October 18, the first Nintendo home video game console went on sale and added to the new video game craze that swept the US.

October 26-November 1, Hurricane Juan was a very erratic tropical storm, it circled in the Gulf of Mexico and passed by Louisiana twice and caused damage mostly from flooding. It caused twelve deaths and $1.5 billion in damages before dissipating.

October 30-November 6, the twenty-second shuttle mission Challenger 9 was launched.

November 15, a package explosion by the Unabomber injured a research assistant at the University of Michigan.

November 18, the popular comic strip *Calvin & Hobbes* appeared for the first time.

November 19, President Reagan arrived in Geneva for meetings with Soviet leader Gorbachev.

November 20, Microsoft introduced Windows 1.0 changing how microcomputers were used by providing user friendly software.

November 23, CIA analyst Larry Wu-tai Chin was arrested in China as a spy.

November 26, President Nixon sold his autobiography to Random house for $3 million. Although Reagan claimed at the time that he had written it himself, it was actually written by ghost writer Richard G. Hubler.

Also November 26-December 3, the twenty-third shuttle mission Atlantis 2 was launched.

December 11, a man was killed by a bomb at a computer store in Sacramento, California. It was the work of the Unabomber.

December 12, a DC 8 crashed in Newfoundland killing 246 American servicemen who were serving as a peacekeeping force in the Sinai.

December 16, two Mafia bosses were killed in front of a steak house in New York City making John Gotti the undisputed boss of the powerful Gambino crime family.

December 24, on Christmas Eve a rightwing Christian extremist, David Lewis Rice, invaded a home in Seattle. He and beat and killed an attorney and his wife, mistakenly believing they were Jewish communists. He was caught and is still serving a life sentence.

December 27, naturalist Dian Fossey was found murdered in Rwanda.

December 31, singer, songwriter and actor Ricky Nelson was killed in a plane crash.

Because of all those caught and convicted for spying in 1985, it is called "The Year of the Spy." Also in 1985 DNA evidence was first used in a criminal case. The Aids disease spread forcing world blood supplies to be tested. Until this year babies were operated on without anesthetic believing that they felt less pain than adults.

The annual inflation rate was 3.55% and the interest rates remained high at 10.75%. The cost of a new house averaged $89,330 and an existing home at $75,500 and monthly rent $375. Average income was $22,200. The average price of a new car was $9,005 with $1.09 for a gallon of gas.

WrestleMania, now *WWE* made its debut with Hulk Hogan and Mr. T defeating Paul Orndorff and "Rowdy" Rodney Piper in the main match. In 1985 television VH1 and the Discovery Channel made their debuts on cable. Elmo made his first appearance on *Sesame Street* and *Nightline* broadcast from troubled South Africa. NBC became the first network television to use satellite broadcast to its affiliates and to introduce stereo sound. Shows making their debuts in 1985 included: *Moonlighting, Mr. Belvedere, National Geographic Explorer, Larry King Live, 227, The Golden Girls, The Equalizer, Spencer for Hire, Growing Pains, McGyver, and Amazing Stories*. Shows ending in 1985 included: *The Dukes of Hazard, V, Alice, Three's a Crowd, Family Feud* (returned in 1988), *The Jeffersons, The Jetsons* (returned in 1987) and *The Charlie Brown & Snoopy Show*.

The Cosby Show and *Cagney & Lacy* won for Best Comedy and Drama at the Emmys. Robert Guillaume in *Benson* and Jane Curtain in *Kate & Allie* won as Best Comedy Actors. William Daniels in *St. Elsewhere* and Tyne daily in *Cagney & Lacy* won for Best Dramatic Actors. Although Paul Michael Glazer was nominated but didn't win for Best Director of a Drama Series his *Miami Vice* episode, *Smuggler's Blues*, with its excellent music soundtrack is considered a classic.

The top songs of 1985 included: *Like a Virgin, Crazy for You, Angel, Dress You Up* and *Material Girl* by Madonna. *Careless Whispers* and *Wake Me Up Before You Go Go* by Wham, *I Want to Know What Love Is* by Foreigner, *Money for Nothing* by Dire Straits, *Take On Me* by a-ha, *Every Time You Go Away* by Paul Young, *We Built This City* by Starship, *Born in the USA* by Bruce Srpingsteen, *Power of Love* by Huey Lewis and the News, *Don't You (Forget About Me)* by Simple Minds, *The Heat is On, You Belong to the City* and *Smuggler's Blues* by Glenn Frey, *Boys of Summer* and *All She wants to Do is Dance* by Don Henley, *Shout* and *Head Over Heels* by Tears for Fears, *Sea of Love* by the Honeydrippers, *A View to Kill* and *Wild Boys* by Duran Duran, *We Belong,* by Pat Benatar, *Neutron Dance* by the Pointer Sisters, *Raspberry Beret* by Prince, *Summer of 69* by Bryan Adams, *Walking on Sunshine* by Katrina and the Wave, *Would I Lie to You?* by the Eurythmics, and *Private Dancer* by Tina Turner.

The Movies of 1985 included the top blockbusters: *Back to the Future, Rambo First Blood Part II, Rocky IV, The Color Purple, Out of Africa, Cocoon, The Jewel of the Nile, Witness, The Goonies, and Spies Like Us*. Other notable films: *The Breakfast Club, A View to Kill, St. Elmo's Fire, Peewee's Big Adventure, Mad Max Beyond Thunder Dome, Mask, The Last Dragon, Prizzi's Honor, Summer Rental, Kiss of the Spider Woman, The Trip to Bountiful* and *Agnes of God*. The Oscars for Best Picture and Director went to *Out of Africa*. Best Actor went to William Hurt for *Kiss of the Spider Woman* and Best Actress Geraldine Page for *The Trip to Bountiful*. Whoppi Goldberg won the Golden Globe Best Actress for *The Color Purple*.

In literature The Bollinger Prize for poetry went to John Ashbery and Fred Chapell. The most popular books were: *Lonesome Dove* by Larry McMurtry which won the Pulitzer Prize, *Maus: A Survivor's Tale* by Art Spiegelman, *The Cider House Rules* by John Irving, *A Handmaid's Tale* by Margaret Atwood, *The Polar Express* by Chris Van Allsburg, *Contact* by Carl Sagan, *Skeleton Crew* by Stephen King, *The Accidental Tourist* by Anne Tyler, *Galápagos* by Kurt Vonnegut Jr., *The Mammoth Hunters* by Jean Auel, *The Postman* by David Brin, *Texas* by James Michener, *Keys to Drawing* by Bert Dodson, *The Beet Queen* by Louise Erdrich, *Queer* by William Burroughs, *Footfall* by Larry Niven, *Lake Wobegon Days* by Garrison Keillor, and *Yeager, An Autobiography* by Chuck Yeager.

CHAPTER 42. 1986: THE CHALLENGER SHUTTLE DISASTER,
CHERNOBYL, THE IRAN-CONTRA SCANDAL AND THE CARTER
CENTER

January 1, Aruba gained its independence from the Netherlands.

January 7, the US announced economic sanctions against Libya for terrorism.

January 9, Kodak lost a patent battle with Polaroid and was forced to give up their instant camera business.

January 10, the tiny Pacific island nation of Palau signed a compact to become a US territory.

January 11, Douglas Wilder of Virginia became the first Black governor.

January 12-18, the twenty-fourth shuttle mission, Columbia 7, carried a crew of seven including the first Hispanic, Franklin Chang-Diaz, future NASA Administrator Charles Bolden, as well as the second member of Congress, Congressman Bill Nelson of Florida.

January 19, the first widespread computer virus, Brain, a program written by two Pakistani brothers, began to infect computers in the US and the United Kingdom.

January 20, the first Martin Luther King Day holiday was celebrated.

Also on January 20, the United Kingdom and France announced plans to construct a tunnel under the English Channel. It became known as "the Chunnel."

January 21, in a chilly 38 degrees Fahrenheit at Perdue University in West Lafayette, Indiana over 100 people participated in the "Nude Olympics and Naked Race." It was banned the following year because of cold weather health concerns.

January 23, the first inductees to the Rock & Roll Hall of Fame included: Elvis Presley, Chuck Berry, James Brown, Ray Charles, Buddy Holly, J.L. Lewis, Fats Domino and the Everly Brothers.

January 24, the space probe Pioneer began its encounter with Uranus discovering new moons.

January 28, the twenty-fifth shuttle Mission, Challenger 10, exploded 73 seconds after liftoff, killing all seven astronauts including school teacher Christa McAuliffe. A large television audience saw the shuttle explode live on television as it was widely televised in school rooms because of McAuliffe going into space. A later study showed that almost 17% of all Americans saw it live and a study showed that over 85% had seen the coverage or heard about the disaster within an hour. It resulted in the shuttle program being shut down for thirty-two months. Also as a result the USAF cancelled all plans to use the shuttle program for further military uses and chose to use the Titan IV program. It remains the worst disaster in the US space program.

February 3, Pixar animation studios opened in California.

February 7, Haitian President for Life Jean-Claude Duvalier, "Baby Doc," was deposed and forced to flee to France.

February 11, Iran began a new offensive against Iraq.

February 19, King Hussein of Jordan severed ties with the PLO.

Also on this date the USSR launched the Mir Space Station.

February 22-26, the People Power Revolution in the Philippines began which would eventually expel the dictator Ferdinand Marcos from power.

February 28, Swedish Prime Minister Olof Palme was assassinated in Stockholm walking home from a late movie with his wife. The murderer was described as a White male between 30 and 50 years of age. He gunned down Palme and left with the murder weapon. It was an assassination and not a robbery. There have been over 134 false claims by those who said they were the murderer. A drug addict was at one time convicted but that was overturned and the man was compensated for false imprisonment. The murder remains unsolved. In late 2016 a new investigation into his murder was undertaken by the government. Palme was a Social Democrat and widely was disliked by the Americans and the British for his neutrality in the Cold War and his strong support for neutral democratic socialist governments. Because of his harsh criticism of the US bombing of Hanoi during the Vietnam War, he caused a temporary freeze in US-Swedish diplomatic relations in 1972. He was a vocal critic of the US and the CIAs meddling in other governments. He was also a fierce critic of both communist and fascist dictators.

March 9, US Navy divers located the remains of the space shuttle challenger and all seven bodies of the astronauts.

March 13, in what now has become known as the Black Sea Incident, the US Navy cruiser the Yorktown and the destroyer Caron claimed the "right of innocent passage" in Soviet waters off Crimea. The incident raised tensions and placed both the US and USSR on a war alert.

Also on March 13, Soyuz T-15 carried the first two cosmonauts to the Mir Space Station.

March 14, the first public offering of Microsoft stock went on sale.

March 20, New York City passed its first legislation making it illegal to discriminate against gays and lesbians.

March 24, the US Navy and Libya clashed in the Gulf of Sidra. In the clash two Libyan ships, a patrol boat and a missile corvette were sunk and two others were damaged and 35 Libyan sailors were killed. The US suffered no casualties or damages. The US also knocked out several Libyan radar sites and damaged several surface to air missile sites.

March 26, an article in the *New York Times* charged that former UN Secretary General Kurt Waldheim was a Nazi war criminal.

April 1, world oil prices dropped below $10 dollars per barrel.

April 2, four US passengers were killed by a terrorist bomb at a TWA ticket counter in Athens.

April 3, the US debt rose to $3 trillion dollars.

April 5, two US soldiers and a Turkish woman were killed by a bomb at a disco club in West Berlin. Libyan terrorists were responsible.

April 8, Clint Eastwood was elected as Mayor of Carmel, California. Eastwood had decided to run for office when he became disgruntled and angry with city zoning laws that clashed with office buildings he was trying to build. His first act as Mayor was to disband the town's planning board.

April 11, in a heavy shoot-out in rural Miami-Dade between two bank robbers and FBI agents, two agents were killed and five wounded. The two robbers, highly trained former soldiers, were also eventually killed.

Also on April 11, Halley's Comet made its closest approach to earth on its eccentric 74 to79 year orbit.

April 13, the first child was born to a non-related surrogate mother.

April 14, Desmond Tutu was elected the Anglican Archbishop of South Africa.

Also on April 15, in Operation El Dorado Canyon, US naval aircraft struck five terrorist targets in Libya and killed fifteen people in response to the West Berlin disco club bombings.

April 16, in response to rumors that he had been killed by the US attacks Libyan leader Muammar Gaddafi appeared on television.

April 17, IBM introduced the first one megabit-chip.

April 18, Robert Gates became the Deputy Director of the CIA. He would become involved in the Iran-Contra scandal, but avoided prosecution and went on to be appointed CIA Director by President George H.W. Bush who also avoided prosecution in the scandal.

April 21, with a huge television build up and fanfare Geraldo Rivera opened Al Capone's "secret vault" on national television only to discover it was empty except for one bottle of bootleg liquor.

April 26, an explosion and fire at the Chernobyl Nuclear Power Plant near Pripyat, Ukraine, then part of the Soviet Union, killed thirty-one and caused radioactive fallout across much of Europe. Outside of the immediate vicinity, Belarus received the worst of the heavy fallout. In a radius of thirty kilometers over 117,000 people and their animals were evacuated within the first week in a because of the radiation. During the next sixteen years the permanent number of evacuees rose to over 350,000 as radiation tests showed other areas of extreme radiation contamination. In 2008 the UN determined that about 64 have died from cancers caused by the radiation and that in total about 4,000 deaths will be attributed to cancers caused by radiation from the accident. Later medical risk models showed this figure to be conservative and predicted deaths from cancer due to radiation exposure up to 41,000 by 2065 according to Greenpeace. An area of about nineteen miles out from the explosion was put into a permanent control zone where it is thought that it will not be safe for human habitation for the next 20,000 years.

Also on April 26, actor Arnold Schwarzenegger married Maria Shriver a member of the Kennedy family.

April 29, over 400,000 books were destroyed by a fire which reached two thousand degrees in the Los Angeles Central Library.

May 6, Donald Pelotte of Gallup, New Mexico, became the first Native American to be a Catholic Bishop.

May 7, Iraq attacked and bombed an Iranian oil refinery.

May 19, the racial violence spread in South Africa. The South African Army attacked the capitals of Botswana, Zimbabwe and Zambia in what military officials said was part of a continuing drive against the guerrillas of the African National Congress.

May 23, led by the Reagan Administration, the US and Western Europe vetoed heavier UN sanctions against South Africa.

Also on May 23, when the Somali President Said Barre went abroad for medical treatment for injuries from a car accident, a Somali opposition group sought to remove him from power which began the Somali Civil War. The war lasted until 1991 causing between 300,000 to 500,000 casualties and displaced over a million people. It sent the region into permanent decline.

May 25, Hands Across America saw 6.5 million people hold hands in a continuous human chain across the entire US. This charity event raised $34 million to fight hunger in Africa and homelessness in the US with people donating up to $10 for their place in the chain. The national event was later marred when the *New York Times* reported that only about $15 million, less than half of the money actually went to charities and that the majority of the money went to the organization USA for Africa, to pay for what they said were their salaries, overhead and operating costs for the event.

May 27, *Dragon Quest*, a Japanese game that developed the template for almost all future computer role playing games was released.

June 4, Jonathan Pollard a Navy Intelligence Analyst pled guilty to spying for Israel. He was later sentenced to life in prison. He was paroled in 2015.

June 8, alleged Nazi war criminal Kurt Waldheim was elected President of Austria.

Also on June 8, Israeli jets attacked Iran's Asadabad Satellite Station.

June 10, an extension of the three year long "state of emergency" was renewed for another year by the White South African Government causing more Black violence and unrest.

June 13, under pressure President Reagan criticized the South African state of emergency.

June 16, a nationwide strike was called in South Africa to protest the White government's actions.

June 23, LISTSERV, the first email management system was developed.

June 18, in defiance of President Reagan, the US House of Representatives approved a bill to impose stricter sanctions on South Africa.

June 23, House Speaker Tip O'Neill refused President Reagan's request to address the Congress. Reagan wanted to persuade them to approve funding for Nicaraguan Contras, but O'Neill said he would only approve an address to Congress if Reagan would answer their questions about Nicaragua and the Contras afterward. Reagan was unwilling to do so.

June 24, Guy Hunt became the first Republican Governor of Alabama in 112 years.

June 24, the US Senate approved Reagan's tax reform package.

June 27, the US informed New Zealand that it would no longer defend it against attack because of their legislation barring US nuclear powered or nuclear armed ships from docking in New Zealand.

Also on June 27, the World Court ruled that any US aid to the Contras was illegal.

July 1, the CSX Transportation Company was established. CSX is one of the largest railroads in the nation serving most of the East and South in the US as well as the Canadian provinces of Ontario and Quebec. It has 21,000 miles of track.

July 2, the US Supreme Court upheld affirmative action but not specific quotas.

July 5-20, the Goodwill Games were held in Moscow.

June 13, British athletes Zola Budd and Annette Cowley were banned from the Goodwill Games because of Britain's opposition to sanctions against South Africa.

July 23, Price Edward married Sarah "Fergie" Ferguson who then became the Duchess of York.

July 27, Iraqi jets attacked the Iranian city of Arak.

August 12, Iran fired missiles on an oil refinery in Bagdad and Iraq took Sirri Island from Iran disrupting Iranian oil exports.

August 20, a disgruntled postal worker in Edmond, Oklahoma shot fourteen of his co-workers before committing suicide.

August 21, a rare natural disaster, a limnic eruption, occurred at Lake Nyos in Cameroon which released a cloud of carbon dioxide gas from the bottom of the lake that killed over 1,700 people.

August 31, a Soviet passenger ship and a freighter collided in the Black Sea killing 398.

Also on this day a cargo ship, Khian Sea left Philadelphia carrying 14,000 tons of toxic waste. It wandered the seas for sixteen months, unable to find a port willing to accept its cargo which was eventually dumped in Haiti.

Also on this date, Gennadi Zakharov, a Soviet employee at the UN in New York was arrested for espionage.

September 2, Nicholas Daniloff, an American journalist, was arrested as a spy in Moscow. The two nations came to an arrangement to swap Daniloff for Gennadi Zakharov. In October the US expelled an additional 100 Soviet diplomats from the US as spies. The Soviets responded by expelling 10

US diplomats in the USSR and withdrew 260 Russian support staff who worked at the US Embassy in Moscow.

September 5, Pan Am Flight 73 was hijacked on the ground in Karachi, Pakistan by five Palestinian terrorists. The pilot and co-pilot were able to escape from a top hatch as the hijackers entered the plane. Their escape prevented the hijackers from forcing the plane off the ground. When the hijacker's demands were not met they killed an American passenger in front of negotiators. The airlines cut off negotiations immediately to prevent more deaths. The frustrated hijackers then decided to commit suicide by blowing up the plane and all on board. The attempt failed when most of the explosives failed to detonate. They then began firing on the passengers who began to escape through emergency exits assisted by flight attendants. When the hijackers ran out of ammunition the Pakistani Special forces captured the plane and took the hijackers into custody. The result was 43 killed and 120 injured with 336 survivors. The casualties were from fourteen different countries. The five hijackers were given death sentences which were later reduced to life in prison. The hijacker who executed the American was extradited to the US in 2001 where he is serving 160 years without parole. The four remaining hijackers in Pakistan escaped from prison in 2008. The FBI has a reward of $5 million for information leading to their capture.

September 12, and American professor, Joseph Cicippio was kidnapped in Beirut. He was mistreated and tortured for five years by Hezbollah until his release in 1991.

September 17, William Rehnquist was confirmed as the sixteenth Supreme Court Justice.

September 19, the drug ATZ became available for AIDS patients.

September 23, Congress selected the rose as the national flower of the US.

October 1, President Carter's Library was dedicated in Atlanta. The Carter Center, a foundation which partners with Emory University, was built adjacent. The Center has improved the lives of people in more than 80 countries by wiping out disease like the Guinea worm, observing and assuring over 103 fair and democratic elections in 39 countries, promoting and negotiating peace, establishing local health systems in poor countries, and promoting human rights. Although now in their nineties, the former President and Rosalynn Carter are active leaders at the center and its activities.

Also on this date the Goldwater-Nichols Act was signed into law. It increased the power of the Chairman of the Joint Chiefs of Staff and made clear the military chain of command. The act was in part in response to the US military's failed attempt to rescue the hostages in Iran in 1980. It was determined that inter-service rivalry between the Army, Navy and Air Force and a lack of a clear chain of command had greatly contributed to the mission's failure.

October, 3 a Soviet submarine, K-19, equipped with missiles and 34 nuclear warheads suffered an explosion and fire near Bermuda. Three Soviet sailors were killed. A fourth bravely died shutting down the nuclear reactor on the sub before it sank. Twenty-five sailors were rescued but two later died of health complications from the incident. In 1988 a Soviet research ship discovered the wreck at the bottom of the Atlantic and saw that the missile silos had been forced open and all the missiles and warheads had disappeared. The Soviets believe that the US Navy took their missiles and warheads.

October 5, *The London Times* reported that Israel was stockpiling nuclear weapons.

October 11-12, Soviet leader Mikhail Gorbachev and President Reagan met for talks about limiting the number of nuclear missiles in Reykjavik, Iceland.

October 14, the Nobel Peace Prize was awarded to Auschwitz survivor Eli Wiesel for his efforts to ensure that the Holocaust be remembered.

October 21, the Marshall Islands signed a compact becoming independent of the US.

October 24, Britain cancelled diplomatic relations with Syria.

November 3, the Lebanese magazine *Ash-Shiraa* reported that the Reagan Administration had sold illegal weapons to Iran to free seven American hostages held by pro-Iranian groups in Lebanon. It was the first report of what would become the Iran-Contra Scandal. It was also a violation of US policy and the World Court. It also broke an election promise Reagan made to never pay for hostages. The US Congress began to question the administration.

Also on this day the Federated States of Micronesia and the Northern Mariana Islands both signed compacts becoming independent of the US.

November 4, in the midterm elections the Democrats regained control of the US House of Representatives for the first time in six years.

November 11, Sperry Rand and Burroughs merged to form Unisys which became the second largest computer company.

November 13, after lying and vehemently denying any sale of illegal weapons to Iran, President Reagan went on national television and shocked the nation when he admitted that his administration had sold weapons to Iran for the release of hostages.

November 14, in his conviction for insider trading Ivan Boesky was given a prison sentence of three and a half years and fined $100 million. Boesky also cooperated with the Security Exchange Commission resulting in the arrest and conviction of Michael Milken, "the Junk Bond King" for fraud and insider trading. Milken would receive ten years in prison and a $600 million fine. Milken also cooperated with the SEC to implicate others and had his jail term later reduced to two years.

November 21, National Security Member Lt. Colonel Oliver North and his secretary Fawn Hall began shredding documents concerning the Reagan Administration's illegal sales of weapons to Iran and their illegal payments to the Contras in Nicaragua.

November 25, US Attorney General Edwin Meese admitted that proceeds from the sale of weapons to Iran went to illegally fund the Contra in Nicaragua.

November 26, Reagan insisted that he knew nothing about the Iran-Contra scandal and appointed former Senator John Tower, former Secretary of State Edmund Muskie, and National Security Advisor Brent Scowcroft to investigate the scandal. It became known as the Tower Commission. The final Tower report later concluded that Reagan was not involved in Iran-Contra but concluded that it was because the President was an absentee president and did not know any of the day to day events or the activities within his own administration and that it was quite likely that Reagan didn't know any of the policies or goals of his administration. It raised more concerns about Reagan's mental capacity.

November 28, Reagan fired Lt. Colonel Oliver North and his National Security Advisor Admiral John Poindexter for their roles in the Iran-Contra scandal.

December 1, the Musée d'Orsay opened in Paris in the former railroad depot. The museum houses the largest collection of impressionist paintings in the world.

December 11, South Africa censored the press.

December 15, the day before he was to testify before Congress about the Iran Contra scandal CIA Director William Casey suffered a cerebral seizure. He never recovered and died the following May.

December 16-19, protests in Almaty, Kazakhstan, called "Jeltoqsan," against the Soviet government erupted over the firing of a popular Kazakhstan leader. The Soviet military was sent in to stop the protests which then became violent. About 200 civilian protestors were killed, another 200 were wounded and about 5,000 were arrested. This event is sometimes seen as the first incident in the breakup of the Soviet Union.

December 19, Soviet physicist and dissident Andrei Sakharov was freed from internal exile.

December 20, the Howard Beach Racial Incident began when a mob of White teenagers in the Howard Beach neighborhood of Queens, New York began assaulting and beating three young Black men. One of the Black victims, Michael Griffith was struck and killed by a motorist while trying to escape.

December 24, Iran began an offensive against the Iraqi islands of Shatt al-Arab.

December 31, a fire in the DuPont Plaza Hotel in San Juan, Puerto Rico killed 97 and injured about another 140.

In 1986 smoking was banned from all forms of public transport including planes, trains and busses. The nicotine patch was invented to aid people to stop smoking. IBM unveiled the first laptop computer and email began with the development of the Internet Mail Access Protocol. The Human genome project began. Laser Tag and the American Girl Dolls were introduced.

Inflation slowed to 1.91% and interest rates fell to 7.5%. The average price of a new house rose to $89,430 with the price of the average existing home at $80,300. Monthly rents averaged $385. The average price of a new car was $9,255 and gas went to 93 cents per gallon.

Television in 1986 saw a merger of News Corporation and Metromedia creating the Fox Broadcasting Network. Metromedia had risen from the ashes of DuMont, the first television network. The NBC Peacock first debuted in May of 1986 and on June 2, regular coverage of the US Senate began on CSPAN. On May 16, Bobby Ewing, a popular character on *Dallas*, intrigued the nation when the show brought him back from the dead in the previous season by calling his death a dream.

Shows that made their debuts in 1986 included: *The Oprah Winfrey Show*, (previously the show had been a local Chicago show which went national in 1896), *Valarie* (later *The Hogan Family*), *Matlock, Perfect Strangers, It's Gary Shandling's Show, Our House, Pee-wee's Playhouse, Siskel & Ebert At the Movies, Head of the Class, Crime Story, LA Law, ALF, Sledge Hammer, Amen, Designing Women, My Sister Sam, The Cavanaughs*. Two shows, *The Hollywood Squares* and *Mama's Family* both returned after being gone for one season.

Shows ending included: *Different Strokes, Benson, The Fall Guy, Let's Make a Deal, Tic Tac Dough, The Love Boat, TJ. Hooker, The Merv Griffin Show, Knight Rider, The Paper Chase, Rip Tide, Trapper John MD*, and the long running soap opera *Search for Tomorrow* which debuted in 1951.

The Golden Girls won the Emmy for Best Comedy Show and *Cagney & Lacy* for Best Drama. Michael J Fox won as Best Comedic Actor in *Family Ties*, and Betty White won in *The Golden Girls*. William Daniels won Best Dramatic Actor in *St Elsewhere* and Sharon Gless in *Cagney & Lacy*.

The top songs of 1986 were dominated by women and included: *Take My Breath Away* by Berlin, *Papa Don't Preach, True Blue* and *Live to Tell* by Madonna, *These Dreams* and *Never* by Heart, *True Colors* by Cyndi Lauper, *Manic Monday* by the Bangles, and *How Will I Know* and *Greatest Love of All* by Whitney Houston. Other hits included: *Addicted to Love* by Robert Palmer, *West End Girls* by the Pet Shop boys, *Kiss* by Prince, *Sledgehammer* by Peter Gabriel, *Sara* by Starship, *When the Going Gets Tough the Tough Get Going* by Billy Ocean, *Danger Zone* by Kenny Loggins, *Walk of Life* by Dire Straits, *Living in America* by James Brown, *Small Town* by John Cougar Mellencamp, *Take Me home* by Phil Collins, and *Say You Say Me* by Lionel Richie.

The movies of 1986 included: *Platoon,Top Gun, Crocodile Dundee, The Karate Kidd II, Star Trek IV: The Voyage Home, Back to School, Aliens, The Golden Child, Ruthless People, Farris Bueller's Day Off, Room with a View, Hannah and Her Sisters, Children of a Lesser God, Mona Lisa, Crimes of the Heart, The Mission, Howard the Duck, Under the Cherry Moon, The Color of Money, Big trouble in Little China, Pretty in Pink, Little Shop of Horrors, 9½ Weeks, Hoosiers, Something Wild, Short Circuit, Peggy Sue Got Married, Heartbreak Ridge, About Last night, The Mosquito Coast, Down and Out in Beverly Hills, Clan of the Cave Bear* and *Iron Eagle*.

The Oscars went to *Platoon* for Best Picture and Director. Paul Newman won Best Actor in *The Color of Money*. Marlee Matlin won Best Actress in *Children of a Lesser God*. Michael Caine and Dianne Wiest won Best Supporting Actors both in *Hannah and Her Sisters* which won Woody Allen the Oscar for Best Original Screenplay. The Raspberry Awards had the Worst Picture as a tie between *Howard the Duck* and Prince's *Under the Cherry Moon*. Prince also won their Worst Director and Actor awards. Madonna won the Worst Actress award.

The books of 1986 included: *The Fatal Shore* by Robert Hughes, *The Prince of Tides* by Pat Conroy, *It* by Stephen King, *The Rising Storm* by Tom Clancy, *A Perfect Spy* by John Le Clarré, *The Blind Watchmaker* by Richard Dawkins, *The Bourne Supremacy* by Robert Ludlum, *The Making of the Atomic Bomb* by Richard Rhodes, *The Sportswriter* by Richard Ford, *Forrest Gump* by Winston Groom, *Strangers* by Dean Koontz, *Unlimited Power: The New Science of Personal Achievement* by Anthony Robbins, *Arctic Dreams* by Barry Lopez, *Whirlwind* by James Clavell, *Driving Miss Daisy* by Alfred Uhry, *The Complete Collected Poems* by Maya Angelou, *You Get So Alone at Times It Just Makes Sense* by Charles Bukowski and *Writing Down the Bones: Freeing the Writer Within* by Natalie Goldberg.

Chapter 43. 1987: More Iran Contra Scandal, Trouble in the Persian Gulf, and a National March for Gay and Lesbian Rights

January 3, Aretha Franklin became the first woman inducted into the Rock & Roll Hall of Fame.

January 4, an AMTRAK train collided with a Conrail engine in Chase, Maryland and killed 16 and injured 164 others. The train was moving at a speed of 108 MPH. The Conrail locomotive crew failed to stop at a signal and also tested positive for marijuana. The Conrail engineer served four years in prison.

January 5, amid a growing controversy concerning the aged president's ability to serve in office, Reagan underwent prostrate surgery.

January 6, the 100th Congress convened. One of its first acts was to form US Senate and House Committees to investigate the Iran-Contra Affair.

January 8, in their continued border wars, China fired about 60,000 artillery shells into Vietnam and launched fifteen divisions against four Vietnamese positions. The Vietnamese claimed to have killed over 1500 Chinese troops. The Chinese claimed to have killed 500 Vietnamese. Both sides claimed the other's reports were inflated.

January 20, hostage negotiator Terry Waite, an Anglican Church representative, was taken hostage while attempting to negotiate the release of hostages from Islamic Jihad. He was not released until 1991. He spent more than four years in captivity, most in solitary confinement.

January 21, blues greats B.B. King and Muddy Waters were inducted into the Rock and Roll Hall of Fame.

January 22, the Pennsylvania Treasurer, Budd Dwyer shot and killed himself at a press conference which was captured by television coverage. Dwyer had been indicted for bribery and fraud and at this press conference it was expected that he would resign.

February 4, President Reagan's veto of the Clean Water Act was overridden by Congress.

February 6, a smoking ban went into effect in all Federal buildings.

February 9, Reagan's National Security Advisor Robert "Bud" McFarlane attempted to commit suicide for his role in the Iran-Contra scandal saying that he "had failed his country." He was later convicted on four counts of lying to Congress in the scandal cover-up.

February 19, anti-smoking ads appeared on television for the first time. The first ads featured an appeal by actor Yul Brynner who died of lung cancer. Brynner had died a year previously and had expressed an interest in making the commercial upon his fatal diagnosis. His words were recorded in 1985 on the *Today Show*, "Now that I'm gone, I tell you: Don't smoke, whatever you do, just don't smoke."

February 20, the Unabomber set off a bomb in a Salt Lake City computer store injuring the owner.

February 27, Donald Regan, President Reagan's Chief of Staff was forced to resign for failing to contain the political fallout of the Iran-Contra scandal and the fall of Reagan's popularity. During the scandal the President's approval ratings from dropped from 67% approval to just 46% according to a *New York Times/CBS News* poll.

March 4, amid rapidly the deteriorating Iran-Contra scandal President Reagan went on television to admit that he had mislead the American people, "A few months ago I told the American people I did not trade arms for hostages. My heart and my best intentions still tell me that's true, but the facts and the evidence tell me it is not." He then claimed that he had no knowledge of the events and that these were "activities undertaken without my knowledge."

Eventually ten of Reagan's Administration officials, including the Secretary of Defense Casper Weinberger and Secretary of State Elliott Abrams were indicted. A White House secretary to aide Lt Colonel Oliver North, and his secretary Fawn Hall who had helped North destroy and shred documents in the cover up was given immunity for her cooperation. Six officials including Weinberger and Abrams were pardoned later by President George H.W. Bush. Vice President Bush was not indicted by the special prosecutor. However, according to a declassified National Security Archive Electronic Briefing Book No. 210 dated November 24, 2006, his diaries of the time show that he was a major player in the scandal. Bush wrote of the weapon sales that he was, "one of the few people that know fully the details."

March 9, American Motors was acquired by the Chrysler Corporation for $1.5 billion.

March 10, the Vatican announced the Catholic Church's formal opposition to test-tube fertilization and called on all governments to put strict limits on "medical interference in human procreation."

March 19, Reverend Jim Bakker the co-host with his wife Tammy Faye of the right-wing Christian television ministry *The 700 Club* and *The PTL Club* resigned when it was discovered that he had paid hush money from *PTL* church funds to Jessica Hahn, his former church secretary, to gain her silence for Bakker's allegedly drugging and raping Hahn. Bakker admitted to having sex with Hahn but denied the drug and rape allegations. Jerry Falwell then took over Bakker's lucrative ministry. Bakker was indicted for misuse of church funds, found guilty and sentenced to forty-five years in prison which was later reduced to eighteen. He served five years before being released.

March 30, Vincent Van Gogh's painting *Sunflowers* sold for $30.9 million to a Japanese business man. It was the highest price paid for a painting at that time.

March 31, British Prime Minister Maggie Thatcher did an interview with Soviet television.

April 7, the National Museum of Women in the Arts opened in Washington, DC.

April 13, in a battle between the oil companies Pennzoil and Texaco, a 1983 Texas jury ruled that Texaco must pay Pennzoil $8.53 billion for interfering with their purchase of the Getty Oil Company. Upon losing their appeals, Texaco, the nation's third largest corporation filed for Chapter 11 bankruptcy protection to allow them to pay the court award.

Also on April 13, Portugal agreed to return Macau to China in 1999.

Also on this date Senator Gary Hart of Colorado announced his intention to run for President in 1988. He was immediately considered to be the Democratic front runner.

April 20, Karl Linnas a former Nazi commandant of a concentration camp, who had been hiding in the US, was exported to the USSR to be sentenced to death as a war criminal. He had been living in New York as a surveyor until his discovery.

April 23, twenty-eight construction workers were killed in an apartment building collapse in Bridgeport, Connecticut.

April 27, the US Justice Department declared former UN Secretary General and Austrian President Kurt Waldheim an undesirable alien for his recently discovered Nazi war crimes. He was refused entry into the US and was persona non grata by the US the rest of his life.

May 3-8, *The Miami Herald* published a story of an affair between presidential candidate Gary Hart and a woman named Donna Rice. *The Herald* also reported that Senator Hart had spent the night and most of the following day with Rice in his Washington, DC townhouse. Hart, who was married, denied the affair as did Rice. On May 8, Hart suspended his campaign after he found out that the *Washington Post* was planning on publishing an account of an alleged affair with another woman. In December after these incidents had come to light Hart began his presidential campaign again but after significant losses in New Hampshire and the Super Tuesday primaries in early 1988 he dropped out of the race.

May 11, Nazi Gestapo war criminal Klaus Barbie, "the Butcher of Lyon," went on trial in Lyon, France. Barbie had been hiding in Bolivia and was extradited to France when he fell out of favor with the Bolivian government. He was convicted and sentenced to life in prison where he died in 1991.

May 16, Mobro 4000, a barge from New York carrying about 3,200 tons of garbage set sail to North Carolina to dump their cargo. When this was discovered by the press and North Carolina officials the barge was ordered to move on with its cargo. The barge sailed as far south as Belize without finding a port willing to accept its cargo. It returned to New York where after legal wrangling the entire barge was burned and its ashes buried where it had begun its journey.

May 17, the USS Stark, a guided missile frigate, was on patrol in the Persian Gulf when it was hit by two Exocet missiles fired from an Iraqi aircraft killing thirty-seven sailors and injuring twenty-one others. The ship didn't return fire. The incident was determined to be an accident. However it remains unknown if this is true. The Captain and Tactical Officer of the Stark were recommended for court-marital, but instead received letters of reprimand and both chose to retire.

May 22, a tornado hit Saragosa, Texas, a town with a population of about 180 people. The tornado killed thirty people and 121 were injured. It destroyed about 80% of the town, causing about $2.5 million in damages.

May 28, the final resting place of the sunken Civil War ship, the Monitor, was discovered by a deep sea robot.

Also on this date an eighteen-year-old West German pilot evaded Soviet air defenses in a small plane and landed in Red Square in Moscow. He was immediately arrested and held until August 1988.

May 29, singer Michael Jackson attempted to buy the remains of the Elephant Man.

May 30, the North American Phillips Company introduced the compact disc video player.

June 8, New Zealand was declared a nuclear free zone.

Also on June 8, after given immunity from prosecution, Oliver North's secretary, Fawn Hall, testified in the Iran-Contra hearings that she and other Reagan Administration officials had hid and destroyed many documents to cover up the Iran-Contra scandal.

June 11, a powerful 5.0 earthquake struck in Lawrenceville, Illinois and was felt in sixteen states and southern Ontario. The quake triggered alarms at the Prairie Island Nuclear Power Plant in Red Wing, Minnesota.

June 12, in the midst of the Iran-Contra scandal, President Reagan needed a popularity boost and appealed to his base by making a speech in West Berlin in front of the Brandenburg gate where he demanded that Soviet leader, Mikhail Gorbachev, "Tear down this wall!"

June 18, an ABC journalist Charles Glass was kidnapped in Lebanon and held for 62 days. He managed to escape in August.

June 19, the US Supreme Court ruled that Louisiana schools teaching evolution do not also have to teach the Christian Creation Theory as then required by the state's law.

June 22, the International Labor Organization meeting in Geneva called for a boycott of South African minerals to punish the White Apartheid government.

June 25, despite strong Jewish and other protests, Pope John Paul II received the Nazi war criminal and Austrian President Kurt Waldheim. Despite the refusal of the US and other diplomats from around the world to participate, the Pope insisted his past be forgiven and that Waldheim should now be received as a diplomatic world leader. The Pope in recognizing Waldheim, who was catholic, rekindled the realization that the Vatican supported the Nazis in Italy and Germany in WWII and reawakened the world to their role in the Ratlines that covered up Nazi crimes and smuggled Nazi war criminals out of Germany at the War's conclusion.

June 28, the Iraqi government dropped mustard gas on an Iranian town. It is the first use of chemical weapons on civilians.

Also on this day, three U.S. troops were killed in an accidental explosion while training in West Germany.

July 1, Robert Bork, a conservative legal scholar who fired the Special Watergate Prosecutor Archibald Cox for Nixon during the Watergate cover-up, was nominated by President Reagan as a Supreme Court Justice. His nomination was rejected by the US Senate in October.

July 7, the Kiwanis Club ended their men only membership requirement.

July 9, Lt. Colonel Oliver North admitted at the Iran-Contra hearings that he and others had destroyed evidence to cover up the scandal.

July 11, the UN announced that the world's Population had reached five billion.

July 12, for the first time in 20 years a Soviet delegation arrived in Israel.

July 17, Iran and France broke off diplomatic relations.

July 22, Soyuz TM-3 was launched with three cosmonauts, two Russians and one Syrian.

Also on July 22, US warships began escorting Kuwaiti oil tankers in the Persian Gulf.

July 25, US Secretary of Commerce Malcolm Baldrige Jr. died of injuries sustained in a rodeo accident when his horse fell on him in a calf-roping competition.

July 31, a clash between Saudi forces and Shia pilgrims in Mecca resulted in over four hundred Shia deaths and thousands of wounded. The clash was seen as a result of growing tensions between Saudi backed Sunni Muslims and Iranian backed Shia Muslims.

August 4, the Federal Communications Commission, with three Reagan appointees and one hold over appointee from Nixon ended the Fairness Doctrine for broadcasters which had been in effect since 1949. The doctrine was ended because of pressure by the Reagan Administration. The doctrine provided that television and radio stations must reserve air time to present controversial public issues and that these issues should be presented in a fair, accurate and equal manner assuring air time for each opposing argument.

The end of the Fairness doctrine has been considered by some historians as one of the causes for the polarization of American political parties and thought. The end of the Fairness Doctrine left television and radio free from having to report both sides fairly or truthfully. In June Congress attempted to codify the Fairness Doctrine assuring its survival and forcing the FCC to continue to enforce it, but the legislation was vetoed by President Reagan. Another attempt was made in 1991 but was abandoned when President Bush threatened to veto any legislation to bring back the Fairness Doctrine. Since this time news organizations and networks have become political and are in some cases promoting certain candidates, parties or political ideologies and presenting opponents unfairly or inaccurately. There is no requirement for television news to be truthful or accurate.

August 11, Donald Harvey, a nurses' aide, was being interrogated by the police in a suspicious death of a patient and suddenly admitted to what he claimed were 87 "mercy killings." The police verified that Harvey killed between 37 and 57 patients under his care from 1970-1987 in various health facilities. He had a nickname at the hospital as "the Angel of Death" because he always seemed to be with a patient when they died. He was sentenced to life in prison in both Ohio and Kentucky where he was killed by another prisoner in 2017.

Also on August 11, Britain and France sent minesweepers to the Persian Gulf to assure safe waters for international shipping.

And on this date Alan Greenspan, who disliked bank regulations, became the nation's top bank regulator as Chairman of the Federal Reserve. He believed banks could regulate themselves which was proven flase in the 2007-2008 economic collapse and he was forced to apologize to Congress.

August 16-24, an astrological event called Harmonic Convergence was organized by some New Age astrologists when eight planets were aligned, in what is called a grand trine, which according some New Age astrological interpretations of Mayan and Aztec cosmology would cause concentrations of psychic power at certain places that were said to be power centers. The New Age astrologers believed that with the force of meditation during this alignment, the world could be changed from war-like to peaceful and from confrontation to cooperation. On this day astrologists organized 144,000 to assemble and meditate near thirty-six designated power centers around the world. They believed this was enough to shift the world from war to peace. At one of these designated power centers, Chaco Canyon National Park in New Mexico, the Associated Press predicted between 5,000 to 20,000 people would come to meditate for the event. It was reported that campgrounds at and near Mt. Shasta in California were also completely booked. Events were also planned in Colorado, South Dakota, and Texas. Michael Coe an expert on Mayan culture at Yale called these New Age interpretations "totally crackpot."

Also on August 16, a Northwest Airline flight crashed on takeoff from Detroit Metropolitan Airport killing 155 of 156 people aboard. The lone survivor was a four-year-old girl.

August 17, the Deputy Fhrer of the Third Reich, Rudolph Hess, the lone prisoner left from the Nuremburg Trials was found dead in what appeared to be a suicide by hanging. He was 93 and in frail health at the time of his death and his family and attorney believed he was incapable of the act and that he was murdered by British Intelligence Agents because he had threatened to reveal British misdeeds during the war. His assigned medical orderly at the time also believed Hess was murdered. Although the British investigated these claims and found no proof, a 2012 report again raised more unanswered questions about his suspicious death.

September 2, real estate mogul Donald Trump took out full page ads addressed "To the American People" in the *New York Times, The Boston Globe* and *The Washington Post.* The ads which cost more than $94,000 were made after Trump's business visit to the Soviet Union and his meeting with Soviet leader Mikhail Gorbachev. A few years earlier Trump had offered himself to Reagan as a nuclear arms negotiator but was rebuffed and he became angry at the President. In the ad he said, "There's nothing wrong with America's Foreign Defense Policy that a little backbone can't cure." And: "For decades, Japan and other nations have been taking advantage of the United States." He said that the US should send a bill to Japan, Germany and other allies to pay for the defense of their nations by the United States. The letter concluded, "Let's not let our great country be laughed at anymore." Trump later went to Portsmouth, New Hampshire where he threatened to run for President as a Republican in 1988.

September 7, the Netherlands sent a minesweeper to the Persian Gulf to help keep the shipping lanes open.

September 10-19, because of harsh criticism from the US, including many US Catholics for the Papal audience with Nazi criminal Kurt Waldheim, Pope John Paul II visited nine cities in the US. It was his fourth trip to the US, however two of those four previous visits were just stopovers in Alaska on his journey to other places. This was his second significant visit to the US since 1979 when he visited seven US cities and met with President Carter.

September 17, the US celebrated 200 years of the US Constitution in Philadelphia.

Also on September 17, televangelist and conservative Christian Pat Robertson announced that he would run as a Republican for president in the 1988 election.

September 21, Belgium sent a minesweeper to the Persian Gulf.

October 1, a 5.9 earthquake struck Southern California killing eight and injuring about two hundred and destroyed about $318 million in property. The quake destroyed or severely damaged 636 homes and 3,387 apartments.

October 4, an early snow storm hit New York and New England dropped as much as a foot of snow in some areas. Over 300,000 homes lost power during the storm.

October 11, protesting inaction by the Reagan Administration in the AIDS crisis, the Supreme Court's action in upholding state laws criminalizing gay sex, and the Reagan Administration's lack of support for gay rights, a National March for Gay and Lesbian Rights was held in Washington, DC. Although organizers and the media projected a crowd of 200,000 protesters, the District of Columbia Police estimated the crowd to actually have been about three quarters of a million people. Speakers included: Caesar Chavez, Jesse Jackson and Whoopi Goldberg. A year later to commemorate the March National Coming Out Day was established.

October 13, Vice President George H.W. Bush announced that he would seek the Republican nomination for President in 1988.

October 14-16, in Midland, Texas, a one and a half-year-old girl, Jessica McClure fell twenty feet down a narrow well. CNNs live coverage and the large audience attracted to the fifty-eight hour rescue made "Baby Jessica" famous. In 1989 ABC made a movie about the accident. With the new age of the twenty-four hour news cycle nearly every story of some significance now played on the television news networks.

October 17, Nancy Reagan underwent a radical mastectomy due to breast cancer.

October 19, an event now called Black Monday occurred when stock markets around the world crashed. The Dow Jones Industrial Average fell 508 points losing over 22% of its value in one day. The crash led to reforms of the financial markets and to Executive Order 12631 in 1988 creating the President's Working Group on Financial Markets, called more frequently the "Plunge Protection Team." This secret group is made up of the Secretary of the Treasury, the Chairman of the Federal Reserve and the Chairman of the Commodities trading Futures Commission. These three people may order banks or any other private entities on behalf of the US government to buy or sell stocks, real estate or any commodities they believe necessary to keep the financial markets from collapsing in crisis. Their work and actions are secret. Many think it was the plunge Protection Team that saved the markets from complete collapse after the 1998 Dot-com bubble crash and the financial 2007-2008 crash.

October 18, after Iran attacked a Kuwaiti oil tanker in the Persian Gulf, the US in retaliation sank two Iranian oil platforms.

November 5, an iceberg as large as Rhode Island broke off from Antarctica raising concerns about global warming.

November 11, Judge Anthony Kennedy was nominated to the Supreme Court.

Also on November 11, another record art sale occurred when Van Gogh's painting *Irises* sold for $53.6 million at auction. It was highest price ever paid for a work of art.

Also on this date the Veterans Day Snow Storm stuck Washington, DC and parts of Maryland dumping over a foot of snow.

November 12, the first Kentucky Fried Chicken opened in China near Tiananmen Square in Beijing.

November 15, in Brasov, Romania workers rioted against the communist government.

November 18, the US House and Senate released their reports about the Iran-Contra Scandal. The reports charged President Reagan with "the ultimate responsibility" for the crimes of his administration.

November 24, the Czechoslovakian Party collapsed and the entire Presidium resigned.

December 1, NASA announced the awarding of contracts to four aerospace companies that would help build Space Station Freedom.

December 2, the US Supreme Court heard the arguments for *Hustler Magazine Inc. v Falwell*. The reverend Jerry Falwell had sued the magazine for a humorous satirical interview depicting him talking about an incestuous relationship with his mother while drunk. The Supreme Court later ruled in favor of Hustler magazine. They found that under the precedent of *Sullivan v New York Times* that Falwell was a public figure subject to political satire and that finding against the magazine would violate their first amendment rights, particularly since any reasonable person would not find the satire believable.

December 7, a disgruntled passenger aboard a Pacific Southwest Airlines flight over Paso Robles, California shot and killed his ex-supervisor on the flight and then killed both pilots. The plane crashed killing all forty-three on the flight.

December 8-10, a Cold War meeting between President Reagan and Mikhail Gorbachev at the White House was held. Both men were suffering from political setbacks at home. Reagan had a stale economy with a faltering stock market and the Iran-Contra Scandal. Gorbachev was experiencing problems with the Politburo and his one-time ally, Boris Yeltsin, who resigned from his government and then severely criticized Gorbachev. The two men sought to negotiate an arms limitations treaty to bolster their sagging images with their constituencies. The Intermediate Range Nuclear Forces Treaty was signed. It eliminated all short range nuclear missiles. By 1991 2,692 missiles were eliminated.

December 8, the Intifada, an uprising of Palestinians in Gaza and on the West Bank against Israel erupted. It was an organized boycott of Israeli businesses, strikes and acts of civil disobedience to protest Israeli treatment of the Palestinians. The protests frequently became violent with both sides blaming the other. In the first 13 months 322 Palestinians were killed by Israeli military and police while only 12 Israelis were killed. Between 23,000 and 30,000 Palestinian children required treatment from beatings in the first two years. The Intifada lasted over five years until September 13, 1993. Over 1,962 Palestinians died compared to 277 Israelis.

December 21, Soyuz TM-4 sent three cosmonauts to the Mir space station.

December 23, Annette "Squeaky" Fromme, a member of the Charles Manson Family who had been imprisoned for the assassination attempt on President Gerald Ford escaped from prison in West Virginia. She was recaptured December 25, and incarcerated in Ft. Worth, Texas.

In other 1987 events the birth rates in the Soviet Union began to fall quickly. Nike pioneered a new athletic shoe, the Nike Air Max. Photoshop was developed by Thomas and John Knoll. The first Starbucks coffee shops were opened outside of Seattle in Vancouver and Chicago. Disposable contact lenses went on sale. The drug Fluoxetine, marketed as Prozac, was approved by the FDA for use as an anti-depressant. A mite called Varroa destructor invaded the US and attacked honey bees and causing hive collapse.

The first legal case testing and ruling upholding the validity of Surrogacy took place in New Jersey over the rights of a child called "Baby M." The US population was estimated just under 245 million.

Gold went to $486.50 per ounce. Yearly inflation was 3.66%. Interest rates were at 8.75%. Average income was $25,300. The average price of a new house was $92,000 and $85,500 for an existing home, with average monthly rents at $395. The average price of a new car was $10, 355 with gas at 89 cents per gallon.

In television for the first time since 1955 and the demise of the DuMont network there were four networks with prime time programming as Fox joined ABC, CBS and NBC in April. Fox showed the first *Simpsons* cartoons which were shorts that had appeared on the *Tracy Ullman Show* before they were spun off as a prime time feature. Shelley Long who played Diane on *Cheers* left the show causing fans to wonder if the show would continue. The show continued successfully until 1993. The show had a history of replacing key popular characters as it did when Nicholas Colasanto who played the bartender Coach died in 1985 and was replaced by Woody Harrelson as Woody Boyd the new bartender. PBS premiered its critically acclaimed series *Eyes on the Prize* about the US Civil Rights movement.

Shows making their debuts in 1987 included: *Unsolved Mysteries, Rescue 911, Houston Knights, Rags to Riches, The Bronx Zoo, The Bold and the Beautiful, Max Headroom, Married with Children, The Tracy Ullman Show, 21 Jump Street, Duet, Mr. President, The Days and Nights of Molly Dodd, Geraldo, Frank's Place, Wiseguy, Out of This World, My Two Dads, Full House, Hooperman, The Slap Maxwell Story, A Different World, Tour of Duty, Jake and the Fat Man, Star Trek: The Next Generation, thirtysomething*, and *Teenage Mutant Ninja Turtles.*

Shows ending their runs included: *Too Close for Comfort, the Love Boat, Silver Spoons, The A Team, Capitol, Remington Steele, Give Me a Break!, Fame, Hill Street Blues, The Scarecrow & Mrs. King, The PTL Club*, and *The Jetsons.*

At the Emmys *The Golden Girls* won Best Comedy and *LA Law* the Best Drama series. Micheal J. Fox and Rue McClanahan won as Best Comedy Actors in *Family Ties* and *The Golden Girls* respectively. Bruce Willis in *Moonlighting* and Sharon Gless in *Cagney & Lacy* won as the Best Dramatic Actors.

The popular tunes of 1987 included more big hits for women: *Walk Like an Egyptian* by The Bangles, *Open Your Heart, Who's That Girl, La Isla Bonita and Causing a Commotion* by Madonna, *I Wanna Dance With Somebody Who Loves Me and Didn't We Almost Have It All?* by Whitney Houston, *Alone and Who Will You Run To* by Heart, *I think We're Alone Now* by Tiffany, *Only in My Dreams* by Debbie Gibson, *Luka* by Susanne Vega, *I heard a Rumor* by Banarama, and *Change of Heart* by Cyndi Lauper. Duets were also popular: *I've Had the Time of My Life* by Bill Medley and Jennifer Warnes, *The Next Time I Fall* by Pete Cetera and Amy Grant and *Somewhere Out There* by Linda Ronstadt and James Ingram. Other hits included: *Bad* by Michael Jackson, *You Got to Fight for Your Right to Party* by the Beastie Boys, *Is this Love* by Survivor, *Rhythm is Going to Get You* by Gloria Estefan and the Miami Sound Machine, *Stand by Me* by Ben E. King, *Carrie* by Europe, *Hip to Be Square, Jacobs Ladder* and *Doing It All for My Baby* by Huey

Lewis and the News, *Keep Your Hands to Yourself* by The Georgia Satellites, *Lean On Me* by Club Nouveau, *The Lady in Red* by Chris de Burgh, *Mony Mony* by Billy Idol, *With or Without You* and *I Still Haven't Found What I'm Looking For* by U2, and *Respect Yourself* by Bruce Willis.

The top grossing movies of 1987 included: *Three Men and a Baby, Fatal Attraction, Beverly Hills Cop II, Good Morning Vietnam, Moonstruck, The Untouchables, The Secret of My Success, Stakeout, Lethal Weapon, and The Witches of Eastwick.* Other 1987 films included: *The Princess Bride, Robocop, Predator, The Lost Boys, Full Metal Jacket, The Running Man, Dirty Dancing, Overboard, La Bamba, The Last Emperor, Empire of the Sun, Broadcast News, Adventures in Baby Sitting, Roxanne, Harry and the Hendersons, Planes Trains and Automobiles, Wall Street,* and *Some Kind of Wonderful.*

At the Oscars *The Last Emperor* won Best Picture and Director. Michael Douglas won Best Actor for *Wall Street*. Cher won Best Actress for *Moonstruck*.

In 1987 literature Russian-American poet, Joseph Brodsky won the Nobel Prize for Literature. *A Summons to Memphis* by Peter Taylor won the Pulitzer Prize for Fiction and August Wilson won the Pulitzer Drama Prize for *Fences*. Other 1987 books included: *Beloved* by Toni Morrison, *Bon Fire of the Vanities* by Tom Wolfe, *The Closing of the American Mind* by Allan Bloom, *Patriot Games* by Tom Clancy, *Misery* and *The Tommy Knockers* by Stephen King, *And the Band Played On* by Randy Shilts, *Sarum* by Edward Rutherford, *The Rise and Fall of Great Powers* by Paul Kennedy, *The Rules of Attraction* by Bret Easton Ellis, *Spy Catcher* by Peter Wright, *Windmills of the Gods* by Sidney Sheldon, *Not Without My Daughter* by Betty Mahmoody, *Trump: The Art of the Deal* by Donald Trump and Tony Schwartz, *The Black Dahlia* by James Elroy, *The Cat Who Played Brahms* and *The Cat who Played Post Office* by Lilian Jackson Brown, *Fried Green Tomatoes at the Whistle Stop Café* by Fannie Flagg, *Postcards from the Edge* by Carrier Fisher, *Watchmen* by Allan Moore, *Sphere* by Michael Crichton, *Outbreak* by Robin Cook, *Weaveworld* by Clive Barker, and *A Brief History of Time* by Stephen Hawking.

CHAPTER 44. 1988: THE 1988 ELECTION, THE S&L SCANDAL, AND RECORD SALES IN ART WORKS

January 2, in response to growing economic concerns in the Soviet Union Mikhail Gorbachev initiated perestroika, a series of economic reforms.

Also on January 2, an Ashland Oil tank ruptured and spilled 3.8 million gallons of oil in Pennsylvania.

In another event on this day the Canada-US Free Trade Agreement was signed.

January 7-8, in the Afghan War 39 Soviet airborne troops fought off an attack by about 250 Mujahideen on hill 3234. A Russian film was later made about this event.

January 8, Governor Evan Mecham of Arizona was indicted on three counts of perjury, two counts of fraud, and one count of failing to report a campaign contribution. A special prosecutor reported his findings to the Arizona House which on February 8, voted to impeach Mecham. On April 4, he was convicted by the Arizona Senate for misusing public funds and removed as governor.

January 11, amid some doubt, the USSR stated they would participate in the Seoul Summer Olympics.

January 15, at a Muslim sacred site in Jerusalem, Israeli police clashed with Muslims and injured seventy.

Also on January 15, CBS television's pro football odds maker, Jimmy "the Greek" Snyder, made on-air racist remarks about NFL Black players and lost his job the next day.

January 16, Czech dissident Válcav Havel was arrested in Prague for protesting the communist government.

January 21, the Amerasian Homecoming Act allowed 30,000 Vietnamese children, the prodigy of American military men serving in Vietnam, and their mothers and siblings, to come to America.

January 25, Vice President George Bush was unpopular with much of the Republican base, so to shore up his support he resorted to pull off a dramatic deception on live television. The Vice President and his aides had agreed in advance that Rather could ask questions about Iran–Contra. During the interview, however, George Bush attacked and yelled at Rather, claiming on-air that Rather and CBS had assured him these "past issues" would not be raised. It was also Bush and his campaign that insisted the interview be broadcast live, so that he could ambush Rather and prove to his Republican base that he (Bush) was not a pushover. Rather was unpopular with Republicans, which also helped Bush generate sympathy and support.

February 3, the US House once again rejected Reagan's request of over $36 million for the Contras.

February 4, Panamanian strongman General Manuel Noriega was indicted by a US Federal Grand Jury in Miami for drug trafficking and racketeering. Noriega's defense was that he had been working for the CIA and the US government and claimed that Vice President Bush and others were aware of and supported his activities.

February 8, in the Republican Iowa Presidential Caucuses the results were Senator Bob Dole 37%, 25% for Christian Conservative Pat Robertson, and only 19% for George Bush. It was a stunning loss for the sitting Vice President. The Democratic results were: Senator Dick Gephardt 31%, Senator Paul Simon had 27%, and Governor Michael Dukakis 22%.

February 10, a three judge panel of the 9th US Circuit Court of Appeals in San Francisco struck down the US Army's ban against homosexuals serving in the Army. It was overturned upon appeal.

February 13-28, the Winter Olympics were held in Calgary, Canada.

February 16, the Democratic Primary results in New Hampshire were 36% for Dukakis, about 20% for Gephardt, and about 17% for Simon. On the Republican side Vice President Bush won with about 38%, Dole had 28%, with 13% for Congressman Kemp.

February 17, US Lt. Colonel William Higgins serving as a UN Truce Observer was kidnapped in Lebanon. He was later killed by his captors.

February 20-March 1, in the Caspian seaside city of Sumgait in Azerbaijan, ethnic clashes broke out between Azerbaijanis and Armenians resulting in a pogrom which targeted the minority Armenian population. There were widespread beatings, rapes and murders and the looting of Armenian homes by gangs of Azerbaijani. The Soviet Military had to quell the riots with tanks and troops to stop the pogrom.

March 6-13, Gallaudet University, established by Congress in 1864 to serve the deaf, selected a hearing person as university president over several well-qualified deaf candidates. The University had never had a deaf president. The University Board of Trustees claimed that the public was not ready for a deaf president with the Board Chair saying as she announced the choice, "The deaf are not yet ready to function in the hearing world." The students and some faculty began a protest that shutdown the campus until their demands were met, one of which was to appoint a deaf president.

The protest ended in celebration when I. King Jordan, became the first deaf university president.

March 9, in the Super Tuesday Primaries which included the state primaries of Texas, Florida, Tennessee, Louisiana, Oklahoma, Mississippi, Kentucky, Alabama, and Georgia, Vice President Bush beat Senator Dole solidifying his lead as the Republican nominee for president. On the Democratic side the states split between Dukakis, Gephardt, Al Gore and the Reverend Jesse Jackson who won in Georgia, Louisiana and Mississippi. These wins placed Jackson in second place overall behind Dukakis.

March 15, Eugene Moreno of Atlanta became the first Black Catholic Archbishop in the US.

Also on March 15, NASA reported the rapid break down of the ozone layer due to chlorofluorocarbons, (CFCs) marketed as "Freon" used in refrigeration, air conditioning units and as aerosol propellants in spray cans.

March 16, the Halabja Massacre occurred when Iraq used chemical weapons on the Kurdish town of Halabja in Northern Iraq. The Iraqi Army attacked the civilian population and killed somewhere between 3,200 to 5,000 inhabitants and injured another 7,000 to 10,000. The Kurds with the support from Iran were attempting to separate from Iraq.

Also on March 16, the First Republic Bank of Texas failed. It was at the time the largest FDIC bank failure.

Also on this date Lt. Colonel Oliver North and Admiral John Poindexter. were indicted for their crimes in the Iran-Contra scandal.

March 22, after a four year effort by Republicans to roll back civil rights laws, Congress passed The Civil Rights Restoration Act of 1987. Reagan vetoed the act. On this date Congress overrode his veto to make the act law.

March 24, a McDonalds opened in Belgrade, Yugoslavia. It was the first in a communist country.

March 25, a candlelight mass demonstration was held against the communist government in Bratislava, Slovakia.

March 26, Jesse Jackson won the Michigan Democratic primary temporarily becoming the front runner over Dukakis. Dick Gephardt withdrew after a poor showing.

April 5, Dukakis won the Wisconsin primary becoming the Democratic front runner again. It was a lead which took him to the nomination.

April 9, the US announced it would place economic sanctions on Panama.

April 12, rock singer Sonny Bono was elected the Mayor of Palm Springs, California.

April 14, the Geneva Accords were signed to settle the conflict in Afghanistan. The USSR announced that it would withdraw all Soviet troops from Afghanistan.

Also on April 14, the USS Samuel B. Roberts while on escort duty in the Persian Gulf struck an Iranian mine. On April 16, the US retaliated by striking two Iranian oil platforms, sinking a frigate, a gun boat, three speed boats and damaging another frigate.

April 23, a federal ban on smoking during domestic flights of two hours or less went into effect.

May 2, the Jackson Pollack painting, *Search,* sold for $4,800,000
May 3, Jasper Johns' painting, *Diver,* sold for $4,200,000.
May 4, the PEPCON rocket plant in Henderson, Nevada exploded. Two people were killed and 372 were injured. The blast was felt ten miles away and did over $100 million in damages.
May 10, Edgar Degas' painting, *Danseresje of 14,* was sold for $10,120,000.
May 14, "the Singing Revolution" began. It would last four years until the Baltic States got their independence from the Soviet Union. On this date thousands of Estonians in Tallinn gathered to sing forbidden patriotic Estonian national songs to protest the Soviet-backed communist government.
Also on May 14, a drunk driver going the wrong way on Interstate 71 near Carrollton, Kentucky killed 27 people on a bus in a church youth outing.
May 16, a report by the Surgeon General C. Everett Koop stated that nicotine has the same addictive properties as heroin and cocaine.
May 29-June 3, the Moscow Summit was held between Reagan and Gorbachev in Moscow, which ratified the Intermediate Range Nuclear Force Treaty.
June 5, the Russian Orthodox Church celebrated its 1,000th Anniversary.
June 6, Vice President Bush in a campaign speech promised to make reparations to Japanese victims of internment during WWII. After his election, he reneged on this promise.
June 7-September 5, Soyuz TM-5 sent three cosmonauts to the Mir Space Station.
June 11, at an event in London called Freedomfest to celebrate the 70th birthday of the antiapartheid leader Nelson Mandela was seen by 600 million worldwide as rock and music stars from the US and Britain entertained the audience. Fox, the new conservative American television network, heavily censured the political aspects of the event and was criticized for its coverage.
June 14, a series of small wildfires spread into Yosemite National Park, becoming a large fire which burned for months. On September 8, the Park was closed for the first time in its history due to the fires. The fires were finally extinguished in late September. Almost 794,000 acres, about 36% of the park was burned.
June 23, NASA scientist James Hansen testified to the US Senate that man-made climate change due to carbon emissions had begun.
June 25, in a summer heat wave Cleveland set an all-time high temperature of 104 degrees Fahrenheit.
June 28, an accident in a metal plating plant in Auburn, Indiana exposed workers to poisonous gases killing five.
June 29, in *Morrison v Olson* the US Supreme Court upheld the law that allows special prosecutors to investigate crimes by White House and executive branch officials. This ruling would become important in the Trump Administration investigations of 2017.
July 1, as the Soviet economy began to disintegrate, the Communist Party of the Soviet Union voted to end their monopoly over the Soviet economy in favor a market based economy.

July 3, an Iranian passenger flight from Tehran to Dubai was misidentified by a US guided missile cruiser and shot down killing 290 passengers and crew. The crew had made ten attempts at contacting the plane on the civilian radio frequencies and fired when they received no response. In 1996 the US and Iran came to an agreement in the International Court of Justice and the US agreed to pay the victims' families $61.8 million.

July 6, in the middle of a heat wave in the Northeast the beaches at Coney Island, Brooklyn and in Monmouth County New Jersey were awash in medical waste including syringes that were possibly contaminated with the aids virus. The beaches in the area had to be closed despite the heat do to these bio-hazards. The medical waste was eventually traced to Fresh Kills landfill on Staten Island. The incident cost the area about $7.7 million in lost tourist revenues for that summer.

Also on July 6, Piper Alpha a North Sea oil platform exploded and burned killing 167 workers and two rescuers.

July 11, after a series of setbacks including firing his manager and accusations of physical abuse of his wife, actress Robin Givens, boxer Mike Tyson hired Donald Trump as an advisor.

July 14, 200,000 demonstrated in Soviet Armenia.

July 18-21 The Democratic Convention nominated Michael Dukakis for President and Senator Lloyd Benson of Texas as Vice President.

July 31, the last Playboy Club closed in Lansing, Michigan.

August 1, rightwing radio host Rush Limbaugh began broadcasting.

August 6, a police riot occurred at Tomkins Square Park in New York City. The riot was a gentrification issue which began when more affluent residents on the west side of the park wanted to curb the after dark use of the park by less affluent residents living east of the park. They managed to get a police curfew on the park. The first protest of the curfew occurred on July 31, without incident. However on August 6, larger crowds began gathering to protest and to watch the protest. Witnesses, including the poet Allen Ginsberg, claimed the police became enraged and began beating protestors and innocent bystanders alike. A film later emerged which verified the witnesses claims of police beatings and brutality.

August 8, an assassination attempt in La Paz, Bolivia was made on Secretary of State George Shultz when a bomb went off in the middle of his motorcade as they were leaving the airport. The windows and tires were blown out on three vehicles and left a large crater in the road but there were no casualties. Another bomb also went off at a US Commissary in La Paz which damaged the entrance but there were no casualties. A Bolivian rebel group who blamed the US for supporting their dictatorial government was responsible. Three rebels were arrested for the incident the following year.

August 11, Al-Qaeda was formed in Pakistan by a Saudi national Osama bin Laden and two Egyptians, Ayman Mohammed Rabie al-Zawahiri and Sayyed Imam Al-Sharif (aka Dr. Fadl). They issued a *fatwā* (a holy war) against the United States.

August 15-18, the Republican National Convention was held in New Orleans. George H.W. Bush was nominated without any real opposition.

However his selection of Senator Dan Quayle raised some objections. It was so unpopular that rather than the customary roll call vote, the Convention confirmed Quayle by a voice vote with many shouting no. Bush's acceptance speech was called "the Thousand Points of Light" where he also made the statement "Read my lips, no new taxes!" It was a statement that would come back to haunt him.

August 17, a plane in Pakistan crashed killing Pakistani President Zia, his senior military staff, the American Ambassador Arnold Raphel and General Herbert Wassom the head of the US Military mission in Pakistan. The reason for the crash has never been proven leading to many conspiracy theories.

August 19, the Civil Liberties Act of 1988 became law which provided for about $20,000 in reparations for each surviving member of the Japanese-Americans interned in prison camps during WWII. The majority of Democrats voted for it while a majority of Republicans voted against it. Vice President Bush who didn't vote sided with the Republicans against it despite his earlier campaign pledge to support it.

August 20, a ceasefire was agreed to by Iran and Iraq ending their eight year war which cost over one million lives.

August 28, at Ramstein US Air Force base in Germany 75, were killed and 346 were injured when three Italian jets collided sending one jet crashing into the crowd during an air show.

August 31-September 4, construction crews caused a short circuit and a subsequent fire in the electrical system which knocked out power for five days in large sections of Seattle, Washington during a ninety-degree heat wave.

September 11, about 300,000 people, a quarter of the Estonian population, gathered at a music festival called "Song of Estonia" to sing national and protest songs and to hear speakers proclaim the Estonian ambition of independence from the USSR.

September 17-October 2, the 1988 Summer Olympics were held in Seoul, Korea.

September 21, the first of the dog whistle "Willie Horton" ads by the Bush campaign against Dukakis appeared on television. William Horton was released from a Massachusetts prison on a weekend furlough and while out of prison raped a woman. The Massachusetts weekend furlough program was enacted by a Republican governor previous to Dukakis, but the Bush campaign made it appear that the program belonged to Dukakis as the incident happened while he was governor. The ad was racially charged noting the woman was White and featured a mug shot of Horton, who was Black. The ad was used to raise White fears of Black rape. William Horton's name was changed to "Willie" in the ad to further emphasize that he was Black. Lee Atwater, Bush's campaign manager, has since admitted the ad was used to raise White racial fears. Both Jesse Jackson and Lloyd Benson publicly called the ads racist. Bush falsely claimed that the ads were run by a political committee and that he and his campaign had no prior knowledge of them. It was a lie as they were at the behest of Lee Atwater. These ads were very effective with White voters. In addition Atwater began to spread other false rumors that Kitty Dukakis had burned an American Flag during an anti-war demonstration and that Dukakis had been treated for mental illness these lies and fabrications were also effective.

On the other side Dukakis played fair and fired his deputy campaign director Donna Brazile for spreading rumors about George Bush's actual affair with his assistant Jennifer Fitzgerald.

September 25, the first presidential debate between George Bush and Michael Dukakis was held in Winston Salem, North Carolina and was seen by over 65 million on television. Dukakis was leading Bush in the election polls throughout the summer, but Bush closed the gap in the fall with the Willie Horton ads and the other lies an rumors spread by Atwater. The first debate was close with each side claiming a win.

September 29-October 3, the Space Shuttle Discovery 7 was launched. It was the first mission of the resumed Space Shuttle Program which had been on hold since the Challenger disaster.

October 5, the Vice Presidential Debate between the Democratic nominee Senator Lloyd Benson and Republican Senator Dan Quayle was held in Omaha, Nebraska. The debate is remembered for Dan Quayle comparing himself to a young John Kennedy and Lloyd Benson responding, "Senator, I served with Jack Kennedy. I knew Jack Kennedy. Jack Kennedy was a friend of mine. Senator, you're no Jack Kennedy."

October 13, the second Presidential Debate was held in Los Angeles and had over 67 million television viewers. Dukakis was hit with a bad bout of the flu and had spent the day of the debate in bed recovering. In what has been called one of the most unfair and loaded questions in presidential debates, the conservative moderator Bernard Shaw asked Dukakis, who was against the death penalty, that if his wife Kitty was raped and murdered would he then favor the death penalty. Dukakis reiterated that he was against the death penalty. This question and answer along with the Willie Horton ads and false rumors about his mental health painted Dukakis as weak and likely cost him the election.

Also on October 13, the Shroud of Turin revered by many Christians as Christ's burial cloth was proven by carbon dating to be a fake made in the Middle Ages.

October 27, the US Embassy in Moscow was ordered to be torn down due to listening devices placed in the walls and floors by the USSR during construction.

October 29-30, about 2,000 anti-abortion protestors were arrested trying to block the entrances to abortion clinics in cities across the US. In Pittsburg 367 were arrested. Large pro-choice demonstrations responded throughout the country with over 2,000 in Boston alone. In Providence, Rhode Island where 300 anti-abortion protestors clashed with an equal number of pro-choice demonstrators, five police officers suffered minor injuries.

October 30, Phillip Morris bought Kraft Foods for $13.1 billion.

November 2, Robert Morris a graduate student created and released the first internet worm infecting thousands of computers making them unusable until the virus was removed. Morris was convicted of a felony.

November 8, the presidential election resulted in the following: George Bush 48.9 million or 54.4% and Dukakis 41.8 million or 45.6%. Dukakis only won eight states and the District of Columbia.

November 15, the state of Palestine was created and over eighty countries recognized the state by the end of 1989.

November 16, President Reagan hosted a state visit by British Prime Minister Maggie Thatcher.

Also on November 16, the Estonian legislature passed the Estonian Sovereignty Act excluding Estonian men from being drafted by the Soviet military. It was the first Soviet republic to defy the Soviet Army.

November 17, Senator John Kerry apologized for repeating a joke about Vice President-Elect Dan Quayle several days earlier while responding to questions about Quayle's intellectual fitness to serve. Kerry had quipped. "Somebody told me the other day that the Secret Service has orders that if George Bush is shot, they're to shoot Quayle."

November 18, in the War on Drugs President Reagan signed a bill giving the death penalty for murderous drug traffickers.

November 23, Reagan vetoed a bill to prohibit lobbying by former federal employees to any agencies where they had prior employment.

November 28, Pablo Picasso's painting *Acrobat and Harlequin* sold for $38.46 million.

November 30, the UN censured the US for refusing PLO leader Arafat a visa to speak to the UN.

Also on November 30, KKR & Company bought RJR Nabisco for $25 billion.

December 2-6, the shuttle Atlantis-3 was launched on a secret military mission. Despite sustaining damages to some heat deflecting tile on liftoff it returned without incident.

December 7, Gorbachev visited the UN in New York and announced the reduction in Soviet military forces by 10%.

Also on December 7, in defiance Estonia changed their official language from Russian back to Estonian.

December 8, President Reagan, President Elect Bush and Gorbachev met to discuss nuclear arms reductions. According to declassified documents at the National Security Archives Gorbachev was ready to enter into agreement on the rapid reduction of nuclear weapons but was met with reluctance by President Elect Bush. The US Ambassador to Moscow, Jack Matlock, later entitled a chapter in his book *Washington Fumbles* in his account of this meeting. Gorbachev's advisor Anatoly Chernyaev called it "the Lost Year" as it would take Bush more than a year to start this discussion.

December 9, federal agents swept into the building taking over the offices of the collapsing Silverado Savings & Loan in Denver. This event brought the Savings and Loan crisis to the attention of the American people. Savings and Loans (S&Ls) were deregulated in the early 1980s by the Reagan Administration. The S&Ls began to develop new lines of business, many in risky real estate ventures involving exotic mortgages and questionable lending. They began getting into trouble in 1986.

The Silverado S&L collapse cost the US taxpayers $1.3 billion to bail it out. At the center of the controversy was President Elect Bush's son Neil Bush who was on the Board of Directors. It was discovered that Bush gave approval of $100 million in bad loans to his two business partners, and had failed to disclose that these were his business partners and that he had profited from the loans. A civil action was brought against Neil Bush and he was banned forever from participating in any banking activities. He was required to pay a $50,000 fine which was later discovered to have been paid by his father's Republican supporters. In a later Resolution Trust Corporation suit against Neil Bush and the other Silverado directors resulted in fines of $26.5 million.

From 1986 to 1991 the Federal Savings and Loan Insurance Corporation was forced to close or resolve the losses from 296 S&Ls resulting in a cost to taxpayers of $125 billion. In 1991 the Resolution Trust Corporations was founded to deal with the S&L crisis and closed or resolved another 742 S&Ls costing billions of dollars.

December 19, NASA released their long range plans for a lunar colony and a manned flight to Mars.

December 21, Pan Am Flight 103 was blown up over Lockerbie Scotland killing 270 people. Libya was thought to be responsible.

Also on December 21, the Wall Street investment banking firm Drexel Burnham Lambert pleaded guilty to insider trading and other financial violations and paid $650 million in penalties.

In 1988 Jimmy Swaggart, the popular rightwing television minister, was involved in a sex scandal with a prostitute that eventually led to his defrocking from the Assemblies of God.

During the year heat waves and drought caused large crop losses across the country causing about $60 billion in farm losses. The heat waves caused between 5,000 and 17,000 heat wave related deaths.

The pot bellied pig became a fashionable pet.

Crack cocaine hit the US, particularly in Los Angeles. It was later learned that this drug trade was organized with the knowledge of the CIA to fund the Contras. (Cockburn and St.Clair)

The first fiber optic transatlantic cables were laid. The first use of laser eye surgery began.

The annual inflation rate rose to 4.08%. Interest rates were at 10.5%. The average income was $24,450. The average price of a new home was $91,600. The average monthly rent was $420. The average price of a new car was $10,400 and the price of a gallon of gas was 91 cents. An IBM PC with 30mb of hard drive and a monochrome monitor and 512k memory sold for $1,249.

In 1988 television: The iconic California Raisin commercials with the song I Heard It Through the Grapevine began showing on television. Mystery Science Theater, which would later go on to be a cable television network cult hit, made its debut as a Minnesota local show on KMTA in the Twin Cities. Magnum PI broadcast a two hour series finale in May. The cable channel TNT made its debut.

Shows that made their 1988 debuts included: 48 Hours, The Wonder Years, America's Most Wanted, Day By Day, In the Heat of the Night, Coming of Age, China

Beach, *Just the Ten of Us*, *Police Academy*, *The American Experience*, *Dear John*, *Empty Nest*, *Roseanne*, *Midnight Caller*, *Paradise*, and *Murphy Brown*.

Shows ending their runs: *My Sister Sam*, *The Facts of Life*, *Cagney & Lacy*, *St. Elsewhere*, *Punky Brewster*, *The Slap Maxwell Story*, *Solid Gold*, *Tales from the Darkside*, *We Got it Made*, and *Magnum PI*.

The Wonder Years won the Emmy for Best Comedy and *thirtysomething* won as best Drama. Michael J. Fox in *Family Ties* and Bea Arthur in *The Golden Girls* won for Best Comedy Actors. Richard Kiley *A Year in the Life* and Tyne Daily in *Cagney & Lacy* won for Best Drama Actors.

Milli Vanilli won the Grammy for best new artists until it was found they had not actually sung their songs, but had lip-synced them and were disqualified. In 1988 music, George Michael had four top hits with *Faith*, *Monkey*, *Father Figure* and *One More Try*. Other hits included: *Need You Tonight*, *New Sensation* and *Devil Inside* by INXS, *Sweet Child o' Mine* by Guns N Roses, *Could've Been* by Tiffany, *Is This Love* by Whitesnake, *Simply Irresistible* by Robert Palmer, *Hungry Eyes* by Eric Carmen, *Love Bites* and *Pour Some Sugar On Me* by Def Leppard, *Angel* by Aerosmith, *A Hazy Shade of Winter* by the Bangels, *Don't Worry Be Happy* by Bobby McFerrin, *Red Red Wine* by UB40, *Bad Medicine* by Bon Jovi, *I'll Always Love You*, *Prove Your Love* and *Tell It to My Heart* by Taylor Dane, *Desire* by U2, *The Loco-motion* by Kylie Minogue, *Candle in the Wind* by Elton John, *I Hate Myself for Loving You* by Joan Jett and the Blackhearts *Cherry Bomb* by John Cougar Mellencamp, and *Kokomo* by the Beach Boys.

The ten top grossing films of 1988 were *Rain Man*, *Who Framed Roger Rabbit*, *Coming to America*, *Big*, *Twins*, *Crocodile Dundee II*, *Die Hard*, *The Naked Gun*, *Cocktail*, and *Beetlejuice*. Other top movies included: *The Accused*, *Midnight Run*, *Bull Durham*, *Mississippi Burning*, *Working Girl*, *Willow*, *A Fish Called Wanda*, *Dirty Rotten Scoundrels*, *Young Guns*, *The Accidental Tourist*, *Hairspray*, *Mystic Pizza*, *Stand and Deliver*, *The Dead Pool*, *The Great Outdoors*, *The Unbearable Lightness of Being*, and *Dangerous Liaisons*.

The Oscars for Best Picture, Director and Actor (Dustin Hoffman) went to *Rain Man*. The Best Actress went to Jodie Foster in *The Accused*. The Best supporting actors went to Kevin Klein in *A Fish Called Wanda* and Geena Davis in *The Accidental Tourist*.

The best books of 1988 included: the Non-Fiction Pulitzer Prize winner about the Vietnam War, *A Bright Shining Lie* by Neil Sheehan, the Pulitzer Prize history winner about the civil rights movement, *Parting the Waters* by Taylor Branch, and another Nobel History Prize winner *Battle Cry of Freedom* by James M. McPherson and the Nobel Prize for Fiction *Breathing Lessons* by Anne Tyler. Other notable 1988 books included: *The Satanic Verses* by Salman Rushdie, *The Silence of the Lambs* by Thomas Harris, *The Alchemist* by Paulo Coelho, *Koko* by Peter Straub, *The Cardinal of the Kremlin* by Tom Clancy, *Alaska* by James Michener, *The Power of Myth* by Joseph Campbell, *The Last Lion Winston Churchill: Alone 1932-1942* by William Manchester, *Dead Poets Society* by N.H. Klienbaum, *Oscar and Lucinda* by Peter Carey, *The Sands of Time* by Sidney Sheldon, *The Icarus Agenda* by Robert Ludlum, and *The Best American Poetry 1988*.

CHAPTER 45. 1989: PROTESTS IN THE EASTERN BLOC, MALL OF AMERICA, BLACK FRIDAY AND THE INVASION OF PANAMA

January 3, while still under indictment for theft from their church ministry, Jim and Tammy Faye Bakker returned to television. Bakker blamed the loss of his PTL Club and his sex scandal on the work of the devil, who he said was jealous of their success. Tammy Faye cried, with thick black mascara running down her face, an image which was carried on many news stations. The program was deemed successful with much of their former audience believing they had been victims of the devil.

January 4, two Libyan MIG 23 Floggers approached two American Navy F-14 Tomcats over the Gulf of Sidra as if they were going to engage. The Tomcats responded and shot down the two Libyan aircraft. Libya accused the US the following day of shooting down two unarmed reconnaissance planes. However US gun camera videos of the incident showed the two MIGs equipped with Apex antiaircraft missiles.

January 5, two French newsmen were arrested for trying to plant three fake bombs at JFK airport to show poor airport security.

January 11, diplomats from 140 nations met in Paris to condemn chemical and biological weapons. By a consensus the nations adopted a nonbinding agreement. The US had hoped to get the nations to agree to a ban on creating and stockpiling these weapons, particularly in Iraq and Libya. The US was condemned by many for hypocritically reserving their right to stockpile chemical and biological weapons and to use them if attacked.

Also on January 11, President Reagan gave his farewell address to the nation.

January 13, a computer virus called the Friday the 13th virus, struck many computers in Britain.

January 14, a large demonstration of Muslims in England burned Salman Rushdie's book *Satanic Verses*.

January 15, a pro-democracy demonstration in Prague was broken up by police.

January 16, the USSR announced plans for a two year manned mission to Mars.

January 17, a gunman killed five children and wounded thirty others before killing himself in a Stockton, California elementary school.

January 18, the Polish Workers Party voted to legalize the trade union, Solidarity.

January 19, President Reagan pardoned New York Yankees owner George Steinbrenner for making illegal campaign contributions to Richard Nixon.

January 20, George H.W. Bush was sworn into office as president.

January 24, the first case of the AIDS virus transmitted orally was recorded.

January 30, the American Embassy in Kabul, Afghanistan was closed.

February 1, arriving to great fanfare Diana Princess of Wales visited New York City.

February 2, the last Soviet troops left Kabul, Afghanistan ending nine years of Soviet occupation.

February 2-6, a cold wave swept the nation plunging fifteen states below zero. Many other states recorded record single temperatures. Denver recorded a minus 22 and Minneapolis also recorded a temperature of minus 22, but with a wind chill of minus 49 degrees. Parts of Texas experienced daytime highs in the twenties for several days in a row.

February 10, Ron Brown was selected the Chairman of the Democratic Party becoming the first American Black to head a major party.

February 11, Barbara Harris became the first woman Episcopal Bishop.

February 14, Union Carbide agreed to pay $470 million to India for the 1984 Bhopal chemical disaster.

Also on February 14, the Ayatollah Khomeini of Iran issued a *fatwā* calling for Salman Rushdie's death.

February 21, in New York City a Chinese drug ring was busted and 820 pounds heroin with a street value of $1 billion was recovered by police. They also recovered $3 million in cash. Nineteen were arrested.

February 23, in a stunning move the US Senate failed to confirm former US Senator John Tower to be George H.W. Bush's Defense Secretary. It was the first cabinet appointment of a new president to be rejected. The primary concerns were Tower's alcohol abuse and womanizing.

February 23-27, President Bush visited Japan, South Korea and China.

February 24, after 44 years the Estonian flag was raised in Tallinn.

Also on February 24, nine passengers were killed when they were sucked out of a United Airlines flight in Honolulu because of uncontrolled decompression.

March 1, Poland began to liberalize its currency exchange in a move towards a market economy.

Also on March 1, the Yugoslavian government imposed a curfew in Kosovo because of claims of intimidation directed toward the Serbian minority. It was the first step of many toward the Kosovo War which would take place in 1998.

March 2, twelve European nations banned the use of chlorofluorocarbons (CFCs) because of their destruction of the ozone layer.

Also on March 2, an oil tanker, Exxon Houston ran aground in Hawaii spilling 117,000 gallons of oil.

March 3, Robert MacFarlane was fined $20,000 and received two years' probation in the Iran Contra Scandal.

March 4, Time Inc. and Warner Communications announced a merger forming Time Warner.

March 9, the Soviet Union proposed that Soviet Bloc countries could submit their disputes to the World Court for binding arbitration. It was the beginning of the Revolutions of 1989 which would see the Eastern European nations reject their communist governments and reject Soviet influence.

March 13, a geomagnetic storm caused a failure of the Hydro-Québec power grid. Six million people in the Northeastern US and eastern Canada were without power for nine hours.

Also March 13-18, Discovery 8, the twenty-eighth shuttle mission was launched.

March 14, President Bush banned the importation of assault rifles for civilian use.

March 15, the US Secretary of Veterans Affairs was established as a cabinet position.

March 16, as economic problems mounted in the Soviet Union the Central Committee of the USSR voted to allow farmers the right to farm outside the collectives, to use state-owned farmland for life and to start making their own farming choices.

March 23, Stanley Pons and Martin Fleischmann claimed to have obtained cold fusion in an experiment. Later experiments showed their experiments to be false.

March 24, the oil tanker Exxon Valdez ran aground when it sailed out of the shipping lanes to avoid ice in Alaska's Prince William Sound. It spilled 10.8 million gallons of crude oil. The spill covered over 1300 miles of coastline and 11,000 square miles of ocean. An Anchorage jury found ExxonMobil negligent and awarded $287 million in actual damages and $5 billion in punitive damages. ExxonMobil then began a series of appeals which eventually reduced the punitive damages down to $507.5 million dollars which was paid out in December 2009. The company paid about $2 billion in cleanup costs but most of this was paid by their insurance.

March 26, in the first free elections in the Soviet Union, the Congress of People's Deputies of the Soviet Union elected both communist and non-communist candidates. The election of candidates from various factions resulted heavy debates about the future of the Soviet Union and the communist party.

March 29, the first Soviet hockey players were permitted to play for the NHL.

April 4-9, tens of thousands of Georgians protested for independence for Georgia from the USSR in Tbilisi. The Georgian Communist Party realizing it had lost control asked that Soviet Troops be sent in to restore order. On April 9, Soviet Armed Personnel carriers and troops surrounded the demonstrators and were given the orders to break up the demonstrations by any means possible. The soldiers advanced on the demonstrators with batons and entrenching tools (spades) and began to swing these at the crowd causing multiple injuries. The first casualty was a sixteen-year-old girl who tried to run away from the soldiers but was caught by two soldiers and beaten to death. Her mother was beaten and badly wounded trying to drag her daughter to safety. As the crowd ran from the soldiers, nineteen protestors, seventeen of them young women, fell and were trampled to death by the crowd. Videos taken at the time showed that the military went into a frenzy beating the crowd. A memorial to the victims was erected in 2004 in Tbilisi to commemorate the victims.

April 5, Solidarity and the Polish government signed an agreement restoring the unions legal status and agreed to hold free elections in Poland in June.

April 7, tens of thousands marched in Washington, DC to protest a shortage of decent affordable housing. The Capitol police estimated that over 70,000 came to protest.

April 14, in the midst of the S&L crisis the US government seized the failed Lincoln Savings and Loan in Irvine, California costing taxpayers $3 billion dollars. Charles Keating the S&L president defrauded investors and managed to keep Federal Home Loan Board regulators at bay for months with the help of five powerful senators who he had paid over $1.5 million in campaign donations. They became known as "The Keating Five." Two of the five senators were American heroes Astronaut John Glenn of Ohio and former POW John McCain of Arizona who later ran for president. The other three were Alan Cranston of California, Dennis DeConcini of Arizona and Donald Riegle of Michigan. After a Senate investigation Cranston was reprimanded, Riegle and DeConcini were cited for acting improperly and Glenn and McCain were criticized for poor judgment. The public was furious with the lenient conclusions. The Senate committee also released its conclusions and decisions at the start of the Gulf War which many thought was done to hide the lenient penalties for the five senators. Regulators were angry that McCain in particular got off too lightly as his wife Cindy also had personal business interests with Charles Keating and had profited from them. Ironically Senator DeConcini who had been the most forceful in blocking the Federal Home Loan Board investigations into Lincoln Savings was in 1995 appointed to this board by President Bill Clinton.

April 15-June 4, the Tiananmen Square protests began and ran through June with an estimated one million Chinese students participating. The protestors called for democracy and freedom of speech and of the press in a post-Mao China. On June 4, Chinese troops moved in and enforced martial law. The Chinese government reported that 215 civilian were killed along with 23 soldiers and police. However the Chinese Red Cross reported about

2,600 civilian deaths and about 50 police and soldiers although this was later retracted at the insistence of the Chinese government according to the *New York Times.*

April 19, in one of the most reported crimes of the 1980s a woman only identified as "The Central Park Jogger" was running in Central Park where she was beaten, stabbed five times, raped and sodomized in an assault which was called "wilding." The young woman, an investment banker, survived and was in a coma for twelve days and has no memory of the incident. Five juvenile males were eventually convicted and served terms of six to thirteen years in prison for the crime. Later a serial rapist admitted to the crime and the five juvenile convictions were overturned when DNA evidence showed the serial rapist was the attacker. New York paid the five wrongfully charged men a $41 million settlement. There were several other robberies and assaults by youth gangs "wilding" in the park that night and authorities thought that this attack was another.

Also on April 19, a gun turret exploded on the USS Iowa killing 47 sailors.

April 19, Vice President Dan Quayle visited American Samoa and in an odd condescending speech he said "You all look like happy campers to me. Happy campers you are, happy campers you have been, and, as far as I am concerned, happy campers you will always be."

April 25, in a stopover in Hawaii the Vice President Quayle confused himself in a speech and said, "Hawaii has always been a very pivotal role in the Pacific. It is in the Pacific. It is a part of the United States that is an island that is right here."

May 2, sometimes called the first crack in the Iron Curtain, Hungary dismantled 150 miles of barbed wire fences along the Austrian border.

May 3, the first McDonalds in Russia began construction. It was opened in January 1990.

May 4, Oliver North was convicted in the Iran-Contra Scandal.

May 4-8, the shuttle Atlantis 4 was launched. It was the first time the general purpose computer failed during a mission. It was successfully replaced with a spare during the flight.

May 9, Dan Quayle made another of his many gaffes as Vice President, when addressing the United Negro College Fund he bungled their motto "A mind is a terrible thing to waste" with "What a waste it is to lose one's mind or not to have a mind is being very wasteful, how true that is."

May 10, Panamanian strongman and President Manuel Noriega declared the presidential election where he lost to his opponent invalid. The following day President Bush ordered 1,900 American troops to the Panama Canal Zone to "protect Americans there."

May 15, Gorbachev visited China. It was the first Sino-Soviet summit in thirty years.

May 26, Vice President Quayle was quoted in the Wall Street Journal saying, "I believe we are on an irreversible trend toward more freedom and democracy, but that could change."

May 26, Republican Congressman Donald "Buzz" Lukens of Ohio was convicted of providing alcohol and having sex with a sixteen-year-old Black child, Rosie Coffman. She allegedly was first abused by Lukens when she was 13, but an all White grand jury chose to only consider the most recent incident. Coffman's mother also testified that afterward Lukens promised to find her a government job for the silence of her and her daughter. Lukens who is White was only convicted of misdemeanors of contributing to the delinquency of a minor and contributing to the unruliness of a minor. He appealed the decision and lost, and later served 30 days in jail and paid a $500 fine. The judge said of Luken that he was "a man with no remorse whatsoever." Lukens remained in Congress and was later accused of fondling and propositioning a female Capitol elevator operator. Lukens lost his Republican primary to John Boehner in 1990 and Boehner would later become Speaker of the US House of Representatives.

May 29, in the wake of the collapsed Argentine economy, food riots and looting erupted. Rampant inflation plagued the nation and was seen as the cause of the problems. The government declared a state of siege and imposed martial law.

May 31, the Democratic Speaker of the House, Jim Wright, resigned as Speaker amid scandal. Wright had violated House rules concerning limits on speaking fees and gifts. He resigned from Congress on June 30, and returned to Texas. He was also under suspicion for using his influence with regulators in the S&L scandal in exchange for campaign donations which may have been further investigated if he had stayed in office. The initial charges were brought by Republican Congressman Newt Gingrich who used the attacks on Wright to propel himself to eventually become the Speaker of the House. Later, Gingrich would later also resign as Speaker of the House, amid a very similar scandal involving speaker fees and gifts.

June 3, the Ayatollah Khomeini died. At his first attempt at a public funeral on June 6, crowds mobbed his coffin and ripped it apart trying to see his body for the last time. At one point Khomeini's body almost crashed to the ground as the crowd fought for a piece of his funeral shroud.

June 4, in Poland's first democratic elections Solidarity and anti-communist candidates won.

June 5, in Tiananmen Square an unknown Chinese protestor called "tank man" by the press stood in front of a tank column temporarily stopping them. The images were shown in media world-wide.

June 12, amid cries of public pornography, Robert Mapplethorpe's gay photography exhibition was removed by the Corcoran Art Gallery in Washington. DC.

June 14, the ground-breaking ceremony for the world's largest shopping mall, "Mall of America" was held in Bloomington, Minnesota on the site of the former Minnesota Vikings and Minnesota Twins Metropolitan Stadium. It would open on August 11, 1992. The mall was 96.4 acres and just under 5 million square feet on four levels, containing more than 520 stores, convention and office space and a large theme park in the middle with adjacent parking ramps for over 12,000 cars, a bus terminal and eventually light rail. Shuttle busses also ran to and from nearby hotels. The Mall of America has since been expanded significantly by more than half again. Although most of the shoppers come from the Midwest and Canada about 20% are other foreign visitors.

Also on June 14, Zsa Zsa Gabor was arrested for assault for slapping a police officer who pulled her over.

June 16, a crowd of over 100,000-250,000 gathered in Budapest for the reburial of Prime Minister Imre Nagy who had been executed by the Soviets as a traitor for the Hungarian Uprising in 1956. This demonstration was the beginning of the end of communist rule in Hungary.

June 21, the US Supreme Court ruled that burning an American flag in protest is protected free speech under the first amendment.

June 24, Jiang Zemin was confirmed as the leader of China.

July 5, South African President Botha met for the first time with Nelson Mandela.

July 9-12, President Bush visited Poland and Hungary to encourage US investment into the two countries.

July 10, 300,000 coal miners in the USSR went on strike for better pay and conditions. It was the largest Soviet strike since unions were outlawed in the 1920s.

July 17, Poland and the Vatican established diplomatic relations for the first time in 50 years.

Also on July 17, the B2 Stealth bomber made its first flight.

July 18, twenty-one-year-old actress and model Rebecca Schaeffer who had starred in the television show *My Sister Sam* was shot and killed by an obsessed fan who had stalked her for three years.

July 19, a United Airlines flight in Sioux City, Iowa crashed killing 111, but 185 survived the crash. The National Transportation Advisory Board determined that inadequate inspections and maintenance was the cause of the crash.

July 31, Hezbollah announced that it had hanged US Marine Lt. Colonel William Higgins in retaliation for Israel's kidnapping of a Hezbollah leader.

Also on July 31, Nintendo released the Game Boy portable video game system in the US.

August 2, NASA confirmed that Voyager II had discovered three more moons of Neptune.

August 7, the presidents of five Central American countries met and concluded that the US backed Contras should be disbanded and that their bases in Honduras destroyed.

August 8-13, space shuttle Columbia 8 was launched on a secret military mission.

August 9, President Bush signed into law The Financial Institutions Reform, Recovery and Enforcement Act of 1989 (FIRREA). It established the Resolution Trust Corporation to close out hundreds of insolvent S&Ls and turned the regulatory powers over to the Office of Thrift Supervision instead of the beleaguered and congressionally influenced Federal Home Loan Bank Board. Many thought this ironic as the President's son Neal Bush had been one of the culprits that led to the S&L crisis.

August 10, General Colin Powell became the first Black Chairman of the Joint Chiefs of Staff.

August 11, Voyager II discovered rings around Neptune.

Also on August 11, speaking on CNN about a possible manned mission to Mars, Vice President Quayle said, "Mars is essentially in the same orbit. Mars is somewhat the same distance from the Sun, which is very important. We have seen pictures where there are canals, we believe and water. If there is water, that means there is oxygen. If oxygen, that means we can breathe."

August 14, the Sega Genesis game system was released in the US.

August 15, President Botha of South Africa resigned. F.W. de Klerk became President and began the negotiations to end apartheid in South Africa. He released Mandela and other political prisoners and ended the ban on the African National Congress (ANC) which led to democratic elections. He would later serve as a deputy to Mandela in the new South African democracy.

August 19, a peace and democracy demonstration was held on both sides of the Hungarian-Austrian Boarder called the Pan-European Picnic.

August 20, two brothers, Lyle and Erik Menendez, murdered their wealthy parents for their money in Beverly Hills, California.

August 21, thousands demonstrated in Prague against the Soviets by condemning the Soviets for crushing the Prague Spring demonstrations on August 21, 1968.

August 23, about two million Estonians, Latvians, and Lithuanians held hands in a 600 km human chain called the Baltic Way to demand freedom and independence from the Soviet Union.

Also on August 23, in Brooklyn, New York three Black teens were chased and beaten by a White gang of youths. One of the Black teens, Yusef Hawkins was shot and killed. Four White youth were eventually convicted and sentenced. The incident lead to some Black violence as well as peaceful protests led by the Reverend Al Sharpton who was stabbed by a White man during one of these protests.

August 24, Tadeusz Mazowiecki became the first non-communist Prime minister of Poland since the communist takeover in 1946.

September 7, former President Jimmy Carter held a summit at the Carter Center in Atlanta, with the leaders of Ethiopia and Eritrean separatists in an attempt to broker a peace in the conflict.

September 10, the Hungarian government opened up its borders to East German refugees attempting to flee their country for the West through Hungary and Czechoslovakia.

September 10-25, Hurricane Hugo blew through the Leeward Islands, Puerto Rico and the Southeastern US, and continued up the east coast killing a total of 107 people and causing over $10 billion in damages.

September 13, Archbishop Desmond Tutu led what was to be the largest anti-apartheid march in South Africa.

September 26, after an eleven year occupation the last Vietnamese soldiers left Cambodia.

Also on September 26, the USSR called for the destruction of all US and Soviet chemical weapons.

Also on this date the Motion Picture Association of America created the NC-17 rating for movies with adult themes.

September 30, West German Foreign Minister Hans-Dietrich Genscher granted 7,000 escaping East Germans free passage to the West in speech from West German embassy balcony in Prague.

October 1, Denmark became the first nation to recognize same sex marriages.

October 3, the East German government closed the border with Czechoslovakia to prevent more escaping East Germans.

October 5, the Dalai Lama won the Nobel Peace Prize.

October 7, the first large demonstration against the communist government in East Germany began in Plauen.

Also on October 7, the Hungarian Communist Party reorganized into a socialist party.

October 9, another large anti-communist protest occurred in Leipzig, East Germany.

October 13, the Friday the 13th stock market crash, sometimes referred to as "Black Friday" was triggered by a breakdown of a $6.75 leveraged buyout for United Airlines which caused the junk bond market to fail. The market plunged by almost 7% in one day.

October 17, the Loma Prieta earthquake struck an area from Salinas to Oakland, California and was broadcast live because it happened during coverage of the World Series. The quake measured 6.9, killing 63 people and injuring 3,757 and caused about $6 billion in property damages. One of the more memorable scenes was the collapse of a double-decker freeway in Oakland, with cars crushed in between the concrete freeway sections. The quake also triggered a tsunami and thousands of landslides. The World Series was delayed for a week.

October 18-23, the shuttle Atlantis 5 was launched. The US launched the Galileo Mission to study Jupiter from the shuttle.

October 18, the National Assembly of Hungary voted to restore a multi-party democracy.

Also on October 18, in the midst of democracy protests the East German communist hard-line leader Erich Honecker stepped down because of health issues.

October 23, the Hungarian Republic was declared replacing the Communist People's Republic.

Also on October 23, a violent explosion and fire at the Phillips petroleum plant on the Houston Ship Canal in Pasadena, Texas killed 23 and injured 314. The blaze took over ten hours to get under control.

October 31, up to a half million East Germans demonstrated for democracy in Leipzig.

November 1, the border between East Germany and Czechoslovakia was reopened. November 3, East Germans began pouring into Czechoslovakia seeking asylum in West Germany.

November 3, hundreds demonstrated for democracy in Sofia, Bulgaria.

November 6, twenty-one Pacific Rim countries, including the US, China and the USSR, established the Asia-Pacific Economic Cooperation (APEC) to promote free trade.

November 7, in the elections Douglas Wilder became the first Black governor of Virginia and David Dinkins became the first Black mayor of New York City.

Also on November 7, the communist government of East Germany resigned.

November 9, it was announced that the check points in the Berlin Wall would be opened for Germans to travel freely between East and West. Crowds swarmed the Wall and began to dance on the top and to dismantle it. Television crews broadcast the event around the world.

November 10, the Bulgarian communist rule came to an end when the Bulgarian Socialist government replaced it.

November 15, Polish Solidarity leader Lech Walesa addressed Congress.

November 16, six Catholic priests were murdered in El Salvador by US trained Salvadorian soldiers.

November 17, a peaceful student demonstration in Prague was violently broken up by police. The event caused even larger demonstrations over the next few days until on November 20, when a half million demonstrated in Prague.

November 24, the Communist Party leaders of Czechoslovakia resigned.

November 28, the Communist Party of Czechoslovakia announced that it would allow free multi-party elections in December.

December 1, Mikhail Gorbachev met with Pope John Paul II and pledged religious freedom for citizens of the USSR.

Also December 1, the East German Parliament abolished the communist party monopoly over the government. The Communists resigned two days later.

Also on this date a military coup against Philippine President Corazon Aquino was put down by US military intervention.

December 3, at a summit in Malta, President Bush and Soviet leader Mikhail Gorbachev met and stated that the Cold War may be coming to an end.

December 6, an anti-feminist radical gunman killed 14 young women at an engineering school in Montreal.

December 7, the communist prime minister of Czechoslovakia resigned.

Also on December 7, Lithuania became the first Soviet Republic to abolish the Communist Party's monopoly on power.

December 10, Mongolia, the second oldest communist country declared that it had peacefully changed from a communist to a democratic country.

December 11, the Trans-Antarctica Expedition of six explorers from six nations (US, USSR, China, France Britain, and Japan reached the South Pole. The team was led by the American explorer Will Steger. The first ever non-mechanized expedition traveled 3,741 miles in 220 days using dog sleds crossing the entire continent. They recorded temperatures as low as minus 113 degrees Fahrenheit.

December 17-25, after an attempt by the Romanian Communist government to evict the dissident Pastor László Tőkés, an ethnic Hungarian, Romania's anti-communist coup began. Protestors broke into the Communist Party headquarters in Timişoara, Romania, and tried to set fire to the building. Riot police drove them back. During the next several days the size of the protesting crowd grew. Romania's communist leader Nicolae Ceauşescu addressed a large crowd in Bucharest on December 21, saying the protestors in Timişoara were fascists. But during his speech loudspeakers mounted behind the large crowd blasted pre-recorded booing and heckling; this represented the start of the coup, which was promoted heavily by Radio Free Europe for days. The police tried to restore order but the crowd became uncontrollable. Ceauşescu retreated as the crowd and police clashed and the military arrived to clear the streets. On December 22, after the suicide of the defense minister, the army began to switch sides and to support the protestors. Ceauşescu's headquarters were attacked; he and his wife Elena fled by helicopter. They were caught on December 23. Two days later, on December 25, Nicolae and Elena were given a summary trial and both sentenced to death on false charges of theft from the Romanian people, and genocide. A firing squad of Romanian soldiers executed them immediately after the trial. The couple insisted they wanted to die together and the Army granted their last request.

December 20-January 31, 1990, the US invaded Panama, in Operation Just Cause, to overthrow the government of Manuel Noriega and to capture and arrest him. During the month long invasion 234 Panamanian military were killed and 1,908 were captured. The US suffered 23 killed, two by friendly fire. The US claims that 516 civilians were killed in the invasion but the Commission for the Defense of Human Rights in Central America (CODEHUCA) estimated 2,500 to 3,000 deaths. A later Panamanian truth commission raised the number of dead and missing to over 3,500. Over 20,000 had their homes destroyed and became refuges as a result. Human Rights Watch's report on the invasion later condemned the US, saying that "The duty to minimize harm to civilians, where doing so would not compromise a legitimate military objective, were not faithfully observed by the invading U.S. forces." The OAS condemned the invasion and Peru withdrew its ambassador over the Invasion. A UN Resolution condemning the US invasion was vetoed by the US and Britain in the Security Council.

One of the main reasons for the invasion was the capture of Noriega who was captured on January 3, 1990 and flown to the US to stand trial for drug trafficking. Noriega was educated in the School of the Americas operated by the US. He was also a CIA asset who they supported with large amounts of cash for many years and was part of the CIAs Iran Contra Operations. He also had alleged ties to then Vice President Bush going back to his CIA days. At his 1992 trial the judge refused allow any testimony about his CIA past and his connections to President Bush saying it was irrelevant. In their book *White Out*, Jeffery St. Clair and Alexander Cockburn claim some of Noriega's drug sales were on behalf of the CIA which used cocaine sales to support the contras. Michael Dukakis also raised Noriega during the 1988 presidential campaign raising the concern that the drug kingpin was a longtime friend of George H.W. Bush. St. Clair and Cockburn and others have speculated that the invasion arrest of Noriega was to protect Bush from further scandal. Noriega has also asserted this, but was not allowed to voice these issues at his Miami trial. The US Army also claimed to have found 50 pounds of cocaine at Noriega's house, which turned out to be tamale flour.

December 22, a cold wave across the Midwest saw temperatures fall below zero as far south as Oklahoma.

December 31, Poland officially became a democratic state and withdrew from the Warsaw Pact.

In 1989 Wal-Mart began to rival Kmart and Sears in the marketplace. The concentration of carbon dioxide in the Earth's atmosphere reached a troubling 350 million parts per million by volume and 1989 was declared the warmest year on record raising concerns about global warming. South Africa dismantled its nuclear weapons. Microsoft Office was introduced. Toyota launched its luxury car the Lexus.

The inflation rate rose to almost 5%. Interest rates were at 10.5%. Average cost of a new home was $120,000 and the average income was $27,450. The average monthly rent was $420. The average price of a new car was $15,350 and the price for a gallon of gas was 97 cents.

In 1989 television *Generations*, the first Black soap opera made its debut in March on NBC. ABC began *TGIF* a prime time block of Friday night sitcoms which would be very popular for the next decade. The Comedy Channel, now Comedy Central, made its debut. CBS aired the 1956 *I Love Lucy Christmas Special* for the first time in many years.

New Shows debuting included: *The Arsenio Hall Show, Inside Edition, Coach, Anything But Love, COPS, Quantum Leap, Generations, The Jim Henson Hour, Rescue 911, Tales from the Crypt, Seinfeld, Saved By the Bell, The Joan Rivers Show, Life Goes On, Major Dad, Hard Copy, Doogie Houser MD, The Young Riders, Baywatch, Family Matters, America's Funniest Videos,* and *The Simpsons* which had started as cartoon shorts on the *Tracy Ullman Show* as a stand alone program.

Shows ending their runs included: *Ryan's Hope, Simon & Simon, Webster, It a Living, Sale of the Century, Dynasty, Family Ties, Moonlighting, The Gong Show, Miami Vice, Kate & Allie, The Cavanaughs, Highway to Heaven, The Equalizer, the Smurfs* and *American Bandstand* which had been on the air since 1952.

After winning four consecutive Emmy's for his comedic role in *Night Court* John Larroquette asked not to be considered again. *Cheers* and *LA Law* won the Emmys for Best Comedy and Drama. Richard Cavanugh for *Empty Nest* and Candice Bergen won the Emmys for Best Comedy Actor and Actress. Carroll O'Connor in *In the Heat of the Night* and Dana Delany in *China Beach* won for Best Dramatic Actor and Actress.

In 1989 music Bobby Brown had top hits with *My Prerogative, Every Little Step* and *On Our Own*, The B 52s had a hit with *Love Shack*, Simply Red with *If You Don't Know Me By Now*, Milli Vanilli had four hits with *Girl You Know Its True, Girl I'm Going to Miss You, Baby Don't Forget My Number* and *Blame It on the*

Rain. Poison had *Every Rose Has Its Thorn*, Paula Abdul had three *Straight Up*, *Forever Your Girl* and *Cold Hearted*. Bette Midler hit with *Wind Beneath My Wings*. Madonna had three *Like a Prayer*, *Express Yourself* and *Cherish*. The Bangles had two with *Eternal Flame* and *In Your Room*. Other hits included: Cher's *If I Could Turn Back Time*, Young MC's *Bust a Move*, Great White's *Once Bitten Twice Shy*, Tone Lōc's *Funky Cold Medina* and *Wild Thing*, Guns N Roses' *Welcome to the Jungle* and *Patience*, and Chicago's *Look Away*.

The ten top grossing films of 1989 were: *Indiana Jones and the Last Crusade*, *Batman*, *Back to the Future Part II*, *look Who's Talking*, *Dead Poets Society*, *Lethal Weapon 2*, *Honey I Shrunk the Kids*, *Ghostbusters II*, *The Little Mermaid*, *and Born of the Fourth of July*. *Other hits of 1989 included: When Harry Met Sally, Driving Miss Daisy, My Left Foot, The Fabulous Baker Boys, Sex Lies and Video Tape, Henry V, Glory, Steel Magnolias, Dangerous Liaisons, The Field of Dreams, The Abyss, Road House, Uncle Buck, National Lampoons Christmas Vacation, Parenthood, Major League, The Burbs, Do the Right Thing, Weekend at Bernie's, Bill & Ted's Excellent Adventure, Turner & Hooch, See No Evil Hear No Evil, Casualties of War,* and *Crimes and Misdemeanors*.

Driving Miss Daisy won the Oscar for Best Picture. Oliver Stone won Best Director for *Born on the Fourth of July*. Best Actor went to Daniel Day-Lewis for *My Left Foot*. Best Actress went to Jessica Tandy for *Driving Miss Daisy*.

Some of the most popular and significant books of 1989 included: E.L. Doctorow's *Billy Bathgate*, Kazuo Ishiguro's *Remains of the Day*, Amy Tan's *The Joy Luck Club*, John Irving's *A Prayer for Owen Meany*, Laura Esquivel's *Like Water for Chocolate*, Tom Clancy's *Clear and Present Danger*, Michael Lewis' *Liars Poker*, Katherine Dunn's *Greek Love*, Martin Amis' *London Fields*, Steven Covey's *The 7 Habits of Highly Effective People*, John LeClarré's *Russia House*, Thomas Friedman's *From Beirut to Jerusalem*, David Fromkin's *A Peace to End All Peace*, James Michener's *Caribbean*, and *Number of Stars* by Lois Lowry. Oscar Hijuelos won the Pulitzer Prize for fiction with *The Mambo Kings Play Songs of Love*. Charles Simic won the Pulitzer Poetry Prize for *The World Doesn't End*. Stanley Karnow won the Pulitzer History Prize for *In Our Image: America's Empire in the Philippines.*

CHAPTER 46. 1990: THE BIRTH OF THE WORLD WIDE WEB, THE
UNIFICATION OF GERMANY AND IRAQ'S INVASION OF KUWAIT

January 1, the first internet companies catering to commercial interests, PSInet and EUnet began selling internet access to commercial customers in the US and Netherlands.

Also January 1, Poland became the first communist country to abolish its socialist economy.

January 7, the Leaning Tower of Pisa was closed because of safety concerns.

January 9-20, the space shuttle Columbia was launched for its ninth mission.

Also on January 9, under the First Amendment the US Supreme court struck down a provision of a Dallas zoning ordinance prohibiting all sexually oriented businesses causing problems in most American city zoning regulations. The court let stand a city's ability to exclude these businesses from some zones, but the cities could not ban them entirely, thereby forcing cities to provide some zone where they are accepted.

January 10, China lifted martial law that was imposed during the Tiananmen Square demonstrations.

January 11, over 300,000 demonstrated in Lithuania for independence.

January 12-19, most Armenians were driven out of Baku, Azerbaijan SSR during a pogrom. On January 20, Soviet troops were sent to restore order. The crowds began an independence protest and over Azerbaijani 130 demonstrators were killed.

January 15, the National Assembly of Bulgaria voted to end socialist rule.

Also on this date in East Berlin thousands raided the secret police (Stasi) headquarters and began destroying government records.

In another event on January 15, a bug in AT&T software caused a telephone blackout, including 911 emergency calls, for nine hours in Atlanta, St. Louis and Detroit and also affected long distance calls.

January 18, Washington, DC Mayor Marion Barry was arrested on drug charges.

January 19, police broke up anti-apartheid protests in South Africa.

January 22, the League of Communists in Yugoslavia voted to give up their monopoly on power. The vote resulted in the messy and violent breakup of Yugoslavia.

January 24, Japan launched the Hiten satellite, which orbited the earth and released a smaller satellite to orbit the moon. The Hiten satellite made ten lunar fly-bys until it was intentionally crashed into the lunar surface in 1993.

Also on this date Moldova sought independence from the USSR. The area where Romania, Ukraine and Moldova meet has had a long and complex history. The ethnic Moldovans (eastern Romanians) of the Moldavian SSR were annexed by the Soviet Union from Romania in 1940. As Moldova began pushing for independence from the Soviet Union, the pro-Soviet populace in the eastern part of the region sought to secede from the Moldavian SSR. By September, they formed an independent Transnistria (officially the Pridnestrovian Moldavian Republic), and their status remains somewhat nebulous to this day.

January 29, Bell Labs in Holmdel, New Jersey, announced the creation of the optical processor, which used light waves instead of electric currents to make much faster calculations and lead to the development of super computers.

January 31, the first McDonalds opened in Moscow.

February 1, smoking was banned on most flights in the United States.

February 2, bowing to world pressure, the South African government promised to free Nelson Mandela and to legalize the African National Congress.

February 7, the Communist Party of the USSR voted to end their monopoly and allow other parties to compete in elections.

February 8, *60 Minutes* commentator Andy Rooney was suspended by CBS for making racist remarks.

February 11, after 27 years in prison anti-apartheid leader Nelson Mandela was released from prison in South Africa.

Also on February 11, Soyuz TM-9 was launched to the Mir Space station. On August 9, they would return to earth.

February 12-13, the Open Skies conference of NATO and Warsaw Pact nations met in Ottawa. They agreed to European troop reductions and the reunification of Germany.

February 12-14, after the Azerbaijani pogroms, 39 Armenian refugees were temporariy settled by the Soviets in Dushanbe, Tajikistan. Rumors fanned fears among the locals that many more Armeinan refugees would come and protests and rioting ensued, with 26 killed and 526 injured by Soviet troops.

February 13, the fifth largest investment bank in the US, Drexel Burnham Lambert, filed for bankruptcy due to their illegal activities in the junk bond market. The bank ceased operations in 1994.

February 14, the *Pale Blue Dot* photograph of Earth by Voyager 1 from 3.5 billion miles away was sent back to Earth.

Also on February 14, Perrier recalled 160 million bottles of sparkling water because of traces of a carcinogen, benzene, in the water.

February 15, Britain and Argentina resumed diplomatic relations after an eight year gap due to Argentina's invasion of the Falkland Islands.

Also on February 15, President Bush met with the presidents of Columbia, Bolivia and Peru in Cartagena to talk about fighting the international drug trade.

February 26, the USSR agreed to remove all Soviet Troops from Czechoslovakia in 1991.

February 28, Nicaragua announced a seize fire with the US backed Contras.

Also February 28-March 4, Atlantis 6, was launched at night on a secret military mission.

March 2, Greyhound Buses went on strike stranding some travelers.

March 3, Carole Gist was crowned the first Black Miss America.

March 4, 1990 the Soviet Union began electing a Congress of People's Deputies. The USSR eventually elected 1,058 Deputies.

March 9, Antonia Novello was sworn in as the first Hispanic Surgeon General.

March 11, Lithuania declared its independence from the USSR and formed a Lithuanian national government.

March 12, the Soviet military began leaving Hungary.

March 13, the Supreme Soviet approved changes to the Soviet Constitution, adding a US-style elected president. On March 15, Mikhail Gorbachev was elected president for a five year term.

March 15, the USSR called Lithuanian independence invalid.

March 18, East Germany and Estonia held their first free elections.

Also on March 18, art thieves posing as police officers stole about $300 million in art work from a museum in Boston. The works included twelve paintings and a Chinese vase. As of this writing they have not been recovered.

March 25, Hungary held its first free multi-party elections since 1948.

March 30, the Estonians declared the Soviet occupation of Estonia illegal and set a schedule to become independent of the USSR.

April 6, Robert Mapplethorpe's show *The Perfect Moment* with nude homoerotic subjects was opened at Cincinnati's Contemporary Arts center amid public protest and accusations of indecency.

April 7, Reagan's National Security Advisor Admiral John Poindexter was convicted of five felonies in the Iran Contra Scandal. The convictions were later nullified on appeal because it was stated that Congress had given him partial immunity in his testimony before them.

April 12, Greyhound Bus hired new drivers to break the strike.

Also on April 12, the newly-elected East German parliament acknowledged the Holocaust and asked for forgiveness.

April 13, the USSR apologized for the Katyn Massacre. The massacre occurred in March of 1940 when about 22,000 Polish officers, police and elected officials were executed in various locations by Soviet troops at the instigation of NKVD chief Lavrentiy Beria. Many were buried in mass graves in Katyn forest. This is a distinct event from the Khatyn tragedy that took place on March 22, 1943, when the entire population of a village in Byelorussia was slaughtered by a Nazi group primarily made up of Ukrainians.

April 22, American educator Robert Polhill, who was held hostage in Lebanon for 39 months, was released.

April 24, East and West Germany agreed that on July 1, they would merge their currencies and economy.

April 24-29, the space shuttle Discovery 10 was launched. The shuttle put the Hubble Telescope into orbit.

April 30, Frank Reed an American educator who had been kidnapped and held prisoner in Lebanon since 1986 was released.

May 2-4, talks about ending apartheid between the South African government and the African National Congress began.

May 4, Latvia declared its independence from the USSR.

May 9, New York *Newsday* reporter Jimmy Breslin was suspended for a racial slur.

May 13, two American airmen were killed by gunmen near Clark Air Force base on the eve before US-Filipino talks about the future of US bases in the Philippines.

May 16, the first Congress of Deputies of the Soviet Union met for the first time.

May 17, the World Health Organization removed homosexuality from its list of mental disorders.

May 20, Romania held its first free elections.

May 23, the government estimated that the S&L crisis had cost the US taxpayer $130 billion.

May 30, President Bush and President Gorbachev began a four day summit in Washington, DC. As part of the summit they signed a treaty and each agreed to destroy their chemical weapons stocks.

June 2, violent storms struck the Midwest producing 88 tornados in Illinois, Indiana, Kentucky, and Ohio.

June 4, Greyhound Bus filed bankruptcy.

Also on June 4, Dr, Jack Kevorkian assisted a woman's suicide in Oregon sparking debate over assisted suicide and the right to die.

Also on this date disagreements over land rights between the Kyrgyz and the Uzbeks ethnic groups in Kirghiz SSR ended in violence.

June 8-9, the first free elections in Czechoslovakia since 1946 were held.

June 8, the 1990 FIFA World Cup in Italy became the first broadcast of HDTV. It was shown live in eight movie theaters.

June 9, Robert Kennedy's daughter Kerry and Andrew Cuomo were wed. The marriage of the two children from important Democratic political families intrigued the press and the American public.

June 13, East Germany began the complete deconstruction of the Berlin Wall.

June 17-30, recently freed Nelson Mandela and his wife Winnie arrived in New York City and began a US and Canadian tour. On June 22, he addressed the United Nations. On June 25, he met with President Bush at the White House.

June 19, the Communist Party of the Russian Soviet Federative Socialist Republic was formed to oppose the Gorbachev reforms.

June 22, the Cold War landmark, Checkpoint Charlie was closed.

July 1, East and West Germany merged their economies. The Deutsche Mark became the currency for both and the border between the two was erased.

July 2, during the Hajj religious pilgrimage a panic stampede occurred in Mecca which saw 1,426 trampled to death.

July 11, "Dart Man" as the press called him was arrested by New York City Police. Over the course of a little over a week Dart Man stabbed 53 women in the buttocks with darts. The women were all described as light-skinned women in business attire. He worked as a bicycle messenger for an ad agency.

July 12, Boris Yeltsin resigned from the Communist Party.

July 19, the Richard Nixon Library opened in Yorba Linda, California.

July 22, the first election ever in Mongolia was held.

July 24, US warships in the Persian Gulf were put on full alert as Iraqi troops massed on the Kuwaiti border.

July, 25, the Bush Administration made a critical mistake when the Bush's Ambassador told Iraq that it would not take sides in the Iraq-Kuwait dispute, sending the signal to Iraq that the US would not defend Kuwait from invasion. The tragic mistake led to the Gulf War.

July 26, the Americans with Disabilities Act became law to protect disabled Americans from discrimination.

July 27, Belarus declared its independence from the Soviet Union. It would become independent in 1991.

July 30, the first Saturn automobile came off the assembly line.

August 1, the computer network RELCOM was formed in the USSR by combining computer networks. Later in August the USSR would link up to the internet.

Also on August 10, Soyuz TM 10, the tenth trip to the Mir space station was launched, with a Japanese reporter aboard.

August 2, Iraq invaded and occupied Kuwait. President Bush ordered US troops to Saudi Arabia.

August 3, the US announced an increase in US Naval forces in the Persian Gulf.

August 4, the European community proposed a boycott against Iraq.

August 6, the UN Security Council voted to begin economic sanctions against Iraq.

August 7, Operation Desert Shield saw the first US forces arrive in Saudi Arabia.

August 8, Iraq formally annexed Kuwait.

August 9, Arab leaders agreed to send forces to protect Saudi Arabia.

August 10, the Magellan Spacecraft landed on Venus.

August 12, to solicit Arab sympathy Saddam Hussein said he would withdraw from Kuwait if Israel withdrew from all occupied territories.

August 20, Saddam Hussein took all Americans and British in Kuwait to Iraq as hostages.

August 22, President Bush called up US Army reservists for active duty.

August 24, the Armenian SSR declared independence from the Soviet Union.

August 28, an F-5 tornado struck the Chicago metro area and killed 29, injured 353, and caused $165 million in damage.

September 5, Saddam Hussein called for all Arabs to rise up against Israel and the West.

September 9, President Bush and Soviet leader Gorbachev met in Helsinki to discuss the Persian Gulf crisis.

Also on September 9, Liberian President Samuel Doe was captured, tortured, and killed by rebels in the on-going civil war. The rebels videotaped his ruthless torture and dismemberment.

September 10-11, Pizza Huts were opened in Moscow and Shenzhen, China.

September 10, Ellis Island was reopened as a museum.

September 11, President Bush addressed the American people saying he would use American force to remove Iraqi troops from Kuwait.

September 15, France announced that it would send 4,000 troops to Saudi Arabia.

September 17, reporter Lisa Olsen was sexually harassed by multiple men, mostly players, in the New England Patriots locker room where she was sent to conduct a player interview.

Also on September 17, Saudi Arabia and the USSR restored diplomatic relations.

September 23, Saddam Hussein announced that Iraq would destroy Israel. He threatened to destroy the Kuwaiti oil fields if the US invaded.

September 24, the Supreme Soviet granted Gorbachev special powers for 18 months to change the USSR from a socialist to a market economy.

Also on September 24, a US Warship stopped and boarded an Iraqi oil tanker.

September 27, the deposed Emir of Kuwait addressed the UN General Assembly. He was invited to the White House the following day.

September 29, US Secretary of State James Baker met with the leaders of Vietnam to discuss the end of a US economic embargo and normalizing diplomatic relations.

October 1, President Bush condemned Iraq before the United Nations. Saddam Hussein said that he may be open to negotiations on Kuwait.

Also On October 1, Serbs in Croatia declared their autonomy.

Also on this date the Rwanda Civil war began.

October 3, the reunification of Germany was formally celebrated with the raising of the German flag over the Brandenburg gate at midnight.

October 6-10, the space shuttle Discovery 11 was launched.

October 7, with concerns about Iraq attacking Israel with poison gas, Israel issued gas masks to all civilians.

October 8, violence erupted in Israel. Police killed 17 Palestinians and wounded over 100 in the clashes.

October 11, Libya's Muammar Gaddafi agreed with Saddam Hussein and said Israel must be destroyed.

October 13, the first Russian Orthodox service in 70 years was held at St. Basil's Cathedral in Moscow's Red Square.

October 15, Mikhail Gorbachev was awarded the Nobel Peace Prize for his efforts to end the Cold War.

Also on October 15, South Africa ended segregation in public facilities.

October 16, US forces in the Persian Gulf reached 200,000.

October 20, anti-war marches began in twenty US cities.

October 23, Iraq released 330 French hostages.

October 30, the first transatlantic fiber optic cable failed greatly slowing the internet traffic between the US and Europe.

November 1, the first portable digital camera was sold in the US.

Also on November 1, President Bush compared Saddam Hussein to Hitler.

November 5, ultra-conservative Rabbi Meir Kahane was assassinated by an Egyptian-American, El Sayyid Nosair, who was later convicted in the first bombing of the World Trade Center in 1993. Nosair later admitted he killed Kahane while in prison.

November 7, the final military parade in Moscow to mark the anniversary of the Great Socialist Revolution took place.

November 8, an additional 100,000 US troops were sent to the Persian Gulf.

November 12, Tim Berners-Lee published a formal proposal for the creation of the World Wide Web.

November 14, Germany and Poland signed a treaty using the Odder-Neisse line as the border between the two.

November 15-20, Atlantis 7 was launched on a secret military mission.

November 20, the USSR refused to endorse the use of force against Iraq.

November 19-21, the US and thirty-three other nations met in Paris to discuss the end of the Cold War.

November 22, President Bush visited US troops in Saudi Arabia.

Also on November 22, British Prime Minister Maggie Thatcher resigned.

November 28, John Major replaced Maggie Thatcher as Prime Minister.

November 29, the UN passed Resolution 678 authorizing military intervention if Iraq did not leave Kuwait by January 15, 1991.

December 2, in the first general election of the reunified Germany Helmut Kohl became Chancellor of Germany.

December 2-10, the space shuttle Columbia 10, was launched with for space telescopes. Along with the cosmonauts at the Mir Space Station it marked the first time that 12 people were in space at the same time.

December 3, Mary Robinson became the first woman President of Ireland.

December 4, Saddam Hussein said that he would withdraw from Kuwait if Iraq could keep control over the Rumailah oil field. On the next day Iraq stated its willingness to negotiate with the US. On December 6, Hussein released all foreign hostages.

December 9, Lech Walesa, the former Solidarity leader was elected President of Poland.

December 11, an 83 vehicle accident due to fog on Interstate 75 near Chattanooga killed 13 people.

December 13, South African President F.W. de Klerk met with Nelson Mandela to discuss the end of Apartheid.

Also on December 13, the US questioned Iraq's seriousness about negotiations.

December 18, President Bush took a no concession stance on Iraqi withdrawal from Kuwait. Two days later the US military told Iraq they were ready to attack on January 15, unless Iraq withdrew.

December 22, Iraq announced that Kuwait was formally a part of Iraq.

December 23, Slovenians voted to secede from Yugoslavia.

December 24, Saddam Hussein stated that if there was war Israel would be its first target.

December 28, two died and 188 were injured in a New York City subway electrical fire.

In 1990 it was discovered that there is an ozone hole over the North Pole as well as the South Pole. The first in-car satellite navigation system went on sale. One of the largest and best preserved Tyrannosaurus Rex fossilized skeletons, named "Sue," was found by paleontologist Sue Hendrickson near Faith, South Dakota. In 1790 Ben Franklin invested $5,000 each for the cities of Boston and Philadelphia with the stipulation they could not withdraw the funds until 1890 and 1990. In this year both Boston and Philadelphia withdrew $20 million.

The US entered a recession. The inflation rate was at 5.39%. The yearend interest rates were at 10%. Average income was $28,960. The average price of a new home was $123,000 and monthly rents averaged $465. The average price of a new car was $15,435 with gasoline at $1.34 per gallon. The price of IBM PS1 computers ranged from $999 to $1999.

In 1990 ABC aired 11 episodes of an ill-fated musical police drama called *Cop Rock* which *TV Guide* called "the most bizarre musical of all time," and dubbed it one of the worst shows in television history. The Sci-fi Channel made its debut. On April 21, the *Cartoon All-stars to the Rescue*, a special anti-drug program for children featuring popular cartoon characters. It was aired simultaneously on all four networks, the USA, BET and Nickelodeon cable channels. The *Brady Bunch* returned to television as *The Bradys*, a drama about the adult Brady children but was cancelled quietly due to poor ratings after only six episodes.

Other shows making their debuts: *Northern Exposure, Carol & Company, Twin Peaks, In Living Color, Wings, Dream On, Parker Lewis Can't Lose, The Fresh Prince of Bel-Air, Law & Order, The Trials of Rosie O'Neil, Evening Shade,* and *Beverly Hills 90210.*

Shows ending their runs included: *Mission Impossible, Mama's Family, Alf, Tour of Duty, My Two Dads, 227, Falcon Crest, Newhart, The Tracy Ullman Show, Pee-Wee's Playhouse* and *Mr. Belvedere*.

At the Emmys *Murphy Brown* was the Best Comedy, *L.A. Law* was the Best Drama. The Best Comedy Actors were Ted Danson in *Cheers* and Candice Bergen in *Murphy Brown*. The Best Dramatic Actors were Peter Falk in *Columbo* and Patricia Wettig in *thirtysomething*.

The top grossing movies of 1990 were: *Ghost, Home Alone, Pretty Woman, Dances with Wolves, Total Recall, Back to the Future Part III, Die Hard 2, Presumed Innocent, Teenage Mutant Ninja Turtles,* and *Kindergarten Cop*. Other significant pictures included: *Goodfellas, Reversal of Fortunes, Misery, Green Card, Dick Tracy, Awakenings, The Hunt for Red October, The Godfather Part III, Predator, Wild at Heart, Days of Thunder, The Night of the Living Dead, The Grifters, Captain America, The King of New York, Bird on a Wire,* and *Joe Versus the Volcano*.

At the Oscars the Best Picture and Director went to *Dances with Wolves*. The Best Actors went to Jeremy Irons in *Reversal of Fortunes* and Kathy Bates in *Misery*. Best Supporting Actors went to Joe Pesci in *Goodfellas* and Whoopi Goldberg in *Ghost*.

In 1990 music their producers admitted that Milli Vanilli did not actually sing their songs. They were stripped of their Grammy. Artists inducted into the Rock & Roll Hall of Fame in 1990 included: Bobby Darin, The Who, The Four Seasons, The Four Tops, Simon & Garfunkel, The Platters, The Kinks, and Hank Ballard.

The top hits of the year included: *Hold On* and *Release Me* by Wilson Phillips, *U Can't Touch This* and *Have You Seen Her* by MC Hammer, *How Am I Supposed to Live without You* by Michael Bolton, *Pump Up the Jam* by Technotronic, *Step by Step* by New Kids On the Block, *We Didn't Start the Fire* by Billy Joel, *Vogue* by Madonna, *The Humpty Dance* by Digital Underground, *Free Fallin'* by Tom Petty, *Opposites Attract* and *The Way That You Love Me* by Paula Abdul and *Vision of Love* by Mariah Carey.

In 1990 Fiction John Updike won a Pulitzer Prize for Fiction for *Rabbit at Rest*. Laurel Thatcher Ulrich won the Pulitzer Prize for History for *A Midwife's Tale*. The Pulitzer Prize for Poetry went to Mona Van Duyn for *Near Changes*. Other notable works included: *The Things They Carried* by Tim O'Brien, *Jurassic Park* by Michael Crichton, *Possession* by A.S. Byatt, *Four Past Midnight* by Stephen King, *The Buddha of Suburbia* by Hanif Kureishi, *Barbarians at the Gate* by Bryan Burrough, *The Mother Tongue: English and How It Got that Way* by Bill Bryson, *Maniac McGee* by Jerry Spinelli, *Get Shorty* by Elmore Leonard, *The Gift of Asher Lev* by Chaim Potok, *L. A. Confidential* by James Ellroy and *The Snapper* by Roddy Doyle.

Chapter 47. 1991: The Gulf War, the Tailhook Scandal, the Fall of Communism and the End of the Soviet Union

January 1, Iraq rejected an Egyptian peace proposal.

Also on January 1, with mounting deficits and a crumbling economy the USSR placed a 5% sales tax on all consumer goods and services.

January 3, after a 23-year gap Israel opened a consulate in the USSR.

January 4, the UN Security Council voted to condemn Israel for its treatment of the Palestinians.

January 5, the South Ossetian War began, with troops from the Soviet Republic of Georgia arriving in tanks to stop the locals seeking to secede and form an autonomous region.

January 7, Saddam Hussein prepared his army for what he said would be a long violent war.

January 9, Secretary of State James Baker met with the Iraqi Foreign Minister in Geneva in an attempt to avoid war. The talks failed.

January 11-13, Soviet troops stormed Vilnius to stop Lithuanian independence, killing 14 civilians and wounding 702.

January 12, Congress passed a resolution authorizing the use of force in Iraq.

January 13-27, in what became known as "The Time of the Barricades," the USSR attempted to put down Latvian independence, mostly in Riga, and the Latvians constructed barricades to protect their capital. During the conflict 6 Latvians were killed and 14 were wounded.

January 13, the UN Secretary General met with Saddam Hussein in a failed attempt to resolve the Kuwaiti issue.

January 17-February 28, Operation Desert Storm, a coalition of 35 nations led by the US began the air assault of Iraq on January 17, which lasted until February 24 when the ground assault began.

January 17, Iraq fired 8 Scud missiles into Israel.

January 18, the US finally acknowledged that Panamanian dictator Manuel Noriega was a CIA and US Army asset and was paid over $320,000 for his service.

January 18, Eastern Airlines ceased operations after 62 years.

January 19, Iraq launched another Scud attack on Tel Aviv.

January 20, the US Patriot missiles were deployed to Israel and became operational, defending Israel from missile attacks.

January 22, another Iraqi missile attack was made on Ramat Gan, Israel.

Also on January 22, Iraq destroyed Kuwaiti oil facilities.

January 26, the civil war in Somalia began.

January 29- February 1, the Iraqis attacked Saudi Arabia at the town of Khafji to try and draw US troops into combat before the air war was over. The attacks were repulsed by US Marines and Army Rangers. US forces suffered 43 dead, 52 wounded, 2 captured and lost 9-12 armored vehicles. Iraq had 71 killed, 148 wounded, 702 missing presumed captured or dead and 186 armored vehicles destroyed.

February 1, the South African government stated that it would repeal all Apartheid laws.

February 5, a Michigan Court banned Dr. Jack Kevorkian from assisting in suicides.

February 7, in the "Troubles," the Irish Republican Army launched a mortar attack on Number 10 Downing Street during a cabinet meeting.

February 10, Lithuanian voters confirmed their desire to gain independence from the USSR. The following day Iceland recognized the independent country of Lithuania.

February 11-August 9, Soyuz TM-9 was launched to the Mir Space Station.

February 13, US bombs hit an air raid shelter in Baghdad, Iraq, killing hundreds of civilians.

February 15, Czechoslovakia, Poland and Hungary signed a cooperation agreement to move their three countries toward a market economy.

February 22, Iraq accepted a Soviet-proposed cease fire agreement — which was rejected by US and coalition forces.

February 25, a Scud missile hit a US barracks in Dhahran, Saudi Arabia, killing 29 and wounding 99 US soldiers.

February 26, Saddam Hussein announced the withdrawal of all Iraqi forces from Kuwait. As the Iraqi forces left they set fire to Kuwaiti oil wells.

February 27, President Bush ordered a ceasefire and declared victory over Iraq.

March 1, the US Embassy in Kuwait was reopened.

March 2, the US Army, despite the ceasefire, destroyed a retreating Iraqi Republican Guard column.

March 3, voters in Latvia and Estonia confirmed their desire for independence from the USSR.

Later on March 3, an amateur video captured Los Angeles Police officers beating an already subdued Black motorist, Rodney King. The officers were tried but were acquitted in 1992; this touched off the Los Angeles Riots.

Also on this date President George H.W. Bush reached his highest approval rating, 82% according to a Gallup Poll. Despite this he would lose his popularity and his bid for a second term in 1992.

March 4, Iraq released all prisoners of war.

March 9, massive pro-democracy demonstrations were held in Belgrade, Yugoslavia and were put down by the military. Two people were killed. In 2006, Montenegro and Serbia became the last of the former Yugoslav republics to declare independence.

March 10, US troops began leaving the Persian Gulf.

March 13, Exxon agreed to pay $1 billion in fines and cleanup for the Exxon Valdez oil spill in Alaska.

March 15, the US and Albania resumed diplomatic relations for the first time since 1939.

March 20, the US forgave $2 billion in loans from economically struggling Poland.

March 22, a New Hampshire high school teacher, Pamela Smart, was found guilty of manipulating her 15-year-old student lover to murder her husband.

March 23, a civil war began in Sierra Leone.

March 31, Albania held their first democratic elections.

Also on March 31, the Georgian SSR voted to be independent from the USSR.

April 1, the Warsaw Pact officially was dissolved.

April 2, the USSR began to double or triple the prices of consumer goods and services.

April 3, the UN passed a resolution requiring Iraq to destroy all biological and chemical weapons and facilities and all missiles with a range greater than 150 km. Iraq agreed on April 5, and began to comply.

April 4, Senator John Heinz of Pennsylvania and six other people were killed when a helicopter and his airplane accidentally collided.

Also on April 4, William Kennedy Smith was charged with raping a woman on the beach while partying in Florida with his uncle Senator Ted Kennedy and his cousin Patrick Kennedy. He claimed the encounter was consensual, despite the fact that several other women then came forward to allege that they too had been raped by Kennedy in the past. He was acquitted after the other women were not allowed to testify. In 2004 an employee accused Smith of sexual assault but this too was dismissed. In 2005 Smith settled with another woman employee who accused him of sexual harassment.

On this date four Vietnamese men botched a robbery and took 41 people hostage in a Good Guys electronic store in Sacramento, California. During the crisis three hostages were killed and 14 others injured. Three of the four of the Vietnamese gunmen were killed and the fourth captured by police.

April 5, former Senator John Tower and 22 others were killed in a plane crash in Georgia.

April 5-11, the space shuttle Atlantis 8 was launched. The mission had two space walks, the first since 1985.

April 12, the US announced the closing of 31 military bases.

April 14, twenty paintings worth more than $500 million were stolen from the Van Gogh Museum in Amsterdam. They were recovered an hour later in a car near the museum.

April 23, the USSR agreed to allow republics to secede under certain conditions.

April 26, over 70 tornados struck the Midwest, killing 17.

April 28-May 6, the space shuttle Discovery 12 was launched on a classified military mission.

April 29, Croatia declared independence from Yugoslavia.

May 4, President Bush was hospitalized with an irregular heartbeat. He was released the following day.

Also on May 4, Congressman Mo Udall of Arizona, a presidential contender in 1976, resigned due to Parkinson's disease.

May 14, Queen Elizabeth II arrived for a 13-day royal visit to the US.

Also on May 14, Winnie Mandela was convicted for her involvement in the kidnapping and killing of a 14-year-old boy. The sentence was never carried out.

May 15, more documents were released showing Manuel Noriega's work for the CIA and his connections to many US officials.

Also on this date President Bush took Queen Elizabeth II to a baseball game.

May 16, Queen Elizabeth II became the first British monarch to address the US Congress.

May 18-October 10, Soyuz TM-12 was launched to the Mir Space Station.

May 20, the USSR approved a law allowing Soviet citizens to travel abroad.

May 25, in a 36-hour period Israel evacuated 14,325 Ethiopian Jews endangered in war-torn Ethiopia.

May 31, a peace treaty was signed ending the Angolan civil war.

June 4, Pope John Paul II created controversy when he equated abortions with Nazi genocide.

Also on June 4, Robert Strauss became the last US Ambassador to the USSR.

June 5-14, the space shuttle Columbia 11 was launched, carrying Spacelab into space.

June 8, the Gulf War Victory Parade was held in New York City.

June 10, Jaycee Dugard, an 11-year-old girl, was kidnapped by a couple and raped and tortured during a confinement lasting until 2009. She had two daughters at the age of 14 and 17 by her rapist. She would later write a memoir, *A Stolen Life*, about her ordeal.

June 12, in Russia's first-ever popular vote, Boris Yeltsin was elected the President of Russia, the USSR's largest republic. (Mikhail Gorbachev was the head of state of the USSR overall.)

June 13, a spectator was killed by lightning at the US Tennis Open.

June 17, President Zachary Taylor's body was exhumed to see if he had been poisoned. No evidence was found.

June 18, Boris Yeltsin arrived in the US for talks.

June 20, Germany decided to move its capital from Bonn to Berlin.

June 25, with the independence of Croatia and Slovenia, Yugoslavia began to collapse.

June 26, Nelson Mandela addressed Congress.

June 27-July 7, the Ten-Day War broke out as Yugoslavian forces attempted to take back Slovenia. It resulted in a successful defense of Slovenian independence.

June 28, the Sierra Madre earthquake struck Southern California killing two, injuring over a hundred and causing about $40 million in damages.

July 1, the telephone service in Washington, DC, Pittsburg, Los Angeles and San Francisco crashed due to a software bug. Twelve million were without telephone service.

July 9, Alan D. Fiers, the CIA Chief of the South American Task Force under President Reagan pled guilty to two counts of withholding information from Congress in the Iran-Contra scandal.

July 10, with the end of Apartheid, the US announced that it was ending the economic boycott against South Africa.

July 11, a total solar eclipse was seen in Hawaii.

July 15, US troops left Northern Iraq.

Also on July 15, Chemical Bank and Manufacturers Hanover Corporation merged in what was then the largest bank merger.

July 16, Mikhail Gorbachev arrived in London to ask the G7 for financial aid.

July 17, Gorbachev and President Bush agreed to terms for the START II Treaty which was signed on July 31.

July 19, boxer Mike Tyson raped 18-year-old Desiree Washington, a Miss Black America contestant. He was convicted in February 1992. Donald Trump defended Tyson before and after the trial claiming that Tyson was the real victim. Trump called the verdict a "travesty" on the Howard Stern Show.

July 22, Jeffrey Dahmer was arrested in Milwaukee after the remains of 11 boys and men were found in his apartment. Dahmer would eventually be charged with 17 murders. Dahmer killed his victims, had sex with the bodies and then ate parts of them while preserving other body parts. Dahmer was later beaten to death in prison by another prisoner in 1994.

July 24, British astronomers announced finding the first planet outside the solar system.

July 26, Paul Reubens (Pee-Wee Hermann) was arrested in Florida for exposing himself in a movie theater.

July 29, a New York City grand jury indicted Bank of Credit and Commerce International for defrauding depositors of $5 billion. It was also accused of money laundering in the Iran-Contra scandal, and for Saddam Hussein, Manuel Noriega, and the Madeline drug cartel. The bank would be forced into closure and described at the time as "the largest bank fraud in world history."

July 31, the US Senate voted to allow women to fly combat aircraft.

Also on July 31, the Soviet special police unit, OMON, assaulted and killed seven Lithuanian border guards.

August 2-11, space shuttle Atlantis 9 was launched.

August 8, the Warsaw radio tower collapsed. At the time it was the tallest manmade structure ever built.

August 13, Super Nintendo went on sale in the US.

Also on August 13, Vice president Dan Quayle made a speech attacking lawyers. Quayle argued that an excess of lawyers, lawsuits and damage awards handicapped the United States in world markets.

August 15, singer/songwriter Paul Simon gave a free concert in Central Park the *New York Times* said the crowd numbered about 600,000.

August 16, President Bush claimed that the US recession would soon end.

August 16-20, Hurricane Bob hit the east coast of the US killing 17 people, and causing $1.5 billion in damages.

August 19, a coup of Soviet hardliners attempted to take over the Soviet Union. Gorbachev was arrested and detained on house arrest. The coup led by Vice President Gennady Yanayev collapsed in less than 72 hours when over a hundred thousand protesting the coup led by Boris Yeltsin surrounded the Soviet parliament building.

August 20-22, Latvia and Estonia declared independence from the Soviet Union and Iceland became the first nation to recognize the two independent Baltic States. On August 25, Denmark and Norway would also recognize them as independent nations. On September 2, the US recognized the Baltic States and reopened embassies there.

August 24, Mikhail Gorbachev resigned as head of the Communist Party of the USSR.

August 24, the Ukraine declared its independence from the USSR.

August 25, Belarus declared independence from the USSR.

August 27, Moldova declared independence from the USSR.

August 29, Boris Yeltsin dissolved the Communist Party of the Soviet Union.

August 30-31, Azerbaijan, Kyrgyzstan and Uzbekistan declared their independence from the USSR.

September 3, a grease fire in a chicken processing plant in North Carolina killed 25 workers.

September 5-7, over 4,000 attendees came to the US Navy's 35th Annual Tailhook Symposium in Las Vegas. During the evening parties 83 women and 7 men were sexually assaulted by US Naval Officers. The Secretary of the Navy and a number of flag officers saw or were made aware of the assaults but chose to ignore them. According to the PBS television show *Frontline* the scandal ultimately resulted in the Secretary of the Navy resigning, 14 admirals resigned or had their careers damaged, as did 300 Navy aviators.

September 6, the USSR formally recognized the independence of the Baltic States.

Also on September 6, the city of Leningrad returned to its original name St. Petersburg. It was named Leningrad by the Soviets in 1924.

September 8, Macedonia voted for independence from Yugoslavia.

September 9, Tajikistan declared independence from the USSR.

September 11, the USSR announced the end of military and economic aid to Cuba.

September 12-18, the Space Shuttle Discovery 13 was launched to put an upper atmosphere satellite into orbit.

September 19, mummified human remains dating from 3,300 BCE, which became known as "Ötzi the Iceman," were discovered in the Alps between Austria and Italy.

September 21, Armenia declared its independence from the USSR.

September 27, the US ended the Cold War 24-hour alert for its B-52 bombers.

September 28, UN weapon inspectors ended a five-day dispute with Iraq.

October 2-March 1992 Soyuz TM-13 was launched to the Mir Space Station.

October 3, Arkansas Governor Bill Clinton announced that he would run for president in 1992.

October 6, Gorbachev condemned anti-Semitism in the USSR.

October 11, Televangelist Jimmy Lee Swaggart was publicly implicated for his involvement with a prostitute.

Also on October 11, the KGB was replaced by the Russian Foreign Intelligence Service, SVR.

October 11-15, when Clarence Thomas was nominated for Supreme Court Justice, law professor Anita Hill accused Thomas of sexual harassment and inappropriate conduct. Despite this, President Bush declared his full support of Thomas. Hill testified before the Senate, but despite the accusations Thomas was approved narrowly 52-48.

October 16, a gunman killed 23 and wounded 27 others before taking his own life at a restaurant in Killeen, Texas.

October 20, the Oakland Hills fire storm in Oakland, California killed 25 and destroyed 3,469 homes and apartments.

Also on October 20, the KKK Grand Wizard David Duke won a preliminary vote in the election for Governor of Louisiana and was placed on the ballot.

October 21, Governor of California Jerry Brown announced that he would run for president in 1992.

Also on October 21, US hostage Jesse Turner, an educator, was released from captivity in Lebanon after five years.

October 27, Turkmenistan declared its independence from the USSR.

October 28-November 4, a small unnamed hurricane in the North Atlantic which became known as "the Perfect Storm" struck New England, causing 13 deaths and $200 million in damage.

October 31,-November 3, the Halloween Blizzard struck the upper Midwest killing 22 and causing $100 million in damage.

November 5, in the Pennsylvania special election to replace John Heinz, who had died in a plane crash, Democratic Senate candidate Harris Wofford came from behind to win.

Also on November 5, after 13 years Vietnam and China restored diplomatic relations which had been cut off during the Sino-Vietnamese War which began in 1979.

November 6, the Communist Party was banned in Russia by Presidential decree.

November 7, the last of the Kuwaiti oil fires from the Persian Gulf War was extinguished.

November 14, British and US officials announced indictments against two Libyan intelligence officers in the bombing of Pan Am Flight 103.

November 18, Serbian paramilitary executed 260 Croatian prisoners of war.

November 23, the Communist Party of Great Britain voted to disband.

November 27, the UN Security Council adopted a resolution to form a peacekeeping force for Yugoslavia.

November 30, a dust storm near San Francisco caused a 93 car and 11 truck accidents which killed 17 people.

December 1, the Ukrainians voted to ratify independence from the USSR.

December 3, President Bush's Chief of Staff John Sununu resigned amid rumors that Bush had asked for his resignation because of Bush's falling poll numbers as the US economy struggled.

December 4, the last and longest held US hostage, Terry Anderson, was freed in Lebanon.

Also on December 4, Pan American World Airways ended operations.

December 12, the new Republic of the Ukraine decriminalized homosexuality.

December 16, Kazakhstan declared independence from the USSR.

December 18, GM announced the closing of 21 plants.

December 25, Mikhail Gorbachev resigned as President of the USSR.

December 26, the Supreme Soviet met for the final time and dissolved the USSR. The Soviet branches of government were to cease operations on December 31. The Russian SFSR became the Russian Federation.

In 1991 the economy was still in recession. Unemployment rose to 6.8% and would continue to rise to 7.5% in 1992. The US Labor Department said 1,623 million jobs were lost from July 1990 to the end of 1991. The recession was the main reason George Bush would lose to Bill Clinton in the election of 1992.

Yearly inflation was 4.25%. The average income was $29,430. The average cost of a new home was $147,200 and average monthly rents rose to $495. The average price of a new car was $15,220 with gas at $1.12 per gallon. In April the minimum wage rose from $3.80 per hour to $4.28.

In 1991 television the first sets with built-in closed captions were made. All prime time television network coverage was suspended for live coverage of the Gulf War. It was announced that Jay Leno would replace Johnny Carson on the *Tonight Show*. The announcement was controversial as David Letterman had expected to replace Carson. Comedy Central debuted in April and CBS' second longest series, *Dallas* ended its run.

Shows making their debuts: *Blossom, Dinosaurs, American Detective, Sisters, Hi Honey I'm Home, Nurses, Home Improvement, Reasonable Doubts, Brooklyn Bridge, Step By Step, Homefront, The Commish, The Jerry Springer Show, Charlie Rose,* and *I'll Fly Away.*

In addition to *Dallas,* shows ending their runs included: *Generations, Tic-Tac-Dough, Doctor Doctor, Hunter, 21 Jump Street, The Days and Nights of Molly Dodd, thirtysomething, DEA, Twin Peaks, Head of the Class, The Hogan Family,* and *China Beach.*

At the Emmys *Cheers* won Best Comedy and *LA Law* won Best Drama. Burt Reynolds won Best Comedy Actor in *Evening Shade.* Kirstie Alley won Best Comedy Actress in *Cheers.* The Best Dramatic Actors were James Earl Jones in *Gabriel's Fire* and Patricia Wettig in *thirtysomething.*

The 1991 top grossing movies were: *Terminator 2 Judgment Day, Robin Hood Prince of Thieves, Beauty and the Beast, Hook, The Silence of the Lambs, JFK, The Addams Family, Cape Fear, Hot Shots!,* and *City Slickers.* Other significant films of 1991 included: *Thelma & Louise, Fried Green Tomatoes, The Commitments, The Prince of Tides, For the Boys, The Fisher King, Boyz N the Hood, Sleeping with the Enemy, Backdraft, Bugsy, My Girl, Drop Dead Fred, The Doors,* and *Regarding Henry.*

At the Oscars *The Silence of the Lambs* swept winning Best Picture, Director, and Actor for Anthony Hopkins and Actress for Jodie Foster.

In 1991 music Freddie Mercury the lead singer of Queen died from complications from AIDS. Some of the top hits of 1991 included: Bryan Adams' *Everything I Do I Do for You* and *Can't Stop This Thing We Started,* Bonnie Raitt's *Something to Talk About,* Amy Grant's *Baby Baby* and *Every Heartbeat,* Nirvana's *Smells Like Teen Spirit,* Metallica's *Enter Sandman,* Roxette's *Joyride* and *Fading Like a Flower,* R.E.M.'s *Losing My Religion* and *Shiny Happy People,* Guns N Roses' *You Could Be Mine* and *Don't Cry,* Prince's *Gett Off* and *Diamonds and Pearls,* Boyz II Men's *Motownphilly,* Michael Jackson's *Black or White,* Mariah Carey's *Emotions,* and Queen's *These Are the Days of Our Lives.*

In literature the Pulitzer Prize for Fiction was won by Jane Smiley for *A Thousand Acres.* The Prize for Poetry was *Selected Poems* by James Tate and the Nonfiction Prize winner James B. Stewart for *Den of Thieves.*

Other significant works included: *Lila: An Inquiry Into Morals* by Robert Pirsig (another Pulitzer Prize finalist), *The Firm* by John Grisham, *The Six Wives of Henry VIII* by Alison Weir, *Needful Things* and *The Waste Lands* by Stephen King, *The Sum of All Fears* by Tom Clancy, *The Kitchen God's Wife* by Amy Tan, *Backlash* by Susan Faludi, *Regeneration* by Pat Barker, *The Third Chimpanzee* by Jared Diamond, *War Time Lies* by Louis Begley, *Me: Stories of My Life* by Katharine Hepburn and *COLD WARRIOR, James Jesus Angleton: The CIA's Master Spy Hunter* by Tom Mangold.

EPILOGUE

> "Cry 'Havoc!' and let slip the dogs of war."
>
> —William Shakespeare's *Julius Caesar*

In history there are few neat boxes and the Cold War is not one of them. The most accepted period for the Cold War is the one I have used in this book 1945 to 1991, the end of WWII to the fall of the USSR. Some would suggest that the real start of the Cold War began with the Siberian and Polar Bear Interventions 1918–1922, when the US along with the English, French and Japanese attacked Northern Russia at Arkhangelsk and in Siberia, occupying Northern Russia for over a year with Siberia occupied by the Americans for four years. Russia had been an ally of the US, Britain and France in WWI, yet it was attacked during the Russian Revolution and civil war. From a Russian or Soviet point of view, the Cold War may have started when it was invaded by its former Western allies in 1918 when they came to the aid of the Czarist White Russians in an attempt to prevent the communist take-over of Russia.

According to the British newspaper *The Telegraph*, in 2008, Stalin made an offer to Britain and France in 1939 to send a million troops to Poland to stop Hitler; some may say that their rejection of this offer was the start of the Cold War. However, Britain, France and Poland claimed they were afraid that if Soviet troops entered Poland, they would never leave. Faced with the refusal of cooperation by the Allies, the Soviets then cut a deal with Hitler proposing to divide Poland and Eastern Europe. However, Hitler broke this treaty and attacked the USSR.

During WWII the Soviet Union and its people were used as an anvil by their Western allies to destroy Hitler's war machine while British and American troops sat safely in Britain until their D Day Invasion in 1944. The Soviets begged them to open a second front from 1942 on, while losing millions to the German assault. Even some military strategists (General

Patton for one) recommended that the US and Britain push up from Italy to join the Soviets in their march toward Berlin. There is every appearance that the US and Britain wanted the Soviets and Germans to vanquish each other. The Cold War tensions began long before 1945.

The Cold War was more than a political and military competition. It changed the culture, people and customs of the United States. It took a once isolationist country and made it internationalist. It took an anti-military and anti-war people and brought them into a permanent state of military readiness and a willingness to enter combat whenever they feel their economic or military hegemony is threatened.

The US is now a xenophobic and jingoistic country that is paranoid about national security and intelligence. America has ignored the advice of General Eisenhower and embraced the military-industrial complex to the extent that a good deal of America makes money when we go to war and we believe we need to defend all American corporate interests worldwide. We are now kept in a permanent state of war readiness. In our eyes, America has become the world's policeman. In the minds of others, America has become the greedy bully and an oppressor.

All wars have consequences, most of them bad. The long Cold War was no exception.

Notes on References

This chronology contains mostly common knowledge events where references are not needed or included. The events can easily be found in many printed or electronic timelines or in most cases as newspaper headlines on these dates.

There are, however, events where the author believes the analysis or details of the event should have references and these are included. These references may appear in their entirety such as "John Prados' book *Unsafe for Democracy: The Secret Wars of the CIA.*" If repeated, they may be referenced as just (John Prados). Most of the references are short, such as "according to the *New York Times* or *Time Magazine*," etc., indicating that a news story appeared on the day or shortly after the event, except where otherwise marked in the text.

Printed in the United States
By Bookmasters